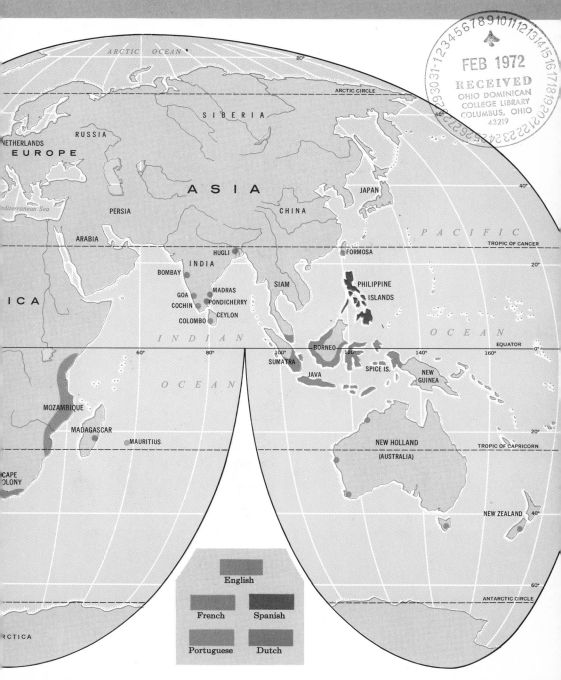

ARCTIC OCEAN

SIBERIA

RUSSIA

NETHERLANDS

EUROPE

ASIA

Mediterranean Sea

PERSIA

CHINA

JAPAN

ARABIA

ARCTIC CIRCLE

TROPIC OF CANCER

PACIFIC

HUGLI

INDIA

BOMBAY

MADRAS

GOA   PONDICHERRY

COCHIN

COLOMBO   CEYLON

SIAM

FORMOSA

PHILIPPINE

ISLANDS

INDIAN

OCEAN

EQUATOR

BORNEO

SUMATRA

JAVA   SPICE IS.   NEW
GUINEA

MOZAMBIQUE

MADAGASCAR

MAURITIUS

CAPE
OLONY

NEW HOLLAND

(AUSTRALIA)

TROPIC OF CAPRICORN

NEW ZEALAND

RCTICA

ANTARCTIC CIRCLE

English

French   Spanish

Portuguese   Dutch

World Civilizations

*Their History
and Their Culture*

FOURTH EDITION

Volume 2

WORLD
CIVILIZATIONS

*from Ancient
to Contemporary*

EDWARD McNALL BURNS

and

PHILIP LEE RALPH

FOURTH EDITION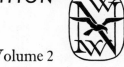

Volume 2

New York · W · W · NORTON & COMPANY · INC ·

To our *Students*

Cartography by Harold K. Faye

Contents

Preface   xvii

Picture Acknowledgments   xxi

Illustrations in Color

(page numbers refer to facing pages)

Illustrations in the Text

Maps

Preface

The time has long since passed when modern man could think of the world as consisting of Europe and the United States. Western culture is, of course, primarily a product of European origins. But it has never been that exclusively. Its original foundations were in Southwestern Asia and North Africa. These were supplemented by influences seeping in from India and eventually from China. From India and the Far East the West derived its knowledge of the zero, the compass, gunpowder, silk, cotton, and probably a large number of religious and philosophical concepts. But especially in recent times the East has increased in importance. It can no longer be thought of as a remote and slumbering world of no concern to anyone in the West except missionaries and manufacturers with surplus goods. The exhaustion of Europe by two World Wars, the revolt of the colored races against Caucasian domination, and the struggle for the world between the Communist powers and the United States have made every part of the earth of vital importance to every other. If peace is indivisible, so are prosperity, justice, and freedom; so, in fact, is civilization itself.

The purpose of this work is to present a compact survey of man's struggle for civilization from early times to the present. No major area or country of the globe has been omitted. Europe, the Commonwealth of Nations, the Middle East, Southeast Asia, Africa, India, China, Japan, and North, Central, and South America have all received appropriate emphasis. Obviously, the history of none of them could be covered in full detail. The authors believe, however, that a broad view of the world as a whole is necessary to understand the basic problems of any of its parts. This thesis acquires additional validity as the nations increase in interdependence. Perspective in history becomes more and more urgent as the momentous problems of our own generation press for solution. If there is any basic philosophical interpretation underlying the narrative, it is the conviction that most of human progress thus far has resulted from the growth of intelligence and respect for the rights of man, and that therein lies the chief hope for a better world in the future.

The First Edition of *World Civilizations* was published in 1955, the Second in 1958, and the Third in 1964. Since the publication of the earlier editions numerous discoveries and reinterpretations have resulted from historical research. To take account of these is one of the major objectives of the present edition. We are now able to see more clearly the revolutionary trends of our times. To describe and assess the significance of such developments as the decline of Western Europe, the ascendancy of the Soviet Union and the United States, the power struggle between East and West, the nationalist revolt against imperialism, the recurring international crises, and the awesome achievements in the fields of thermonuclear energy, cybernetics, and space exploration a new edition of *World Civilizations* becomes necessary. But the present edition is not a mere enlargement of its predecessors. Much new material has ben added, but substantial portions of the old have been eliminated, and rewriting has been done throughout. Notable changes include: an increased amount of political history, especially of the medieval and modern periods, and of Russia; new assessments of India, China, and Japan and the emerging nations of Africa and Southeast Asia; new chapters on the Industrial Revolutions of the nineteenth and twentieth centuries; division and reorganization of the chapter on Democracy and Nationalism in the nineteenth century; abandonment of the chapter on the Return to International Anarchy and insertion of chapters on New Power Relationships and the Revolution of Our Time. The Fourth Edition of *World Civilizations* has been entirely remapped by the noted cartographer, Harold K. Faye. Illustrations in most cases have been enlarged, with the addition of numerous new ones from archives both Western and Oriental. The color plates, which so greatly enhanced the value of the previous edition, have been retained and improved in clarity and brightness. Available for use with the new edition is a Teacher's Manual and a new Study Guide, whose distinctive feature is the inclusion of many extracts from original sources.

As its title indicates, this work is not exclusively or even primarily a political history. Political narrative is recognized as important, but it is not the whole substance of history. In the main, the facts of political history are subordinated to the development of institutions and ideas or are presented as the groundwork of cultural, social, and economic movements. The authors consider the effects of the Industrial Revolutions to be no less important than the Napoleonic Wars. They believe it is of greater value to understand the significance of Newton, Darwin, and Einstein than it is to be able to name the kings of France. In accordance with this broader conception of history, more space has been given to the teachings of John Locke and John

Stuart Mill than to the military exploits of Gustavus Adolphus or the Duke of Wellington.

In preparing this revision the authors have benefited from the assistance and counsel of many individuals whose services no words of appreciation can adequately measure. Professor Ardath W. Burks of Rutgers University has read and criticized the material on the Far East. Professor James L. Shirley of Northern Illinois University has thoroughly examined the chapters on the Middle and Far East, and also those on early Europe and the Commonwealth of Nations. All of the chapters on Europe and the United States have been critically reviewed by Professors David L. Cowen of Rutgers University and Eugen Weber of the University of California at Los Angeles. In addition, various sections of the material have been carefully criticized by able specialists in their fields. They are: Professor Gene Brucker of the University of California, Berkeley, for the early modern chapters, and Professor Lancelot L. Farrar of the University of Washington for the chapters on later modern history and the contemporary world. Professor Paul Henry Lang of Columbia University, distinguished historian of music, has rewritten the sections on music. Professor Earle Field of San Fernando Valley State College has reviewed the maps and made valuable recommendations for additions and improvements. Mrs. Lynn Masciarelli has rendered efficient service in typing and proofreading. The help of Professor Remigio U. Pane of Rutgers University with the Spanish and Italian pronunciations; of Dr. F. Gunther Eyck with the German pronunciations; of Mrs. Eric Wendelin with the Spanish and Portuguese pronunciations; and of Dr. Madeleine Charanis, Dr. Lucy Huang, and Professor Ardath W. Burks with the French, Chinese, and Japanese pronunciations, respectively, is gratefully acknowledged. Finally, the authors are indebted to their wives for their aid with the laborious tasks of typing, checking, proofreading, and indexing, and for their patience, devotion, and understanding.

EDWARD McNALL BURNS
PHILIP LEE RALPH

Picture Acknowledgments

The corporations, public agencies, and individuals listed below have generously provided photographs or other materials to illustrate *World Civilizations*. Specific contributions are indicated in the list of illustrations by the name of the donor in full or by code letters after the title of the picture furnished.

American Museum of Natural History (AMNH)
American Philosophical Society
American School of Classical Studies, Athens (Agora Excavations)
American Telephone and Telegraph Company
Anderson, Rome
Wayne Andrews
Arab Information Bureau
Arabian-American Oil Company
Arena Chapel, Padua
Australian News and Information Bureau (ANIB)
Baltimore & Ohio Railroad (B&O RR)
Bayeux Public Library
John Barrington Bayley
Belgian Government Tourist Bureau (BGTB)
Bethlehem Steel Corporation
J. David Bowen
John P. Bradford
Brazilian Government Trade Bureau
British Information Services (BIS)
British Museum (BM)
British Transport Commission
British Travel Association (BTA)
John Bryson, *Saturday Evening Post*
Canadian Pacific Railway
Chase Manhattan Bank Museum of Moneys of the World (Chase)
Chinese News Service
Stephen C. Clark
Columbia National Tourist Bureau (CNTB)
Creole Petroleum

Electronic Music Center of Columbia and Princeton Universities
Ford Motor Company
Henry Ford Museum, Dearborn
Fitzwilliam Museum, Cambridge
Foreign Operations Administration
Alison Frantz
Free Europe Press
French Embassy, Press and Information Division (FEPI)
French Government Tourist Office (FGTO)
French National Railroad (FNR)
Marcel Gautherot
Philip Gendreau, New York
Germanic Museum, Nuremberg
German Railroads
German Tourist Information Office (GTIO)
Ghana Information Services
Greek Information Office (GIO)
Henry E. Huntington Library and Art Gallery (Huntington)
Iglesia San Tomé, Toledo, Spain
Government of India Tourist Office (GITO)
Information Service of India (ISI)
International Harvester Company
Israel Government Tourist Office (IGTO)
Israel Office of Information (IOA)
Italian State Tourist Office (ISTO)
Consulate General of Japan, New York
Japan National Tourist Organization (JNTO)
Japan Tourist Association

PICTURE ACKNOWLEDGMENTS

Japan Travel Information Office (JTIO)
Jewish Museum of New York, Frank J. Darmstaedter (JMNY)
P. Kidson and U. Pariser, *Sculpture at Chartres* (Alec Tiranti, Ltd.)
Kuwait Oil Company
Robert Lehman
Lever Brothers
His Highness the Prince of Liechtenstein
Marshall MacDuffie
Mauritshuis, The Hague
Metropolitan Museum of Art, New York (MMA)
Mexican National Tourist Council
Minneapolis Institute of Art
Mitsubishi-Nippon Heavy Industries, Ltd.
Morgan Library, New York (Morgan)
Museum of Fine Arts, Boston
Museum of Modern Art, New York (Modern)
National Archives
National Gallery of Art
National Geographic Magazine
National Museum, Naples
Joseph Needham, Oxford University Press
Richard J. Neutra
New York Academy of Medicine (NYAM)
New York Public Library, Picture Collection and Print Collection (NYPL)
Oriental Institute, University of Chicago

Pakistan Consulate General
Pan American Union (PAU)
Philadephia Museum of Art (PMA)
Phillips Memorial Gallery
Pitti Palace, Florence
Prado, Madrid
Press Information Bureau, Government of India (PIBI)
Her Majesty the Queen
Rutgers University, Department of Art (Rutgers)
Santa Maria della Grazie, Milan
Seattle World's Fair
A. A. Schechter Associates
Sistine Chapel
South African Information Service
Spanish Tourist Office (STO)
Sperry-Rand Corporation
Standard Oil Company of New Jersey
Olli Steltzer
Swiss National Tourist Office
Tennessee Valley Authority
Alec Tiranti, Ltd.
Trans World Airlines (TWA)
Uffizi Gallery, Florence (Uffizi)
United China Colleges (UCC)
United Nations
USAID
United States Army
United States Lines Company
United States Marine Corps
United States Navy
University Prints (UP)
V. W. van Gogh
Victoria and Albert Museum
Whitney Museum of American Art
Yale University Press

FROM SPECIAL COLLECTIONS AND GIFTS IN THE METROPOLITAN MUSEUM OF ART, NEW YORK

BEQUEST OF BENJAMIN ALTMAN, 1913: Arm chair upholstered in Beauvais tapestry after design by Berain.
BEQUEST OF WILLIAM K. VANDERBILT, 1920: Secretaire: ebony with black marble top; black and gold lacquer panels; ormolu mounts, with the cipher of Marie Antoinette.
BEQUEST OF MRS. H. O. HAVEMEYER, 1929. THE H. O. HAVEMEYER COLLECTION: *Portrait of a Young Man*, Bronzino; *Boy with a Greyhound*, Veronese; *Portrait of a Gentleman*, Ingres; *Pink and Green*, Degas; *Montagne Sainte Victoire with Aqueduct*, Cézanne; *Still Life*, Cézanne.
GIFT OF HENRY PAYNE BINGHAM, 1937: *Venus and Adonis*, Peter Paul Rubens.
GIFT OF ANN PAYNE BLUMENTHAL, 1941: Arm chair *(bergère)*.
JULES S. BACHE COLLECTION: *Madonna and Child*, Luca della Robbia; *Portrait of a Young Man*, Bellini (1949); *Portrait of a Lady*, Domenico Veneziano (1949).
THE ALFRED STIEGLITZ COLLECTION, 1949: *Sea and Gulls*, John Marin.
BEQUEST OF SAMUEL A. LEWISOHN, 1951: *Ia Orana Maria*, Gauguin.
BEQUEST OF MARY WETMORE SHIVELY IN MEMORY OF HER HUSBAND, HENRY L. SHIVELY: *Portrait of Louis XV as a Child, in Royal Costume*, Hyacinthe Rigaud.

FROM SPECIAL COLLECTIONS AND GIFTS IN THE MUSEUM OF MODERN ART, NEW YORK

MRS. SIMON GUGGENHEIM FUND: *Piano Lesson*, Henri Matisse; *Three Musicians*, Pablo Picasso; *I and the Village*, Marc Chagall.
ACQUIRED THROUGH THE LILLIE P. BLISS BEQUEST: *The Starry Night*, Vincent van Gogh; *The Table*, George Braque.
MRS. JOHN D. ROCKEFELLER, JR., FUND: *Around the Fish*, Paul Klee.

World Civilizations

*Their History
and Their Culture*

FOURTH EDITION

Volume 2

PART ONE

The Early Modern World, 1400-1789

By a paradox of history the brilliant age of cultural revival in Europe known as the Renaissance was accompanied by the rise of absolute government. The relationship, however, was not one of cause and effect. By little more than a coincidence the Renaissance was built on the ruins of a crumbling feudalism. And it was the need for strong government to replace the anarchy of decaying feudalism that brought the new absolute monarchs to the height of their power. Some monarchs of this era were benevolent or "enlightened" despots and attempted to govern as "first servants of the state." But, unfortunately, for every wise, dedicated ruler there were at least two or three who concerned themselves exclusively with their own welfare. No one could guarantee that a benevolent despot would not be succeeded by a pig-headed or incompetent son. Not only was such the case in Europe, but almost identical conditions prevailed in India. The Mogul ruler Akbar was a worthy contemporary of Queen Elizabeth I of England, but stupid and vicious successors brought the Mogul dynasty to an early decline. China, also, enjoyed stability and prosperity under K'ang Hsi and his enlightened grandson, Ch'ien Lung, but stagnated as the later Manchu emperors imposed a narrow conservatism upon their subjects. In Japan no absolute monarchy came into existence in this period. Theoretically, feudalism remained intact, but the rise of the Tokugawa Shoguns in 1603 established the substance if not the form of absolute government. In contrast with Western Europe, both Chinese and Japanese despotism survived into the twentieth century.

1

A Chronological Table

	WESTERN EUROPE	EASTERN AND CENTRAL EUROPE

1500

The domestic system, 1400–1750

Tudor Dynasty in England, 1485–1603

Sir Francis Bacon, 1561–1626
Shakespeare, 1564–1616
Beginning of international law: Hugo
    Grotius, 1583–1645
Spanish Armada, 1588
Bourbon dynasty in France, 1589–1792
Edict of Nantes, 1598

1600

Mercantilism, 1600–1789

Thirty Years' War, 1618–1648
Colbert, 1619–1683
Deism, 1630–1800
Rationalism in philosophy, 1630–1700
Puritan Revolution in England, 1640–1649
Beginning of modern state system, 1648
Commonwealth and Protectorate in Eng-
    land, 1649–1659

Classicism in literature and the arts, 1600–
    1750
Cameralism, 1600–1800

1650

Restoration of Stuart dynasty, 1660–1688

The Enlightenment, 1680–1800

Revocation of Edict of Nantes, 1685

Newton's law of gravitation, 1687
Glorious Revolution in England, 1688–
    1689
John Locke, *Two Treatises of Civil Gov-
ernment*, 1690

Peter the Great, 1682–1725

1700

Physiocrats, 1750–1800
Romanticism, 1750–1830
Seven Years' War, 1756–1763
Rousseau, *The Social Contract*, 1762
Beginning of factory system, *ca.* 1770

Joseph Priestley discovers oxygen, 1774

Age of Enlightened Despots, 1740–1796
Frederick the Great, 1740–1786

Mozart, 1756–1791
Catherine the Great, 1762–1796

1775

Adam Smith, *Wealth of Nations*, 1776

Romanticism, 1780–1830
Kant, *The Critique of Pure Reason*, 1781

Goethe, *Faust*, 1790–1808

Edward Jenner develops vaccination for
    smallpox, 1796

THE AMERICAS

INDIA AND THE FAR EAST

Voyages of discovery and exploration, 1450–1600

Conquest of Mexico, 1522
Conquest of Peru, 1537

Arrival of Portuguese traders in China and Japan, 1537–1542
Jesuit missionaries active in China and Japan, 1550–1650
Akbar the Great Mogul, 1556–1605

1500

Founding of Jamestown, 1607

Landing of Pilgrims, 1620

British East India Co. chartered, 1600
Tokugawa Shogunate, 1603–1867

1600

Taj Mahal, 1632–1647
Japanese isolation, 1637–1854

Manchu Dynasty in China, 1644–1912
Maratha Confederacy in India, 1650–1760

1650

Decline of Mogul Empire in India, 1700–1800

1700

Benjamin Franklin, 1706–1790

French and Indian War, 1754–1763

The Stamp Act, 1765

American War for Independence, 1775–1783
Declaration of Independence, 1776

1775

Constitutional Convention (Philadelphia), 1787
U.S. Constitution goes into effect, 1789

Bill of Rights, 1791

CHAPTER 1

The Age of Absolutism (1485-1789)

There are four essential characteristics or qualities of royal authority.
First, royal authority is sacred.
Second, it is paternal.
Third, it is absolute.
Fourth, it is subject to reason.

—Jacques Bossuet, *Politics Drawn from the Very Words of Holy Scripture*

It becomes necessary now to go back and attempt to analyze the major political developments which accompanied the birth of modern civilization. During the fourteenth and fifteenth centuries the decentralized feudal regime of the Middle Ages broke down and was gradually replaced by dynastic states with governments of absolute power. For this there were numerous causes, some of which have already been discussed.[1] The position of the nobles was weakened by the growth of an urban economy, by the decay of the manorial system, and by the effects of the Crusades, the Black Death, and the Hundred Years' War. But these factors would not necessarily have laid the foundations for absolute monarchy. They might just as conceivably have resulted in chaos or in the democratic rule of the masses. We must therefore look for other causes to account for the rise of despotic governments. Apparently the most significant of these causes were the wars of the sixteenth and seventeenth centuries. These wars were themselves a product of a variety of factors. With the decay of feudalism, great struggles occurred between the forces of centralization and the forces of localism or decentralization. Ambitious kings sought to eliminate powerful princes and dukes who in some cases were their overlords. Struggles for empire also resulted from the geo-

The rise of the new absolutism

[1] See especially the paragraphs on the decline of feudalism in the chapter on The Later Middle Ages: Political and Economic Institutions.

graphic expansion incident to the Commercial Revolution. From the colonies and into the royal coffers flowed wealth which was used in many cases to build navies and to hire professional soldiers. To organize and equip armies and fleets, large bureaucracies of civil servants became necessary. These also aided in the consolidation of monarchical power. Finally, the Protestant Revolution contributed not a little to the growth of royal omnipotence. It broke the unity of the Christian Church, abolished papal overlordship over secular rulers, fostered nationalism, revived the doctrine of the Apostle Paul that "the powers that be are ordained of God," and encouraged the kings of northern Europe to extend their authority over religious as well as over civil affairs.

I. THE GROWTH AND DECAY OF ABSOLUTE GOVERNMENT IN ENGLAND

The real founders of despotic government in England were the Tudors. The first of the kings of this line, Henry VII, came to the throne in 1485 at the end of the Wars of the Roses, in which rival factions of nobles had fought each other to the point of exhaustion. So great was the disgust on account of the turmoil of these wars that many of the citizens welcomed the establishment of absolute monarchy as an alternative to anarchy. The middle class, especially, desired the protection of consolidated government. This factor more than anything else accounts for the remarkable success of the Tudors in regulating the consciences of their subjects and in binding the nation to their will. It should be added that the most celebrated members of the dynasty, Henry VIII (1509–1547) and Elizabeth I (1558–1603), gained some of their power through shrewdly maintaining a semblance of popular government. When they desired to enact measures of doubtful popularity, they regularly went through the formality of obtaining parliamentary approval. Or when they wanted more money, they manipulated procedure in such a way as to make the appropriations appear to be voluntary grants by the representatives of the people. But the legislative branch of the government under these sovereigns was little more than a rubber stamp. They convoked Parliament irregularly and limited its sessions to very brief periods;[2] they interfered with elections and packed the two houses with their own favorites; and they cajoled, flattered, or bullied the members as the case might require in order to obtain their support.

In 1603 Elizabeth I, the last of the Tudors, died, leaving no direct descendants. Her nearest relative was her cousin, King James VI of Scotland, who now became the sovereign of both England and Scotland under the name of James I. His accession marks the beginning of the troubled history of the Stuarts, the last of

Absolutism in England founded by the Tudor monarchs

The establishment of divine-right monarchy by James I

---

[2] During Elizabeth's reign it was in session on the average only three or four weeks out of the year.

Queen Elizabeth I (1558–1603). In this regal portrait the queen is shown armed with the two symbols of power and justice, the scepter and the orb. A touch of cynicism seems to be revealed in her face.

the absolute dynasties in England. A curious mixture of stubbornness, vanity, and erudition, King James was appropriately called by Henry IV of France "the wisest fool in Christendom." Though he loved to have his courtiers flatter him as the English Solomon, he did not even have sense enough to emulate his Tudor predecessors in being satisfied with the substance of absolute power; he insisted upon the theory as well. From France he appropriated the doctrine of the divine right of kings, contending that "as it is atheism and blasphemy to dispute what God can do, so it is presumption and high contempt in a subject to dispute what a king can do." In his speech to Parliament in 1609, he declared that "Kings are justly called gods, for they exercise a manner of resemblance of Divine power upon earth." [3]

That such ridiculous pretensions to divine authority would arouse opposition among the English people was a result which even James himself should have been able to foresee. Despite the clever machinations of the Tudor sovereigns and the desire of the middle class for stable government, England still had traditions of liberty which could not be ignored. The feudal ideal of limited government expressed in Magna Carta had never been entirely destroyed. Moreover, the policies of the new king were of such a character as to antagonize even some of his most conservative subjects. He insisted upon supplementing his income by modes of taxation which had never been sanctioned by Parliament; and when the leaders of that

The high-handed policies of James I

[3] Quoted by R. G. Gettell, *History of Political Thought*, p. 201.

body remonstrated, he angrily tore up their protests and dissolved the two houses. He interfered with the freedom of business by granting monopolies and extravagant privileges to favored companies. He conducted foreign relations in disregard for the economic interests of some of the most powerful citizens. Ever since the days of Hawkins and Drake, English merchants had been ambitious to destroy the commercial empire of Spain. They openly desired a renewal of the war, begun during Elizabeth's reign, for that purpose. But James made peace with Spain and entered into negotiations for the marriage of his son to the daughter of the Spanish king. When the Spanish princess rejected him because of his unwillingness to turn Catholic, the English people went wild with joy. Their rejoicing, however, was premature, for a short time later, in accordance with his father's wishes, the prince married the sister of the king of France.

It was not marriage alliances alone that involved King James in religious troubles. The Elizabethan Compromise, which brought the Reformation in England to a close, had not been satisfactory to the more radical Protestants. They believed that it did not depart widely enough from the forms and doctrines of the Roman Church. During the reign of Queen Mary many of them had been in exile in France and had come under the influence of Calvinism. When Elizabeth's compromise policy took shape, they denounced it as representing too great a concession to Catholicism. Gradually they came to be called Puritans from their desire to "purify" the Anglican church of all traces of "Popish" ritual and observances. In addition, they preached an ascetic morality and condemned the episcopal system of church government. However, they did not form a united group. One faction believed that it could transform the Anglican church by working within that organization. The other preferred to withdraw from the Anglican fold and establish separate congregations where they could worship as they pleased. The members of this latter group came to be designated Separatists. They achieved fame in American history as the so-called Pilgrims, who founded Plymouth Colony.

Any brand or faction of Puritans was anathema to King James. Though not much interested in theology, he distrusted any religion that did not fit in with his own ideas of relations between church and state. In his estimation the Puritans, by repudiating the episcopal system of church government, were threatening to pull down one of the chief pillars of monarchy itself. Refusal to submit to the authority of bishops appointed by the king was identical in his mind with disloyalty to the sovereign. For this reason he regarded the Puritans as the equivalent of traitors and threatened to "harry them out of the land." He showed little more wisdom or discretion in his dealings with the Catholics. For the most part, he favored them, though he could not resist the temptation to levy fines upon them from time to time for violating the severe code which came down

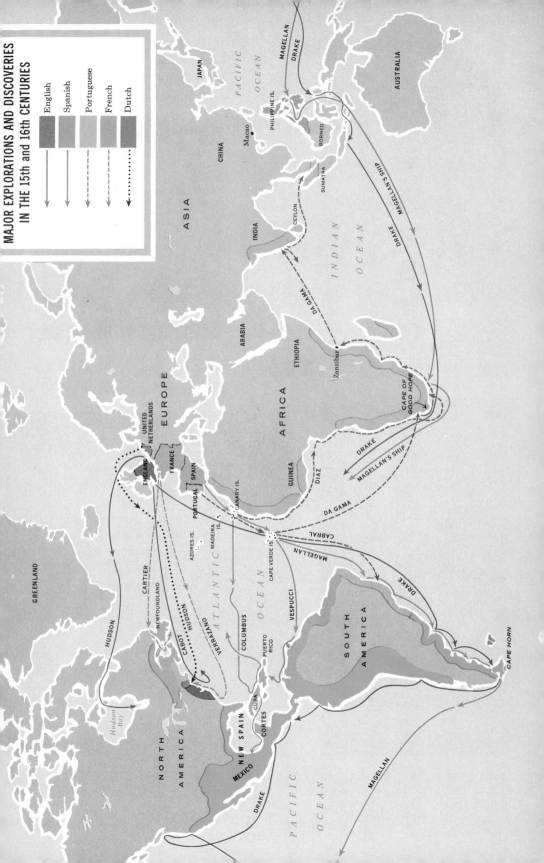

MAJOR EXPLORATIONS AND DISCOVERIES
IN THE 15th and 16th CENTURIES

English
Spanish
Portuguese
French
Dutch

Burial of the Count of Orgaz, El Greco (1541–1614). El Greco's masterpiece immortalizes the character of the people among whom he dwelt. The elongated figures, gaunt faces, and bold and dramatic colors are typical of his work. (Iglesia S. Tomé, Toledo, Spain)

The Marchessa Durazzo, Anthony Van Dyck (1599-1641). This portrait of a Genoese noblewoman suggests the Italian Renaissance sophistication admired by the Flemish burghers. (MMA)

Queen Mariana of Austria, Diego Velásquez (1599–1660). Velasquez's portraits celebrate the pomp and power of the Spanish court, but also emit the breath and life of real people. (Prado)

England and Scotland Crowning Charles I, Peter Paul Rubens (1577–1640). This voluptuous scene with classical setting was part of a series painted by Rubens in Whitehall Palace, London, to glorify the Stuart family. (Minneapolis Inst. of Art) from the Reformation. In 1605 a group of fanatical adherents of the Roman faith organized the Gunpowder Plot. They planned to blow up the Parliament building while the king and the legislators were assembled in it, and in the resulting confusion, seize control of the government. The plot was discovered, and Parliament enacted even more stringent laws against the Catholics. James, however, allowed the measures to go unenforced. Needless to say, his persistent leniency antagonized his Protestant subjects and made him more unpopular than ever.

From 1611 to 1621 King James ruled virtually without Parliament. But this did not mean that his troubles were over. In 1613 the rights of the people found a new champion when Sir Edward Coke was appointed Chief Justice. Coke was no democrat, but he did have a profound reverence for the common law and for the basic liberties inferred from Magna Carta. Moreover, he was a staunch defender of the privileged position of lawyers and judges. When the king insisted that he also had the faculty of reason and could interpret the law as well as the judges, Coke reminded him that he was not learned in the law, and that causes which concerned the lives and fortunes of his subjects were not be be decided by natural reason but only on the basis of long study and experience. Furthermore, the Chief Justice developed a rudimentary concept of judicial review. In the celebrated Dr. Bonham's case, he held that "when an act of Parliament is against common right and reason, or repugnant, or impossible to be performed, the common law will control it, and adjudge such act to be void." [4] There is evidence that this opinion was highly regarded in colonial America, and that it was one of the factors which later gave rise to the idea that the Supreme Court of the United States has the authority to nullify laws of Congress which conflict with the Constitution.

The first of the Stuart kings died in 1625 and was succeeded by his son as Charles I (1625–1649). The new monarch was more regal in appearance than his father, but he held the same inflated notions of royal power. As a consequence he was soon in hot water with the Puritans and the leaders of the parliamentary opposition. As in the case of his father, the conflict was precipitated by questions of taxation. Soon after his accession to the throne Charles became involved in a war with France. His need for revenue was desperate. When Parliament refused to make more than the customary grants, he resorted to forced loans from his subjects, punishing those who failed to comply by quartering soldiers upon them or throwing them into prison without a trial. The upshot of this tyranny was the famous Petition of Right, which Charles was compelled by the leaders of Parliament to agree to in 1628. This document, which ranks with Magna Carta as the second great charter of English liberties, declared all taxes not voted by Parliament illegal. It condemned also

---

[4] Quoted by George H. Sabine, *A History of Political Theory*, p. 452.

The continued
tyranny of
Charles I

the quartering of soldiers in private houses and prohibited arbitrary imprisonment and the establishment of martial law in time of peace.

But acceptance of the Petition of Right did not end the conflict. Charles soon resumed his old tricks of raising money by various irregular means. He revived obsolete feudal laws and collected fines from all who violated them. He compelled rich burghers to apply for knighthood and then charged them high fees for their titles. He sold monopolies at exorbitant rates and admonished his judges to increase the fines in criminal cases. But the most unpopular of all his expedients for raising revenue was his collection of ship money. Under an ancient custom the English seaboard towns had been required to contribute ships for the royal navy. Since the needs of the fleet were now provided for in other ways, Charles maintained that the towns should contribute money; and he proceeded to apply the new tax not merely to the coastal cities but to the inland counties as well. The levies of ship money were particularly irritating to the middle class and served to crystallize the opposition of that group to monarchical tyranny. Many refused to pay, and the king's attorney-general finally decided to prosecute. A wealthy squire by the name of John Hampden was haled into court in a test case. When convicted by a vote of seven to five, he acquired a sort of martyrdom. For years he was venerated by the middle class as a symbol of resistance to royal autocracy.

Conflict with
the Calvinists

Like his blundering father before him, Charles also aroused the antagonism of the Calvinists. He appointed as Archbishop of Canterbury a clergyman by the name of William Laud, whose sympathies were decidedly high-Anglican. He outraged the Sabbatarianism of the Puritans by authorizing public games on Sunday. Worse still, he attempted to impose the episcopal system of church government upon the Scottish Presbyterians, who were even more radical Calvinists than the Puritans. The result was an armed rebellion by his northern subjects.

The outbreak
of civil war

In order to get money to punish the Scots for their resistance, Charles was finally compelled in 1640 to summon Parliament, after more than eleven years of autocratic rule. Knowing full well that the king was helpless without money, the leaders of the House of Commons determined to take the government of the country into their own hands. They abolished ship money and the special tribunals which had been used as agencies of tyranny. They impeached and sent to the Tower the king's chief subordinates, Archbishop Laud and the Earl of Strafford. They enacted a law forbidding the monarch to dissolve Parliament and requiring sessions at least every three years. Charles replied to these invasions of his prerogative by a show of force. He marched with his guard into the House of Commons and attempted to arrest five of its leaders. All of them escaped, but the issue was now sharply drawn between king and Parliament, and an open conflict could no longer be averted. Both sides

The Trial of Charles I, King of Great Britain and Ireland, 1625–1649. His armies defeated by the forces of Cromwell and himself a prisoner, Charles was tried by a special court in Westminster Hall and convicted of treason "by levying war against the parliament and kingdom of England." Soon afterward he was beheaded. His dignity in his last hours fitted Shakespeare's lines: "Nothing in his Life became him, like the leaving it."

collected troops and prepared for an appeal to the sword.

These events ushered in a period of civil strife, which lasted from 1642 to 1649. It was a struggle at once political, economic, and religious. Arrayed on the side of the king were most of the chief nobles and landowners, the Catholics, and the staunch Anglicans. The followers of Parliament included, in general, the small landholders, tradesmen, and manufacturers. The majority were Puritans and Presbyterians. The members of the king's party were commonly known by the aristocratic name of Cavaliers. Their opponents, who cut their hair short in contempt for the fashionable custom of wearing curls, were called in derision Roundheads. At first the party of the royalists, having obvious advantages of military experience, won most of the victories. In 1644, however, the parliamentary army was reorganized, and soon afterward the fortunes of battle shifted. The Cavalier forces were badly beaten at Marston Moor and at Naseby, and in 1646 the king was compelled to surrender. The struggle would now have ended had not a quarrel developed within the parliamentary party. The majority of its members, who were now Presbyterians, were ready to restore Charles to the throne as a limited monarch under an arrangement whereby the Presbyterian faith would be imposed upon England as the state religion. But a radical minority of Puritans, made up principally of Separatists but now

Cavaliers and Roundheads

11

more commonly known as Independents, distrusted Charles and insisted upon religious toleration for themselves and all other Protestants. Their leader was Oliver Cromwell (1599–1658), who had risen to command of the Roundhead army. Taking advantage of the dissension within the ranks of his opponents, Charles renewed the war in 1648 but after a brief campaign was forced to concede that his cause was hopeless.

The defeat and execution of the king

The second defeat of the king gave an indisputable mastery of the situation to the Independents. Cromwell and his friends now resolved to put an end to "that man of blood," the Stuart monarch, and remodel the political system in accordance with their own desires. They conducted a purge of the legislative body by military force, ejecting 143 Presbyterians from the House of Commons; and then with the "Rump Parliament" that remained—numbering about sixty members—they proceeded to eliminate the monarchy. An act was passed redefining treason so as to apply to the offenses of the king. Next a special High Court of Justice was established, and Charles was brought to trial before it. His conviction was a mere matter of form. On January 30, 1649, he was beheaded in front of his palace of Whitehall. A short time later the House of Lords was abolished, and England became an oligarchic republic. The first stage in the so-called Puritan Revolution was now completed.

The Commonwealth and Protectorate

The work of organizing the new state, which was given the name of the Commonwealth, was entirely in the hands of the Independents. Since the Rump Parliament continued as the legislative body, the really fundamental change was in the nature of the executive. In place of the king there was set up a Council of State composed of forty-one members. Cromwell, with the army at his back, soon came to dominate both of these bodies. However, as time went on he became exasperated by the attempts of the legislators to perpetuate themselves in power and to profit from confiscation of the wealth of their opponents. Accordingly, in 1653, he marched a detachment of troops into the Rump and ordered the members to disperse, informing them that the Lord Jehovah had no further use for their services. This action was followed by the establishment of a virtual dictatorship under a constitution drafted by officers of the army. Called the Instrument of Government, it was the nearest approach to a written constitution Britain has ever had. Extensive powers were given to Cromwell as Lord Protector for life, and his office was made hereditary. At first a Parliament exercised limited authority in making laws and levying taxes, but in 1655 its members were abruptly dismissed by the Lord Protector. Thereafter the government was but a thinly disguised autocracy. Cromwell now wielded a sovereignty even more despotic than any the Stuart monarchs would have dared to claim. In declaring his authority to be from God he even revived what practically amounted to the divine right of kings.

That Cromwell's regime would have its difficulties was certainly to be expected, since it rested upon the support of only a small minority of the British nation. He was opposed not only by royalists and Anglicans but by various dissenters more radical than he. Like all upheavals of a similar character, the Puritan Revolution tended to move farther and farther in an extremist direction. Many of the Puritans became Levellers, who derived their name from their advocacy of equal political rights and privileges for all classes. Expressly disclaiming any intention of equalizing property, they confined their radicalism to the political sphere. They insisted that sovereignty inheres in the people and that government should rest upon the consent of the governed. Long in advance of any other party, they demanded a written constitution, universal manhood suffrage, and the supremacy of Parliament. The Levellers were especially powerful in the army and through it exerted some influence upon the government. Still farther to the left were the Diggers, so called from their attempt to seize and cultivate unenclosed common land and distribute the produce to the poor. Though in common with the Levellers the Diggers appealed to the law of nature as a source of rights, they were more interested in economic than in political equality. They espoused a kind of primitive communism based upon the idea that the land is the "common treasury" of all. Every ablebodied man would be required to work at productive labor, and all persons would be permitted to draw from the common fund of wealth produced in proportion to their needs. The church would be transformed into an educational institution and the clergy would become schoolmasters, giving instruction every seventh day in public affairs, history, and the arts and sciences. "To know the secrets of nature is to know the works of God" was one of the Digger mottoes.

But Cromwell's difficulties emanated from numerous sources. Before the Commonwealth had been in existence a year, trouble brewed in Ireland and Scotland. Ireland had been a hotbed of rebel- lion since 1641, and the dissatisfied elements now refused to recognize Cromwell's government. In Scotland Prince Charles, the oldest son of Charles I, had been proclaimed king, and royalists throughout the British Isles were making his cause their own. Within a few months Cromwell suppressed the revolt of the Irish, declaring upon his return to London in 1650 that the frightful butcheries he had perpetrated at Drogheda and Wexford were "the righteous judgment of God upon the barbarous wretches" who had rebelled. Next he routed the Scottish army and forced Prince Charles to seek refuge on the Continent. Cromwell also had his troubles with religious factions. His policy of granting toleration to all except Anglicans and Catholics continued to be opposed by the majority of the Puritans and the Presbyterians, both of whom desired a state church. That he succeeded in maintaining his regime in power as **13** long as he did was due mainly to three factors: (1) the strength of the army; (2) the commercial advantages he bestowed upon the middle class, especially through the Navigation Act of 1651 and the treaties with Holland and France; and (3) his victories in wars with the Spaniards and Dutch.

Downfall of the
Protectorate
and restoration
of the Stuarts

In September 1658, the stout-hearted Protector died. He was succeeded by his well-meaning but irresolute son Richard, who managed to hold office only until May of the following year. Perhaps even a man of much sterner fiber would also have failed eventually, for the country had grown tired of the austerities of Calvinist rule. Neither the Commonwealth nor the Protectorate had ever had the support of a majority of the English nation. Royalists regarded the Independents as usurpers. Republicans hated the disguised monarchy which Oliver Cromwell had set up. Catholics and Anglicans resented the branding of their acts of worship as criminal offenses. Even some members of the middle class gradually came to suspect that Cromwell's war with Spain had done more harm than good by endangering English commerce with the West Indies. For these and similar reasons there was general rejoicing when in 1660 a newly elected Parliament proclaimed Prince Charles king and invited him to return to England and occupy the throne of his father. The new king had gained a reputation for joyous living and easy morality, and his accession was hailed as a welcome relief from the somber rule of soldiers and zealots. Besides, he pledged himself not to reign as a despot, but to respect Parliament and to observe Magna Carta and the Petition of Right; for he admitted that he was not anxious to "resume his travels." England now entered upon a period known as the Restoration, covered by the reigns of Charles II (1660–1685) and his brother James II (1685–1688). Despite its auspicious beginning, many of the old problems had not really been solved but were simply concealed by the fond belief that the nation had regained its former stability.

The failure
of the Puritan
Revolution
paves the way
for the Glori-
ous Revolution
of 1688–1689

Toward the end of the seventeenth century England went through a second political upheaval, the so-called Glorious Revolution of 1688–1689. Several of the causes were grounded in the policies of Charles II. That amiable sovereign was extravagant and lazy but determined on occasion to let the country know whose word was law. His strongly pro-Catholic attitude aroused the fears of patriotic Englishmen that their nation might once again be brought into subservience to Rome. Worse still, he showed a disposition, in spite of earlier pledges, to defy the authority of Parliament. In 1672 he suspended the laws against Catholics and other Dissenters and nine years later resolved to dispense with the legislative branch entirely. The policies of Charles II were continued in more insolent form by his brother, who succeeded him in 1685. King James II was an avowed Catholic and seemed bent upon making that faith the established religion of England. He openly violated an act of Parliament requiring that all holders of public office should adhere to the Anglican church, and proceeded to fill important positions in the army and the civil service with his Romanist followers. He continued his brother's practice of exempting Catholics from the disabilities imposed upon them by Parliament, even going so far as to demand that the Anglican bishops should read his decrees for this purpose in their churches. As long as his opponents could expect that James II would be succeeded by one of his two Protestant daughters, they were inclined to tolerate his arbitrary rule, lest the country be plunged again into civil war. But when the king acquired a son by his second wife, who was a Catholic, the die of revolution was cast. It was feared that the young prince would be inoculated with his father's doctrines, and that, as a consequence, England would be fettered with the shackles of despotic and papist rule for an indefinite time to come. To forestall such a result it seemed necessary to depose the king.

The "Glorious Revolution" of 1688–1689 was an entirely bloodless affair. A group of politicians from both the upper and middle classes secretly invited Prince William of Orange and his wife Mary, the elder daughter of James II, to become joint rulers of England.[5] William crossed over from Holland with an army and occupied London without firing a shot. Deserted even by those whom he had counted as loyal supporters, King James took refuge in France. The English throne was now declared vacant by Parliament and the crown presented to the new sovereigns. But their enthronement did not complete the revolution. Throughout the year 1689 Parliament passed numerous laws designed to safeguard the rights of Englishmen and to protect its own power from monarchical invasion. First came an act requiring that appropriations should be made for one year only. Next the Toleration Act was passed, granting religious liberty to all Christians except Catholics and Unitarians. Finally, on the sixteenth of December the famous Bill of Rights was enacted into law. It provided for trial by jury and affirmed the right of Englishmen to petition the government for a redress of grievances. It condemned excessive bail, cruel punishments, and exorbitant fines. And it forbade the king to suspend laws or to levy taxes without the consent of Parliament. More sweeping in its provisions than the Petition of Right of 1628, it was backed by a Parliament that now had the power to see that it was obeyed.

Results of the Glorious Revolution

The significance of the revolution of 1688–1689 would be almost impossible to exaggerate. Since it marked the final triumph of Parliament over the king, it therefore spelled the doom of absolute monarchy in England. Never again was any crowned head in Britain

Significance of the Glorious Revolution

[5] There is evidence that William himself was a party to the secrets of the dissatisfied Englishmen, and he may even have inspired the invitation. Threatened with war by the king of France, he could make very good use of the resources and military power of England.

able to defy the legislative branch of the government as the Stuart monarchs had done. The revolution also dealt the *coup de grâce* to the theory of the divine right of kings. It would have been impossible for William and Mary to have denied the fact that they received their crowns from Parliament. And the authority of Parliament to determine who should be king was made more emphatic by the passage of the Act of Settlement in 1701. This law provided that upon the death of the heiress-presumptive Anne, younger sister of Mary, the crown should go to the Electress Sophia of Hanover or to the eldest of her heirs who might be Protestant.[6] There were some forty men or women with a better claim to the throne than Sophia, but all were eliminated arbitrarily by Parliament on the ground of their being Catholics. Finally, the Glorious Revolution contributed much to the American and French revolutions at the end of the eighteenth century. The example of the English in overthrowing absolute rule was a powerful inspiration to the opponents of despotism elsewhere. It was the British revolutionary ideal of limited government which furnished the substance of the political theory of Voltaire, Jefferson, and Paine. And a considerable portion of the English Bill of Rights was incorporated in the French Declaration of the Rights of Man in 1789 and in the first ten amendments to the American Constitution.

2. ABSOLUTE MONARCHY IN FRANCE AND SPAIN

The development of absolutism in France followed a course quite similar in some respects to that in England. Although France remained Catholic, her rulers had to contend with a Calvinist (Huguenot) opposition almost as formidable as that of the Puritans in England. They also had a prosperous middle class to which they could look for support, on occasions, against the nobility. Both nations had their staunch defenders of absolutism among lawyers and political philosophers. But there was one notable difference. England enjoyed an advantage of geographic isolation that sheltered her from foreign danger. Her soil had not been invaded since the Norman Conquest in 1066. As a consequence her people felt secure, and her rulers found it difficult to justify a huge professional army. They did, of course, maintain large fleets of war vessels, but a "bluewater" navy could not be used in the same manner as an army stationed in inland garrisons to overawe subjects or to stifle incipient revolutions. France, on the other hand, like most Continental nations, faced almost constant threats of invasion. Her northeastern and eastern frontiers were poorly protected by geographic barriers and had been penetrated several times. As a result, it was easy for

Contrasting conditions in England and France

---

[6] In this way the House of Hanover, the ruling dynasty until 1901, came to the English throne. The first Hanoverian king was Sophia's son, George I (1714–1727).

the French kings to argue the need for massive armies of professional soldiers. And such troops could readily be utilized to nip domestic disturbances in the bud. It would doubtless be a mistake to give all of the credit to this difference in geographic position for the longer persistence of absolute government in France, but it was certainly a major factor.

The growth of royal despotism in France was the product of a gradual evolution. Some of its antecedents went back to the reigns of Philip Augustus, Louis IX, and Philip IV in the thirteenth and fourteenth centuries. These kings solidified royal power by hiring mercenary soldiers, subsituting national taxation for feudal dues, arrogating to themselves the power to administer justice, and restricting the authority of the Pope to regulate ecclesiastical affairs in their kingdom. The Hundred Years' War (1337–1453) produced an even further accretion of power for the kings of France. They were now able to introduce new forms of taxation, to maintain a huge standing army, and to abolish the sovereignty of the feudal nobles. The members of this latter class were gradually reduced to the level of courtiers, dependent mainly upon the monarch for their titles and prestige.

The trend toward absolutism was interrupted during the sixteenth century when France was involved in a war with Spain and torn by a bloody struggle between Catholics and Huguenots at home. Ambitious nobles took advantage of the confusion to assert their power and contested the succession to the throne. Peace was restored to the distracted kingdom in 1593 by Henry of Navarre (1589–1610), who four years before had proclaimed himself king as Henry IV. He was the founder of the Bourbon dynasty. Though at one time a leader of the Huguenot faction, Henry perceived that the nation would never accept him unless he renounced the Calvinist religion. Flippantly remarking that Paris was worth a Mass, he formally adopted the Catholic faith. In 1598 he issued the Edict of Nantes, guaranteeing freedom of conscience and political rights to all Protestants. With the grounds for religious controversy thus removed, Henry could turn his attention to rebuilding his kingdom. In this work, he had the able assistance of his chief minister, the Duke of Sully. Grim, energetic, and penurious, Sully was a worthy forerunner of Colbert in the seventeenth century. For years the king and his faithful servant labored to repair the shattered fortunes of France. Sully devoted his efforts primarily to fiscal reform, so as to eliminate corruption and waste and bring more revenue into the royal treasury. He endeavored also to promote the prosperity of agriculture by draining swamps, improving devastated lands, subsidizing stock-raising, and opening up foreign markets for the products of the soil. The king gave most of his attention to fostering industry and commerce. He introduced the manufacture of silk into France, encouraged other industries by subsidies and monopolies, and made favorable commercial treaties with England and Spain. But Henry did not stop with economic reforms. He was deeply concerned with crushing the renascent power of the nobility, and so successful were his efforts in this direction that he restored the monarchy to the dominant position it had held at the end of the Hundred Years' War. He was active also in sponsoring the development of a colonial empire in America. During his reign the French acquired a foothold in Canada and began their exploration in the region of the Great Lakes and the Mississippi Valley. His rule was intelligent and benevolent but none the less despotic.

The reign of Henry IV was brought to an end by the dagger of a crazed fanatic in 1610. Since the new king, Louis XIII, was only nine years old, the country was ruled by his mother, Marie de Médicis, as regent. In 1624 Louis XIII, no longer under the regency, entrusted the management of his kingdom to a brilliant but domineering cleric, Cardinal Richelieu, whom he made his chief minister. Richelieu dedicated himself to two objectives: (1) to destroy all limitations upon the authority of the king; and (2) to make France the chief power in Europe. In the pursuit of these aims he disciplined both himself and the nation and allowed nothing to stand in his way. He ruthlessly suppressed the nobility, destroying its most dangerous members and rendering the others harmless by attaching them as pensioners to the royal court. Though he fostered education and patronized literature, he neglected the interests of commerce and allowed graft and extravagance to flourish in the government. His main constructive achievements were the creation of a postal service and the establishment of a system under which *intendants*, or agents of the king, took charge of local government. Both were conceived as devices for consolidating the nation under the control of the crown, thereby eradicating surviving traces of feudal authority.

Richelieu's ambitions were not limited to domestic affairs. To make France the most powerful nation in Europe required an aggressive diplomacy and eventual participation in war. France was still surrounded by what Henry IV had referred to as a "Hapsburg ring." On her southern border was Spain, ruled since 1516 by a branch of the Hapsburg family. To the north, less than 100 miles from Paris, were the Spanish Netherlands. Other centers of Hapsburg power included Alsace, the Franche-Comté, Savoy, Genoa, and Milan, and still farther to the east the great Austrian Empire itself. Cardinal Richelieu eagerly awaited an opportunity to break this ring. As we shall see, he finally found it in the Thirty Years' War. Though engaged in suppressing Protestants at home, he did not hesitate to ally himself with Gustavus Adolphus, king of Sweden and leader of a coalition of Protestant states. Long before his death in 1642 the great cardinal-statesman had forged to the front as the most powerful individual in Europe.

*Cardinal
Richelieu*

*Richelieu's
foreign
policy*

Portrait of Louis XIV, "Le Grand Monarque." Garbed in resplendent robes of ermine and velvet, with undergarments and stockings of silk.

Absolute monarchy in France attained its zenith during the reigns of the last three Bourbon kings before the Revolution. The first of the monarchs of this series was Louis XIV (1643–1715), who epitomized the ideal of absolutism more completely than any other sovereign of his age. Proud, extravagant, and domineering, Louis entertained the most exalted notions of his position as king. Not only did he believe that he was commissioned by God to reign, but he regarded the welfare of the state as intimately bound up with his own personality. The famous phrase imputed to him, *l'état c'est moi* (I am the state), may not represent his exact words, but it expresses very clearly the conception he held of his own authority. He chose the sun as his official emblem to indicate his belief that the nation derived its glory and sustenance from him as the planets do theirs from the actual sun. Perhaps it can be said to the credit of Louis that no man worked harder at the "trade of a king." He gave personal supervision to every department and regarded his ministers as mere clerks with no duty but to obey his orders. In general, he followed the policies of Henry IV and Richelieu in consolidating national power at the expense of local officials and in trying to reduce the nobles to mere parasites of the court. But any possible good he may have done was completely overshadowed by his extravagant wars and his reactionary policy in religion. In 1685 he revoked the Edict of Nantes, which had granted freedom of conscience to the Huguenots. As a result, large numbers of his most intelligent and prosperous subjects fled from the country.

Until the beginning of the Revolution in 1789 the form of the French government remained essentially as Louis XIV had left it.

19

His successors, Louis XV (1715–1774) and Louis XVI (1774–1792), also professed to rule by divine right. But neither of these kings had the desire to emulate the Grand Monarch in his enthusiasm for work and his meticulous attention to the business of state. Louis XV was lazy and incompetent and allowed himself to be dominated by a succession of mistresses. Problems of government bored him incredibly, and when obliged to preside at the council table he "opened his mouth, said little, and thought not at all." His grandson, who succeeded him, the ill-fated Louis XVI, was weak in character and mentally dull. Indifferent to politics, he amused himself by shooting deer from the palace window and playing at his hobbies of lock-making and masonry. On the day in 1789 when mobs stormed the Bastille, he wrote in his diary "Nothing." Yet both of these monarchs maintained a government which, if not more despotic, was at least more arbitrary than had ever been the case before. They permitted their ministers to imprison without a trial persons suspected of disloyalty; they suppressed the courts for refusing to approve their decrees; and they brought the country to the verge of bankruptcy by their costly wars and by their reckless extravagance for the benefit of mistresses and worthless favorites. If they had deliberately planned to make revolution inevitable, they could scarcely have succeeded better.

The growth of absolute monarchy in Spain was swifter and less interrupted than was true of its development in France. As late as the thirteenth century what is now Spain was divided into five parts. Four Christian kingdoms—Aragon, Castile, León, and Navarre—maintained a precarious existence in the north, while the southern half of the country was in the possession of the Moors. Before 1250 León had been absorbed by Castile, and some 200 years later further progress toward unification was accomplished by the marriage of Ferdinand of Aragon and Isabella of Castile. Though ruling nominally as independent monarchs, for all practical purposes they were sovereigns of a united Spain. Like their predecessors, they continued the crusade against the Moors, completing as their major achievement the conquest of Granada, last stronghold of Moorish power on the Iberian peninsula. The surviving Moors were expelled from the country, along with the Jews, for in the desperate struggle to drive out an alien invader all forms of non-Christian belief had come to be regarded as treason.

Queen Isabella died in 1504, and King Ferdinand in 1516. Their entire kingdom was inherited by their daughter Joanna, who had married into the Hapsburg family. Her son succeeded to the throne of Spain as Charles I in 1516. Three years later he was elected Holy Roman Emperor as Charles V, thereby uniting Spain with Central Europe and southern Italy. Charles was interested not merely in the destinies of Spain but in the welfare of the Church and in the politics of Europe as a whole. He dreamed that he might be the instrument

El Escorial, Palace and Monastery near Madrid. Built by Philip II, it contains one of the finest art collections in the world. Shown is the sacristy of the monastery.

of restoring the religious unity of Christendom, broken by the Protestant Revolution and of making the empire over which he presided a worthy successor of Imperial Rome. Though successful in holding his disjointed domain together and in fighting off attempts of the French to conquer his Italian possessions and of the Turks to overrun Europe, he failed in the achievement of his larger objectives. At the age of fifty-six, overcome with a sense of discouragement and futility, he abdicated and retired into a monastery. The German princes chose his brother, Ferdinand I, to succeed him as Holy Roman Emperor. His Spanish and Italian possessions, including the colonies overseas, passed to his son, who became king as Philip II.

21

Greatness and
decay under
Philip II

Philip II came to the throne of Spain at the height of its glory. But he also witnessed, and to a considerable extent was responsible for, the beginning of its decline. His policies were mainly an intensification of those of his predecessors. He was narrow, despotic, and cruel. Determined to enforce a strict conformity in matters of religion upon all of his subjects, he is reputed to have boasted that he would gather faggots to burn his own son if the latter were guilty of heresy. Reference has already been made to the horrors of the Spanish Inquisition and of the war for suppression of the revolt in the Netherlands. Philip was equally shortsighted in his colonial policy. Natives were butchered or virtually enslaved. Their territories were greedily despoiled of their gold and silver, which were

Philip II, King of Spain, 1556–1598. The famous protruding chin and lower lip which were distinctive marks of the Hapsburgs are clearly evident in this figure.

dragged off to Spain in the mistaken belief that this was the surest means of increasing the nation's wealth. No thought was given to the development of new industries in either the colonies or the mother country. Instead, the gold and silver were largely squandered in furthering Philip's military and political ambitions. It can be said, however, in the king's defense that he was following the accepted theories of the time. Doubtless most other monarchs with a like opportunity would have imitated his example. Philip II's crowning stupidity was probably his war against England. Angered by the attacks of English privateers upon Spanish commerce, and frustrated in his schemes to bring England back into the Catholic faith,

The destruction
of the Armada

he sent a great fleet in 1588, the "Invincible Armada," to destroy Queen Elizabeth's navy. But Philip had little knowledge of either the new techniques of naval warfare or of the robust patriotism of the English. A combination of fighting seamanship and disastrous storms sent all but 50 of the 132 ships to the bottom of the Channel. **22** Spain never recovered from the blow. Though a brilliant afterglow,

The Defeat of the Spanish Armada, 1588. From an engraving by John Pine. The situation of the Armada, with some of its ships burning and others dashed on the rocks by a storm, is made to appear hopeless.

exemplified in the work of the Renaissance artists and dramatists, continued for some years, the greatness of Spain as a nation was approaching its end.

3. ABSOLUTISM IN CENTRAL EUROPE

The chief countries of Central Europe where despotism flourished on its most grandiose scale were Prussia and Austria. The founder of absolute rule in Prussia was the Great Elector, Frederick William, a contemporary of Louis XIV. Not only was he the first member of the Hohenzollern family to acquire full sovereignty over Prussia, but he brought all three of his dominions—Prussia, Brandenburg, and Cleves—under centralized rule, abolishing their local Diets and merging their petty armies into a national military force. The work of the Great Elector was continued and extended by his grandson, known as Frederick William I (1713–1740), since he now had the title of *King* of Prussia.[7] This miserly monarch ruled over his people like a Hebrew patriarch, regulating their private conduct and attending personally to the correction of their shortcomings. His consuming passion was the army, which he more than doubled in size and drilled to a machinelike efficiency. He even sold the furniture in the palace to hire recruits for his famous regiment of Potsdam Giants. Those whom money could not buy he is alleged to have kidnaped. He traded musicians and prize stallions for sol-

The beginning of absolute monarchy in Prussia

[7] Originally the title was King *in* Prussia, probably for the reason that there was another Prussia, West Prussia, which still belonged to Poland.

The "enlight-
ened" despotism
of Frederick
the Great

diers who were well over six feet in height.

The most noted of the Prussian despots was Frederick II (1740–1786), commonly known as Frederick the Great. An earnest disciple of the reformist doctrines of the new rationalist philosophy, Frederick was the leading figure among the "enlightened despots" of the eighteenth century. Declaring himself not the master but merely the "first servant of the state," he wrote essays to prove that Machiavelli was wrong and rose at five in the morning to begin a Spartan routine of personal management of public affairs. He made Prussia in many ways the best-governed state in Europe, abolishing torture of accused criminals and bribery of judges, establishing elementary schools, and promoting the prosperity of industry and agriculture. He fostered scientific forestry and imported crop rotation, iron plows, and clover from England. He opened up new lands in Silesia and brought in hundreds of thousands of immigrants to cultivate them. When wars ruined their farms, he supplied the peasants with new livestock and tools. As an admirer of Voltaire, whom he entertained for some time at his court, he tolerated all sorts of religious beliefs. He declared that he would build a mosque in Berlin if enough Moslems wished to locate there. Yet he was perversely anti-Semitic. He levied special taxes on the Jews and made efforts to close the professions and the civil service to them. Moreover, such benevolence as he showed in internal affairs was not carried over into foreign relations. Frederick robbed Austria of Silesia, conspired with Catherine of Russia to dismember Poland, and contributed at least his full share to the bloody wars of the eighteenth century.

Absolutism in
Austria

The full bloom of absolutism in Austria came during the reigns of Maria Theresa (1740–1780) and Joseph II (1780–1790). Under the rule of the beautiful but high-strung empress a national army was established, the powers of the Church were curtailed in the interest of consolidated government, and elementary and higher education was greatly expanded. Unlike the despots of most other countries, Maria Theresa was sincerely devoted to Christian morality. Though she participated in the dismemberment of Poland to make up for the loss of Silesia, she did so with grave misgivings—an attitude which prompted the scornful remark of Frederick the Great: "She weeps, but she takes her share." The reforms of Maria Theresa were extended, at least on paper by her son Joseph II. Inspired by the teachings of French philosophers, Joseph determined to remake his empire in accordance with the highest ideals of justice and reason. Not only did he plan to reduce the powers of the Church by confiscating its lands and abolishing monasteries, but he gave Jews and heretics equal privileges with Catholics. In addition, he aspired to humble the nobles and improve the condition of the masses. He decreed that the serfs should become free men and promised to relieve them of the feudal obligations owed to their masters. He aimed to make education universal and to force the nobles to pay their proper share of taxes. But most of his magnificent plans ended in failure. He met defeat in his foreign wars. He antagonized not merely the nobles and clergy but also the proud Hungarians, who were deprived of all rights of self-government. He alienated the sympathies of the peasants by making them liable to compulsory military service. He was scarcely any more willing than Louis XIV or Frederick the Great to sacrifice personal power and national glory, even for the sake of his lofty ideals.

4. ABSOLUTISM IN RUSSIA

Russia at the beginning of the early modern age was a composite of European and Oriental characteristics. Much of her territory had been colonized by the Norsemen in the early Middle Ages. Her religion, her calendar, her system of writing had been derived from Byzantium. Even her feudal regime, with its boyars, or magnates, and serfs, was not greatly dissimilar to that of western Europe. On the other hand, much of Russia's culture, and many of her customs, were distinctly not European. Her arts were limited almost entirely to icon painting and an onion-domed religious architecture. There was no literature in the Russian language, arithmetic was barely known, Arabic numerals were not used, and bankers and merchants made their calculations with the abacus. Nor were manners and customs comparable to those of the West. Women of the upper classes were veiled and secluded. Flowing beards and skirted garments were universal for men. Knives and forks were considered superfluous. Seasons of wild revelry alternated with periods of repentance and morbid atonement. Geographically, also, Russia had an Asiatic orientation. The Russian heartland looked out upon Siberia, Persia, and China, with Europe in the rear. Swedes barred the approaches to the Baltic just as Tartars and Turks prevented access to the Black Sea and the Mediterranean. It would be a mistake, however, to suppose that Russia was totally cut off from Europe. As early as the fourteenth century, German merchants of the Hanse conducted some trade in Russian furs and amber. In the 1550's English merchants discovered the White Sea and made Archangel a port of entry through which military supplies could be exchanged for a few Russian goods and even products from Persia and China. But with Archangel frozen most of the year, the volume of this trade was undoubtedly small.

Russia at the beginning of the modern age

As late as the thirteenth century Russia was a collection of small principalities. They were besieged from the west by Swedes, Lithuanians, Poles, and the Teutonic Knights, or members of the Teutonic Order. The Teutonic Order was one of several religious and military organizations that sprang from the Crusades. Established originally for charitable purposes, it developed into a military

Foreign invaders; the Mongols

25

club whose members adopted as their mission the conquest of lands on Germany's eastern frontier. Their operations set a precedent for the famous *Drang nach Osten* (Drive to the East) which later occupied such a prominent place in German history. From the east Russia was threatened by the Mongols (Tartars) or the Golden Horde, who had established a great empire in central Asia, eventually including both northern India and China. In 1237 the Mongols began an invasion which led to their conquest of nearly all of Russia. Though brutal conquerors, their rule was comparatively mild. They allowed the principalities to manage their own affairs so long as they paid tribute to the Mongol khan. Religion and local customs were not molested. Nevertheless, Mongol rule was in several ways a disaster for Russia. It marked the development of a stronger Asiatic orientation. Henceforth Russia turned more and more away from Europe and looked beyond the Urals as the arena of her future development. Her citizens intermarried with Mongols and adopted many elements of their way of life.

The rise of Moscow; Ivan the Great

Eventually, Mongol power declined, in accordance with the common fate of vast empires. In 1380 a Russian army defeated the Tartars and thus initiated a movement to drive them back into Asia. The state which assumed the leadership of this movement was the Grand Duchy of Moscow. Under strong rulers it had been increasing its power for some time. Located near the sources of the great rivers flowing both north and south, it had geographic advantages surpassing those of the other states. Moreover, it had recently been made the headquarters of the Russian church. The first of the princes of Moscow to put himself forward as Tsar (Caesar) of Russia was Ivan the Great (1462–1505). Taking as his bride the niece of the last of the Byzantine Emperors, who had perished in the capture of Constantinople in 1453, he proclaimed himself his successor by the grace of God. He adopted as his insignia the Byzantine double-headed eagle and imported Italian architects to build him an enormous palace, the Kremlin, in imitation of the one in Constantinople. Avowing his intention to recover the ancient lands that had been lost to foreign invaders, he forced the Prince of Lithuania to acknowledge him as sovereign of "all the Russias" and pushed the Tartars out of northern Russia and beyond the Urals.

Peter the Great

The first of the Tsars to attempt the Europeanization of Russia was Peter the Great (1682–1725). He stands out as the most powerful and probably the most intelligent autocrat yet to occupy the Russian throne. With a reckless disregard for ancient customs, Peter endeavored to force his subjects to change their ways of living. He forbade the Oriental seclusion of women and commanded both sexes to adopt European styles of dress. He made the use of tobacco compulsory among the members of his court. He summoned the great nobles before him and clipped their flowing beards with his own hand. In order to make sure of his own absolute power he abolished

St. Basil's Church in Moscow, Built in the 16th Century. The tent-shaped tower in the center exemplifies the first major departure from Byzantine models and the beginning of a Russian national style. The church is now a public museum.

all traces of local self-government and established a system of national police. For the same reason he annihilated the authority of the patriarch of the Orthodox church and placed all religious affairs under a Holy Synod subject to his own control. Profoundly interested in Western science and technology, he made journeys to Holland and England to learn about shipbuilding and industry. He imitated the mercantilist policies of Western nations by improving agriculture and fostering manufactures and commerce. In order to get "windows to the west" he conquered territory along the Baltic shore and transferred his capital from Moscow to St. Petersburg, his new city at the mouth of the Neva. But the good that he did was greatly outweighed by his extravagant wars and his fiendish cruelty. He put thousands to death for alleged conspiracies against him, and the heads that rolled in the dust of the palace square were frequently chopped off by the arm of the great Tsar himself. He murdered his own son and heir because the latter boasted that when *he* became Tsar he would return Russia to the ways of her fathers. To raise money for his expensive wars he debased the currency, sold valuable concessions to foreigners, established government monopolies on the production of salt, oil, caviar, and coffins, and imposed taxes on almost everything, from baths to beehives. **27**

The significance of Peter the Great is not easy to evaluate. He did not singlehandedly transform Russia into a Western nation. Western influences had been seeping into the country as a consequence of trade contacts for many years. But Peter accelerated the process and gave it a more radical direction. Evidence abounds that he really did aim to remake the nation and to give it at least a veneer of civilization. He sent many of his countrymen abroad to study. He simplified the ancient alphabet and established the first newspaper to be published in Russia. He ordered the publication of a book on polite behavior, teaching his subjects not to spit on the floor or to scratch themselves or gnaw bones at dinner. He encouraged exports, built a fleet on the Baltic, and fostered new industries such as textiles and mining. Though a reaction set in after Peter's death against many of his innovations, some of them survived for at least two centuries. The church, for example, continued as essentially an arm of the state, governed by a Procurator of the Holy Synod appointed by the Tsar himself. Serfdom not only survived but continued in the extended forms required or authorized by Peter. No longer were serfs bound to the soil; they could be bought and sold at any time, even for work in factories and mines. Finally, the absolutism developed by Peter showed few signs of abating until the twentieth century. It was an absolutism based upon force, with a secret police, an extensive bureaucracy, and a subordinated church as instruments for imposing the autocrat's will.

The other most noted of the Russian monarchs in the age of absolutism was Catherine the Great (1762–1796), who before her marriage was a German princess. Frequently classified as one of the "enlightened despots," Catherine corresponded with French philosophers, founded hospitals and orphanages, and expressed the hope that someday the serfs might be liberated. Ambitious to gain for herself a place in the Enlightenment, she purchased Diderot's library and rose at five in the morning to dabble in scholarship. She wrote plays, published a digest of Blackstone's *Commentaries on the Laws of England*, and even began a history of Russia. Her accomplishments as a reformer, however, had only a limited scope. She took steps toward a codification of the Russian laws, restricted the use of torture, and remodeled and consolidated local government. Any plans she may have had, however, for improving the lot of the peasants were abruptly canceled after a violent serf rebellion in 1773–1774. Landlords and priests were murdered and the ruling classes terrified as the revolt swept through the Urals and the valley of the Volga. Catherine responded with stern repression. The captured leader of the peasants was drawn and quartered, and as a guaranty against future outbreaks, the nobles were given increased powers over their serfs. They were permitted to deal with them virtually as if they were chattel slaves. Catherine's chief significance lies in the fact that she continued the work of Peter the Great in introducing Russia to Western ideas and in making the country a formidable power in European affairs. She managed to extend the boundaries of her country to include not only eastern Poland but lands on the Black Sea.

5. THE WARS OF THE DESPOTS

Between 1485 and 1789 the years of peace in Europe were actually outnumbered by the years of war. The earlier conflicts were largely religious in character and have already been dealt with in the chapter on the Reformation. The majority of the wars after 1600 partook of the nature of struggles for supremacy among the powerful despots of the principal countries. But religion was also a factor in some of them, and so was the greed of the commercial classes. In general, nationalistic motives were much less important than in the wars of the nineteenth and twentieth centuries. Peoples and territories were so many pawns to be moved back and forth in the game of dynastic aggrandizement.

Character of the wars in the age of the despots

The major warfare of the seventeenth century revolved around a titanic duel between Hapsburgs and Bourbons. Originally the rulers of Austria, the Hapsburgs had gradually extended their power over Hungary and Bohemia as well. In addition, the head of the family enjoyed what was left of the distinction of being Holy Roman Emperor. Since the time of Charles V (1519–1556) branches of the Hapsburgs had ruled over Spain, the Netherlands, the Franche-Comté, Alsace, Savoy, Genoa, Milan, and the Kingdom of the Two Sicilies.[8] For many years this expansion of Hapsburg power had been a source of profound disturbance to the rulers of France. They regarded their country as encircled and longed to break through the enclosing ring. But tensions were building up in other parts of Europe also. The princes of Germany looked with alarm upon the growing power of the Holy Roman Emperor and sought opportunities to restrict him in ways that would increase their own stature. The kings of Denmark and Sweden were also developing expansionist ambitions, which could hardly be realized except at the expense of the Hapsburg Empire. Finally, the seeds of religious conflict, sown by the Reformation, were about ready to germinate in a new crop of hostilities. In 1608–1609 two opposing alliances had been formed, based upon principles of religious antagonism. The first was the Evangelical Union headed by Frederick, the Calvinist Elector of the Palatinate. The other was an alliance of Catholic princes under

Underlying causes of conflict

[8] Charles V was the grandson of Ferdinand and Isabella of Spain and became king of that country as Charles I in 1516. Three years later he was made Holy Roman Emperor. He was also the grandson of Maximilian I of Austria and therefore a Hapsburg. When Charles abdicated as Emperor in 1556, his realm was divided. The Spanish and Italian dominions and the colonies in America went to his son Philip II and his central European possessions to his brother, Ferdinand I.

the leadership of Maximilian, Duke of Bavaria. The existence of these mutually hostile leagues added to the tension in central Europe and contributed toward making an eventual explosion almost a certainty. The conflict that followed, known as the Thirty Years' War (1618–1648), was one of the most tragic in history.

The Thirty Years' War

The immediate cause of the Thirty Years' War was an attempt of the Holy Roman Emperor, Matthias, to consolidate his power in Bohemia. Though the Hapsburgs had been overlords of Bohemia for a century, the Czech inhabitants of the country had retained their own king. When the Bohemian throne became vacant in 1618, Matthias conspired to obtain the position for one of his kinsmen, Duke Ferdinand of Styria. By exerting pressure he induced the Bohemian Diet to elect Ferdinand king. The Czech leaders resented this. Both nationalist and Protestant traditions were strong in the country, and Ferdinand was known to be a staunch champion of militant Catholicism. The upshot was the invasion by Czech noblemen of the Emperor's headquarters in Prague and the tossing of his representatives out of the window. Czech leaders then proclaimed Bohemia an independent state with Frederick, the Calvinist Elector Palatine, as king. The war now began in earnest. The success of the Hapsburgs in suppressing the Bohemian revolt and in punishing Frederick by seizing his lands in the valley of the Rhine galvanized the Protestant rulers of northern Europe into action. Not only the German princes but King Christian IV of Denmark and Gustavus Adolphus of Sweden joined the crusade against Austrian aggression —with the additional purpose, of course, of expanding their own dominions. In 1630 the French intervened with donations of arms and money to the Protestant allies, and after 1632, when Gustavus Adolphus was killed in battle, France bore the brunt of the struggle. The war was no longer a religious conflict, but essentially a contest between the Bourbon and Hapsburg houses for mastery of the Continent of Europe. The immediate objectives of Cardinal Richelieu, who was directing affairs for Louis XIII, were to wrest the province of Alsace from the Holy Roman Empire and to weaken the hold of the Spanish Hapsburgs on the Netherlands and on Italy. For a time the French armies suffered reverses, but the organizing genius of Richelieu and of Cardinal Mazarin, who succeeded him in 1643, ultimately brought victory to France and her allies. Peace was restored to a distracted Europe by the Treaty of Westphalia in 1648.

*See color map
at page 40*

Results of the Thirty Years' War

Most of the results of the Thirty Years' War were unmitigated evils. By the Treaty of Westphalia France was confirmed in the possession of Alsace and the bishoprics of Metz, Toul, and Verdun; Sweden received territory in Germany; the independence of Holland and Switzerland was formally acknowledged; and the Holy Roman Empire was reduced to a mere fiction, since each of the German princes was now recognized as a sovereign ruler with power to make war and peace and to govern his state as he chose. But most of these changes merely laid the foundations for bitter international squabbles in the future. In addition, the war wrought terrible havoc in central Europe. Probably few military conflicts since the dawn of history had ever caused so much misery to the civilian population. It is estimated that fully one-third of the people in Germany and Bohemia lost their lives as a consequence of famine and disease and the marauding attacks of brutal soldiers. The armies of both sides pillaged, tortured, burned, and killed in such manner as to convert whole regions into veritable desert. In Saxony one-third of the land went out of cultivation, and packs of wolves roamed through areas where thriving villages once had stood. In the midst of such misery, education and intellectual achievement of every description were bound to decline, with the result that civilization in Germany was retarded by at least a century.

The Thirty Years' War did not even end the rivalry of Bourbons and Hapsburgs. Though France had made notable gains under the Treaty of Westphalia, she was still confronted on her borders by several possessions of her enemy. Spain on the south, the Belgian Netherlands to the north, the Franche-Comté to the east, and the Kingdom of the Two Sicilies continued to be ruled by the Spanish Hapsburgs, while their Austrian kinsmen had never relinquished title to their provinces in the valley of the Rhine. When Louis XIV took personal charge of affairs in France after the death of Mazarin in 1661, he determined to revise these boundaries. First he made an attempt to conquer the Belgian Netherlands, which involved him in a war not only with Spain but eventually with Holland, the Austrian emperor, and the Elector of Brandenburg. When Louis endeavored to supplement his modest conquests in this war by diplomatic intrigue, a powerful alliance was formed against him by the Emperor Leopold of Austria. The war which followed, known as the War of the League of Augsburg (1688–1697), represented a new stage in the struggle between Hapsburg and Bourbon. In his previous contests Louis XIV had been able to count on the neutrality of England because of the traditional rivalry between that country and Holland. But now, since the Glorious Revolution, England had a new king in the person of William III, erstwhile Stadholder of Holland and implacable enemy of France. William promptly enlisted under the banner of the League of Augsburg, along with Sweden, Austria, Spain, and a number of the German states. With so strong a combination against him, Louis was finally compelled to sue for peace.

In 1700 the French king saw what appeared to be a new opportunity. In that year Charles II, king of Spain, died with neither children nor brothers to succeed him, and willed his dominion to the grandson of Louis XIV. The Austrians denounced this settlement,

Final stage: the
War of the
Spanish Suc-
cession

and formed a new alliance with England, Holland, and Brandenburg. The War of the Spanish Succession, which broke out in 1702
when Louis attempted to enforce the claim of his grandson, was the
last important stage in the struggle between Bourbons and Hapsburgs.[9] By the Peace of Utrecht (1713–1714) the grandson of
Louis XIV was permitted to occupy the Spanish throne, on condition that France and Spain should never be united. Nova Scotia and
Newfoundland were transferred to England from France, and
Gibraltar from Spain. The Belgian Netherlands, Naples, and Milan
were given to the Austrian Hapsburgs.

Significance of
the War of the
Spanish Succes-
sion

It would be difficult to exaggerate the significance of the War of
the Spanish Succession. Since it involved most of the nations of Europe and also the lands overseas, it was the first of what can be
called "world wars." It was fought, however, not by mass armies
but chiefly by professional soldiers. It was the prototype, therefore,
of most of the wars of the eighteenth century. These were wars
among kings, in which the masses of the people were little involved.
Among large-scale conflicts the War of the Spanish Succession was
the first in which religion played almost no part. Secular rivalries
over commerce and sea power were the major bones of contention.
The war disposed of the claims of the smaller states to equal rank
with their larger neighbors. Brandenburg and Savoy were the only
important exceptions. The first came to be called Prussia and the
second, Sardinia. Aside from Sardinia, the rest of the Italian states
dwindled into insignificance. Austria henceforth was overshadowed
by Prussia. Holland suffered such a strain from the war that she
ceased to be a prime factor in the competition for world power. With
a Bourbon king on the throne, Spain was reduced to subservience to
France. Her Bourbon dynasty continued to rule, with brief interrup-
tions, until the overthrow of Alphonso XIII in 1931. The War of the
Spanish Succession left France and Great Britain as the two major
powers in Europe. Of these, the latter was the principal victor. Not
only did she acquire valuable possessions, but she muscled her way
into the Spanish commercial empire. By an agreement known as the
Asiento she gained the privilege of providing Spanish America with
African slaves. This privilege opened the way to the smuggling of all
kinds of goods into the Spanish colonies, and contributed toward
making Great Britain the richest nation on earth.

The Seven
Years' War

The most important of the wars of the despots in the eighteenth
century was the Seven Years' War (1756–1763), known in American history as the French and Indian War. The causes of this struggle were closely related to some of the earlier conflicts already
discussed. One of the chief factors in the wars of the League of

---

[9] The War of the Austrian Succession (1740–1748), in which France fought
on the side of Prussia against Great Britain and Austria, also involved a struggle
between Bourbons and Hapsburgs. But the results for France were indecisive:
the war was mainly a duel between Prussia and Austria.

Augsburg and the Spanish Succession had been commercial rivalry
between England and France. Each had been striving for supremacy
in the development of overseas trade and colonial empires. The
Seven Years' War was simply the climax of a struggle which had
been going on for nearly a century. Hostilities began, appropriately
enough, in America as the result of a dispute over possession of the
Ohio valley. Soon the whole question of British or French domination of the North American continent was involved. Eventually,
nearly every major country of Europe was drawn in on one side or
the other. Louis XV of France enlisted the aid of his kinsman, the
Bourbon king of Spain. A struggle begun in 1740 between Frederick
the Great and Maria Theresa over possession of Silesia was quickly
merged with the larger contest. The Seven Years' War thus reached
the proportions of what virtually amounted to a world conflict, with
France, Spain, Austria, and Russia arrayed against Great Britain and
Prussia in Europe, and with English and French colonial forces
striving for mastery not only in America but also in India.

The outcome of the Seven Years' War was exceedingly significant for the later history of Europe. Frederick the Great won a
decisive victory over the Austrians and forced Maria Theresa to
surrender all claims to Silesia. The acquisition of this territory increased the area of Prussia by more than a third, thereby raising the
Hohenzollern kingdom to the status of a first-rank power. In the
struggle for colonial supremacy the British emerged with a sensational triumph. Of her once magnificent empire in America, France
lost all but two tiny islands off the coast of Newfoundland, Guade-
loupe and a few other possessions in the West Indies, and a portion
of Guiana in South America. [10] She was allowed to retain her trading privileges in India, but she was forbidden to build any forts or
maintain any troops in that country. France was now crippled almost beyond hope of recovery. Her treasury was depleted, her
trade almost ruined, and her chances of dominance on the Continent
of Europe completely shattered. These disasters, brought on by the
stupid policies of her rulers, had much to do with preparing the
ground for the great revolution of 1789. By contrast, Britain was
now riding the crest of the wave—in a literal as well as a figurative
sense, for her triumph in the Seven Years' War was a milestone in
her struggle for supremacy on the seas. The wealth from her expanded trade enriched her merchants, thereby enhancing their prestige in political and social affairs. But perhaps most important of all,
her victory in the struggle for colonies gave her an abundance of
raw materials which enabled her to take the lead in the Industrial
Revolution.

[10] All of the territory given up by the French was acquired by Great Britain,
with the exception of Louisiana, which France turned over to Spain as a reward for her part in the war.

6.   THE POLITICAL THEORY OF ABSOLUTISM

The autocratic behavior of the despots in the sixteenth, seventeenth, and eighteenth centuries was not all of their own making. As indicated at the beginning of this chapter, they were encouraged by various economic and political factors for which they were not solely responsible. To these causes must be added another: the influence of political theory. Several of the Stuart and Bourbon kings, for example, derived justification for their policies from philosophers who expressed the prevailing ideas of their time in systematic and forceful writings. These ideas were, of course, not those of the common people, but they did reflect the desires of those whom John Adams used to call "the rich, the well-born, and the able."

The influence of political philosophers in buttressing absolute rule

One of the first of the philosophers to lend encouragement to the absolutist ambitions of monarchs was Jean Bodin (1530–1596), whose zeal in the persecution of witches had earned for him the title of "Satan's Attorney-General." Bodin was not quite so extreme as some of his colleagues in exalting monarchical power. He agreed with the medieval philosophers that rulers were bound by the law of God, and he even acknowledged that the prince had a moral duty to respect the treaties he had signed. But Bodin had no use for parliaments of any description. He emphatically denied the right of a legislative body to impose any limits upon royal power. And while he admitted that princes who violated the divine law or the law of nature were tyrants, he refused to concede that their subjects would have any right of rebellion against them. The authority of the prince is from God, and the supreme obligation of the people is passive obedience. Revolution must be avoided at all costs, for it destroys that stability which is a necessary condition for progress. The main contribution of Bodin, if such it can be called, was his doctrine of sovereignty, which he defined as "supreme power over citizens and subjects, unrestrained by the laws." By this he meant that the prince, who is the only sovereign, is not bound by man-made laws. There is no *legal* restriction upon his authority whatever—nothing except obedience to the natural or moral law ordained by God.

Jean Bodin

The most noted of all the apostles of absolute government was the Englishman Thomas Hobbes (1588–1679). Writing during the Puritan Revolution and in close association with the royalists, Hobbes was disgusted with the turn which events had taken in his native country and longed for a revival of the monarchy. However, his materialism and his doctrine of the secular origin of the kingship made him none too popular with the Stuarts. For the title of his chief work Hobbes chose the name *Leviathan*, to indicate his conception of the state as an all-powerful monster.[11]   All associations

Thomas Hobbes

[11] In the Book of Job, Leviathan is the monster that ruled over the primeval chaos. Job 41:1.

within the state, he declared, are mere "worms in the entrails of Leviathan." The essence of Hobbes' political philosophy is directly related to his theory of the origin of government. He taught that in the beginning all men lived in a state of nature, subject to no law but brutal self-interest. Far from being a paradise of innocence and bliss, the state of nature was a condition of universal misery. Every man's hand was against his neighbor. Life for the individual was "solitary, poor, nasty, brutish, and short." [12] In order to escape from this war of each against all, men eventually united with one another to form a civil society. They drew up a contract surrendering all of their rights to a sovereign, who would be strong enough to protect his subjects from violence. Thus the sovereign, while not a party to the contract, was made the recipient of absolute authority. The people gave up *everything* for the one great blessing of security. In contrast with Bodin, Hobbes did not recognize any law of nature or of God as a limitation upon the authority of the prince. Absolute government, he maintained, had been established by the people themselves, and therefore they would have no ground for complaint if their ruler became a tyrant. On the basis of pure deduction, without any appeal to religion or history, Hobbes arrived at the conclusion that the king is entitled to rule despotically—not because he has been appointed by God, but because the people have *given* him absolute power.

In a sense the great Dutchman, Hugo Grotius (1583–1645), may also be considered an exponent of absolutism; though with him the question of power within the state was more or less incidental to the larger question of relations among the states. Living during the period of religious strife in France, the revolt of the Netherlands, and the Thirty Years' War, Grotius was impressed by the need for a body of rules that would reduce the dealings of governments with one another to a pattern of reason and order. He wrote his famous *Law of War and Peace* to prove that the principles of elemental justice and morality ought to prevail among nations. Some of these principles he derived from the Roman *jus gentium* and some from the medieval law of nature. So well did he present his case that he has been regarded ever since as one of the chief founders of international law. His central doctrine was the idea that every independent state, regardless of its size, must be treated as fully sovereign and entitled to equal rights. This sovereignty must never be infringed by any other power. But Grotius' revulsion against turbulence also inspired him to advocate despotic government. He did not see how order could be preserved within the state unless the ruler possessed unlimited authority. He maintained that in the beginning the people had either surrendered to a ruler voluntarily or had been compelled to submit to superior force; but in either case, having once established a government, they were bound to obey it unquestion-

Hugo Grotius

[12] *Leviathan* (Routledge ed.), p. 81.

ingly forever.

The theories just discussed were not simply those of a few ivory-tower philosophers, but rather the widely accepted ideas of an age when order and security were considered more important than liberty. They reflected the desire of the commercial classes, especially, for the utmost degree of stability and protection in the interest of business. Mercantilism and the policies of the despots went hand in hand with the new theories of absolute rule. The dictum, "I am the state," attributed to Louis XIV, was not just the brazen boast of a tyrant, but came close to expressing the prevailing conception of government—in Continental Europe at least. Those who had a stake in society really believed that the king *was* the state. They could hardly conceive of a government able to protect and assist their economic activities except in terms of centralized and despotic authority. Their attitude was not so far different from that of some people today who believe that a dictatorship of one form or another is our only means for security and plenty.

7. SIGNIFICANCE OF THE AGE OF ABSOLUTISM

The age of absolutism was important not merely for the establishment of absolute monarchies. It bears even greater significance for its effects upon international relations. It was during this period that the modern state system came into existence. During the era of approximately 1000 years after the fall of Rome, states, in the sense in which we now understand the term, scarcely existed in Europe west of the Byzantine Empire. True, there were kings in England and France, but until almost the end of the Middle Ages, their relations with their subjects were essentially those of lords with their vassals. They had *dominium* but not sovereignty. In other words, they had the highest proprietary rights over the lands which constituted their fiefs; they did not necessarily possess supreme political authority over all the persons who lived on their lands. Only through extension of the taxing power, the judicial power, and the establishment of professional armies did such rulers as Philip Augustus of France, Henry II of England, and Frederick II of the Holy Roman Empire take steps toward becoming sovereigns in the modern sense. Even so, their domains continued their essentially feudal character for several more centuries. In yet another respect these rulers were not sovereign: they were not free from external control. In theory, they were subject to the Holy Roman Emperor, who was supposed to have a universal secular authority over Western Christendom. More important, they were responsible for their personal conduct and even for their relations with their subjects to the spiritual authority of the Pope. For example, Pope Innocent III compelled King Philip Augustus of France, by means of an interdict on his kingdom, to take back the wife he had repudiated. The same Pope forced

King John of England to acknowledge England and Ireland as fiefs of the papacy.

By some historians the beginnings of the modern state system are considered to date from the invasion of Italy in 1494 by King Charles VIII of France. Involved in this war for conquest of foreign territory were considerations of dynastic prestige, the balance of power, elaborate diplomacy, and alliances and counteralliances. It was in no sense a religious or ideological war but a struggle for power and territorial aggrandizement. Other historians conceive of the Reformation as the primary cause of the modern state system. The Protestant Revolution broke the unity of Western Christendom. It facilitated the determination of kings and princes to make their own power complete by repudiating the authority of a universal Church. As early as 1555 the Peace of Augsburg gave to each German prince the right to decide whether Lutheranism or Catholicism should be the faith of his people. It was probably the Treaty of Westphalia, however, that played the dominant role in making the modern state system a political reality. This treaty, which ended the Thirty Years' War in 1648, transferred territories from one rule to another with no regard for the nationality of their inhabitants. It recognized the independence of Holland and Switzerland and reduced the Holy Roman Empire to a fiction. Each of the German princes was acknowledged as a sovereign ruler with power to make war and peace and to govern his domain as he chose. Finally, the treaty introduced the principle that *all* states, regardless of their size or power, were equal under international law and endowed with full and complete control over their territories and inhabitants.

Causes of the rise of the state system

Whatever its origins, the modern state system may be considered to embody the following elements: (1) the equality and independence of all states; (2) the right of each state to pursue a foreign policy of its own making, to form alliances and counteralliances, and to wage war for its own advantage; (3) the use of diplomacy as a substitute for war, often involving intrigue, espionage, and treachery to the extent necessary for political advantage; (4) the balance of power as a device for preventing war or for assuring the support of allies if war becomes necessary. Most of these elements of the state system have continued to the present day. Even the establishment of the League of Nations and the United Nations brought no substantial change, for both were founded upon the principle of the sovereign equality of independent states. Some observers believe that there will be no genuine prospect of world peace until the system of sovereign independent states is recognized as obsolete and is replaced by a world community of nations organized on a federal basis.

Elements of the modern state system

SELECTED READINGS

HISTORICAL AND BIOGRAPHICAL

· *Items so designated are available in paperbound editions.*

Adams, G. B., *Constitutional History of England,* New York, 1921. A standard work, still highly regarded.

· Aylmer, G. E., *A Short History of Seventeenth-Century England,* New York, 1963 (Mentor).

· Beloff, Max, *The Age of Absolutism,* New York, 1962 (Torchbook).

Bruun, Geoffrey, *The Enlightened Despots,* New York, 1929. The best short treatise.

Carston, F. L., *The Origins of Prussia,* London, 1954.

Clark, G. N., *The Later Stuarts, 1660–1714,* Oxford, 1934.

· Elliott, J. H., *Imperial Spain, 1469–1716,* New York, 1964 (Mentor).

· Elton, G. R., *The Tudor Revolution in Government,* New York, 1959 (Cambridge University Press). A thoughtful interpretation.

· Ford, Franklin L., *Strasbourg in Transition, 1603–1714,* Cambridge (Norton Library).

· Gardiner, S. R., *Oliver Cromwell,* New York, 1901 (Collier).

Gipson, L. H., *The Great War for the Empire,* New York, 1954.

· Harris, R. W., *A Short History of Eighteenth-Century England,* New York, 1963 (Mentor).

· Hill, Christopher, *The Century of Revolution, 1603–1714,* London, 1963 (Norton Library).

Holborn, Hajo, *A History of Modern Germany: 1648–1840,* New York, 1964.

· Keir, D. L., *The Constitutional History of Modern Britain, Since 1485,* Princeton, 1960 (Norton Library). An excellent introductory survey.

· Neale, J. E., *Queen Elizabeth,* New York, 1931 (Anchor).

Nowak, Frank, *Medieval Slavdom and the Rise of Russia,* New York, 1930.

Ogg, David, *Louis XIV,* New York, 1951. A good brief account.

Packard, L. B., *The Age of Louis XIV,* New York, 1929. An excellent short treatise.

· Pares, Sir Bernard, *A History of Russia,* New York, 1965 (Vintage).

Petrie, C., *Earlier Diplomatic History, 1492–1713,* New York, 1949. Valuable for origins of the state system.

· Pollard, A. F., *Henry VIII,* New York, 1951 (Torchbook).

Riasanovsky, N. V., *A History of Russia,* New York, 1963.

Schenk, W., *The Concern for Social Justice in the Puritan Revolution,* New York, 1948. Valuable and interesting.

Scherger, G. L., *The Evolution of Modern Liberty,* New York, 1904.

· Sumner, B. H., *Peter the Great and the Emergence of Russia,* London, 1950 (Collier).

· Trevelyan, G. M., *England under the Stuarts,* New York, 1904 (Barnes & Noble). Thoughtful and very readable.

· ———, *The English Revolution 1688–1689,* London, 1938 (Galaxy). Emphasizes results.

Trevor-Davies, R., *The Golden Century of Spain,* London, 1937. A good brief account.

Vernadsky, George, *Ancient Russia,* New Haven, 1945.

· Wedgwood, C. V., *The Thirty Years' War,* London, 1938 (Anchor). A complete and well-reasoned account.

———, *Richelieu and the French Monarchy,* New York, 1950.

· Wolf, John B., *The Emergence of the Great Powers, 1685–1715*, New York, 1951 (Torchbook).

Zeeveld, Gordon, *Foundations of Tudor Policy*, Cambridge, 1948.

POLITICAL THEORY

· Allen, J. W., *History of Political Thought in the Sixteenth Century*, New York, 1928 (Barnes & Noble). The standard work, still unsurpassed.
· Figgis, J. N., *The Divine Right of Kings*, Cambridge, 1922 (Torchbook).
· Friedrich, C. J., *The Age of the Baroque, 1610–1660*, New York, 1952 (Torchbook). Emphasizes political theory.

Sabine, G. H., *A History of Political Theory*, New York, 1961. Especially good on sixteenth and seventeenth centuries.

SOURCE MATERIALS

Bodin, Jean, *Six Books Concerning the State*, especially Book I, Chs. I, VI, VIII, X, Cambridge, 1962.
· Grotius, Hugo, *The Law of War and Peace*, especially Prolegomena and Book I, Ch. I, New York, 1963 (Library of Liberal Arts).
· Hobbes, Thomas, *Leviathan*, Part I, Chs. XIII–XV; Part II, Chs. XIII, XVIII, XIX, XXI, XXVI, New York (Library of Liberal Arts and others).

James I, *The Trew Law of Free Monarchies*.

Webster, Hutton, *Historical Selections*, pp. 640–42, "The Bill of Rights."

39

Austria

Brandenburg-
Prussia

The Church

Spain

Boundary of the Holy Roman Empire

RUSSIA

Kiev

POLAND

Warsaw

Vistula R.

E. PRUSSIA

Danzig

BALTIC SEA

Stockholm

Copenhagen

DENMARK

NORTH SEA

SCOTLAND

Edinburgh

IRELAND

Dublin

Liverpool

ENGLAND

London

Bristol

English Channel

ATLANTIC OCEAN

FRANCE

Paris

Seine R.

Loire R.

Bordeaux

Garonne R.

Rhône R.

SPAIN

Madrid

Tagus R.

PORTUGAL

Lisbon

Strait of Gibraltar

BALEARIC ISLANDS

Marseilles

AVIGNON

SAVOY

PIEDMONT

SWITZ.

FRANCHE-COMTE

LORRAINE

SPANISH NETH.

Amsterdam

UNITED PROVINCES

Rhine

Hamburg

HANOVER

MECKLEN-BURG

Berlin

BRANDENBURG

SAXONY

Elbe R.

HESSE

WÜRTEN-BERG

BAVARIA

AUSTRIA

Vienna

HUNGARY

Budapest

Danube R.

MILAN

GENOA

MODENA

PARMA

TUSCANY

Florence

PAPAL STATES

Rome

VENICE

Zara
(To Venice)

Ragusa

Cattaro

Adriatic Sea

CORSICA
(To Genoa)

SARDINIA
(To Spain)

Naples

KINGDOM OF THE TWO SICILIES

MEDITERRANEAN SEA

ALGERIA

TUNIS

OTTOMAN EMPIRE

BLACK SEA

Constantinople

AEGEAN SEA

CYPRUS
(To Ottoman Empire)

CRETE
(To Venice)

To Venice

500 miles

0

The Blue Boy, Thomas Gainsborough (1727–1788). Though the costume suggests the romantic ideal of Prince Charming, the face is a penetrating study of the moodiness and uncertainty of adolescence. (Huntington Library)

Sarah Siddons as the Tragic Muse, Sir Josh Reynolds (1723–1792). Mrs. Siddons, a famo actress of the XVIII cent., is here portrayed the Queen of Tragedy, in accordance with R nolds' habit of depicting wealthy patrons in i pressive classical poses. (Huntington Library)

Le Mezzetin, Antoine Watteau (1684–1721). Mezzetin was a popular character in Italian comedy who was much liked in France. Watteau enjoyed portraying the make-believe world of the court with its festivals and formalized elegance. (MMA)

CHAPTER 2

The Intellectual Revolution
of the Seventeenth and
Eighteenth Centuries

I wish we could derive the rest of the phenomena of nature . . .
from mechanical principles, for I am induced by many reasons
to suspect that they may all depend upon certain forces by which
the particles of bodies, by some causes hitherto unknown, are
either mutually impelled towards one another, and cohere in regular figures, or are repelled and recede from one another. These
forces being unknown, philosophers have hitherto attempted the
search of Nature in vain; but I hope the principles here laid down
will afford some light either to this or some truer method of
philosophy.
—Sir Isaac Newton, Preface to the First Edition,
Mathematical Principles (*Principia Mathematica*)

By one of the strangest ironies of history, the period when arrogant
despots bestrode the nations of the European continent was a period
of stupendous intellectual achievement. To one who understands the
underlying forces at work in this and in preceding ages, however,
the cultural progress of the seventeenth and eighteenth centuries is
not particularly mysterious. The absolute monarchs, of course, had
nothing to do with it. Though a few, like Frederick the Great, dabbled in philosophy and science, not one of them could accurately be
described as a patron of learning. The intellectual advance of their
time was due rather to factors growing out of the principal economic and cultural movements in European history after the end of
the Middle Ages. Characteristic examples were the influence of the
Renaissance, the increasing prosperity of the middle and lower
classes, and the widened intellectual horizons produced by the new
knowledge of distant lands and strange peoples.

Causes of intel-
lectual advance
in the 17th and
18th centuries

The achievements in philosophy and science in the seventeenth and eighteenth centuries, together with the new attitudes resulting therefrom, constitute what is commonly known as the Intellectual Revolution. But to speak of this revolution as if it were an event without precedent in the records of man leads to an erroneous conception of history. On several occasions before this, developments had occurred which went quite as far in upsetting old habits of thinking as did any of the discoveries of the seventeenth and eighteenth centuries. Illustrations may be found in the radicalism and individualism of the Sophists in fifth-century Athens and in the profoundly disturbing effects of the revival of paganism and worldliness in the later Middle Ages. Nevertheless, the Intellectual Revolution of the seventeenth and eighteenth centuries was somewhat broader in scope than any of these earlier upheavals, and its results were perhaps more significant for our own generation.

1. PHILOSOPHY IN THE SEVENTEENTH CENTURY

Perhaps without straining the imagination too much, we can say that the Intellectual Revolution had a triple paternity. Its fathers were René Descartes, Sir Isaac Newton, and John Locke. More will be said later about Newton and Locke. For the present we need to examine the teachings of the renowned Frenchman who initiated the dominant philosophic trend of the seventeenth century. René Descartes (1596–1650), soldier of fortune, mathematician, and physicist, was an unswerving advocate of rationalism in philosophy. He was, of course, not the first exponent of reason as the pathway to knowledge; but his rationalism differed from that of most earlier thinkers—the medieval Scholastics, for instance—in his rigid exclusion of authority. He scorned reliance upon books, no matter how venerable the reputation of their authors. Convinced that both traditional opinion and the ordinary experiences of mankind are untrustworthy guides, he determined to adopt a new method entirely unprejudiced by either. This method was the mathematical instrument of pure deduction. It would consist in starting with simple, self-evident truths or axioms, as in geometry, and then reasoning from these to particular conclusions. Descartes believed that he had found such an axiom in his famous principle: "I think, therefore I am." From this he maintained that it is possible to deduce a sound body of universal knowledge—to prove, for example, that God exists, that man is a thinking animal, and that mind is distinct from matter. These "truths," he declared, are just as infallible as the truths of geometry, for they are products of the same unerring method.

But Descartes is important not only as the father of the new rationalism. He was also partly responsible for introducing the conception of a mechanistic universe. He taught that the whole world of matter, organic and inorganic alike, could be defined in terms of extension and motion. "Give me extension and motion," he once boldly declared, "and I will construct the universe." The entire mass of physical substance, he asserted, is continually moving in a series of whirlpools or vortices, some of them infinitely small and others large enough to carry the planets around their suns. Every individual thing—a solar system, a star, the earth itself—is a self-operating machine propelled by a force arising from the original motion given to the universe by God. Descartes did not even exclude the bodies of animals and of men from this general mechanistic pattern. The whole world of physical nature is one. The behavior of animals and the emotional reactions of men flow automatically from internal or external stimuli. He insisted, however, that man is distinct from all other creatures in the possession of a reasoning faculty. Mind is not a form of matter, but an entirely separate substance implanted in the body of man by God. Its seat is the pineal gland, located in the upper region of the skull. Along with this dualism of mind and matter, Descartes also believed in *innate* ideas. He taught that self-evident truths having no relation to sensory experience must be inherent in the mind itself. Man does not learn them through the use of his senses, but perceives them instinctively because they have been part of his mental equipment from birth.

Of the several teachings of Descartes the new rationalism and mechanism were by far the most influential. In fact, these two doctrines were almost sufficient in themselves to have produced a revolution, for they involved the rejection of nearly all the theological bias of the past. No longer need the philosopher pay homage to revelation as a source of truth; reason was now held to be the solitary fount of knowledge, while the whole idea of spiritual meaning in the universe was cast aside like a worn-out garment. Descartes' principles of rationalism and mechanism were adopted in some form or other by the majority of the philosophers of the seventeenth century. The most noted of his intellectual successors were the Dutch Jew Benedict Spinoza and the Englishman Thomas Hobbes, whom we have already encountered as a political theorist. Benedict (or Baruch) Spinoza was born in Amsterdam in 1632 and died an outcast from his native community forty-five years later. His parents were members of a group of Jewish immigrants who had fled from persecution in Portugal and Spain and had taken refuge in the Netherlands. At an early age Spinoza came under the influence of a disciple of Descartes and as a result grew critical of some of the dogmas of the Hebrew faith. For this he was expelled from the synagogue, cursed by the chief priests and elders, and banished from the community of his people. From 1656 till his death he lived in various cities of Holland, eking out a meager existence by grinding lenses. During these years he developed his philosophy, incorporating the rationalism and mechanism but not the dualism of Descartes.

Descartes' conception of a mechanistic universe

Descartes' intellectual successors

Benedict Spinoza

Spinoza maintained that there is only one essential substance in the universe, of which mind and matter are but different aspects. This single substance is God, who is identical with nature itself. Such a conception of the universe was, of course, pure pantheism; but it was grounded upon reason rather than upon faith, and it was intended to express the scientific notions of the unity of nature and the continuity of cause and effect. It is not without significance that one of the greatest of modern scientists, Albert Einstein, declared that his idea of God was the same as that of Spinoza.

Spinoza's ethical philosophy

Much more than Descartes, Spinoza was interested in ethical questions. Having come to the conclusion early in life that the things men prize most highly—wealth, pleasure, power, and fame—are empty and vain, he set out to inquire whether there was any perfect good which would give lasting and unmitigated happiness to all who attained it. By a process of geometric reasoning he attempted to prove that this perfect good consists in "love of God"—that is, in worship of the order and harmony of nature. If men will but realize that the universe is a beautiful machine, whose operation cannot be interrupted for the benefit of particular persons, they will gain that serenity of mind for which philosophers have yearned through the ages. We can only be delivered from impossible hopes and cringing fears by acknowledging to ourselves that the order of nature is unalterably fixed, and that man cannot change his fate. In other words, we gain true freedom by realizing that we are not free. But with all his determinism, Spinoza was an earnest apostle of tolerance, justice, and rational living. He wrote in defense of religious liberty and, in the face of cruel mistreatment, set a noble example in his personal life of kindliness, humanity, and freedom from vengeful passions.

Thomas Hobbes

The third of the great rationalists of the seventeenth century was Thomas Hobbes. Born before either Descartes or Spinoza, he actually outlived both. Hobbes agreed with his two contemporaries in the belief that geometry furnished the only proper method of discovering philosophic truth. But he denied the doctrine of innate ideas, maintaining that the *origin* of all knowledge is in sense perception. He likewise refused to accept either the dualism of Descartes or the pantheism of Spinoza. According to Hobbes, absolutely nothing exists except matter. Mind is simply motion in the brain or perhaps a subtle form of matter, but in no sense a distinct substance. God, also, if we can believe that He exists, must be assumed to have a physical body. There is nothing spiritual anywhere in the universe of which the mind can conceive. This was the most thoroughgoing materialism to make its appearance since the days of Lucretius. Naturally it was combined with mechanism, as materialism usually is. Hobbes contended that not only the universe but man himself can be explained mechanically. All that man does is determined by appetites or aversions, and these in turn are either inherited or acquired through experience. In similar fashion, Hobbes maintained that there are no absolute standards of good and evil. Good is merely that which gives pleasure; evil, that which brings pain. Thus did Hobbes combine with materialism and mechanism a thoroughgoing philosophy of hedonism.

2. THE ENLIGHTENMENT

The climax of the Intellectual Revolution in philosophy was a movement known as the Enlightenment. Beginning in England about 1680, it quickly spread into most of the countries of northern Europe and was not without influence in America. The supreme manifestation of the Enlightenment, however, was in France, and the period of its real importance was the eighteenth century. Few other movements in history have had such profound effects in molding men's thoughts or in shaping the course of their actions. The philosophy of the Enlightenment was built around a number of significant concepts, chief among which were the following:

The chief philosophical concepts of the Enlightenment

(1) Reason is the only infallible guide to wisdom. All knowledge has its roots in sense perception, but the impressions of our senses are but the raw material of truth, which has to be refined in the crucible of reason before it can have value in explaining the world or in pointing the way to the improvement of life.

(2) The universe is a machine governed by inflexible laws which man cannot override. The order of nature is absolutely uniform and not subject in any way to miracles or to any other form of divine interference.

(3) The future is bright with promise if men will abandon old superstitions and prejudices and live in accordance with the dictates of reason. The leaders of the Enlightenment believed in the possibility of a "heavenly city" delivered from ignorance, intolerance, and oppression. It would be purged also of artificiality and enslavement to outworn conventions. Religion, government, and economic institutions would be reduced to their simplest and most natural forms in order to lessen the possibility of tyranny and greed.[1]

(4) There is no such thing as original sin. Men are not inherently depraved but are driven to acts of cruelty and meanness by scheming priests and war-making despots. The infinite perfectibility of human nature, and therefore of society itself, would become easily realized if men were free to follow the guidance of reason and their own instincts.

The inspiration for the Enlightenment came partly from the rationalism of Descartes, Spinoza, and Hobbes, but the real founders of the movement were Sir Isaac Newton (1642–1727) and John Locke (1632–1704). Although Newton was not a philosopher in the ordinary sense, his work has the deepest significance for the his-

The founders of the Enlightenment: (1) Sir Isaac Newton

[1] The political and economic doctrines of the Enlightenment will be treated more fully in the chapter on the French Revolution.

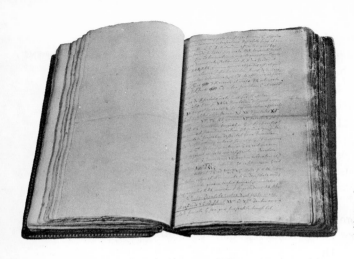

The Manuscript of Newton's *Philosophia Naturalis Principia Mathematica*. The first edition was published in 1687.

tory of thought. His majestic achievement was to bring the whole world of nature under a precise mechanical interpretation. His celebrated principle that "every particle of matter in the universe attracts every other particle with a force varying inversely as the square of the distance between them and directly proportional to the product of their masses" was held to be valid not only on this earth but throughout the endless expanse of solar systems. From this it was an easy step to the conclusion that every event in nature is governed by universal laws, which can be formulated as precisely as mathematical principles. The discovery of these laws is the chief business of science, and the duty of man is to allow them to operate unhindered. Gone was the medieval conception of a universe guided by benevolent purpose; men now dwelt in a world in which the procession of events was as automatic as the ticking of a watch. Newton's philosophy did not rule out the idea of a God, but it deprived Him of His power to guide the stars in their courses or to command the sun to stand still.

(2) John Locke

The influence of John Locke was quite different from that of Newton, but it was scarcely any less important. Locke was the father of a new theory of knowledge, which served as the keynote of the philosophy of the Enlightenment. Rejecting Descartes' doctrine of innate ideas, he maintained that all of man's knowledge originates from sense perception. This theory, known as sensationalism, had already been asserted by Hobbes; but Locke was the first of modern philosophers to develop it in systematic form. He insisted that the human mind at birth is a blank tablet, a "white paper," upon which absolutely nothing is inscribed. It does not even contain the idea of a God or any notions of right and wrong. Not until the newborn child begins to have experiences, to perceive the external world with its senses, is anything registered in its mind. But the simple ideas which result directly from sense perception are merely the foundations of knowledge; no human being could live intelligently on the basis of them alone. These simple ideas must be integrated and fused

46

into *complex ideas*. This is the function of the reason or understanding, which has the power to combine, coordinate, and organize the impressions received from the senses and thus to build a usable body of general truth. Sensation and reason are both indispensable—the one for furnishing the mind with the raw materials of knowledge and the other for working them into meaningful form. It was this combination of sensationalism and rationalism which became one of the basic elements in the philosophy of the Enlightenment. Locke is significant also for his defense of religious toleration and for his liberal political theory, which will be discussed in the chapter on the French Revolution.

The Enlightenment blossomed forth in its fullest glory in France during the eighteenth century under the leadership of Voltaire and other like-minded critics of the established order. Voltaire, or François Marie Arouet as he was originally named, epitomized the Enlightenment in somewhat the same way as Luther did the Reformation or Leonardo da Vinci the Italian Renaissance. A son of the bourgeoisie, Voltaire was born in 1694 and, despite his delicate physique, lived to within eleven years of the outbreak of the French Revolution. He developed a taste for satiric writing early in his life and got himself into numerous scrapes by his ridicule of noblemen and pompous officials. As a consequence of one of his lampoons he was sent to the Bastille and afterwards exiled to England. Here he remained for three years, acquiring a deep admiration for British institutions, and composing his first philosophic work, which he entitled *Letters on the English*. In this work he popularized the ideas of Newton and Locke, whom he had come to regard as two of the greatest geniuses who ever lived. Most of his later writings—the *Philosophical Dictionary, Candide*, his histories, and many of his poems and essays—were also concerned with exposition of the doctrine that the world is governed by natural laws, and that reason and concrete experience are the only dependable guides for man to follow. Voltaire had contempt for the smug optimism which taught that the ills of each make up the good of all, and that everything is for the best in the best of all possible worlds. He saw, on the contrary, universal misery, hatred, strife, and oppression. Only in his utopia of El Dorado, which he placed somewhere in South America, were freedom and peace conceivable. Here there were no monks, no priests, no lawsuits, and no prisons. The inhabitants dwelt together without malice or greed, worshiping God in accordance with the dictates of reason, and solving their problems by logic and science. But this idyllic life was made possible only by the fact that the land was cut off by impassable mountains from the "regimented assassins of Europe."

Voltaire is best known as a champion of individual freedom. He regarded all restrictions upon liberty of speech and opinion as utterly barbarous. In a letter to one of his opponents he wrote what

has often been quoted as the highest criterion of intellectual tolerance: "I do not agree with a word that you say, but I will defend to
the death your right to say it." [2] But if there was any one form of
repression that Voltaire abhorred more than others, it was the
tyranny of organized religion. He blasted with fire and brimstone
against the monstrous cruelty of the Church in torturing and burning intelligent men who dared to question its dogmas. With reference to the whole system of persecuting and privileged orthodoxy,
he adopted as his slogan, "Crush the infamous thing." He was almost
as unsparing in his attacks upon political tyranny, especially when it
resulted in the slaughter of thousands to glut the ambitions of
despots. "It is forbidden to kill," he sarcastically asserted: "therefore
all murderers are punished unless they kill in large numbers and to
the sound of trumpets." [3]

Among the other philosophers of the Enlightenment in France
were Denis Diderot and Jean d'Alembert, both of whom lived in the
latter part of the eighteenth century. Diderot and d'Alembert were
the chief members of a group known as the Encyclopedists, so-
called from their contributions to the *Encyclopedia*, which was
intended to be a complete summation of the philosophic and scientific knowledge of the age. In general, both of them agreed with the
rationalism and liberalism of Voltaire. Diderot, for example, maintained that "men will never be free till the last king is strangled with
the entrails of the last priest." D'Alembert, while accepting the rationalist and individualist tendencies of the Enlightenment, differed
from most of his associates in advocating a diffusion of the new doctrines among all the people. The general attitude of his contempo-

[2] E. B. Hall, *Voltaire in His Letters*, p. 65.
[3] *Philosophical Dictionary*, article on "War."

Voltaire, by Jean Antoine
Houdon (1741–1828). The noted French sculptor seems to
have captured the sardonic attitude of the great foe of superstition and unreason. In front
of Théâtre Français, Paris.

raries, notably Voltaire, was to despise the common man, to regard him as a mere clodhopper beyond redemption from ignorance and grossness. But for d'Alembert the only assurance of progress lay in universal enlightenment. Accordingly, he maintained that the truths of reason and science should be taught to the masses in the hope that eventually the whole world might be freed from darkness and tyranny.

Although the Enlightenment was of much less importance in Germany than in France or England, it did give birth to some progressive ideas. The most widely recognized of its German leaders was Gotthold Lessing (1729–1781), primarily a dramatist and critic but also a philosopher of humane and far-sighted views. The essence of his philosophy is tolerance, founded upon a sincere conviction that no one religion has a monopoly of truth. In his play, *Nathan the Wise*, he expounded the idea that nobility of character has no particular relation to theological creeds. He maintained that, historically, men of charitable spirit were as often found among Jews and Moslems as among Christians. Largely for this reason he condemned adherence to any one system of dogma and taught that the development of each of the world's great religions (Christianity included) was simply a step in the spiritual evolution of mankind. One of Lessing's friends and disciples turned out to be the foremost Jewish philosopher of the Enlightenment. His name was Moses Mendelssohn (1729–1786), and he was a sickly product of the ghetto in the German town of Dessau. Agreeing with Lessing that religions should be judged by their effects upon the conduct of their followers, Mendelssohn urged his Jewish brethren to give up their notion of themselves as the Chosen People of God. They should look upon Judaism merely as one of a number of good religions. He recommended also that Jews should renounce their clannishness, that they should cease to long for a return to Zion, and that they should adapt themselves to the civic requirements of the countries in which they lived. His teachings, along with those of Moses Maimonides, the great rationalist Jew of the twelfth century, were among the principal sources of what has since come to be known as Reform Judaism.

Two other philosophers are commonly given a place in the Enlightenment—the Scotsman David Hume (1711–1776) and the Frenchman Rousseau (1712–1778).[4] Neither, however, was in full agreement with the majority of his contemporaries. Hume is noted above all for his skepticism. He taught that the mind is a mere bundle of impressions, derived exclusively from the senses and tied together by habits of association. That is, we learn from experience to associate warmth with fire and nourishment with bread. If we had never actually experienced the sensation of warmth, no reasoning faculty in our minds would enable us to draw the conclusion

[4] By birth Rousseau was French Swiss, a native of Geneva, but he lived the greater part of his life in France.

that fire produces heat. But constant repetition of the fact that when we see a flame we generally experience warmth leads to the habit of associating the two in our minds. Impressions and associations are all that there is to knowing. Since every idea in the mind is nothing but a copy of a sense impression, it follows that we can know nothing of final causes, the nature of substance, or the origin of the universe. We cannot be sure of any of the conclusions of reason except those which, like the principles of mathematics, can be verified by actual experience. All others are likely to be the products of feelings and desires, of animal urges and fears. In thus denying the competence of reason, Hume placed himself almost entirely outside the main intellectual trend of the Enlightenment. As a matter of fact, he helped to prepare its death.

In similar measure Jean Jacques Rousseau repudiated many of the basic assumptions which had stemmed from Newton and Locke. A hopeless misfit wallowing in the mire of his emotions, Rousseau would have been a marvel indeed if he had championed the rationalist doctrines of the Enlightenment. Whole segments of his personality appear to have been out of joint. He failed in nearly every occupation he undertook. He preached lofty ideals of educational reform, but abandoned his own children to a foundling asylum. He quarreled with everybody and reveled in morbid self-disclosures. Undoubtedly it was these qualities of temperament which were largely responsible for his revolt against the coldly intellectual doctrines of his contemporaries. He maintained that to worship reason as the infallible guide to conduct and truth is to lean upon a broken reed. Reason, of course, has its uses, but it is not the whole answer. In the really vital problems of life it is much safer to rely upon feelings, to follow our instincts and emotions. These are the ways of nature and are therefore more conducive to happiness than the artificial lucubrations of the intellect. The "thinking man is a depraved animal." [5] Yet notwithstanding his contempt for reason, Rousseau was in other ways thoroughly in agreement with the viewpoint of the Enlightenment. He extolled the life of the "noble savage" even more fervently than did any of his associates. In his prize-winning essay, the *Discourse on the Arts and Sciences,* he contrasted the freedom and innocence of primitive men with the tyranny and wickedness of civilized society, even insisting that the progress of learning is destructive of human happiness. He shared the impatience of the Enlightenment with every sort of restriction upon individual freedom, though he was much more concerned about the liberty and equality of the masses than were the other reformers of his time. He regarded the origin of private property as the primary source of misery in human society.

It would be almost impossible to fix limits to the influence of Rousseau. As the first significant writer to uphold the validity of

50   [5] *A Discourse on the Origin of Inequality* (Everyman Library ed.), p. 181.

conclusions dictated by emotion and sentiment he is commonly considered the father of romanticism. For fifty years after his time Europe was bathed in literary tears, and it was difficult to find a philosopher who would boldly assert the inerrancy of reason. His slogan, "Back to nature," furnished the foundation for a veritable cult dedicated to the pursuit of the simple life. The new fashion spread even to the simpering courtiers at Versailles. The queen herself designed a dainty rural village in a corner of the palace grounds and diverted herself by playing milkmaid. But Rousseau's influence was not limited to the founding of romanticism and the encouragement of sentimental devotion to nature. His dogmas of equality and popular sovereignty, though frequently misinterpreted, became the rallying cries of revolutionaries and of thousands of more moderate opponents of the existing regime. And, as the chapter on the French Revolution will show, it was Rousseau's political philosophy that provided the real inspiration for the modern ideal of majority rule.

The most typical religious philosophy of the Enlightenment was deism. The originator of this philosophy appears to have been an Englishman by the name of Lord Herbert of Cherbury (1583–1648). In the eighteenth century deistic doctrines were propagated by such men as Voltaire, Diderot, and Rousseau in France; Alexander Pope, Lord Bolingbroke, and Lord Shaftesbury in England; and Thomas Paine, Benjamin Franklin, and Thomas Jefferson in America. Not satisfied with condemning the irrational elements in religion, the deists went on to denounce every form of organized faith. Christianity was spared no more than the others. Institutionalized religions were branded as instruments of exploitation, devised by wily scoundrels to enable them to prey upon the ignorant masses. As Voltaire expressed it, "the first divine was the first rogue who met the first fool." [6] But the aims of the deists were not all destructive. They were interested not merely in demolishing Christianity but in constructing a simpler and more natural religion to replace it. The fundamental tenets of this new religion were about as follows: (1) there is one God who created the universe and ordained the natural laws that control it; (2) God does not intervene in the affairs of men in this world: He is not a capricious deity, like the God of the Christians and Jews, making "one vessel unto honour and another unto dishonour" in accordance with His peculiar whims; (3) prayer, sacraments, and ritual are mere useless mumbo jumbo; God cannot be wheedled or bribed into setting aside natural law for the benefit of particular persons; (4) man is endowed with freedom of will to choose the good and avoid the evil; there is no predestination of some to be saved and others to be damned, but rewards and punishments in the life hereafter are determined solely by the individual's conduct on earth.

[6] *Philosophical Dictionary*, article on "Religion."

THE
ENLIGHTENMENT

The influence
of Rousseau

The religious
doctrines of the
Enlightenment:
deism

Naïve though many of its assumptions were, the influence of the Enlightenment was tremendous. No other movement, with the possible exception of humanism, had done more to dispel the accumulated fogs of superstition and illogical restraint that still enveloped the Western world. The rationalism of the Enlightenment helped to break the shackles of political tyranny and to weaken the power of conscienceless priests. Its ideal of religious freedom was a leading factor in the ultimate separation of church and state and in the liberation of the Jews from ancient restrictions. The humanitarianism implied in the opposition to oppression carried over into agitation for penal reform and for the abolition of slavery. The desire for a natural order of society contributed to a demand for the overthrow of relics of feudalism and for the destruction of monopoly and unearned privilege. If there was any evil result of the Enlightenment, it probably consisted in an exaggerated development of individualism. Liberty of the individual against political and religious tyranny was unfortunately too easily translated into the right of the strong to satisfy economic greed at the expense of the weak.

3.   REVOLUTIONARY SCIENTIFIC DISCOVERIES

The major scientific interests of the Intellectual Revolution followed very largely the paths marked out during the late Renaissance. Accordingly, primary attention was given to the physical sciences. Unquestionably the most illustrious physicist of the Intellectual Revolution was Sir Isaac Newton. His conclusions molded men's thinking in philosophy for a hundred years. His influence upon science was even more lasting; the Newtonian physics stood virtually unchallenged until the twentieth century. It was in 1687 that Newton published his renowned law of universal gravitation. Based in part upon the work of Galileo, this law provided a single unifying principle for the entire world of matter. Besides, it removed all doubt as to the validity of the Copernican hypothesis and placed the study of celestial mechanics on a firm scientific foundation. But Newton's researches in physics were not confined to the problem of gravitation. He devised a series of tables, of great value to navigation, by which the changing positions of the moon among the stars could be accurately predicted. He invented the sextant for measuring these positions and thereby determining latitude and longitude. His achievements in spectrum analysis proved of substantial value in paving the way for later discoveries regarding the nature of light. He shares with Galileo the honor of being the father of modern physics.

Some preliminary progress was made during the Intellectual Revolution in connection with the understanding of electrical phenomena. At the beginning of the seventeenth century the Englishman William Gilbert (1540–1603), discovered the properties of lodestones and introduced the word "electricity" into the language.[7] Other scientists quickly became interested, and sensational results were anticipated from experiments with the marvelous "fluid." A learned Jesuit even suggested that two persons might communicate at a distance by means of magnetized needles which would point simultaneously to identical letters of the alphabet. Late in the eighteenth century Alessandro Volta (1745–1827) constructed the first battery and proved the identity of "animal magnetism" with electricity. Still another important achievement in electrical physics was the invention in 1746 of the Leyden jar for the storage of electric energy. It was mainly as a result of this invention that Benjamin Franklin was able to show that lightning and electricity are identical. In his celebrated kite experiment in 1752 he succeeded in charging a Leyden jar from a thunderstorm.

Almost as spectacular as the progress in physics was the development of chemistry. If any one scientist can be called the founder of modern chemistry, the title must be given to Robert Boyle (1627–1691). The son of an Irish nobleman, Boyle achieved distinction in 1661 with the publication of his *Sceptical Chymist, or Chymico-Physical Doubts and Paradoxes*. In this work he rejected the theories not only of the alchemists but also of the medico-chemists who followed in the footsteps of Paracelsus.[8] He thereby contributed much toward the establishment of chemistry as a pure science. In addition, he distinguished between a mixture and a compound, learned a great deal about the nature of phosphorus, produced alcohol from wood, suggested the idea of chemical elements, and revived the atomic theory. No scientist before his time had foreshadowed so much of the knowledge of modern chemistry.

Despite the work of Boyle, little further development of chemistry occurred for almost 100 years. The reason lay partly in the wide acceptance of errors concerning such matters as heat, flame, air, and the phenomenon of combustion. The most common of these errors was the so-called phlogiston theory. Phlogiston was the fire substance. When an object burned, phlogiston was given off. The object minus the ash was, therefore, phlogiston. In the second half of the eighteenth century a number of important discoveries were made which ultimately overthrew this theory and cleared the way for a true understanding of some of the most familiar chemical reactions. In 1766 Henry Cavendish, one of the richest men in England, reported the discovery of a new kind of gas obtained by treating iron, zinc, and other metals with sulphuric acid. He showed that this gas, now known as hydrogen, would not of itself support combustion, and yet would be rapidly consumed by a fire with access to the air. In

---

[7] "Electric" comes from the Greek word for amber. Gilbert and others had observed that amber rubbed on fur will attract paper, hair, straw, and various other things. Preserved Smith, *A History of Modern Culture*, I, 63–64.

[8] See pp. 570–71, Volume 1

Lavoisier Demonstrating the Principle of Oxidation.

1774 oxygen was discovered by Joseph Priestley, who had managed for some years to squeeze enough time out of his profession of Unitarian minister to perform some extensive experiments in natural science. He found that a candle would burn with extraordinary vigor when placed in the new gas—a fact which indicated clearly that combustion was not caused by any mysterious principle in the flame itself. A few years after this discovery Cavendish demonstrated that air and water, long supposed to be elements, are a mixture and a compound, respectively, the first being composed principally of oxygen and nitrogen and the second of oxygen and hydrogen.

Lavoisier

The final blow to the phlogiston theory was administered by Antoine Lavoisier (1743–1794), one of the greatest of all scientists of the Intellectual Revolution. By some he has been called "the Newton of Chemistry." Lavoisier proved that both combustion and respiration involve oxidation, the one being rapid and the other slow. He provided the names for oxygen and hydrogen, demonstrated that the diamond is a form of carbon, and argued that life itself is essentially a chemical process. But undoubtedly his greatest accomplishment was his discovery of the law of the conservation of mass. He found evidence that "although matter may alter its state in a series of chemical actions, it does not change in amount; the quantity of matter is the same at the end as at the beginning of every operation, and can be traced by its weight." This "law" has, of course, been modified by later discoveries regarding the structure of the atom and the conversion of some forms of matter into energy. It is hardly too much to say that as a result of Lavoisier's genius chemistry became a true science. To the lasting shame of the French Revolutionists, he was put to death on the guillotine at the age of fifty-one, a victim of the Reign of Terror.

Although it was the physical sciences that received the major attention in the Intellectual Revolution, the biological sciences were by no means neglected. One of the greatest of the early biologists was Robert Hooke (1635–1703), the first man to see and describe the cellular structure of plants. This achievement was soon followed by the work of Marcello Malpighi (1628–1694) in demonstrating the sexuality of plants and in comparing the function of vegetable leaves with that of the lungs of animals. About the same time a Dutch businessman and amateur scientist, Anthony van Leeuwenhoek (1632–1723), discovered protozoa and bacteria and wrote the first description of human spermatozoa. The seventeenth century also witnessed some progress in embryology. About 1670 the Dutch physician, Jan Swammerdam (1637–1680), carefully described the life history of certain insects from the caterpillar stage to maturity and compared the change of tadpole into frog with the development of the human embryo.

The biological
scientists:
Hooke, Malpi-
ghi, Leeuwen-
hoek, and
Swammerdam

In many ways the end of the seventeenth century appeared to mark a decline of originality in the sciences that deal with living things. During the next 100 years biologists were inclined more and more to center their efforts upon description and classification of knowledge already in existence. The most brilliant classifier of biological knowledge was the Swedish scientist, Carl von Linné (1707–1778), more commonly known by his Latinized name of Linnaeus. In his *System of Nature* and in his *Botanical Philosophy* Linnaeus divided all natural objects into three kingdoms: stone, animal, and vegetable. Each of these kingdoms he subdivided into classes, genera, and species. He invented the system of biological nomenclature still in use, by which every plant and animal is designated by two scientific names, the first denoting the genus and the second the species. Thus he called man *Homo sapiens*. Though some people condemned Linnaeus for presuming to rename the animals that Adam had named, his classification was nevertheless widely adopted even in his own time. Despite certain defects which have had to be corrected, it still has its value.

The second great genius of descriptive biology in the eighteenth century was the Frenchman Georges Buffon (1707–1788). His *Natural History* in forty-four volumes, though intended as a summation of practically all science, dealt mainly with man and other vertebrates. While much of the material in this work was taken from the writings of other scientists and from the accounts of travelers, the author did have a unique ability in reducing a vast body of knowledge to orderly arrangement and in enlivening it with his own interpretations. The chief importance of Buffon to us lies in his recognition of the close relationship between man and the higher animals. Though he could never quite bring himself to accept the full implications of the evolutionary theory, he was nonetheless strongly impressed by the striking resemblances among all of the higher species. He admitted the possibility that the entire range of organic forms had descended from a single species.

The development of physiology and medicine progressed rather slowly during the seventeenth century. Among the several reasons, one was the inadequate preparation of physicians, many of whom had begun their professional careers with little more training than a kind of apprenticeship under an older practitioner. Another was the common disrepute in which surgery was held as a mere trade, like that of barber or blacksmith.[9] Perhaps the most serious of all was the prejudice against dissection of human bodies as a basis of anatomical study. As late as 1750 medical schools which engaged in this practice were in danger of destruction by irate mobs. Despite these obstacles some progress was still possible. About 1670 Malpighi and Leeuwenhoek confirmed the famous discovery of Sir William Harvey by observing the actual flow of blood through the network of capillaries connecting the arteries and veins. At approximately the same time an eminent physician of London, Thomas Sydenham, proposed a new theory of fever as nature's attempt to expel diseased material from the system. The substance of this theory is still quite generally accepted; in fact, new evidence has been discovered which strongly confirms it.

The paucity of
medical
achievements in
the 17th century

Medical progress during the eighteenth century was somewhat more rapid. Among the noteworthy achievements were the discovery of blood pressure, the founding of histology or microscopic anatomy, the development of the autopsy as an aid to the study of disease, and the recognition of scarlet fever as a malady distinct from smallpox and measles. But the chief milestones of medical advancement in this period were the adoption of inoculation and the development of vaccination for smallpox. Knowledge of inoculation came originally from the Near East, where it had long been employed by the Saracens. Information concerning its use was relayed to England in 1717 through the letters of Lady Montagu, wife of the British ambassador to Turkey. The first systematic application of the practice in the Western world, however, was due to the efforts of the great Puritan leaders, Cotton and Increase Mather, who implored the physicians of Boston to inoculate their patients in the hope of curbing an epidemic of smallpox which had broken out in 1721. By the middle of the century inoculation was quite generally employed by physicians in Europe and in America. In 1796 the milder method of vaccination was discovered by Edward Jenner. It was now revealed that direct inoculation of human beings with the deadly virus of smallpox was unnecessary: a vaccine manufactured in the body of an animal would be just as effective and much less

[9] As a matter of fact, surgery in northern Europe was very commonly left in the hands of barbers. Surgeons in England are still referred to as "Mr."

0   500 miles

NORTH SEA

SCOTLAND

ADAM SMITH, 1723
△ Edinburgh
HUME, 1711
BURNS, 1759

GOLDSMITH, 1728

ENGLAND

IRELAND

Dublin
SWIFT, 1667
Liverpool

PRIESTLEY, 1733
NEWTON, 1642

RICHARDSON, 1689
S. JOHNSON, 1709
DRYDEN, 1631
PAINE, 1737
WREN, 1632
GAINSBOROUGH, 1727
LOCKE, 1632
FIELDING, 1707
London
HOBBES, 1588

BACON, 1561
DEFOE, 1659
GIBBON, 1737
MILTON, 1608
POPE, 1688

ATLANTIC OCEAN

NETHERLANDS
VERMEER, 1632
REMBRANDT, 1606
Delft
Leiden

VAN DYCK, 1599

WATTEAU, 1684

Seine R.

VOLTAIRE, 1694
LAVOISIER, 1743
Paris

DESCARTES, 1596

DIDEROT, 1713

Dijon

Loire R.

FRANCE

PASCAL, 1623

ROUSSEAU, 1712
Geneva
SWITZ.

MONTESQUIEU, 1689

Bordeaux

Garonne R.

Toulouse

Rhine R.

HOLY ROMAN EMPIRE

Göttingen
RUBENS, 1577
BACH, 1685
HANDEL, 1685

Berlin

Erfurt

Prague

GOETHE, 1749
Frankfurt
Nuremberg
Mannheim

Danube R.

KEPLER, 1571
Munich
Salzburg
MOZART, 1756

Vienna

HAYDN, 1732

AUSTRIA

HUNGARY

Rhone R.

Verona △

Turin △
Genoa
Bologna △
Florence △
GALILEO, 1564

ITALY

Marseilles

DENMARK

Copenhagen

KANT, 1724
Königsberg

Hamburg

Elbe R.

POLAND

Vistula R.

Oder R.

OTTOMAN EMPIRE

ADRIATIC SEA

Rome △

CORSICA

BERNINI, 1598
Naples

Barcelona

PORTUGAL
Tagus R.
Lisbon

Madrid

SPAIN

BALEARIC
ISLANDS

SARDINIA

VELAZQUEZ, 1599
Seville

MEDITERRANEAN SEA

SICILY

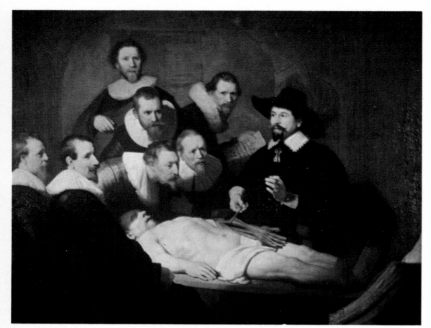

The Anatomy Lesson, Rembrandt van Rijn (1606–1669). Rembrandt scorned the classical themes of most of his contemporaries and turned to character analysis and the portrayal of life. (Mauritshuis, The Hague)

Execution of the Rioters, Francisco Goya (1746–1828). Unlike most artists of his time, Goya dealt unflinchingly with suffering, violence, fear, and death. Depicted here is the execution of Spanish rebels by Napoleon's soldiers in 1808. This harshness caused the rebellion to spread over the whole peninsula. (Prado)

likely to have disastrous results. Vast possibilities were thus opened up for the elimination of contagious diseases.

4. CLASSICISM IN ART AND LITERATURE

In so far as there was any one purpose dominating the art and literature of the seventeenth and eighteenth centuries, it was the desire to preserve or recapture the spirit of ancient Greece and Rome. The artists and writers of the Intellectual Revolution strove to imitate classical models. They chose classical titles and themes for many of their works and embellished them wherever possible with allusions to antique mythology. Deploring the destruction of ancient civilization by "Christian barbarians," they were unable to see much value in the cultural achievements of later centuries. In particular, they despised the Middle Ages as a long night of barbaric darkness. Doubtless most of them would have agreed with the dictum of Rousseau that the Gothic cathedrals were "a disgrace to those who had the patience to build them." In all of these attitudes the men of the Intellectual Revolution were following in the footsteps of the humanists. Devotion to the achievements of classical antiquity was at least one important element of Renaissance culture that had not yet died out. Nevertheless, it must not be forgotten that the classicism of the seventeenth and eighteenth centuries was by no means exactly the same as that of the humanists. As a rule, it was more sentimental, grandiose, and extravagant. Besides, it was less sincere, since it was frequently employed for the glorification of cynical monarchs and their corrupt and frivolous dependents. Finally, classicism was now perhaps even less a universal theme than it had been during the age of the Renaissance. A number of the great artists and writers of the seventeenth and eighteenth centuries sought to escape from its influence entirely.

The nature of the new classicism

The leading arts to be developed during the age of the Intellectual Revolution were architecture and painting. Sculpture ceased to be an independent art, as it had been in the Renaissance, and was relegated to its earlier function of a mere aid to the adornment of buildings. The prevailing style of architecture in the seventeenth century was the so-called baroque. Originating in Italy, it spread to France, England, and Spain and was eventually adopted for churches, palaces, opera houses, museums, and government buildings in practically every Western country. In European capitals to this day it meets the eye in every direction. Among its celebrated monuments still standing are the Luxembourg palace and the main palaces at Versailles in France, St. Paul's Cathedral in London, the government buildings in Vienna and Brussels, and the palaces of the Tsars at Peterhof near Leningrad in Russia. The most noted of the baroque architects were Giovanni Lorenzo Bernini (1598–1680), who de-

Classicism in architecture: the baroque style

Altar of S. Peter's Church in Vienna. This lavishly sculptured alcove is one of the finest examples of a baroque interior.

signed the colonnade and square in front of St. Peter's Church in Rome, and Sir Christopher Wren (1632–1723), whose masterpiece was St. Paul's Cathedral. The baroque style was supposed to be founded upon the architecture of ancient Rome, but it was much more lavish than anything the Romans produced. Its principal features were hugeness, artificiality, extravagance of ornamentation, and the extensive use of such "classical" elements as the column, the dome, and sculptured representations of mythological scenes. So much detail was added to the surface of the buildings that they often give the impression of having been carved, like the altars in medieval churches. A similar passion for splendor and magnificence was reflected in the enrichment of interiors with gilt and silver, flashing mirrors, and colored marble. Originally, baroque architecture was a style inspired by the Catholic Reformation. It represented an attempt by the Church to strengthen its hold upon Catholics through manifestations of grandeur and magnificence. Later it was used by rulers of the chief dynastic states to symbolize their power and opulence.

During the eighteenth century the heavy and pompous architectural style of the age of Louis XIV gave way to still other adaptations of the classical. The first to be developed was the rococo architecture in France, so called from the fantastic scrolls and shell-like designs which were commonly employed for ornamentation. The rococo differed from the baroque not only in being lighter but also in the impression of grace and sumptuous refinement it was intended to create. In place of a struggle for dynastic power and for colonial empire, it was now the indolent ease and elegant manners of the court of Louis XV which set the standard for French society. A

The rococo and Georgian styles

more delicate and effeminate architecture seemed to be necessary to accompany this change. Well-known examples of the rococo style are the Petit Trianon at Versailles and the palace of Sans Souci at Potsdam, built by Frederick the Great. About the middle of the eighteenth century a reaction set in against both the rococo and the baroque, and efforts were made to produce a truer and less flamboyant imitation of the classical. Perhaps the best results were achieved in England and in the American colonies with the development of the so-called Georgian style, named for the era when the four Georges reigned successively as kings of England (1714–1830) and known on this side of the ocean as colonial architecture. Though the Georgian retained certain elements of the baroque—the columns, the dormer windows, and often the cupola or dome—it at least had the classical merit of simplicity.

To a certain extent the evolution of painting during the seventeenth and eighteenth centuries paralleled that of architecture. The greatest of the painters who may be considered to have expressed the baroque tradition were the Flemings, Peter Paul Rubens (1577–1640) and Anthony Van Dyck (1599–1641), and the Spaniard, Diego Velázquez (1599–1660). Rubens was not merely the outstanding genius among these three, but he was the greatest of all the Flemish painters. In such famous works as *The Fates Spinning*

Classicism in painting: the baroque tradition

See color plates at page 9

Versailles. The colossal palace of Louis XIV was nearly a third of a mile long and was surrounded by formal gardens decorated with baroque statuary and fountains.

THREE MASTER PAINTERS OF THE SEVENTEENTH CENTURY

Anthony Van Dyck, *Portrait of a Sitting Man* (opposite page, top left). Like his master Rubens, Van Dyck frequently portrayed rulers and nobles.

Peter Paul Rubens, *Portrait of His Two Sons* (opposite page, top right) and *Venus and Adonis* (opposite page, bottom). Rubens often painted classical themes which he conceived on a grand scale and executed with sweeping vigor.

Rembrandt van Rijn, *Old Woman in an Armchair* (at right) and *Aristotle Contemplating the Bust of Homer* (below). The most philosophical of Dutch painters, Rembrandt is noted for his profound studies of human nature.

and *Venus and Adonis* he combined classical themes with the sumptuous color and richness so pleasing to the affluent burghers and nobles of his day. The pink and rounded flesh of his full-blown nudes is thoroughly in keeping with the robust vitality of the age. Both Rubens and his gifted pupil, Anthony Van Dyck, are noted for their portraits of rulers and nobles. These were done in highly aristocratic fashion with full attention to the gorgeous details of elegant apparel and opulent furnishings in the background. Van Dyck's best-known portraits are those of the English kings, James I and Charles I, and their families. Velázquez, the third great artist of the baroque tradition, was the court painter to Philip IV of Spain. Much of his work consisted of paintings of royal faces, suffused in soft and silvery light but empty of meaning or emotional expression.

All of the painters mentioned thus far were exponents in some degree of the classical influence. But there were others in both the seventeenth and eighteenth centuries who refused to be bound by the prevailing artistic conventions. Foremost among them was Rembrandt van Rijn (1606–1669), now universally acclaimed as one of the greatest painters of all time. The son of a well-to-do miller of Leyden, Rembrandt was allowed to begin his artistic education at an early age. Under a series of native masters he learned the technique of subtle coloring and skillful depiction of the unusual in nature. Famous by the time he was twenty-five, he fell upon evil days later in his life, mainly as a consequence of bad investments and the failure of critics to appreciate his more recondite works. In 1656 he was stripped by his creditors of all he possessed, even to his table linen, and driven from his house. Apparently these reverses served mainly to broaden and deepen his philosophy, for in this very same year he produced some of his greatest achievements. As a painter Rembrandt surpassed all the other members of the Dutch school and deserves to be ranked with the great masters of the High Renaissance in Italy. No artist had a keener understanding of the problems and trials of human nature or a stronger perception of the mysteries of this life. His portraits, including those of himself, are imbued with an introspective quality and with a suggestion that the half is not being told. The subjects he delighted to paint were not the incidents of classical mythology but solemn rabbis, tattered beggars, and scenes from the Old and New Testaments, rich in drama and in human interest. Some of his best-known works include *The Good Samaritan*, *The Woman Taken in Adultery*, *The Marriage of Samson*, and *The Night Watch*.

Two other noted artists of the period of the Intellectual Revolution also departed widely from the classical tradition. The first was the Dutchman Frans Hals (1580–1666) and the second was the Spaniard Francisco Goya (1746–1828). Like his great contemporary Rembrandt, Hals insisted upon choosing the subjects he liked, regardless of whether they conformed to the notions of

*The painters who defied classical conventions:
(1) Rembrandt*

See color plates at page 57

(2) Hals and Goya

62

genteel critics. Most of his works are realistic portraits. He loved to depict the imbecilic grin in the face of the tavern drunkard, the naïve enthusiasm of itinerant singers and players, or the bewildered misery of some beaten and hopeless derelict. Goya was not merely a rebel against accepted artistic standards but a political and social revolutionary as well. He detested the aristocracy, despised the Church, and ridiculed the hypocrisy of respectable society. But he reserved his deepest contempt for absolute monarchy. His *Charles IV on Horseback* has been called "the most impudent portrait of royalty ever painted." Goya also made use of his talents to indict the cruelty of war, especially during the period when Europe was ravaged by Napoleon's armies.

See color plates at page 57

The history of literature in the seventeenth and eighteenth centuries exhibited tendencies quite similar to those of art. The most popular literary ideal was classicism, which generally meant not only a studied imitation of classical forms but also an earnest devotion to reason as a way of life, on the assumption that the Greeks and Romans had been rationalists above everything else. Although classicism was not confined to any one country, its principal center was France. Here lived during the reign of Louis XIV a distinguished company of poets and dramatists, who gave more genuine luster to their country than had ever been won by the Grand Monarch in his boldest exploits of diplomacy and war. The most noted member of this company was Jean-Baptiste Poquelin (1622–1673), who is much better known by his adopted name of Molière. Much of the work of these writers was marked by qualities similar to those of the baroque in art: it was decorative, turgid, affected, artificial, and in general expressive of a tendency to subordinate content to form. The writings of Molière, however, stand out as a brilliant exception. Less respectful of ancient formalism than any of his associates, Molière was the most original of French comedians. Few keener critics of human nature have ever lived. "The business of comedy," he once declared, "is to represent in general all the defects of men and especially of the men of our time." The mortal weakness he delighted most to ridicule was pretentiousness. But with all of his penchant for satire, Molière had a measure of pity for the evil fortunes of men. In a number of his plays sympathy and even melancholy go hand in hand with clever wit and pungent scorn. His genius was probably broader in scope than that of any other dramatist since Shakespeare.

Classicism in literature: the French poets and dramatists

England also had a luxuriant growth of literary effort in the classical style. The first great master of this style as applied to English literature was the renowned Puritan poet, John Milton (1608–1674). The leading philosopher of the Puritan Revolution, Milton wrote the official defense of the beheading of Charles I and later on held the position of Secretary for Foreign Tongues under Cromwell's Commonwealth. Nearly all of his writings were phrased in

John Milton

the rich and stately expression of the classical tradition, while many of the lesser ones revolved about themes from Greek mythology. But Milton was as much a Puritan as he was a classicist. He could never quite get away from the idea that the essence of beauty is morality. Moreover, he was deeply interested in theological problems. His greatest work, *Paradise Lost*, is a synthesis of the religious beliefs of his age, a majestic epic of the Protestant faith. In spite of the fact that Milton was a Puritan, his views in this work departed widely from Calvinist dogma. Its principal themes are the moral responsibility of the individual and the importance of knowledge as an instrument of virtue. Paradise is lost repeatedly in human life to the extent that man allows passion to triumph over reason in determining the course of his actions. Milton also threw Calvinist doctrine to the winds in his *Areopagitica*, perhaps the most eloquent defense of freedom of speech in the English language.

Classicism in English literature reached its zenith in the eighteenth century in the poetry of Alexander Pope (1688–1744) and in the writings of a score of masters of prose. Pope was the great exponent in verse of the mechanistic and deistic doctrines of the Enlightenment. In such works as his *Essay on Man* and his *Essay on Criticism* he set forth the view that nature is governed by inflexible laws, and that man must study and follow nature if he would bring any semblance of order into human affairs. The chief masters of prose who wrote under classicist influence were the journalist and writer of popular fiction Daniel Defoe (1660?–1731); the satirist Jonathan Swift (1667–1745); and the historian Edward Gibbon (1737–1794), author of *The Decline and Fall of the Roman Empire*.

Alexander Pope and the masters of English prose

The age of classicism in English prose was also the period that witnessed the origin of the modern novel. To some extent the new literary form was anticipated in Spain by the picaresque tale recounting the adventures of a young rogue and in England by Daniel Defoe's *Robinson Crusoe*, a story based upon the fictional adventures of a shipwrecked sailor who had spent five years on a desolate island off the coast of Chile. But the true modern novel, with its more or less elaborate plot of human behavior and its psychological analysis of life and love, springs from the work of Samuel Richardson (1689–1761) and Henry Fielding (1707–1754). In 1740 Richardson published his *Pamela, or Virtue Rewarded*, an involved and priggish account of the attempts of a Mr. B. to seduce his virtuous serving maid. Nine years later came Fielding's *The History of Tom Jones*, acclaimed by some critics as the greatest novel in the English language. Rich in humor and in colorful description of manners and customs, it is also free from the sentimentality of Richardson's works. The novels of Richardson and Fielding provided the inspiration for innumerable others, not only in England but on the Continent of Europe as well.

The origin of the modern novel

Earlier in this chapter we learned that the rationalistic and mechanistic philosophy of the Enlightenment was followed by a romantic revolt, expressed first of all in the teachings of Rousseau. We have now to observe that an almost identical development took place in literature. Beginning about 1750 a reaction set in against the intellectualism and high-flown formalism involved in the classical tradition. A group of writers now demanded a return to simplicity and naturalism with less attention to man as a rational creature and more to his instincts and feelings. No longer was it considered disgraceful for the poet to show sympathy or pity or to display any other of his deepest emotions; the heart should rule the head, at least in all cases where problems vital to man's happiness were concerned. No longer was nature regarded as a cold, automatic machine but worshiped as the embodiment of beauty, sublimity, and charm, or tenderly revered as a source of protection and solace. God now ceased to be a mere First Cause and came to be identified with the universe itself or mystically adored as the soul of nature. Still another element in the romantic ideal was glorification of the common man, often accompanied by a generous compassion for the weak and oppressed. Although some of this regard for the lowly had been implied in the humanitarianism of the Enlightenment, most of the leaders of that movement had little respect for the masses. Now under the influence of romanticism the humble herdsman and peasant were given a recognition in literature long overdue.

Though literary romanticism had its roots in France in such sentimental works as *Émile* and *The New Héloïse* of Rousseau, the movement attained its most vigorous development in Great Britain and Germany. Among the eighteenth-century romantic poets in Britain were Thomas Gray (1716–1771), author of the *Elegy Written in a Country Churchyard;* and, to a certain extent, Oliver Goldsmith (1728–1774), who celebrated the rustic innocence of Auburn, "loveliest village of the plain." The most original of them all, however, was the Scotsman Robert Burns (1759-1796). In his homely dialect verse the romantic feeling for nature and sympathy for the common man received their finest expression. No writer has inspired more tenderness for the humblest things of this earth or filled the world with a deeper respect for those who toil for their bread. Moreover, Burns was unique among poets of his age in combining an extraordinary pathos with a delicate touch of humor. He had the rare gift of being passionately earnest without being solemn. In the very last years of the eighteenth century two other romantic poets began their literary activities on British soil. Their names were William Wordsworth and Samuel Taylor Coleridge. But since most of the work of these men was done in the nineteenth century, they can be discussed more appropriately in a later chapter.

The romantic movement in German literature developed primarily under the brilliant guidance of Friedrich Schiller (1759–1805) and Johann Wolfgang von Goethe (1749–1832). Schiller grew up

during the period of the *Sturm und Drang* (Storm and Stress),
when writers all over Germany were denouncing restraints and
conventions and attempting to free the culture of their country
from foreign domination. As a consequence his romanticism generally embraced as its important elements the idealization of heroic
deeds and the glorification of struggles for freedom. While a strong
quality of individualism pervades a number of his plays, especially
The Robbers and *The Maid of Orleans,* Schiller's conception of
liberty seems to have been closely akin to nationalism. This is revealed quite clearly in his *William Tell,* a drama of the struggle of
the Swiss against Austrian tyranny. This nationalistic aspect of
Schiller's work was probably the one which had the major influence
upon later German writers.

The greatest name in the history of German literature is unquestionably that of Schiller's older contemporary, Johann Wolfgang
von Goethe. The two men were associated for a number of years at
the court of the Duke of Weimar. Born in Frankfurt, the son of a
family of ample means, Goethe was educated for the law but soon
found the limits of knowledge in that profession unsatisfying. His
indefatigable spirit drove him to the study of medicine, and then
of the fine arts and the natural sciences.[10] His first important literary
production was *The Sorrows of Young Werther,* a romantic novel
about a love-sick youth who takes his own life with the pistol of his
rival and friend. Written in dashing sentimental style, it attained an
enormous popularity not only in Germany but also in England and
France. Though·the author apparently intended that it should express the idea that weakness of character is the greatest of sins, it
came to be taken as a symbol of profound dissatisfaction with the
world and as a basis of fiery revolt. In 1790 Goethe published the
first part of his drama *Faust,* which he finally completed in 1831, a
year before his death. Universally acknowledged as his grandest
achievement, *Faust* not only epitomizes the personal philosophy of
the author but expresses the spirit of the modern age as few other
writings have done. Part I reflects some of the quality of rebellion in
the *Sturm und Drang,* but in Part II the conviction grows that freedom from restraint is not enough; the individual must go on in an
endless quest for mastery of all knowledge and for enrichment of
life through unlimited experience. Considered as a whole, the drama
is a symbol of perpetual unrest, of that ceaseless yearning for the
fullness of life which has come to be one of the most distinctive
traits of modern civilization.

[10] Goethe's achievements as a scientist were by no means insignificant. His
studies of the development of plants and animals contributed much to our
knowledge of comparative morphology. About 1785 he discovered that a formation in the human jawbone is analogous to the corresponding formation in
the jaw of the higher apes. Long before Darwin and even before Lamarck, he
convinced himself by his own researches that organic evolution is a fact.

5. MUSIC IN THE SEVENTEENTH AND EIGHTEENTH CENTURIES

As was observed in a preceding chapter,[11] the sixteenth century marked the culmination of a long era of music illustrated by choral works of polyphonic structure. The seventeenth opens with a general rebellion against polyphony, a rebellion so powerful and pervasive that the Palestrinian style became completely archaic within twenty-five years of the death of its creator. The new ideal, a primary voice *accompanied* by one or several instruments, which swept Italy in an incredibly short time, became known as *monody*. One of the main reasons for this radical change was the Italians' powerful dramatic instinct; they realized that the feelings of an individual cannot be expressed by a many-voiced chorus. The same trends that created modern theater and the dramatic architecture of the Jesuits invaded music and led to the creation of opera, which reached its first magnificent manifestation in *Orfeo* (1607) by Claudio Monteverdi (1567–1643), the dominating musical personality in the first half of the new century. Within a generation operas were performed in most important cities in Italy, and by 1736 Venice boasted an opera house for every parish. Now the already respectable instrumental music of the Renaissance began to make rapid gains and a fine literature arose for beautifully constructed instruments—organ, harpsichord, and the various string and wind instruments. In the last third of the century instrumental music created the concerto, along with opera one of the greatest original stylistic accomplishments of the Italian baroque. Both opera and concerto spread beyond the Alps and conquered every country, producing national offshoots. In the meantime the Germans, still adhering to their polyphonic tradition, fostered a distinguished school of Lutheran composers. In France, Jean Baptiste Lully (1632–1687), the creator of French lyric tragedy, was a true contemporary of Racine, while in England Henry Purcell (*ca.*1659–1695) crowned the century with his fine anthems and engaging theater music. Though the seventeenth century was preoccupied with experiments, it created an impressive synthesis upon which the first half of the eighteenth century could build the final great edifices of the late baroque.

The late baroque culminated in two towering figures: Johann Sebastian Bach (1685–1750) and George Frederick Handel (1685–1759). Though both of them were born in Saxony, Bach became the epitome of German musical genius, while Handel, who lived for almost half a century in London and became a British subject, embodied an English national style. Bach combined an unbounded imagination and a capacious intellect with heroic powers of discipline

The birth of opera and the concerto

Johann Sebastian Bach

---

[11] See § 6 in the chapter on The Expansion of the Renaissance.

and an unquenchable zeal for work. By lifelong study he made himself the master of most existing types and styles of music, from little dance pieces for the clavichord to gigantic choral works. Being a church musician, Bach's duty was to provide new music for the elaborate Sunday and holy day services. Therefore the bulk of his work is made up of cantatas (over 200 preserved), oratorios, Passions, and Masses. His settings of the Gospel according to St. John and St. Matthew represent the unsurpassable peak of this genre. Fundamentally, though, Bach was an instrumental composer, the creator of tremen-

Johann Sebastian Bach (1685–1750).

dous works for the organ and harpsichord. Then there are his spacious concertos, sonatas for various combinations of instruments, and suites for orchestra. Bach was still steeped in an almost medieval German Protestant mysticism that no longer fitted the age of the Enlightenment. Thus it happened that soon after his death he was overshadowed by a musical world devoted to more mundane aims. But when the nineteenth century rediscovered him his influence became paramount; to this day composers "return" to Bach for inspiration and guidance.

Handel was the absolute antithesis of his great fellow-Saxon. George Frederick Handel After four years spent in Italy he completely absorbed Italian techniques and modes of composition, subsequently settling in England where for years he ran an opera company that produced

nothing but Italian operas, mostly his own. Though many of these are masterpieces that we are just beginning to appreciate, the fact remains that Italian opera did not suit the taste of the large English middle class public, and after decades spent in composing and producing dozens of operas, Handel finally realized that he must turn to something more acceptable to the English mind. This he found in the "oratorio," a rather loose definition for the English music drama intended for an ideal theater. With the exception of *Messiah*, the most famous of the oratorios, these works were not religious music, although the themes came from the Old Testament. Undoubtedly one reason for Handel's success in his adopted country was the fact that his virile and heroic oratorios symbolized the English people, their pride in their institutions and their attainment of national greatness. Handel lived in circumstances wholly different from those permitted to Bach and most other Continental composers. He was not a salaried artisan but a free citizen, an English squire who ran his own business and left behind a respectable estate.

After a transition era in music led by J.S. Bach's gifted sons we reach the period dominated by the Viennese School, so called because its leading masters were active in or near the Austrian capital. By about 1770 a remarkable stylistic synthesis reconciled baroque weightiness, rococo charm, and pre-romantic excitement. This peace between warring extremes created an island in the romantic stream, an art that truly deserves the term applied to it: classicism. Vienna now assimilated every musical thought, from Naples to Hamburg. Christoph Willibald Gluck (1714–1787) reformed the declining "serious" opera into a noble drama that recalls the tone of classical antiquity. But the mischievous, Italian comic opera, the *opera buffa*, was victorious in the end and forced a fusion with the serious opera which reached its unsurpassable height in the operas of Wolfgang Amadeus Mozart (1756–1791), while chamber and orchestral music reached a new formal and expressive level under the leadership of Joseph Haydn (1732–1809).

The eighteenth century was full of music, but its social organization was as cruel to the creative artist as is our own free society. If the artist was not employed by a court, noble house, church, or municipality, if he was not an internationally acclaimed virtuoso or a renowned teacher, he was ground up in the effort to make a living. Mozart was among the first to shed the security of the "musical lackey" and try the free artistic economy of the metropolis. While a child prodigy he was adored and admired, but when he left the employ of the Archbishop of Salzburg to take up the career of a free lance artist in Vienna, a shadow fell over him that he was not able to elude. The remaining ten years of his life were spent in bountiful productivity. Yet he had to live from hand to mouth—the world was not yet ready for the independent artist.

When appraising the music of the classical era we must realize that in spite of the magnificent sonatas and symphonies, the stylistic

The birth of classicism in music

Mozart; his early life

core of the era was still in dramatic music. This classical music, with its clear, absolute forms, emphasized on the stage everything that is permanent and finite. Mozart used these forms to shape the characters, fates, and conflicts of human beings in a way that they too became permanent and finite. Drama and melody, characterization and absolute form evolve simultaneously on Mozart's stage. Each great opera—*The Marriage of Figaro, Don Giovanni, The Magic Flute*—provides a center around which cluster piano sonatas, quartets, quintets, concertos, and symphonies. The nineteenth century's likening of Mozart to Apollo was neither an accident nor a mistake, but men failed to understand that hidden behind the Appollonian poise and smile were deep wounds.

Haydn was carved from harder timber than Mozart; his peasant background made him tenacious and stubborn. If Mozart embodied the aristocratic spirit, Haydn did that of the liberated plebeian. It was because of their diametrically opposed personalities that the two musicians got along so well; they complemented each other, learned from each other, and fulfilled the hopes and aspirations of the second half of the eighteenth century. Haydn had a sharp intellect and he acquired his extensive knowledge of music through incessant study and experimentation. His art conveys the impressions of the village and the countryside, but also the elegance of the princely household that employed him for many years, as well as the solemnity of the cathedral. Haydn's compositions are so numerous that a complete edition of them has never been made. They include many operas and Masses, oratorios, concertos, over eighty string quartets, and more than 100 symphonies. It was Haydn who firmly established the technical and stylistic principles of symphonic construction, creating, with Mozart, the pattern of the symphony orchestra which remained the basis for all future developments.

6. SOCIAL IDEALS AND REALITIES DURING THE AGE OF THE ENLIGHTENMENT

A movement as profoundly disturbing to Western society as the Intellectual Revolution was bound to have its effects upon social customs and individual habits. These effects were especially discernible during the bloom of the Enlightenment in the eighteenth century. Of course, not all of the social progress of this time can be traced to intellectual influences; much of it derived from the bulging prosperity induced by the expansion of trade in the Commercial Revolution. Nevertheless, the progress of philosophy and science had more than incidental effects in clearing away the cobwebs of ancient prejudice and in building a more liberal and humane society.

Causes of the
social changes
of this period

Mention has already been made of the influence of the Enlightenment in promoting the cause of social reform. A characteristic expression of this influence was agitation for revision of drastic criminal codes and for more liberal treatment of prisoners. In regard to both, the need for reform was urgent. Penalties even for minor offenses were exceedingly severe in practically all countries, death being the punishment for stealing a horse or a sheep or for the theft of as little as five shillings in money. During the first half of the eighteenth century no fewer than sixty crimes were added to the capital list in England. The treatment accorded to bankrupts and debtors was also a standing disgrace. Beaten and starved by cruel jailers, they died by the thousands in filthy prisons. Conditions such as these eventually challenged the sympathies of several reformers. Foremost among them was Cesare Beccaria, a jurist of Milan, who had been deeply influenced by the writings of French rationalist philosophers. In 1764 he published his famed treatise on *Crimes and Punishments,* in which he condemned the common theory that penalties should be made as horrible as possible in order to deter potential offenders. Insisting that the purpose of criminal codes should be the prevention of crime and the reform of the wayward rather than vengeance, he urged the abolition of torture as unworthy of civilized nations. He likewise condemned capital punishment as contrary to the natural rights of man, since it cannot be revoked in case of error. Beccaria's book created a veritable sensation. It was translated into a dozen languages, and it stimulated efforts to improve conditions in many lands. By the end of the eighteenth century considerable progress had been made in reducing the severity of penalties, in relieving debtors from punishment, and in providing work and better food for prisoners.

The humanitarian spirit of the Enlightenment found an outlet also in other directions. Several of the scientists and philosophers, notably Buffon and Rousseau, denounced the evils of slavery. Many more condemned the slave trade. The efforts of intellectuals in this regard were warmly seconded by the leaders of certain religious groups, especially by prominent Quakers in America. Even John Wesley, conservative as he was on many social issues, branded slavery as an abomination. Pacifism was another ideal of many of the new liberal thinkers. Voltaire's strictures on war, which have already been related, were by no means the only example of such sentiments. Even the sentimental Rousseau could perceive the illogic in Grotius' attempt to draw a distinction between just and unjust wars. From the pens of other *philosophes* emanated various ingenious plans for insuring perpetual peace, including a scheme for a league of nations with power to take concerted action against aggressors.[12]

Perhaps it was natural that humanitarian agitation for reform should be accompanied by an increase of sympathy for the lower classes. This was especially true during the final stage of the Enlightenment. With the progress of reason and the increasing emphasis upon the natural rights of man, the strong reaction against the

Social idealism: (1) the reform of criminal codes

(2) opposition to slavery and war

(3) increase of sympathy for the lower classes

[12] This was the famous scheme of the Abbé de Saint-Pierre (1658–1743).

evils of slavery and war was eventually translated into a protest against every form of suffering and oppression. Thus the hardships of the poor came in for a larger share of attention than they had received since the time of the Sophists. Besides, the middle class, in the pursuit of its ambition to dethrone the aristocracy, needed the support of the peasants and urban workers. Out of such factors there developed a tendency on the part of leading thinkers to espouse the cause of the common man. In some quarters, it became popular to despise aristocratic lineage or royal birth. Thomas Paine echoed the sentiments of many when he declared that a single honest plowman was worth more than all the crowned ruffians who ever lived. The great Scottish economist, Adam Smith, deplored the habit of feeling more pity for a royal scoundrel like Charles I than for the thousands of common citizens slaughtered in the civil war. Several of the French philosophers of the Enlightenment went considerably farther in professions of sympathy for the masses. Gabriel de Mably (1709–1785), the Marquis de Condorcet (1743–1794), and Rousseau advocated an absolute equality of freedom and privileges for every man. Mably and Condorcet, at least, perceived that this could not be attained except by a redistribution of wealth. While they did not propose socialism, they nevertheless argued that landed property should be held in substantially equal amounts, so that exploitation of the poor by the rich would be practically impossible.

The attempt to
discover a new
basis for
morality

The majority of the philosophers of the Enlightenment inclined to the view that morality is rooted in the psychological instincts of the individual or in considerations of social utility. Those who held to the doctrine of an instinctive basis argued that all human conduct is determined by self-interest, by the pursuit of pleasure and the avoidance of pain. They believed that proper education would enable each individual to perceive that his own self-interest lay in not hurting others, and that ultimately very little restraint would be necessary. David Hume and Adam Smith evolved a somewhat broader theory, contending that morality is determined largely by reflective sympathy. Man, they declared, has a tendency to project himself into the situation of persons around him and to imagine how he would feel under similar circumstances. If the condition of others is wretched, he himself experiences pain, while happiness in others gives rise to sensations of pleasure. Consequently men are impelled by nature to do those things which will promote the happiness of their fellow creatures and especially to avoid those things which will cause suffering. This ethical philosophy was developed most fully in Adam Smith's *Theory of Moral Sentiments* (1759).

The revolt against the moral ideals expounded by theologians was reflected not only in the books of the philosophers; it was also revealed in the principal customs and social practices of the time. The eighteenth century, in particular, was an age of pampered elegance and gracious living decidedly at variance with the ascetic taboos of

Canvassing for Votes, by William Hogarth (1697–1764). For our knowledge of social life in the eighteenth century we are indebted to the satirical engravings of Hogarth. Bribery seems to be the chief lubricant of the electoral process depicted here.

the church. The houses of the nobles were resplendently furnished with shining mirrors, crystal chandeliers, and graceful sofas and chairs richly upolstered in brocaded silk. Men of the upper classes arrayed themselves in powdered wigs, velvet coats with lace at the cuffs, silk stockings, and knee breeches of delicate hue. Not since the days of the Renaissance had fashion played so dominant a part in the lives of both sexes. Habits of personal behavior were also characterized by similar qualities of elegance and artificiality. Form was everything; motive, nothing. The ladies and gentlemen of the best society addressed even those whom they cordially hated with the most fulsome compliments and groveled disgustingly in the presence of higher rank. In a satirical treatise on etiquette, published about 1750, the courtly ceremony of bowing was described, with some measure of truth, as "departing from the perpendicular little by little until the whole spine is presented to the person one is bowing to, as much as to say to him, 'Will your lordship do me the honor of cudgelling me?' " [13]

Actually, among the upper classes, manners very largely took the

Morality as exemplified in the customs and practices of the upper classes

[13] Quoted by Preserved Smith, *A History of Modern Culture*, II, 607.

The more vio-
lent and brut-
ish aspects of
18th-century
society

place of morals. The ladies and gentlemen who danced the stately minuet and deported themselves with such charming grace quite commonly ridiculed married love as a relic of a benighted past. Adultery became fashionable and almost a virtue. A husband sometimes lived on friendly terms with his wife's lovers, for no one in this cultivated society would be so uncouth as to display any sentiment of jealousy. Prostitution had not only its apologists but also its defenders, and brothels were quite commonly permitted to remain open on Sundays, though theaters had to be closed. The prevailing attitude toward relations between the sexes appears to have been that of Buffon, who declared that "there is nothing good in love but the physical."

Eighteenth-century society also had its more violent and brutish aspects, which were largely survivals from the turbulent days of the Renaissance. Despite the severity of penal laws, vicious crimes were still very common. In many large cities bands of hooligans roamed the streets at night, while footpads infested the highways in the open country. In London such hoodlums were known as Mohawks, and their favorite diversions, aside from robbery, were beating constables, "turning women upside down," and gouging out the eyes of any who tried to restrain them. Drunkenness continued in much the same measure as before, though the consumption of hard liquor by the poorer classes appears to have increased. About this time gin became popular, especially in England, as the poor man's drink. Gambling and cruel games and sports likewise survived unabated. Yet another of the prevailing vices of this period was dueling, although it was confined primarily to the upper and middle classes. The gentleman of spirit was still supposed to avenge any real or imaginary insult by challenging the offender to a mortal combat with sword or pistol. Even so prominent a statesman as William Pitt the younger felt obliged to meet an opponent on the so-called field of honor.

It is necessary to observe, however, that the picture of social conditions in the eighteenth century was not altogether dark. For one thing, there was a definite improvement in the standard of living, certainly for the middle classes and probably even for some of the poor. This is evidenced by the increasing per capita consumption of sugar, chocolate, coffee, and tea, which were not merely substituted for other foods and beverages but were additions to the average diet. The growing demand for linen and cotton cloth, and for such articles of luxury as mahogany furniture designed by such masters as Chippendale, Hepplewhite, and Sheraton, may be taken as a further indication of rising prosperity. Such evidences applied, however, only to a small proportion of the population, chiefly to the nobles and to the merchants, bankers, and lawyers in the larger cities. The life of the peasants, with a few exceptions, was still one of privation. In England large tenant farmers enjoyed some luxuries, but the condition of the small, independent yeomen was far from prosperous. Because of instability of prices, increasing taxes, and the costs of new farming methods, many were forced down into the ranks of agricultural wage earners. In France the peasants constituted about 80 per cent of the population, but less than one-twentieth of them owned their land. The remainder were serfs, tenant farmers, and *métayers,* who were required to surrender half of the produce of the lands they occupied to the lord. Most wretched of all were the peasants of eastern Europe. In East Prussia peasants often had to work from three to six days a week for their lord, and some had only late evening or night hours to cultivate their own lands. In Russia landlords had the power of life and death over their serfs, and could sell them apart from the land and even apart from their families.

The other of the more favorable aspects of social life during the age of the Enlightenment was a sharp reduction of the death rate. This came about as the result of several causes. Probably the most important was the effective control of smallpox as a consequence of inoculation and vaccination. A second factor was the establishment of maternity hospitals, which, in combination with improved obstetrical methods, reduced the mortality among infants in the second half of the century by more than 50 per cent and among mothers by an even larger proportion. Finally, advancement in sanitation, together with the adoption of more hygienic habits by people of all classes, contributed not a little to the conquest of various diseases and to lengthening the span of life.

Improvements in health and sanitation

SELECTED READINGS

PHILOSOPHY

· *Items so designated are available in paperbound editions.*

· Artz, F. B., *From the Renaissance to Romanticism: 1300–1820,* Chicago, 1962 (Phoenix).

· Becker, C. L., *The Heavenly City of the Eighteenth Century Philosophers,* New Haven, 1932 (Yale University Press).

Brandes, Georg, *Voltaire,* New York, 1930, 2 vols. A brilliant evaluation by a distinguished critic.

Bury, J. B., *History of the Freedom of Thought,* New York, 1913.

· Cassirer, Ernest, *Philosophy of the Enlightenment,* Princeton, 1952 (Beacon). A difficult book, but the student who studies it carefully will find it rewarding.

Chapman, J. W., *Rousseau—Totalitarian or Liberal?* New York, 1956.

· Church, W. F., *The Influence of the Enlightenment on the French Revolution,* New York, 1964 (Heath).

Green, F. C., *Jean-Jacques Rousseau: A Critical Study of His Life and Writings,* New York, 1955.

· Hazard, Paul, *European Thought in the Eighteenth Century,* New York, 1954 (Meridian).

Hearnshaw, Fossey, ed., *The Social and Political Ideas of Some Great French Thinkers of the Age of Reason*, London, 1930. Sketchy but interesting evaluations.

Hibben, J. G., *The Philosophy of the Enlightenment*, Princeton, 1910.

Kropotkin, Peter, *Ethics: Origin and Development*, New York, 1924. Stimulating and suggestive.

Lecky, W. E. H., *History of the Rise and Influence of the Spirit of Rationalism in Europe*, New York, 1914, 2 vols. A classic.

· Lovejoy, Arthur, *Essays in the History of Ideas*, Baltimore, 1948 (Capricorn). Includes good chapters on the Intellectual Revolution.

· McGiffert, A. C., *Protestant Thought before Kant*, New York, 1915 (Torchbook). An excellent survey.

· Manuel, Frank E., *The Age of Reason*, Ithaca, 1951 (Cornell).

· Martin, Kingsley, *The Rise of French Liberal Thought*, New York, 1954, 2d rev. edn. A brilliant but somewhat biased account. Also available in paperback under the title, *French Liberal Thought in the Eighteenth Century: A Study of Political Ideas from Bayle to Condorcet* (Torchbook).

Morais, H. M., *Deism in Eighteenth Century America*, New York, 1934.

Morley, John, *Rousseau*, New York, 1891, 2 vols.

———, *Voltaire*, New York, 1871.

Mowat, R. B., *The Age of Reason*, New York, 1934. A good general account.

· Muller, H. J., *Religion and Freedom in the Modern World*, Chicago, 1963 (Phoenix).

Randall, J. H., Jr., *The Making of the Modern Mind*, New York, 1926. Chs. XI, XII, XVI.

Rowe, Constance, *Voltaire and the State*, New York, 1955.

· Rudé, George, *The Crowd in History: A Study of Popular Disturbances in France and England, 1730–1848*, New York, 1964 (Wiley).

Schapiro, J. S., *Condorcet and the Rise of Liberalism in France*, New York, 1934.

· Smith, Preserved, *A History of Modern Culture*, New York, 1934, Vol. II (Collier).

· Snyder, L. L., *The Age of Reason*, Princeton, 1953 (Anvil). Includes a good interpretive essay as well as selections from original sources.

· Stephen, Leslie, *History of English Thought in the Eighteenth Century*, New York, 1927 (Harbinger, 2 vols.).

Vaughan, C. E., *The Romantic Revolt*, New York, 1930.

SCIENCE

· Butterfield, Herbert, *The Origins of Modern Science*, New York, 1951 (Collier).

· Hall, A. R., *The Scientific Revolution, 1500–1800*, Boston, 1956 (Beacon).

· Hogben, Lancelot, *Mathematics for the Million*, New York, 1937 (Pocket Book).

Nordenskiöld, Erik, *The History of Biology*, New York, 1928.

Singer, Charles, *A Short History of Medicine*, New York, 1928.

· Smith, Preserved, *History of Modern Culture*, New York, 1934, Vol. II (Collier).

Taylor, Frank, *Galileo and the Freedom of Thought*, London, 1938.

LITERATURE, ART, AND MUSIC

Bukofzer, Manfred F., *Music in the Baroque Era*, New York, 1947.

Davenport, Marcia, *Mozart*, New York, 1932.

· Guérard, A. L., *France in the Classical Age: Life and Death of an Ideal*, New York, 1928 (Torchbook).

Lang, Paul, *Music in Western Civilization*, New York, 1941.

———, *George Friedrich Handel*, New York, 1966.

Machlis, Joseph, *The Enjoyment of Music*, rev. ed., New York, 1963. Excellent.

Robertson, J. G., *A History of German Literature*, New York, 1930.

· Schweitzer, Albert, *J. S. Bach*, London, 1923, 2 vols. (Bruce Humphries, 2 vols.).

· Stephen, Leslie, *English Literature and Society in the Eighteenth Century*, New York, 1907 (Barnes & Noble).

Vaughan, C. E., *The Romantic Revolt*, New York, 1930.

Wright, C. H. C., *French Classicism*, Cambridge, Mass., 1920.

SOURCE MATERIALS

Baumer, F. L. V., *Main Currents of European Thought*, New York, 1952.

· Descartes, René, *Discourse on Method*, Parts I, II, V (Library of Liberal Arts and others).

· Milton, John, *Areopagitica; The Tenure of Kings and Magistrates* (Appleton-Century-Crofts, Inc.).

Newton, Sir Isaac, *Principia, Third Book*. Rules of Reasoning in Philosophy.

Spinoza, Benedict, *A Theological-Political Treatise*.

Voltaire, *Philosophical Dictionary; Candide; Essay on Toleration*.

· Redman, B. R., ed., *The Portable Voltaire*, New York, 1949 (Viking).

CHAPTER 3

India and the Far East during the Early Modern Era (*ca.* 1500-1800)

Fuji-ichi was a clever man, and his substantial fortune was amassed in his own lifetime. . . . In addition to carrying on his regular business, he kept a separate ledger, bound from odd scraps of paper, in which, as he sat all day in his shop, pen in hand, he entered a variety of chance information. As the clerks from the money exchanges passed by he noted down the market ratio of copper and gold; he inquired about the current quotations of the rice brokers; he sought information from druggists' and haberdashers' assistants on the state of the market at Nagasaki; for the latest news on the prices of ginned cotton, salt, and saké, he noted the various days on which the Kyoto dealers received dispatches from the Edo branch shops. Every day a thousand things were entered in his book, and people came to Fuji-ichi if they were ever in doubt. He became a valuable asset to the citizens of Kyoto.

—I. Saikaku, *The Tycoon of All Tenants* (1688)

Between the sixteenth and the nineteenth centuries a reinvigorated Indian empire headed by a new dynasty attained the rank of a major power; China, under the last of a long series of imperial dynasties, waxed even stronger, becoming the largest and most populous country in the world; and Japan adapted her feudal institutions to the requirements of a despotic government. In both India and China, and to a lesser degree in Japan, splendor and magnificence reflected the tastes of wealthy societies and mighty rulers, as was also true in much of Europe during this same period. In the long run, however, the great Asian states found themselves at a disadvantage because they played a passive rather than an active role in the Commercial Revolution. As Western European nations turned to empire-building and expanded their naval forces, they established direct contacts with the coastal regions of Asia, took over the bulk of the trade between East and West, and frequently

Impact of the West upon the East

79

threatened the independence of non-European peoples. For several centuries the principal Eastern states were strong enough to protect themselves against the threat of aggression from the West. Faced with rigid trade restrictions in China and almost totally excluded from Japan, the seafaring Europeans turned to other quarters. In the 1570's the Spanish occupied the Philippines, subduing the native tribes and the communities of Chinese colonists in the Islands. A few years later the Dutch, through their East India Company, laid the foundations of a rich empire in Indonesia, dislodging the Portuguese who had preceded them by almost a century. The British and French somewhat belatedly turned their attention to the mainland of India, where they secured valuable trading posts in the course of the seventeenth century.

1. INDIA UNDER THE MOGUL DYNASTY

In the sixteenth century a new invasion of India by Moslem forces from the north produced very different results from those that had accompanied the Turkish inroads and the institution of the Delhi Sultanate. It led to the establishment of the dynasty known as the Mogul—a Persian variant of the word "Mongol"—which created an efficient and, on the whole, successful pattern of government and, most significant, demonstrated the possibility of an integration of the Indian people regardless of religious profession. Actually, the ruling family and the administrative officers were far from pure-blooded Mongols. Babur ("the Tiger"), the founder of the dynasty, was descended on his father's side from Timur (of Turkish stock) and on his mother's side from the Mongol conqueror Genghis Khan. His own descendants were of mixed parentage, including Turkish, Persian, and Indian strains. Babur, like many another conqueror, began his career as the head of a small state in Turkestan. By advancing into Afghanistan he secured control of the frontier mountain passes commanding the route to the Punjab. Within the space of five years (ended by his death in 1530) he conquered the greater part of Hindustan, while retaining his territories in Afghanistan and southern Turkestan. His conquest was facilitated by the fact that he possessed artillery and match-fired muskets of European manufacture, although these guns were very primitive. The empire which Babur had begun to mark out was fully established and also given its most distinctive character by his grandson, Akbar.

Akbar, deservedly termed "the Great Mogul," was truly remarkable both as a personality and as a sovereign. He is generally considered India's greatest ruler, although he evidently fell short of the noble idealism exemplified by Asoka some 1800 years earlier. Perhaps the scarcity of records for Asoka's reign makes a comparison unfair. At any rate, enough data are available for Akbar's period to

Babur "the Tiger"

Akbar, the Great Mogul

show that he was unquestionably one of the world's outstanding
political figures in the sixteenth century. His reign was a long
one—from 1556 to 1605 (the dates almost coincide with the reign
of Elizabeth I of England). Much of it was devoted to schemes of
conquest, unsuccessfully in the Deccan but resulting in the extension of Mogul authority over all northern India and the neighboring portion of Afghanistan. Far more important was Akbar's determination to conciliate and secure the support of the Hindu population, a decision to which he adhered inflexibly throughout his
reign. For his large harem (said to number over 5000) he chose
wives of several different nationalities, partly with an eye toward
political expediency. By contracting marriage alliances with the
proud Rajput clans (whose spirit had never been broken by the
Turks) he hoped to win their allegiance. (Akbar's favorite wife
and the mother of his successor to the throne was a Rajput princess.) Early in his reign he took the important step of abolishing the
special taxes on non-Moslems, and he appointed Hindus—especially
Rajputs—to civil and military office. A Hindu raja served in the
highly responsible post of minister of finance. Akbar abandoned
entirely all attempts to win converts to Islam by coercion and introduced a policy of religious toleration, although he tried to discourage those Hindu practices which he considered reprehensible,
such as animal sacrifice, child marriage, and suttee.

Akbar's administration was bureaucratic and relatively efficient.
At the head of each of the provinces and districts into which he
divided the state he placed a military governor who was paid a   Akbar's
generous salary but was required to maintain a prescribed number administrative
of troops and was held to a strict accountability for his actions. methods
Thus the government was not feudal in basis, although there was a
nobility of various grades (including some Hindus and Indian Moslems as well as Moguls). While Akbar was unable to keep an adequate check on every part of his large dominions, he made a
sincere effort to enforce justice among his mixed population, and
he severely punished officials whose corruption was detected. The
criminal code was a savage one, but not more barbarous than in
most European countries of that day. Civil law was based largely
upon Islamic tradition and the Koran. Akbar's chief source of
revenue was a land tax, assessed upon the fields actually under cultivation and amounting to one-third of the annual value of the
crop, based on the average yield over a ten-year period. Undoubtedly the rate of assessment was exorbitant, imposing a heavy
burden upon the cultivators; but it was applied uniformly, receipts
were issued to the taxpayers, and there were safeguards against the
cupidity of local officials.

The latter part of Akbar's long reign was generally peaceful, and,
in spite of the invasions and the murderous strife of preceding centuries, a high level of prosperity seems to have been reached in **81**

India. Akbar maintained a sound currency, typified by gold coins of extraordinary fineness. Commerce throve, cities expanded, and a substantial middle class of traders and skilled artisans flourished. Common laborers, however, were far from prosperous, and many were slaves. The country villagers also, who made up the majority of the population, apparently subsisted on a very low standard of living. Great wealth and lavish display were confined to large landowners and officials and were most conspicuous in the court of the emperor. It is estimated that Akbar's total revenue from all sources was equal to more than $200,000,000 a year.

Prosperity for the rich, hardships for the poor

Akbar's unusual personality and rare combination of interests left their mark upon all aspects of his reign. Endowed with a superb physique, he loved feats of strength and dangerous exploits, sometimes risking his life in the most reckless fashion by attacking a lion singlehanded or by riding wild elephants. In a fit of temper he could be pitilessly cruel, but he was generally fair in judgment and frequently generous to a defeated opponent. This high-strung emperor was endowed with lively intellectual curiosity and a capacious mind. He is credited with several inventions, chiefly in connection with the improvement of artillery. Although he stubbornly

Abkar's personality and his cultural interests

Turkish Prisoners Before Timur. Indian painting from the period of Akbar (1556-1605). The use of Arabic script as a decorative device reflects the Moslem influence.

THE MOGUL EMPIRE IN INDIA

THE MOGUL EMPIRE:

Under Akbar, 1556-1605

Expansion under Shah Jahan, 1627-1658
and Aurangzeb, 1658-1707

refused to learn to read or write, he was fond of literature and
metaphysical speculation and collected a huge library. A gifted
musician, he not only acquired skill as a performer (especially on a
type of kettle drum) but also became versed in the highly intricate
theory of Hindu vocalization. The promotion of art and architecture was another of his ardent pursuits.

The Mogul rulers did not lack heirs, but each reign usually
ended with princes revolting against their father and joining in
fratricidal strife with one another. Nevertheless, the administrative
system and policies of Akbar were retained substantially for half a
century after his death. The most renowned of his successors was **83**

**The sumptuous
tastes of Akbar's
successors**

Shah Jahan, whose reign extended from 1627 to 1658. Shah Jahan devoted much of his resources to peaceful pursuits, especially the erection of costly buildings to gratify a sumptuous but exquisite taste. He established his chief royal residence at Delhi, where he laid out a new city and named it after himself. Both Delhi and Agra in the seventeenth century were among the world's greatest cities in respect to number of inhabitants and impressive public buildings. Agra, with a population of 600,000, was divided into separate sections for the different types of merchants and artisans and contained seventy great mosques and 800 public baths. The new Delhi was protected by walls rising 60 feet above the river. Here was constructed a huge royal palace that beggars description. It housed the famous Peacock Throne, inlaid with precious metals and jewels, the value of which has been estimated as in excess of $5,000,000. Shah Jahan's most celebrated monument is the Taj Mahal, located at Agra and designed as a mausoleum and memorial to his favorite wife (who died while bearing her fourteenth child to the emperor). The Taj engaged the labor of 20,000 workmen and was some fifteen years in construction. The design of the building is of dubious architectural integrity; its charm lies largely in its setting, amid shaded walks, lakes, and gardens.

**The Maratha
Confederacy**

Before the Moguls had completed their cycle of power, they were confronted with a hostile Hindu confederacy known as the Marathas, located in the hilly region of the western Deccan. The Maratha tribesmen, reputedly of the lowest (*sudra*) caste, were a sturdy people who, under the leadership of their wily and resourceful king Sivaji, became a scourge to the Moguls' supremacy. Masters of guerilla tactics, the Marathas could not be crushed, even though their strongholds were taken and the "Mountain Rat"

The Taj Mahal at Agra. Built by Shah Jahan in memory of Mumtaz Mahal, it is considered one of the finest examples of Indian Moslem architecture.

Left: *Mumtaz Mahal ("Ornament of the Palace")*. Favorite wife of Shah Jahan, who died in childbirth in 1631 at the age of 39.
Right: *Shah Jahan (1627-1658)*. The Mogul Emperor was famous for his luxurious court and his magnificent buildings.

(Sivaji) was himself held captive for a time. The confederacy became a state within the state, collecting taxes and governing a large section of the Deccan, apparently with greater satisfaction to the inhabitants than under the Mogul administration.

Another Hindu element which acquired an undying hatred for the Moguls was the Sikhs of the Punjab. In origin the Sikhs were a religious group with progressive and idealistic convictions. The sect **The Sikhs** had been founded in the fifteenth century by Nanak, a philanthropic and spiritually minded preacher who sought to establish a common bond between Hindus and Moslems. The essence of his teaching was the brotherhood of man, the oneness of God, and the duty of acts of charity:

> Make love thy mosque; sincerity thy prayer-carpet; justice thy Koran;
> Modesty thy circumcision; courtesy thy Kaaba; truth thy Guru; charity thy creed and prayer;
> The will of God thy rosary, and God will preserve thine honor, O Nanak.[1]

Thus Nanak's religion was a blend of Islamic and Hindu doctrines but rejected formal scriptures and mechanical rites. Because he utterly repudiated caste he gained many adherents from among the depressed classes of Hindus. Akbar had treated the Sikhs kindly and made a grant of land to their Guru (spiritual teacher), but the

[1] Quoted in H. G. Rawlinson, *India, A Short Cultural History*, p. 378. **85**

hostility of later Moguls goaded them to fury. The sect which had begun as a peaceful reformist movement was gradually transformed into a military order. Its members were initiated by a rite called "Baptism of the Sword," and many of them adopted the surname Singh, meaning "Lion." While they retained an antipathy toward caste and subscribed to a strict code of personal discipline, they lost much of the generous idealism of their early leaders. Appearing sometimes as no better than brigands, they showed particular relish for slaughtering Moslems. Thus at the opening of the eighteenth century the Mogul power was menaced not only by the usual court intrigues but also by the spirited defiance of powerful Hindu groups—Rajputs, Marathas, and Sikhs.

Aurangzeb

The long and calamitous reign of Shah Jahan's son Aurangzeb (1658–1707) pushed the empire to its farthest territorial limits but drained it of much of its strength. A man of tremendous energy, sobriety, and fanatical piety, Aurangzeb sacrificed almost every principle of prudent statesmanship in a futile attempt to establish religious conformity and orthodoxy. He demolished Hindu temples and revived the hated poll tax on non-Moslems which Akbar had wisely rescinded. He waged wars not only against Hindu princes but also against heretical Moslem states in the Deccan. Although he devoted some 25 years to military campaigns and won many victories, he created enemies faster than he could subdue them and he left the Marathas—whom he had tried to destroy—more firmly united than ever.

The sack of Delhi (1739)

One further catastrophe robbed the Mogul Dynasty of most of its remaining vitality, although the Moguls were accorded the formal dignity of ruling sovereigns until long after the British had entrenched themselves in India. In 1739 a usurper to the throne of Persia, Nadir Shah, invaded India and sacked Delhi with terrific carnage. He carried off an enormous quantity of booty, including the Peacock Throne, and left much of the city in ruins.

Cultural advancement: architecture

The Mogul period in India was one of considerable activity in intellectual and artistic fields. The emperors were generally cosmopolitan in outlook and welcomed both commercial and cultural intercourse with foreign states. A fusion of Indian, Turkish, Arabic, and Persian elements took place as manifested in literature, the arts, and the general tone of society. As might be expected, architecture illustrates most perfectly the interaction of Hindu and Islamic motifs. Moslem builders introduced the minaret or spire, the pointed arch, and the bulbous dome; Hindu and Jain traditions emphasized horizontal lines and elaborate ornamentation. Because Indian stonemasons and architects were frequently employed even on Moslem religious edifices, there was bound to be a fruitful interchange of ideas, and this culminated in the sixteenth and seventeenth centuries in the production of a distinctive Indo-Moslem architectural style. Some of Akbar's constructions at Agra, of durable red sandstone, are still standing; and so is most of an entire city which he conceived and had completed at a site a few miles west of Agra and then abandoned only five years later. But Akbar's forts and government halls lacked the choice materials, the refinement, and the sensuous beauty of the buildings executed for Shah Jahan a half-century later. In place of sandstone, these employed the finest marbles, agate, turquoise, and other semi-precious stones, and were frequently decorated with inlays of gold and silver. Shah Jahan's dazzling structures, contrasting markedly with the robustness of Akbar's work, betray an excessive elegance bordering on decadence.

The Islamic taboos against pictorial representation were almost totally disregarded by the Mogul rulers, who were enthusiastic collectors and connoisseurs of painting. Reflecting the influence of contemporary Persian art, the most typical examples of painting were miniatures, including landscapes and especially portraits, executed with realism and meticulous detail. Calligraphy also enjoyed the status of a fine art, and many manuscripts were illuminated with pictures as in medieval Europe. Texts from the Koran were employed as decorative devices on screens and the façades of buildings, in keeping with a general practice in Moslem countries.

Painting and calligraphy

Probably the most significant expression of Indian creative talent during the Mogul period was literature, which was stimulated by royal patronage and also by the fact that several languages could be drawn upon. Both Turkish and Persian were spoken in court circles; familiarity with Arabic, the language of the Koran, was a necessity for educated Moslems; and a knowledge of the native

Languages and the foundations of literature

Great Mosque in Lahore, Pakistan. Built under the Mogul emperor Aurangzeb, this mosque of red sandstone with marble-covered domes shows Persian influence.

dialects of northern India was essential for administrators. A permanent result of the intermingling between Turko-Persian and Indian cultures was the rise of a variety of speech known as Urdu ("the camp language"). While Urdu in its vocabulary includes many Persian and Arabic words and is written in Arabic script, its grammatical structure is basically the same as that of Hindi, the most prevalent Aryan vernacular of northern India. Both Urdu and Hindi came to be standard mediums of communication throughout northern India. (Urdu is now confined chiefly to Pakistan.)

While the Mogul rulers fostered a cosmopolitan atmosphere at court, attracting thither many Persian scholars and poets, the literary works of most enduring value were produced by Hindus, especially during the tolerant regime of Akbar. This emperor showed great interest in India's literary treasures as well as in her art and music, and he had Persian translations made from the *Vedas* and the Epics. Tulsi Das, one of India's greatest poets, lived during Akbar's reign. His principal work was an idealized and highly spiritual version of the ancient epic, the *Ramayana*. This poem, which combines fine craftsmanship with a warm and fervent moral earnestness, was written in the vernacular tongue rather than in Sanskrit, although its author was a Brahman.

The reigns of Akbar's later successors, so disastrous to the political fortunes of the Mogul state, were also marked by social unrest and cultural decline. The fanatical Aurangzeb frowned upon art as idolatrous and discouraged literature on the ground that it exalted human vanity. He banished music from his court and, in his extreme mania for orthodoxy, even replaced the Persian solar calendar with the clumsier lunar calendar because the latter had been used by Mohammed. Mogul culture at its best, however, had always been largely a phenomenon of the court and nobility, with few roots among the mass of the populace. Consequently its decline, which was rapid in the eighteenth century, had little effect upon the great body of Hindu society. In many parts of India skillful craftsmanship and exacting artistic standards were carried on much as they had been before the Moslem invasions. Particularly notable was the so-called Rajput school of painting, which was fostered at the courts of native princes in Rajputana and which was more vigorous and less sensuous than the Mogul school.

One aspect of the Mogul period which was bound to have tremendous consequences for the future was the coming of Europeans to India. Although the trading settlements which they established at various points on the coast were small and seemingly insignificant, they denoted the awakening of Europeans to the commercial possibilities of the Far East. The maritime enterprise so highly developed by the Indian states in earlier times had fallen into decay; and even the Mogul empire, for all its splendor, did not long maintain an effective navy. The rise of powerful Western European

CHINA UNDER
THE MANCHU
(CH'ING)
DYNASTY

The Portuguese
and British
footholds

states ended the control of Eastern waters by Arab navigators and brought direct pressure to bear on Indian territory.

In the early sixteenth century the Portuguese acquired and fortified several ports on the Indian coast and in Ceylon. Although they lost most of these to more powerful European rivals, they managed to retain Goa, Damão, and Diu until forcibly dispossessed by the Government of independent India in December 1961. More significant for the future was the activity of the British East India Company, which was chartered in 1600 and a few years later acquired a port at Surat (north of Bombay on the western coast). This was the fruit of patient negotiation carried on with officials of the Mogul emperor, for whose power the British agents necessarily felt a healthy respect. The Moguls were reluctant to offend the Portuguese as long as the latter commanded the sea routes which Moslem pilgrims used in traveling to Mecca; consequently, only minor concessions were granted to the English in the beginning. William Hawkins, a swashbuckling adventurer, and the more sedate Sir Thomas Roe served successively as English representatives at the court of the Mogul Jahangir, and each wrote a lively account of this eccentric and self-indulgent emperor, who showered hospitality upon his foreign visitors but shrewdly avoided committing himself to a formal treaty. Sir Thomas Roe, while resolutely upholding the dignity of his station before the Mogul courtiers, at the same time warned his own countrymen not to repeat the Portuguese policy of seizing territory and attempting to found colonies in India. The English, he urged, should seek profit "at sea and in quiet trade," remembering that "war and traffic are incompatible." This advice was little heeded in the subsequent history of the East India Company. Before the close of the seventeenth century the company had secured three locations, of strategic as well as commercial importance, in widely separated regions of India: the island of Bombay off the western coast (given by Portugal in 1661 when the English king, Charles II, married a Portuguese princess), Madras on the southeastern coast, and Fort William (Calcutta) at the mouth of the Ganges.

2. CHINA UNDER THE MANCHU (CH'ING) DYNASTY

With the disintegration of the Ming Dynasty it was China's fate to succumb, for the second time in her history, to conquest by a foreign invader. By the early seventeenth century a strong military organization had been formed in the Amur River region by the Manchus, kinsmen of the Juchên who had divided China with the Sung emperors 500 years before. Taking advantage of China's weakness and factional strife, the Manchu forces pushed southward through Manchuria and occupied Peking in 1644. A few years pre-

Establishment of
Manchu rule

viously their chieftain had exchanged his tribal title of khan for that of emperor and assumed a Chinese dynastic name—Ch'ing, meaning "Clear" or "Pure." While the Manchu (or Ch'ing) Dynasty, which lasted until the Revolution of 1911, is dated from 1644, it was not firmly established until considerably later. Northern China was occupied with little opposition, but many campaigns were required to subdue the stubbornly resisting southern Chinese. Near the end of the seventeenth century a rebellion led by Chinese generals was so nearly successful that it threatened to detach southern China from Manchu rule entirely, but it was finally crushed in 1681 by the young Manchu emperor, K'ang Hsi. Not until 1683 was the last anti-Manchu regime overthrown in Formosa, which was then incorporated into the Chinese empire. K'ang Hsi took steps to make revolt more difficult in the future. He strengthened the control of the central government at Peking over the provinces and distributed the authority in each province among several officials so that each could exercise a check upon the others. Instead of uprooting Chinese political institutions, he adapted them to the requirements of a uniform and centralized administrative system and laid the foundations for a long period of internal peace.

From the material standpoint the Manchu Dynasty, which proved to be the last of China's imperial ruling houses, was one of the most successful of all. The state was larger than at any other time in its history except for the brief period in the thirteenth cen-

Ch'ien Lung (1736-1796). The great Manchu Emperor under whom the Ch'ing Dynasty reached its climax. (Painting on silk by a nineteenth-century artist.)

tury when China was part of the pan-Asian Mongol empire. It included Manchuria, Mongolia, Sinkiang, and Formosa, while Tibet was a protectorate, and Korea, Burma, Nepal, and parts of Indochina were tributary dependencies. The government was also remarkably efficient during the first century and a half of the dynasty's history, partly because most of this period was covered by the reigns of two very able and long-lived emperors. K'ang Hsi, who while still a youth had broken the rebellion in south China, reigned for sixty-one years (1661–1722). He was therefore a contemporary of King Louis XIV of France, but he was far more of a statesman than the celebrated "Sun King." Under K'ang Hsi's grandson, Ch'ien Lung, who ruled for another sixty years (1736–1796), the dynasty reached the climax of its prestige and effectiveness. Thus, while Europe was in a condition of turbulence and shaken by the wars of rival despots, China enjoyed the advantages of unity and peace under a government which was stable if not entirely benevolent. That Chinese society was generally prosperous is indicated by a phenomenally rapid growth in population under the Manchus. It is no exaggeration to say that in the eighteenth century China was one of the best governed and most highly civilized states in the world, besides being the largest in territory and in the number of its inhabitants.

Obviously, the Manchu Dynasty was by no means a repetition of the Mongol, even though it was founded by northern invaders of nomadic origin. From the outset the Manchu emperors attempted to identify themselves with the culture and institutions of their Chinese subjects and to rule in accordance with accepted traditions. As a safeguard against rebellion they stationed garrisons in various parts of the country (composed of Chinese and Mongol troops as well as Manchu). They required Chinese men to braid their hair in a queue after the Manchu fashion and to adopt the Manchu style of dress as a token of submission. At the same time they preserved the ancient administrative framework, continued the civil-service examinations, and exalted the state cult of Confucius by requiring temples to be maintained in every district and by elevating the spirit of the ancient sage to the highest rank of official deities. In appointments to office the Manchus showed partiality to their own national group, but nothing like the extreme discrimination which had characterized the Mongol rule. More than 80 per cent of the lower governmental offices were filled by Chinese. The top administrative posts were divided about equally between Manchus and Chinese, with half of the Chinese quota going to northerners and half to southerners. Unfortunately, this seemingly equitable arrangement was somewhat unfair to southern China because this region was the more heavily populated.

The substantial material progress that took place during the Manchu period was not an unalloyed benefit to the entire nation.

Nothing equivalent to an industrial revolution occurred, but there were sufficient social and economic changes to create serious problems for the future. While Chinese society remained basically unaltered in organization and structure between the tenth and the nineteenth centuries, it experienced a great increase in numbers.

Problems of
population growth

From time to time the imperial government had taken a census of the population, and the returns—though probably incomplete and inaccurate—indicate an upward trend, especially during the period of Manchu rule. By the early twelfth century, under the Sung, the number of Chinese people had grown to about 100 million. Following the Mongol conquest there was an appreciable decline, but this was only temporary. During the first two centuries of the Manchu Dynasty the population seems to have increased about threefold. It is estimated that by the middle of the nineteenth century the Empire included approximately 300 million Chinese, besides 10 million Manchus. The causes of this rapid growth are not entirely clear, but it is certain that before the end of the Manchu Dynasty, China was feeling acute distress from the pressure of population upon food supply. The lack of sufficient arable land to support such large numbers led to the clearing and cropping of areas in the upper river valleys which had hitherto been covered with forest. Deforestation eventually produced soil erosion and increased the danger of floods and droughts, thus aggravating China's agrarian problem in the modern era.

Although the Chinese were basically one people in their fundamental institutions and cultural heritage, significant sectional differences, which augured trouble for the Manchu regime, had developed between the northern and the southern portions of the country. The sectional contrasts were largely the result of geographic and climatic differences between north and south, but they were intensified by historic factors. The Yangtze valley and the southeastern coastal region were by far the most productive agricultural areas and also contained the largest cities, which had long been centers of international commerce. The inhabitants of these areas were characterized by a breadth and diversity of interests and frequently by an independence of spirit which stemmed not so much from an extreme individualism as from a strong sense of family solidarity. Southern Chinese resented the fact that they paid the greater share of taxation, and yet the government seemed to spend most of its money for the benefit of the Peking region. They also felt that they were discriminated against in the competitive examinations, so that the leadership which they might have supplied was denied adequate recognition. In spite of their efforts toward conciliation, the Manchu emperors were never able to repose complete confidence in the loyalty of the southern Chinese, and the revolution which finally overthrew the dynasty had its origin in the south.

Conflicts between
north and south

Not the least among the problems with which the Manchu regime ultimately had to contend was that caused by the penetration
of Europeans into the Far East, although as long as the dynasty
remained vigorous it experienced little difficulty in holding the
foreigners within bounds. The overseas expansion of the Western
nations during the Commercial Revolution affected China as well as
India and other Eastern lands. By the early sixteenth century the
Portuguese had occupied Malacca, and one of their trading vessels
reached Canton in 1516. The Chinese authorities, long accustomed
to peaceful commercial intercourse with Arabs and other foreigners, at first had been disposed to grant the normal privileges to the
newcomers. Portuguese adventurers, however, pillaged Chinese
ships engaged in trade with the Indies and raided coastal cities, looting and massacring the inhabitants. Such actions convinced the
Chinese that Europeans were no better than pirates; nor was their
opinion favorably revised with the arrival, a little later, of the
Dutch and the English. The wanton depredations perpetrated by
these early Western seafarers were responsible for the unflattering
name which the Chinese came to apply to Europeans—"Ocean
Devils." The government finally determined to exclude Europeans
from the coastal cities but allowed the Portuguese to maintain a
trading center and settlement at Macao in the far south. Established
in 1557, this post has been retained by the Portuguese to the present day. As a security measure, the local officials constructed a
wall blocking off the Portuguese settlement on the island of Macao
and imposed rigid restrictions upon the activities of the foreigners.
The trade was too profitable for the Chinese to want to abolish it
altogether, and the Portuguese were soon extended the privilege of
docking at Canton at prescribed times and under strict supervision.

Thus, before the Manchu conquest of China, precedents had
already been set for dealing with Western traders. When the
Manchus attacked the Ming empire, the Portuguese assisted the
Ming court, supplying artillery and some military personnel. This
intervention was a portent of things to come, suggesting the
ominous possibilities of European interference in Chinese affairs;
but its immediate effect was to implant in the Manchu rulers a
prejudice against the meddling "Ocean Devils" at the very time
when the new regime was being inaugurated. Nevertheless, as the
Manchu emperors succeeded in strengthening their position, they
were willing to allow European trade to continue, though restricting it chiefly to Canton. Meanwhile, the suspicion attaching to
Europeans had been partially dispelled through contacts with Christian missionaries, especially the Jesuits, who had been active in the
Far East since the sixteenth century. Many of these Catholic missionaries impressed the Chinese with their breadth of scholarship,
their respect for Chinese culture, and their sincere interest in the

people among whom they had come to work. Consequently they were permitted to win converts to Christianity and were welcomed into intellectual circles. The early Manchu emperors were generally cordial to Christian missionaries, particularly the French Jesuits, whom they employed at court in such various capacities as instructors in science, mathematics, and cartography.

While the maritime expansion of Western nations was bringing Portuguese, Spanish, French, and others into the Far East, China came into more direct contact with another European power as Russia extended the frontier of her empire overland toward the Pacific. By the latter seventeenth century the Russians were encroaching on the Manchurian border. The success of the Manchus in meeting this threat from the north illustrates the strength of the state at this time, in decided contrast to the weakness which it exhibited before the great Western powers a century and a half later. In 1689 a treaty negotiated with Russian officials defined the boundary between the two countries, provided for a limited commercial intercourse, and arranged for the reciprocal extradition of criminals. This treaty (and subsequent ones negotiated during the eighteenth century) in no way impaired the sovereignty or prestige of China. Her day of humiliation under the impact of Western imperialism was yet to come.

In cultural fields the Manchu period was one of abundant productivity but little originality. It is probably correct to say that the over-all trend was toward sterility or even decadence. Chinese culture was still of high level and even brilliant, but it was largely an echo of the genius of earlier centuries. This does not mean that the Chinese had deteriorated in vitality or innate capacity. The decline was partly due to the rigidity of their social institutions and to the fact that they had developed an extreme veneration for ancient authorities, which fostered an attitude of stiff conservatism. More directly it was the result of the government's policy of encouraging docility among the people and frowning upon all innovation. Under the Manchu emperors more than under any native Chinese dynasty the accumulated dogmas of orthodox Confucianism (the Neo-Confucianism of Chu Hsi) were upheld inflexibly and perpetuated in the civil-service examinations through which officials were recruited. Inevitably, as the bureaucracy grew ever more conventional and inelastic in its thinking, it was ill-prepared to cope with new problems as they arose. The exalting of orthodoxy above every other virtue led slowly but surely to a state of intellectual stagnation.

Examples can be found, however, of vigorous and independent thinkers among the Chinese of this period, even in the field of philosophy. Valuable contributions were made by a school of critical scholars who pioneered in the objective and scientific study of ancient classics. The prime objective of this school was to purge

Chinese philosophy of the Buddhist and Taoist influences which had encrusted it during the Sung period. Hence, in spite of their perceptiveness and their defiance of conventions, the "Han Learning" scholars were attempting to rehabilitate the distant past rather than to deal directly with the needs of the present. While they were unable to dislodge the narrow conservatism that prevailed in high quarters, the movement was not devoid of results. That such was the case is indicated by the decline of Buddhism as an intellectual force in China even though it remained a popular religion.

If freshness and originality were lacking in most fields of expression, a notable exception was provided by the novel, which continued to be a successful literary medium and reached an even higher state of excellence than it had under the Ming. The best Chinese novels of this period readily bear comparison with significant prose works of other nations, Eastern or Western. As under the Ming, the novel was sometimes a vehicle for satire or trenchant criticism of governmental policies. One early nineteenth-century novel embodied an attack upon the subjection of women and advocated sweeping social and educational reforms.

During the early Manchu period Chinese culture—retrogressive as it may have been—created a more distinct impression upon the civilized nations of the West than had ever been true before. In the eighteenth century especially, Chinese-style gardens, pagodas, and pavilions became fashionable among the wealthy classes of Western Europe. Other items borrowed from China included sedan chairs, lacquer, and incense, while the craze for Chinese porcelain reached such proportions that it had the unfortunate effect of lowering the quality of the product. In addition, largely through translations and commentaries prepared by the Jesuits, European intellectuals were introduced to Chinese thought and literature. European acquaintance with these subjects was, of course, limited and superficial, but it was sufficient to arouse curiosity and admiration. Spokesmen of the Enlightenment upheld the somewhat mythical "Chinese sage" as an example of how man could be guided by reason, and fragments of Confucian texts were cited in support of deism.

The Manchu rulers had demonstrated their ability to adapt themselves to the institutions and traditions of their subjects. At the same time, they proved their inability to escape the enfeebling influences that tended to undermine every successful Chinese dynasty. By the nineteenth century their leadership had degenerated seriously, control was slipping into the hands of palace eunuchs, and the court was becoming the scene of soft living and intrigue. As the rulers grew less effectual, they were inclined to compensate for their own deficiencies by appearing more stern and arrogant than their predecessors. Occasionally they instigated persecution of the Christians, and they displayed a haughty and overbearing attitude toward the few European delegations which sought an audi-

English Plate with Pseudo-Chinese Design. From the Chelsea pottery factory (eighteenth century).

Chinese Porcelain. Decorated with "famille verte," a vivid green enamel typical of the K'ang Hsi period (1661-1722).

CHINESE-JAPANESE INFLUENCE ON WESTERN APPLIED ARTS

English "Chinese" Chippendale Settee. (About 1775).

ence with the emperor. Meanwhile, domestic discontent was manifest in rebellions—both incipient and overt—in various parts of
China. Secret societies, hostile to the Manchu government, were
organized. The dynasty was probably doomed even before friction
with the Western powers later in the nineteenth century created
new and distressing problems.

3. JAPAN UNDER THE TOKUGAWA SHOGUNATE

The most turbulent period of Japanese feudalism was ended
rather abruptly at the close of the sixteenth century when a series
of military campaigns forced the *daimyo* (great lords) to acknowledge the authority of a single ruler. The rise of the *daimyo*[2] had
led to the establishment of fairly effective government within their
individual domains, some of which were large enough to include
several of the ancient provinces. Hence, when the great lords were
brought under a common central authority, the way was open for
a genuine unification of the country, and Japan entered upon an
era of comparative peace and stability which brought her to the
threshold of modern times. Hideyoshi, a man of low birth who had
worked his way up to a high military command under one of the
leading *daimyo*, almost succeeded in unifying Japan, but he diverted his energies to the ambitious project of conquering China.
Although he invaded Korea, he met with stiff opposition from
Korean and Chinese forces, and he lacked sufficient naval support
to control the supply lines between Japan and the mainland. He
died in 1598 with his dream unfulfilled. Hideyoshi's work in Japan,
however, was ably completed by his former vassal Ieyasu, who
smashed the remnants of opposition and transferred the fruits of
victory to his own family, the Tokugawa. Ieyasu assumed the
office of Shogun, but he made it a much more efficient instrument
of government than it had ever been before.

Under the Tokugawa Shogunate (1603–1867), Japan's feudal
institutions remained intact, but they were systematized and made
to serve the interests of a strong central government. Ieyasu
founded his capital at Edo (now Tokyo), where he built a great
castle surrounded with moats and an elaborate series of outer defenses. The great domains of central and eastern Japan were held
by members of the Tokugawa or by men who had helped Ieyasu in
his campaigns. These trusted supporters of the regime were known
as "hereditary *daimyo*," while the lords who had acknowledged
Ieyasu's supremacy only when forced to do so were called "outer
daimyo." The members of both groups were hereditary vassals of
the Shogun and were kept under careful surveillance lest they
should try to assert their independence. The Shogun employed a
corps of secret police to report any signs of disaffection through-

Rise of
the Tokugawa

Centralization
of authority

[2] See Vol. I, p. 521.

Five-Storied Pagoda at Nikko, in Central Japan. It was built in 1636 and dedicated to Tokugawa Ieyasu, founder of the Tokugawa Shogunate. The structure (about 100 feet high) is ornately carved, painted, and lacquered, but is given a magnificent natural setting by the surrounding forest.

out the country. As a special precaution he required all *daimyo* to maintain residences in Edo and spend part of each year there, and also to leave close relatives as hostages when they returned to their own estates. The system which Ieyasu devised was so well organized and thorough that it did not depend on the personal ability of the Shogun for its operation and continuance. For the first time Japan had a durable political framework, which remained undisturbed in the hands of the Tokugawa for two and a half centuries.

It should be noted that the Japanese government was still dual in form. The imperial family and a decorative court nobility continued to reside at Kyoto, while the real power was lodged in the Bakufu, the military hierarchy headed by the Shogun at Edo. The Tokugawa Shoguns cultivated the fiction that they were carrying out the will of a divine emperor. By emphasizing the emperor's sanctity they added an aura of invulnerability to their own position, and by keeping him in seclusion they rendered him harmless. The shadow government at Kyoto was now entirely dependent upon the Shogun even for its financial support, but it was carefully and respectfully preserved as a link with Japan's hallowed past.

Persistence of dual government

The most serious problem of the early Tokugawa period concerned relations with Europeans. Before the close of the sixteenth century both the Portuguese and the Spanish were carrying on considerable trade in Japan, and the Dutch and the British secured trading posts early in the following century. Europeans had been accorded a favorable reception by the Japanese, who seemed eager to learn from them. Firearms, acquired from the Portuguese, came

Relations with Europeans

into use for the first time in Japan and played a part in the feudal battles of the late sixteenth century. The introduction of gunpowder had the effect temporarily of stimulating the construction of heavy stone castles by the *daimyo*, a practice which was carefully regulated by the Tokugawa after they had seized the Shogunate.

Along with the Western traders came missionaries, who at first encountered little hostility. Vigorous proselyting by Portuguese Jesuits and Spanish Franciscans met with remarkable success in winning converts to the Catholic faith among all classes of the population, including some of the feudal nobles. By the early seventeenth century there were close to 300,000 Christian converts in Japan, chiefly in the south and west where the European trading centers were located. Eventually, however, the Shoguns decided that Christianity should be proscribed, not because they objected to the religion as such but because they were afraid it would divide the country and weaken their authority. They were annoyed by the bickering between rival European groups and also feared that their subjects were being enticed into allegiance to a foreign potentate, the Pope. The first persecutions were mild and were directed against Japanese Christians rather than against the Europeans; but when the missionaries refused to halt their work they were severely dealt with, and many were executed. Finally, in 1637, when a peasant revolt against oppressive taxation developed into a Christian rebellion, the Shogun's forces conducted a real war against the Christian strongholds in southwestern Japan and, in spite of the most heroic resistance, wiped out the Christian communities and exterminated the religion almost completely.

The expulsion of
Europeans and the
adoption of
isolationism

Following this bloody purge, the Shoguns adopted a policy of excluding all Europeans from Japanese settlement. That they were able to enforce it shows how strong their government had become. Reluctant to cut off Western trade entirely, they made a slight exception in the case of the Dutch, who seemed to be the least dangerous politically. The Dutch were permitted to unload one ship each year at the port of Nagasaki in the extreme western corner of Japan, but only under the strictest supervision. Going even farther along the line of reaction, the Shogun next forbade his Japanese subjects to visit foreign lands on pain of forfeiting all their rights and commanded that no ship should be built large enough to travel beyond the coastal waters of the island empire. Although traffic with China was continued, the Shoguns forced upon their country a policy of almost complete isolationism, thus reversing the course which had been followed advantageously during many centuries preceding.

The Tokugawa regime gave Japan a long period of peace and orderly government, in which the ideal of a harmonious society seemed to be realized. By the early eighteenth century population **99**

Japanese Bronze (Eighteenth Century). The figure depicted is Kuan Ti, Chinese "God of War" —actually a deified military hero of the early third century A.D. Regarded as the patron of military officials, he was particularly revered in China during the late Ch'ing (Manchu) period.

Prosperity and
stability;
exaltation of the
warrior

had reached a total of about 30 million; thenceforth it increased but slightly for a century and a half. The country as a whole was prosperous; industry and internal trade continually expanded, even though foreign commerce had been curtailed. Hence the fact that population remained almost stationary does not signify a condition of stagnation. Nevertheless, the rigidity of institutions under the Tokugawa administration in the long run paved the way for the downfall of the Shogunate. Great emphasis was placed upon observing clear distinctions between the social classes and their respective functions. Theoretically, the social structure was arranged in accordance with the classes of China, which ranked, in order of importance: (1) scholar-officials, (2) farmers, (3) artisans, (4) merchants, and (5) soldiers, bandits, and beggars. In Japan, however, the realities of a feudalized society produced a peculiar distortion of the ideal arrangement (which was somewhat fanciful even in China). The warrior, who had enjoyed a position of leadership for centuries, was elevated from the lowest category to the highest. In return for the place of honor assigned to him, he was expected to exhibit the qualities of the scholar also, and to a considerable extent he did. The *daimyo* and the *samurai* were no longer the uncouth lawless ruffians of early feudal days but refined aristocrats, who took pride in the rigorous discipline to which they were bred, and cultivated literature and the arts. Still, their preeminence had been won in the first instance by force, and their position was regarded as a hereditary right, not to be challenged by men of superior ability who had been born to a lower class.

The administrative and legal code of the Tokugawa, although it was supposed to embody the ethical principles of Confucius, was actually repressive, inequitable, and aimed at holding each group to its designated station. Penalties for offenses were adjusted to the rank of the offender, the most cruel and revolting punishments being reserved for the humble laboring folk. Further to emphasize class distinctions, sumptuary laws prescribing diet and costume were issued, although it was found impossible to enforce them. A tragic incident of the year 1651 illustrates the harshness of a regime which exalted privilege above the claims of ordinary humanity. A poor farmer presented a memorial to the Shogun protesting the mistreatment which he and his fellow tenants were suffering at the hands of their overlord. The Shogun punished the guilty *daimyo*, but he also beheaded the children of the farmer and then crucified the man and his wife for the crime of daring to criticize a superior.[3]

The artificial class structure of Tokugawa Japan proved to be a detriment to the health of society, although it could not prevent social changes from taking place. In spite of the lip service paid to the farmer's honorable state, the peasants, who of course formed the majority of the population, were the most flagrantly exploited group of all. They were obliged to support the feudal aristocracy and, because the tax system was based almost exclusively upon agricultural assessments, they also furnished the bulk of the state's revenue. The *samurai* were officially rehabilitated as a distinguished class of warriors, but their position became more and more anomalous. While they possessed a monopoly of the profession of arms, they found little opportunity to practice it because the Shogun discouraged feudal quarrels and there were no foreign wars. Thus the *samurai* became, by and large, a group of respectable parasites, although many of them as individuals displayed both talent and energy. On the other hand, the merchants, who were ranked at the bottom of the social pyramid, steadily accumulated wealth, exerted an increasing influence over the whole national economy, and inevitably imparted a bourgeois tone to society in the bustling cities.

During the Tokugawa period Japanese culture, being largely cut off from outside contacts, acquired a distinctive national character. In spite of rigid social controls, some freedom of action and expression was possible for the privileged groups within the confines of their own class. Even in the political sphere the regime was not centralized to the point of being totalitarian. Having set up adequate precautions against rebellion, the Shoguns allowed a measure of autonomy to the *daimyo* in governing their fiefs and also to the associations of wholesale city merchants and manufacturers which gradually replaced the older and more restrictive guilds. The *samurai*, who in their military capacity were almost superfluous, were often employed in administrative functions by the *daimyo*. *Samurai* often took over the management of a great domain so completely that the *daimyo* was reduced to little more than a figurehead.

[3] G. B. Sansom, *Japan, a Short Cultural History*, pp. 518–19.

An important aspect of the intellectual life of the period was the growing interest in Chinese philosophy. This resulted partly from the fact that a number of Chinese scholars had fled to Japan when the Ming Dynasty was overthrown by the Manchus. More directly it resulted from the Shoguns' policy of encouraging the study of the Chinese Confucian classics, particularly among the aristocracy, because they thought it would help to instill habits of discipline in their subjects. These writings, of course, had long been honored in Japan, but now they were diligently examined for the purpose of developing a native school of philosophers who, through their example and through their position as administrators, could inculcate the principles of virtue—especially obedience—among all classes of the population. The ascendancy of Confucian philosophy among intellectuals had the effect of weakening the influence of Buddhism, even though the Shogun, when engaged in his campaign to exterminate Christianity in Japan, had made it a point to encourage Buddhist forms of worship.

The most significant cultural changes were those related to the growth of large cities, such as Edo, Osaka, and Kyoto, where men of wealth were creating an atmosphere of comfort and gaiety in contrast to the restrained decorum of the feudal nobility. In these populous commercial and industrial centers the trend in art and literature and especially in the field of entertainment was toward a distinctly middle-class culture, which was sometimes gaudy but appealing in its exuberance and spontaneity. In the pleasure quarters of the cities an important figure was the *geisha* girl, who combined the qualities of a modern beauty queen with the talents of a night-club entertainer. Trained in the art of conversation as well as in song and dance, she provided the sparkling companionship which men too often missed in their own homes because of the habits of docility and self-effacement that they instilled into their wives and daughters. Prostitution, also, was prevalent on a large scale in the towns, in spite of attempts by the authorities to curtail the evil. Inherently sordid as was the practice, it took on a specious refinement under the patronage of the well-to-do, and some courtesans acquired an enviable standing in the loose but highly sophisticated society which flouted established conventions. Not only merchants and business men but even *samurai* and *daimyo* were attracted by the gay diversions of city life, and surreptitiously exchanged the boredom of their routine existence for the delights of a "floating world" of pleasure and uninhibited self-expression.

The culture of the
middle and lower
classes

The dissolute society of the Tokugawa cities was by no means utterly degenerate. Some of the best creative talents in Japan catered to bourgeois appetites, just as they did in Italy during the Renaissance. Racy novels, satirizing contemporary figures and piquant with gossip, innuendo, and scandal, came into vogue. Previously art had been chiefly aristocratic and religious, except for

Woman Weaving Cloth.

the exquisitely designed articles of ordinary household use produced by the various handicrafts. Now a type of folk art was appearing which mirrored society realistically and also was enlivened with humor and caricature. Its chief medium was the wood-block color print, which could be produced cheaply enough to reach a wide public and which has ever since been a popular art form. Another proof of the influence that urban tastes were exerting in the aesthetic sphere is seen in the evolution of the *Kabuki* drama. In contrast to the *No*, the highly stylized and austere dance-drama that had been perfected a few centuries earlier under the patronage of the aristocracy, the *Kabuki* offered entertainment appealing to the middle and lower classes of the towns. Although it owed something to traditional dance forms, the *Kabuki* drama was derived more immediately from the puppet theater and, unlike the *No*, it was almost entirely secular in spirit. As developed in the seventeenth and eighteenth centuries, the *Kabuki* drama attained a high degree of realism, with exciting plots, lively action, and effective stage devices. In the opinion of some theatrical experts, it deserves to rank as the greatest drama any civilization has ever produced.

The Art of Tile Making. A wood-block by Hokusai (1760-1849), an artist famous for landscapes.

Economic changes

Various forces were at work in Japan which tended to undermine the foundations of Tokugawa institutions, in spite of the outward appearance of calm. Of these forces, the most potent were economic. The partial transformation of Japan's economy from an agrarian to a mercantile basis, which enhanced the importance of men engaged in manufacture, trade, and transport, rendered feudalism obsolete and at the same time imposed heavier burdens upon the peasants. Most alarming from the viewpoint of the Tokugawa bureaucracy was the fact that the feudal classes began to feel the pinch of adversity. Although money had been in circulation for many centuries, the incomes of *daimyo* and of their *samurai* retainers were still computed in measures of rice, the chief agricultural staple. The merchants who provisioned such great cities as Edo and Osaka controlled the marketing of a large proportion of the rice crop; hence they were able to foresee fluctuations in price and sometimes even to induce fluctuations for their own benefit. Naturally, the *daimyo* and *samurai* were at a disadvantage in a period of unstable prices, because their incomes were from land rents, and because their necessities were increasingly supplied by articles that had to be purchased in the cities. Often the price of rice was considerably below the general price level, and even when it was high the middleman appropriated most of the profit. The landed aristocrats found their real incomes diminishing while low-born traders and brokers grew richer and richer.

Kabuki Actor (Matsumoto Ko-shiro). Portrayed here as a fishmonger by Sharaku, a wood-block artist noted for his caricatures of actors (1794 or 1795).

Woman Playing the Flute. The flutist is by Harunobu (1724-1770), earliest master of the multi-colored-print technique.

Inevitably, class lines began to break down, just as they did in Western Europe under similar conditions during the period of the Commercial Revolution. Wealthy Japanese merchants purchased *samurai* rank and title, while nobles adopted children of bourgeois families or contracted marriage alliances with this class in an effort to recoup their fortunes. Feeling honor-bound to maintain their accustomed style of living—at least in appearances—the aristocrats borrowed recklessly. As early as 1700 the indebtedness of the *daimyo* class was reputed to have reached a figure one hundred times greater than the total amount of money in Japan. Impoverished *samurai* pawned their ceremonial robes and even the swords which were their badge of rank. While townspeople in large numbers were entering the lower grades of *samurai*, *samurai* and farmers were flocking to the towns, where the more successful ones merged into the bourgeois class.

The disruption of classes

There was ample evidence of mounting social unrest in the latter part of the Tokugawa period. As the nobles sank more deeply into debt, they tightened the exactions upon their own subordinates to the limit of endurance, justifying this extortion with the argument that peasants were merely seeds to be pressed or cattle to be driven. In the eighteenth and nineteenth centuries agrarian uprisings were frequent, although they were almost always suppressed with extreme cruelty. Abortion and infanticide became prevalent in some of the rural areas of Japan, not only among the peasants but among poorer members of the *samurai* class as well. These distressing

Economic oppression and dislocation

105

symptoms, however, do not mean that there was general economic stagnation. Even Japanese agriculture was vastly more progressive than in earlier centuries. The amount of land under cultivation doubled, new crops were introduced, better fertilizers and tools came into use, and irrigation was extended through the co-operative efforts of farm villages. In agricultural organization the general trend was away from large family combinations to smaller units which could be run more efficiently. The spread between prosperous and impoverished peasants consequently widened, and there was an increase in tenantry as opposed to individual farm ownership. At the same time the emergence of a mobile class of wage earners stimulated the growth of village industries—processing silk, cotton, tobacco, and sugar cane—and constituted a reserve labor force which eventually contributed to the rapid industrialization of Japan in the post-Tokugawa period. Peasant discontent, riots, and local rebellions were not an indication of utter misery, but they were a challenge to the inequities of the tax system and to the arbitrary and antiquated class structure. It is significant that conditions were much better in the lands of the "outer lords" of western and southern Japan than in the regions directly under Tokugawa control and more demoralized by city influences. In many of these outer fiefs the peasants were relatively prosperous, the *samurai* sober and industrious, and loyalty to the *daimyo* still deep rooted. And these strong outer *daimyo* were the natural rivals of the Tokugawa family.

The critical
position of the
Shogunate and
the approaching
end of isolation

The unrest generated by economic dislocation was further augmented by cultural trends in the later Tokugawa period. As a national spirit developed, it was accompanied by a renewal of interest in Japan's past. Shintoism, the ancient cult over which the imperial family presided, had been largely eclipsed by Buddhism. Gradually, however, its popularity revived, and several new Shinto sects obtained an enthusiastic following. The study of ancient records (historical and mythological) stimulated reflection on the origins of the imperial government and directed attention to the fact that the Shogunate was a comparatively recent innovation or actually a usurpation, not an authentic part of the ancient political structure. At the same time, familiarity with China's political heritage—induced by the vogue of Confucian scholarship which the Shoguns themselves had promoted—raised doubts among Japanese intellectuals as to the merits of a dual administrative system or of feudal institutions. Moreover, Western books and ideas were seeping into Japan through the port of Nagasaki where the Dutch were permitted a very limited trade. Even before Japan was "opened" in the nineteenth century, considerable interest had been aroused in Western guns, ships, watches, glassware, and scientific instruments. Thus Japan's insulation from the outside world was beginning to develop cracks at the same time that internal discontent had reached a dangerous point. By the opening of the nineteenth century the Shogun's position was precarious, unlikely to withstand the shock of a severe crisis, especially since other powerful families were eagerly watching for any sign of weakness on the part of the Tokugawa.

SELECTED READINGS—INDIA

· *Items so designated are available in paperbound editions.*

Archer, J. C., *The Sikhs*, Princeton, 1946.

· Brown, D. M., *The White Umbrella: Indian Political Thought from Manu to Gandhi*, Berkeley, 1953 (California). A brief sketch.

Cambridge History of India, Vol. IV.

Garratt, G. T., ed., *The Legacy of India*, Oxford, 1937.

Moreland, W. H., and Chatterjee, A. C., *A Short History of India*, 4th ed., London, 1957.

Philips, C. H., *India*, London, 1949. A useful survey.

· Rawlinson, H. G., *India, a Short Cultural History*, New York, 1952 (Praeger). An excellent interpretive study.

Smith, V. A., *Akbar the Great Mogul*, Oxford, 1917.

Spear, Percival, *India: A Modern History*, Ann Arbor, 1961.

——, ed., *The Oxford History of India*, 3rd ed., New York, 1958. A thorough revision of a standard older history.

——, *Twilight of the Mughuls*, Cambridge, 1951.

· Wolpert, Stanley, *India*, Englewood Cliffs, N.J., 1965 (Spectrum).

—CHINA

Buck, Pearl, *The Chinese Novel*, New York, 1939.

· Creel, H. G., *Chinese Thought from Confucius to Mao Tse-tung*, Chicago, 1953 (Mentor).

Fitzgerald, C. P., *China, a Short Cultural History*, 3rd ed., New York, 1961 (Praeger).

· Fung Yu-lan, *A Short History of Chinese Philosophy* (Derk Bodde, ed.), New York, 1948 (Macmillan).

· Goodrich, L. C., *A Short History of the Chinese People*, 3rd ed., New York, 1959 (Torchbooks). Brief but informative.

Ho Ping-ti, *Studies on the Population of China, 1368–1953*, Cambridge, Mass., 1959. A masterful survey of population trends and related social and economic problems.

Honour, Hugh, *Chinoiserie: The Vision of Cathay*, New York, 1962. An account of the rise of European interest in the arts and crafts of the Orient.

· Hudson, G. F., *Europe and China: A Survey of Their Relations from the Earliest Times to 1800*, London, 1930 (Beacon).

Latourette, K. S., *The Chinese, Their History and Culture*, 4th ed., 2 vols. in one, New York, 1964. Comprehensive in scope; extensive bibliographies.

Lattimore, Owen, and Onon, U., *Nationalism and Revolution in Mongolia*, New York, 1955.

Lin Yutang, *Imperial Peking: Seven Centuries of China*, New York, 1961. A richly illustrated popular account of the great capital under successive dynasties.

Michael, Franz, *The Origin of Manchu Rule in China*, Baltimore, 1942.

Munsterberg, Hugo, *Short History of Chinese Art*, New York, 1949.

Nivison, D. S., and Wright, A. F., eds., *Confucianism in Action*, Stanford, 1959.

Reischauer, E. O., and Fairbank, J. K., *East Asia: The Great Tradition (A History of East Asian Civilization*, Vol. I), Boston, 1960. The best one-volume text in English to date for the history of China and Japan to the opening of the nineteenth century; illustrated.

Rowbotham, A. H., *Missionary and Mandarin: The Jesuits at the Court of China*, Berkeley, 1942.

Scott, A. C., *The Classical Theater of China*, New York, 1957.

Shryock, J. K., *The Origin and Development of the State Cult of Confucius*, New York, 1932.

Sickman, L., and Soper, A., *The Art and Architecture of China*, Baltimore, 1956. Reliable, richly illustrated.

Sullivan, Michael, *An Introduction to Chinese Art*, Berkeley, 1961.

Sun, E. Z., and De Francis, John, *Chinese Social History*, Washington, 1956. Translations of articles by modern Chinese scholars.

—JAPAN

Anesaki, Masaharu, *Art, Life and Nature in Japan*, Boston, 1933.

Bellah, R. N., *Tokugawa Religion: The Values of Pre-Industrial Japan*, Glencoe, Ill., 1957.

Dore, R. P., *Education in Tokugawa Japan*, Berkeley, 1965. Scholarly and insightful.

Embree, J. F., *The Japanese Nation*, New York, 1945. A brilliant and well-balanced study by an anthropologist.

· Ernst, Earle, *The Kabuki Theatre*, New York, 1956 (Evergreen).

· Keene, Donald, *Japanese Literature: An Introduction for Western Readers*, New York, 1955 (Evergreen).

———, *The Japanese Discovery of Europe*, London, 1952.

Reischauer, E. O., *Japan Past and Present*, rev. ed., New York, 1953. A very lucid and well-organized summary of the main strands in Japanese history.

Sadler, A. L., *The Maker of Modern Japan: The Life of Tokugawa Ieyasu*, London, 1937.

Sansom, G. B., *Japan, a Short Cultural History*, rev. ed., New York, 1952. A substantial but highly readable work by an eminent British scholar.

———, *The Western World and Japan*, New York, 1950.

Sheldon, C. D., *The Rise of the Merchant Class in Tokugawa Japan, 1600–1868: An Introductory Survey*, Locust Valley, N.Y., 1958.

· Smith, T. C., *The Agrarian Origins of Modern Japan*, Stanford, 1959 (Atheneum).

Swann, Peter C., *An Introduction to the Arts of Japan*, New York, 1958.

· Warner, Langdon, *The Enduring Art of Japan*, Cambridge, Mass., 1952 (Evergreen).

Yukio, Y., *Two Thousand Years of Japanese Art*, New York, 1958.

SOURCE MATERIALS

· de Bary, W. T., ed., *Sources of Chinese Tradition*, Chaps. XXII, XXIII (Columbia).

· ———, ed., *Sources of Indian Tradition*, "Islam in Medieval India"; "Sikhism" (Columbia).

· ———, ed., *Sources of Japanese Tradition*, "The Tokugawa Period" (Columbia).

Gallagher, L. J., tr., *China in the Sixteenth Century. The Journals of Matthew Ricci: 1583–1610.*

· Hibbett, Howard, *The Floating World in Japanese Fiction* (Evergreen).

· Keene, Donald, ed., *Anthology of Japanese Literature* (Evergreen).

Markham, C. R., ed., *The Hawkins' Voyages.*

Morse, H. B., ed., *The Chronicles of the East India Company Trading to China,* 5 vols.

Smith, V. A., ed., *F. Bernier: Travels in the Mogul Empire* A.D. *1656–1668.*

Wang, C. C., tr., *Dream of the Red Chamber* (Chinese novel).

PART TWO

The Later Modern World,
1789-1914

The period 1789–1914 marked a climax in the world's history. Accumulated tendencies of the past four centuries reached their peak and wrought miracles of change unheard of since the time of the Greeks. The French Revolution gathered together a number of these tendencies and made them vital forces in the world for more than 100 years. This was notably true of nationalism, individualism, equalitarianism, and opposition to absolute monarchy. Advances in medical science and improvements in food supply made possible a doubling of the population of the globe in little more than a century. The Commercial Revolution and the need for mechanized production brought about Industrial Revolutions that affected the course of history more deeply than all the "decisive battles" since the days of the Pharaohs. The individualism of the Renaissance and the rationalism of the Enlightenment prepared the way for the liberalism and democracy of the nineteenth and twentieth centuries. So great was the appeal of these forces that they were not confined to Europe and the Americas but spread ultimately to the Far East. Thus the great lords of Japan, in adopting a constitution in 1889, saw fit to establish the forms of cabinet government, while the leader of the Chinese Revolution of 1911 made "democracy" one of his shibboleths. But the most powerful current reaching its climax between 1800 and 1914 was undoubtedly nationalism. More new states were created in this period than in any other era of world history. They multiplied especially in Europe and in Latin America. Asia lagged behind the West, but portents of restiveness had begun to appear, and it was only a matter of time until the peoples of the Middle and Far East would strike out boldly for control of their own destinies.

A Chronological Table

THE AMERICAS	INDIA, THE MIDDLE AND FAR EAST
Great Awakening, 1740–1810	Manchu Dynasty in China, 1644–1912

1775

American Revolution, 1775–1783
Declaration of Independence, 1776

Adoption of the Constitution of the U.S.,
1787
John Fitch's steamboat, 1787

The Bill of Rights, 1791
Thomas Paine, *The Rights of Man*, 1791

1800

Jeffersonian Revolution, 1800–1801

Latin American wars for independence,
1808–1826

Independence of Argentina, 1816

Independence of Brazil, 1822
Independence of Mexico, 1822
Monroe Doctrine, 1823

1825

Jacksonian Revolution, 1828–1837

Mechanization of agriculture, 1835–

Anglo-Chinese War (Opium War), 1839–1842

Use of ether as an anesthetic, 1842
Telegraph, 1844

1850

Taiping Rebellion, 1851–1864

Opening of Japan, 1854
Great Mutiny in India, 1857–1858
British Crown assumes rule in India, 1858

First oil well, 1859

BRITAIN AND WESTERN EUROPE	CENTRAL AND EASTERN EUROPE
Physiocrats, 1750–1800	
Development of steam engine, 1769	Beethoven, 1770–1827
William Wordsworth, 1770–1850	
Beginning of factory system, *ca.* 1770	
Adam Smith, *The Wealth of Nations*, 1776	
Classical economics, 1776–1880	
	Immanuel Kant, *Critique of Pure Reason*, 1781
	Friedrich List, 1789–1846
French Declaration of Rights of Man, 1789	
French Revolution, 1789–1799	
Utilitarianism, 1790–1870	
Edward Jenner develops vaccination for smallpox, 1796	Franz Schubert, 1797–1828
Coup d'état of Napoleon, 1799	
Romanticism in literature and arts, 1800–1900	
Victor Hugo, 1802–1885	
First Empire in France, 1804–1814	
Revival of atomic theory, 1810	
Charles Dickens, 1812–1870	
	Richard Wagner, 1813–1883
Battle of Waterloo, 1815	Congress of Vienna, 1814–1815
	Carlsbad Decrees, 1819
	Feodor Dostoievski, 1821–1881
First railroad, 1825	
Henrik Ibsen, 1828–1906	Leo Tolstoi, 1828–1910
	Independence of Greece, 1829
July Revolution in France, 1830	
Realism in literature and arts, 1830–1914	
Independence of Belgium, 1831	
First Reform Act, 1832	Unification of Germany, 1833–1871
Chartist Movement, 1838–1848	
Émile Zola, 1840–1902	Tchaikovsky, 1840–1893
Repeal of Corn Laws, 1846	Law of conservation of energy, 1847
February Revolution in France, 1848	*Communist Manifesto*, 1848
Second Republic in France, 1848–1852	Unification of Italy, 1848–1870
Law of dissipation of energy, 1851	
Second Empire in France, 1852–1870	Crimean War, 1854–1856
Bessemer process, 1856	
Charles Darwin, *Origin of Species*, 1859	
J. S. Mill, *On Liberty*, 1859	

THE AMERICAS	INDIA, THE MIDDLE AND FAR EAST

Civil War, 1861–1865
Empire of Maximilian in Mexico, 1862–
    1867

Sun Yat-sen, 1866–1925
Meiji Restoration, 1867
End of Shogunate in Japan, 1867
Mahatma Gandhi, 1869–1948
End of feudalism in Japan, 1871

1875

Telephone, 1876

Pragmatism, 1880–1930

Organization of Indian National Congress, 1885

Republic of Brazil, 1889
Beginning of finance capitalism, 1890
Populism, 1890–1897

Adoption of Constitution in Japan, 1889
Jawaharlal Nehru, 1889–1964
Sino-Japanese War, 1894–1895

William James, *The Will to Believe*, 1897
Spanish-American War, 1898

Open-door policy in China, 1899

1900

Progressive movement, 1901–1916
First airplane flight, 1903
Roosevelt Corollary to Monroe Doctrine, 1904

Boxer Rebellion, 1900

Russo-Japanese War, 1904–1905

Model T Ford, 1908

Young Turk Revolution, 1908

Madero Revolution in Mexico, 1911

Revolution in China, 1911

BRITAIN AND
WESTERN EUROPE

Antiseptic surgery, 1865

Second Reform Act, 1867
Franco-Prussian War, 1870–1871
Impressionism, 1870–1890
Paris Commune, 1871

Development of dynamo, 1873
Germ theory of disease, 1875
Third Republic in France, 1875–1940

Herbert Spencer, *Data of Ethics*, 1879

Third Reform Act, 1884

Post-impressionism, 1890
Dreyfus affair, 1894–1905
Discovery of X-ray, 1895

First Hague Conference, 1899
Boer War, 1899–1902

Hugo DeVries, mutation theory, 1901
Cubism, 1903–
Entente Cordiale, 1904
Separation of church and state in France,
1905

Second Hague Conference, 1907
Triple Entente, 1907
Discovery of protons and electrons, *ca.*
1910
Parliament Act of 1911

CENTRAL AND EASTERN
EUROPE

Emancipation of serfs in Russia, 1861

Austro-Prussian War, 1866
Ausgleich establishes Dual Monarchy,
1867

Law of Papal Guaranties, 1871
German Empire, 1871–1918
Kulturkampf, 1872–1886

Internal-combustion engine, 1876
Russo-Turkish War, 1877–1878
Congress of Berlin, 1878

Triple Alliance, 1882–1914

Berlin-to-Baghdad Railway, 1890–1907

Ivan Pavlov discovers conditioned reflex,
ca. 1895
Diesel engine, 1897

Wireless telegraph, 1899

Russo-Japanese War, 1904–1905
Founding of psychoanalysis, *ca.* 1905
Russian Revolution of 1905
Einstein theories, 1905–1910

Young Turk Revolution, 1908
Bosnian crisis, 1908

Balkan wars, 1912–1913

1875

1900

CHAPTER 4

The French Revolution (1789-1799)

Today the third estate is everything, the nobility but a word. . . .
—Abbé Sieyès, *What Is the Third Estate?*

France, when she let loose the reins of regal authority, doubled
the licence of a ferocious dissoluteness in manners, and of an insolent irreligion in opinions and practices; and has extended
through all ranks of life, as if she were communicating some
privilege, or laying open some secluded benefit, all the unhappy
corruptions that usually were the disease of wealth and power.
—Edmund Burke, *Reflections on the Revolution in France*

Profound changes were wrought in the political history of the
Western world in the latter part of the eighteenth century. This
period witnessed the death throes of that peculiar system of govern- **The era of rev-**
ment and society which had grown up during the age of the **olution**
despots. In England this system had already been largely overthrown by 1689, but in other nations of Europe it lingered on,
growing more and more ossified and corrupt with the passing of the
years. It flourished in every major country of Europe under the
combined influence of militarism and the ambitions of monarchs to
consolidate their power at the expense of the nobles. But scarcely
anywhere did it exist in so deplorable a form as in France during
the reigns of the last three Bourbon kings. Louis XIV was the supreme incarnation of absolute rule. His successors, Louis XV and
Louis XVI, dragged the government to very low depths of extravagance and irresponsibility. Moreover, their subjects were sufficiently enlightened to be keenly aware of their disadvantages. Yet
the French Revolution was not an isolated event. In many ways it
was simply the French aspect of a great Western revolution which
had begun in the American Colonies in the 1770's, had spread to Ireland in 1782–1783, to the Low Countries, to Hungary and Poland,
and to some of the cantons of Switzerland. The French outbreak
was the climax of this widespread Western revolution. Moreover, it **117**

was the broadest and most significant. It involved not merely the king and the nobility but the middle class, the peasants, and even the "little people" of the cities and towns.

I. THE CAUSES OF THE FRENCH REVOLUTION

For convenience we can divide the causes of the French Revolution into three main classes: political, economic, and intellectual. Naturally, this division is somewhat arbitrary, for none of these classes was entirely distinct. The intellectual causes, for example, and to some extent the political also, were largely economic in origin. Nevertheless, for purposes of simplification it will be best to keep them separate. One of the major political causes has already been mentioned. This was the despotic rule of the Bourbon kings. For nearly 200 years government in France had been largely a one-man institution. During the fourteenth, fifteenth, and sixteeth centuries a kind of parliament known as the Estates General, composed of representatives of the clergy, the nobility, and the common people, had met at irregular intervals. But after 1614 it was no longer summoned. Henceforth the king was the sole repository of sovereign power. In a very real sense the king was the state. He could do almost anything his imperious will might dictate, without fear of impeachment or legislative restrictions of any kind. No questions of constitutionality or the natural rights of his subjects need trouble him. He could throw men into prison without a trial by means of royal orders, or *lettres de cachet*. He could prevent any criticism of his policies by clamping a rigid censorship on the press or by restricting freedom of speech. It must be conceded, however, that the tyranny of the French kings has often been exaggerated. In actual practice there was comparatively little interference with what men wrote or said, particularly during the reigns of Louis XV and Louis XVI. No action of these monarchs inhibited the mordant wit of Voltaire or suppressed the radical books of Rousseau.[1] On the contrary, the attacks by these and other philosophers increased in virulence the nearer the Revolution approached. The explanation, of course, is not to be found in any liberalism of Louis XV and his dull-witted grandson but rather in their indifference to politics.

A second political cause of the French Revolution was the illogical and unsystematic character of the government. Confusion reigned in nearly every department. The political structure was the product of a long and irregular growth extending back into the Middle Ages. New agencies had been established from time to time to meet some particular condition, with a total disregard for those

---

[1] Voltaire was imprisoned for a time and afterwards exiled to England for one of his vitriolic lampoons, but this was early in his career. Most of his trenchant criticisms of the government and the Church were written *after his return* from England.

Portrait of Louis XV, Dressed as a Child in Royal Costume by a French Artist of the Eighteenth Century.

already in existence. As a result there was much overlapping of functions, and numerous useless officials drew salaries from the public purse. Conflicts of jurisdiction between rival departments frequently delayed action on vital problems for months at a stretch. Almost everywhere inefficiency, waste, and graft were the ruling qualities of the system. Even in financial matters there was no more regularity than in other branches of public policy. Not only did the government have no budget, but accounts were seldom kept; and there was no clear-cut distinction between the income of the king and the income of the state. Worse still was the fact that the collection of public revenues was exceedingly haphazard. Instead of appointing official collectors, the king employed the old Roman system of farming out the collection of taxes to private corporations and individuals, permitting them to retain as profit all that they could gouge from the people in excess of a stipulated amount. Similar disorganized conditions prevailed in the realm of law and judicial procedure. Nearly every province of France had its special code based upon local custom. As a consequence an act punishable as a crime in southern France, where the Roman influence was strongest, might be no concern of the law in a central or northern province. **119**

This lack of uniformity was especially galling to the business classes, who were often involved in transactions in distant parts of the country.

(3) the costly
wars of the
French kings

Probably the most decisive of the political causes was the disastrous wars into which France was plunged during the eighteenth century. Revolutions are not made by sporadic attacks upon a system still in its prime, no matter how oppressive some of its policies may be. Before a great political and social upheaval (which is the way we must define a true revolution) can occur, it seems to be necessary that there shall be a near collapse of the existing order. Something must happen to produce a condition of chaos, to reveal the incompetence and corruption of the government, and to create such disgust and hardship that many of those who formerly supported the old regime shall now turn against it. Nothing could be better calculated to achieve these ends than conflict with foreign powers resulting in humiliating defeat or at least in serious reverses. As a matter of fact, it is almost impossible to conceive of any of the great revolutions of modern times except as a consequence of long and disastrous wars.[2] The first of the wars that prepared the ground for the French Revolution was the Seven Years' War (1756–1763), fought during the reign of Louis XV. In this struggle France was pitted against England and Prussia and, in spite of aid from Austria and also for a time from Russia, went down to overwhelming defeat. As a result, the French were compelled to surrender nearly all of their colonial possessions. It was natural and, on the whole quite justifiable, that the blame for this catastrophe should be placed on the incompetence of the government. The effects of this blow were made worse when Louis XVI decided in 1778 to intervene in the American War for Independence. Though France was now on the winning side, the cost of maintaining fleets and armies in the Western Hemisphere for more than three years virtually bankrupted the government. As we shall see, it was this condition of financial helplessness in the face of an impossible burden of debt which led directly to the quarrel between the king and the middle class and the consequent outbreak of revolution.

The French
Revolution not
the result of
misery and
poverty among
the people

In turning to the economic causes of the French Revolution, we must note first of all that universal wretchedness among the mass of the people was not one of them. The popular notion that the Revolution occurred because the majority of the people were starving for want of bread, and because the queen said, "Let them eat cake," is far from historically accurate. Despite the loss of her colonial empire, France on the eve of the Revolution was still a rich and prosperous nation. Some conditions were critical, however. The government was so close to bankruptcy that it could pay its debts only by

[2] A distinction, of course, must be drawn between true revolutions and those of the "palace" variety, so common in Africa, Southeast Asia, and in Latin America, which are really very little more than substitutes for elections.

borrowing money at ruinous rates of interest. Though some industries were prospering, others were scraping the bottom of the barrel to make ends meet. The textile industries were suffering from the severe drought of 1785. Wine-making, a chief pillar of export trade, was in the doldrums. Because of drought and crop failures, farmers were no longer able to pay their hired workers. These flocked into the cities to join the ranks of the jobless industrial workers. Yet the masses in the cities were too beaten and unorganized to take definite steps for their own benefit. As for the bulk of the rural population, it is the opinion of some modern scholars that the French peasants in the eighteenth century were better off than the rural folk in any other country of Europe except England.[3] Only about one-twentieth of the French population still languished in serfdom, and the proportion was gradually diminishing. What the downtrodden classes did in 1789 was not to initiate the Revolution, but to provide an army of followers after it had been started by others. The fact cannot be emphasized too strongly that the French Revolution was launched as a middle-class movement. Its original objectives were primarily for the benefit of the bourgeoisie. Since the leaders of this class needed the support of a larger percentage of the people, they naturally took some notice of the grievances of the peasants, and eventually of the proletarians.

What then were the real economic causes? Perhaps we should place at the head of the list the rise of the middle class to a position of extraordinary affluence and prestige. The emergence of a new economic group with a sense of grievances and a consciousness of its own strength and importance seems to be a necessary condition to the outbreak of any revolution. This class is never composed of miserable dregs of humanity—wretched, starving, and hopeless. On the contrary, its ranks must be permeated by a sense of confidence inspired by previous success and strengthened by the belief that additional effort will being greater gains in the future. During the years preceding the Revolution the French bourgeoisie had grown to be the dominant economic class. Aside from the land, nearly all of the productive wealth was in its hands. It controlled the resources of trade, manufacturing, and finance. Moreover, its members appear to have been growing richer year by year. In 1789 the foreign commerce of France reached the unprecedented total of 1,153,000,000 francs.[4] But the chief effect of this rising prosperity was to sharpen bourgeois discontent. No matter how much money a merchant, manufacturer, banker, or lawyer might acquire, he was still excluded from political privileges. He had almost no influence at the court; he could not share in the highest honors; and, except in the choice of a few petty local officers, he could not even vote. Besides, he was looked down upon as an inferior by the idle and frivolous

The real economic causes: (1) the rise of the middle class

[3] L. R. Gottschalk, *The Era of the French Revolution*, pp. 30–31.
[4] *Ibid.*, p. 44.

nobility. Occasionally some snobbish count or duke would consent to the marriage of his son to the daughter of a rich burgher; but one who did so often made a practice of referring to the marriage as "manuring [his] land." As the middle class rose in affluence and in consciousness of its own importance, its members were bound to resent such attempts at social discrimination. But above all it was the demand of the commercial, financial, and industrial leaders for political power commensurate with their economic position that made the bourgeoisie a revolutionary class.

(2) opposition
to mercantilism

A demand for political power was not the only consequence of the growing prosperity of the middle class; there was also an increasing clamor for the abandonment of mercantilist policies. In earlier times mercantilism had been welcomed by merchants and manufacturers because of its effects in procuring new markets and fostering trade. But those times were at the beginning of the Commercial Revolution when business was still in its swaddling clothes. As commerce and industry flourished through succeeding centuries, the bourgeoisie became increasingly confident of its ability to stand on its own collective feet. The result was a growing tendency to look upon the regulations of mercantilism as oppressive restrictions. Merchants disliked the special monopolies granted to favored companies and the interference with their freedom to buy in foreign markets. Manufacturers chafed under the laws controlling wages, fixing prices, and restricting the purchase of raw materials outside of France and her colonies. These were only a few of the more annoying regulations enforced by a government operating under the twin objectives of paternalism and economic self-sufficiency. Perhaps it is not strange that the middle class should have come to think of pure economic liberty as a paradise, worthy to be gained at terrific cost. At any rate, it can scarcely be doubted that the desire of businessmen to be rid of mercantilism was one of the principal causes of the French Revolution.

(3) the survival of privilege: the first estate

A third factor, mainly economic in character, which contributed much to the outbreak of the French Revolution was the system of privilege entrenched in the society of the *ancien régime*. Prior to the Revolution the population of France was divided into three great classes or estates: the first was composed of the clergy; the second, of the nobles; and the third, of the common people. The first estate really included two different ranks: (1) the higher clergy, made up of cardinals, archbishops, bishops, and abbots; and (2) the lower clergy or parish priests. Though all of these servants of the Church were supposed to be members of a privileged group, in actual fact a wide gulf separated the two ranks. The lower clergy were frequently as poor as their humblest parishioners and were generally disposed to sympathize with the common man. By contrast, the higher clergy lived on the fattest fruits of the land and moved in the gay and sophisticated circle of the king and his court.

Including no more than 1 per cent of the total population, they nevertheless owned about 20 per cent of all the land, to say nothing of vast wealth in the form of castles, paintings, gold, and jewels. Several of the bishops and archbishops had incomes running into hundreds of thousands of francs. Naturally, most of these gilded prelates gave little attention to religious affairs. Some of them dabbled in politics, aiding the king in maintaining his absolute rule. Others gambled or devoted their energies to more scandalous vices. Though it cannot be assumed that all of them were depraved and neglectful of their professional duties, a sufficient number were corrupt, domineering, and vicious to convince many people that the Church was rotten to the core and that its leaders were guilty of robbing the people and wasting the nation's resources.

The second estate, comprising the secular nobility, was also divided into two subordinate castes. At the top were the *nobles of the sword*, whose titles went all the way back to the feudal suzerains of the Middle Ages. Beneath them were the *nobles of the robe*, whose immediate ancestors had acquired some judicial office conferring a title of nobility; the "robe" was the magistrate's or judge's gown. Though commonly despised by their brethren of more ancient lineage, the nobles of the robe were by far the most intelligent and progressive members of the upper classes. Several of their number became ardent reformers, while a few played prominent roles in the Revolution itself. Their ranks included such famous critics of the established order as Montesquieu, Mirabeau, and Lafayette. It was the nobles of the sword who really constituted the privileged class in the second estate. Together with the higher clergy they monopolized the leading positions in the government, usually delegating the actual work to subordinates. While they owned vast estates, they customarily resided at Versailles and depended upon stewards or bailiffs to extort enough from the peasants to provide for their luxurious needs. Few, indeed, of these high-born wastrels performed any useful function. They acted as if they believed that their only responsibilities to society were to flatter the king, to cultivate the graces of courtly life, and occasionally to patronize the decadent classical art. In a very real sense, most of them were worthless parasites consuming the wealth which others labored hard to produce.

Among the most valuable privileges of clerics and nobles were those relating to taxation. And the inequitable system of taxation may well be considered a fourth economic cause of the French Revolution. Taxes in France, long before 1789, had come to consist of two main types. First, there were the direct taxes, which included the *taille*, or tax on real and personal property; the *capitation*, or poll tax; and the *vingtième*, or tax on incomes, originally at the rate of 5 per cent, but in the eighteenth century more commonly 10 or 11 per cent. The indirect taxes, or taxes added to the price of commodities and paid by the ultimate consumer, embraced mainly the tariffs on articles imported from foreign countries and the tolls levied on goods shipped from one province of France to another. In addition, the *gabelle*, or tax on salt, may also be considered a form of indirect tax. For some time the production of salt had been a state monopoly in France, and every individual inhabitant was required to buy at least seven pounds a year from the government works. To the cost of production was added a heavy tax, with the result that the price to the consumer was often as much as fifty or sixty times the actual value of the salt. While exceedingly burdensome, the indirect taxes were not as a rule unfairly distributed. It was difficult, of course, for anyone, regardless of his social status, to avoid paying them. The case of most of the direct taxes, however, was far otherwise. The clergy, by virtue of the medieval rule that the property of the Church could not be taxed by the state, escaped payment of both the *taille* and the *vingtième*. The nobles, especially those of higher rank, made use of their influence with the king to obtain exemption from practically all direct levies. As a result, the main task of providing funds for the government fell upon the common people, or members of the third estate. And since few of the artisans and laborers had much that could be taxed, the chief burden had to be borne by the peasants and the bourgeoisie.

A final economic cause of the Revolution was the survival of relics of feudalism in France as late as 1789. While the feudal system itself had long since become extinct, vestiges of it remained and served as convenient instruments for maintaining the power of the king and the privileged position of the nobles. In some backward areas of the country serfdom still lingered, but the prevalence of this institution must not be exaggerated. The highest estimate ever given of the number of peasants who were serfs is 1,500,000, out of a total rural population of at least 15,000,000. The vast majority of the peasants were free men. A considerable proportion owned the lands they cultivated. Others were tenants or hired laborers, but the largest percentage appear to have been sharecroppers, farming the lands of the nobles for a portion of the harvest, generally ranging from a third to a half. However, even those peasants who were entirely free were still required to perform obligations which had come down from the later Middle Ages. One of the most odious of these was the payment of an annual rental to the lord who had formerly controlled the land. Another was the donation to the local noble of a share of the price received whenever a tract of land was sold. In addition, the peasants were still required to contribute the *banalités*, or fees supposedly for the use of various facilities owned by the noble. During the Middle Ages *banalités* had been paid for the use of the lord's flour mill, his wine press, and his bake oven. In spite of the fact that by the eighteenth century many of the peasants owned such equipment themselves and no longer benefited by the services provided by the noble, the *banalités* were still collected

(5) the survival of relics of feudalism

Le Hameau, A Rustic Villa Constructed in English Style on the Grounds of Le Petit Trianon at Versailles. Here ladies of the Court led a mimic peasant life. The villa was one of the favorite spots of Marie Antoinette.

in the original amounts.

Probably the most exasperating of all the relics of feudalism were the *corvée* and the hunting privileges of the nobility. The *corvée*, formerly a requirement of labor on the lord's demesne and in the building of roads and bridges on the manorial estate, was now an obligation to the government. For several weeks each year the peasant was forced to put his own work aside and devote his labor to maintaining the public highways. No other class of the population was required to perform this service. Even greater inconvenience was suffered by the rural citizens as a result of the hunting privileges of the nobles. From time immemorial the right to indulge in the diversions of the chase had been regarded as a distinctive badge of aristocracy. The man of gentle birth must have unlimited freedom to pursue this exciting pastime wherever he wished. Naturally, nothing so trivial as the property rights of the peasants should be allowed to stand in the way. In some parts of France the peasants were forbidden to weed or mow in breeding time lest they disturb the nests of the partridges. Rabbits, crows, and foxes could not be killed regardless of how much damage they did to the crops or to domestic fowl and young animals. Furthermore, the peasant was supposed to resign himself to having his fields trampled at any time by the horses of some thoughtless crew of noble hunters.

Every great social upheaval of modern times has developed out of

The corvée and the hunting privileges of the nobility

125

a background of intellectual causes. Before a movement can reach the proportions of an actual revolution, it is necessary that it be supported by a body of ideas, providing not only a program of action but a glorious vision of the new order that is finally to be achieved. To a large extent these ideas are the product of political and economic ambitions, but in time they take on the significance of independent factors. Originally secondary or derivative causes, they ultimately become primary causes. Eventually the fulfillment of the ideas is accepted as an end in itself and draws the allegiance of men like the gospel of a new religion. The intellectual causes of the French Revolution were mainly an outgrowth of the Enlightenment. This movement produced two interesting political theories, which have exerted influence ever since. The first was the *liberal* theory of such writers as Locke and Montesquieu; and the second was the *democratic* theory of Rousseau. While the two were fundamentally opposed, they nevertheless had elements in common. Both were predicated upon the assumption that the state is a necessary evil and that government rests upon a contractual basis. Each had its doctrine of popular sovereignty, although with contrasting interpretations. And, finally, both upheld in some measure the fundamental rights of the individual.

The father of the liberal theory of the seventeenth and eighteenth centuries was John Locke (1632–1704). Locke's political philosophy is contained chiefly in his *Second Treatise of Civil Government*, published in 1690. In this he developed a theory of limited government which was used to justify the new system of parliamentary rule set up in England as a result of the Glorious Revolution. He maintained that originally all men had lived in a state of nature in which absolute freedom and equality prevailed, and there was no government of any kind. The only law was the law of nature, which each individual enforced for himself in order to protect his natural rights to life, liberty, and property. It was not long, however, until men began to perceive that the inconveniences of the state of nature greatly outweighed its advantages. With every individual attempting to enforce his own rights, confusion and insecurity were the unavoidable results. Accordingly, the people agreed among themselves to establish a civil society, to set up a government, and to surrender certain powers to it. But they did not make that government absolute. The only power they conferred upon it was the executive power of the law of nature. Since the state is nothing but the joint power of all the members of society, its authority "can be no more than those persons had in a state of nature before they entered into society, and gave it up to the community." [5] All powers not expressly surrendered are reserved to the people themselves. If the government exceeds or abuses the authority explicitly granted in the political contract, it becomes tyrannical; and the people then have

126   [5] *Second Treatise of Civil Government* (Everyman Library ed.), p. 184.

the right to dissolve it or to rebel against it and overthrow it.

Locke condemned absolutism in every form. He denounced despotic monarchy, but he was no less severe in his strictures against the absolute sovereignty of parliaments. Though he defended the supremacy of the law-making branch, with the executive primarily an agent of the legislature, he nevertheless refused to concede to the representatives of the people an unlimited power. Arguing that government was instituted among men for the preservation of property (which he generally defined in the inclusive sense of life, liberty, and estate),[6] he denied the authority of any political agency to invade the natural rights of a single individual. The law of nature, which embodies these rights, is an automatic limitation upon every branch of the government. Regardless of how large a majority of the people's representatives should demand the restriction of freedom of speech or the confiscation and redistribution of property, no such action could legally be taken. If taken illegally it would justify effective measures of resistance on the part of the majority of citizens. Locke was much more concerned with protecting individual liberty than he was with promoting stability or social progress. If forced to make a choice, he would have preferred the evils of anarchy to those of despotism in any form.

Locke's condemnation of absolutism

The influence of few political philosophers in the history of the world has exceeded that of Locke. Not only were his doctrines of natural rights, limited government, and the right of resistance against tyranny an important source of French Revolutionary theory, but they found ready acceptance in American thought as well. They furnished most of the theoretical foundation for the colonial revolt against British oppression. They were reflected so clearly in the Declaration of Independence that whole passages of that document might almost have been copied from the *Second Treatise of Civil Government*. Lockian principles also influenced the drafting of the Constitution and especially the arguments advanced by Hamilton, Madison, and Jay in the *Federalist* urging its ratification. Later, when the new government enacted the Alien and Sedition laws, it was mainly on the basis of Lockian theory that Madison and Jefferson in the Virginia and Kentucky Resolutions appealed to the several States to resist the usurpation of power.

Locke's influence

In France the foremost exponents of the liberal political theory were Voltaire (1694–1778) and Baron de Montesquieu (1689–1755). As was indicated earlier, Voltaire considered orthodox Christianity to be the worst of the enemies of mankind, but he reserved plenty of contempt for tyrannical government. During his exile in England he had studied the writings of Locke and had been deeply impressed by their vigorous assertions of individual freedom. Returning to France while still a comparatively young man, he devoted a large part of the remainder of his life to the fight for intel-

The liberal political theory of Voltaire

[6] *Ibid.*, p. 159.

lectual, religious, and political liberty. In common with Locke he conceived of government as a necessary evil, with powers which ought to be limited to the enforcement of natural rights. He maintained that all men are endowed by nature with equal rights to liberty, property, and the protection of the laws. But Voltaire was no democrat. He was inclined to think of the ideal form of government as either an enlightened monarchy or a republic dominated by the middle class. To the end of his life he continued to be more than a little afraid of the masses. He was even fearful that his attacks upon organized religion might serve to incite the multitude to deeds of violence. It is related that after he had been robbed by some peasants, he attended church for a season in order to persuade the country bumpkins that he still believed in God.

The influence
of Montesquieu

A more systematic political thinker than Voltaire was his older contemporary, Baron de Montesquieu. Though, like Voltaire, a student of Locke and an ardent admirer of British institutions, Montesquieu was a unique figure among the political philosophers of the eighteenth century. In his celebrated *Spirit of Laws* he brought new methods and new conceptions into the theory of the state. Instead of attempting to found a science of government by pure deduction, he followed the Aristotelian method of studying actual political systems as they were supposed to have operated in the past. He denied that there is any one perfect form of government suitable for all peoples under all conditions. He maintained, on the contrary, that political institutions in order to be successful must harmonize with the physical conditions and the level of social advancement of the nations they are intended to serve. Thus he declared that despotism is best suited to countries of vast domain; limited monarchy to those of moderate size; and republican government to those of small extent. For his own country, France, he was disposed to think that a limited monarchy would be the most appropriate form, since he regarded the nation as too large to be made into a republic unless on some kind of federal plan.

The separation
of powers and
checks and
balances

Montesquieu is especially famous for his theory of the separation of powers. He avowed that it is a natural tendency of man to abuse any extent of power entrusted to him, and that consequently every government, regardless of its form, is liable to degenerate into despotism. To prevent such a result he argued that the authority of government should be broken up into its three natural divisions of legislative, executive, and judicial. Whenever any two or more of these are allowed to remain united in the same hands, liberty, he declared, is at an end. The only effective way to avoid tyranny is to enable each branch of the government to act as a check upon the other two. For example, the executive should have the power by means of the veto to curb the encroachments of the lawmaking branch. The legislature, in turn, should have the authority of impeachment in order to restrain the executive. And, finally, there

should be an independent judiciary vested with power to protect individual rights against arbitrary acts of either the legislature or the
executive. This favorite scheme of Montesquieu was not intended,
of course, to facilitate democracy. In fact, its purpose was largely
the opposite: to prevent the absolute supremacy of the majority, expressed as it normally would be through the people's representatives
in the legislature. It was a typical illustration of that strong dislike
which the bourgeoisie had come to have for despotic government in
any form, whether of the few or of the many. Montesquieu's principle of the separation of powers was none the less influential. It was
incorporated in the first of the governments set up during the
French Revolution, and it found its way with very few changes indeed into the Constitution of the United States.[7]

The second of the great political ideals which occupied an important place in the intellectual background of the French Revolution
was the ideal of democracy. In contrast with liberalism, democracy, **The democratic**
in its original meaning, was much less concerned with the defense of **political theory**
individual rights than with the enforcement of popular rule. What
the majority of the citizens wills is the supreme law of the land, for
the voice of the people is the voice of God. It is generally assumed
that under democracy the minority will continue to enjoy full
liberty of expression, but this assumption does not necessarily hold.
The only sovereign right of the minority is the right to become the
majority. As long as a particular group remains a minority, its members cannot claim any rights of individual action beyond the control
of the state. Many exponents of democracy in the present generation deny that this statement is true and stoutly maintain their devotion to freedom of speech and freedom of the press as rights which
the government cannot legally infringe. But this attitude springs
from the fact that the current ideal is generally combined with
liberalism. Indeed, democracy and liberalism have now come to be
used as if they were identical in meaning. Originally, however, they
were entirely separate ideals. Historic democracy also included a belief in the natural equality of all men, opposition to hereditary privilege, and an abiding faith in the wisdom and virtue of the masses.

The founder of democracy as described above was Jean Jacques
Rousseau (1712–1778). Since Rousseau was also the father of
romanticism, we can expect that sentiment should have deeply col- **Rousseau, the**
ored his political judgments. Consistency, moreover, was not always **founder of de-**
a crowning virtue of his reasoning. The most significant of his writ- **mocracy**
ings on political theory were his *Social Contract* and his *Discourse
on the Origin of Inequality*. In both of these he upheld the popular
thesis that men had originally lived in a state of nature. But in contrast with Locke he regarded this state of nature as a veritable para-

[7] For the influence of Montesquieu upon the founders of the American government, see E. M. Burns, *James Madison: Philosopher of the Constitution*, pp.
180–83.

dise. No one suffered inconvenience from maintaining his own rights against others. Indeed, there were very few chances of conflict of any sort; for private property did not exist for a long time, and every man was the equal of his neighbor. Eventually, however, evils arose, due primarily to the fact that some men staked off plots of land and said to themselves, "This is mine." It was in such manner that various degrees of inequality developed; and, as a consequence, "cheating trickery," "insolent pomp," and "insatiable ambition" soon came to dominate the relations among men.[8] The only hope of security was now for men to establish a civil society and to surrender all of their rights to the community. This they did by means of a social contract, in which each individual agreed with the whole body of individuals to submit to the will of the majority. Thus the state was brought into existence.

Jean-Jacques Rousseau, from a contemporary painting.

Rousseau's
conception of
sovereignty

Rousseau developed an altogether different conception of sovereignty from that of the liberals. Whereas Locke and his followers had taught that only a portion of sovereign power is surrendered to the state, the rest being retained by the people themselves, Rousseau contended that sovereignty is indivisible, and that all of it became vested in the community when civil society was formed. He insisted further that each individual in becoming a party to the social contract gave up all of his rights to the people collectively and agreed to submit absolutely to the general will. It follows that the sovereign power of the state is subject to no limitations whatever. The general will, expressed through the vote of the majority, is the court of final appeal. What the majority decides is always right in the political sense and is absolutely binding upon every citizen. The state, which in actual practice means the majority, is legally omnipotent. But this does not really imply, according to Rousseau, that the liberty of the individual is entirely destroyed. On the contrary, subjec-

[8] *Discourse on the Origin of Inequality* (Everyman Library ed.), p. 207.

tion to the state has the effect of enhancing *genuine* liberty. Individuals in surrendering their rights to the community merely exchange the animal liberty of the state of nature for the true freedom of reasoning creatures in obedience to law. Compelling an individual to abide by the general will is therefore merely "forcing him to be free." It must be understood, also, that when Rousseau referred to the state he did not mean the government. He regarded the state as the politically organized community, which has the sovereign function of expressing the general will. The authority of the state cannot be represented, but must be expressed directly through the enactment of fundamental laws by the people themselves. The government, on the other hand, is simply the executive agent of the state. Its function is not to formulate the general will but merely to carry it out. Moreover, the community can set the government up or pull it down "whenever it likes." [9]

THE CAUSES

The influence of Rousseau's political theory would be hard to exaggerate. His dogmas of equality and the supremacy of the majority were the chief inspiration for the second stage of the French Revolution. Doctrinaire radicals like Robespierre were among his most fervent disciples. But Rousseau's influence was not confined to his own country. Some of his theories made their way to America and found an echo in certain of the principles of Jacksonian Democracy—although, of course, it is extremely improbable that many of Jackson's followers had ever heard of Rousseau. The German Romantic Idealists, who, in the early nineteenth century, glorified the state as "God in history," would also appear to have been indebted to the philosophy of *The Social Contract*. From Rousseau's doctrines that the state is legally omnipotent, and that true liberty consists in submission to the general will, it was not a very difficult step to exalting the state as an object of worship and reducing the individual to a mere cog in the political machine.[10] Even though Rousseau suggested that the majority would be limited by moral restraints and insisted upon the right of the people to "pull down" their government, these limitations were not enough to counteract the effect of his stress upon absolute sovereignty.

The influence of Rousseau

As a final intellectual cause of the French Revolution, the influence of the new economic theory must be given at least passing attention. In the second half of the eighteenth century a number of brilliant writers began attacking the traditional assumptions in regard to public control over production and trade. Their special target of criticism was mercantilist policy. To a large extent the new economics was founded upon the basic conceptions of the Enlightenment, particularly the idea of a mechanistic universe governed by inflexible laws. The notion now came to prevail that the

The influence of the new economic theory

[9] *The Social Contract* (Everyman Library ed.), p. 88.
[10] For a discussion of the political theory of the Romantic Idealists see § 3 in the chapter on The Age of Romanticism and Reaction.

sphere of the production and distribution of wealth was subject to laws just as irresistible as those of physics and astronomy. The new economic theory may also be regarded as the counterpart of political liberalism. The cardinal aims of the two were quite similar: to reduce the powers of government to the lowest minimum consistent with safety and to preserve for the individual the largest possible measure of freedom in the pursuit of his own devices.

The first of the leading champions of a revised attitude toward economic problems were members of a group known as the Physiocrats. The most eminent among them were François Quesnay (1694–1774), author of the *Tableau Économique*, the bible of Physiocracy; Dupont de Nemours (1739–1817), ancestor of the Dupont family in the United States; and Robert Jacques Turgot (1727–1781), finance minister for a brief period under Louis XVI.[11] From the outset the Physiocrats condemned mercantilist doctrine. One of their chief aims was to prove that the *natural* enterprises of agriculture, mining, and fishing are more important to national prosperity than commerce. Nature, they held, is the real producer of wealth, and therefore those industries which actually exploit the resources of nature and make them yield things of value to man are most to be prized. Trade is essentially sterile, since it merely transfers goods already in existence from one person to another. As time went on, these doctrines were subordinated to another idea which the Physiocrats came to regard as paramount to everything else. This was the liberation of economic activity from the suffocating restraints imposed by the state. The Physiocrats demanded that the government should refrain from all interference with business except in so far as might be necessary for the protection of life and property. Nothing should ever be done to hinder the operation of natural economic laws. This doctrine was neatly summed up in the picturesque maxim, *Laissez faire et laissez passer, le monde va de lui-même* (Let do and let alone, the world goes on of itself). The ideal of laissez faire soon came to embody such notions as the sanctity of private property and the rights of freedom of contract and free competition. It was thus the very antithesis of the restrictive policy of mercantilism.

The greatest of all the economists of the age of the Enlightenment and one of the most brilliant of all time was Adam Smith (1723–1790). A native of Scotland, Smith began his career as a lecturer on English literature at the University of Edinburgh. From this he was soon advanced to a professorship of logic at Glasgow College. He first won fame in 1759 with the publication of his *Theory of Moral Sentiments*. Although he had been interested for some time in problems of political economy, this interest was effectively stimulated by

[11] Another economist, Vincent de Gournay (1712–1759), influenced the Physiocrats, but he was never actually a member of the school. He is commonly credited with having originated the phrase, laissez faire.

two years of residence in France while serving as tutor to the young Duke of Buccleuch. Here he became acquainted with the leading members of the Physiocratic school and was delighted to find that some of their theories agreed with his own. He described the economics of Quesnay, "with all its imperfections," as "the nearest approximation to truth that has yet been published on the principles of that science." But Smith never enlisted under the standard of the Physiocrats, despite the undoubted influence of many of their doctrines upon him. In 1776 he published his *Inquiry into the Nature and Causes of the Wealth of Nations*, generally considered the foundation of modern economic theory. In this work he maintained that labor, rather than agriculture or the bounty of nature, is the real source of wealth. While in general he accepted the principle of *laissez faire*, avowing that the prosperity of all can best be promoted by allowing each individual to pursue his own interest, he nevertheless recognized that certain forms of governmental interference would be desirable. The state should intervene for the prevention of injustice and oppression, for the advancement of education and the protection of public health, and for the maintenance of necessary enterprises which would never be established by private capital. Notwithstanding these rather broad limitations upon the principle of laissez faire, Smith's *Wealth of Nations* was adopted as Holy Writ by the economic individualists of the eighteenth and nineteenth centuries. Its influence in causing the French Revolution was indirect but none the less profound. It furnished the final answer to mercantilist argument and thereby strengthened the ambition of the bourgeoisie to have done with a political system which continued to block the path to economic freedom.

2. THE DESTRUCTION OF THE *Ancien Régime*

Early in the year 1789 the volcano of discontent in France burst forth into revolution. The immediate causes were a series of economic troubles for which no one seemed to be able to find an acceptable remedy. As a consequence of bad harvests bread prices almost doubled. Commercial treaties recently negotiated with Britain resulted in an influx of British manufactured goods and sharply curtailed French production. In December 1788, 80,000 workers were reported unemployed in Paris. Most serious of all was the near bankruptcy of the French government. To meet the mounting deficit, the king's finance ministers proposed new taxes, notably a stamp duty and a direct tax on the annual production of the soil. Meanwhile, such earlier impositions as the *taille* and the *gabelle* would continue in effect. Additional taxation might well have provided the government with the revenue it so desperately needed had there not been confusion and discord in the administration of fiscal policies. Every proposed reform threatened the interests of some

The immediate causes of the French Revolution

133

ENGLAND

HOLY ROMAN EMPIRE

Rhine R.

AUSTRIAN

ENGLISH CHANNEL

FLANDERS AND HAINAUT

ARTOIS

PICARDY

PALATINATE

Rouen

Varennes ●

METZ AND VERDUN

ISLE OF

NORMANDY

Versailles ● Paris ★

CHAMPAGNE

AND

BRIE

LORRAINE

WÜRTTEMBERG

FRANCE

Seine R.

NETH.

ALSACE

BRITTANY

MAINE

ORLÉANAIS

ANJOU

TOURAINE

SAU-
MUROIS

BERRY

NIVERNAIS

Loire R.

BURGUNDY

FRANCHE COMTÉ

SWISS
CONFEDERATION

POITOU

BOURBONNAIS

ATLANTIC

AUNIS

MARCHE

SAINTONGE AND

ANGOUMOIS

LIMOUSIN

AUVERGNE

LYONNAIS

DUCHY
OF
SAVOY

KINGDOM OF SARDINIA

OCEAN

● Bordeaux

Rhone R.

DAUPHINY

GUIENNE AND GASCONY

PROVENCE

● Toulouse

LANGUEDOC

● Marseilles

BEARN

FOIX

ROUSSILLON

MEDITERRANEAN

CORSICA

ANDORRA

SPAIN

SEA

0   200 miles

FRANCE IN 1789 • THE "GOVERNMENTS"

powerful group. As a result, pressure was brought upon the king to
dismiss the minister responsible. Conditions moved rapidly from bad
to worse as the government continued its makeshift policy of borrowing and spending. Prices rose so rapidly that the cost of bread
alone consumed more than 50 per cent of the poor man's income. In
1787 the king summoned an Assembly of Notables in the hope that
the chief magnates of the realm might consent to bearing a larger
share of the fiscal burden. Factional discord soon split the Assembly.
The nobles of the sword and the higher clergy staunchly supported
the monarchy and demanded retention of their privileges. The
judicial oligarchy, or nobles of the robe, took a broader view. Inspired by the philosophy of the Enlightenment and the American

134 Revolution, they argued not merely in favor of fiscal revision but of governmental reform. Specifically, they demanded convocation of the Estates General to deal with the national crisis.

Although the Estates General had not met for 175 years, the belief prevailed widely that it alone could save the country in a dire emergency. This was the burden of the numerous *cahiers de doléances,* or statements of grievances, drawn up by all classes for submission to local and national agencies. They not only condemned extravagance and fiscal abuses, the arbitrary acts of ministers, and *letters de cachet,* but they insisted upon the authority of the Estates General to enact laws and levy taxes. As its name implies, the Estates General was supposed to represent the three great estates or classes of the nation. During the period when it was convoked more or less regularly, the representatives of each estate had met and voted as a body. Generally this meant that the first and second estates combined against the third. By the late eighteenth century the third estate had attained such importance that it was not willing to tolerate such an arrangement. Consequently its leaders demanded that the three orders should sit together and vote as individuals. Leaving this issue unresolved, King Louis XVI, in the summer of 1788, yielded to popular clamor and summoned the Estates General to meet in May of the following year. After weeks of wrangling, the third estate, on June 17, boldly proclaimed itself the National Assembly and invited the representatives of the privileged orders to join in its work. Many of them actually did so. Within two days a majority of the clergy went over and a sprinkling of the nobles also. But then the king intervened. When the rebellious deputies assembled at their hall on the morning of June 20, they found its doors guarded by troops. There were now no alternatives but to submit or to defy the sovereign power of the monarch himself. Confident of the support of a majority of the people, the commoners and their allies withdrew to a near-by hall, variously used as a riding academy and a tennis court. Here under the leadership of Mirabeau and the Abbé Sieyès they bound themselves by a solemn oath not to separate until they had drafted a constitution for France. This Oath of the Tennis Court, on June 20, 1789, was the real beginning of the French Revolution. By claiming the authority to remake the government in the name of the people, the Estates General was not merely protesting against the arbitrary rule of Louis XVI but asserting its right to act as the highest sovereign power in the nation. On June 27 the king virtually conceded this right by ordering the remaining delegates of the privileged classes to meet with the third estate as members of a National Assembly.

The course of the French Revolution was marked by three great stages, the first of which extended from June 1789 to August 1792. During most of this period the destinies of France were in the hands of the National Assembly, dominated by the leaders of the third estate. In the main, this stage was a moderate, middle-class stage. The masses had not yet gained any degree of political power, nor

The first stage of the Revolution

The triumph of the third estate

were they in a position to seize control of the economic system. Aside from the destruction of the Bastille on July 14, 1789, and the murder of a few members of the royal guard, there was comparatively little violence in Paris or Versailles. In certain of the country districts, however, a more unruly spirit prevailed. Many of the peasants grew impatient over the delay in granting reforms and determined to deal with the situation directly. Arming themselves with pitchforks and scythes, they set out to destroy what they could of the *ancien régime.* They demolished *châteaux* of hated nobles, plundered monasteries and residences of bishops, and murdered some of the miserable lords who offered resistance. Most of this violence occurred during the summer of 1789 and had much to do with frightening the upper classes into surrendering some of their privileges.

Achievements
of the first
stage: (1) the
destruction of
feudal privi-
leges

The most significant developments of the first stage of the Revolution were the achievements of the National Assembly between 1789 and 1791. The initial one of these achievements was the destruction of most of the relics of feudalism. This came about largely as a result of the rebellious temper displayed by the peasants. By the beginning of August 1789, such alarming reports of anarchy in the

The Storming of the Bastille, July 14, 1789. The mob has seized the Governor and has begun the attack on the prison. Though this event is celebrated by the French as their national holiday, it was merely a belated confirmation of the real beginning of the Revolution with the Oath of the Tennis Court on June 20.

EUROPE · 1789

Hapsburg possessions

Boundary of the Holy Roman Empire

Volga R.

RUSSIAN EMPIRE

Sea of Azov

BLACK SEA

Constantinople

OTTOMAN EMPIRE

AEGEAN SEA

Athens

SWEDEN

Stockholm

BALTIC SEA

Dnieper R.

POLAND

Dniester R.

Warsaw

Vistula R.

PRUSSIA

Budapest

Danube R.

Oder R.

Berlin

Elbe R.

Prague

HOLY ROMAN

Vienna

EMPIRE

SEA

DENMARK

Rhine R.

Berne

SWITZ.

Po R.

Venice

VENETIAN REP.

ADRIATIC SEA

PAPAL STATES

Rome

IONIAN IS.
(To Venice)

KINGDOM

OF THE

TWO SICILIES

NORTH SEA

UNITED NETHERLANDS

Amsterdam

Brussels

GREAT BRITAIN

London

Thames R.

Seine R.

Paris

FRANCE

GENOA

(Fr.)

KINGDOM OF SARDINIA

MEDITERRANEAN

OTTOMAN EMPIRE

IRELAND
(Br.)

Dublin

English Channel

Loire R.

Garonne R.

Bay of Biscay

ATLANTIC OCEAN

Madrid

Tagus R.

SPAIN

Gibraltar (Br.)

PORTUGAL

Lisbon

Strait of Gibraltar

500 miles

Portrait of a Gentleman, Jean Auguste Ingres (1780–1867). A student of David, Ingres was a devoted admirer of classical antiquities. But he was also influenced by romanticism. (MMA)

A Woman Reading, Camille Corot (1796–1875). Corot was predominantly a naturalist, a painter of lifelike scenes of innocence and simplicity. He shared the romanticists' sentimental worship of woods and fields. (MMA)

Madame Recamier, Jacques Louis David (1748–1825). David was the exponent of a new classicism during and after the French Revolution. The couch, the lamp, and the costume are copied from Rome and Pompeii. (Louvre)

villages had reached the National Assembly that an urgent need for concessions soon came to be recognized by many of the members. On the fourth of August a certain noble proposed in an eloquent speech that all of his brethren should renounce their feudal privileges. His plea stirred the Assembly to a wild enthusiasm, compounded partly of fear and partly of revolutionary zeal. Nobles, churchmen, and burghers vied with each other in suggesting reforms. Before the night had ended, numerous remnants of the hoary structure of vested rights had been swept away. Ecclesiastical tithes and the *corvée* were formally abolished. Serfdom was eliminated. The hunting privileges of the nobles were declared at an end. Exemption from taxation and monopolies of all kinds were sacrificed as contrary to natural equality. While the nobles did not surrender all of their rights, the ultimate effect of these reforms of the "August Days" was to annihilate distinctions of rank and class and to make all Frenchmen citizens of an equal status in the eyes of the law.[12]

Following the destruction of privilege the Assembly turned its attention to preparing a charter of liberties. The result was the Declaration of the Rights of Man and of the Citizen, issued in September 1789. Modeled in part after the English Bill of Rights and embodying the teachings of liberal political philosophers, the French Declaration was a typical middle-class document. Property was declared to be a natural right as well as liberty, security, and "resistance to oppression." No one was to be deprived of anything he possessed except in case of public necessity, and then only on condition that he should have been "previously and equitably indemnified." Proper consideration was also to be given to personal rights. Freedom of speech, religious toleration, and liberty of the press were held to be inviolable. All citizens were declared to be entitled to equality of treatment in the courts. No one was to be imprisoned or otherwise punished except in accordance with due process of law. Sovereignty was affirmed to reside in the people, and officers of the government were made subject to deposition if they abused the powers conferred upon them. Nothing was said about any right of the common man to an adequate share of the wealth he produced or even to protection by the state in case of inability to earn a living. The authors of the Declaration of Rights were not socialists, nor were they interested particularly in the economic welfare of the masses.

(2) the Declaration of the Rights of Man

The next of the main accomplishments of the National Assembly was the secularization of the Church. Under the *ancien régime* the higher clergy had been a privileged caste, rewarding the king for his favors by a staunch support of absolute rule. As a result, the Church had come to be regarded as an instrument of greed and oppression almost as odious as the monarchy itself. Moreover, the ecclesiastical

(3) the secularization of the Church

[12] Along with these reforms in connection with the destruction of monopolies and feudal privileges, the guilds were also abolished and workers were forbidden to form unions.

institutions were the possessors of vast estates, and the new Revolutionary government was desperately in need of funds. Accordingly, in November 1789, the National Assembly resolved to confiscate the lands of the Church and to use them as collateral for the issue of *assignats*, or paper money. In July of the following year the Civil Constitution of the Clergy was enacted, providing that all bishops and priests should be elected by the people and should be subject to the authority of the state. Their salaries were to be paid out of the public treasury, and they were required to swear allegiance to the new legislation. The secularization of the Church also involved a partial separation from Rome. The aim of the Assembly was to make the Catholic Church of France a truly national institution with no more than a nominal subjection to the papacy. Since the Pope condemned this arrangement and forbade any bishop or priest to accept it, the result was to divide the clergy of France into two different groups. A minority took the oath of allegiance to the Civil Constitution and were henceforth known as the "juring" clergy. Some of the "non-jurors" fled from the country, but many remained and united with reactionary nobles in stirring up hatred for the whole Revolutionary program.

Not until 1791 did the National Assembly manage to complete its primary task of drafting a new constitution for the nation. Too many other problems of more immediate concern had absorbed its attention. Besides, autocratic government was already a thing of the past. The constitution as it finally emerged gave eloquent testimony to the dominant position now held by the bourgeoisie. France was not made a democratic republic, but the government was converted merely into a limited monarchy, with the supreme power virtually a monopoly of the well-to-do. The privilege of voting was restricted to those who paid a direct tax equal to three days' wages, while eligibility for holding office was limited to citizens of comparative wealth. As to the structure of the government, the principle of the separation of powers was to be the basic feature. For this the founders of the new system went back to Montesquieu's idea of independent legislative, executive, and judicial departments. The lawmaking powers were bestowed upon a Legislative Assembly chosen indirectly by the people through a process somewhat similar to that by which the President of the United States was originally supposed to be selected. The king was deprived of the control he had formerly exercised over the army, the Church, and local government. His ministers were forbidden to sit in the Assembly, and he was shorn of all power over the legislative process except a suspensive veto, which in fact could be overridden by the issuance of proclamations. Thus the new system, although far removed from absolute monarchy, was decidedly not a government the masses could claim as their own.

In the summer of 1792 the French Revolution entered a second

(4) the Constitution of 1791

138

The Execution of Louis XVI. The event took place on what is now the Place de la Concorde in Paris, on January 21, 1793.

stage, which lasted for about two years. This stage differed from the first in a number of ways. To begin with, France was now a republic. On the tenth of August the Legislative Assembly voted to suspend the king and ordered the election, by universal manhood suffrage, of a National Convention to draft a new constitution. Soon afterward Louis XVI was brought to trial on charges of plotting with foreign enemies of the Revolution, and on January 21, 1793, he was beheaded. In addition to its republican character, the second stage differed from the first in the fact that it was dominated by the lower classes. No longer was the course of the Revolution dictated by relatively conservative members of the bourgeoisie. Instead, it was extremists representing the proletariat of Paris who were largely responsible for determining the nature of the movement. The liberal philosophy of Voltaire and Montesquieu was now replaced by the radical, equalitarian doctrines of Rousseau. Yet another difference was the more violent and bloody character of the second stage. This was the period not only of the execution of the king but also of the September massacres (1792) and of the Reign of Terror from the summer of 1793 to the summer of 1794.

The second or radical stage of the Revolution

What factors may be taken to explain this spectacular transition from a comparatively moderate, middle-class phase to a stage of radicalism and turmoil? First of all may be mentioned the disappointed hopes of the proletariat. The Revolution in its beginning had held out what appeared to be glorious promises of equality and

Causes of the transition to a radical stage

139

justice for every citizen. Hope had been built particularly on the Declaration of Rights, in spite of its emphasis upon the sanctity of private property. But now after more than three years of social and political upheaval it was just as hard for the urban worker to earn his bread as it had been before. In actual fact, it was probably harder. In the spring of 1791 the government abolished the public workshops which had provided employment for thousands who had been left jobless by the disruption of business. Moreover, new laws were passed prohibiting the formation of unions, collective bargaining, picketing, and strikes. Another disappointment developed when the common man discovered after the adoption of the Constitution of 1791 that he was not even to be allowed to vote. Ever more clearly the realization dawned that he had simply exchanged one set of masters for another. In such a state of mind he was bound to be attracted by the preaching of extremists, who offered to lead him into the Promised Land of security and plenty. A second cause of the transition to a radical stage was the accumulated momentum of the Revolution itself. Every great movement of this kind generates an atmosphere of discontent, which is breathed more deeply by some men than by others. The result is the emergence of a kind of professional revolutionist, who is eternally dissatisfied no matter how much has been accomplished. He denounces the leaders of the revolution in its preliminary stage even more scathingly than he condemns the adherents of the old order. For him, no price of slaughter and chaos is too great to pay in order to purchase the fulfillment of his own ideals. He will murder his closest associates, the moment they disagree with him, just as readily as he will consign the most hated reactionary to outer darkness. He is the political counterpart of the religious fanatic who believes that sword and faggot are proper instruments for hastening the reign of God's righteousness and peace.

Yet perhaps the most important cause of the triumph of the radicals was the outbreak of war between France and foreign states. In several European countries the progress of the French Revolution was coming to be viewed with increasing alarm by reactionary rulers. The fear was particularly strong in Austria and Prussia, where numerous *émigrés*, or French royalists, had taken refuge and were convincing the monarchs of those countries of the danger that the Revolution might spread. Besides, the French queen, Marie Antoinette, was a member of the Hapsburg family and was making frenzied appeals to the Emperor to come to the aid of her husband. In August 1791, the Austrian and Prussian rulers joined in issuing the Declaration of Pillnitz, in which they boldly avowed that the restoration of order and of the rights of the monarch in France was a matter of "common interest to all sovereigns of Europe." Naturally this pronouncement was keenly resented by the French, since it could hardly be interpreted in any other way than as a threat of intervention. Moreover, there was a tendency on the part of many of the revolutionists to welcome a conflict with a foreign enemy. While the moderate faction expected that military success would solidify the loyalty of the people to the new regime, many of the radicals were clamoring for war in the secret hope that the armies of France would suffer defeat, and that the monarchy would thereby be discredited. A republic could then be set up, and the heroic soldiers of the people would turn defeat into victory and carry the blessings of freedom to all the oppressed of Europe. With such considerations in mind, the Assembly voted for war on April 20, 1792. As the radicals had hoped, the forces of the French met serious reverses. By August the allied armies of Austria and Prussia had crossed the frontier and were threatening the capture of Paris. A fury of rage and despair seized the capital. The belief prevailed that the military disasters had been the result of treasonable dealings with the enemy on the part of the king and his conservative followers. As a consequence, a vigorous demand arose for drastic action against all who were suspected of disloyalty to the Revolution. It was this situation more than anything else which brought the extremists to the fore and enabled them to gain control of the Legislative Assembly and to put an end to the monarchy.

From 1792 to 1795—that is, during the second stage of the Revolution and for more than a year longer—the governing power of France was the National Convention. Originally elected as a constituent assembly, this body was supposed to draft a new constitution and then surrender its authority to a regular government. In 1793 a new constitution was actually drawn up, the most democratic in history thus far. It provided for universal manhood suffrage and the right of referendum. It declared that society owes a living to the poor, either by finding work for them or giving them the means of subsistence. It made the provision of education an obligation of the state. Never before had the needs of social democracy been so clearly recognized in an instrument of government. But on account of the disordered conditions of the time, the Constitution of 1793 was never put into effect. With the justification that a national emergency existed, the Convention simply prolonged its life from year to year. After the spring of 1793 it delegated its executive functions to a group of nine (later twelve) of its members, known as the Committee of Public Safety. This agency conducted foreign relations, supervised the command of the armies, and enforced the Reign of Terror. The Convention itself was composed of a number of factions representing various shades of radical opinion. The most important were the Girondists and the Jacobins. The Girondists drew their support largely from regions outside of Paris and were inclined to distrust the proletariat. They were republicans but not extreme democrats. Their Jacobin opponents were among the most thoroughgoing radicals of the Revolution.[13] Though most of them sprang from the middle class, they were ardent disciples of Rousseau and militant champions of the urban workers. They accused the Girondists of desiring an "aristocratic republic" and of plotting to destroy the unity of France by putting into effect some kind of federal plan in which the *départements* or provinces would be exalted at the expense of Paris.

Leadership in the National Convention was furnished by some of the most interesting and dramatic personalities of modern history. Famous among those who usually identified themselves with the Girondists were Thomas Paine (1737–1809) and the Marquis de Condorcet (1743–1794). Following his brilliant work as a pamphleteer in the American Revolution, Paine sailed for England, determined to open the eyes of the people of that country "to the madness and stupidity of the government." In 1791 he published his celebrated *Rights of Man*, a blistering attack upon Edmund Burke's *Reflections on the Revolution in France*, issued the previous year. *The Rights of Man* created a sensation, especially after the bungling attempts of the government to suppress it. The author was indicted for treason, but he escaped to France before he could be seized for trial. In 1792 he was elected to the National Convention and immediately began an active career as one of the more moderate leaders of that body. He urged the destruction of the monarchy but opposed the execution of the king on the ground that it would alienate American sympathy. Ultimately he incurred the suspicion of some of the extremists and escaped the guillotine by the sheerest accident.

A man of milder temperament than Paine but of similar philosophic interests was the Marquis de Condorcet. Originally a disciple of Voltaire and Turgot, he eventually went considerably beyond these bourgeois liberals in his demands for reform. He condemned not only the evils of absolutism, mercantilism, slavery, and war, as did many of the enlightened thinkers of his time, but he was one of the first to insist that the elimination of poverty should be a cardinal purpose of statecraft. He thought that this end could be largely attained through the destruction of monopoly and privilege and the abolition of primogeniture and entail. The removal of these obstacles would permit a wide distribution of property, especially land, and thereby enable most individuals to achieve economic independence. He also advocated old-age pensions and cooperative banking to provide cheap credit.[14] At the height of the Terror, Condorcet was outlawed for denouncing the violence of the Jacobins and was compelled to flee for his life. Disguised as a carpen-

The moderate leaders in the National Convention: (1) Thomas Paine

(2) Condorcet

---

[13] The Jacobin Club had not always been radical. During the earlier years of the Revolution it had numbered among its members such well-known moderates as Mirabeau, Sieyès, and Lafayette. In 1791, however, it had come under the domination of extremists led by Maximilien Robespierre.

[14] J. S. Schapiro, *Condorcet and the Rise of Liberalism*, pp. 142–55.

ter, he wandered half-starved through the country until one night he aroused suspicion, was apprehended, and thrown into prison. The next morning he was found dead on the floor. Whether he collapsed from suffering and exposure or swallowed poison he was supposed to have carried in a ring is unknown.

Foremost among the leaders of the extremist factions were Marat, Danton, and Robespierre. Jean Paul Marat (1743–1793) was educated as a physician, and, by 1789, had already earned enough distinction in that profession to be awarded an honorary degree by St. Andrews University in Scotland. Almost from the beginning of the Revolution he stood as a champion of the common people. He opposed nearly all of the dogmatic assumptions of his middle-class colleagues in the Assembly, including the idea that France should pattern her government after that of Great Britain, which he recognized to be oligarchic in form. He was soon made a victim of persecution and was forced to find refuge in sewers and dungeons, but this did not stop him from his efforts to rouse the people to a defense of their rights. In 1793 he was stabbed through the heart by Charlotte Corday, a young woman who was fanatically devoted to the Girondists. In contrast with Marat, Georges Jacques Danton (1759–1794) did not come into prominence until the Revolution was three years old, but, like Marat, he directed his activities toward goading the masses into rebellion. Elected a member of the Committee of Public Safety in 1793, he had much to do with organizing the Reign of Terror. As time went on he appears to have wearied of ruthlessness and displayed a tendency to compromise. This gave his opponents in the Convention their opportunity, and in April 1794, he was sent to the guillotine. Upon mounting the scaffold he is reported to have said: "Show my head to the people; they do not see the like every day."

The most famous and perhaps the greatest of all the extremist leaders was Maximilien Robespierre (1758–1794). Born of a family reputed to be of Irish descent, Robespierre was trained for the law and speedily achieved a modest success as an advocate. In 1782 he was appointed a criminal judge, but soon resigned because he could not bear to impose a sentence of death. Of a nervous and timid disposition, he was never able to display much executive ability, but he made up for this lack of talent by fanatical devotion to principle. He had adopted the belief that the philosophy of Rousseau held the one great hope of salvation for all mankind. To put this philosophy into practice he was ready to employ any means that would bring results, regardless of the cost to himself or to others. This passionate loyalty to a gospel that exalted the masses eventually won him a following. Indeed, he was so lionized by the public that he was allowed to wear the knee breeches, silk stockings, and powdered hair of the old society until the end of his life. In 1791 he was accepted as the oracle of the Jacobin Club, now purged of all but its most radical elements.

Maximilien Robespierre. After
a drawing from life by François
Gérard (1770–1837).

Later he became president of the National Convention and a member of the Committee of Public Safety. Though he had little or nothing to do with originating the Reign of Terror, he was nevertheless responsible for enlarging its scope. He actually came to justify ruthlessness as a necessary and therefore laudable means to revolutionary progress. In the last six weeks of his virtual dictatorship, no fewer than 1285 heads rolled from the scaffold in Paris. But sooner or later such methods were bound to bring his own doom. On July 28, 1794, he and twenty-one of his lieutenants were beheaded, after no more pretense of a trial than Robespierre himself had allowed to his opponents.

The extent of violence during the second stage

The actual extent of violence during the second stage of the Revolution will probably never be known. Many of the stories of horrible butchery that circulated then and later were highly exaggerated. No streets ran red with blood and no rivers were clogged with corpses. Nevertheless, an appalling amount of bloodshed did actually occur. During the period of the Terror, from September 1793 to July 1794, the most reliable estimates place the number of executions at approximately 20,000 in France as a whole. A law of September 17, 1793, made every person who had been identified in any way with the Bourbon government or with the Girondists an object of suspicion; and no one who was a suspect or who was suspected of being a suspect was entirely safe from persecution. When some time later the Abbé Sieyès was asked what he had done to distinguish himself during the Terror, he responded dryly, "I lived." Yet when all is said, it must be conceded that the slaughter during the French

Revolution was much less than that which has accompanied most civil and international wars. The 20,000 victims of the Reign of Terror can hardly be compared, for example, to the hundreds of thousands slain during the American War between the States. Napoleon Bonaparte, whom many people worship as a hero, was responsible for at least twenty times as many deaths as all of the members of the Committee of Public Safety. This comparison is not meant to condone the savagery of the Terror, but it may serve to correct a distorted picture.

Despite the violence of the Reign of Terror, the second stage of the French Revolution was marked by some worthy achievements. Such leaders as Robespierre, fanatical though they might have been, were nevertheless sincere humanitarians, and it was not to be ex-

Reforms achieved during the second stage

The Goddess of Reason carried through the Streets of Paris, 1793. During the second stage of the French Revolution the government attempted to supplant Christianity by worship of the Goddess of Reason.

pected that they would ignore the opportunity to inaugurate reforms. Among their most significant accomplishments were the abolition of slavery in the colonies; the prohibition of imprisonment for debt; the establishment of the metric system of weights and measures; and the repeal of primogeniture, so that property might not be inherited exclusively by the oldest son but must be divided in substantially equal portions among all of the immediate heirs. The Convention also attempted to supplement the decrees of the National Assembly in abolishing the remnants of feudalism and in providing for greater freedom of economic opportunity. The property of enemies of the Revolution was confiscated for the benefit of the government and the lower classes. Great estates were broken up and offered for sale to poorer citizens on easy terms. The indemnities hitherto promised to the nobles for the loss of their privileges were abruptly canceled. To curb the rise in the cost of living, maximum prices for grain and other necessities were fixed by law, and mer-

145

chants who profiteered at the expense of the poor were threatened with the guillotine. Still other measures of reform were those in the sphere of religion. At one time during the Terror an effort was made to abolish Christianity and to substitute the worship of Reason in its place. In accordance with this purpose a new calendar was adopted, dating the year from the birth of the republic (September 22, 1792) and dividing the months in such a way as to eliminate the Christian Sunday. When Robespierre came to power, he supplanted this cult of Reason by a deistic religion dedicated to the worship of a Supreme Being and to the belief in the immortality of the soul. Finally, in 1794, the Convention took the more sensible step of making religion a private concern of the individual. It was decided that church and state should be entirely separate, and that all beliefs not actually hostile to the government should be tolerated.

The end of the second stage: the Thermidorian Reaction

In the summer of 1794 the Reign of Terror came to an end, and soon afterward the Revolution passed into its third and final stage. The event which inaugurated the change was the Thermidorian Reaction, so called from the month of Thermidor (heat month—July 19 to August 18) in the new calendar. The execution of Robespierre on July 28, 1794 represented the completion of a cycle. The Revolution had now devoured its own children. One after another the radical giants had fallen—first Marat, then Hébert and Danton, and now finally Robespierre and Saint-Just. The only remaining leaders in the Convention were men of moderate sympathies. As time went on they inclined toward increasing conservatism and toward any kind of political chicanery which would serve to keep them in power. Gradually the Revolution came once more to reflect the interests of the bourgeoisie. Much of the extremist work of the radicals was now undone. The law of maximum prices and the law against "suspects" were both repealed. Political prisoners were freed, the Jacobins were driven into hiding, and the Committee of Public Safety was shorn of its despotic powers. The new situation made possible the return of priests, royalists, and other *émigrés* from abroad to add the weight of their influence to the conservative trend.

The third stage: the conservative Constitution of the Year III

In 1795 the National Convention adopted a new constitution, which lent the stamp of official approval to the victory of the prosperous classes. The new organic law, known as the Constitution of the Year III, granted suffrage to all adult male citizens who could read and write, but they were permitted to vote only for electors, who in turn would choose the members of the Legislative Body; and in order to be an elector, one had to be the proprietor of a farm or other establishment with an annual income equivalent to at least 100 days of labor. It was thus made certain that the authority of the government would actually be derived from citizens of considerable wealth. The Legislative Body was to be composed of two houses, a

lower house or Council of Five Hundred and a senate or Council of

Ancients. Since it was not practicable to restore the monarchy, lest the old aristocracy also come back into power, executive authority was vested in a board of five men known as the Directory, to be nominated by the Council of Five Hundred and elected by the Council of Ancients. The new constitution included not only a bill of rights but also a declaration of the *duties* of the citizen. Conspicuous among the latter was the obligation to bear in mind that "it is upon the maintenance of property . . . that the whole social order rests."

The third stage of the French Revolution was of little historical importance compared with the other two. In general it was a period of stagnation, wholesale corruption, and cynicism. The burning zeal for reform that had characterized the other two stages now disappeared into thin air. The members of the new government were interested much more in opportunities for personal profit than in the shining ideals of philosophers for remaking the world. Graft was a familiar accompaniment of the levying and collecting of taxes and the disbursement of public funds. Even some members of the Directory coolly demanded bribes as the price of favors which the duties of their office should normally have required them to bestow. This cynical greed in high places was bound to have its effect upon the tone of society. It is therefore not surprising that the age of the Directory should have been a period of riotous extravagance, dissipation, and frenzied pursuit of wealth. Speculation and gambling tended to crowd legitimate business into a secondary place. While famine stalked the slums of Paris, profiteers accumulated fortunes and flaunted their gains at the expense of the people in senseless display. Thus were the glorious promises of the Revolution trailed in the mud, even by some who had originally sworn to uphold them.

The corrupt
and cynical
character of the
third stage

In the fall of 1799 the Revolution in France came to a close. The event that marked its end was the *coup d'état* of Napoleon Bonaparte on the eighteenth Brumaire (November 9). This, however, was merely the final blow. For some time the regime set up by the Constitution of the Year III had been hovering on the verge of collapse. Though for a while it was bolstered up by victories in the war which was still going on against foreign enemies of the Revolution, eventually even this support was torn away. In 1798–1799 the aggressive policy of the Directory had involved France in a struggle with a new combination of powerful foes—Great Britain, Austria, and Russia. The fortunes of battle soon shifted. One after another the satellite states the French had erected on their eastern frontier collapsed. The armies of the republic were driven from Italy. Soon it appeared as if all the gains of previous years were to be blotted out. Meanwhile the Directory had been suffering an even greater loss of prestige from its conduct of internal affairs. Thousands of people were disgusted with the shameful corruption of public officials and their heartless indifference to the needs of the poor. To

The end of the
Revolution: the
coup d'état of
Napoleon
Bonaparte

make matters worse, the government was partly responsible for a serious financial crisis. In order to defray the cost of wars and to make up for the extravagance of incompetent officials, the issuance of *assignats* or paper money was increased. The inevitable results were wild inflation and utter chaos. Within a short time the *assignats* had depreciated until they were actually worth no more than 1 per cent of their face value. By 1797 conditions had grown so hopeless that the only alternative was to repudiate all of the outstanding paper currency. During the period of financial chaos millions of cautious and respectable citizens who had managed to accumulate some property were reduced to the level of proletarians. The effect was naturally to turn them into bitter enemies of the existing government.

Under these deplorable circumstances the accession of Napoleon Bonaparte was rendered comparatively easy. Disgust with the banality and indifference of the Directory, resentment on account of the hardships suffered from the inflation, the sense of being humiliated as a result of defeat in the war—these were the factors which encouraged a widespread conviction that the existing regime was intolerable, and that only the appearance of a "man on horseback" could save the nation from ruin. In other words, Napoleon rose to power under conditions quite similar to those which presided at the birth of more recent dictatorships in Germany and Italy. But, of course, young Bonaparte was a military hero, which Hitler and Mussolini were not. In 1795 he had endeared himself to the friends of law and order by defending the National Convention with a "whiff of grapeshot" against an uprising of Parisian insurgents. Later he had come trailing clouds of glory from his campaigns in Italy and in Egypt. True, his reports of success in the latter country were slightly colored, but they convinced patriotic Frenchmen that here at last was a general in whose skill they could place absolute trust. Besides, no one could doubt the fact that he had driven the Austrians from Italy and had added Savoy and Nice and the Austrian Netherlands to France. It is no wonder that he should have come to be regarded as the man of the hour. His name became a symbol of national greatness and the glorious achievements of the Revolution. And as the revulsion of feeling against the Directory increased, he was hailed more than ever as the incorruptible hero who would deliver the nation from shame and disaster.

3. THE GOOD AND EVIL FRUITS OF THE REVOLUTION

While the coming to power of Napoleon Bonaparte as a military dictator marked the beginning of a new era, it by no means erased the influence of the French Revolution. Indeed, as will subsequently be shown, Napoleon himself preserved quite a few of the

Revolutionary achievements and posed as an embattled champion of
Equality and Fraternity, if not of Liberty. But even if he had done
none of these things, the heritage of the Revolution would most certainly have survived. No movement which had so thoroughly
shaken the foundations of society could ever have passed into history without leaving a train of momentous results. Its influence
reverberated through most of the years of the nineteenth century
and was felt in a score of nations of the Western world. The new
passion for liberty was the activating force behind numerous insurrections and so-called revolutions which punctuated the period
between 1800 and 1850. First came the uprising of the Spaniards
against Joseph Bonaparte in 1808. This was followed by a veritable
epidemic of revolutionary disturbances between 1820 and 1831 in
such countries as Greece, Italy, Spain, France, Belgium, and Poland.
Finally, the revolutionary movements of 1848 were far from unrelated to the great French upheaval of 1789, since most of them were
infused with the same nationalist enthusiasm and with similar ideals
of political liberty.

DESTRUCTION OF
THE OLD
REGIME

The influence
of the French
Revolution

The French Revolution also had other results of more enduring
character and of greater benefit to mankind as a whole. It dealt, first
of all, a powerful blow to absolute monarchy. Thenceforth few
kings dared to claim an unlimited authority. Even though a Bourbon
was restored to the throne of France in 1814, he made no pretensions to a divine appointment to rule as he liked. Secondly, the
French Revolution was responsible for the destruction of most of
the remnants of a decadent feudalism, including serfdom and the
feudal privileges of the nobles. The guilds also were abolished, never
to be revived. Though a few of the elements of mercantilism still
survived, its days as a recognized policy of governments were numbered. Although the separation of church and state, accomplished in
1794, was eventually nullified by Napoleon, it nevertheless furnished a precedent for an ultimate divorce of religion from politics,
not only in France but in other countries as well. Among the remaining beneficial results of the Revolution may be mentioned the
abolition of slavery in the French colonies, the elimination of imprisonment for debt, the overthrow of the rule of primogeniture,
and a wider distribution of land through the breaking up of great
estates. Finally, the groundwork of two of Napoleon's most significant achievements, his educational reforms and his codification of
the laws, was actually prepared by Revolutionary leaders.

The more en-
during results
of the French
Revolution

On the other hand, the fact cannot be ignored that the French
Revolution bore some bitter fruit. It was largely responsible for the
growth of jingoistic nationalism as a dominant ideal. Nationalism, of
course, was nothing new. It can be traced almost as far back as the
unfoldment of the earliest civilizations. It manifested itself in the
Chosen People belief of the Hebrews and in the racial exclusiveness
of the Greeks. Nevertheless, nationalism did not really become a

The legacy of
evil results

virulent and all-pervading force until after the French Revolution. It was the pride of the French people in what they had achieved and their determination to protect those achievements that gave rise to a fanatical patriotism exemplified in the stirring battle song, the *Marseillaise*. For the first time in modern history a whole nation was girded for war. In contrast to the relatively small professional armies of former days, the National Convention in 1793 enrolled a force of nearly 800,000 men, while millions behind the lines devoted their energies to the gigantic task of suppressing disaffection at home. Workers, peasants, and bourgeois citizens alike rallied to the slogan of "Liberty, Equality, and Fraternity" as to a holy cause. The cosmopolitanism and pacifism of the philosophers of the Enlightenment were completely forgotten. Later this militant patriotism infected other lands, contributing the weight of its influence to exalted notions of national superiority and to racial hatreds. Finally, the French Revolution resulted in a deplorable cheapening of human life. The butchery of thousands during the Reign of Terror, often for no crime at all but merely as a method of striking fear into the hearts of enemies of the Revolution, tended to create the impression that the life of a man was of very small worth compared to the noble aims of the faction in power. Perhaps this impression helps to explain the comparative indifference with which France accepted, a few years later, the sacrifice of hundreds of thousands of her citizens to satisfy the boundless ambitions of Napoleon.

SELECTED READINGS

· *Items so designated are available in paperbound editions.*

Aldridge, A. D., *Man of Reason: the Life of Thomas Paine*, London, 1960.
· Arendt, Hannah, *On Revolution*, New York, 1963 (Compass).
Barber, E. G., *The Bourgeoisie in Eighteenth-Century France*, Princeton, 1955.
· Brinton, C. C., *A Decade of Revolution, 1789–1799*, New York, 1934 (Torchbook). Stimulating and critical.
——, *The Jacobins: An Essay in the New History*, New York, 1930.
Cobban, Alfred, *In Search of Humility; the Role of the Enlightenment in Modern History*, London, 1960.
· Ford, Franklin, *Robe and Sword: The Regrouping of the French Aristocracy after Louis XIV*, Cambridge, Mass., 1953 (Torchbook).
Gershoy, Leo, *The French Revolution, 1789–1799*, New York, 1932. A dependable summary.
——, *The French Revolution and Napoleon*, New York, 1933.
· ——, *From Despotism to Revolution*, New York, 1944 (Torchbook). Valuable for background of the Revolution.
· Geyl, Pieter, *Napoleon, For and Against*, New Haven, 1949 (Yale University Press).
· Gooch, G. P., *English Democratic Ideas in the Seventeenth Century*, New York, 1962 (Torchbook).
Gooch, R. K., *Parliamentary Government in France, Revolutionary Origins, 1781–1791*, Ithaca, N.Y., 1960.

Gottschalk, L. R., *The Era of the French Revolution*, New York, 1929.
———, *Jean Paul Marat; a Study in Radicalism*, New York, 1927.
Hampson, Norman, *A Social History of the French Revolution*, Toronto, 1963.
Kerr, W. B., *The Reign of Terror, 1793–94*, Toronto, 1927.
· Lefebvre, Georges, *The Coming of the French Revolution*, Princeton, 1947 (Vintage). An excellent study of the causes and early events of the Revolution.
Madelin, Louis, *Figures of the Revolution*, New York, 1929.
· Martin, Kingsley, *French Liberal Thought in the Eighteenth Century*, Boston, 1929 (Torchbook).
· Mathiez, Albert, *The French Revolution*, New York, 1928 (Universal Library). A liberal interpretation.
Moore, J. M., *The Roots of French Republicanism*, New York, 1962.
Palmer, R. R., *The Age of the Democratic Revolution: A Political History of Europe and America, 1760–1800*, Princeton, 1964.
· ———, *Twelve Who Ruled*, Princeton, 1941 (Atheneum). Excellent biographical and interpretive studies.
· Rudé, George, *The Crowd in History: A Study of Popular Disturbances in France and England, 1730–1848*, New York, 1964 (Wiley).
Schapiro, J. S., *Condorcet and the Rise of Liberalism in France*, New York, 1934. A splendid study of revolutionary idealism.
Sée, Henri, *Economic and Social Conditions in France during the Eighteenth Century*, New York, 1927.
Sydenham, M. J., *The Girondins*, London, 1961. A reinterpretation of the significance of this faction.
Thompson, J. M., *Leaders of the French Revolution*, New York, 1929.
· ———, *Robespierre and the French Revolution*, New York, 1953 (Collier). An excellent short biography.

SOURCE MATERIALS

Higgins, E. L., *The French Revolution as Told by Contemporaries*, Boston, 1938.
Locke, John, *Second Treatise on Civil Government* (Everyman Library ed.), London, 1924.
· Montesquieu, Baron de, *The Spirit of Laws*, especially Books, I, II, III, XI (Hafner Library of World Classics).
Rousseau, J. J., *The Social Contract* (Everyman Library ed.), London, 1913.
Sieyès, Abbé, *What Is the Third Estate?*
Smith, Adam, *The Wealth of Nations*, Introduction and Books I, IV.
Stewart, J. H., *A Documentary Survey of the French Revolution*, New York, 1951.
· Tocqueville, Alexis de, *The Old Regime and the French Revolution*, Garden City, L. I., 1955 (Anchor).
University of Pennsylvania Translations and Reprints, Vol. I, No. 5, Declaration of the Rights of Man and of the Citizen.
———, *Translations and Reprints*, Vol. I, No. 5, Decree Abolishing the Feudal System.
Young, Arthur, *Travels in France during the Years 1787, 1788, 1789*, New York, 1929. A contemporary account of the life of the peasants.

CHAPTER 5

The Age of Romanticism and Reaction (1800-1830)

The principle of non-intervention is very popular in England; false in its essence, it may be maintained by an island-state. New France has not failed to appropriate this principle and to proclaim it loudly. It is brigands who object to police, and incendiaries who complain about firemen. We can never admit a claim as subversive as this is of all social order; we recognize, however, that we always have the right to answer any appeal for help addressed to us by a legitimate authority, just as we recognize that we have the right of extinguishing the fire in a neighbor's house in order to prevent its catching our own.

—Prince Metternich, 1830

The century that followed the French Revolution was a period of rapid and tremendous change. By comparison, life in preceding ages seems almost static. Never before in so short a time had there been such radical alteration of modes of living or such wholesale destruction of venerable tradition. As a result of a welter of inventions the speed of living was accelerated to a pace which would have startled Leonardo da Vinci or Sir Isaac Newton. The population of Europe increased from 180 million at the close of the French Revolution to the almost incredible total of 460 million by 1914. Never before in little more than a century had anything like such an increase occurred. As a result of these and similar changes, life for modern man took on a degree of complexity and variety hitherto unknown. New political and social ideals multiplied in bewildering confusion. The entire age was an age of flux, of conflicting tendencies and sharp disagreements over the problems of society. We must not suppose, however, that the nineteenth century was totally unrelated to preceding periods. Although Napoleon declared after his *coup d'état* of 1799 that the great aims of the years of turbulence had been accomplished

Character of the new age

153

and that now the revolution was over, such was not really the case. In the minds of a great many people the objectives of the French Revolution remained as goals worth striving for. Through a period of thirty years and more the Western world was disturbed by what virtually amounted to a civil war between the defenders of those goals and those who would repudiate freedom and equality and force men back under obedience to authority. It was a condition not unlike that which followed the Russian revolution of 1917 when a conflict between Communists and their opponents fanned out into other countries and eventually took on global dimensions.

I. THE SIGNIFICANCE OF NAPOLEON

We have seen that the *coup d'état* of the eighteenth Brumaire dealt what seemed to be a final blow to the French Revolution.

Napoleon not a
true son of the
French Revo-
lution

Therefore, the period of Napoleon's rule, from November 1799 to April 1814 and during the Hundred Days from March until June 1815, may properly be regarded as the initial stage of the nineteenth-century reaction against the liberal ideals which had made the Revolution possible. To be sure, Napoleon professed to be in sympathy with some of these ideals, but he established a form of government scarcely compatible with any of them. His real aim, so far as it concerned the work of the Revolution, was to preserve those achievements which comported with national greatness and with his own ambitions for military glory. In other words, he fostered and strengthened Revolutionary patriotism and continued those accomplishments of his predecessors which could be adapted to the purposes of concentrated government. But liberty in the sense of the inviolability of personal rights meant nothing to him; in fact, he declared that what the French people needed was not liberty but equality. Moreover, he interpreted equality as meaning little more than a fair opportunity for all regardless of birth. That is, he did not propose to restore serfdom or to give back the land to the old nobility, but neither did he plan any restrictions upon the economic activities of the rich.

In order to understand the historical significance of Napoleon, it is necessary to know something of his personal life and of the part

The early ca-
reer of Napo-
leon

he played in the dramatic events preceding his rise to power. Born in 1769 in a little town in Corsica just a year after the island had been ceded to France, Napoleon was the son of a proud but impoverished family that held a title of nobility from the republic of Genoa. In 1779 he entered a school at Brienne in France and five years later was admitted to the military academy in Paris. As a student he appears to have led an unhappy existence, abstaining from all social pleasures, eating dry bread to save expenses, and growing ever more bitter against the French, whom he accused of enslaving his fellow Corsicans. He achieved no distinction in any academic subject except mathematics, but he applied himself so assiduously to military science that he won a commission as a sub-lieutenant of artillery at the age of sixteen. The progress of the Revolution and the outbreak of foreign war brought rapid promotion, since many of the officers appointed under the *ancien régime* fled from the country. By 1793 he had become Colonel Bonaparte and had been entrusted with the difficult task of expelling the British from Toulon. Soon afterward he was rewarded with a promotion to brigadier-general. In 1795 he defended the National Convention against an uprising of reactionaries in Paris and was placed in command the following year of the expedition against the Austrians in Italy. His brilliant success in this campaign elevated him to the status of a national hero. His name was on everybody's lips. Politicians feared him and tumbled over one another to grant his every desire. While the comfortable classes adored him as a bulwark against radicalism, many ordinary folk were deceived by his honeyed pledges of devotion to Revolutionary doctrine. To all whose emotions had been set aflame by the new patriotism he loomed as the symbol of victory and of hope for a glorious future.

Had conditions in France been more stable than they were in 1799, it is probable that Napoleon Bonaparte would have lived out his days as no more than a talented army officer. But we have seen that conditions in this and in preceding years were exceedingly chaotic. Corruption, profiteering, and financial ruin added to the woes of a people already bowed down by the miseries of a long revolution. So profound was the mood of despair that thousands welcomed a new despotism as the only hope of relief. Besides, the government of the Directory was shot through with intrigue. One of its members, the Abbé Sieyès, was actually conspiring to overthrow it and was casting about for a popular hero to assist him. Napoleon had the advantage of being married to the mistress of one of the Directors, but his triumph was due also to certain qualities of his own personality. He was shrewd, egotistical, and unscrupulous. He had the sagacity to perceive that the people were tired of disorder and corruption, and that they longed for the return of stability. Convinced that destiny had touched his brow, he determined to let nothing stand in the way of fulfillment of his lofty ambitions. Moreover, he was endowed with an indefatigable energy. He is alleged to have insisted that two hours of sleep were normal for a man, four hours for a woman, and "eight for a fool." He endeared himself to his soldiers by his ability to withstand hardships and by his infinite capacity for personal attention to every detail necessary to the success of a military campaign. Lastly, Napoleon had a keen instinct for the dramatic, a gift of eloquence, and a magnetic ability to exact from his followers the highest measure of devotion. He knew how to make the most of an inspiring setting and to fill the imaginations of all around him with magnificent visions of glory and power.

The new regime set up by Napoleon after the *coup d'état* of the eighteenth Brumaire was a thinly disguised autocracy. The constitution, drafted by the conspirators themselves, provided for a form of government known as the Consulate. Executive powers were vested in three Consuls, who were to appoint a Senate. The Senate, in turn, was to designate members of the Tribunate and the Legislative Body from lists of candidates chosen by popular vote. The First Consul, who of course was Bonaparte himself, was given authority to propose all laws, in addition to his power to appoint the entire administration and to control the army and the conduct of foreign affairs. The Tribunate was to discuss the laws without voting on them, after which the Legislative Body would accept or reject the laws without the privilege of debating them. Final approval of legislative measures would be determined in many cases by the Senate, which was to decide all questions of constitutionality. Thus the whole system depended in last analysis upon the will of the First Consul. But the framers of the constitution made a pretense of deferring to popular sovereignty, since the principle of universal manhood suffrage was revived. In December 1799, the new instrument of government was submitted to a popular referendum and was approved by a stupendous majority. When the votes were finally counted, it was found (or at least it was claimed) that only 1562 out of more than 3,000,000 had been cast in the negative. However, 4,000,000 eligible voters had abstained. The constitution thus adopted went into effect on January 1, 1800; but since the Revolutionary calendar was still technically in force, it is known as the Constitution of the Year VIII.

Though Napoleon was now an absolute monarch in nearly everything but name, he still was not satisfied. In 1802 he obtained the consent of the people to extend his term of office as First Consul from ten years to life. All that then remained was to make his position hereditary. In 1804 by another plebiscite he won permission to convert the Consulate into an empire. Soon afterward, in the midst of impressive ceremonies in the Cathedral of Notre Dame, he placed a crown upon his own head and assumed the title of Napoleon I, Emperor of the French. His action in making this change was influenced partly by the growth of opposition. Several attempts had recently been made to take his life, and royalist plots were being hatched against him. Napoleon proceeded against the conspirators with characteristic ruthlessness. Scores were arrested upon mere suspicion, and some of the most prominent were singled out for execution. Having thus disposed of his chief enemies, Napoleon evidently concluded that the best way to guard against future trouble of this kind would be to establish a dynasty of his own and thereby cut the ground from under all Bourbon pretenders. Especially if he could obtain for his rule the benediction of the Church, there would be few who would dare to oppose him. For this reason, he brought

Pope Pius VII all the way from Rome to officiate at his coronation, though he was careful to produce the impression that His Holiness was acting as the mere agent of God and not as an international sovereign who could create and depose the emperor.

It is unfortunately true that most of the fame of Napoleon Bonaparte rests upon his exploits as a soldier. His work as a statesman was much more important. In the latter capacity he made at least a few notable contributions to civilization. He confirmed the redistribu-

Napoleon's constructive work as a statesman

Napoleon Crowning Josephine, 1804. Though Napoleon brought Pius VII from Rome to grace his coronation, he took the crown from the Pope's hands and placed it upon his own head, then crowned the Empress. Detail from the painting by Jacques Louis David, in the Louvre.

tion of land accomplished by the Revolution, thereby permitting the average peasant to remain an independent farmer. He eliminated graft and waste from the government, reformed the system of taxation, and established the Bank of France to promote a more efficient control over fiscal affairs. He drained marshes, enlarged harbors, built bridges, and constructed a network of roads and canals. Most of these achievements were completed mainly for military purposes, but partly also in order to win the support of the commercial classes. In addition, he centralized the government of France, dividing the country into uniform districts or *départements*, each under a prefect taking orders from Paris.[1] Perhaps his accomplishment of

[1] The *départments* were originally established by the Revolutionary National Assembly, but not under a centralized arrangement. Their officers were to be elected by the people.

greatest significance was his completion of the educational and legal reforms begun during the Revolution. He ordered the establishment of *lycées* or high schools in every important town, and a normal school in Paris for the training of teachers. To supplement these changes, he brought the military and technical schools under control of the state and founded a national university to exercise supervision over the entire system. But he was never willing to allocate more than a small fraction of his budget for educational purposes, with the consequence that only a tiny proportion of the children of France received instruction at the expense of the state. In 1810, with the aid of a staff of jurists, he completed his famous Code Napoléon, a revision and codification of the civil and criminal laws on the basis of plans worked out by the National Convention. Despite its harsh provisions—the death penalty, for example, was retained for theft, parricides were to have their hands cut off before execution, and slavery was reestablished in the colonies—the Code Napoléon was hailed as the work of a second Justinian. With modifications it remained the law of France and Belgium for more than a century, and substantial portions of it were incorporated in the legal systems of Germany, Italy, Switzerland, Japan, and the French colony of Louisiana, where it was to persist even after the purchase of that territory by the United States.

Other results
of Napoleon's
statecraft

Napoleon's work as a statesman included many other changes in the political system of France. For one thing, he restored the union between the Catholic Church and the state. In 1801 he signed a Concordat with the Pope, which provided that bishops be nominated by the First Consul and that the salaries of the clergy be paid by the government. Even if the Catholic Church did not regain the legal monopoly it had enjoyed under the *ancien régime*, since other religions were also to be tolerated, it was nevertheless placed in a position of decided advantage and was thereby able to increase its power in succeeding years. Not until 1905, when the Concordat of 1801 was finally broken, was Catholicism again reduced to equality with other faiths. Napoleon was responsible also for curtailing the liberties of his subjects almost from the moment he came into power. He abolished trial by jury in certain cases, imposed a strict censorship on the press, and suspended many journals that he suspected of being hostile toward his policies. So effective was his control over the entire nation that not a single French newspaper mentioned the disastrous defeat which Napoleon's navy suffered at Trafalgar until after the collapse of the empire, more than eight years later. In addition to all this, Napoleon perverted education to patriotic purposes and to the glorification of his personal ambitions. He ordered that children be taught in the schools to love and obey their emperor and to offer "fervent prayers for his safety."

Although a detailed account of Napoleon's campaigns must be left to the military historian, the subject cannot be ignored. His exploits as a military commander had considerable effect in shaping the course of history. To his credit it should perhaps be said that the wars in which he engaged were not all of his own making. Upon his accession to power in 1799 he inherited from the Directory the struggle with the Second Coalition, composed of Great Britain, Austria, and Russia.[2] By flattery and intrigue he quickly procured the withdrawal of Russia and then turned against Austria with all the forces he could muster. Leading his choicest battalions through the treacherous passes of the Alps in the spring of 1800, he fell upon the Austrians in the Po valley and crushed them as in the jaws of a vise. Soon afterward the Hapsburg Emperor sued for peace. By 1801 Great Britain was the only enemy still in the war. Lacking a powerful navy, Bonaparte concluded that the British were beyond his reach and decided to negotiate rather than fight. In 1802 he accepted the Peace of Amiens, whereby Great Britain agreed to give up the colonial possessions seized during the war, exclusive of the islands of Trinidad and Ceylon. Napoleon was now free to devote his time to consolidating his power at home.

But the Peace of Amiens turned out to be no more than a truce. For various reasons England and France again came to grips in 1803. The British were alarmed by Napoleon's extension of influence over Italy and the Netherlands and by his conclusion of an alliance with Spain. Napoleon was irritated by the British refusal to withdraw from Malta in accordance with the Treaty of Amiens. But the chief reason for the renewal of the war was undoubtedly the economic ambitions of both the English and the French. The merchants and manufacturers of Britain feared that Napoleon might soon grow strong enough to reconquer the colonial empire which France had lost in the Seven Years' War. In similar fashion the wily Corsican was counting upon the destruction of British prosperity as the surest way of winning the applause of the French bourgeoisie, whom he reckoned as his most valuable supporters. Though war was declared in May 1803, hostilities did not actually begin for some time. Both sides spent more than a year in preparation—the French in amassing a fleet for an invasion of England, and the British in acquiring a string of allies. By 1805 the Third Coalition against France had been brought into being—this time composed of Great Britain, Austria, Russia, and Sweden.

Napoleon now resumed his old tactics of attempting to annihilate his Continental enemies first of all. Abandoning for the time being the invasion of England, he hurled an army against the Austrians near the town of Ulm in October 1805, and soon afterward captured Vienna. In December of the same year he won a decisive vic-

[2] The First Coalition was the original combination of European powers formed in opposition to the French Revolution. It was organized in 1793 and was made up of Austria, Prussia, Great Britain, Spain, Holland, and some lesser states.

tory over a combined army of Austrians and Russians at Austerlitz. The result was the elimination of Austria from the war under the terms of a peace which deprived her of three million of her subjects and reduced her to a second-rate power. Seized with panic lest she meet a similar fate, Prussia now threw down the challenge to France. Napoleon lost no time in accepting, and, before another year had passed, the armies of Frederick William III had been driven from the field. The Corsican marched through Berlin in triumph and subjected the greater part of the country to the rule of his generals. Next he turned his attention to the Russians. Defeating them at Friedland in June 1807, he impressed upon Tsar Alexander I the wisdom of peace. Napoleon and Alexander met in July at the Prussian town of Tilsit to draft the terms of a settlement. Curiously, the two emperors decided to become allies. They drew up what amounted to a virtual partnership to control the destinies of Europe between them. In return for a pledge to cooperate in excluding British trade from the Continent, Napoleon agreed that Alexander should be free to do as he liked with Finland and to take certain territories from Turkey. At the same time Prussia was loaded with a staggering punishment. She was robbed of half her territory, saddled with a huge indemnity, and practically reduced to a vassal state of France.

The star of the Little Corporal was now at its zenith. He was master of nearly all of the Continent of Europe west of Russia. He had

Napoleon at the
zenith of his
power

destroyed what was left of the Holy Roman Empire and had brought most of the German states outside of Austria into a Confederation of the Rhine of which he himself was Protector. He had not only extended the boundaries of France, but he had created as

*See color map
at page 168*

his personal domain a new kingdom of Italy including the Po valley and what had once been the republic of Venice. In addition, he had placed relatives and friends on several of the remaining thrones of Europe. His brother Joseph had been made king of Naples, his brother Louis king of Holland, and his brother Jerome king of Westphalia. He had selected his friend, the king of Saxony, to be the ruler of the duchy of Warsaw, a new Poland created mainly out of territories taken from Prussia. Not since the days of Charles V had so much of Europe been dominated by any one man. Yet Napoleon's position was far from secure, for he still had the "contemptible nation of shopkeepers" across the English Channel to deal with. Having lost to the British in the great naval battle of Trafalgar (October 1805), he determined to wear them down by the indirect method of ruining their commerce. In 1806 and the years following he established his famous Continental System, a scheme by which his various puppet states were obliged to cooperate with France in excluding British goods from the whole of Continental Europe. By depriving the English nation of its markets, Napoleon hoped that he could eventually sap its wealth to such a degree that the people would turn against their government and force it to capitulate. By the Treaty of Tilsit, as already noted, he even managed to bring Russia into the scheme.

The story of Napoleon's career from 1808 to 1815 is a record of the gradual decay of his fortunes. From his overthrow of the Directory in 1799 to the Peace of Tilsit in 1807 he had steadily climbed to an eminence which even an Alexander or a Caesar might well have envied. But soon after the latter event his difficulties began to multiply until finally they overwhelmed him in disaster. The explanation is to be found in several factors. First of all, with the passage of the years, he grew more egotistical, and therefore less inclined to accept advice even from his most capable subordinates. He kept nurturing the idea that he was a man of destiny until it developed into an obsession, a superstitious fatalism that destroyed the resiliency of his mind. Second, his aggressive militarism provoked an inevitable reaction among its victims. The more it became evident that Napoleon's conquests were the sordid fruits of a maniacal ambition for power, the stronger was the determination of the vanquished to regain their freedom. Peoples that had at one time mistakenly welcomed him as an apostle of Revolutionary liberty now turned against him as a hated foreign oppressor. In addition, militarism was producing its

The Battle of Trafalgar, by the English painter Joseph M. W. Turner (1775–1851). This battle is regarded by the British as one of the decisive events in their history, for it destroyed Napoleon's naval power and demolished any hopes he might have had of conquering Britain. The painting hangs in the Royal Maritime Museum at Greenwich.

effect upon France itself. The bones of hundreds of thousands of the best young men of the nation had been strewn in the dust of battlefields all over Europe. The problem not merely of filling their places in the ranks of the army but also of maintaining the levels of agricultural and industrial production was becoming more and more serious. Finally, the Continental System proved to be a boomerang. It actually inflicted more damage upon France and her allies than it did upon England. Napoleon found it impossible to enforce the exclusion of British products from the Continent, since most of the countries he dominated were agricultural nations and insisted upon trading the things they produced for manufactured goods from England. Moreover, the British retaliated with a series of Orders in Council making all vessels trading with France or her allies subject to capture. The effect was to cut Napoleon's empire off from sources of supply in neutral countries.

The first episode of Napoleon's downfall was the Spanish revolt which broke out in the summer of 1808. In May of that year Napoleon had tricked the Spanish king and the crown prince into resigning their claims to the throne and had promoted his brother Joseph from king of Naples to king of Spain. But scarcely had the new monarch been crowned than the people rose in revolt. Though Napoleon sent an army against them, he was never able to crush the rebellion entirely. With encouragement and assistance from the British, the Spaniards kept up a series of guerilla attacks which caused no end of expense and annoyance to the great warlord of France. Furthermore, the courage of Spain in resisting the invader promoted a spirit of defiance elsewhere, with the result that Napoleon could no longer count upon the docility of any of his victims.

The second stage in the downfall of the Corsican adventurer was the disruption of his alliance with Russia. As a purely agricultural country, Russia had suffered a severe economic crisis when she was no longer able, as a result of the Continental System, to exchange her surplus grain for British manufactures. The consequence was that the Tsar Alexander began to wink at trade with Britain and to ignore or evade the protests from Paris. By 1811 Napoleon decided that he could endure this flouting of the Continental System no longer. Accordingly, he collected an army of 600,000 men and set out in the spring of 1812 to punish the Tsar. The project ended in horrible disaster. The Russians refused to make a stand, thereby leading the French farther and farther into the heart of their country. Not until the enemy was nearing Moscow did they finally give battle at Borodino. Defeated in this engagement, they permitted Napoleon to occupy their ancient capital. But on the very night of his entry, fire of suspicious origin broke out in the city. When the flames subsided, little but the blackened walls of the Kremlin remained to shelter the invading troops. Hoping that the Tsar would eventually surrender, Napoleon lingered amid the ruins for more

than a month, finally deciding on October 22 to begin the home-
ward march. The delay was a fatal blunder. Long before he had
reached the border, the terrible Russian winter was upon him.
Swollen streams, mountainous drifts of snow, and bottomless mud
slowed the retreat almost to a halt. To add to the miseries of bitter
cold, disease, and starvation, Cossacks rode out of the blizzard to
harry the exhausted troops. Each morning the miserable remnant
that pushed on left behind circles of corpses around the campfires of
the night before. On December 13 a few thousand broken, starved,
and half-demented soldiers crossed the frontier into Germany—a
miserable fraction of what had once been proudly styled the
Grande Armée. The lives of nearly 300,000 men had been sacrificed
in the Russian adventure.

The disastrous outcome of the Russian campaign destroyed the
myth that Napoleon was invincible. Soon the Prussians and the Austrians regained their courage and, with Russian aid, joined in a War
of Liberation. Napoleon hastily collected a new army and marched
to suppress the revolts. He won a few modest victories in the spring
and summer of 1813 but was finally cornered at Leipzig by an allied
army of 500,000 men. Here on October 16–19 was fought the celebrated Battle of the Nations, in which Napoleon was decisively
beaten. His grand empire now collapsed like a house of cards; his
vassal states deserted him; and France itself was invaded. On
March 31, 1814, the victorious allies entered Paris. Thirteen days
later Napoleon signed the Treaty of Fontainebleau, renouncing all
of his claims to the throne of France. In return he was granted a
pension of two million francs a year and full sovereignty over the
island of Elba, located in the Mediterranean Sea within sight of his
native Corsica. The victors then took up with the French Senate the
problem of reorganizing the government of France. It was agreed
that the Bourbon line should be restored in the person of Louis
XVIII, brother of the king who had been sent to the guillotine in
1793. It was carefully stipulated, however, that there was not to be a
full restoration of the *ancien régime*. Louis XVIII was made to
understand that he must not interfere with the political and economic
reforms which still survived as fruits of the Revolution. In accordance with this requirement the new sovereign issued a charter con-
firming the Revolutionary liberties of the citizen and providing for
a limited monarchy.

But the restoration of 1814 proved to be short-lived. The exiled
emperor was growing impatient with his tiny island kingdom and
eagerly awaiting the first opportunity to escape. His chance came in
the spring of 1815. At this time the allies were quarreling among
themselves over the disposition of Poland and Saxony. The French
people were showing signs of disgust with the prosaic rule of Louis
XVIII and with the effrontery of returning nobles of the *ancien
régime*. Under these circumstances Napoleon slipped away from Elba

and landed on the coast of southern France on March 1. Everywhere he was received by peasants and former soldiers in a delirium of joy. Officers sent to arrest him went over to his side with whole regiments of his former comrades in arms. On March 20, after a journey of triumph across the country, Napoleon entered Paris. Louis XVIII, who had sworn that he would die in defense of his throne, was already on his way to Belgium. But Napoleon was not to enjoy his new triumph long. Almost immediately upon learning of the escape from Elba, the allies abandoned their bickerings, proclaimed the Corsican an outlaw, and prepared to depose him by force. On June 12, 1815, Napoleon set out from Paris with the largest army he could gather in the hope of routing the enemy forces before they could invade his country. Six days later at Waterloo in Belgium he suffered a crushing defeat at the hands of the Duke of Wellington in command of an army of British, Dutch, and Germans. With all hope lost, Napoleon returned to Paris, abdicated his throne a second time, and made plans to escape to America. Finding the coast too heavily guarded, he was compelled to take refuge on a British ship. He was subsequently exiled by the British government to the rocky South Atlantic island of St. Helena. There he died, on May 5, 1821, a lonely and embittered man.

The significance
of Napoleon

In attempting a final estimate of the significance of Napoleon Bonaparte, we must not lose sight of the fact that his name has been richly embellished with legend. The myth-mongering of patriots and hero-worshipers has raised his reputation almost to supernatural proportions. With the single exception of Jesus of Nazareth, he is actually the most written-about figure in history. But whether he deserves so exalted a fame is at least a debatable question. He was by no means a universal genius with a mastery of all knowledge or a patent on wisdom. Aside from mathematics, he knew little about any of the sciences, and his grasp of economics was too feeble to save him from the colossal errors of the Continental System. Though he was undoubtedly a clever tactician, the blunders of his Russian campaign indicate that even in military affairs he was not infallible. But worse than any other of his shortcomings were his defects of character. He was unscrupulous and unprincipled and capable of the basest trickery even against his friends. Moreover, his boundless egotism made him as coldly indifferent to the shedding of blood as a beast of the jungle crushing the bones of its prey. His real significance lies in the fact that he helped to preserve some of the major results of the French Revolution. Though he might easily have done so, he refused to restore the regime of privilege which had flourished in the days of the Bourbons. He confirmed the abolition of serfdom and the repeal of primogeniture, and he allowed the peasants to keep the lands they had acquired through the breakup of the great estates. What is more, he was at least indirectly responsible for spreading Revolutionary ideals into other countries. For exam-

ple, it was his smashing defeat of Prussia in 1806 which finally persuaded the leading men of that nation of the necessity of adopting
the main reforms of the French Revolution as the only means by
which their state could rise again to smite the oppressor. Under
Baron vom Stein and Chancellor Hardenberg, the Prussian government in 1807–1808 abolished serfdom and threw open the various
occupations and professions to men in all ranks of society. Unfortunately these measures were accompanied by an outburst of extreme
nationalism, which found characteristic expression in the adoption
of compulsory military service, one of the tyrannical devices employed by Napoleon himself. True, he did not invent it. It had been
initiated by the Revolution before him. But he continued it, as he
did the whole Revolutionary concept of a nation in arms and of war
as a mass endeavor rather than a game of kings and generals.

2. THE CONGRESS OF VIENNA AND THE CONCERT OF EUROPE

Following the overthrow of Napoleon, an overwhelming desire
for peace and order seized the minds of the conservative classes in
the victorious countries. Nearly everything that had happened since *The movement*
the Corsican had come into power now came to be regarded as a *to return to*
horrible nightmare. In some quarters there was a desire to return to *the status quo*
the *status quo* of 1789, to undo the work of the Great Revolution,
and to revive the power and the glamour of the *ancien régime*. The
government of the Papal States proceeded to abolish street lighting
in Rome as a dangerous novelty, while the Elector of Hesse restored
pigtails to the freshly-powdered heads of his faithful soldiers. The
leading statesmen realized, however, that a complete restoration of
the old order would not be possible. For example, it was perfectly
evident that the French people would not tolerate a revival of serfdom or the return of confiscated lands to the nobles and clergy.
Therefore, while the portly Louis XVIII was put back on the
throne, it was understood that he would continue to rule in conformity with the Charter of 1814. Furthermore, some of the victorious powers were not ready to give up the conquests they had
made at the expense of France. Hence it was found necessary to
modify suggestions frequently made for redrawing the map of Europe in accordance with the form it had had in the days of Louis
XVI.

Most of the work of deciding the fate of Europe at the conclusion
of the long war which had involved nearly the whole of the Western world was done at the so-called Congress of Vienna. To refer to *The Congress*
this body as a "Congress" is to be guilty of a misnomer, for, as a *of Vienna*
matter of fact, no plenary session of all the delegates was ever held.
As in the drafting of the Versailles Treaty more than a hundred
years later, the vital decisions were really made by small commit-

tees. Nevertheless, the assemblage at Vienna was staged with such pomp and splendor that even the most neglected member was made to feel that he was participating in events of epochal importance. The Austrian government, in the capacity of host, is reputed to have spent some $15,000,000 in providing a gorgeous array of banquets, balls, and military reviews. The chief delegates, however, composed such a galaxy of titled magnificence that the humbler representatives were easily pushed into the background. No fewer than six monarchs attended: the Tsar of Russia, the Emperor of Austria, and the kings of Prussia, Denmark, Bavaria, and Württemberg. Great Britain was represented by Lord Castlereagh and the "Iron Duke" of Wellington. From France came the subtle intriguer Talleyrand, who had served as a bishop under Louis XVI, as foreign minister at the court of Napoleon, and who now stood ready to espouse the cause of reaction.

The dominant roles at the Congress of Vienna were played by Alexander I and Metternich. The dynamic Tsar was one of the most baffling figures in history. Reared at the voluptuous court of Catherine the Great, he imbibed the doctrines of Rousseau from a French Jacobin tutor. In 1801 he succeeded his murdered father as Tsar and for the next two decades disturbed the dreams of his fellow sovereigns by becoming the most liberal monarch in Europe. After the defeat of Napoleon in the Russian campaign, his mind turned more and more into mystical channels. He conceived of a mission to convert the rulers of all countries to the Christian ideals of justice and peace. But the chief effect of his voluble expressions of devotion to "liberty" and "enlightenment" was to frighten conservatives into suspecting a plot to extend his power over all of Europe. He was accused of intriguing with Jacobins everywhere to substitute an all-powerful Russia for an all-powerful France.

Alexander I

The most commanding figure at the Congress was Klemens von Metternich, born in 1773 at Coblenz in the Rhine valley, where his father was Austrian ambassador at the courts of three small German states. As a student at the University of Strassburg the young Metternich witnessed some excesses of mob violence connected with the outbreak of the French Revolution, and to these he attributed his life-long hatred of political innovation. After completing his education he entered the field of diplomacy and served for nearly forty years as Minister of Foreign Affairs. He was active in fomenting discord between Napoleon and the Tsar Alexander, after the two became allies in 1807, and he played some part in arranging the marriage of Napoleon to the Austrian archduchess, Marie Louise. In 1813 he was made a hereditary prince of the Austrian Empire. At the Congress of Vienna Metternich distinguished himself for charm of manner and skillful intrigue. His two great obsessions were hatred of political and social change and fear of Russia. Actually the two were related. It was not simply that he feared revolutions as

Metternich

such; he feared even more revolutions inspired by the "Jacobin" Tsar for the sake of establishing Russian supremacy in Europe. For this reason he favored moderate terms for France in her hour of defeat, and was ready at one time to sponsor the restoration of Napoleon as Emperor of the French under the protection and overlordship of the Hapsburg monarchy.

The basic idea that guided the work of the Congress of Vienna was the principle of *legitimacy*. This principle was invented by Talleyrand as a device for protecting France against drastic punishment by her conquerors, but it was ultimately adopted by Metternich as a convenient expression of the general policy of reaction.

The Congress of Vienna, 1814–1815. The figure standing to the left of center is Prince Metternich; seated at the right with his arm on the table is Talleyrand.

Legitimacy meant that the dynasties of Europe that had reigned in pre-Revolutionary days should be restored to their thrones, and that each country should regain essentially the same territories it had held in 1789. In accordance with this principle Louis XVIII was recognized as the "legitimate" sovereign of France, and the restoration of the House of Orange in Holland, of the House of Savoy in Piedmont and Sardinia, and of the Bourbon rulers of Spain and the Two Sicilies was also confirmed. France was compelled to pay an indemnity of 700,000,000 francs, but her boundaries were to remain essentially the same as in 1789. Other territorial arrangements likewise adhered to the idea of a return to the *status quo*. The Pope was allowed to recover his temporal possessions in Italy; Switzerland was **167** restored as an independent confederation under guaranties of neutrality by the principal powers; while the Polish kingdom set up by Napoleon was abolished and the country again divided among Russia, Austria, and Prussia.

But the Congress of Vienna was a bit cynical in applying the principle of legitimacy. Before the lace-cuffed princes had gone very far in restoring the old map of Europe, they diluted the principle of legitimacy with their curious system of compensations. The real purpose of this system was to enable certain of the major powers to gratify their hunger for spoils. For example, Great Britain was permitted to keep the valuable territories she had taken from the Dutch, who had fought for a time on the side of France. Among these rich prizes were South Africa, a portion of Guiana in South America, and the island of Ceylon. Then to compensate the Dutch for the loss of so large a part of their empire, provision was made for transferring the Austrian Netherlands, or Belgium, to Holland. Since this involved a sacrifice on the part of Austria, the Hapsburgs were rewarded with an extensive foothold in Italy. They received the republic of Venice and the duchy of Milan, and members of the family were placed on the thrones of Tuscany, Parma, and Modena. Thus Austria profited by gaining a compact empire occupying a commanding position in central Europe. A similar series of compensations was provided to reward Russia for her part in conquering Napoleon. The Tsar was allowed to retain Finland, which he had seized from Sweden in 1809. Sweden, in turn, was compensated by the acquisition of Norway from Denmark. All of these arrangements were put through with a total disregard for the interests of the peoples concerned. Despite the fact that the Belgians were altogether different in culture and religion from the Dutch, they were nevertheless forced to submit to the rule of Holland. Nor were the interests of the Norwegians considered in the slightest in transferring them to the sovereignty of Sweden.

One of the cardinal purposes of Metternich and his conservative colleagues was to erect the Vienna settlement into a permanent bulwark of the *status quo*. With this end in view they established the Quadruple Alliance of Great Britain, Austria, Prussia, and Russia as an instrument for maintaining the settlement intact. In 1818 France was admitted to the combination, thereby making it a Quintuple Alliance. For some years this aggregate of powers functioned as a kind of League of Nations to enforce the system of Metternich. It is also frequently referred to as the Concert of Europe, for its members were pledged to cooperate in suppressing any disturbances which might arise from the attempts of peoples to throw off their "legitimate" rulers or to change international boundaries. In the minds of liberals and nationalists of this period the Quintuple Alliance was often confused with another combination that also grew out of the settlement at Vienna. This was the so-called Holy

Alliance, a product of the sentimental idealism of the Tsar Alex-

THE EMPIRE OF NAPOLEON
AT ITS GREATEST EXTENT · 1812

French territory — Allied with Napoleon
French dependencies — Independent states
✕ Battle sites

SWEDEN

NORWAY

DENMARK
Copenhagen

RUSSIA

Moscow
Borodino
NAPOLEON, 1812

BALTIC SEA

Tilsit
Friedland ✕
PRUSSIA
Berlin
DUCHY OF WARSAW
Warsaw

NORTH SEA

HOLLAND
Amsterdam
CONFEDERATION OF THE RHINE
Leipzig
Elbe R.
Austerlitz ✕
Vienna
AUSTRIAN EMPIRE

ENGLAND
London

IRELAND

English Channel

Brussels
Waterloo ✕
★ Paris
FRENCH EMPIRE
Bordeaux

Rhine R.
Ulm
HELVETIC REPUBLIC
KINGDOM OF ITALY
Po R.
ILLYRIAN PROVINCES
ADRIATIC SEA

Marseilles

CORSICA
KDM. OF SARDINIA

PAPAL STATES
Rome
KINGDOM OF NAPLES
Naples

KDM. OF SICILY

BLACK SEA

OTTOMAN EMPIRE

AEGEAN SEA

MEDITERRANEAN SEA

ATLANTIC OCEAN

KDM. OF PORTUGAL
Lisbon

Madrid
SPAIN

500 miles

Liberty Leading the People, Eugene Delacroix (1798–1863). Delacroix was a colorful painter of dramatic and emotional themes, as exemplified by this imaginary scene from the Revolution of 1830. (Louvre)

Salisbury Cathedral from the Bishop's Garden, John Constable (1776–1837). This British romanticist is best known for his idealizations of nature in her quiet and peaceful moods. (MMA)

The Flight into Egypt, William Blake (1757–1827). A poet as well as a painter, Blake lived in a world of dream and fantasy. He attributed to divine inspiration his talent for expressing delicate simplicity. (MMA)

Lady Lillith, Dante Gabriel Rossetti (1828–1882). The chief figure in the Pre-Raphaelite movement, Rossetti cared more for the expression of ideas than for technical perfection. (MMA)

Grand Canal, Venice, Joseph M. W. Turner (1775–1851). Turner's complete absorption in light, color, and atmosphere helped to prepare the way for the French impressionists. (MMA)

EUROPE AFTER THE CONGRESS OF VIENNA
1815

Boundary of the
Germanic Confederation

Austrian Empire

France

Prussia

ATLANTIC OCEAN

NORTH SEA

BALTIC SEA

BLACK SEA

ADRIATIC SEA

MEDITERRANEAN SEA

RUSSIAN EMPIRE

OTTOMAN EMPIRE

AUSTRIAN EMPIRE

KINGDOM OF FRANCE

KINGDOM OF SPAIN

KINGDOM OF PORTUGAL

KINGDOM OF THE TWO SICILIES

KINGDOM OF SARDINIA

KINGDOM OF NORWAY AND SWEDEN

KINGDOM OF DENMARK

KINGDOM OF THE NETHERLANDS

GREAT BRITAIN

P R U S S I A

POLAND

HUNGARY

MOLDAVIA

WALLACHIA

REPUBLIC OF CRACOW

SAXONY

BAVARIA

HANOVER

MECK-LENBURG

HOLSTEIN

SCHLESWIG

HESSE

WÜRTEM-BERG

BADEN

SWISS CONFED.

LOMBARDY-VENETIA

PAPAL STATES

TUSCANY

MODENA

PARMA

LUCCA

CORSICA

MONTENEGRO

ALSACE

LORRAINE

LUXEMBOURG

BELGIUM

ENGLAND

SCOTLAND

IRELAND

ALGERIA

TUNISIA

MOROCCO

BALEARIC ISLANDS
(To Spain)

Moscow

Kiev

Constantinople

Copenhagen

Berlin

Hamburg

Amsterdam

Vienna

Budapest

Berne

Milan

Rome

Naples

Palermo

Munich

Paris

Bordeaux

Marseilles

Barcelona

Madrid

Lisbon

London

Liverpool

Birmingham

Edinburgh

Dublin

500 miles

0

ander I. In September 1815, Alexander proposed that the monarchs of Europe should "take as their sole guide . . . the precepts of Justice, Christian Charity, and Peace," and that they should base international relations as well as the treatment of their subjects "upon the sublime truths which the Holy Religion of our Savior teaches. . . ." But none of the Tsar's fellow sovereigns took him seriously. Though most of them signed the agreement he proposed, they were inclined to regard it as so much mystical verbiage. As a matter of fact, the Holy Alliance was never anything more than a series of pious pledges. The real weapon for preserving the triumph of reaction was not the Holy Alliance but the Quintuple Alliance.

The purposes of the Quintuple Alliance were achieved primarily through a series of international congresses which met between 1818 and 1822. It was at the second of these conferences, the Congress of Troppau, that the true character of the Alliance was most clearly revealed. Here the assembled delegates drew up an agreement avowing the intention of the great powers to intervene by force of arms to suppress any revolution that might threaten the stability of Europe. In two different instances the policy of intervention was actually carried out. After an uprising in the Kingdom of the Two Sicilies, in which the Bourbon monarch, Ferdinand I, was compelled to swear allegiance to a liberal constitution, Metternich convoked the Congress of Laibach in 1821. King Ferdinand was summoned before it, commanded to disavow his oath, and persuaded to invite an Austrian army to march into Naples. As a result, the constitution was revoked, and Ferdinand was restored to his position as an autocratic sovereign. In 1822 the Congress of Verona was summoned to deal with an insurrection in Spain, which also had had the effect of forcing the king to subscribe to a liberal constitution. After considerable wrangling among the powers as to the measures which should be taken to crush the revolt, it was finally decided that the king of France should send an army into Spain to support his Bourbon kinsman. Not only was the revolt speedily crushed, but intervention was followed by the blackest reaction Europe had yet seen. Hundreds of devoted liberals were put to death; even greater numbers were chained in the vilest of prisons. And it is not without interest that some of the ruthless measures of the Spanish king were the result of direct encouragement from the leaders of the Quintuple Alliance.

Although foreign intervention was confined to Spain and the Kingdom of the Two Sicilies, these were by no means the only countries where violent conflicts occurred between liberals and conservatives. The system of Metternich involved a regime of stern repression in domestic affairs by the governments of the great powers as well as the suppression of revolutions in the lesser states. But the more blind and bitter the policy of repression, the greater was the number of uprisings against it. In Great Britain the rule of

The activities
of the Quintuple Alliance

The clash
of liberals and
conservatives:
(1) in Great
Britain and
France

170

the Tories for the benefit of the landed aristocracy evoked powerful opposition from intellectual radicals like William Godwin, from the poets Shelley and Byron, and from the new industrial classes. When the protests of these groups were silenced by laws prohibiting public meetings and muzzling the press, some of the more desperate leaders organized the Cato Street Conspiracy in 1820 to murder the whole Tory Cabinet. Discovery of the plot was a foregone conclusion, and five of the conspirators were hanged. In France the modest compromise with progressive ideas which Louis XVIII incorporated in his Charter of 1814 proved to be more than his die-hard followers were willing to stand. As a result, the years between 1815 and 1820 were fraught with savage and sometimes bloody strife between Ultra-Royalists and their liberal and moderate opponents. In 1820 the assassination of the king's nephew by a fanatical liberal so frightened the people that the Ultra-Royalists were swept into control of Parliament. Then followed a series of reactionary laws which pushed France farther back into the mire of the *ancien régime*. In 1824 the victory of the forces of reaction was strengthened still further when Louis XVIII died and was succeeded by his brother, Charles X, the leader of the Ultra-Royalists.

Similar struggles occurred in central and eastern Europe with almost identical results. In Germany students in the universities organized secret societies and participated in stormy agitation against **(2) in Germany** hated regimes. These activities convinced Metternich, who dominated the Germanic Confederation, that all of central Europe was about to be engulfed by a radical revolution. Accordingly, he forced through the federal Diet a program of repressive measures known as the Carlsbad Decrees (1819). By the terms of these it was provided that every university should have a government supervisor; rebellious professors were to be removed from their positions; student societies were ordered to be dissolved; and the press was to be subject to a strict censorship. Vigorous enforcement of the Carlsbad Decrees put the liberal movement in Germany under a cloud, from which it did not emerge until 1848.

Meanwhile, the change in the attitude of the Tsar Alexander I had produced some rumblings of discontent in benighted Russia. Time was when Alexander had been one of the most enlightened monarchs of Europe. He had founded schools and universities. He had **(3) in Russia** emancipated a few of the serfs and had considered plans for freeing the remainder. He had even toyed with the idea of granting a written constitution. But after 1818 he turned reactionary and repented the liberal sins of his youth in sackcloth and ashes. This change of heart of the Tsar was the signal for the growth of an opposition movement among officers of the army and the intellectual classes. When Alexander died in 1825, the leaders of this movement determined to prevent the reaction from going any farther. They organized the Dekabrist revolt (from the Russian word for December) to compel the accession to the throne of the liberal Grand Duke Constantine in place of his hard-shell brother, Nicholas. Unfortunately Constantine would have nothing to do with the rebellion, and Nicholas speedily crushed it. The ensuing reign was one of the worst in Russian history. Not only did Nicholas abolish freedom of the press, but he established a system of secret police and converted the nation into a huge military camp where every move of the citizen could be watched and controlled by the government.

In spite of what semed to be enduring victories for the cause of reaction, by 1830 the system of Metternich had begun to break down. The initial step in the process was the withdrawal of Great Britain from the Quintuple Alliance. As early as 1822 the British refused to participate in Metternich's scheme for suppression of the revolution in Spain. Soon afterward they flatly repudiated the entire policy of intervention in the internal affairs of foreign states. It was not that the British of this time were more liberal than their allies on the Continent; it was rather that the Industrial Revolution was forcing Britain to seek new markets for the things she produced. Therefore she was strongly opposed to a foreign policy that would antagonize other nations and cut off her channels of trade. She had developed a lucrative commerce with the states of Central and South America, which had lately thrown off their allegiance to Spain, and she was fearful that the system of Metternich might be used to force these former colonies back under Spanish rule.

About the same time that Great Britain was weakening her ties with the Concert of Europe, Russia began to develop ambitions which also threatened the supremacy of Metternich's system. For some years the Russians had been greedily awaiting the breakup of the Ottoman Empire in the hope that that would pave the way for an easy expansion into the Balkans. The Russian opportunity came after 1821 when the Greeks launched a rebellion against Turkish rule. Since the Tsar Alexander I was still bound by loyalty to the doctrine of legitimacy, nothing was done until after his death in 1825. His successor, Nicholas I, entertained no such scruples. Especially when he observed in England and France expressions of the profoundest sympathy for the Greeks in their heroic struggle against an infidel oppressor, he determined to go to their rescue. Accordingly, in 1828, he declared war against Turkey. In a little more than a year a Russian army fought its way almost to the gates of the Turkish capital and forced the Sultan to sign the Treaty of Adrianople. By the terms of this treaty Turkey was compelled to acknowledge the independence of Greece, to grant autonomy to Serbia, and to permit the establishment of a Russian Protectorate over the provinces which later became the kingdom of Rumania. In thus contributing to the dismemberment of the empire of a "legitimate" ruler, Russia, with considerable encouragement from England and France, dealt a powerful blow to the system of political stagnation which Metternich was striving to maintain. For all practical purposes the empire of the Tsars had ceased to be a member of the Quintuple Alliance.

The system of Metternich was weakened still further by the series of revolutions that broke out in western Europe in 1830. The first in the series was the July Revolution in France, which resulted in the overthrow of Charles X, the last of the regular line of Bourbon kings. As was indicated previously, Charles X, who had succeeded Louis XVIII in 1824, was the perfect embodiment of the spirit of reaction. His stubborn and vindictive attitude inspired relentless hatred, especially among the ranks of the bourgeoisie, who resented his reduction of the interest on government bonds and his attempt to disfranchise three-fourths of the voters. As evidence accumulated that the king was determined to rule in complete defiance of Parliament, barricades were thrown up in the streets. After futile efforts to quell the insurrection with a remnant of loyal troops, Charles abdicated his throne and fled to England. The leaders of the bourgeoisie then chose as his successor Louis Philippe, a member of the Orleanist branch of the Bourbon family and a former Jacobin who had taken an active part in the revolution of 1789. The new government was proclaimed to be a constitutional monarchy founded upon the principle of popular sovereignty; and the white flag of the Bourbons was replaced by the tricolor originally invented by the apostles of Liberty, Equality, and Fraternity.

(3) the July
Revolution in
France

Soon after the July Revolution in France a revolt broke out in the Belgian Netherlands. It will be recalled that in the Vienna settlement of 1815 the Belgian or Austrian Netherlands had been subjected to the rule of Holland in defiance of the obvious differences of language, nationality, and religion between the Belgians and the Dutch. An additional basis of friction was the divergent economic interests of the two peoples. Whereas the Dutch were engaged primarily in commerce and agriculture, the occupations of the Belgians were largely industrial. These differences, combined with the stupid tyrannies of the Dutch king, incited the Belgians in the fall of 1830 to strike a blow for independence. The revolt was regarded with favor by the new government in France and also by the British, who hoped that it might benefit their trade. Consequently, the following year, an international agreement was signed in London that recognized the independence of Belgium as a constitutional monarchy. The Dutch had no alternative but to acquiesce in an accomplished fact. In 1839 the independence and neutrality of Belgium were guaranteed by all the great powers.

(4) the revolt
of the Belgians

The revolutionary movement of 1830 spread into a number of other countries, but the results were not so successful. In Italy revolts were staged in the Papal States against Gregory XVI, a zealous reactionary and friend of the Hapsburgs, and also in Parma and Modena against the Austrian puppets who ruled there. But in each of these cases Austrian troops were rushed to the scene and quickly restored the deposed governments. The only permanent results were to stimulate Italian nationalism and to nourish a morbid hate of the Austrians. In the Germanies, uprisings in several of the duchies and lesser kingdoms bore fruit in moderate constitutions, but the governments of the two most important German states— Prussia and Austria—were now so powerful that opposition groups were completely cowed. The only remaining revolt of serious dimensions was the insurrection of the Poles in 1831, a desperate attempt of that harassed people to regain independence from Russia. Had the Poles been as fortunate as the Belgians in obtaining aid from foreign nations, they might have won. But the British and the French were now too busy with affairs in western Europe and gave nothing more than verbal support. As a consequence, the Tsar Nicholas I was able to crush the revolt with murderous severity. Hundreds of the rebellious leaders were shot or exiled to the dreary wastes of Siberia, and Poland was governed henceforth as a conquered province.

3. THE PREDOMINANCE OF INTELLECTUAL CONSERVATISM

Just as there was a struggle in the years from 1800 to 1830 between liberals and conservatives in the political sphere, so there was a similar clash in the realm of ideas. And the outcome of this second struggle was not so far different from that of the first. In general, throughout the period, the doctrines of intellectual conservatives enjoyed supremacy. Order was exalted above liberty. The interests of groups, of society, and especially of the state were given precedence over those of the individual. An emphasis upon faith, authority, and tradition superseded the eighteenth-century belief in the primacy of reason and science. A group of French philosophers under the leadership of Joseph de Maistre (1754–1821) sought to inaugurate a Catholic revival in which mystical piety, supernaturalism, and the belief in an infallible Church would serve as the lamps to guide men's feet from the pitfalls of skepticism and anarchy. Maistre acclaimed obedience as the first political virtue and regarded the executioner as the bulwark of social order.

Revulsion
at excesses
of French
Revolution;
Edmund
Burke

For this ascendancy of conservative patterns of thought various factors were responsible. There was, of course, the tendency, common in all ages, of many writers and thinkers to take their cue from the dominant political trend, which in this period was conservative. But probably the major factor, in the beginning at least, was the strong revulsion of feeling which had set in against the horrors of the French Revolution. All who had been frightened by the violence of that movement were inclined to blame it on the rationalism, materialism, and individualism of the age of the Enlightenment. Hence they were disposed to swing to the opposite extreme of glorifying faith, authority, and tradition. Such in particular was the attitude expressed by Edmund Burke (1729–1797), the renowned British orator and Whig statesman of the late eighteenth century. Although he did not live to see the end of the French Revolution, Burke denounced that movement with all the fiery eloquence he could command. To him the Revolution was an attempt to repudiate the accumulated wisdom of the ages. This world, he averred, cannot be made over in a single night. No one generation has the right to set itself up as the judge of society's future needs. The institutions and traditions which have come down to us from the past have an enduring value. To lay violent hands upon them is to threaten the vital elements of civilization itself.

The body of thought that stands as the most perfect expression of the age of reaction was the German philosophy of Romantic Idealism. This philosophy derives its name from the fact that it was a combination of the romanticist theory of truth with the idealist conception of the universe. That is, it was neither rationalistic nor materialistic in the strict meaning of those terms. Instead, it recognized the validity of intuitive or instinctive knowledge in addition to that which comes from reason, and it sought to explain the universe in a sense at least partly spiritual. The Romantic Idealists also deviated sharply from the individualism and humanism of eighteenth-century philosophy. They regarded the individual as totally devoid of significance except insofar as he was a member of some social group. Therefore, they argued, the welfare of the group must come first, and that of the individual will automatically follow. Society and the state are social organisms, products of a *natural* evolution, and not the artificial creations of man himself for his own convenience. No such thing as a state of nature ever existed, nor was political society founded by a social compact. Consequently the individual cannot claim any inviolable sphere of rights beyond the jurisdiction of organized society. His duty is rather to submerge his own interests in those of the group and thereby gain the true liberty which consists in obedience to law and in respect for accumulated tradition.

Romantic Idealism

The philosopher who provided the original inspiration for Romantic Idealism was a methodical little German who lived most of his life in the eighteenth century. His name was Immanuel Kant, and he was born in Königsberg in 1724; there he died in 1804 without once having left his native city, except for a brief period of tutoring in a neighboring village. Devoting most of his life to teaching, he matured his philosophic ideas very slowly. When well along toward middle age he could still refer with scorn to the metaphysicians as those who dwelt on the high towers of abstruse cogitation, "where there is usually a great deal of wind." Not until he was fifty-seven years old did he finish his first great work, the *Critique of*

Romantic Idealism founded by Immanuel Kant

Pure Reason. As a philosopher, Kant owed considerable to the great minds of the Enlightenment. They contributed particularly to his political ideas. Unlike most of his followers, he believed in the natural rights of man and even defended the separation of powers as a necessary protection for the liberty of the citizen. But in the field of general philosophy Kant departed widely from the rationalism of the eighteenth century. He divided the entire universe into two worlds: one, the realm of physical nature, or the world of *phenomena;* and the other, the realm of ultimate reality, or the world of *noumena.* The methods of knowing applicable to these realms are entirely different. Sense perception and reason can give us knowledge only of the realm of *phenomena,* of the world of physical things. But in the higher realm of the spiritual, which is the world of ultimate reality, such methods are of no avail. Since all ordinary knowledge rests in final analysis upon sense perception, we cannot prove by reason or science that God exists, that the human will is free, or that the soul is immortal. Nevertheless, we are justified in assuming that these things are true. In the realm of *noumena,* faith, intuition, and deep conviction are just as valid instruments of knowledge as logic and science in the realm of *phenomena.*

Other Romantic Idealist philosophers: Fichte

The immediate disciples of Kant generally inclined toward a more abstract and metaphysical philosophy than that of their master. Such was notably the case of Johann Gottlieb Fichte (1762–1814). Fichte and his associates taught that the world of mind or spirit is the real world, and that the individual realizes his true nature only by bringing himself into harmony with the universal purpose. The human mind can know nothing of reality except insofar as the mind is informed and guided by the supreme ego or universal intelligence. The philosophy of Fichte evolved into a kind of spiritual pantheism with a world-spirit directing all life and activity toward a final goal of sublime perfection. Fichte is also of more than trivial importance as a political philosopher. He was one of the earliest apostles of collectivistic nationalism in Germany. During the years of the Napoleonic invasions he proclaimed to his countrymen the ideal of a united and powerful Germany with a mission to assume the leadership of the civilized world. He taught that this state should rule with an eye single to justice and prosperity for all its subjects.

Hegel

Undoubtedly the most influential philosopher of the Romantic Idealist movement was Georg Wilhelm Hegel (1770–1831). Professor of philosophy for a considerable period at the University of Berlin, Hegel won a great number of adherents, and through them exerted a potent force in shaping intellectual currents for many years. The central doctrine of Hegel's philosophy is the idea of purposive evolution. He regarded the universe as in a condition of flux, with everything tending to pass over into its opposite. In particular, each institution or social or political organism grows to maturity, fulfills its mission, and then gives way to something different. But

Georg Wilhelm Friedrich Hegel (1770–1831).

the old itself is never entirely destroyed; the clash of opposites results eventually in a fusion, in the creation of a new organism made up of elements taken from the two opposites themselves. Then the process is repeated over and over again with each new stage representing an improvement over that which has gone before. But Hegel's conception of evolution was not mechanistic. He believed the whole process to be guided by the universal reason or God. Evolution, he maintained, is the unfoldment of God in history. Further, he argued that the war of opposites would ultimately lead to a beneficent goal. This goal he described as the perfect state, in which the interests of every citizen would be perfectly blended with the interests of society. Actually, Hegel worshiped the state in a much more ecstatic fashion than did any of the other Romantic Idealists. He held that true liberty consists in subjection to political society, and that the individual has no rights which the state is bound to respect, for without the state the individual would be nothing but an animal. "The State is the Divine Idea as it exists on earth." [3]

Romantic Idealism cast its influence in many directions. In one or another of its forms it was adopted as the principal gospel of nearly all in the conservative camp. Churchmen who had been disturbed by the attacks of deists and skeptics were delighted to find a philosophy that recognized the merits of faith and exalted the world of spirit. People with a stake in the maintenance of order rejoiced in the new worship of tradition and authority and in the implied con-

The influence of Romantic Idealism

[3] Hegel, *Philosophy of History* (J. Sibree, trans.), p. 87.

177

demnation of revolution. Especially pleasing to the ruling class were the political teachings of Hegel, who enjoyed such prestige at the Prussian court that his enemies called him "the official philosopher." The doctrines of Hegel and Fichte strengthened the rising tide of nationalism and ultimately contributed their quota to the devastating flood of fascism.[4] But Romantic Idealism also bore certain other fruits not exactly to the liking of its principal exponents. One of their younger contemporaries, Arthur Schopenhauer (1788–1860), developed the notion of a universal force, directing all growth and movement, into a philosophy of stark pessimism. He taught that this force is *will*—a blind, unconscious craving of individuals and species to survive. Since the will to live is present in all animate forms, and since it leads the strong to devour the weak, this world is the worst of all possible worlds. Selfishness, pain, and misery are inseparable from life, and therefore the only road to happiness for man consists in as complete a denial of life as possible after the manner of an Oriental ascetic. Still another of the strange offshoots of Romantic Idealism was the philosophy of history of Karl Marx. For his celebrated doctrine of dialectical materialism, Marx was heavily indebted to Hegel. Both believed in a progressive evolution through a clash of opposing systems, resulting finally in a perfect society. But whereas Hegel assumed that the ultimate goal would be a perfect state, Marx argued that it would be communism. It was the proud boast of the great socialist leader that he turned Hegel right side up.

Romantic Idealism was most popular in Germany. In other countries, especially in England and France, where the influence of the Enlightenment had taken deeper root, philosophy was generally more liberal in tone. The leading system of thought in England in the early nineteenth century was Utilitarianism, founded by Jeremy Bentham (1748–1832). Despite a frail and nervous physique, Bentham displayed prodigious intellectual talent throughout the greater part of his long life. He began the study of Latin when he was only three years old and was graduated from Oxford at the age of fifteen. When he was nearly seventy he was still propounding schemes for prison reform and for cutting canals across the Isthmus of Panama and the Isthmus of Suez. His chief philosophical work, the *Principles of Morals and Legislation*, was published in 1789. Bentham's Utilitarianism derives its name from his cardinal teaching that the supreme test to which every belief and institution should be made to conform is the test of utility or usefulness. This test he defined as contributing to the greatest happiness of the greatest number. Any doctrine or practice which fails to meet this requirement should be rejected forthwith, regardless of how much hoary tradition may stand behind it. Despite its social connotations, Bentham's ideal was the acme of individualism. Not only did he maintain that

Utilitarianism,
founded by
Jeremy Ben-
tham

---

[4] Hegelian ideas influenced the growth of fascism not only in Germany but also in Italy. See H. W. Schneider, *Making the Fascist State,* pp. 20–24.

the interest of the community is simply the sum of the interests of the several members who compose it, but he was quite frank in admitting that the motives of individuals are purely selfish. The mainspring of human action is the desire to secure pleasure and to avoid pain. Therefore society should leave to each of its members complete freedom to follow his own enlightened self-interest. Since every individual knows better than anyone else what constitutes his own good, the welfare of society can best be promoted by allowing to each of its members the maximum liberty of action. Bentham was firmly convinced that granting this concession would not mean a reversion to the ways of the jungle. He insisted that every man would be obliged to respect his neighbor's rights through fear of retaliation; that men would obey the laws for the simple reason that the "probable mischiefs of obedience are less than the probable mischiefs of disobedience." [5]

Bentham's most faithful disciple was James Mill (1773–1836), but the greatest of all the Utilitarian philosophers was James Mill's oldest son, John Stuart Mill (1806–1873). Educated exclusively by his father, John Stuart Mill surpassed even Bentham as an intellectual prodigy. He learned the Greek alphabet at the age of three, and by the time he was eight had read all of Herodotus and a considerable portion of Plato in the original. When scarcely thirteen he had completed a rigorous course of training in history, Scholastic logic, and Aristotelian philosophy. His greatest works are his *Logic*, his *Principles of Political Economy*, his essay *On Liberty*, and his *Representative Government*. As a philosopher, John Stuart Mill summed up nearly all of the major tendencies in English thought initiated by Locke, Hume, and Bentham. He was a sensationalist, a skeptic in regard to final truth, and a champion of the liberal and practical point of view. But he was also an original and independent thinker and made a number of distinct contributions of his own. He founded a new system of logic, based upon experience as the original ground of all knowledge. All of the so-called self-evident truths, even the axioms of mathematics, he argued, are simply inferences derived from the observed facts that nature is uniform and that every effect has a cause. Knowledge comes neither from inborn ideas nor from mystic intuition. Though Mill agreed with the general purport of Bentham's teachings, he rejected the doctrine that the pursuit of pleasure and the avoidance of pain are the sole determinants of human conduct (the "pig philosophy," as Thomas Carlyle once called it). According to Mill the conduct of individuals is often influenced by mere habit and by the desire for unity with their fellow beings. Further, he maintained that pleasures themselves differ in quality, arguing that it is better to be "Socrates dissatisfied than a fool satisfied." In his later years Mill also modified much of Bentham's individualism. While repudiating socialism on the ground

[5] W. A. Dunning, *History of Political Theories*, III, 216.

that it would involve the destruction of personal liberty, he never-theless advocated a considerable degree of intervention by the state for the benefit of its less fortunate members. He looked forward to a time "when society will no longer be divided into the idle and the industrious; when the rule that they who do not work shall not eat, will be applied not to paupers only, but impartially to all. . . ." [6]

The nearest approach to a liberal and practical philosophy on the Continent of Europe was the Positivism of Auguste Comte (1798–1857). Positivism takes its name from Comte's doctrine that the only knowledge of any value is *positive* knowledge, or knowledge which comes from the sciences. Comte's philosophy may therefore be placed, along with Utilitarianism, in the classification of *empirical* philosophies, which includes those deriving all truth from experi-ence or from observation of the physical world. Comte rejected metaphysics as utterly futile; no man can discover the hidden essences of things—why events happen as they do, or what is the ultimate meaning and goal of existence. All that we know is how things happen, the laws which control their occurrence, and the re-lations existing between them. If there was any one purpose preemi-nent over others in Comte's philosophy, it was to devise means for improving relations among men. He did not agree with Bentham that the actions of individuals are motivated exclusively by self-interest. He avowed, on the contrary, that men are influenced by nobler impulses of *altruism*, or feelings for others, as well as by in-stincts of selfishness. The great object of all social teaching should be to promote the supremacy of altruism (a word invented by Comte) over egoism. Believing that this purpose could be achieved only through an appeal to the emotions of love and self-sacrifice, Comte developed what he called the Religion of Humanity, which was supposed to bring men together in a common devotion to jus-tice, charity, and benevolence. Although this religion included no belief in the supernatural, it was provided with an extensive ritual and even with a Trinity and a priesthood. Ridiculed by its critics as "Catholicism minus Christianity," it nevertheless represented an at-tempt to build a system of belief dedicated to the aim of social progress.

4· ROMANTICISM IN LITERATURE AND THE ARTS

In the chapter on the Intellectual Revolution it was observed that toward the end of the eighteenth century a romantic revolt set in against the dominant classical tendencies in literature. The essence of romanticism was the glorification of the instincts and emotions as opposed to a worship of the intellect. Included in it also were such elements as a deep veneration for nature, a contempt for formalism, a sentimental love for humble folk, and often a flaming zeal to re-

[6] J. S. Mill, *Autobiography* (Uniform Library ed.), p. 231.

make the world. Among the leaders of the new movement in its infancy were Rousseau, Thomas Gray, Oliver Goldsmith, Robert Burns, and Friedrich Schiller. Romanticism flourished after the beginning of the nineteenth century, attaining the zenith of its growth about 1830. No longer was it confined to literature; it was a vital force in painting and to a considerable extent also in music. Though it still had to compete in some fields with classicism, especially in France during the era of Napoleon, it was by far the most vigorous literary and artistic influence in the first three decades of the nineteenth century.

Romanticism in literature had its deepest and longest roots in England. Its two great prophets at the beginning of the nineteenth century were the poets William Wordsworth (1770–1850) and Samuel Taylor Coleridge (1772–1834). Wordsworth is noted for his mystical adoration of nature, not alone in its surface beauties but especially as the embodiment of a universal spirit which unites all living things in a kinship of divinity. He believed that a sensuous worship of nature would bring man to a deeper awareness of the nobility of life, that it would enable him to hear "the still sad music of humanity" and thereby increase his love and compassion for his fellow creatures. The special gift of Coleridge was an ability to make the weird and fantastic credible. Though he sometimes wandered into the dense jungles of metaphysics, he succeeded in the magic stanzas of *The Ancient Mariner* in producing some of the most colorful imaginative writing in the English language. This work reveals his unusual power of combining tender, almost womanly sentiment with witching descriptions of strange, supernatural terrors, of phantoms and specters that rise out of the murky depths of the emotions to torment man with a sense of his helplessness. *Romanticism in English literature: Wordsworth and Coleridge*

Perhaps the most typical of the English romantic poets were John Keats (1795–1821), Percy Bysshe Shelley (1792–1822), and George Gordon, Lord Byron (1788–1824). Keats differed from most of his contemporaries in identifying beauty with intellectual passion in somewhat the same way as the Greeks identified the beautiful with the good. The substance of his creed is expressed in the well-known lines from the *Ode on a Grecian Urn:* "Beauty is truth, truth beauty,—that is all ye know on earth, and all ye need to know." His conception was one of ideal beauty, which endures independently of the fading of the flower or the passing of the loveliness of youth. The other two short-lived poets of the English romantic circle were much more interested in political and social questions. In spite of their upper-class origins, both were rebels against stubborn conservatism and employed their talents in passionate appeals for justice and freedom. Shelley was expelled from Oxford on a charge of atheism and then for some years was a disciple of William Godwin, the philosophical anarchist. Though he eventually modified some of his youthful radicalism and allowed his *Keats, Shelley, and Byron* thoughts to wander more and more into vaporous abstractions, he never relinquished his hatred of injustice or his hopes for a golden dawn of happiness and freedom. Lord Byron, who inherited the title of baron at the age of ten, was even more than Shelley a poet of stormy defiance, of romantic daring, and of sardonic laughter at the hypocrisy and arrogance of the human race. Not only in the qualities of his proud personality, but also in the scandals which enveloped his career and in the directness and audacity of his poetic style he typified for the age the spirit of romantic man. His death while aiding the Greeks in their war for independence was a fitting climax to his brief, adventurous life.

Sir Walter Scott

Not all of the romantic writers in Great Britain confined their efforts to poetry. The most noted of those who achieved an enduring reputation in both poetry and prose was the learned but none too subtle Tory, Sir Walter Scott (1771-1832). Nurtured on family pride from his early life and fascinated by the rich legends of his ancestral heritage, Scott never succumbed to the rebellious tendencies which frequently characterized the romantic tradition. So far as political ideals were concerned, he accepted things as they were and even gloried in the advantages of wealth and social position. His interest as a writer was distinctly antiquarian. Both in his poetry and in his prose he sought to revive the heroic and picturesque legends of his Scottish background. His thirty-two Waverly novels deal mainly with the history of medieval Scotland, in an age as remote as the twelfth century. The chief historical importance of Sir Walter Scott consists in the fact that he introduced a new element into literary romanticism—that of worshipful reverence for the past. His novels, which were undoubtedly the most popular and influential fiction of the early nineteenth century, served to cast a glamour upon the Middle Ages, to rescue that epoch from the scorn with which it had been treated as a consequence of the classical prejudices of the Enlightenment.

Romanticism in
Germany:
Heinrich Heine

Except for the dramas of Schiller and Goethe, discussed in a preceding chapter,[7] romantic literature in Continental countries is scarcely to be compared with that in England. The only other important writer in Germany was Heinrich Heine (1797-1856), born of orthodox Jewish parents but later a convert to Christianity for the sake of expediency. Like Shelley and Byron, Heine was an individualist and a relentless critic of entrenched conservatism. He devoted nearly the whole of his active life to what he loved to call "humanity's war of liberation." But he was not merely a witty satirist and pungent critic of smugness and reaction. In his *Book of Songs* he displayed lyric gifts of tenderness and melancholy and a haunting charm of melody which few other poets of his day could surpass. He has been aptly called "a nightingale nesting in the wig of a Voltaire."

[7] See pp. 65–66.

Romanticism in France as in England wavered between a mystic irrationalism, on the one hand, and a gallant defense of individual liberty and social reform on the other. The chief exponent of the irrational tendency was François de Chateaubriand (1768–1848), a kind of stepfather of French romanticism. Chateaubriand found in the mysteries of Christianity and in the "holy innocence" of simple folk the sublimest beauty in the universe. Along with Joseph de Maistre and others he was the prophet of a Catholic revival designed to guide men back to an age of faith and thus save them from the perils of reason. The libertarian and individualist aspect of French romanticism was best exemplified by the work of George Sand (1804–1876) and Victor Hugo (1802–1885). The former, whose real name was Aurore Dupin, wrote novels of country life with an idyllic charm that has endeared them to countless readers. She was one of the first to make peasants and humble laborers the heroes of fiction. Later she became a zealous advocate of republicanism and of the rights of women to a love untrammeled by marital convention. A novelist of much wider influence was Victor Hugo, who for many years was the living voice of French romanticism. Intensely interested in public affairs, he was an eloquent champion of political freedom and of justice for those who were caught in the web of fate. His best-known work is *Les Miserables*, an epic of the redemption of a soul purified by heroism and suffering and a powerful indictment of social cruelty.

In attempting to judge the importance of literary romanticism as a factor of social and intellectual progress, we should note, first of all, its grave limitations. The disdain for reason and scientific analysis by even the most liberal of the romanticists was certainly a handicap to any permanent solution of humanity's problems. Furthermore, their exaggerated emotionalism occasionally made a mockery of some of their most laudable intentions. Excesses of sentimentality are not easily controlled. To allow free reign to the emotions in one direction is to run the risk of an impairment of judgment in others. Thus we find Victor Hugo hurling bitter invectives against Napoleon III, whom he called "Napoleon the Little," but singing paeans of praise to Napoleon I. It was perhaps for this reason also that the liberalism of so many of the romanticists eventually gave way to nationalism, as in the case of Schiller, or even to hopeless reaction, as in the case of Wordsworth. Yet, notwithstanding these weaknesses, literary romanticism accomplished no small amount of good in combating repression in many of its forms and in proclaiming the nobility of the common man. And probably it is safe to say that it was these elements of strength which really survived to influence the work of such writers as Dickens, George Eliot, and John Ruskin in the middle and later years of the nineteenth century.

The growth of a romantic movement in art was scarcely notice-

See color plates
at page 137

able until after the downfall of Napoleon. This was especially true in France. With the outbreak of the French Revolution a strong reaction set in against the elegant rococo style of the old order. But instead of launching a new tradition, the artists of the Revolution simply went back to what was supposed to be a *pure* classicism, on the assumption that this would be in harmony with the rationalist ideals of the new order. The advent of Napoleon made no perceptible change. The Little Corporal liked to think of himself as a modern Caesar or Alexander the Great. Accordingly, he adopted the Roman imperial eagle as one of his emblems, invested his son with the title of King of Rome, and erected arches, columns, and temples of triumph in the city of Paris. Under such influences it is not surprising that a classicist movement in art of more than ordinary vitality should have crystallized in France in the first two decades of the nineteenth century. It reached its apex in painting under the leadership of Jacques David (1748–1825) and Jean Auguste Ingres (1780–1867). The work of both of these men was characterized by order and restraint, by a strict attention to form, and by a liberal choice of themes from Greek and Roman mythology.

Notwithstanding the vigor of the classical revival, the force of the romantic influence, overflowing from the channels of literature and philosophy, was not to be denied. After the defeat of Napoleon at Waterloo the period of the Enlightenment and the Revolution was definitely accepted as a closed chapter. There seemed to be no longer any reason for trying to preserve the ideals of a bygone age. As a consequence, classicism in painting was quickly supplanted by romanticism. The foremost champion of the new style in France was Eugène Delacroix (1798–1863), who gloried in portraying struggles for freedom and other dramatic and sometimes violent scenes from history. In place of the restraint and sobriety of classical painting, he substituted an emotionalism in some cases as overwrought as that of Michelangelo. Inspired also by Rubens and the Venetians, he employed small strokes of pure color that seem to merge into the actual flesh of his living or dying subjects. The work of Delacroix was paralleled to a certain distance by that of the romantic landscape painters. Their chief representative was Camille Corot (1796–1875), leader of the Barbizon school, so called from the village of Barbizon near Paris. Among others who followed the same tradition was the Englishman J. M. W. Turner (1775–1851). The romantic landscape painters were just as addicted to effusive displays of emotionalism as Delacroix, but it was an emotionalism of a quieter tone. They were poets of nature who suffused forests and streams and mountains with a gentle haze of tender worship.

From what we have learned about the influence of romanticism upon literature and painting, we should normally expect that architecture also would be deeply affected. Such, however, was not the case. While it is true that, under romantic inspirations, a movement was started about 1840 to revive the medieval Gothic, the results were only moderately significant. A large number of churches with soaring spires and pointed arches were built, and even some government buildings also; but not infrequently what was supposed to be pure Gothic turned out to be a crude eclecticism made up of elements taken only partly from the Gothic. In general, the classical influence was still too strong to be overcome, with the result that throughout the greater part of the nineteenth century variations of the baroque continued to be the most popular building styles. Not until about 1900 was there much evidence of a desire to create a new and original architecture more truly expressive of our own civilization.

In music, as in painting and literature, the first decades of the nineteenth century saw the rise of romanticism, though many of the precepts of the preceding classical period were by no means abandoned. The romanticists regarded music not essentially as objective beauty but mainly as a medium for expressing man's inner moods. It must not merely please but must stir a sympathetic vibration in the listener. Attempts were made to capture in tone the various aspects of nature and, above all, human sentiments and passions. To some extent the composers, like the poets, responded to the exciting political drama about them. It is significant that at first musical romanticism found its congenial expression in lyricism—piano pieces and songs. This represents a rebellion against the logical architecture of the large symphonic forms. Since the redoubtable guardian of the latter, indeed the one who carried them to their final flowering, Ludwig van Beethoven (1770–1827) stood there as a formidable sentinel, the spirit of romanticism moved into chamber and orchestral music only gradually.

Ludwig van Beethoven was born in the west German town of Bonn but spent most of his productive years in Vienna, then regarded as the musical capital of Europe. His life seems to bear out the adage that great art is the product of suffering. Poverty and a harsh father made his childhood unhappy, and his adult life was a succession of difficulties, largely occasioned by his impractical nature and irascible temper. He was not only coarse in manner, careless in dress, and blunt to the point of rudeness, but overly sensitive and suspicious, frequently injuring his closest friends because of resentment toward some imaginary slight. In spite of such traits he was able to retain the loyalty of his friends and to fascinate and humble the Viennese aristocracy, both male and female. The bold independence of thought and action which he carried off successfully in a staid aristocratic society augured the transition to a new age. The crowning source of Beethoven's suffering was his deafness, which began to trouble him before he was thirty and became total in his later years. As a result, he was not only forced to give up playing in public, but was never able to hear many

Architecture not greatly affected by romanticism

The beginning of romanticism in music

Ludwig van Beethoven

185

Beethoven's
works

See color plates
at page 169

of his greatest works.

The first two decades of Beethoven's life in Vienna saw the composition of dozens of piano sonatas, much chamber music, eight symphonies, overtures, one opera, and one Mass. While the composer's development was steady in this large output, the most remarkable thing about these works is their uniqueness: each represents a new solution of the problems of the respective genre. In the Fifth Symphony Beethoven reaches the summit of symphonic logic, the Sixth is a glorification of nature, the Seventh a Dionysian revelry, the Eighth a genial conjuring up of the spirit of the eighteenth-century symphony. Then Beethoven embarks on his last artistic journey; the deaf composer takes us into the world of visions, though everything remains ordered by an iron will. Five piano sonatas, five string quartets, the Ninth Symphony and the great Mass called *Missa Solemnis* constitute his final legacy. They fill the listener with awe not so much because of their unusual form or their vast proportions, but because of their tone, a tone altogether new in the history of music. It expresses boundless will and power and ecstasy, the tone of unspeakable solitude breaking into the open. It is this tone and harnessed power that made Beethoven the Titan of music.

Franz
Schubert

Franz Schubert (1797–1828), the Viennese schoolteacher's son, does not fit very well into any scheme or schedule. He was no one's disciple; he just assimilated music that was around him and by his eighteenth year composed masterpieces—surely the embodiment of what is called "God-given" natural talent. But this was a dangerous precocity. Perhaps Schubert felt that he must hasten, for he died in his thirty-first year. After he left the paternal home he lived a romantic bohemian life with a group of like-minded poets, painters,

Ludwig van Beethoven (1770–1827).

and singers, eternally poor, eternally working, and eternally hoping. In this genial company perhaps three friends shared one hat and five one purse, but the world was wrong in construing from this care-free existence the parochial picture of unfortunate derelicts perishing in the adventure. These people lived a life congenial to them, but it was a life that did not agree with the pattern set by the ruling Biedermeier bourgeoisie. They did not need much, they got together in the evenings to make music, and on nice days went out into the country where Schubert would compose on the back of a country-inn menu half a dozen songs and waltzes in one afternoon. It is thus that Schubert's music came to reflect Vienna's grace and the rhythm of its life. Schubert was the greatest of song composers, but he was also the only one of the age who could be ranked next to Beethoven as an instrumental composer. Though they lived in the same town, Schubert was so overawed by Beethoven that he never dared to address him. Among his eight symphonies and numerous chamber music works and piano sonatas there are many incomparable masterpieces. He also composed great Masses; only his operas failed to show the full weight of his genius.

SELECTED READINGS

THE AGE OF NAPOLEON

· *Items so designated are available in paperbound editions.*

· Brinton, Crane, *The Lives of Talleyrand*, New York, 1932 (Norton Library).

· Bruun, Geoffrey, *Europe and the French Imperium*, New York, 1938 (Torchbook).

Dard, Emile, *Napoleon and Talleyrand*, New York, 1937. A good study based on original sources.

Fisher, H. A. L., *Napoleon*, New York, 1913. A brief study of Napoleon as a personality and as a soldier and ruler.

Gershoy, Leo, *The French Revolution and Napoleon*, New York, 1933. A brief but excellent account.

· Gayl, Pieter, *Napoleon, For and Against*, New Haven, 1949 (Yale University Press).

Gottschalk, L. R., *The Era of the French Revolution, 1715–1815*, New York, 1929. Thorough and scholarly.

Kircheisen, F. M., *Napoleon*, New York, 1932.

Tarle, Eugene, *Napoleon's Invasion of Russia*, New York, 1942. An exciting account.

Thompson, J. M., *Napoleon Bonaparte*, New York, 1952. A recent evaluation.

THE AGE OF REACTION

· Artz, F. B., *Reaction and Revolution, 1814–1832*, New York, 1934 (Torchbook).

· Gulick, E. V., *Europe's Classical Balance of Power*, Ithaca, N.Y., 1955 (Norton Library).

Herman, A., *Metternich*, New York, 1932.

· Kissinger, Henry A., *A World Restored: Europe After Napoleon*, Gloucester, Mass. (Universal Library).

· May, A. J., *The Age of Metternich, 1814–1848*, New York, 1933 (Holt, Rine-
  hart & Winston). A good summary.
· Nicholson, Harold, *The Congress of Vienna*, London, 1946 (Compass).
· Webster, C. K., *The Congress of Vienna, 1814–1815*, New York, 1919 (Barnes
  & Noble). The standard work.

INTELLECTUAL AND ARTISTIC DEVELOPMENTS, 1800–1830

Artz, F. B., *France under the Bourbon Restoration, 1814–1830*, New York,
  1963. Emphasizes social and intellectual developments.

Bell, Clive, *Landmarks in Nineteenth Century Painting*, New York, 1927.

Boas, George, *French Philosophies of the Romantic Period*, Baltimore, 1934.

Brandes, Georg, *Main Currents in Nineteenth Century Literature*, New
  York, 1901–06.

· Brinton, Crane, *English Political Thought in the Nineteenth Century*, New
  York, 1962 (Torchbook). A new edition.

———, *Political Ideas of the English Romanticists*, London, 1926.

Davidson, W. L., *Political Thought in England from Bentham to Mill*, New
  York, 1916.

Einstein, Alfred, *Music in the Romantic Era*, New York, 1947.

Lang, Paul, *Music in Western Civilization*, New York, 1941.

Machlis, Joseph, *The Enjoyment of Music*, rev. ed., New York, 1963.

· Merz, J. T., *History of European Thought in the Nineteenth Century*, New
  York, 1911–14 (Dover, 4 vols.).

Randall, J. H., Jr., *The Making of the Modern Mind*, New York, 1926. Chs.
  XVI, XVII.

Wenley, R. M., *Kant and His Philosophical Revolution*, New York, 1911.

Wright, C. H. C., *A History of French Literature*, New York, 1925.

SOURCE MATERIALS

Bentham, Jeremy, *A Fragment on Government*.

———, *Principles of Penal Law*, Part II, Book II, Ch. XII.

· Burke, Edmund, *Reflections on the Revolution in France* (Holt, Rinehart &
  Winston and others).

· de Caulaincourt, A. A. L., *With Napoleon in Russia*, New York, 1935 (Universal Library). An eye-witness account by one of Napoleon's officers.

· Herold, J. C., ed., *The Mind of Napoleon*, New York, 1955 (Collier).

Johnston, R. M., ed., *The Corsican: A Diary of Napoleon in His Own Words*.

· Kant, Immanuel, *Plan for Perpetual Peace* (Library of Liberal Arts).

· Mill, John Stuart, *Autobiography*, New York, 1924 (Library of Liberal Arts
  and others).

Thompson, J. M., ed., *Napoleon Self-Revealed*, Boston, 1934.

CHAPTER 6

The First Industrial Revolution
(1760-1860)

During the period from 1300 to about 1700 modern civilization
passed through its first great economic upheaval. This was the Commercial Revolution, which annihilated the semistatic economy of
the Middle Ages and replaced it with a dynamic capitalism dominated by merchants, bankers, and shipowners. But the Commercial
Revolution was only the beginning of swift and decisive changes in
the economic sphere. It was soon followed by an Industrial Revolution, which not only enlarged the scope of business in the field of
commerce but extended it into the realm of production as well. Insofar as it is possible to reduce it to a compact formula, the Industrial Revolution may be said to have embraced the following: (1)
the mechanization of industry and agriculture; (2) the application
of power to industry; (3) the development of the factory system;
(4) a sensational speeding-up of transportation and communication;
and (5) a marked increase of capitalistic control over nearly all
branches of economic activity. Although the Industrial Revolution
began as early as 1760, it did not gain its full momentum until the
nineteenth century. Many historians divide the movement into two
great stages, with the year 1860 marking the approximate boundary
line between them. The stage from 1860 to 1914 is often referred to
as the Second Industrial Revolution.

**The meaning of
the Industrial
Revolution**

189

I. THE COMPLEX OF CAUSES

The First Industrial Revolution sprang from a multitude of causes, some of them much more remote than is usually suspected. It may be well to consider first the early improvements in technology. The marvelous inventions of the late eighteenth century did not spring full-blown like Athena from the brow of Zeus. On the contrary, there had been a more or less fruitful interest in mechanical innovations for some time. The period of the Commercial Revolution had witnessed the invention of the pendulum clock, the thermometer, the air pump, the spinning wheel, and the stocking frame, to say nothing of improvements in the techniques of smelting ores and making brass. About 1580 a mechanical loom was devised, capable of weaving several strands of ribbon at the same time. There were also important technological advances in such industries as glass blowing, clock making, wood finishing and shipbuilding. Several of the early inventions made necessary the use of factory methods. For example, the silk-throwing machine invented in Italy about 1500 had to be housed in a large building and required a considerable corps of workers. In the Temple Mills on the Thames above London, according to a description by Daniel Defoe in 1728, brass was beaten into kettles and pans by enormous hammers operated by water power. These early technological improvements are hardly to be compared in significance with those made after 1760, but they do indicate that the machine age did not burst upon the world out of a clear sky.

Among other causes of paramount importance were certain more direct consequences of the Commercial Revolution. That movement brought into existence a class of capitalists who were constantly seeking new opportunities to invest their surplus wealth. At first this wealth could be readily absorbed by trade or by mining, banking, and shipbuilding ventures; but as time went on the opportunities in such fields became limited. As a consequence more and more capital was made available for the development of manufacturing. But a rapid development of manufacturing would scarcely have occurred had there not been a growing demand for industrial products. This demand grew largely from the establishment of colonial empires and from the marked increase in the population of Europe. It will be recalled that one of the primary objects in the acquisition of colonies was to expand the market for manufactured goods from the mother country. At the same time the potential markets at home were being rapidly enlarged by the large increase of population in western European countries. In England the number of inhabitants rose from 4,000,000 in 1600 to 6,000,000 in 1700 and to 9,000,000 by the end of the eighteenth century. The population of France grew from 17,000,000 in 1700 to 26,000,000 about a hundred years later. How much of this increase was due to the advancement of medicine in the eighteenth century and how much of it was the product of a more ample food supply resulting from the expansion of trade is a debatable question. Certainly the influence of the second of these factors cannot be ignored. Finally, the Commercial Revolution gave a stimulus to the growth of manufactures through its basic gospel of mercantilism. The mercantilist policy was designed, as much as for any other purpose, to increase the quantity of manufactured goods available for export and thereby to ensure a favorable balance of trade.

Despite the importance of the causes already mentioned, the Industrial Revolution would undoubtedly have been delayed had there not been a need for fundamental mechanical improvements in certain fields of production. By 1700 the demand for charcoal for smelting iron had so depleted the resources of timber that several of the nations of western Europe were threatened with deforestation. A partial solution was found about 1709 when Abraham Darby discovered that coke could be used for smelting. But in order to obtain sufficient coke it was necessary that coal be mined in much larger quantities than ever before. Since the chief obstacle to the extraction of coal was the accumulation of water in the mines, the need for the new fuel led to a search for some convenient source of power to drive the pumps. Various experiments in connection with this search finally resulted in the invention of the steam engine. An even more crucial need for mechanization existed in the textile industry. With the increasing popularity of cotton clothing in the seventeenth and eighteenth centuries, it was simply impossible to provide enough yarn with the primitive spinning wheels still in use. Even when every available woman and child was pressed into service, the demand could not be met. In Germany the soldiers in the barracks were actually put to work spinning cotton thread. As the need grew more and more urgent, rewards were offered by scientific societies and business organizations for improved methods of producing yarn. In 1760, for example, the English Society of Arts offered a prize for the invention of a machine which would enable one person to spin six threads at once. The result of all this attention to mechanical needs was the development a few years later of the spinning jenny and the water frame, the forerunners of a series of important inventions in the textile industry. As the practicability of these machines was soon demonstrated, mechanization was bound to be extended to other manufactures.

2. WHY THE INDUSTRIAL REVOLUTION BEGAN IN BRITAIN

At first thought it may seem rather strange that a small island kingdom should not only have become the industrial leader of the world but should have held that leadership for more than a century. **191**

The relative
poverty
of Britain
until well into
the 18th century

A modern philosopher makes the claim that Britain until well into the eighteenth century was "the poorest country in Western Europe." [1] Certainly she had no remarkable variety of products within her borders. She was not nearly so capable of approaching self-sufficiency as France or Germany. Her agricultural resources were no longer adequate to provide for her needs, and the exhaustion of her forests had been noted since the time of the Stuarts. Her coal and iron, generally considered her richest assets, did not assume great industrial importance until the nineteenth century. But side by side with these adverse conditions there were other factors more than sufficient to tip the balance in Britain's favor.

Favorable factors operating in Britain

Possibly we should place at the head of the list of favorable conditions the fact that Britain had profited most from the Commercial Revolution. Though it is true that about 1750 France had a foreign trade 25 per cent larger than that of Britain, it must be remembered that the French population was at least three times as large as the British. Moreover, France had reached her limit of imperial aggrandizement, while much of the profit of her world trade was being diverted through loans and taxes to the upkeep of a costly army and a frivolous and extravagant court. Britain, on the other hand, was just on the brink of a golden age of power and prosperity. She had already acquired the most valuable colonies in the Western Hemisphere, and she was soon to clinch her imperial and commercial supremacy by defeating the French in the Seven Years' War. In addition, a much larger proportion of Britain's gains from overseas trade was available for productive investment. Her government was comparatively free from corruption and wasteful expenditure. Her military establishment cost less than that of the French, and her revenues were much more efficiently collected. As a result, her merchants and shipowners were left with a larger share of surplus earnings, which they were eager to invest in any conceivable business venture that might be the source of additional profit.

Britain the
leading capitalist nation

In view of these facts it is not strange that Britain should have emerged as the leading capitalist nation in the early eighteenth century. Nowhere was the joint-stock company more highly developed. Trading in securities was organized as a legitimate business when the London Stock Exchange was chartered in 1698. By 1700 London was able to compete with Amsterdam as the financial capital of the world. Britain, moreover, had perhaps the best banking system in Europe. At its apex was the Bank of England, founded in 1694. Though established for the purpose of raising funds for the government, it was organized as a private corporation. Its stock was privately owned, and its management was not subject to any official control by the state. Nevertheless, it always operated in close association with the government, and even in its early days served as an important stabilizing factor in public finance. With the financial sta-

[1] José Ortega y Gasset, *The Revolt of the Masses*, p. iii n.

bility of the government thus assured, leaders of business enterprise could carry on their activities unhindered by fear of national bankruptcy or ruinous inflation. It may be pertinent to add in this connection that little semblance of order prevailed in French finances until the establishment of the Bank of France during the era of Napoleon.

There is evidence that political and social factors were not unimportant in accounting for the beginning of the Industrial Revolution in Britain. Although the British government of the eighteenth century was far from democratic, it was at least more liberal than most of the governments on the Continent. The Glorious Revolution of 1688–1689 had done much to establish the conception of limited sovereignty. The doctrine was now widely accepted that the power of the state should extend no farther than the protection of man's natural rights to liberty and to the enjoyment of property. Under the influence of this doctrine Parliament repealed old laws providing for special monopolies and interfering with free competition. Mercantilist principles continued to be applied to trade with the colonies, but in the sphere of domestic business many restrictions were gradually abolished. Furthermore, Britain was already coming to be recognized as a haven for refugees from other countries. More than 40,000 Huguenots settled in her villages and cities after being driven from France in 1685 by the revocation of the Edict of Nantes. Thrifty, energetic, and ambitious, these people instilled new vigor into the British nation. Thomas Huxley declared, many years later, that a drop of Huguenot blood in the veins was worth thousands of pounds sterling. Social conditions also were distinctly favorable to the industrial development of Britain. Her nobility had ceased to be a hereditary caste exclusively and was rapidly becoming an aristocracy of wealth. Almost anyone who had made a fortune could rise to the highest levels of social distinction. William Pitt the younger declared that every man with an income of £10,000 a year should have a right to a peerage, no matter how humble his origin. Conditions such as these placed a premium upon business success.

A few other causes must be added to complete the picture. First may be mentioned the fact that the damp climate of the British Isles was singularly favorable for the manufacturing of cotton cloth, since the thread would not become brittle and break easily when woven by machines. And it is sufficient to call to mind that it was the mechanization of the textile industry which ushered in the age of machines. Second, the guild system of production, with its elaborate restrictions, had never become so firmly implanted in Britain as on the Continent. Even the regulations that were established had been thrown off, especially in the northern counties, by the end of the seventeenth century. Lastly, since wealth was more evenly distributed in Britain than in most other nations at that time, her manufacturers could devote their attention to the production of large

See color map at page 56

quantities of cheap and ordinary wares instead of to the making of limited supplies of luxury goods. This factor had considerable influence in promoting the adoption of factory methods in the hope of achieving a larger output. In France, by contrast, the demand was for articles *de luxe* to gratify the tastes of a small class of elegant wastrels. Since quality of workmanship was a primary consideration in this type of goods, there was little incentive to invent machines.

3. MEN AND MACHINES IN THE EARLY DAYS

The application
of machinery
to cotton man-
ufactures

The initial stage of the Industrial Revolution, from about 1760 to 1860, witnessed a phenomenal development of the application of machinery to industry that laid the foundations for our modern mechanical civilization. As we have seen, the first of the branches of industry to be mechanized was the manufacture of cotton cloth. This was not one of the staple pursuits of Englishmen but was a young enterprise, in which every entrepreneur was free to employ almost any methods he pleased. Furthermore, it was a business in which profits depended upon quantity production. If the industry were to make any progress at all, some means had to be devised of turning out a greater volume of yarn than could ever be accomplished with the primitive implements still in use. The first of the contrivances developed in response to this need was the spinning jenny, invented by James Hargreaves in 1767. The spinning "jenny," so called from the name of the inventor's wife, was really a compound spinning wheel, capable of producing sixteen threads at once. Unfortunately the threads it spun were not strong enough to be used for the longitudinal fibers, or warp, of cotton cloth. It was not until the invention of the water frame by Richard Arkwright about two years later that quantity production of both kinds of cotton yarn became possible. Finally, in 1779, another Englishman, Samuel Crompton, combined features of both the spinning jenny and the water frame in a hybrid contraption which he appropriately called the mule. This machine was gradually improved, until about twenty years later it was capable of spinning simultaneously 400 strands of the finest quality of yarn.

The power
loom and the
cotton gin

The problems of the cotton industry were still not entirely solved. The invention of spinning machines had more than made up for the deficiency of yarn, but now there was a scarcity of weavers. Those who followed this occupation were able to command such high wages that they were alleged to be strutting about with five-pound notes stuck in their hat bands and to be eating roast goose for their Sunday dinners. It soon became obvious that the only remedy for this shortage of weavers would be the invention of some kind of automatic machine to take the place of the hand loom. Many declared such a contrivance impossible, but a Kentish clergyman, the Reverend Edmund Cartwright, was not to be discouraged so easily.

He reasoned that if automatic machinery could be applied to spinning, it could be just as logically extended to weaving. Knowing little about mechanics himself, he hired a carpenter and a smith to put his ideas into effect. The result was the power loom, which Cartwright patented in 1785. A good many years elapsed, however, before it was sufficiently improved to be more than a modest success. Not until about 1820 did it largely displace more primitive methods of weaving. Meanwhile, the invention of a machine for separating the seeds from the cotton fiber made possible a much more abundant supply of raw cotton at a lower price. This machine was the cotton gin, invented by a Yankee schoolteacher, Eli Whitney, in 1792.

Several of the new inventions in the textile industry contributed to the growth of the factory system. The water frame, the spinning mule, and the automatic loom were large and heavy machines which could not possibly be set up in the cottages of individual workers. All were eventually designed to be driven by power, and, besides, they cost so much that no one but a wealthy capitalist could afford to buy them. It was therefore inevitable that they should be installed in large buildings, and that the workers employed to operate them should be brought under the supervision of the owner or of a manager acting for him. Such were the essentials of the factory system in its original form. Appropriately enough, the real founder of this system was Richard Arkwright, inventor of the water frame. By indomitable perseverance and shrewd management, Arkwright rose from the status of an obscure barber and wigmaker to that of a captain of industry. Commonly working from five in the morning until nine at night, he struggled against obstacles for years. His shops were gutted by mobs of irate workers who feared that machines would deprive them of their jobs. He was accused, perhaps with some truth, of stealing his ideas for the water frame from others. Altogether he is said to have spent some $60,000 before his plans brought him any profit. He established his first factory, operated by water power, in 1771.

Origin of the factory system

It is difficult to believe that the factory system would ever have assumed much importance had it not been for the perfection of the steam engine. Water wheels were slow, and streams of sufficient force to turn them were not always available. Other sources of power were also tried, but with even less satisfactory results. The original power loom invented by Cartwright was operated by a cow, while some of his successors used horses and even a Newfoundland dog. That steam could be employed as a means of power had been known for centuries. Crude steam engines had been devised by Hero of Alexandria in the first century B.C., by Leonardo da Vinci during the Renaissance, and by various individuals in the early modern period. None of these, however, had been put to any definite use except to turn the spit in royal kitchens and to perform

Newcomen's steam engine

miracles in ancient temples. The first man to apply the power of steam to industrial purposes was Thomas Newcomen, who in 1712 devised a crude but effective engine for pumping water from the British coal mines. By the middle of the century nearly 100 of his engines were in use.

Though of great value to the coal mining industry, Newcomen's engine suffered from defects which prevented its being widely used for general industrial purposes. For one thing, it wasted both fuel and power. It was constructed in such a way that after each stroke of the piston, the steam had to be condensed by spraying cold water into the cylinder. This meant that the cylinder had to be heated again before the next stroke, and this alternate heating and cooling

Newcomen's
engine greatly
improved by
James Watt

The Steam Engine, invented by James Watt (1736–1819).

greatly retarded the speed of the engine. In the second place, Newcomen's "Miner's Friend" was adaptable only to the straight-line motion necessary for pumping; the principle of converting the straight-line action of the piston into a rotary motion had not been discovered. Both of these defects were eventually remedied by James Watt, a maker of scientific instruments at the University of Glasgow. In 1763 Watt was asked to repair a model of the Newcomen engine. While engaged in this task he conceived the idea that the machine would be greatly improved if a separate chamber were added to condense the steam, so as to eliminate the necessity of cooling the cylinder. He patented his first engine incorporating this device in 1769. Later he invented a new arrangement of valves which permitted the injection of steam into both ends of the cylinder, thereby making the piston *work* on the backward as well as on the forward stroke. In 1782 he devised a means of converting the action of the piston into a circular motion and thus made the engine available for driving machinery in factories. Unfortunately Watt's genius as an inventor was not matched by his business ability. He admitted that he would "rather face a loaded cannon than settle a disputed account or make a bargain." As a consequence he fell into debt in attempting to place his machines on the market. He was rescued by Matthew Boulton, a wealthy hardware manufacturer of Birmingham. The two men formed a partnership, with Boulton providing the capital. By 1800 the firm had sold 289 engines for use in factories and mines.

Few single inventions have had greater influence upon the history of modern times than the steam engine. Contrary to popular opinion, it was not the initial cause of the Industrial Revolution; instead, it was partly an effect. Watt's engine, at least, would never have become a reality if there had not been a demand for an effective source of power to operate the heavy machines already invented in the textile industry. On the other hand, the perfection of the steam engine was certainly a cause of the more rapid growth of industrialization. It raised the production of coal and iron to a new importance. It made possible a revolution in transportation. It provided almost unlimited opportunities for accelerating the manufacture of goods, thereby making the industrialized nations the richest and most powerful in the world. Before the development of the steam engine, the resources of power were largely at the mercy of the weather. In time of drought, low water in the streams would probably force the mills to curtail operations or even to shut down entirely. Ships on ocean voyages might be delayed for weeks by lack of wind. Now, however, there was a constant supply of energy, which could be tapped and used when needed. It is therefore not too much to say that the invention of Watt's engine was the real beginning of the age of power.

The importance of the steam engine

One of the industries that owed its rapid development to the improvement of the steam engine was the manufacture of iron and iron products. While many of the new machines, such as the spinning jenny and the water frame, could be constructed of wood, steam engines required a more substantial material. Moreover, the cylinders of these engines needed to be bored as accurately as possible in order to prevent a loss of power. This made necessary a considerable advance in the production of machine tools and in scientific methods of iron manufacture. The pioneer in this work was John Wilkinson, a manufacturer of cannon. In 1774 Wilkinson patented a method of boring cylinders which reduced the percentage of error to a very small amount for that day. Even more important than the achievements of Wilkinson were the accomplishments of another Englishman, Henry Cort, a naval contractor. In 1784 Cort devised the method of puddling, or stirring the molten iron to eliminate a larger percentage of its carbon content. This process made possible the production in quantity of the tougher grade of metal known as wrought iron. Two years later Cort invented the rolling mill for the manufacture of sheet iron. These two achievements revolutionized the industry. Within less than twenty

Early development of the iron industry

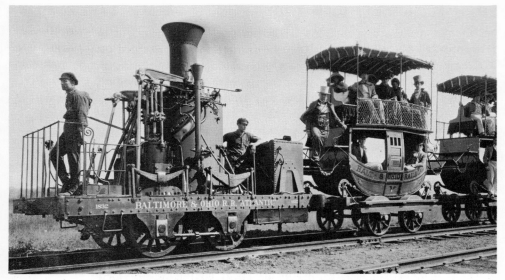

The First Train to Enter the City of Washington. The locomotive was built for the Baltimore and Ohio by Phineas Davis, a watchmaker of York, Pennsylvania, in 1832. It accumulated a service of 60 years.

years the production of iron in England quadrupled, and the price dropped to a fraction of what it had been.

Early developmentments in transportation: (1) roads and canals

The fundamental changes in modes of production just described were soon followed by momentous developments in transportation. The first signs of a definite improvement in methods of travel began to appear about 1780. It was about that time that the construction of turnpikes and canals in England was started in earnest. By 1830 nearly all of the highways had been drained and covered with a surface of broken stone, while the principal streams had been linked together by a network of 2500 miles of canals. The improvement of roads made possible a faster stagecoach service. In 1784 the postmaster general inaugurated a mail service with coaches that ran continuously day and night, covering a distance of 120 miles in twenty-four hours. By the end of the century special stages, known as "flying machines," operated between all of the principal cities, sometimes achieving the sensational speed of nine or ten miles per hour.

(2) the first railroads

But the really significant progress in transportation did not come until after the steam engine had been generally accepted as a dependable source of power. Attempts were first made to adapt the use of steam to stagecoaches, and several of these ancestors of the modern automobile were actually put on the highways. The most successful was one built about 1800 by Richard Trevithick, which managed to run ninety miles over the road from London to Plymouth. Gradually the opinion grew that it would be more profitable to use the steam engine to draw a train of cars over iron rails. A number of such railroads were already in existence for the purpose of transporting coal, but the cars were drawn by horses. The man primarily responsible for the first steam railway was George Ste-

198

phenson, a self-made engineer who had not even learned to read until he was seventeen years of age. While employed as an enginewright at a colliery he devoted his leisure hours to experiments with locomotives. In 1822 he convinced a group of men who were projecting a coal railroad from Stockton to Darlington of the merits of steam traction, and was appointed engineer for the line with full liberty to carry out his plans. The result was the opening three years later of the first railway operated entirely by steam. The locomotives he built for this line attained a speed of fifteen miles an hour, the fastest rate at which human beings had yet traveled. In 1830 he designed his famous *Rocket,* which thundered over the

Model of First-class Carriage, Liverpool and Manchester Railway, 1834. There were three compartments, each resembling a stage coach.

tracks of the Manchester and Liverpool Railroad at nearly twice the speed of the earlier models. Before Stephenson died in 1848, nearly 6000 miles of railroad had been built in England and a similar amount in the United States.

Meanwhile the steam engine was being gradually applied to water transportation. Here it was Americans rather than Englishmen who took the lead. Precisely who should receive credit for inventing the steamboat is a matter of dispute. There is evidence that a number of men had something to do with it. About 1787 an American metal worker, John Fitch, constructed a boat that actually carried passengers on the Delaware for several months. Fitch's steamboat is particularly significant because it embodied a crude screw propeller instead of the paddle wheel universally employed by the other inventors. But Fitch was never able to make his craft a financial success. After vainly attempting to persuade governments to adopt

(3) the beginning of steam navigation

199

his invention, he committed suicide in 1798. Another American, Robert Fulton, is given the credit for having made the steamboat commercially successful. That Fulton was any more ingenious than Fitch is open to doubt, but he was a good enough salesman and promoter to secure the backing of a wealthy capitalist, and he knew how to keep himself in the public eye. In 1807 he was acclaimed as a national hero when his *Clermont,* equipped with a Boulton and Watt engine and a paddle wheel, traveled the entire distance from New York to Albany under its own power. This was the beginning of an era of steam navigation. Soon paddle-wheel craft similar to Fulton's were chugging over rivers and lakes not only in America but in Europe. In April 1838, the first steamships, the *Sirius* and the *Great Western,* crossed the Atlantic. Two years later Samuel Cunard founded the famous Cunard Line, providing a regular transoceanic service with vessels propelled entirely by steam.

The one significant improvement in communications, during the first stage of the Industrial Revolution was the invention of the telegraph. As early as 1820 the French physicist Ampère discovered that electromagnetism could be used for sending messages by wire between distant points. About all that remained was to devise effective instruments for transmitting and receiving the messages. Experiments for this purpose were carried on by a number of individuals. Three of them succeeded almost simultaneously. During the year 1837 systems of electric telegraphy were invented by the German Karl Steinheil, by the Englishman Charles Wheatstone, and by the American Samuel Morse. It was not until 1844, however, that the first telegraph line efficient enough for commercial purposes was established. This was the line between Baltimore and Washington, which Morse succeeded in having built on the strength of improvements in his own invention. Once started, telegraph systems multiplied all over the world. Soon all important cities were linked, and by 1851 a cable had been laid under the English Channel. The crowning achievement of all was the laying of the first Atlantic cable in 1866 under the direction of the American capitalist, Cyrus Field.

The Industrial Revolution also had its agricultural aspects. They were especially noticeable in the first sixty years of the nineteenth century. Among them were the production of better breeds of livestock; the introduction of new crops, such as the sugar beet, which was now being extensively cultivated in Germany and France; and the development of agricultural chemistry by Justus von Liebig, which made possible the production of artificial fertilizers. Agriculture in this period also came under the influence of mechanization. Better plows and harrows were designed, and the threshing machine was quite generally adopted. In 1834 the American farmer, Cyrus McCormick, patented his mechanical reaper and soon afterward began its manufacture in Chicago. By 1860 these machines were being sold at the rate of 20,000 a year. As a result of these various im-

The invention
of the telegraph

Improvements
in agriculture

The Guitarist, Edouard Manet. *The Guitarist* is no more impressionistic than is the portrait of Zola. Instead, it reflects the technique of fully modeled figures in somber style which Manet acquired from Hals and Goya. (MMA)

Émile Zola, Édouard Manet (1832–1883). Though Manet is called the "father of impressionism," he was also a rebel against the traditions of sweetness and artificiality that dominated the XIX cent. He liberated painting, as his friend Zola emancipated literature. (Louvre)

Girl Burning Weeds, Jean François Millet (1814–1875). Millet painted the men and women who toiled in the fields and their struggles against poverty and the whims of nature. His sympathies sometimes led him to a romantic idealization. (MMA)

The Third-Class Carriage, Honoré Daumier (1808–1879). Though Daumier was noted for his realistic caricatures and satires, his attitude toward common folk was one of sympathy and understanding. (MMA)

Village Girls, Gustave Courbet (1819–1877). One of the first of the realists, Courbet often portrayed life in a bitter and disparaging light. He eschewed imagination and painted only what he saw. (MMA)

ENGLAND AT THE START OF THE INDUSTRIAL REVOLUTION

(dotted)	Population centers
●	Principal manufacturing cities
(shaded)	Coal fields
✕✕✕	Iron ore deposits

SCOTLAND

• Glasgow
• Edinburgh

NORTHUMBERLAND

Newcastle
Gateshead
CUMBERLAND
DURHAM
Middlesbrough
WESTMORELAND
Ouse R.

NORTH SEA

YORK
York

I. OF MAN

IRISH SEA

Hull

Leeds
LANCASTER
Wakefield
Manchester
Liverpool
Rotherham
Northwich
CHESTER
DERBY
NOTTINGHAM
Trent R.
Lincoln
LINCOLN

Grimsby

ANGLESEY

Stoke
STAFFORD
Nottingham

WALES

Cardigan Bay

Walsall
Aston Manor
Birmingham
SALOP
LEICESTER
Leicester
RUTLAND

Norwich
NORFOLK
Great Yarmo

WORCESTER
WARWICK
NORTHAMPTON
HUNTINGDON
CAMBRIDGE
SUFFOLK

HEREFORD
Avon R.
Northampton
BEDFORD
Ipswich

MONMOUTH
Gloucester
GLOUCESTER
OXFORD
BUCKING-HAM
HERTFORD
ESSEX

Swansea
Newport
Oxford

Cardiff
Bristol
BERKS
MIDDLESEX
London
Thames R.

Bristol Channel
Bath
WILTS
Reading
SURREY
Chatham
KENT

• Devizes

SOMERSET

Taunton
HANTS
Southampton
SUSSEX
Brighton
Hastings
Portsmouth
Eastbourne

DEVON
DORSET
I. OF WIGHT
Strait of

Bournemouth

CORNWALL
Plymouth

ENGLISH CHANNEL

| 0 | 50 | 100 miles |

The World's First Reaper. Invented by Cyrus McCormick in 1831, the machine would cut 6 to 8 acres of grain in a day. It did not bind the grain into sheaves, but left this process to be done by hand.

provements, agriculture all over the world rejoiced in an unprecedented prosperity, which lasted until the great depression of 1873.

4. NEW SOCIAL AND ECONOMIC DOCTRINES

The First Industrial Revolution produced its full complement of economic theory—part of it to justify the new order, part of it for critical analysis, and the remainder as a gospel of social reform. No sooner had the factory system been well established and profits begun to flow into the coffers of the new lords of creation than some of the more articulate and belligerent among them rose up to defend their privileges. In doing so they often displayed a coldness toward the plight of the masses and a confidence in their own right to inherit the earth which the nobles of the *ancien régime* might well have envied. Indeed, some of the apologists for the new system evolved into a type of economic Bourbons, learning nothing from the past and closing their eyes to the dangers of the future. This attitude was expressed in the doctrines that private property is sacred, that every man has a right to do what he will with his own, and that poverty is invariably the result of laziness and incompetence. Several of the high priests of the new capitalism went so far as to declare that poverty was a good thing for the masses since it taught them to respect their superiors and to be grateful to Providence for such blessings as they did receive.

Economic
Bourbonism

But some of the economic theory in defense of the capitalist ideal was more disinterested. Of this type were the teachings of the classical economists, or economic liberals, as they are often called. The founder of classical economics was Adam Smith, whose work was discussed in a preceding chapter. Though Smith wrote before industrial capitalism had reached its full stature, and though some of his teachings did not harmonize well with a strict interpretation of laissez faire, there was nevertheless enough in the general implica-

The theory of
the classical
economists

201

tions of his theory to cause him to be acclaimed the prophet of capitalist ideals. The specific doctrines of classical economics, however, were largely the work of Smith's disciples—including such eminent writers as Thomas R. Malthus, David Ricardo, James Mill, and Nassau Senior. The chief elements in the theory subscribed to by most of these men may be summarized as follows:

(1) Economic individualism. Every individual is entitled to use for his own best interests the property he has inherited or acquired by any legitimate method. Each person must be allowed to do what he likes with his own so long as he does not trespass upon the equal right of others to do the same.

(2) Laissez faire. The functions of the state should be reduced to the lowest minimum consistent with public safety. The government should shrink itself into the role of a modest policeman, preserving order and protecting property, but never in any wise interfering with the operation of economic processes.

(3) Obedience to natural law. There are immutable laws operating in the realm of economics as in every sphere of the universe. Examples are the law of supply and demand, the law of diminishing returns, the law of rent, and so on. These laws must be recognized and respected; failure to do so is disastrous.

(4) Freedom of contract. Every individual should be free to negotiate the best kind of contract he can obtain from any other individual. In particular, the liberty of workers and employers to bargain with each other as to wages and hours should not be hampered by laws or by the collective power of labor unions.

(5) Free competition and free trade. Competition serves to keep prices down, to eliminate inefficient producers, and to ensure the maximum production in accordance with public demand. Therefore no monopolies should be tolerated, nor any price-fixing laws for the benefit of incompetent enterprisers. Further, in order to force each country to engage in the production of those things it is best fitted to produce, all protective tariffs should be abolished. Free international trade will also help to keep prices down.

Several of the disciples of Adam Smith made distinctive contributions of their own. For example, Thomas R. Malthus (1766–1834) introduced the element of pessimism which caused the new economics to be branded as "the dismal science." A clergyman of the Anglican church, rector of a small parish in Surrey, Malthus published his memorable *Essay on Population* in 1798. Issued originally in pamphlet form, the *Essay* grew out of some discussions which the author had with his father concerning the perfectibility of man. The elder Malthus was a disciple of Rousseau, but he was so impressed with his son's arguments against the superficial optimism of the Frenchman that he urged him to put them in writing. The pamphlet created an immediate sensation and provoked discussion for many years afterward. In 1803 it was expanded into a book on the basis of extended researches which the author undertook to refute his critics. The substance of the Malthusian theory is the contention that nature has set stubborn limits to the progress of mankind in happiness and wealth. Because of the voracity of the sexual appetite there is a natural tendency for population to increase more rapidly than the means of subsistence. To be sure, there are powerful checks, such as war, famine, disease, and vice; but these, when they operate effectively, augment still further the burden of human misery. It follows that poverty and pain are inescapable. Even if laws were to be passed distributing all wealth equally, the condition of the poor would be only temporarily improved; in a very short time they would begin to raise larger families, with the result that the last state of their class would be as bad as the first. In the second edition of his work Malthus advocated postponement of marriage as a means of relief, but he continued to stress the danger that population would outrun any possible increase in the means of subsistence.

The main teachings of Malthus were taken over and elaborated by David Ricardo (1772–1823), one of the keenest if not one of the broadest intellects of the nineteenth century. Ricardo was an Eng- lish Jew who embraced Christianity at the age of twenty-one and married a Quaker. By the time he was twenty-five he had accumulated a fortune on the Stock Exchange and soon became one of the richest men in Europe. As an economist Ricardo is famous, first of all, for his subsistence theory of wages. According to this theory, wages tend toward a level which is just sufficient to enable the workers "to subsist and perpetuate their race, without either increase or diminution." This he held to be an iron law, from which there is no escape. If wages should rise temporarily above the subsistence standard, the population would increase, and the ensuing competition for jobs would quickly force the rate of pay down to its former level. Ricardo is noted, in the second place, for his teachings in regard to rent. He maintained that rent is determined by the cost of production on the poorest land that must be brought under cultivation, and that consequently as a country fills up with people an ever-increasing proportion of the social income is taken by the landlords. Though a great proprietor himself, he denounced the recipients of rent as the real enemies of both the capitalists and the workers. Finally, Ricardo is important for his labor theory of value, which influenced one of the main doctrines of the Marxian socialists. However, he attached some significance also to the role of capital in determining value—an idea which was abhorrent to Marx.

In his later years Ricardo frequently associated himself with an interesting group of reformers in England known as the philosophical radicals. The foremost economist among them was James Mill (1773–1836), who, as already mentioned, enjoyed some reputation as a Utilitarian philosopher. While the teachings of James Mill would now be considered far from radical, they were nevertheless liberal enough to show that the classical economics was not hopelessly benighted and reactionary. The doctrines he incorporated in his *Elements of Political Economy* included the following: (1) the chief object of practical reformers should be to prevent the population from growing too rapidly, on the assumption that the wealth available for productive purposes does not naturally increase as fast as the number of inhabitants; (2) the value of commodities depends entirely upon the quantity of labor necessary to produce them; and (3) the unearned increment of land, or the increase in the value of land which comes exclusively from social causes, such as the building of a new factory in the vicinity, should be heavily taxed by the state. This last doctrine, based upon Ricardo's theory of rent, was destined for a wide popularity in England. In modified form it became part of the gospel of the Liberal party in the early 1900's, and it was a feature of the celebrated Lloyd George budget of 1909.

Probably the ablest of the classical economists who came after Ricardo was Nassau William Senior (1790–1864). The first professor of political economy at Oxford, he was also a distinguished lawyer and served on a number of royal commissions. Like most of his predecessors, Senior regarded economics as a deductive science. He maintained that its truths could all be derived from a limited number of great abstract principles. His main contribution was his theory that *abstinence* creates a title to wealth. He admitted that labor and natural resources are the primary instruments of value, but he contended that abstinence is a secondary instrument. Therefore he argued that the capitalist who has refrained from enjoying all of his wealth in order to accumulate a surplus for investment has a claim on the profits of production. His abstinence involves sacrifice and pain just as does the work of the laborer. Consequently it is unfair to give the entire reward to the latter. The evil reputation of Senior comes primarily from the fact that he condemned the demands of the trade unions for a reduction of the working day. He had an honest but mistaken conviction that the whole net profit of an industrial enterprise is derived from the last hour of operation. Hence to shorten the working day would eliminate profits and thereby result in closing the factories. For this doctrine he was dubbed by his critics "Last Hour" Senior.

Most of the leading classical economists or economic liberals were citizens of Great Britain. This was true partly because economic liberalism harmonized well with political liberalism, which was stronger in Britain than in any other European country, and partly because British industrialists were beginning to perceive notable advantages from a policy of free trade with the rest of the world. On the Continent of Europe, however, conditions were entirely different. There the old traditions of strong government still lingered. Moreover, Continental manufacturers were attempting to build up industrial establishments which would be able to compete with the

Critics and
opponents
of the classical
economics:
(1) John Stuart
Mill

British. To achieve this, it was desirable to have the patronage and protection of the state. Hence we should not be surprised to find that the majority of the opponents of economic liberalism were natives of countries on the Continent. Nevertheless, at least one of its abler critics was an Englishman—the brilliant Utilitarian philosopher, John Stuart Mill (1806–1873). Though Mill as an economist is often considered a member of the classical school, he actually repudiated a number of its most sacred premises. First, he rejected the universality of natural law. He admitted that there are unchangeable laws governing the field of production, but he insisted that the distribution of wealth can be regulated by society for the benefit of the majority of its members. Second, he advocated more radical departures from laissez faire than any recommended by his forerunners. He did not oppose legislation, under certain conditions, for shortening the working day, and he believed that the state might properly take preliminary steps toward the redistribution of wealth by taxing inheritances and by appropriating the unearned increment of land. In the fourth book of his *Principles of Political Economy* he urged the abolition of the wage system and looked forward to a society of producers' cooperatives in which the workers would own the factories and elect the managers to run them. On the other hand, it should not be forgotten that Mill was too much of an individualist ever to go very far in the direction of socialism. He distrusted the state, and his real reason for advocating producers' cooperatives was not to exalt the power of the proletariat but to give to the individual worker the fruits of his labor.

The most noted of the German economists who wrote in direct opposition to the theories of the classical school was Friedrich List (1789–1846), who derived inspiration for some of his ideas from seven years' residence in America. List condemned the doctrines of laissez faire and freedom of international trade. Contending that the wealth of a nation is determined less by natural resources than by the productive powers of its citizens, he declared that it is the duty of governments to further the arts and sciences and to see to it that every individual makes the most of his talents in cooperating for the general good. He stressed the well-rounded development of the nation as all-important regardless of the effects upon the immediate fortunes of particular citizens. Holding that manufactures are essential to such a development, he demanded protective tariffs until the new industries should be able to compete with those of any other country. List was the forerunner of a long line of German economists who proposed to make the state the guardian of the production and distribution of wealth. Their object was less that of justice to the individual than the idea of consolidating the unity and increasing the strength of the nation. They believed that the government should not only impose protective tariffs, but should regulate and plan the development of industry so as to balance production and consumption. By a curious contradiction some of them were also imperialists. List demanded a German customs union which would extend "over the whole coast from the mouth of the Rhine to the frontier of Poland including Holland and Denmark." [2] He insisted also that Germany had a mission to lead in world affairs and to civilize barbaric and benighted countries. He was one of the earliest exponents of German expansionism and of Germany's destiny as a world power.

We come next to a group of theorists who were more interested in social justice than in discovering economic laws or in laying the foundations of national prosperity. The earliest exemplars of this more radical attitude were the utopian socialists, who take their name from the fact that they proposed idealistic schemes for co-operative societies, in which all would work at their appropriate tasks and share the results of their common efforts. To a considerable extent the utopian socialists were the heirs of the Enlightenment. Like the philosophers of that movement they believed that all crime and greed were the results of an evil environment. If men could be freed from vicious custom and from a social structure which facilitates enslavement of the weak by the strong, then all might live together in harmony and peace. Accordingly, the utopian socialists recommended the establishment of model communities, largely self-contained, where most of the instruments of production would be collectively owned and where government would be mainly on a voluntary basis. Among the original propagators of such plans was the Frenchman Charles Fourier (1772–1837),[3] but the soundest and most realistic of them all was Robert Owen (1771–1858). A native of Wales, Owen rose from an artisan apprentice to co-proprietor and manager of a great cotton mill at New Lanark in Scotland. Here he built new houses for his workers, reduced their hours of work from fourteen to ten, and established free schools for their children. The severe depression that followed in the wake of the Napoleonic wars convinced him that the economic order was in urgent need of reform. Like many others since his day, he concluded that the profit system was the cause of all the trouble. The existence of profit, he maintained, makes it impossible for the worker to buy all the things he has produced. The result is overproduction, periodic crises, and unemployment. As a solution, Owen proposed the organization of society into cooperative communities, in which the sole reward to each member would be payment in pro-

---

[2] S. S. Lloyd (trans.), *The National System of Political Economy*, p. 143.

[3] Count Henri de Saint-Simon is also commonly considered a founder of utopian socialism, but about all that he actually proposed was the abolition of class distinctions and the control of society by industrial experts. Some of his followers taught that the state should be made the sole inheritor of property, which would then be allotted to individuals in proportion to their ability to use it for the advantage of the community. See Charles Gide and Charles Rist, *A History of Economic Doctrines*, pp. 198–225.

Karl Marx (1818–1883). The photograph shows the prophet of socialism at the peak of his career, in the 1870's.

portion to his actual hours of labor. A number of such communities were set up, the most famous being the ones at Orbiston, Scotland, and New Harmony, Indiana. For a variety of reasons all of them failed within a very short time.

A more influential form of socialism was the so-called "scientific socialism" of Karl Marx (1818–1883). The son of a Jewish lawyer who had turned Christian for professional reasons, Marx was born at Trèves near Coblenz in the Rhineland. His father planned for him a career as a conventional bourgeois lawyer and, with that end in view, sent him to the University of Bonn. But young Marx soon displayed a distaste for the law and abandoned his legal studies for the pursuit of philosophy and history. After a year at Bonn he went to the University of Berlin, where he fell under the influence of a group of disciples of Hegel who were giving the teachings of their master a slightly radical twist. Though Marx earned the degree of doctor of philosophy at the University of Jena in 1841, his critical views prevented him from realizing his ambition of becoming a university professor. He turned to journalism, editing various radical periodicals and contributing articles to others. In 1848 he was arrested on a charge of high treason for participating in the revolutionary movement in Prussia. Though acquitted by a middle-class jury, he was soon afterward expelled from the country. In the meantime he had formed an intimate friendship with Friedrich Engels (1820–1895), who remained his lifelong disciple and *alter ego*. In 1848 the two men issued the *Communist Manifesto*, the "birth cry of modern socialism." From then until his death in 1883 Marx spent nearly all of his years in London, struggling against poverty, occasionally writing a few articles (some of which he sold to the New York *Tribune* for $5 apiece), but giving most of his time to poring over dusty manuscripts in the British Museum, gathering material for a great work on political economy. In 1867 he

(4) the Marxian socialists

207

published the first volume of this work under the title of *Das Kapital*. Two other volumes were issued after his death from manuscripts revised and edited by some of his disciples.

Not all of the teachings of Karl Marx were entirely original. For some of his ideas he was indebted to Hegel; for others to the French socialist, Louis Blanc (1811–1882), and probably to Ricardo. Nevertheless, it was Marx who first combined these ideas into a comprehensive system and gave them full-bodied meaning as an explanation of the facts of political economy. Since Marxist theory has been one of the most influential bodies of thought in modern times, it is necessary to understand its doctrines. Fundamental among them are the following:

(1) The economic interpretation of history. All of the great political, social, and intellectual movements of history have been determined by the economic environment out of which they arose. Marx did not insist that the economic motive is the sole explanation of human behavior, but he did maintain that every fundamental historical development, regardless of its character on the surface, has been the result of alterations in methods of producing and exchanging goods. Thus the Protestant Revolution was essentially an economic movement; the disagreements over religious belief were mere "ideological veils," concealing the actual causes.

(2) Dialectical materialism. Every distinct economic system, based upon a definite pattern of production and exchange, grows to a point of maximum efficiency, then develops contradictions or weaknesses within it which produce its rapid decay. Meanwhile the foundations of an opposing system are being gradually laid, and eventually this new system displaces the old, at the same time absorbing its most valuable elements. This dynamic process of historical evolution will continue by a series of victories of the new over the old, until the perfect goal of communism has been attained. After that there will doubtless still be change, but it will be change within the limits of communism itself.

(3) The class struggle. All history has been made up of struggles between classes. In ancient times it was a struggle between masters and slaves and between patricians and plebeians; in the Middle Ages it was a conflict between guild-masters and journeymen and between lords and serfs; now it has been narrowed down to a struggle between the class of capitalists and the proletariat. The former includes those who derive their chief income from *owning* the means of production and from exploiting the labor of others. The proletariat includes those who are dependent for their living primarily upon a wage, who must sell their labor power in order to exist.

(4) The doctrine of surplus value. All wealth is created by the worker. Capital creates nothing, but is itself created by labor. The value of all commodities is determined by the quantity of labor power necessary to produce them. But the worker does not receive

the full value which his labor power creates; he receives a wage, which ordinarily is just enough to enable him to subsist and reproduce his kind. Most of the difference between the value he produces and what he receives is *surplus value*, which goes to the capitalist. In general, it consists of three elements: interest, rent, and profits. Since the capitalist creates none of these things, it follows that he is a robber, who appropriates the fruits of the laborer's toil.

(5) The theory of socialist evolution. After capitalism has received its death blow at the hands of the workers, it will be followed by the stage of socialism. This will have three characteristics: the dictatorship of the proletariat; payment in accordance with work performed; and ownership and operation by the state of all means of production, distribution, and exchange. But socialism is intended to be merely a transition to something higher. In time it will be succeeded by communism, the perfect goal of historical evolution. Communism will mean, first of all, the classless society. No one will live by owning, but all men solely by working. The state will now disappear; it will be relegated to the museum of antiquities, "along with the bronze ax and the spinning wheel." Nothing will replace it except voluntary associations to operate the means of production and provide for social necessities. But the *essence* of communism is payment in accordance with needs. The wage system will be completely abolished. Each citizen will be expected to work in accordance with his faculties and will be entitled to receive from the total fund of wealth produced an amount in proportion to his needs. This is the acme of justice according to the Marxist conception.

The influence of Karl Marx upon the nineteenth and twentieth centuries can only be compared with that of Voltaire or Rousseau upon the eighteenth. His doctrine of the economic interpretation of history is a popular theory even among historians who are not his followers. He numbers his disciples in every civilized nation of this planet and in a great many underdeveloped countries besides. He is almost a god in Russia, where his dogma of dialectical materialism is accepted not only as a foundation of economics but as a test to which science, philosophy, and art must also conform. In every industrialized nation before World War I there was a socialist political party of considerable importance, the one in Germany having the largest representation in the Reichstag after 1912. Nearly everywhere the growth of socialism was a vital influence in furthering the enactment of social insurance and minimum wage laws and in promoting taxation of incomes and inheritances for the purpose of redistributing wealth. Marx, of course, was not interested in these things as ends in themselves, but the ruling classes were eventually persuaded to adopt them as a convenient tub to be thrown to the socialist whale. Socialists have also quite generally lent their support to the co-operative movement, to government ownership of rail-

Revisionists
and
strict Marxists

roads and public utilities, and to innumerable schemes for protecting workers and consumers against the power of monopoly capitalism.

Toward the end of the nineteenth century the followers of Marx split into two factions. The majority in most countries adhered to the doctrines of a group known as the revisionists, who, as their name implies, believed that the theories of Marx should be *revised* to bring them into line with changing conditions. The other faction was made up of the strict Marxists, who insisted that not one jot or tittle of the master's teachings should be modified. In addition to this cleavage in general attitude there were also specific differences. Whereas the revisionists advocated the attainment of socialism by peaceful and gradual methods, the strict Marxists were revolutionists. The revisionists concentrated their attention upon immediate reforms, with the slogan, "Less for the better future and more for the better present"; the strict Marxists demanded the dictatorship of the proletariat or nothing. The leaders of the majority faction were willing to recognize the interests of separate nations; they were prone to talk about duty to the fatherland, and they frequently supported the demands of their governments for increased armaments and for lengthened terms of military service. The strict Marxists, on the other hand, were uncompromising internationalists; they held to the contention of Marx that the world proletariat is one great brotherhood, and they frowned upon patriotism and nationalism as capitalist devices to throw dust in the eyes of the workers. On the whole, it was the revisionists who gained control of the socialist parties in the majority of Western nations. The Social Democratic party in Germany, the Unified Socialist party in France, and the Socialist party in the United States were all largely dominated by the moderate faction. In Britain leadership of the Labour party was supplied in most cases by the Fabian socialists, so named from their policy of delay in imitation of the tactics of Fabius, a Roman general in the wars against Carthage. Prominent among the Fabians were Beatrice and Sidney Webb, the novelist H. G. Wells, and the dramatist George Bernard Shaw.

The transition
from strict
Marxism to
Communism

About 1918 most of the strict Marxists withdrew altogether from the socialist parties and have since been known generally as Communists. But "strict Marxism" in its communist form has often shown a tendency in recent years to abandon the internationalism of Marx and to glorify patriotism and defense of the fatherland. This was particularly true of Russia and some of her satellites during World War II and the years following.

Anarchism

Many of the social idealists of the nineteenth and early twentieth centuries were torn between the desire to improve the welfare of society by collectivist means and the hope of gaining for the individual a maximum of personal freedom. We have seen that even the Marxists proposed eventually to abolish the state. But the collectivist-individualist issue received much more attention from the anarchists. Strictly defined, anarchism means opposition to all government based upon force. The followers of this philosophy have generally conceded that some form of social organization is necessary, but they condemn the coercive state as absolutely incompatible with human liberty. As to the problem of what should be done with the economic system, the anarchists have sharply disagreed. Some have been pure individualists, holding that man's right to acquire and use property should be subject only to the laws of nature. The father of anarchism, William Godwin (1756–1836), believed that if the land were made as free as the air, no further change in the economic structure would be necessary. In the judgment of the French anarchist, Pierre Proudhon (1809–1865), an arrangement whereby society would provide every man with free and unlimited credit would be a sufficient means of ensuring economic justice. Such a plan, he thought, would prevent anyone from monopolizing the resources of the earth and would guarantee to the citizen who was thrifty and industrious the full reward of his labors.

But the first of the anarchists to exert much influence were those who combined their hatred of the state with a definite philosophy of collectivism. Foremost among them were the three Russian aristocrats, Mikhail Bakunin (1814–1876), Peter Kropotkin (1842–1921), and Leo Tolstoi (1828–1910). Though often classified as a communistic anarchist, Bakunin was really much closer to socialism. Indeed, for a time he was associated with the followers of Marx in the International Workingmen's Association, organized in London in 1864. His program for a new society included collective ownership of the means of production, abolition of surplus value, and payment in accordance with work performed. In other words, it was much like that of the socialist stage of the Marxists, except, of course, that it did not involve the preservation of the state. Bakunin is also sometimes regarded as the father of terroristic anarchism. Advocating the overthrow of the state and of capitalism by violence, he inspired what later came to be called "propaganda by the deed"—that is, attracting attention to the anarchist cause by murdering a few prominent public officials and hated exploiters. It was followers of Bakunin who were alleged to have been responsible for assassinating President McKinley, President Carnot of France, and King Humbert I of Italy. But the more intelligent anarchists of the collectivist school condemned these tactics. For example, Prince Kropotkin denounced the use of individual violence under any conditions. He believed that a final revolutionary effort would be necessary, but he certainly preferred that the state should be weakened by peaceful methods, by gradually convincing people that it is an unnecessary evil, that it breeds wars, and that it exists primarily to enable some men to exploit others. From the standpoint of economic reform, Kropotkin was a communist. He insisted that all property except articles of personal use should be socially owned, and that

The collectivistic anarchists: Bakunin and Kropotkin

Leo Tolstoi

payment should be on the basis of need.

The most noted of all the collectivistic anarchists and one of the most interesting figures of modern times was Count Leo Tolstoi. Best known for his novels, which will be discussed in a later connection, Tolstoi was also one of the greatest of Russian philosophers. His ideas were born of strenuous emotional conflict and of an almost despairing search for a way of life that would satisfy his restless intellect. He indulged for a time in fashionable dissipation, attempted to relieve his troubled mind by philanthropic activities, and then finally abandoned it all for the life of a simple peasant. He came to the conclusion that no progress could be made in remedying the ills of society until the upper classes renounced their privileges and adopted the humble existence of men who toil for their bread. Yet this would be only a beginning. In addition, all selfish individualism must disappear, all wealth must be surrendered to a common fund, and all agencies of force must be abolished. Tolstoi based much of his philosophy upon the New Testament, especially upon the Sermon on the Mount. He found in Jesus' teachings of meekness, humility, and nonresistance the essential principles of a just society. Above all, he condemned the use of violence, regardless of the purpose for which it is employed. Violence brutalizes man; it places its user in the hands of his enemies; and, as long as force is available as a weapon, reliance upon civilized methods is almost impossible.

Syndicalism

A third of the great radical philosophies produced by the Industrial Revolution was syndicalism, whose chief exponent was Georges Sorel (1847–1922). Syndicalism demands the abolition of both capitalism and the state and the reorganization of society into associations of producers. It resembles anarchism in its opposition to the state; but whereas the anarchist demands the abolition of force, the syndicalist would retain it, even after the state has been destroyed. Syndicalism also resembles socialism in that both would involve collective ownership of the means of production; but instead of making the state the owner and operator of the means of production, the syndicalist would delegate these functions to associations of producers. Thus all the steel mills would be owned and operated by the workers in the steel industry, the coal mines by the workers in the coal industry, and so on. Further, these associations or syndicates would take the place of the state, each one governing its own members in all of their activities as producers. In all other matters the workers would be free from interference. On the other hand, Sorel entertained no illusions as to the capacity of the masses for self-government. He regarded the average man as very much of a sheep, fit only to be a follower. He believed, therefore, that the ruling authority in the syndicates should be exercised quite frankly by the intelligent few.

Last of all, we must not overlook the Christian socialists, the least radical among all the critics of capitalist economics. The founder of Christian socialism was Robert de Lamennais (1782–1854), a French Catholic priest who sought to revive the Christian religion as an aid to reform and social justice. From France the movement spread to England and was adopted by a number of Protestant intellectuals, especially by the novelist Charles Kingsley (1819–1875). In its early days Christian socialism was little more than a demand for application of the teachings of Jesus to the problems created by industry, but in later years it began to assume more tangible form. In 1891 Leo XIII, "the workingman's Pope," issued his famous encyclical *Rerum novarum*, in which he revived with a modern slant the liberal economic attitude of St. Thomas Aquinas. Though the encyclical expressly recognized private property as a natural right and vigorously repudiated the Marxist doctrine of the class war, at the same time it strongly discountenanced unlimited profits. It appealed to employers to respect the dignity of their workers as men and as Christians and not to treat them as "chattels to make money by, or to look upon them merely as so much muscle or physical power." By way of specific proposals to mitigate the harshness of the industrial regime, it recommended factory legislation, the formation of labor unions, an increase in the number of small landowners, and limitation of hours of employment.[4] The issuance of this encyclical gave a mighty impulse to the growth of Christian socialism among liberal Catholics. In European countries before World War I, Catholic parties frequently played an active role, sometimes in combination with the moderate Marxists, in furthering the movement for social legislation.

Christian socialism

SELECTED READINGS

THE FIRST INDUSTRIAL REVOLUTION

· *Items so designated are available in paperbound editions.*

· Ashton, T. S., *The Industrial Revolution, 1760–1830*, New York, 1948 (Galaxy). A clear introductory account of the First Revolution.

Bowen, Frank, *A Century of Atlantic Travel*, Boston, 1930.

Day, Clive, *Economic Development in Modern Europe*, New York, 1933. Interesting and well-written.

Dewey, D. R., *Financial History of the United States*, New York, 1922.

Dietz, F. C., *The Industrial Revolution*, New York, 1927. Good on technological progress.

Heaton, Herbert, *Economic History of Europe*, New York, 1936, Chs. 21–30.

· Mantoux, Paul, *The Industrial Revolution in the Eighteenth Century*, New York, 1947 (Torchbook).

[4] The substance of Leo's encyclical was reaffirmed in 1931 by Pope Pius XI in a new encyclical, *Quadragesimo Anno*.

· Mumford, Lewis, *Technics and Civilization*, New York, 1934 (Harbinger). Stimulating.

Ogg, F. A., and Sharp, W. R., *Economic Development of Modern Europe*, New York, 1929.

Reid, W. S., *Economic History of Great Britain*, New York, 1956.

· Tawney, R. H., *The Acquisitive Society*, New York, 1920 (Harvest).

Taylor, George, *The Transportation Revolution, 1815–1860*, New York, 1956.

Toynbee, Arnold, *Lectures on the Industrial Revolution of the Eighteenth Century in England*, London, 1937. Valuable for the early history.

NEW ECONOMIC DOCTRINES

Bell, John F., *A History of Economic Thought*, New York, 1956.

Cole, G. D. H., *What Marx Really Meant*, New York, 1934.

Ferguson, J. M., *Landmarks of Economic Thought*, New York, 1938. A good summary, clearly written.

Gide, Charles, and Rist, Charles, *A History of Economic Doctrines*, Boston, 1948. A good summary.

Ginzberg, Eli, *The House of Adam Smith*, New York, 1934. Authoritative.

Hook, Sidney, *Towards the Understanding of Karl Marx*, New York, 1933. A stimulating analysis, though difficult in some places.

Laidler, H. W., *History of Socialist Thought*, New York, 1927.

Newman, P. C., *The Development of Economic Thought*, New York, 1952. An elementary survey.

Russell, Bertrand, *Proposed Roads to Freedom*, New York, 1919.

· Schumpeter, Joseph, *Capitalism, Socialism, and Democracy*, New York, 1942 (Torchbook). A provocative analysis.

Wagner, D. O., ed., *Social Reformers: Adam Smith to John Dewey*, New York, 1934.

· Wilson, Edmund, *To the Finland Station*, Garden City, N.Y., 1953 (Anchor). An interesting and provocative survey of the history of Marxism.

SOURCE MATERIALS

· Malthus, T. R., *An Essay on Population*, especially Books I and IV (Richard D. Irwin and others).

· Marx, Karl, *Critique of the Gotha Program*, New York, 1933 (International Publishers).

· ————, and Engels, F., *The Communist Manifesto* (Appleton-Century-Crofts and others).

· Mill, J. S., *Autobiography*, New York, 1924 (Library of Liberal Arts and others).

Owen, Robert, *A New View of Society*, New York.

————, *Report to the County of Lanark*.

· Tolstoi, Count Leo, *The Kingdom of God Is Within You*, New York, 1905 (Noonday Press).

Webster, Hutton, *Historical Selections*, pp. 776–80, Children in Factories.

CHAPTER 7

The Ascendancy of Nationalism
(1830-1914)

I am sure of one thing . . . that is, in those matters of foreign
policy, whatever may be your feelings, our conscience tells us that
we have not fulfilled a single act, not written a single line, not
uttered a single word that was not inspired by a warm love for
the fatherland, by a very keen desire to promote its interests and
to increase its honor. . . . We were guided constantly by the inflexible intention of maintaining intact the national dignity, of
preserving pure of all stain . . . that glorious tricolored flag which
a generous sovereign has entrusted to our care.
> —Count Camillo Benso di Cavour, Speech to the
> Piedmontese Chamber of Deputies, April 16, 1858

The history of the world from 1830 to 1914 was marked by a vigorous growth of nationalism and its logical offshoot, an extensive and
arrogant imperialism. Nationalism may be defined as a program or
ideal based upon a consciousness of nationhood. The feeling or consciousness of nationhood may depend upon a number of factors. A
people may consider themselves a nation because of peculiarities of
race, language, religion, or culture. In most cases, however, the factors which weld diverse groups together are a common history and
common aspirations for the future or a belief in a common destiny.
Only such elements as these can explain the fact that Belgium, Switzerland, Canada, and the United States are nations, since in all four
there are major differences in language, in religion, or in both—to
say nothing of different ethnic backgrounds. Although nationalism
was in some respects a beneficent force, particularly in the early
days when it often took the form of struggles for liberty, in the
main it was and still is an evil influence. It is especially evil when it
expresses itself in jingoism, in militarism, and in ambitions to conquer and dominate.

The meaning of nationalism

215

Without question nationalism was one of the most powerful forces that molded the history of the Western world between 1830 and 1914. From a vague sentiment during the early centuries of the modern era it grew into a veritable cult. For millions of deluded folk it became a stronger force than religion, surpassing Christianity in its appeal to the emotions and to the spirit of sacrifice in a holy cause. Men died for the honor of the flag as cheerfully as any martyrs had ever laid down their lives for the Cross. Though often coexistent with democracy and liberalism, militant nationalism was more powerful than either, and frequently thwarted or stifled both.

The evolution of nationalism

Nurtured by the French Revolutionary ideal of Fraternity, modern nationalism evolved through two stages. From 1800 to about 1848 it was little more than an emotional loyalty to a cultural and linguistic group and a yearning for deliverance from foreign oppression. After 1848 it developed into an aggressive movement for national greatness and for the right of each people united by cultural and ethnic ties to determine its own destinies. Its more extreme manifestations were exemplified by a frenzied worship of political power and a slavish devotion to doctrines of racial superiority and illusions of national honor. In such forms it was virtually synonymous with chauvinism, that species of vainglorious patriotism expressed in the sentiment, "My country, right or wrong."

The stages of nationalism

I. NATIONALISM IN FRANCE

The revolution of 1830

Since France was the home of a great outpouring of national feeling during the Revolution of 1789 and during the era of Napoleon, it was inevitable that worship of national greatness should continue as a vigorous force in that country. Nearly every major event that followed reflected in some measure the power of that force. The July Revolution of 1830, for example, though primarily a revolt of the bourgeoisie against the reactionary policies of Charles X, was inspired also by a desire to return to the banners and shibboleths associated with the glory of France when she wielded supremacy over most of Europe. Of much greater importance as a manifestation of nationalism was the February Revolution of 1848. As in 1830, the movement began as a revolt against reactionary policies. King Louis Philippe had grown indifferent to the demands of the masses, and his ministers were cynical and corrupt. Moreover, he turned a deaf ear to zealous patriots who wanted France to go to the relief of northern Italians who longed to throw off Austrian rule and of Poles who hated the tyranny of Russia.

The Revolution of 1848

The strength of nationalism showed itself even more clearly in the election that followed the deposition of Louis Philippe. France had been made a republic with a constitution modeled after that of the United States. This meant a powerful executive with the title of President. December 10, 1848, was set as the date of the Presidential election. Four candidates competed in this election: a moderate republican, a socialist, a Catholic, and a man who had something for everybody—Louis Napoleon Bonaparte. More than 7,000,000 votes were cast; and out of this total nearly 5,500,000 went to Louis Napoleon. Who was this man, who enjoyed such amazing popularity that he could poll more than twice as many votes as the other three candidates combined? Louis Napoleon Bonaparte (1808–1873) was the

Napoleon III, Emperor of the French, 1852–1870.

nephew of Napoleon I, his father being Louis Bonaparte, who for a brief period was king of Holland. After his uncle's downfall, Louis Napoleon went into exile, spending most of his time in Germany and in Switzerland. Returning to France after the July Revolution of 1830, he was imprisoned a few years later for attempting to provoke an uprising at Boulogne. But in 1846 he escaped to England, where he was liberally supplied with funds by both British and French reactionaries. By the summer of 1848 the situation in France was such that he knew it was safe to return. In fact, he was welcomed with open arms by men of all classes. Conservatives were looking for a savior to protect their property against the onslaughts of the radicals. Proletarians were beguiled by his glittering schemes for prosperity in his book, *The Extinction of Pauperism*, and by the fact that he had corresponded with Louis Blanc and with Pierre Proudhon, the anarchist. In between these two classes was a great multitude of patriots and hero-worshipers to whom the very name Napoleon was a matchless symbol of glory and greatness. It was chiefly to this multitude that the nephew of the Corsican owed his astounding triumph. As one old peasant expressed it: "How could I help voting for this gentleman—I whose nose was frozen at Moscow?"

Louis Napoleon
as dictator and
then Emperor

With grandiose dreams of emulating his uncle, Louis Napoleon was not long content to be merely *President* of France. Almost from the first he used his position to pave the way for a higher calling. He enlisted the support of the Catholics by permitting them to regain control over the schools and by sending an expedition to Rome to restore the Pope to his temporal power in central Italy. He threw sops to the workers and to the bourgeoisie in the form of old-age insurance and laws for the encouragement of business. In 1851, alleging the need for extraordinary measures to protect the rights of the masses, he proclaimed a temporary dictatorship and invited the people to grant him the power to draw up a new constitution. In the plebiscite held on December 21, 1851, he was authorized by an over-whelming majority (7,500,000 to 640,000) to proceed as he liked. The new constitution, which he put into effect in January 1852, made the President an actual dictator. His term of office was length-ened to ten years, and he was given the exclusive power to initiate legislation and to make war and peace. Although the legislative branch was preserved in name, it could not initiate or amend bills or even change any specific provisions in the budget. Still the little Caesar was not satisfied; he would be content with nothing less than the imperial dignity which had graced the shoulders of his famous uncle. After exactly one year Louis Napoleon Bonaparte ordered another plebiscite and, with the approval of over 95 per cent of the voters, assumed the title of Napoleon III, Emperor of the French.

The regime of
Napoleon III

The Second Empire in France endured from December 1852, to September 1870. Its creator and preserver ruled by methods not dis-similar to those of other Caesars both before and since. He stimu-lated an imposing prosperity by draining swamps, building roads, improving harbors, subsidizing railroads, and constructing a mag-nificent system of boulevards in Paris. He cultivated the favor of the lower classes by mouthing Revolutionary phrases and by schemes for social welfare. At the same time he strove to make sure that rad-icals would not become troublesome. He subjected the press to strict surveillance and controlled elections by paying the expenses of *official* candidates and by requiring all others to take an oath of fi-delity to the Emperor. Nor did he neglect opportunities to add lus-ter to his regime by an aggressive foreign policy. He annexed Alge-ria in northern Africa and established a protectorate over Indochina. In 1854 he plunged into the Crimean War with Russia under the pretext of protecting Catholic monks in Turkey. Since Napoleon had the aid of Great Britain and Turkey and also for a time of Sar-dinia, he managed to emerge from this war on the victorious side. Now more than ever he could rejoice in the plaudits of the mob and pose as the arbiter of the destinies of Europe.

By 1860 the glamour of Napoleon's reputation had begun to wear thin. The first great blow to his prestige was a result of the outcome of his Italian adventure. In 1858 he had formed an alliance with the

IN FRANCE

The decline and
fall of the
Second Empire

Italian nationalists to help them expel the Austrians; but as soon as he saw that his erstwhile friends were bent upon consolidating the whole Italian peninsula into a nation-state and upon destroying the temporal sovereignty of the Pope, he promptly deserted them. By so doing, he antagonized thousands of his more liberal followers, who reproached him for abandoning a gallant people to Austrian oppression. In 1862 Napoleon intervened in Mexico. He sent an army into that country to establish an empire and then offered the throne to the Archduke Maximilian of Austria. But at the conclusion of the American Civil War the government of the United States compelled the withdrawal of the French troops, and soon afterward Maximilian was captured and shot by the Mexicans. As a consequence of this tragic adventure, opposition to Napoleon's rule markedly increased. After the elections of 1869 he decided that it would be expedient to make some concessions. He granted to the Assembly the right to initiate laws and to criticize and ratify or reject the budget. But in 1870 he resolved to gamble once more on a bold stroke of foreign policy to retrieve his fortunes. Shortly before this the government of Spain had been overturned, and the revolutionists had offered the crown to Prince Leopold of Hohenzollern, a cousin of the King of Prussia. Militarists and fire-eating "patriots" in France professed to see in this a threat to the security of the French nation. Napoleon himself probably did not desire a war. He apparently assumed that vigorous diplomatic measures would give France all she needed in the way of a glorious triumph. But he allowed himself to be dominated by a militant clique that surrounded the Empress Eugénie and included several of his ministers. Members of this clique emphasized the rapid growth of the Prussian nation and its commanding position in central Europe. Accordingly, they advocated a preventive war. Now or never was their motto. France must seize the initiative while she still had an equality in numbers and a superiority, they believed, in military power. They maneuvered Napoleon into sending the French ambassador to meet with King William I of Prussia at the spa of Ems and there to demand that the king *never* allow a member of the Hohenzollern family to become a candidate for the Spanish throne. Though annoyed by this demand, King William wanted peace. But even less than Napoleon III was he master in his own house. The real dictator of policy in Prussia was the minister-president, Otto von Bismarck. And Bismarck lusted for war, if for no other reason than to rally the south German states behind the Prussian standard and unite all Germans in one great nation. France was badly defeated in the ensuing war, which lasted only a few weeks. After the battle of Sedan (September 2, 1870) Napoleon himself was taken prisoner, and two days later his government was overthrown by a group of republicans in Paris.

Following the collapse of Napoleon's empire a provisional government was organized to rule the country until a new constitution

219

could be drafted. Elections were held in February 1871 for a national constituent assembly, resulting in the choice of some 500 monarchists and only about 200 republicans. The explanation lies in the fact that during the electoral campaign the republicans had urged a renewal of the war, while the monarchists took the attitude that France was already defeated, and that she might as well negotiate with her conquerors for the best terms she could get. It was not that the French people overwhelmingly preferred a monarchy, but rather that they longed for peace. Fortunately the monarchists were hopelessly divided. Angry discord among them postponed for almost four years a definite decision as to the permanent form the French government should take. Finally, in January 1875 the National Assembly adopted the first of a series of constitutional laws recognizing the government as republican in form. This action signified the formal establishment of the Third Republic in France.

France in this era was not destined to have a happy future. It was almost torn apart by nationalist discord and social conflict from the beginning. The first episode of this type was the Paris Commune, an uprising of patriots and radicals in the spring of 1871. Its causes included: (1) a feeling of shame on account of defeat in the war and the humiliating peace terms accepted by the provisional government; (2) the misery of the poorer classes; and (3) resentment against the preponderant influence of the provinces in the provisional government, a reversal of the time-honored supremacy of Paris. The Communards forced the provisional government to take refuge in Versailles and held control of the capital for two months. The leaders of the provisional government gradually marshaled their forces for a reconquest of the city. The effort was attended by horrible brutality, especially during the Bloody Week of May 21–28. After their slaughter and defeat the Communards were branded as enemies of law and order and exemplars of the kind of violence the world could expect from the triumph of disciples of Marx. Though the Communards did, indeed, commit acts of violence, including the killing of hostages, only a minority of Communards were Marxists. The majority were not socialists at all but really Jacobins who wanted a republic of small, independent shopkeepers and craftsmen. They were not interested in abolishing private property but in distributing it more widely.

The collapse of the Paris Commune did not end the troubles of France that grew out of her defeat in the Franco-Prussian War. Monarchists and clericals charged the Republic with weakness and corruption and longed for a more autocratic government to lead the nation back to the path of glory. Illustrative of this movement was the Boulanger episode of 1887–1889. Georges Boulanger was a general in the army and a former minister of war who developed Napoleonic ambitions. Appealing to the injured pride of patriotic Frenchmen, he won enthusiastic applause by clamoring for a war of re-

The Paris Commune. Organized by Marxists and other radicals, the Commune of Paris was intended to be the supreme governing body of the French capital and the nucleus around which other communes would eventually be formed. Proclamation of the Commune on March 26, 1871, led to a bloody civil war that raged for two months.

venge against Germany. By harping on scandals recently exposed in the republican regime, he endeared himself to the monarchists and also to conservative Catholics, who hated the Republic for its anti-clerical program. Soon he was the most popular man in France. Everywhere mobs clamored for their "brave general" under the illusion that a new Bonaparte had risen in their midst. Flattered and emboldened by this adulation, Boulanger determined upon a national plebiscite as more tangible proof of the people's support. He stood for election to the Chamber of Deputies in every available district and won by substantial margins ten times in six months. In January 1889 he crowned his exploits by rolling up a triumphant majority in radical Paris. It seemed now that nothing could stop him from riding into power as a military dictator. But fortunately for the Republic, this god who had been worshiped by the rabble and by the ladies in the salons turned out to have feet of clay. When the government finally mustered enough courage to order his arrest on charges of conspiracy, he fled ingloriously to Belgium. Two years later he blew out his brains on the grave of his mistress.

The inglorious end of the Boulangist movement did not terminate the attempts to discredit the Republic. In the 1890's the reactionaries adopted anti-Semitism as a spearhead for the advancement of their aims. The fact that certain Jewish bankers had recently been involved in scandalous dealings with politicians lent color to the monarchist charge that the government was shot through with corruption and that money-grabbing Jews were largely to blame. Catholics

The Dreyfus affair

221

were persuaded to believe that Jewish politicians had dictated the anticlerical legislation of the republican regime. With such charges befouling the air, it is not strange that anti-Semitism should have flared into a violent outbreak. In 1894 a Jewish captain of artillery, Alfred Dreyfus, was accused by a clique of monarchist officers of selling military secrets to Germany. Tried by court-martial, he was convicted and sentenced for life to Devil's Island. At first the verdict was accepted as the merited punishment of a traitor; but in 1897 Colonel Picquart, a new head of the Intelligence Division, announced his conclusion that the documents upon which Dreyfus had been convicted were forgeries. A movement was launched for a new trial, which the War Department promptly refused. Soon the whole nation was divided into friends and opponents of the luckless captain. On the side of Dreyfus were the radical republicans, the socialists, people of liberal and humanitarian sympathies, and such prominent literary figures as Émile Zola and Anatole France. The anti-Dreyfusards included the monarchists, the clericals, the Jew-baiters, the militarists, and a considerable number of conservative workingmen and sincere but mistaken patriots. Dreyfus was finally set free by executive order in 1899, and six years later he was cleared of all guilt by the Supreme Court and restored to the army. He was immediately promoted to the rank of major and decorated with the emblem of the Legion of Honor. The outcome of the Dreyfus affair effectively squelched the monarchist movement in France. Thereafter its adherents were gradually reduced to political insignificance—a mere "handful of old nuts rattling in a bag."

As already intimated, the Dreyfus affair was an element in a broader struggle over the issue of church and state, which also had nationalist implications. From the beginning of its history the Third Republic had been tinctured with anticlericalism. Its founders were not necessarily atheists, but they did believe that a powerful church with ambitions to extend its political and social influence was a threat to republican government. The aims of the anticlericals were to curb this influence, to reduce the economic privileges of the Catholic Church, and to break the stranglehold the clergy had gained upon education. The roots of anticlericalism extended in several directions. In part, it was a result of the Industrial Revolution, which fostered materialistic interests and intensified the struggle between the bourgeoisie and the *ancien régime*, with which the Church was usually identified. It was also a product in some measure of the growth of science and of skeptical and liberal philosophies, which were often employed as primary weapons in fighting religious conservatism. Probably the main cause of its growth was the rise of a militant nationalism. The Catholic Church was not only committed to an internationalist outlook, but as late as the 1860's Popes were still asserting their rights to temporal power and pour-

The roots of
anticlericalism

ing out their anathemas upon rulers who would establish omnipotent states. Wherever nationalism gathered powerful momentum, clericalism was almost certain to be regarded as a primary enemy.

Anticlericalism in France reached the peak of its fury between 1875 and 1914. The great majority of the leaders of the Third Republic were hostile to the Church; and naturally so, for the Catholic hierarchy was aiding the monarchists at every turn. Clericals conspired with monarchists in backing Boulanger and even more actively with militarists and anti-Semites in attempting to discredit the Republic during the Dreyfus affair. But in the end they overreached themselves. The outcome of the Dreyfus affair not only sounded the knell of monarchism but led to a furious attack upon the Church. In 1901 the government passed the Associations Act, prohibiting the existence of any religious order in France not authorized by the state. This was followed in 1904 by an act forbidding all members of religious orders to teach in either public or private schools. Finally, in 1905, the Separation Law was passed, which, as its name indicates, dissolved the union of Church and state. For the first time since 1801 the adherents of all creeds were placed on an equal basis. No longer were the Catholic clergy to receive their salaries from the public purse. Although some of these measures were modified in later years, clericalism remained in the minds of most Frenchmen under a heavy cloud of suspicion.

2. NATIONALISM IN CENTRAL, SOUTHERN, AND EASTERN EUROPE

The February Revolution in France touched off a series of revolts in central Europe, beginning with an uprising in Austria on March 13. Mobs of students and workingmen rioted in Vienna and forced the resignation of that last great pillar of the *ancien régime*, Prince Metternich. Frightened by the refusal of his troops to fire upon the rebels, the Emperor promised a constitution for Germanic Austria, excluding Hungary and the Italian possessions. The constitution as finally adopted provided for a cabinet responsible to parliament and for a liberal franchise, and the assembly which drew it up also abolished the remaining feudal obligations of the peasants. Almost immediately the Hungarians took advantage of the turmoil in Vienna to establish a liberal government, and in April 1849, under the leadership of Louis Kossuth, they proclaimed the independence of the Hungarian Republic. But neither of these revolutions was permanently successful, for the reason that they soon became entangled in the discords of nationalism. The Hungarian liberals were no more willing than the Austrians to grant the privileges to subject nationalities that they claimed for themselves. As a consequence, the Hapsburgs were able to stir up ill feeling among the Slavs and to use them to good advantage in curbing the ambitions of the dominant

223

nationalities. By the summer of 1849 the Emperor had succeeded in overthrowing the Hungarian Republic and in revoking the Austrian constitution. The discontent, however, continued until a compromise known as the *Ausgleich* was finally worked out between the Austrians and the Hungarians in 1867. The *Ausgleich* established a dual monarchy, with the head of the House of Hapsburg serving as both Emperor of Austria and King of Hungary. Each of the two parts of the empire was made practically autonomous, with its own cabinet and parliament. Three joint ministers, of war, finance, and foreign affairs, looked after the interests of the state as a whole in their respective spheres. Enabling both the Magyars in Hungary and the Germans in Austria to rule as master races, this arrangement survived until the Dual Monarchy was broken into fragments in 1918.

The revolutionary
movement in
Germany

Within a week after the revolutionary movement of 1848 began in Vienna, it spread to the states of Germany. Since 1815 the German states together with Austria had constituted the thirty-eight members of the Germanic Confederation. The several princes guarded their semi-independence jealously, but among many of the people there was a growing sentiment in favor of union into a nation-state. Businessmen urged it under the conviction that trade would flourish. Nationalists demanded it on the basis of cultural and racial unity. During the month of March 1848, concessions were extorted from nearly every one of the German rulers—in some cases promises of constitutions, in others, liberal ministries or freedom of speech and of press. In May of the same year liberals and nationalists convoked a great national convention at Frankfurt to draft a constitution for a united Germany. This was the celebrated Frankfurt Assembly, composed of high-minded delegates from all the states of the Confederation. The Assembly succeeded in adopting a bill of rights but soon fell into a hopeless tangle over other constitutional issues. When the majority of the delegates agreed that the new Germany should be a limited monarchy, the republicans bolted. There was also heated discussion over the question whether Austria should be included, and over the problem of who should be monarch. When it was decided that only the *German* provinces of Austria should be admitted, the Austrian government commanded its delegates to come home. Still hopeful of effecting a union on a less ambitious scale, the Assembly offered the crown to King Frederick William IV of Prussia. But that weak-willed monarch refused to accept for fear of antagonizing Austria and also because he was reluctant to have anything to do with a revolutionary body. Soon afterward the Frankfurt Assembly dispersed in disgust, with absolutely nothing to show for its efforts. Most of the reforms which had been secured outside of the Assembly likewise gradually melted away, and thousands of the revolutionaries emigrated from the country and took refuge in the United States.

224

The unification of Germany was now left to be achieved by the hard realism of Bismarck. Otto von Bismarck (1815–1898) was born into the class of Junkers, or landed aristocrats, who for centuries had furnished the Prussian state with the bulk of its bureaucrats and high army officers. After a session at the Universities of Göttingen and Berlin as an indifferent student but a capable duelist and rake, he entered government service, only to be dismissed a short time later for his irregular and dissolute habits. During the revolutionary movement of 1848 he served in the Prussian Parliament as a staunch upholder of divine-right monarchy. He was one of a group of intransigent aristocrats who urged the Prussian king not to accept a "crown of shame" from the Frankfurt Assembly. Later Bismarck was instrumental in organizing the Conservative party, dedicated to protecting the interests of the Junker class, the established church, and the army, and to the building of a powerful Prussia as the nucleus of a German nation. In 1862 he was summoned by King William I to become Minister-President of his beloved Prussia.

In consolidating the German states into a united nation, Bismarck followed a succession of steps of almost diabolical cleverness. First he plotted to eliminate Austria from her commanding position in the Germanic Confederation. As a preliminary means to this end he entered into a dispute with Denmark over possession of Schleswig and Holstein. Inhabited largely by Germans, these two provinces had an anomalous status. Since 1815 Holstein had been included in the Germanic Confederation, but both were subject to the personal overlordship of the King of Denmark. When, in 1864, the Danish king attempted to annex them, Bismarck invited Austria to participate in a war against Denmark. A brief struggle followed, at the end of which the Danish ruler was compelled to renounce all his claims to Schleswig and Holstein in favor of Austria and Prussia. Then the very sequel occurred for which Bismarck ardently hoped: a quarrel between the victors over division of the spoils. The upshot was that in 1866 Prussia and Austria plunged into war. Since Bismarck knew that the Hapsburgs would have the help of the south German states, he formed an alliance with Italy, promising to reward her, in the event of victory, with the cession of Venetia. The conflict which followed, known as the Seven Weeks' War, ended in an easy triumph for Prussia. Austria was forced to give up her claims to Schleswig and Holstein, to surrender Venetia to Italy, and to acquiesce in the dissolution of the Germanic Confederation. Immediately following the war Bismarck proceeded to unite all of the German states north of the Main River into the North German Confederation. The constitution of this union, which the great Minister-President boasted he wrote in a single night, provided that the King of Prussia should be the hereditary President of the Confederation, and that there should be an upper house representing the governments of the several states and a lower house elected by universal

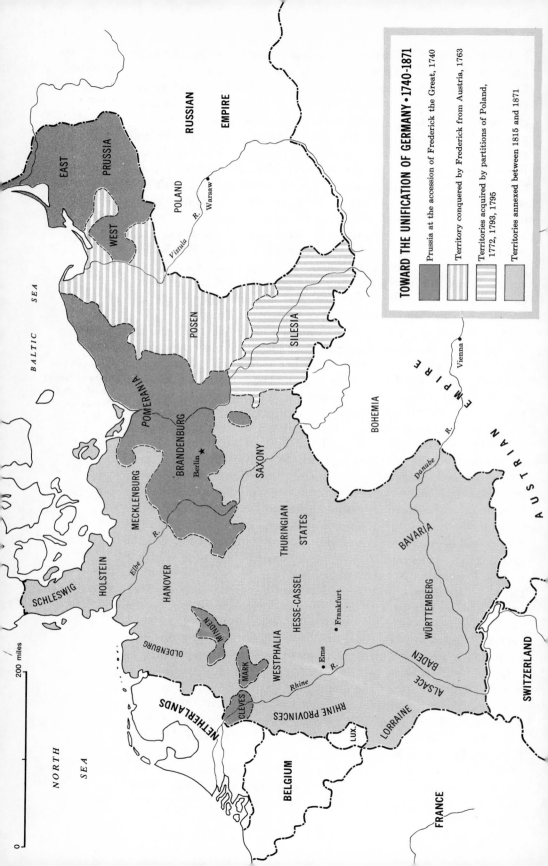

TOWARD THE UNIFICATION OF GERMANY · 1740-1871

Prussia at the accession of Frederick the Great, 1740

Territory conquered by Frederick from Austria, 1763

Territories acquired by partitions of Poland, 1772, 1793, 1795

Territories annexed between 1815 and 1871

RUSSIAN EMPIRE

AUSTRIAN EMPIRE

BALTIC SEA

NORTH SEA

EAST PRUSSIA

WEST PRUSSIA

POLAND

Warsaw

Vistula R.

POSEN

SILESIA

BOHEMIA

Vienna

Danube R.

POMERANIA

BRANDENBURG

Berlin

SAXONY

MECKLENBURG

Elbe R.

THURINGIAN STATES

BAVARIA

HOLSTEIN

SCHLESWIG

HANOVER

OLDENBURG

MINDEN

MARK

CLEVES

WESTPHALIA

HESSE-CASSEL

Frankfurt

Ems

R.

Rhine

RHINE PROVINCES

WÜRTTEMBERG

BADEN

ALSACE

LORRAINE

LUX.

SWITZERLAND

NETHERLANDS

BELGIUM

FRANCE

200 miles

0

manhood suffrage.

The final step in the completion of German unity was the Franco-Prussian War. We have learned of the part played by French politicians in provoking a crisis with Prussia over the question of succession to the Spanish throne. The attitude of Bismarck was just as provocative. He knew that a war with France would be the best possible means to kindle a *German* nationalism in Bavaria and Württemberg and in the remaining states south of the Main. When he received a dispatch sent by King William I from Ems informing him that the demand of the French for perpetual exclusion of the Hohenzollern family from the Spanish throne had been refused, he

Bismarck, Thiers, and Favre Arranging the Peace Terms at the End of the Franco-Prussian War. Otto von Bismarck was Chancellor of the new German Empire. Louis-Adolphe Thiers and Jules Favre represented the provisional government set up after the overthrow of Napoleon III. The arrogance of the Imperial Chancellor and the dejection of the French representatives could hardly be more graphically portrayed.

decided that the time for action had come. He determined to release the telegram from Ems in such a form as to make it appear that King William had insulted the French ambassador. Bismarck's prediction that this would have the effect of "a red rag upon the Gallic bull" was speedily borne out. When the garbled report of what happened at Ems was received in France, the whole nation was immediately in an uproar. On July 15, 1870, when Napoleon's ministers requested the legislative body to approve a declaration of war, there were only ten dissenting votes. No sooner had the struggle begun than the south German states rallied to the side of Prussia in the belief that she was the victim of aggression. Such was the beginning of a war that was destined to have tremendous effects upon the subsequent history of Europe. From the start the Prussians had the advantage. The disciplined efficiency of their military machine stood out in bold contrast to the ineptitude of the French. Supplies for Napoleon's troops were woefully inadequate, and one of his generals was unable for a time to locate the army he was supposed to command. The result could have been foretold from the beginning. After the capture of Napoleon at Sedan in September 1870 and the conquest of Paris after a desperate siege four months later, the war was officially ended by the Treaty of Frankfurt. France surrendered the major portions of Alsace and Lorraine and agreed to pay an indemnity of 5 billion francs.

Meanwhile events in Italy had been running a course almost parallel to that which had led to the unification of Germany. Italy before 1848, it should be remembered, was a patchwork of petty states. The most important of those possessing independence were the Kingdom of Sardinia in the north, the Papal States in the central region, and the Kingdom of the Two Sicilies in the south. The former republics of Lombardy and Venetia were held by Austria, and Hapsburg dependents ruled in Tuscany, Parma, and Modena. As the revolutionary fervor of 1848 swept across the peninsula, one ruler after another granted democratic reforms. Charles Albert of Sardinia outdistanced all the others with his celebrated Fundamental Statute providing for civil liberties and a parliamentary form of government. But it soon became evident that the Italians were more interested in nationalism than in democracy. For some years romantic patriots had been dreaming of the *Risorgimento*—the resurrection of the Italian spirit—which would restore the nation to the position of glorious leadership it had held in ancient times and during the age of the Renaissance. To achieve this, it was universally agreed that Italy must be welded into a single state. But there was difference of opinion as to the form the new government should take. Young idealists followed the leadership of Giuseppe Mazzini (1805–1872), who labored with sincere devotion for the founding of a republic. Religious-minded patriots believed that the most practicable solution would be to federate the states of Italy under the presidency of the Pope. The majority of the more moderate nationalists advocated a constitutional monarchy built upon the foundations of the Kingdom of Sardinia. The aims of this third group gradually crystallized under the leadership of a shrewd Sardinian nobleman, Count Camillo di Cavour (1810–1861). In 1850 he was appointed Minister of Commerce and Agriculture of his native state and in 1852 Prime Minister.

The movement
to establish a
nation-state in
Italy

The campaign for unification of the Italian peninsula began with efforts to expel the Austrians. In 1848 revolts were organized in the territories under Hapsburg domination, and an army of liberation marched from Sardinia to aid the rebels; but the movement ended in failure. It was then that Cavour, as the new leader of the campaign, turned to less heroic but more practical methods. In 1855, to attract

the favorable attention of Great Britain and France, he entered the
Crimean War on their side despite the fact that he had no quarrel
with Russia. In 1858 he held a secret meeting with Napoleon III and
prepared the stage for an Italian War of Liberation. Napoleon
agreed to cooperate in driving the Austrians from Italy for the price
of the cession of Savoy and Nice by Sardinia to France. A war with
Austria was duly provoked in 1859, and for a time all went well for
the Franco-Italian allies. But after the conquest of Lombardy, Napoleon suddenly withdrew, fearful of ultimate defeat and afraid of
antagonizing the Catholics in his own country by aiding an avow-
edly anticlerical government. Thus deserted by her ally, Sardinia
was unable to expel the Austrians from Venetia. Nevertheless, she
did make some extensive gains: she annexed Lombardy, and the
duchies of Tuscany, Parma, and Modena while the northern portion
of the Papal States voted in a burst of nationalist enthusiasm for
union with her. Sardinia was now more than twice her original size
and by far the most powerful state in Italy.

The second step in consolidating the unity of Italy was the conquest of the Kingdom of the Two Sicilies. This kingdom was ruled
by a Bourbon, Francis II, who was thoroughly hated by his Italian   The completion
subjects. In May 1860 a romantic free-lance adventurer by the name   of Italian uni-
of Giuseppe Garibaldi set out with his famous regiment of 1000   fication
"red shirts" to rescue his fellow Italians from oppression. Within
three months he had conquered the island of Sicily and had then
marched to the deliverance of Naples, where the people were already in revolt. By November the whole kingdom of Francis II had
fallen to the gay buccaneer. Garibaldi at first apparently intended to
convert the territory into an independent republic but was finally
persuaded to surrender it to the Kingdom of Sardinia. With most of
the peninsula now united under a single rule, Victor Emmanuel II,
King of Sardinia, assumed the title of King of Italy (March 17,
1861). Venetia was still in the hands of the Austrians, but in 1866
they were forced by the Prussians to cede it to Italy as a reward for
her part in the Seven Weeks' War. All that remained to complete
the unification of Italy was the annexation of Rome. The Eternal
City had resisted conquest thus far largely because of the military
protection accorded to the Pope by Napoleon III. But in 1870 the
outbreak of the Franco-Prussian War compelled Napoleon to withdraw his troops. The opportunity was too good to be overlooked. In
September 1870 Italian soldiers occupied Rome, and in July of the
following year it was made the capital of the united kingdom.

The occupation of Rome brought the kingdom of Italy into conflict with the papacy. Indeed, the whole movement for unification
had been characterized by hostility to the Church. Such was inevita-   Anticlericalism
bly the case, with the Pope ruling in the manner of a secular prince   in Italy
over the Papal States and hurling the thunders of his wrath against
those who would rob him of his domain for the sake of a united

THE RISORGIMENTO

Top left: *Giuseppe Mazzini* (1805–1872). Italian idealist and patriot, he strove in vain for the unification of his country as a republic.

Top right: *Count Camillo di Cavour* (1810–1861). First Prime Minister of the United Kingdom of Italy.

Right: *Giuseppe Garibaldi* (1807–1882). Italian patriot, conqueror of the Kingdom of the Two Sicilies.

Below: *The Battle of San Martino* (June, 1859). The Battle of San Martino was an event in the Italian War of Liberation against Austria.

SWITZERLAND   AUSTRIA

SAVOY
To France in 1860)

LOMBARDY   VENETIA

KINGDOM OF
SARDINIA

• Milan

Venice

Po R.

Turin

FRANCE   PARMA

MODENA   Bologna

Genoa   ROMAGNA

LUCCA   Florence

Arno R.

CORSICA
(To France)

TUSCANY

UMBRIA

PAPAL STATES

Tiber R.

Rome ★

A D R I A T I C   S E A

KINGDOM OF SARDINIA

T Y R R H E N I A N

S E A

KINGDOM

OF

THE

TWO

★ Naples

SICILIES

0   200 miles

M E D I T E R R A N E A N   Palermo   • Messina

SICILY   S E A

THE UNIFICATION OF ITALY

Italy. Following the occupation of Rome in 1870 an attempt was made to solve the problem of relations between the state and the papacy. In 1871 the Italian Parliament enacted the Law of Papal Guaranties purporting to define the status of the Pope as a reigning sovereign. He was to be granted full authority over the Vatican and Lateran buildings and gardens and the right to send and receive ambassadors. In addition, he was to have free use of the Italian postal, telegraph, and railway systems and was to be paid an annual indemnity of about $645,000. This law the reigning pontiff, Pius IX, promptly denounced on the ground that issues affecting the Pope could be settled only by an international treaty to which he himself was a party. Whereupon he shut himself up in the Vatican and refused to have anything to do with a government which had so **231**

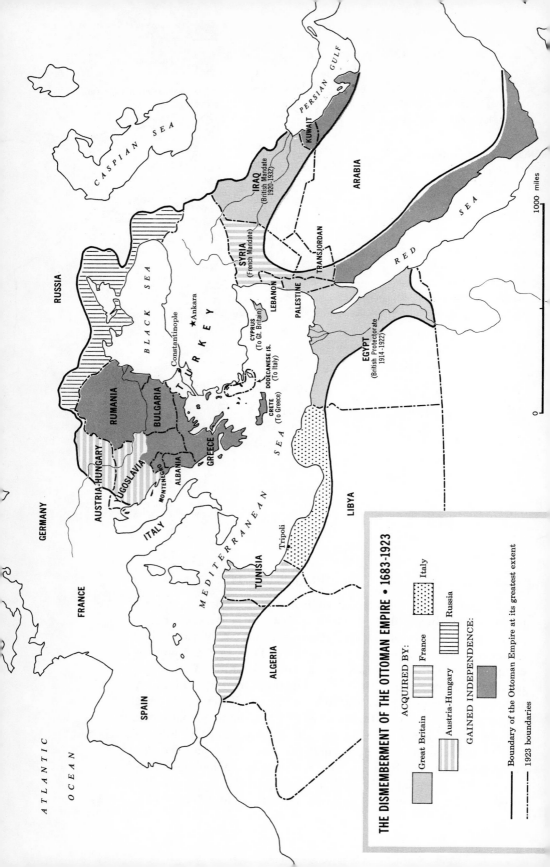

THE DISMEMBERMENT OF THE OTTOMAN EMPIRE • 1683-1923

ACQUIRED BY:

Great Britain

France

Austria-Hungary

GAINED INDEPENDENCE:

Italy

Russia

Boundary of the Ottoman Empire at its greatest extent

1923 boundaries

shamefully treated Christ's Vicar on earth. His successors continued this practice of voluntary imprisonment until 1929, when a series of agreements between the Fascist government and Pius XI effected what appeared to be a satisfactory settlement of the dispute.

In southeastern Europe during the nineteenth century nationalism partook primarily of a liberation character. This was particularly true of the lands of the Balkans. Before 1829 the entire Balkan peninsula—bounded by the Aegean, Black, and Adriatic Seas—was controlled by the Turks. But during the next eighty-five years a gradual dismemberment occurred of the Turkish empire in the Balkans. In some instances the slicing away of territories was perpetrated by rival European powers, especially by Russia and Austria; but generally it was the result of nationalist revolts by the Sultan's Christian subjects. In 1829, at the conclusion of the first Russo-Turkish War, the Ottoman Empire was compelled to acknowledge the independence of Greece and to grant autonomy to Serbia and to the provinces of Wallachia and Moldavia under Russian protection. At the end of the Crimean War, Russia was forced to relinquish her domination of Moldavia and Wallachia, with the result that in 1862 the two provinces were united as a virtually independent Rumania. As the years passed, resentment against Ottoman rule spread through other Balkan territories. In 1875–1876 there were uprisings in Bosnia, Herzegovina, and Bulgaria, which the Sultan suppressed with murderous vengeance. Reports of atrocities against Orthodox Christians gave Russia an excuse for renewal of her age-long struggle for domination of the Balkans. In this second Russo-Turkish War (1877–1878) the armies of the Tsar won a smashing victory. The Treaty of San Stefano, which terminated the conflict, provided that the Sultan surrender nearly all of his territory in Europe, except for a remnant around Constantinople. But at this juncture the great powers intervened. Austria and Great Britain, especially, were opposed to letting Russia assume jurisdiction over so large a portion of the Near East. Consequently the Tsar was obliged to submit to a revision of the Treaty of San Stefano at the Congress of Berlin in 1878. The Treaty of Berlin, which was thereupon adopted, returned most of the conquered territory to Turkey, except for Bessarabia, which Russia was allowed to retain; Thessaly, which was given to Greece; and Bosnia and Herzegovina, which were placed under the administrative control of Austria. Seven years later the Bulgars, who had been granted some degree of autonomy by the Treaty of Berlin, seized the province of Eastern Rumelia from Turkey and in 1908 established the independent Kingdom of Bulgaria.

In the very year when this last dismemberment occurred, Turkey herself was engulfed by the tidal wave of nationalism. For some time her more enlightened citizens had been growing increasingly disgusted with the weakness and incompetence of the Sultan's government. In particular, those who had been educated in the univer-

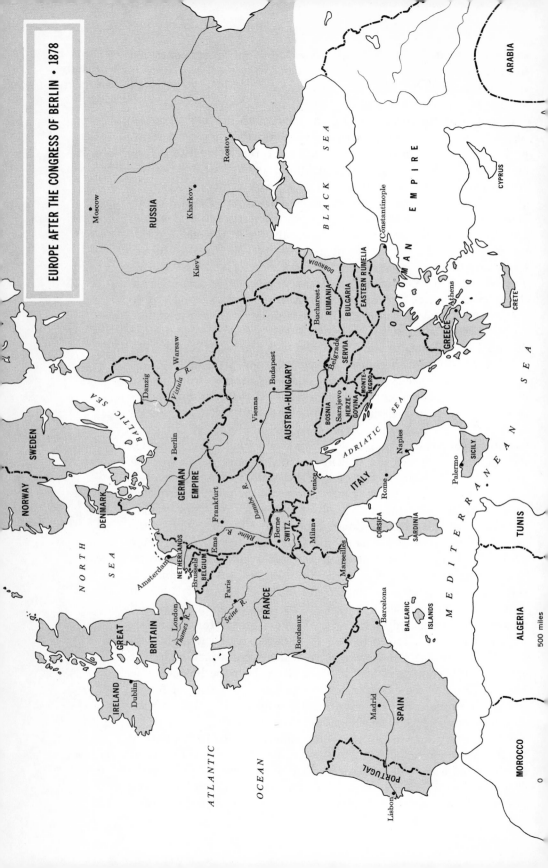

EUROPE AFTER THE CONGRESS OF BERLIN · 1878

ARABIA

CYPRUS

B L A C K   S E A

RUSSIA

Moscow

Kharkov

Kiev

Rostov

OTTOMAN EMPIRE

Constantinople

DOBRUDJA

Bucharest

RUMANIA

BULGARIA

EASTERN RUMELIA

Belgrade

SERVIA

MONTE-NEGRO

BOSNIA   Sarajevo

HERZE-GOVINA

GREECE

Athens

CRETE

Warsaw

Vistula R.

Danzig

BALTIC SEA

Berlin

GERMAN EMPIRE

Vienna

Budapest

AUSTRIA-HUNGARY

ADRIATIC SEA

Venice

Naples

SICILY

Palermo

SWEDEN

NORWAY

DENMARK

NORTH SEA

Frankfurt

Danube R.

Ems

Rhine R.

Berne   SWITZ.

Milan

Marseilles

ITALY

Rome

CORSICA

SARDINIA

M E D I T E R R A N E A N   S E A

TUNIS

Amsterdam

NETHERLANDS

Brussels

BELGIUM

Paris

Seine R.

FRANCE

Bordeaux

Barcelona

BALEARIC ISLANDS

ALGERIA

500 miles

GREAT BRITAIN

London

Thames R.

IRELAND

Dublin

ATLANTIC OCEAN

Madrid

SPAIN

PORTUGAL

Lisbon

MOROCCO

0

sities of England and France were becoming more and more convinced that their country should be rejuvenated by the introduction
of Western ideas of science, patriotism, and democracy. Organizing
themselves into a society known as the Young Turks, they forced
the Sultan in 1908 to establish constitutional government. The following year, when a reactionary movement set in, they deposed the
reigning Sultan, Abdul Hamid II, and placed on the throne his wit-
less brother, Mohammed V, as a titular sovereign. The real powers
of government were now entrusted to a grand vizier and ministers
responsible to an elected parliament. Unfortunately this revolution
did not mean increased liberty for the non-Turkish inhabitants of
the empire. Instead, the Young Turks launched a vigorous movement to Ottomanize all of the Christian subjects of the Sultan. At
the same time the disturbances preceding and accompanying the
revolution opened the way for still further dismemberment. In 1908
Austria annexed the provinces of Bosnia and Herzegovina, which
the Treaty of Berlin had allowed her merely to administer, and in
1911–1912 Italy made war upon Turkey for the conquest of
Tripoli.

3. THE NEW IMPERIALISM

Not long after the beginning of the nineteenth century the type
of imperialism fostered by the Commercial Revolution gradually
died out. There were few men any longer in public life who rose to
defend it; some even roundly condemned it on the ground that colonies were not worth what it cost to acquire and defend them. The
causes of this change in attitude are to be found in such factors as
the decline of mercantilism and the absorbing interest in internal development which accompanied the early stages of the Industrial Revolution. Following the decay of this early imperialism there was
a decided lull in the scramble for external possessions until about
1870, when expansionist activity was renewed on a more vigorous
and extensive scale. In addition to quantitative differences, the new
imperialism bore other striking contrasts with the old. Whereas the
struggle for empire during the Commercial Revolution had been
confined mainly to the Western Hemisphere and the tropical islands, the theaters of imperialism after 1870 were chiefly in Africa
and in Asia. The imperialism of mercantilist days had been carried
on largely to magnify the power and wealth of the state—to bring
bullion into the treasury—which would enable the government to
maintain armies and equip navies; the new imperialism operated for
the benefit of leading *citizens* of the mother country, to provide
them with markets for their goods and opportunities for investment
of their surplus capital. The raw materials most keenly desired by
the imperialists of earlier days had been gold and silver, tropical
products, and naval stores; the later imperialists paid scant regard to

The new imperial-
ism contrasted
with the old

any of these but greedily coveted territories rich in iron, copper, petroleum, manganese, and wheat. As a last difference, under the old imperialism large-scale emigration to the colonies had been generally discouraged, but a primary purpose of the new imperialism was to acquire colonies as homes for surplus inhabitants of the mother country.

Causes of the
revival of imper-
ialism after 1870

Undoubtedly the major factors responsible for the revival of imperialism after 1870 were to be found in the Second Industrial Revolution. The spread of industrialization to many other countries in addition to Great Britain produced an intense competition for markets and for new sources of raw materials. Despite the problem of finding outlets for surplus manufactured products, the governments of most countries eventually yielded to capitalist pressure for protective tariffs. The result was still higher production and a consequent greater demand for colonies as dumping grounds for articles the home market could not absorb. Under such conditions it became virtually impossible for the regime of international free trade, which had seemed to promise so much for the peace and prosperity of the world, to continue. As noted, some Continental countries adopted protective tariffs during the 1880's. The United States, also, was closing the door more and more tightly to foreign manufactures. Perhaps nothing did more to stimulate the imperialism of European powers than the fear that their accustomed markets in neighboring countries and in America would soon be lost. But not all of the motives for the new imperialism were economic. By 1870 or soon after, the population of a number of industrialized nations had begun to expand to uncomfortable limits; hence there was a desire of governments to acquire territories where surplus inhabitants might settle and still remain citizens and potential soldiers of the fatherland. Finally, the new imperialism was the product in considerable measure of nationalism and of the development of an extensive program of missionary activity by the churches of Europe and America.

The beginning of
the scramble for
African territory

If any one man could be called the father of the new imperialism, he was probably Leopold II, King of the Belgians. In 1876 Leopold took possession of the rich Congo River territory in central Africa (about ten times the size of Belgium) and held it practically as his personal domain until 1908, when he sold it for a stiff indemnity to the Belgian government. It was not long after the Belgian king had set the example that Great Britain and France took a deeper interest than they had ever shown before in the dismemberment of Africa. The former established a protectorate over Egypt about 1882 and subsequently took possession of the Egyptian Sudan, Rhodesia, Uganda, and British East Africa as colonies. In 1902 the British succeeded after a three-year war in conquering the Boer republics (the Orange Free State and the Transvaal), which were united in 1909 with the Cape Colony and Natal to form the self-governing dominion of South Africa. Designs of the French upon African territory

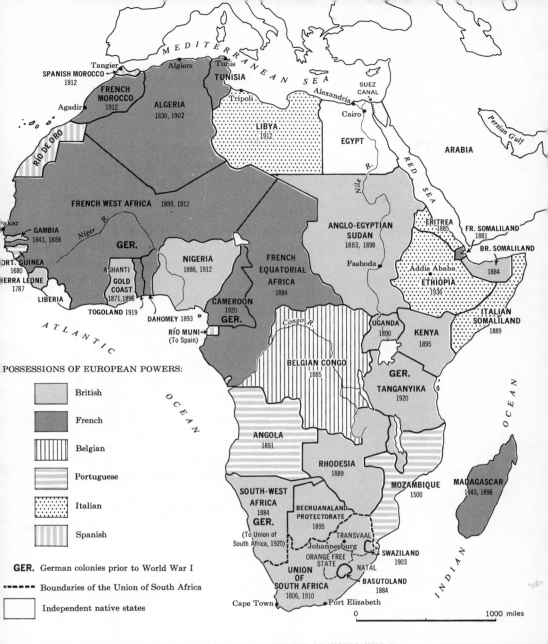

POSSESSIONS OF EUROPEAN POWERS:

British

French

Belgian

Portuguese

Italian

Spanish

GER. German colonies prior to World War I

------ Boundaries of the Union of South Africa

Independent native states

0   1000 miles

IMPERIALISM IN AFRICA TO THE EVE OF WORLD WAR II

were evidenced as early as 1830 when they established control over
a number of Algerian ports. By 1857 they had succeeded in conquering and annexing the remainder of Algeria. But the efforts of
the French to carve out an empire on the Dark Continent did not
really begin on an extensive scale until 1881. In that year they occupied Tunis and then gradually took possession of the Sahara, the
French Congo, French Guinea, Senegal, and Dahomey. By 1905
nearly all of the choicest territories in Africa had been monopolized
by the Belgians, the British, and the French.

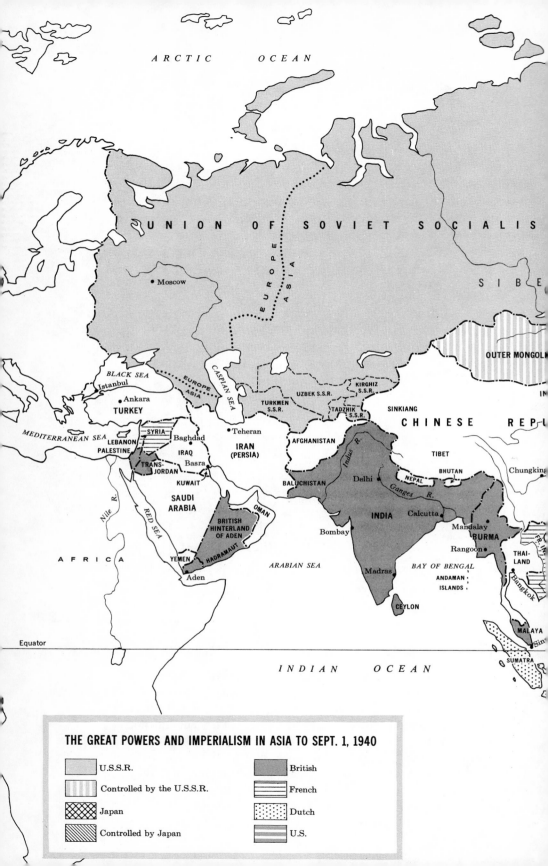

THE GREAT POWERS AND IMPERIALISM IN ASIA TO SEPT. 1, 1940

U.S.S.R.

Controlled by the U.S.S.R.

Japan

Controlled by Japan

British

French

Dutch

U.S.

ARCTIC   OCEAN

REPUBLICS

ALASKA

BERING SEA

SEA OF
OKHOTSK

A

MANCHUKUO

Amur R.

Harbin

GOLIA

Vladivostok

SEA OF JAPAN

Peiping

Tientsin

CHOSEN
(KOREA)

JAPAN

Tokyo

C

Yokohama

Osaka

Nanking

gtze R

Shanghai

Wenchow

E. CHINA SEA

Foochow

PACIFIC

Amoy

TAIWAN
(FORMOSA)

ton

Swatow

OCEAN

Hong Kong (Br.)

NAN

CHINA SEA

PHILIPPINE

Manila

ISLANDS

0   1000 miles along the equator

WAK

RNEO

CELEBES

MOLUCCAS
(SPICE ISLANDS)

NEW GUINEA

AUSTRALIA

The entry of
Germany and
Italy into the
African scramble

The entrance of Germany and Italy into the scramble for colonies in Africa was delayed by the complexity of domestic problems. Both nations had just completed long campaigns for unification and were still deeply involved in troubles with the papacy. Besides, the rulers of neither country were much interested in outlying possessions. Bismarck, for example, was ambitious to consolidate his empire at home and to hold the position of leadership which Germany had won in Continental European affairs. He once declared that the friendship of Great Britain was worth more to him than "twenty marshy colonies in Africa." [1] However, even Bismarck was eventually persuaded by merchants, industrialists, and shipping magnates to enter the race for African empire. In 1884 he proclaimed a protectorate over Southwest Africa and then took over in rapid succession German East Africa, the Kamerun, and Togoland. About 1888 the Italians decided that they also must have a share of what was left of Africa. They established a foothold in Somaliland on the eastern coast and then attempted to reduce the adjacent country of Abyssinia to a protectorate. The result was one of the most disastrous defeats ever suffered by a modern nation. The Italian forces were so badly shattered by the Abyssinians at Adowa in 1896 that Italy made no further attempts to conquer the Lion of Judah until 1935. Her only important acquisitions of African territory between 1896 and 1914 were Tripoli and Cyrenaica, which she conquered from Turkey in 1912 and combined under the new name of Libya.

Meanwhile European powers were beginning to stake out new claims for themselves on the continent of Asia. Long before 1870 a number of European nations had engaged in land-grabbing exploits in the Orient. As early as 1582 the Russians had crossed the Ural Mountains, and in less than a century they had reached the Pacific. In 1763, after eliminating the French as rivals for possession of India, the British had begun the subjugation and development of that country, most of which they converted into a possession of the crown in 1858. At the end of the so-called Opium War in 1842 Great Britain forced the Chinese to cede to her the island of Hong Kong. (The Opium War had grown out of a conflict between the ambitions of British traders and the efforts of a Chinese commissioner to curb the importation of opium.) A few years after the British acquisition of Hong Kong the French established a protectorate over Indochina. In 1858 Russia took possession of everything north of the Amur River and soon afterward founded the city of Vladivostok (Ruler of the East), also upon territory wrested from China. But it was not until about 1880 that the chief military and industrialized nations began to dream of carving the whole of Asia into colonies and spheres of influence. The richest prize of all, of course, was the Chinese empire with its 400,000,000 inhabitants and its area as large as that of Europe. Great Britain may be said to have

[1] W. O. Aydelotte, *Bismarck and British Colonial Policy*, p. 21.

initiated the process by annexing Burma in 1885. Ten years later occurred the first Sino-Japanese War (1894–1895), as a result of which Japan obtained the island of Formosa and the surrender of Chinese claims to Korea, which she eventually annexed and renamed Chosen. During the closing years of the nineteenth century several of the European powers that had recently protested against Japanese aggression proceeded to help themselves to additional slices of the Chinese melon. By 1898 the independence of China appeared doomed to extinction. It was commonly assumed by Europeans, at least, that the southeastern portion of the empire would fall to France as her sphere of influence, that Great Britain and Germany would divide the central portion, and that Russia and Japan would scramble for what was left in the north.

About the turn of the century, imperialism in China was checked temporarily by three extraordinary developments. The first and least important was the proclamation in 1899 of the Open Door policy by the United States. Although this policy was little more than an empty phrase so far as other governments were concerned, it undoubtedly raised the hopes of China that the United States would resent and possibly oppose the imperialist aggressions of other powers. Much more influential was a display of violent resistance by the Chinese themselves. In 1900 the Society of Harmonious Fists, commonly called the Boxers, organized a movement to oust the "foreign devils" from the country. Much property was destroyed, the legations in Peking were besieged, and hundreds of foreigners, including the German minister, were killed. Though supported by the Chinese government, the rebellion was finally suppressed by an expedition-

The Boxer Rebellion. The Chicu Mun Gate in Peking, just after the Boxers partially destroyed it.

ary force of British, Russians, Japanese, Germans, Frenchmen, and Americans. The third and most important cause of the temporary decline of imperialism in China was rivalry among the despoilers themselves. Several of the great powers became suspicious that their competitors were attempting to get more than their proper share of the booty. The distrust was especially keen among Great Britain, Russia, Germany, and Japan. In 1902 the British and the Japanese concluded an alliance to protect certain areas they hoped to develop against the encroachments of the Russians and the Germans. When, in 1904, it became evident that Russia intended to swallow Manchuria, the Japanese took up arms. The conflict ended in 1905 in a decisive victory for Japan. Russia was forced to surrender Port Arthur to her rival and to acknowledge Japanese supremacy in Korea. But these developments merely delayed the spoliation of China. In 1912 the same old imperialistic activities were revived when Great Britain assumed what virtually amounted to sovereign rights in Tibet. The following year Russia established a protectorate over the enormous province of Outer Mongolia, which the Soviet government still retains in a dependent status. Thus on the eve of World War I the independence of China was still very far from secure against the cupidity of nations professing to represent a superior level of culture.

SELECTED READINGS

· *Items so designated are available in paperbound editions.*

NATIONALISM

· Binkley, R. C., *Realism and Nationalism*, New York, 1935 (Torchbook). A stimulating account of the period 1852–1871.

Dawson, William, *The German Empire, 1867–1914, and the Unity Movement*, London, 1919, 2 vols. Masterly and complete.

· Eyck, Erich, *Bismarck and the German Empire*, London, 1950 (Norton Library). The best one-volume study of the Iron Chancellor.

Gewehr, W. M., *The Rise of Nationalism in the Balkans, 1800–1930*, New York, 1931. Brief but scholarly.

Griffith, G. O., *Mazzini, Prophet of Modern Europe*, New York, 1932.

Guérard, A. L., *Napoleon III*, New York, 1958. A laudatory account.

Hayes, C. J. H., *The Historical Evolution of Modern Nationalism*, New York, 1931.

——, *Essays on Nationalism*, New York, 1933.

· Kohn, Hans, *The Idea of Nationalism*, New York, 1944 (Macmillan). A perceptive analysis.

· ——, *Basic History of Modern Russia*, New York, 1957 (Anvil).

Lord, Robert, *The Origins of the War of 1870*, Cambridge, Mass., 1924. The beginnings of the Franco-Prussian war.

Noether, E. P., *Seeds of Italian Nationalism, 1700–1815*, New York, 1951.

Siegfried, A., *France, a Study in Nationality*, New Haven, 1930. An interesting interpretation.

Simpson, F. A., *The Rise of Louis Napoleon*, New York, 1925.

———, *Louis Napoleon and the Recovery of France, 1848–1856*, London, 1923.

Snyder, L. L., *From Bismarck to Hitler*, Williamsport, Pa., 1935. A thorough and scholarly account.

• ———, *Basic History of Modern Germany*, New York, 1957 (Anvil).

Thayer, William, *The Life and Times of Cavour*, Boston, 1914. Lively and thorough.

• Thompson, J. M., *Napoleon and the Second Empire*, Oxford, 1954 (Norton Library.

• Whyte, A. J., *The Evolution of Modern Italy*, Oxford, 1944 (Norton Library). A good introductory study.

IMPERIALISM

Angell, Norman, *The Great Illusion*, New York, 1933.

Carroll, E. M., *Germany and the Great Powers, 1866–1914*, New York, 1938.

Chubb, O. E., *20th Century China*, New York, 1964.

Clark, Grover, *The Balance Sheets of Imperialism*, New York, 1936. A good study of results.

• Feis, Herbert, *Europe, the World's Banker, 1870–1914*, New Haven, 1930 (Norton Library). An interesting economic analysis.

Fraser, H. F., *Foreign Trade and World Politics*, New York, 1926.

Harris, N. D., *Europe and Africa*, New York, 1927.

———, *Europe and the East*, New York, 1926.

Hoffman, Ross, *Great Britain and the German Trade Rivalry, 1875–1914*. Philadelphia, 1933. A perceptive account.

Hoskins, H. L., *European Imperialism in Africa*, New York, 1930.

Langer, W. L., *The Diplomacy of Imperialism*, New York, 1950. A standard work.

Moon, P. T., *Imperialism and World Politics*, New York, 1926.

Owen, D. E., *Imperialism and Nationalism in the Far East*, New York, 1929.

Somervell, D. C., *The British Empire*, London, 1948.

Tan, C. C., *The Boxer Catastrophe*, New York, 1955. The most recent scholarly account.

Willcox, W. B., *Star of Empire*, New York, 1950.

SOURCE MATERIALS

Bismarck, Otto von, *Bismarck, the Man and the Statesman, Written and Dictated by Himself*, London, 1899, 2 vols.

Renan, Ernest, *What Is a Nation?*

Ruskin, John, *The Crown of Wild Olive*.

Schurz, Carl, *Reminiscences*, pp. 163–65. Failure of the Frankfort Assembly.

Silone, Ignazio, *The Living Thoughts of Mazzini*, New York, 1929.

Tocqueville, Alexis de, *Recollections*, pp. 79–89, February Revolution in France, New York, 1949 (Meridian).

CHAPTER 8

The Maturing of Democracy
(1830-1914)

The will of the people . . . practically means the will of the
most numerous or the most active *part* of the people—the majority, or those who succeed in making themselves accepted as the
majority; the people, consequently, *may* desire to oppress a part
of their number; and precautions are as much needed against this
as against any other abuse of power. . . . "The tyranny of the
majority" is now generally included among the evils against which
society requires to be on its guard.
— John Stuart Mill, *On Liberty*

After the revolutions of 1830 many nations of the Western world
experienced a rebirth of democracy. In Europe, Great Britain took
the lead while France, Germany, and Italy lagged behind. But even
Spain, Turkey, and the Balkan kingdoms ultimately adopted at least
some of the forms of democratic rule. What most of these countries
were interested in was governmental or political democracy, exemplified by parliaments, universal manhood suffrage, and the cabinet
system. Not until after the beginning of the twentieth century was
there much concern with social or economic democracy.

The rebirth of
democracy

In order to understand the true meaning of democracy, we need
to consider its historical origins. As a political ideal, democracy had
its roots in the philosophy of Rousseau. It was Rousseau's doctrine
of the absolute sovereignty of the majority, together with his and
the other romanticists' deification of the common man, which more
than anything else gave us our ideal of the voice of the people as the
voice of God. Historically, political democracy meant, above all,
that the majority of the people should be entitled to speak for the
entire nation, and that in forming that majority the votes of all the
citizens should be equal. The machinery of the democratic state
therefore included universal suffrage and such provisions as fre-

The meaning of
political demo-
cracy

245

quent elections and adequate popular control over the officers of
government. In order that this machinery operate effectively, the
citizens must have the right to organize political parties and to
choose freely among them. Freedom of speech and freedom of the
press were also considered essential components of the democratic
ideal. But none of these rights was regarded as absolute and beyond
the control of the majority. To be sure, if they were destroyed entirely, democracy would cease to exist; but the majority could most
certainly limit them when there was a clear and immediate danger to
the public safety. Historically, all that democracy has really required is that all ideas unaccompanied by threat of violence be tolerated and that *peaceful* minorities be allowed to strive to become
the majority. The political ideal which affirms the *absolute* right of
the citizen to write or speak or live as he pleases, so long as he does
no actual harm to his neighbor, is not democracy but individualism,
or, as some would call it, liberalism.

I. THE EVOLUTION OF DEMOCRACY
IN GREAT BRITAIN

The evolution of democracy in Great Britain includes primarily
three different elements: the extension of the suffrage, the development of the cabinet system of government, and the growth of the
supremacy of the House of Commons. Prior to 1832 the system of
voting and representation in England was exceedingly undemocratic. Only in a very few boroughs could the majority of the citizens vote. In the rural areas the franchise was restricted to a mere
handful of the larger proprietors. Out of a total membership of
about 650 in the House of Commons no more than a third could be
said to have been elected in any proper sense. The rest were appointed by local magnates or selected by petty groups of the richest
property-holders or by members of favored guilds. In some cases
the positions were openly sold or offered for rent for a term of
years. To make matters worse, the distribution of seats had been
thrown out of balance by the shift of population to the industrial
centers of the north. While many of the new cities, such as Birmingham and Manchester, with more than 100,000 people in each,
were denied representation entirely, villages in the south which had
been almost depopulated continued to send as many as two and
three members to the House of Commons. One of these villages
(Old Sarum) was a deserted hill; another (Dunwich) had slipped
beneath the waves of the sea; yet both were still represented in Parliament, by that remarkable British capacity for preserving a fiction
long after the facts have disappeared.[1]

The undemocratic
character of the
British govern-
ment in the early
19th century

[1] The prize example of these "rotten boroughs" was the village of Bute in
Scotland. Here there was only one inhabitant left who was qualified to vote,
but the village retained its right to send a representative to Parliament. On

Interior of the House of Commons. The government and opposition members sit on opposite sides of this chamber. Those supporting the government, or cabinet, sit to the right of the Speaker, who occupies the canopied throne. Her Majesty's Loyal Opposition sits on the Speaker's left. The cabinet and the "shadow cabinet" of the opposition sit on the front benches.

Despite the smug assurance of the Duke of Wellington that the political system described above was "perfectly satisfactory," there was much agitation against it. Not only the common people but also members of the middle class were thoroughly dissatisfied with an arrangement which gave almost a monopoly of power to the landed aristocracy. Emboldened by the success of the July Revolution of 1830 in France, the British Whigs under the leadership of Lord John Russell and Earl Grey inaugurated a movement for electoral reform. Strong opposition and vigorous agitation forced Wellington to resign as Prime Minister. Earl Grey then formed a new ministry, and the famous Reform Bill of 1832 became a law. Though its provisions were much more moderate than many of the radicals would have liked, it was still a noteworthy gain. The bill enfranchised most of the adult males of the middle class and nearly all of the smaller landholders and tenant farmers; but the great masses of agricultural laborers and industrial workers in the cities were still excluded from the suffrage. The proportion of voters was increased from about 1 out of every 100 inhabitants to 1 out of 32. In addition, the bill provided for some sweeping reforms in representation. Villages with a population of less than 2000 were deprived of their right to elect representatives to the House of Commons, while towns of slightly larger size had their representation cut in half. The seats in the Commons thus set free were distributed among the great industrial cities of the north.

The movement for political reform

election day this solitary voter regularly appeared at the polling place, "moved and seconded his own nomination, put the question to the vote, and was unanimously elected" to a seat in the House of Commons.

The Reform Act of 1832 definitely established the supremacy of the middle class. In the elections that followed soon afterward, the Whigs, who now began to call themselves Liberals, captured a majority of seats in the House of Commons. The Tories, henceforth more commonly known as Conservatives, also began to bid for capitalist support. The result was a wave of parliamentary enactments distinctly favorable to bourgeois interests. One appropriated money to private societies for the maintenance of schools, to the end that the sons of the poor might be trained in the virtues of diligence. Another, the celebrated Poor Law of 1834, abolished "outdoor" relief, except for the sick and the aged, and provided that all able-bodied paupers be compelled to earn their keep in workhouses. This law was based upon the theory that poverty is a man's own fault, and that consequently the poor should be forced to work as a punishment for their shiftlessness. The crowning achievement of this period of bourgeois legislation was the repeal of the Corn Laws in 1846. The Corn Laws were a form of protective tariff for the benefit of the landowning class. As revised in 1822, they provided that no foreign grain might be imported unless the price of British wheat was at least 70s. per quarter (about $2.19 per bushel). If the price rose above that figure, wheat from foreign countries was allowed to be admitted under a heavy duty. The effect was to give a rich bounty to the British landowners and at the same time to keep the price of bread exceedingly high. For more than twenty years industrial capitalists had clamored for repeal of these tariffs, on the double ground that they necessitated the payment of higher wages and limited the sale of British manufactures in foreign markets. It was not, however, until 1846 that their efforts were successful. The repeal of the Corn Laws started Britain on the road to her free-trade policy, which was continued in force until after World War I.

None of these results of middle-class supremacy conferred much immediate benefit upon the proletariat. Hours in the factories were till unconscionably long; and, despite the rapid expansion of industry, periods of hard times still punctuated the rising prosperity. Moreover, Parliament was deaf to all the pleas of the lower classes for a share in the franchise. The great Liberal statesman, Lord John Russell, flatly declared that the reforms granted in 1832 were "final." In the face of such resistance as this, many urban workers decided that the only hope of relief was to strive for a complete democratization of the British government. Accordingly, they enlisted with great enthusiasm under the banner of Chartism, a movement organized in 1838 under the leadership of Feargus O'Connor and William Lovett. Chartism derived its name from its celebrated People's Charter, a program of six points. They included: (1) universal manhood suffrage; (2) equal electoral districts; (3) the secret ballot; (4) annual Parliaments; (5) abolition of property qualifications for members of the House of Commons; and (6) payment of salaries to members of Commons. Though some of the Chartists advocated violence, most of them confined their activities to mass demonstrations and to the drafting of petitions to be presented to Parliament. In 1848, under the stimulus of the February Revolution in France, the leaders prepared for a giant effort. A procession of 500,000 workers was to march to the Houses of Parliament for the purpose of presenting a monster petition and overawing the members into granting reforms. The ruling classes were badly frightened. The pugnacious old Duke of Wellington was again summoned to command the troops. In addition to the regular army, he was provided with a special force of 170,000 constables—one of whom was Napoleon's slippery nephew, soon to become Emperor of France. But on the day scheduled for the demonstration (April 10, 1848) there was a heavy downpour of rain. Instead of the 500,000 workers who were to march in the parade, only a tenth of that number appeared. When the petition was presented to Parliament, it was found to contain less than half of the vaunted 6,000,000 signatures, and some of these were fictitious.

Though Chartism ended in failure, the spirit it represented lived on. It is significant that all of the six points, with the single exception of the demand for annual Parliaments, have since been incorporated in the British constitution. In the years following the fiasco of 1848 the forces of democracy gradually recouped their strength and succeeded under the guidance of more practical leaders in achieving considerable progress. In 1858 they wrung from the Conservative government of Lord Derby the abolition of property qualifications for members of the House of Commons. By 1866 the democratic movement had gained such headway that the leaders of both parties were ready to compete with each other for popular support. The result was the Reform Act of 1867, maneuvered through Parliament by the Conservative Benjamin Disraeli when the old generation of Liberals refused to go along with William E. Gladstone in enacting the more moderate bill of the preceding year. The Reform Act of 1867 conferred the franchise upon all men in towns and cities who occupied separate dwellings, regardless of their value, and also upon all who occupied tenements with an annual rental of at least £10.

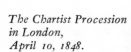

The Chartist Procession in London, April 10, 1848.

Since only the poorest of the industrial workers were unable to fulfill these conditions, the bulk of the proletariat automatically became entitled to vote. In 1884 the Liberals had a turn at extending the franchise. The Reform Act of that year, the third in the series of great electoral reform measures, was sponsored by Gladstone. Its main provision was to extend the voting requirements hitherto adopted for the cities and towns to the counties. The result was to enfranchise nearly all the agricultural laborers. All that remained was to give the suffrage to women, migratory laborers, and the very poor who could not meet any of the residence or property requirements previously set up. These final concessions were not made until 1918.

The second of the chief factors in the evolution of democracy in Great Britain was the development of the cabinet system. Without the growth of this system Britain might well have remained simply a limited monarchy. It must be understood that the cabinet is not merely a council of ministers but is the supreme organ of the government. It is a committee of Parliament, responsible to the House of Commons, which exercises in the name of the crown the supreme legislative and executive authority. Not only does it decide all questions of general policy, but it originates nearly all legislation; and, as long as it remains in office, it determines what bills shall be passed. If it is defeated in the House of Commons on a fundamental issue, it must either resign forthwith or "go to the country"—that is, dissolve Parliament and order a new election to test the opinion of the voters. In other words, the cabinet has full responsibility for the management of public affairs, subject only to the will of the people and to that of their representatives in the House of Commons. When Englishmen speak of "His (or Her) Majesty's Government," it is the cabinet they have in mind. When the party in power loses an election and thereby control of the House of Commons, the leader of the opposition party immediately forms a new cabinet. While awaiting his turn to become Prime Minister he receives a salary as leader of His (or Her) Majesty's Loyal Opposition.

As almost everyone knows, the cabinet system was the product of a slow evolution of precedent. No statute or great charter brought it into being, and to this day it rests solely upon custom. Its history goes back no farther than the Glorious Revolution. Not until after the supremacy of the king had been superseded by the supremacy of Parliament was the principle established that the chief ministers of the crown should be responsible to Parliament. Upon coming to the throne in 1689, William and Mary acceded to the demand that their choice of advisers should be satisfactory to the legislature. For a time they selected their ministers from both of the major parties, but as the need for harmonious relations with Parliament grew more urgent, they gradually restricted their choice to the party which held the majority. In this way the precedent was set that all the

The early evolu-
tion of the
cabinet system

chief ministers should possess the confidence of the dominant group in Parliament. But the cabinet was not yet a very powerful body. It did not become so until the reign of George I (1714–1727). George was a dull-witted prince from the German state of Hanover. Since he could neither speak nor understand the English language, he entrusted the whole work of governing to his ministers. He stayed away from meetings of the cabinet entirely and allowed that body to pass under the direction of Sir Robert Walpole. Though he persistently disclaimed the title, Walpole was the first Prime Minister in the modern sense. He was the first to perform the double function of head of the cabinet and leader of the majority party in the House of Commons. He established his headquarters at No. 10 Downing Street, which remains to this day the official residence of British prime ministers. When in 1742 he suffered defeat in the House of Commons, he resigned immediately, notwithstanding the fact that he still possessed the full confidence of the king.

Such was the early evolution of the cabinet system. Though most of the precedents upon which it rests had already been set by the middle of the eighteenth century, it still had a rocky road to travel. Some members of Parliament disliked the system, since it appeared to involve a partial surrender of Parliamentary supremacy. Not until about the middle of the nineteenth century was the cabinet system universally accepted or fully comprehended as an integral part of the British constitution. Its operation was first clearly described by Walter Bagehot in his *English Constitution*, published in 1867. In more recent years a number of new precedents were added, the most important of them being that when the cabinet is defeated in the House of Commons, the Prime Minister and his colleagues shall have the option of resigning immediately or of dissolving Parliament and appealing to the country in a great national referendum.

Scarcely less important in the evolution of political democracy in Great Britain was the emergence of the House of Commons as the more powerful branch of Parliament. Down to the eighteenth century the House of Lords, composed of hereditary peers and the princes of the church, enjoyed much greater dignity and influence. The first step toward the supremacy of the representative chamber was the establishment of the principle, during Walpole's ministry, that the cabinet should be responsible exclusively to the Commons. In the early nineteenth century the precedent became fixed that the lower house should have final authority over matters of finance. But still the Lords had enormous power. They had a veto over general legislation, which was limited only by the fear of public resentment and by the authority of the Prime Minister in an emergency to threaten the creation of new peers.[2] Furthermore, since the upper

[2] In Britain the monarch has the authority to elevate an unlimited number of men to the peerage. But since the crown acts only upon the advice of the Prime Minister, it is this official who has the actual power to create new

chamber was invariably a Tory stronghold, the favorite schemes of Liberal cabinets were often balked. Matters reached a crisis in 1909 when the Lords threw out the budget prepared by David Lloyd George, Chancellor of the Exchequer, and backed by the Asquith cabinet. The Prime Minister dissolved Parliament and appealed to the voters. Though his party won but a modest victory, he was convinced that the nation was on his side and began preparation of a bill to clip the wings of the House of Lords. The measure, known as the Parliament Act of 1911, was finally passed after a threat to swamp the upper house with a majority of Liberal peers. The Parliament Act provided that money bills should become laws one month after they had been passed by the House of Commons, whether the Lords approved them or not; in the case of other legislation the House of Lords was given only a suspensive veto: if ordinary bills were passed by the Commons in three consecutive sessions, they became laws at the end of two years, despite the opposition of the upper house. It is therefore accurate to say that the popularly elected branch of Parliament was henceforth, for all practical purposes, the real legislative body in Great Britain.[3]

2.   THE GROWTH OF DEMOCRACY IN FRANCE

The government of Louis Philippe, set up after the July Revolution of 1830, was a considerable improvement over that of his predecessor, Charles X, but it was still far from representative of the rule of the people. Louis Philippe took his cue from the bourgeoisie and systematically ignored the lower classes. Qualifications for the suffrage were indeed reduced, but still only 200,000 Frenchmen were entitled to vote. When leaders of the masses appealed to the Premier, François Guizot, for a liberalization of the franchise, he cynically replied, "Get rich." By 1848 the king and his ministers had so aroused the disgust of a large number of their subjects that the latter were ready to incur the risks of a new revolution to overthrow the monarchy.

The insignificant progress of democracy in France before 1848

The French revolution of 1848 is known as the February Revolution. Its causes were several. One was the demand of all but a small minority of the people for more democracy. Another was disgust with the corruption of Louis Philippe and his intimate circle; convinced, like Louis XV in an earlier day, that soon would come the deluge, they strove to enrich themselves as fast as possible at public expense. A third cause was discontent of Catholics with the apparent anticlerical bias of the Citizen King. He had appointed as his chief minister the Protestant Guizot and had allowed him to discriminate against Catholic schools. A fourth cause was the spread of

Causes of the Revolution of 1848

members of the House of Lords. If necessary, he could use this power to pack the upper house with his own followers.

[3] See p. 679. for later revision of the Parliament Act.

socialism through the ranks of the industrial proletariat. During the lean months of the depression which began in 1847, many of the workers had been converted to the socialism of Louis Blanc, with its scheme for national workshops to give employment and prosperity to all. But the February Revolution was also a product of nationalism, and in the end this factor was destined to dwarf all the others. As "king of the bourgeoisie" Louis Philippe had placed business above everything else. His chief capitalist supporters were determined that France should not become involved in any war lest their trade and investments be imperiled. Consequently they refused to yield to the clamor for intervention on behalf of the Poles against Russia or of the Italians against Austria. This angered patriotic Frenchmen who thirsted for national glory and for the restoration of France to a position of leadership among the powers of Europe.

By 1847 the government of Louis Philippe had alienated the sympathies of nearly all but a wealthy minority of its subjects. However, the most defiant opposition came from patriotic republicans **The overthrow of** and monarchists and from the socialists. In 1847 these groups organ- **Louis Philippe** ized a campaign of huge demonstrations designed to impress upon the king the need for reform. When the government took alarm and prohibited a demonstration scheduled for February 22, 1848, barricades were thrown up in the streets, and two days later Louis Philippe was forced to abdicate. A provisional government of republicans and socialists took over control of the state, and in April elections were held for a constituent assembly. The results of the voting were a disappointment to the socialists, for the reactionaries and middle-class parties had combined to protect the interests of private property. Angry and disillusioned, the radical workers of Paris again tore up the pavements. For three terrible June days there was bloody fighting in the slums of the capital. The insurrection was finally crushed, its leaders were shot, and 4000 of their followers were deported to the colonies. The way was now cleared for the bourgeois majority in the Constituent Assembly to complete a constitution for the Second Republic. The document as it finally emerged was copied in part from that of the United States. It contained a bill of rights and provided for universal manhood suffrage and for the separation of powers. There was to be a President elected by the people for a four-year term, and the people were also to choose a single-chambered legislative assembly. Having finished their work, the authors of the constitution set December 10, 1848, as the date for the election of the first President.

As we learned in a previous chapter, the outcome of this election was the choice of Louis Napoleon Bonaparte, nephew of Napoleon I, as President. Though he had ample powers as a constitutional ex- **Beginning of the** ecutive, he was not satisfied with a less grandiose title than that of **Third Republic** his famous uncle. Accordingly, in 1851, he made himself dictator and a year later Emperor of France. Thereafter most remnants of **253** democracy disappeared, though following the collapse of his Mexican venture the Emperor found it expedient to restore to the Assembly the power to initiate laws and to ratify or reject the budget. Further concessions might also have been made in time had it not been for the Franco-Prussian War. Napoleon III allowed himself to be dragged into this war, with disastrous results. Following the defeat of his armies in the Battle of Sedan (September 2, 1870) and his capture soon afterward, his government was overthrown by an uprising in Paris. A National Assembly was elected and a provisional republic set up which later came to be called the Third Republic.

The constitution of the Third Republic consisted of three organic laws adopted by the National Assembly in 1875. Though amendments and precedents effected some changes, its essential form continued until the dissolution of the Third Republic on July 9, 1940. The government established by this constitution was about as democratic as any in the world. There was a parliament, with a lower house elected by universal manhood suffrage, and a President chosen by parliament. The cardinal feature, however, was the cabinet system, copied in part from Great Britain. The most important powers of the government were exercised by a ministry responsible to parliament. The President was about the nearest approach to a nonentity that it would be possible to find among heads of state. His every official act had to be countersigned—which is to say, approved—by a member of the ministry. On the other hand, there were several important differences between the cabinet system in France and that in Great Britain. The French cabinet was responsible not only to the lower house or Chamber of Deputies but also to the Senate, which was elected indirectly by the people; the cabinet in Great Britain was responsible exclusively to the House of Commons. The most important difference consisted in the fact that the French Premier had no effective authority to dissolve parliament. This meant that members of parliament could overturn cabinets at will, with no risk of being forced to stand for reelection. If defeated on the floor of either house, the Premier and his colleagues had no alternative but to resign. With the possible exception of the multiplicity of parties, nothing contributed so much to the instability of the French system. Cabinets were sometimes unable to hold the support of a majority in parliament for more than a few weeks or even a few days. Although this instability was often deplored, it was really the product of a natural reaction of the French people against previous dictatorial regimes.

3. DEMOCRACY IN GERMANY, ITALY, AND THE SMALLER STATES

The Franco-Prussian War destroyed one empire and created another. We have seen that after Napoleon III was captured at Sedan, his government was overthrown in Paris and a provisional republic set up. Beyond the Rhine the great explosion of patriotic enthusiasm made it possible for Bismarck to absorb the south German states into the North German Confederation. Treaties negotiated during the course of the war stipulated that all of Germany should be united into a Hohenzollern empire. These agreements were given formal effect by an impressive ceremony staged in the palace of Louis XIV at Versailles on January 18, 1871, in which King William I of Prussia was invested with the title of German Emperor. Bismarck, now raised to the dignity of prince, became the first Imperial Chancellor. With no more than the necessary changes, the constitution of the North German Confederation was accepted as the constitution of the new Empire. The government thus created had only two features which could positively be considered democratic. First, there was universal manhood suffrage in national elections; second, there was a parliament with a lower house, or Reichstag, elected by popular vote. In other respects the system was well adapted to conservative rule. In place of the cabinet system, the Chancellor and the other ministers were responsible solely to the Emperor. The Emperor himself was no figurehead; he was vested with extensive authority over the army and navy, over foreign relations, and over the enactment and execution of the laws. Besides, he could declare war if the coasts or territory of the Empire were attacked, and as King of Prussia he controlled one-third of the votes in the upper house, or Bundesrat, of the imperial parliament.

Yet the government of the German Empire was not a complete autocracy. Although the Kaiser could influence the enactment of legislation, he had no veto power. All treaties he negotiated had to be approved by the Bundesrat, and he could get no money without the consent of the Reichstag. Indeed, the latter body was far from a mere debating society, as was so often alleged by Germany's enemies during World War I. On the contrary, it had law-making powers virtually the equivalent of those of the Bundesrat, and it was strong enough to extort concessions from several Chancellors.

It should be recognized, further, that the government of the German Empire was a constitutional government and not a party dictatorship like that of the Nazis in the twentieth century. The laws were extensive and complete and, for the most part, were strictly observed. Every little bureaucrat had a code to follow, and no one, not even the Emperor, was above the law. The chief defect of the system, aside from the absence of ministerial responsibility to parliament, was the inability of the representatives of the people to originate legislation. Their power was essentially negative: they could veto proposals of the Kaiser and his ministers, but they could rarely initiate measures of their own. Finally, it should be borne in mind that the German Empire was a federal state. Though it was described by President A. Lawrence Lowell of Harvard as a union

The establishment of the German Empire

Limitations on autocracy

The German Empire a constitutional government

comprising "a lion, a half-dozen foxes, and a score of mice," the division of powers made by the constitution was essentially the same as in the United States. That is, all powers not granted to the central government were reserved to the states. All of the states had control over their own forms of government, relations of church and state, public education, highways, and police. In addition, certain of the larger southern states were given special privileges when they entered the Empire. Even the enforcement of the laws was left primarily in the hands of the state governments, since the government of the Empire had no courts or police and no other machinery for applying the laws against individuals.

Anticlericalism
in Germany: the
Kulturkampf

Like the republic of France, the new German Empire also had trouble with the Catholic Church. The German anticlerical movement in the nineteenth century was given the pretentious name of *Kulturkampf*, or "struggle for civilization," and it was initiated by Bismarck, with some help from intellectual liberals, in 1872. Bismarck's motives were almost exclusively nationalistic. He was neither a skeptic nor a materialist but a staunch Lutheran. Nevertheless, he perceived in some Catholic activities a threat to the power and stability of the Empire he had just created. He resented, first of all, the support Catholic priests continued to give to the states'-rights movement in southern Germany and to the grievances of Alsatians and Poles. He was alarmed also by recent assertions of the authority of the Pope to intervene in secular matters and by the promulgation in 1870 of the dogma of papal infallibility. In addition, he was anxious to win the more ardent support of the bourgeois National Liberals in strengthening the foundations of the new Empire. For these reasons he resolved to deal such a blow to Catholic influence in Germany that it would never again be a factor in national or local politics. His weapons were a series of laws and decrees issued between 1872 and 1875. First, he induced the Reichstag to expel all the Jesuits from the country. Next, he forced through the Prussian Landtag the so-called May Laws, which placed theological seminaries under state control and permitted the government to regulate the appointment of bishops and priests. No one was allowed to be appointed to any position in the Church unless he was a German citizen and then only after a state examination. At the same time civil marriage was made compulsory, even though a religious ceremony had already been performed. In the enforcement of these measures, six of the ten Catholic bishops in Prussia were imprisoned, and hundreds of priests were driven from the country.

The failure of the
Kulturkampf

Although Bismarck won some of the chief battles of the *Kulturkampf*, he lost the war. The causes of his failure were several. First, he antagonized his progressive followers by refusing to consider their demands for ministerial responsibility. Second, the Catholic or Center party appealed so effectively on behalf of the persecuted clergy and adopted so enlightened an economic program that it grew into the largest political party in Germany. In the elections of

1874 it captured nearly a fourth of the seats in the Reichstag. Third, Bismarck was alarmed by the growth of socialism, and he was even more dismayed when the chief sponsors of this philosophy, the Social Democrats, formed an alliance with the Centrists. At their current rate of growth these two parties would soon have a majority in the Reichstag. In the hope of forestalling such a result, Bismarck gradually relaxed his persecution of the Catholics. Between 1878 and 1886 nearly all of the obnoxious legislation was repealed, and the *Kulturkampf* passed into the limbo of statesmen's blunders. The Catholic Church was thus restored practically to its former position in Germany.

As in Germany, the advancement of democracy in Italy was closely tied in with a nationalist movement for unification. By a series of revolutions, wars, and diplomatic maneuvers, this movement attained its goal, accomplished, as we have seen, between 1848 and 1871. As the revolutionary fervor of 1848 swept across the peninsula, one ruler after another granted reforms. Charles Albert, King of Sardinia, outdistanced all the others with his celebrated Fundamental Statute providing for civil liberties and a parliamentary form of government. Ultimately, this Statute became the constitution of a united Italy, as the various states were brought under the rule of the House of Savoy, the reigning dynasty of the Kingdom of Sardinia.

Democracy in
Italy

Some of the smaller states of central and west central Europe actually made more progress in democracy than did most of their large neighbors. For example, all had the cabinet system of government by the eve of World War I. In addition, universal manhood suffrage had been adopted in Switzerland, in Belgium, and in the Scandinavian countries. Norway and Denmark had taken the next logical step of extending the franchise to women. Belgium, Sweden, and Switzerland had adopted proportional representation, and Switzerland had made extensive use of the initiative and referendum. Proportional representation is a device for guaranteeing representation to minorities as well as to the majority. Each political party is awarded a number of representatives in the legislative body in direct proportion to its voting strength. The initiative and referendum are instruments of direct democracy. Under the initiative a certain percentage of the voters can initiate legislation and compel a legislature or parliament to take action upon it. The referendum is a device for submitting legislation to the people for their final approval or rejection. With the exception of proportional representation, which was adopted for limited use in local elections in Great Britain, none of these devices produced much appeal in the larger countries.

Democracy in the
smaller states

4. THE PERSISTENCE OF CONSERVATISM IN EASTERN EUROPE

To speak of democratic progress in the countries of eastern Europe before World War I would be to invite derision. In Russia, for

The period of
reform in Russia:
the emancipation
of the serfs

example, the government of the Tsarist empire in 1914 was not
much different from what it had been 100 years earlier. Nevertheless, Russian history after 1850 did witness some remarkable improvements. Though many of them were social and economic
rather than political, they did mean a better life for the common
people and can justifiably be considered here. The first great period
of reform was the reign of Alexander II (1855–1881). In his devotion to duty and in his interest in the welfare of his subjects, Alexander was undoubtedly one of the best of Russian Tsars. He had no
intention of surrendering despotic power, but he was at least determined to exercise that power in a benevolent fashion. His reforms were of three main types: economic, political, and educational. The first took the form of freeing the peasants from subjection to the nobles. A tiny beginning in this direction had already
been made by Alexander I (1801–1825) in the Baltic provinces, but
the vast majority of the Russian peasants remained in a condition of
serfdom. On March 3, 1861, the sixth anniversary of his accession to
the throne, Alexander II issued a decree that swept the whole system into the dustbin of history. The serfs were made free men, no
longer bound to the soil or obligated to work for the nobles. During
the next few years the government arranged to purchase from the
nobles portions of their estates to be turned over to the peasants.
These lands were not given to individuals, but were allotted to the
village communities or *mirs* to be parceled out for the use of their
members. The *mirs* were required to collect from their members
enough money to repay the government in installments over a period of forty-nine years for its purchase of the land. For this reason
it is sometimes said that Alexander liberated the peasants from the
nobles and made them serfs of the state. There is evidence, however,
in the increasing yield of the peasants' holdings that the *muzhik* had
not simply exchanged one master for another.

Alexander II's
political and
educational re-
forms

Of less significance but by no means unimportant were Alexander's political and educational reforms. In 1862 he abolished the judicial powers of the old bureaucracy and established a system of
courts on the Western model with professional judges and trial by
jury. In 1864 he accorded to each province the right to elect a
zemstvo, or provincial assembly, to be composed of the chief landowners and of delegates chosen by the townsfolk and peasants. The
zemstvos were to have authority to legislate on such matters as
roads, education, public health, and the care of the poor. Alexander's educational reforms consisted of government aid for the establishment of elementary schools and technical institutes, the relaxation of censorship, and the introduction of science into the curricula
of the universities. He planned much more in most of these directions than he was able to accomplish.

After 1865 Alexander II succumbed to reaction and proceeded to
nullify much of his earlier work as a benevolent prince. He sub-

jected the acts of the *zemstvos* to the veto of the imperial governors. He instilled new vigor into the secret police and restored the old methods of arbitrary punishment of persons accused of political crimes. He revived censorship and ordered the universities to purge their curricula of the sciences and to direct the attention of their students toward subjects less provocative of questioning and doubt. How can this reversal of attitude by the great "Liberating Tsar" be explained? In part it was an expression of disillusionment resulting from the indifference of many of the people his reforms were designed to help. Besides, some radical intellectuals and leaders of the masses in the cities scoffed at the Tsar's enlightened endeavors as mere palliatives. But weightier reasons for Alexander's change of heart were a series of attacks upon his life and the Polish revolt of 1863. Conservatives at his court took advantage of every opportunity to persuade him that these manifestations were the direct results of his liberal policies. They gradually convinced him that any further concession to rebellious elements would wreck the entire system. It would be difficult to conceive of advice more stupid. Instead of frightening malcontents into silence, the revival of the old methods of repression simply incited revolutionary activity on a wider scale than before. As the years passed, Alexander himself became aware that this was true and decided to return once more to the path of reform. But his conversion came too late. On the very day in 1881 when he signed a decree authorizing commissions to prepare new liberal plans, he was killed by a terrorist bomb.

The years that followed the death of Alexander II marked the flood tide of reaction against the entire policy of reform. The new Tsar, Alexander III (1881–1894), governed under the theory that Russia had nothing in common with western Europe, that her people had been nurtured on despotism and mystical piety for centuries and would be utterly lost without them. Such Western ideals as rationalism and individualism would undermine the childlike faith of the Russian masses and would plunge the nation into the dark abyss of anarchy and crime. In like manner, Western institutions of trial by jury, parliamentary government, and free education could never produce other than the most hideous fruits if planted in Russian soil. With such doctrines as these as his guiding principles, Alexander III enforced a regime of stern and vengeful repression. He curtailed in every way possible the powers of the *zemstvos*, increased the authority of the secret police, and even subjected the governments of the *mirs* to wealthy nobles selected by the state. These policies were continued, though in somewhat less rigorous form, by his son, Nicholas II, who was a very much weaker man. Both Tsars were ardent proponents of Russification and used it with a vengeance to strengthen their power. Russification was simply the more ruthless counterpart of similar nationalistic movements in various countries. Its purpose was to extend the language, religion, and culture of

Siberia under the Tsars: On the Long Road to Exile. Between 1823 and 1898, 700,000 criminals and "political undesirables" were exiled by the Tsar's government. In 1904 the practice was resumed but was suspended by the Bolsheviks in 1917. During the forced collectivization of agriculture in the 1930's the Soviet government established "corrective labor camps" in Siberia, and some 5,000,000 resisting peasants were sent there.

Great Russia, or Russia proper, over all of the subjects of the Tsar and thereby to simplify the problem of governing them. It was aimed most of all at the Poles, the Finns, and the Jews, since these were the nationalities considered most dangerous. Inevitably it resulted in some cruel oppression. The Finns were deprived of their constitution; the Poles were compelled to study their own literature in Russian translations; and high officials in the Tsar's government connived at *pogroms* against the Jews. In the worst of these mob attacks—the one at Kishinev in 1903—hundreds of Jews were butchered by fanatical Christians, goaded to a frenzy by foul propaganda.

The barbarities of Russification had much to do with the outbreak of the revolutionary movement of 1905. But there were also other underlying causes. The Industrial Revolution, which had been under way since about 1890, led to congestion in the cities, to the growth of a militant working class, and to a succession of sharp economic crises. A second cause, closely related to this, was the multiplication of radical parties. The oldest of these parties, if such it can be called, was made up of the nihilists. The nihilists were mainly intellectuals who were so thoroughly disgusted with Russian civilization that they believed the whole political and social structure should be razed to the ground. Glorifying reason and science, they professed to believe in nothing that rested upon faith. It was from this that their name was derived—from the Latin *nihil*, nothing. Whereas the nihilists were generally individualists, their successors were mainly collectivists. The most important of the collectivist

The revolutionary movement of 1905

groups were the anarchists—followers of Bakunin and later of Kropotkin and Tolstoi; [4] the Social Revolutionaries; and the Social Democrats. The last two differed from each other in a number of ways. The Social Revolutionaries were essentially a peasant party, though most of their leaders came from the intelligentsia. With the slogan, "the whole land to the whole people," they demanded that the great estates be broken up and distributed among the *mirs*. Many of them also advocated terrorism as a means of forcing the upper classes to grant their demands. By contrast, the Social Democrats were a Marxist group espousing the interests of the proletariat and urging united action by the masses in place of individual terrorism. In 1903 this party broke into two factions: the Bolsheviks, or majority, who believed that Russia was ready for a socialist revolution in the immediate future, and the Mensheviks, or minority, who contended that the completion of a bourgeois capitalist stage was a necessary condition for the establishment of socialism.

The growth and
decline of the
revolutionary
movement

The immediate cause of the revolutionary movement was the calamitous outcome of Russia's war with Japan. As reports came in telling how the armies of the Tsar had been routed time after time on the fighting front in Manchuria, it was impressed upon the Russian people as never before that the system of irresponsible tyranny under which they lived was rotten and incompetent. Members of the middle class, who had hitherto refrained from association with the revolutionists, now joined in the clamor for change. Radical workingmen organized strikes and held demonstrations in every important city. By the autumn of 1905 nearly the whole urban population had enlisted in a strike of protest. Merchants closed their stores, factory owners shut down their plants, lawyers refused to plead cases in court, and even valets and cooks deserted their wealthy employers. It was soon evident to the slow-witted Tsar that the government would have to yield. On October 30, he issued his famous October Manifesto pledging guaranties of individual liberties, promising a moderately liberal franchise for the election of a Duma, or national legislature, and affirming that henceforth no law would be valid unless it had the Duma's approval. This was the high-water mark of the revolutionary movement. During the next two years Nicholas issued a series of sweeping decrees which made the October Manifesto virtually a dead letter. In 1906 he deprived the Duma of control over foreign affairs, over the army and navy, and over constitutional questions, and abolished its power to punish the ministers by withholding approval of the budget. In 1907 he decreed that the Duma be elected indirectly on a class basis by a number of electoral colleges. Thereafter the legislative body was pretty well packed with obedient followers of the Tsar.

The reasons for this setback to the revolutionary movement are not hard to discover. In the first place, the army remained loyal to

[4] See Chapter 6.

its commander-in-chief. Consequently, after the termination of the war with Japan in 1905, the Tsar had an enormous body of troops who could be counted upon if necessary to decimate the ranks of the revolutionists. An even more important reason for the decline of the movement was the split in the ranks of the revolutionists themselves. After the issuance of the October Manifesto, large numbers of the bourgeoisie became frightened at threats of the radicals and declared their conviction that the revolution had gone far enough. Withdrawing their support altogether, they became known henceforth as Octobrists. The more liberal merchants and professional men, under the name of Constitutional Democrats, or Cadets, maintained that opposition should continue until the Tsar had been forced to establish a government modeled after that of Great Britain. This fatal division rendered the middle class politically impotent. Finally, disaffection appeared within the ranks of the proletariat. Many of the workers lost heart and deserted their radical leaders. Further attempts to employ the general strike as a weapon against the government ended in disaster.

But the Russian revolutionary movement of 1905 was not a total failure. The cruel vengeance taken by the bloodhounds of the Tsar convinced many people that their government was not a benevolent autocracy, as they had been led to believe, but a stubborn and brutal tyranny. The uprising revealed to the masses their principal mistakes and taught them what sources of strength they should rely upon for success in the future. Even a few of the concessions actually obtained were not completely wiped out. The Duma, for instance, was not abolished. It continued to serve as a means by which at least scattered remnants of opponents of reaction could make themselves heard. Significantly enough, the revolution of 1917 actually began in the Duma. But this was not all. The revolt of 1905 persuaded some of the more sagacious advisers of the Tsar that last-ditch conservatism was none too safe. The result was the enactment of a number of reforms designed to conciliate the troublesome classes. Among the most significant were the agrarian reforms sponsored by Premier Stolypin between 1906 and 1911. These included: (1) the transfer of 5,000,000 acres of crown lands to the peasants; (2) permission for the peasant to withdraw from the *mir* and set himself up as an independent farmer; and (3) cancellation of the remaining installments owed by the peasants for their land. Nor were the working classes altogether forgotten. Decrees were issued permitting the formation of labor unions, providing for a reduction of the working day (to not more than ten hours in most cases), and establishing sickness and accident insurance. Yet the hopes of some liberals that Russia was on the way to becoming a progressive nation on the Western model proved illusory. The Tsar remained stubbornly autocratic. Few of the peasants had enough money to buy the crown lands offered for purchase. In view of the rising cost of

living, the factory workers considered their modest gains insufficient and lapsed into a sullen passivity. A new revolutionary outbreak merely awaited the opportune moment.

5. MOVEMENTS FOR SOCIAL REFORM

Toward the end of the nineteenth century the idea gained ground
that political democracy was not enough. That cabinets should be
responsible to parliaments, and that every citizen should be entitled
to vote, seemed to be matters of comparatively small moment so
long as workers were at the mercy of a ruthlessly competitive industrial system. Consequently, in a number of countries, agitation
began for what is sometimes called economic democracy or the
welfare state. As generally defined, economic democracy implies
that all men shall have a substantially equal opportunity to make the
most of their latent abilities, and that no one shall suffer needlessly
from the misfortunes of life. It is not synonymous with the old liberal concept of equality before the law, which, as Anatole France
scornfully remarked, "forbids the rich man as well as the poor man
to sleep under bridges, to beg in the streets, and to steal bread."
Economic democracy means that little children shall not be herded
into factories to be exploited by selfish employers, that old people
shall not be thrown on the human scrap heap when the energy has
been drained from their bodies, and that workers shall not be compelled to bear the whole burden of industrial accidents, unemployment, and disease. In short, it involves a somewhat drastic modification of the ideal of laissez faire, which appeared to be so firmly entrenched during the second half of the nineteenth century.

The Russian Revolution of 1905. A painter's conception of a barricade in the
streets of Moscow.

THE MATURING
OF DEMOCRACY
(1830–1914)

Reasons for the
decline of
laissez faire

On the other hand, it should be remembered that the decline of laissez faire was not exclusively the result of the movement for economic democracy. The original form which modification of laissez faire often took on the Continent of Europe was protectionism, prompted by the desire of the rising industrial bourgeoisie to stave off competition from England. Protectionism was sometimes followed by outright subsidies, illustrated by the bounties given by the Italian and French governments to the silk industry and to various branches of agriculture. In such nations as Germany, Italy, and Russia the railroads and telegraph and telephone lines were either built by the state, or nationalized afterwards, primarily for purposes of military efficiency. In France the tobacco and match manufacturing industries were taken over by the state as sources of public revenue, and were operated as government monopolies. Even a great deal of the social legislation enacted in Continental countries was inspired by factors of nationalism, militarism, and paternalism. Governments desired to win the loyalty of all classes of their subjects and to make sure of a healthy supply of cannon fodder in time of war.

Bismarck's pro-
gram of social
legislation in
Germany

The first of the great powers to enact a comprehensive program of social legislation was Germany, under the guidance of her shrewd but domineering Chancellor, Prince von Bismarck. The reasons why Germany should have taken the lead are not difficult to fathom. Unlike Great Britain and France she had never been deeply affected by eighteenth-century liberalism; hence she had no strong traditions of individualism or laissez faire. While her political philosophers were persistently affirming the subjection of the individual to the state, her economists were preaching doctrines of national self-sufficiency and paternalism. Bismarck himself maintained that it was the duty of the state to regulate all functions of society in the national interest and to look after the weaker citizens, "that they may not be run over and trampled under foot on the highway of life." But he had other reasons also for engaging in what appeared to be a defense of the workers' rights. He was anxious to undermine the growing popularity of socialism by stealing a portion of its thunder. In a speech in the Reichstag he frankly avowed his purpose of insuring the workingman against sickness and old age so that "these gentlemen [the Social Democrats] will sound their bird call in vain." In addition, he had military purposes in mind. He was desirous of making the German proletarian a loyal soldier and of safeguarding his health in some measure from the debilitating effects of factory labor. Bismarck's program of social legislation was initiated in 1883–1884 with the adoption of laws insuring workmen against sickness and accidents. These acts were soon followed by others providing for rigid factory inspection, limiting the employment of women and children, fixing maximum hours of labor, establishing public employment agencies, and insuring workers against incapacity on account of old age. By 1890, when Bismarck was forced to retire,

Germany had adopted nearly all the elements, with the exception of unemployment insurance, in the pattern of social legislation that has since become familiar in the majority of Western nations.

Other countries on the Continent of Europe soon followed the German example. A French law of 1892 not only regulated the employment of women and children but prescribed a maximum day of ten hours for all workers; in 1905 this limit was reduced to nine hours. Other acts of the French parliament ensured free medical attendance for laborers and their families, accorded protection to the activities of labor unions, and compelled employers to compensate workers for injuries. The capstone of this system of legislation was added in 1910 with the passage of a law providing old-age pensions, not only for industrial workers, in accordance with the usual practice, but for domestic servants and farm laborers as well. The series of laws enacted in Italy was much the same, except for the absence of the provision regarding free medical attention. The Italian laws were supplemented, however, by an act of 1912 providing for nationalized life insurance and also by measures encouraging cooperative stores.

Social legislation in France and in Italy

Because of her strong individualist traditions, Great Britain lagged behind the other great powers in western Europe. To be sure, there had been some early progress, illustrated by laws prohibiting the employment of women and children in underground labor in the mines. But the British government adopted no extensive measures of social reform until after the rejuvenated Liberal party came into power in 1905. The old generation of Liberals under Gladstone, representing primarily the business classes, had been committed to principles of laissez faire. Their energies had been absorbed very largely in problems of political reform and of home rule for Ireland. But in 1898 Gladstone died, and control over his party passed into younger hands. Several of the new leaders—Herbert Asquith, David Lloyd George, John Morley, and Winston Churchill—were enthusiastic idealists, resolved to wage "implacable warfare" against misery and squalor. Upon coming to power in 1905 these ardent reformers determined to throw the old-fashioned doctrines of their party to the winds and transform Britannia into a paradise of fair treatment for all. During the years that followed, down to the beginning of World War I, they succeeded in having written into the statutes the most remarkable schedule of reform legislation since the Glorious Revolution. First came the Workmen's Compensation Act of 1906 and the Old Age Pensions law of 1908. Next came the Trade Boards Act of 1909, authorizing special commissions to fix the minimum pay for workers in sweatshops; three years later the principle that the government could establish minimum wages was extended to the coal-mining industry. In 1911 the Liberal cabinet procured the passage of the great National Insurance Act introducing a system of contributory insurance against sickness for all wage earners

Social reform in Britain, 1905–1914

and providing unemployment insurance for workers in the construction and building trades. The unemployment provisions of the Act applied to more than 2,000,000 workers in industries especially susceptible to the effects of depressions.

To this list of more conventional social reforms of the Liberal government must be added certain others for which there was almost no precedent. In 1909 the Liberal Parliament enacted a law permitting the clearance of slum areas and authorizing local authorities to provide respectable housing for the poor. This law set a precedent for an enormous amount of public housing construction in later years, especially in the period after 1918. Among the most significant of all the social reforms of the Liberal regime were certain provisions incorporated in the Lloyd George budget of 1909. In this remarkable fiscal program David Lloyd George proposed not only to increase the regular income taxes but to levy in addition a super-tax on the incomes of the rich. He recommended also that the government should confiscate 20 per cent of the unearned increment of land values, and that a heavy tax should be imposed on all undeveloped land appraised in excess of £ 50 per acre. The object of these measures was twofold: to raise revenue for old-age pensions and for various forms of social insurance and to level down great fortunes. It was hoped that the tax on unearned increment and on undeveloped lands would help to break the land monopoly of the richer nobles—of such magnates as the Duke of Westminster, who owned 600 acres in London, and the Marquess of Bute, who owned one-half of the area of Cardiff. Thrown out by the House of Lords, the Lloyd George budget was finally enacted into law after the Liberals were returned to power in the January election of 1910.

*New departures
in economic and
social reform*

SELECTED READINGS

Items so designated are available in paperbound editions.

DEMOCRACY

Brogan, D. W., *France under the Republic*, New York, 1940.
· Cole, G. D. H., and Postgate, R., *The British Common People, 1746–1946*, New York, 1947 (Barnes & Noble).
· Derry, J. W., *A Short History of Nineteenth-Century England*, New York, 1963 (Mentor).
Fife, R. H., *The German Empire between Two Wars*, New York, 1916.
Graham, Stephen, *Tsar of Freedom: The Life and Reign of Alexander II*, New Haven, 1935.
Hovell, M., *The Chartist Movement*, New York, 1925.
Karpovich, M., *Imperial Russia, 1801–1917*, New York, 1932. An excellent short treatise.
Lindsay, A. D., *The Essentials of Democracy*, Philadelphia, 1929.

——, *The Modern Democratic State*, New York, 1947.

· Maynard, John, *Russia in Flux*, New York, 1948 (Collier).

· Mayo, H. B., *An Introduction to Democratic Theory*, New York, 1960 (Oxford).

Neumann, Robert G., *European and Comparative Government*, New York, 1960.

· Pares, Bernard, *A History of Russia*, New York, 1928 (Vintage). A standard work.

Postgate, Raymond, *1848: Story of a Year*, London, 1955.

Reid, J. H. S., *The Origins of the British Labour Party*, Minneapolis, 1955.

Riasanovsky, N. V., *A Short History of Russia*, New York, 1963.

Robinson, G. T., *Rural Russia under the Old Regime*, New York, 1932.

Seymour, Charles, *Electoral Reforms in England, 1832–1885*, New Haven, 1915.

Somervell, D. C., *Disraeli and Gladstone*, New York, 1926.

· Thompson, J. M., *Louis Napoleon and the Second Empire*, New York, 1955 (Norton Library). A valuable summary based on scholarly works.

SOCIAL REFORM

Dawson, W. H., *Bismarck and State Socialism*, New York, 1891.

· Hobsbawm, E. J., *Primitive Rebels*, London, 1959 (Norton Library).

Keep, J. L. H., *The Rise of Social Democracy in Russia*, New York, 1963.

Laski, H. J., *The Rise of Liberalism*, New York, 1936. A critical study from a Marxist viewpoint.

Orth, S. P., *Socialism and Democracy in Europe*, New York, 1913.

Pipkin, C. W., *The Idea of Social Justice*, New York, 1928.

——, *Social Politics and Modern Democracies*, New York, 1931.

· Robertson, Priscilla, *Revolutions of 1848: A Social History*, Princeton, 1952 (Torchbook). A stimulating account written from the viewpoint of the people who lived at that time.

· Thompson, E. P., *The Making of the English Working Class*, New York, 1964 (Vintage).

Woodward, Ernest, *The Age of Reform, 1815–1870*, Oxford, 1938. Great Britain during the Age of Democracy.

CHAPTER 9

The Rise of the United States

I doubt too whether any other Convention we can obtain may be able to make a better Constitution. For when you assemble a number of men to have the advantage of their joint wisdom, you inevitably assemble with those men all their prejudices, their passions, their errors of opinion, their local interests, and their selfish views. From such an assembly can a perfect production be expected? It therefore astonishes me, Sir, to find this system approaching so near to perfection as it does . . .

—Benjamin Franklin, Speech to the
Constitutional Convention, 1787

The country we call the United States of America began its history as an appendage of Europe. Except for the American Indians and the slaves brought over from Africa, all of its earliest inhabitants were Europeans. They spoke European languages and brought with them European habits, ideas, and achievements. For years many of them thought of America as a place in which to pick up gold and silver or reap a rich harvest from tobacco or indigo plantations and then return to the Old World to live a life of ease and luxury. By the eighteenth century, however, Americans had begun to think of their country as unique, as a nation with a character and destiny of its own. As time went on, the sense of national independence increased, and more and more modifications were made in the European cultural pattern. American civilization was never divorced from its Old World origins, but it acquired an expanding number of unique characteristics as the nation grew and waxed in power. By 1914 America had surpassed most European countries in the achievement of a democratic society and was at least their equal in devotion to concepts of national greatness.

Relations with
Europe

1. THE YOUTH OF THE NATION

By the middle of the eighteenth century the thirteen British colonies in America, established between 1607 and 1682, had outgrown **269**

A New England Town Meeting. The town meeting, dating from the founding of the New England colonies, survives to this day as a major example of direct democracy in the United States.

their swaddling clothes. Their interests were no longer predominantly those of colonists. Their ideals and habits of thinking, in many cases, had diverged from those of the mother country. Their economic system had attained a maturity which gave them a feeling of self-reliance and an unwillingness to be tied any longer to the apron strings of British authority. The British, moreover, had abetted this self-reliance by following for a considerable period a policy of "salutary neglect" with respect to the colonies. Small wonder, therefore, that they should have drifted steadily toward independence. Many years after independence had been formally established, John Adams accurately appraised the situation when he wrote that "the revolution was effected before the war commenced. The revolution was in the minds and hearts of the people." [1]

The causes of the American Revolution are fairly well known. It should be recognized, at the outset, that the revolt in the American colonies was part of a great wave of revolution that swept over the Western world in the seventeenth and eighteenth centuries. Crests of this wave included also the Glorious Revolution of 1688–1689 in England and the French Revolution of 1789–1799, to say nothing of minor revolts in Holland, Austria, Poland, and Switzerland. None of these revolts was exclusively political. They reflected primarily the rise of a middle class against a dominant aristocracy that owed its privileges to an obsolete feudalism.

The American Revolution not an isolated phenomenon

But there were also specific causes peculiar to the American Revolution. Prominent among them was opposition to the mercantilist policies of the British government. These were exemplified by various acts for the regulation of trade and the raising of revenue passed by the British Parliament. The oldest were the Acts of Trade and Navigation (1651, 1660–1672), which prohibited trade between England and the colonies in other than English-owned or English-built ships, and forbade the exportation of certain "enumerated articles," such as tobacco, sugar, and cotton to any country except England. Much of the time enforcement of these acts remained rather lax and haphazard, but in 1764 Parliament attempted, by means of the so-called Sugar Act, to tighten up the system. The Sugar Act

Specific causes of the American Revolution: (1) Britain's mercantilist policies

[1] Letter to Mr. Niles, January 14, 1818.

reduced the tariff on certain imports but levied additional duties on sugar, wines, coffee, silks, and linens brought into the colonies from the French and Spanish West Indies. More important, it reformed the customs service and provided more stringent regulations for the collection of duties. New England merchants, who had grown accustomed to lax enforcement, were incensed because they saw their opportunities for bringing in sugar and molasses from the Spanish and French West Indies about to be cut off. A profitable trade had developed in such commodities, which could be sold in large quantities to distillers to be made into rum.

The Sugar Act of 1764 was designed not merely to regulate but also to increase revenues. The Seven Years' War, or French and Indian War as it was called in America, had left the British treasury burdened with debt. Since the war had benefited America, many British statesmen contended that the colonies should pay a share of the debt. Accordingly, George Grenville, Chancellor of the Exchequer, introduced into Parliament a number of colonial taxation measures culminating in the fateful Stamp Act of 1765. The Stamp Act required that revenue stamps costing from a half penny to twenty shillings be affixed to all newspapers, pamphlets, commercial bills, legal documents, and similar papers. The tax would not prove particularly burdensome, although merchants feared a heavy drain of hard money, since every bill of lading would be taxed and the stamps could be purchased only for specie. Nevertheless, the Act aroused a violent storm of opposition participated in by nearly all classes. Lawyers, bankers, land speculators, and newspapermen vented their wrath in denunciations and encouraged the boycotting of British goods. A mob surged through the crooked streets of Boston and gutted the mansion of Lieutenant-Governor Hutchinson. From New Hampshire to Georgia the Act was flouted, the agents who sold the stamps were driven from their offices, and the stamps themselves were publicly burned.

Of capital importance also as a cause of the Revolution was British interference with the interests of land-hungry colonists in the West. A Royal Proclamation of 1763 organized all territory acquired by Britain in the French and Indian War into four regions: Grenada (including several West Indian islands), East Florida, West Florida, and Quebec. More serious, it reserved all the western territory between the Alleghenies and the Mississippi, and between the Floridas and Quebec, for the exclusive use of the Indians. The colonists were forbidden to make any purchases or settlements whatever in that region. At a single stroke all the Western land claims that the colonies had cherished for years were wiped out. In 1774 Parliament sought to amend matters by passing a new Western land act, the so-called Quebec Act. This law was intended to correct certain errors in the Proclamation of 1763, but it seemed only to make matters worse by annexing all of the territory north of the Ohio River to

(5) conflicting
theories of
representation
and the sover-
eignty of Par-
liament

the Province of Quebec. The Western claims of four colonies in this region were thereby swept away.

Like all revolutions, the one that occurred in America between 1775 and 1781 had its ideological basis. For reasons not altogether clear, colonial political leaders drew their inspiration from the English philosophers of the seventeenth century rather than from those of their own time. It was Locke, Harrington, Milton, and to some extent Sir Edward Coke who provided Samuel Adams, Thomas Paine, and Thomas Jefferson with their sharpest intellectual weapons. From such sources they drew the idea that Englishmen, no matter where they might live, had fundamental rights on which the British government must not infringe. From such sources also came the doctrines of the state of nature, the social contract, the law of nature, no taxation without representation, and the right of revolution.

Most fundamental of all the ideological causes, perhaps, were the conflicting theories of representation and the sovereignty of Parliament. Colonial leaders maintained that a true representative must be an *actual* representative, that is, he must live in the district whose interests he purported to represent. For the British the prevailing theory was that of "virtual representation," which meant representation of classes rather than of geographical areas. According to this theory every aristocrat in the empire was *virtually* represented by the British nobility, and every commoner by the members of the House of Commons regardless of the location of the districts which happened to elect them. On the issue of the sovereignty of Parliament disagreement was equally sharp. Colonial philosophers, in accordance with seventeenth-century theory, rejected the doctrine of absolute sovereignty, whether of parliaments, kings, or anyone else. British constitutionalists had gradually evolved the theory that Parliament was legally omnipotent. As their noted leader, Sir William Blackstone, expressed it, "The power and jurisdiction of Parliament is so transcendent and absolute that it cannot be confined, either for causes or persons, within any bounds. . . . It can, in short, do every thing that is not naturally impossible." [2] This conception was given legal effect in 1766 with the enactment of the Declaratory Act asserting in sweeping terms the authority of Parliament to "make laws and statutes of sufficient force and validity to bind the colonies in all cases whatsoever."

The incidents which precipitated the actual outbreak of the American Revolution are too well known to require much comment. In March 1770, a company of British soldiers stationed in Boston for the protection of British officials became panicky and opened fire on a disorderly mob. When the smoke had cleared away, four Americans lay dead in the snow. This event was the

[2] *Commentaries*, Book I, Ch. II, 160–61.

celebrated Boston Massacre. In December 1773 occurred the Boston Tea Party, when a band of citizens disguised as Indians dumped tea into the harbor in resentment against a monopoly in that commodity which the British government had granted to the powerful East India Company. Britain retaliated by closing the port of Boston until the tea was paid for, by increasing the power of the king's subordinates in Massachusetts, and by ordering the transportation of political offenders to England for trial. General Gage, commander of the British garrison in Boston, was charged with the enforcement of these "Intolerable Acts," as the colonists called them. In the spring of 1775 he learned that Massachusetts patriots were collecting munitions at Concord. On the night of April 18 he sent a detachment of troops to confiscate them. But the patriots learned of the plan and made preparations to defeat it. When the British arrived in Lexington the next morning, they found a determined band of minutemen lined up across the common. In the resulting confusion and panic someone fired a shot. Soon the firing became general, and the Americans were dispersed, leaving eight of their number dead on the green. The British continued their march to Concord, but on the return to Boston they were assailed by minutemen from behind stone walls, trees, and houses. When the frightened detachment stumbled into Boston, it had lost 247 of its members in killed and wounded. The battles of Lexington and Concord marked the beginning of the Revolution.

The American Revolution had a multiple aspect. In the beginning it was a violent protest against the alleged tyrannies of the British government. Scarcely anyone thought as yet of independence, although some had visions of reorganizing the empire under a common sovereign, with autonomy for the various regions. In less than a year a demand for independence had become dominant, and a Declaration proclaiming that "these United Colonies are, and of right ought to be, free and independent states" was signed on July 4, 1776. But the Revolution also had something of the character of a political and social upheaval. In many states radicals like Samuel Adams and Thomas Paine had influence enough to accomplish far-reaching reforms. The new constitutions adopted in 1776 did not simply provide for a replacement of British by colonial rule. They deprived the governors of veto power, reduced their terms to one year, and subjected them to the supremacy of the legislature. In some states elaborate checks and balances were erected to prevent any form of despotism. Pennsylvania, Vermont, and Georgia went to the extent of establishing unicameral legislatures. That these political reforms would be accompanied by efforts in the direction of social reform was almost inevitable. A few states attacked the foundations of aristocracy—primogeniture, tithes, quit-rents, and entail. Others abolished their state churches or wiped out religious qualifications for holding office. Radical economic legislation was also

The political and social revolution

enacted. Several of the states confiscated crown lands and the princely estates of wealthy loyalists and divided them up among small farmers and war veterans. After the war the radicals in some states gained enough power to pass laws for the benefit of the debtor classes. These measures took the form of *stay* laws, suspending the payment of interest and principal on mortgages; *tender* laws, requiring the acceptance of land or produce at fixed prices as legal tender in payment of debts; and paper-money laws. In 1786 an armed rebellion for the benefit of debtors swept over central Massachusetts. Led by Daniel Shays, a former army captain, its objective was to prevent the courts from sitting and rendering judgments for the collection of debts. It was finally put down, but not until after an infuriated mob had threatened to besiege the state capitol.

The menace of economic radicalism combined with the weakness of both state and central governments led to a demand for drastic revisions in the national constitution. Since 1781 the colonies as a group had been governed under the Articles of Confederation. These, as their name implies, provided for a confederate, not a federal or centralized government. All power was derived from and could be exercised only through the state governments. The central authority could take no action against individuals. Its "great and radical vice," as Alexander Hamilton pointed out, was its power to legislate only for "states or governments in their corporate or collective capacities as contradistinguished from the individuals of which they consist." [3] This resulted in critical handicaps when it came to raising revenue or obtaining soldiers to serve in the army. By 1786 the threat to the security of property and to orderly and stable government was so serious that most of the conservative leaders of the country were ready for drastic changes. In September of that year a convention to consider problems of interstate commerce was convoked at Annapolis. But with only five states represented, Madison and Hamilton induced the delegates to issue a call for a new convention to assemble in May of the following year. The new convention was to deal with the much broader problem of revising the Articles of Confederation to render them "more adequate to the exigencies of the Union."

The convention of 1787 met in Philadelphia from May to September behind closed doors. Since the leading delegate, James Madison, kept copious notes, we have what seems to be a full and accurate record of what took place. From the outset the majority of the delegates showed an inclination to scrap the Articles of Confederation and write a new instrument. The Constitution which the convention finally produced bore few of the earmarks of a revision of the Articles. The new government was given a sphere of sovereign authority which the states were powerless to invade. The foundations of the system would rest in part on the people themselves, at least inso-

The movement for a new constitution

Adoption of the Constitution

[3] *Federalist* No. 15.

far as they chose the members of the House of Representatives and
participated in the selection of the Electoral College. A powerful
executive was created with authority to veto acts of Congress and to
use his own agents to enforce the laws. Provision was made also for
a federal judiciary, and at least some of the leaders of the convention intended that the Supreme Court should exercise the power of
judicial review, that is, nullify acts of Congress and of the state
legislatures allegedly in conflict with the Constitution. Finally, the
Constitution itself, and the laws and treaties made in pursuance
thereof, were declared to be the supreme law of the land. The
judges in every state were to be bound thereby, regardless of any
conflicting provisions in the state constitutions or laws.

The adoption of the Constitution of 1787 is regarded by some
writers as having accomplished a counterrevolution in the United
States. True it is that most of the delegates who took a prominent
part in the work of the convention were men of substance and conservative views. None of the old firebrands like Samuel Adams,
Patrick Henry, Thomas Paine, and John Hancock were present.
Thomas Jefferson was absent from the country as minister to
France. Of the delegates who attended, the majority seemed to
think of democracy as virtually synonymous with mob rule. Edmund Randolph declared that all the evils from which the country
had recently suffered were traceable to the "turbulence and follies
of democracy." James Madison thought the people were too prone
to impetuous and violent impulses ever to be trusted with unlimited
power. The primary aim of the fathers of our government was not
to enthrone the masses but to establish a *republic* that would promote stability and protect the rights of property against the leveling
tendencies of majorities. For this reason they adopted elaborate
checks and balances, devised the Electoral College for choosing the
President, created a powerful judiciary, and entrusted the selection
of senators to the legislatures of the several states. These principles
reflected a definite reaction against the extreme democracy of the
Revolutionary period and the years immediately following. No
longer dominant were the Revolutionary ideals of glorification of
the common people, defense of the rights of man, and distrust of the
courts and executive power. Nevertheless, the political system the
fathers created was liberal in comparison with other governments of
that time. The President at least was not a monarch, nor was the
Senate a chamber of nobles.

The first decades in the history of the United States under its new
Constitution were marked by phenomenal growth and expansion.
When the first census was taken in 1790, the country had a total
population of 3,900,000. By 1830 this had increased to 12,800,000
and by 1860 to 31,000,000. In 1790 the Union comprised 17 states
with a total area of 890,000 square miles. By 1830 there were 27
states with more than double the original area. By 1860 the number

*Counterrevolu-
tionary tenden-
cies*

*Growth of the
United States;
improvements in
transportation*

275

of states had increased to 33 and the area to more than three times its original size. The period was characterized also by feverish activity in the extension of transportation facilities. First came the era of canal building. New York State set the precedent by beginning the construction of the Erie Canal in 1817 to connect Lake Erie with the Hudson River. Completed in 1825, it reduced the cost of freight from Buffalo to New York from $120 a ton to $14. Soon other states caught the fever. Pennsylvania projected a canal—with horse railroads and inclined planes in the mountainous regions—to link Philadelphia with Pittsburgh. Some states plunged so deeply into the canal-construction business that they went bankrupt. But even if they had been financially successful, inland waterways would never have provided a complete transportation system. Facilities for land transportation were also necessary. Recognizing this need, Congress made a small appropriation in 1806 to start a great national road, eventually to extend from Cumberland, Maryland, to St. Louis. Renewed appropriations were made grudgingly, however, and the road was not finished for nearly fifty years. Many more miles of highways were built by the states but never enough to meet the need. In 1825 a movement was initiated which was destined to eclipse in importance all other transportation construction projects. This was the building of the Baltimore and Ohio Railroad, which was opened to horse-drawn railcar traffic in 1830. Throughout the remainder of the nineteenth century railway construction absorbed as large a proportion of the nation's resources and manpower as did any other economic activity.

The growth of
democracy

Growth and expansion in the early decades were not confined to material things. There was notable advancement also of democracy. From 1789 to 1801 the Federalists held the reins of power, representing the big landowners, the money power, and the conservatives generally. In the latter year the Democratic-Republicans gained control as a result of the election of Thomas Jefferson to the Presidency in 1800. This event is often referred to as the Jeffersonian Revolution, on the supposition that Jefferson was the champion of the masses and of the political power of the underprivileged. There is danger, however, in carrying this interpretation too far. In several respects Jefferson's ideas were far removed from democracy in its historic meaning. Instead of being a follower of Rousseau, he was a disciple of Locke. He believed that that government is best which governs least, and he strenuously opposed the unlimited sovereignty of the majority. His conception of an ideal political system was an aristocracy of "virtue and talent," in which respect for personal liberty would be the guiding principle. Furthermore, he compared the mobs of great cities to sores on the human body and despised the mass of industrial workers as "panders of vice, and the instruments by which the liberties of a country are generally overturned." [4]

[4] *Writings of Jefferson* (Washington ed.), I, 403.

Yet it cannot be denied that the Jeffersonian movement had a number of democratic objectives of cardinal importance. Its leaders were vigorous opponents of special privilege, whether of birth or of wealth. They worked for the repeal of primogeniture and entail and the abolition of established churches. They led the campaign for the addition of a Bill of Rights to the Federal Constitution and were almost exclusively responsible for its success. Although professing devotion to the principle of the separation of powers, they actually believed in the supremacy of the representatives of the people and viewed with abhorrence the attempts of the executive and judicial

Thomas Jefferson. Portrait by Thomas Sully of the great apostle of liberty at the age of 78.

branches to increase their power. Three of the most typical ideals of Jefferson himself were decentralized government, periodic revisions of constitutions and laws, and the importance of public education. He stressed the value of local government to the extent of advocating primary assemblies similar to the New England town meetings for the exercise of a large proportion of the public powers. He urged that constitutions and laws be submitted to the people for their approval or rejection every nineteen or twenty years, on the theory that no one generation has the right to bind its successors for the indefinite future. In later life he completed plans for an elaborate system of public education. There was to be free instruction for all children in the elementary schools, and scholarships were to be provided in district colleges and in the state university for a limited number of students selected on the basis of intelligence and achievement. By this method Jefferson sought to ensure opportunity for all, not simply for the well-born and the rich. The persons thus educated would be available for selection as natural aristocrats by enlightened citizens who had received enough knowledge to recognize good men when they saw them.

By the end of the War of 1812 the force of Jeffersonian Democracy was almost entirely spent. Any democratic movement of the future would have to proceed from different premises and rest upon new foundations. Not only did the war create new problems and divert men's interests from the need for reform, but the economic aspect of the country had undergone numerous changes. The common people in the cities had grown conscious of their political importance and had begun to demand privileges. More important, the dominance of the Old South, the stronghold of Jeffersonian Democracy, had passed into history. As a result of the Louisiana Purchase and the settlement of the Northwest Territory, a new frontier had come into existence. Life in the new areas was characterized by a rugged freedom and independence that left no room for snobbishness or class distinctions. In the struggle to survive, the things that counted most were hard work and sharp wits. Birth and education were of little value. As a consequence, a new democracy, which eventually found its leader in Andrew Jackson, rapidly crystallized around the major principle of equality. The Jacksonian Democrats considered all men politically equal, not merely in rights but in privileges. They therefore stood for universal manhood suffrage, for making all public offices elective, and for rotation in office. Since they considered one man as good as another, they rejected the idea that special knowledge or ability was required for government positions. They even threw open to ordinary citizens such offices as county surveyor and superintendent of schools. Paradoxically, the Jacksonian Democrats approved of a strong executive. They restored the veto power to the state governors, lengthened their terms of office, and acclaimed the President of the United States as the real representative of the people's will. The explanation seems to lie in the fact that they had come to regard legislative bodies as strongholds of "special interests."

2. THE REAL AMERICAN REVOLUTION

As was noted earlier, the term American Revolution applied to the events of 1775–1781 was partly a misnomer. The struggle of those years took the form chiefly of a war for independence. True, there were some indications of political and social upheaval, especially in the new state constitutions and in the measures against loyalists and aristocrats, but there was no displacement of classes such as occurred during the French Revolution or during the Russian Revolution of 1917. In the main, the same classes continued in power after independence as before. Men of substance like Robert and Gouverneur Morris, John Hancock, and Alexander Hamilton were no less active in the Revolution than financial failures like

Samuel Adams and Thomas Paine.

A much more radical transformation of American society took place in less than a century after independence had become a fact. The event that ushered in this transformation was the Civil War, or War of Secession, or War between the States, as it is variously called. Before the Civil War, as Charles A. Beard pointed out, the most powerful class in America was the Southern planter aristocracy. Nine of the sixteen Presidents were native Southerners. So were 14 of the 24 Secretaries of State, 15 of the 26 Speakers of the House, and 21 of the 35 Justices of the Supreme Court. The Democratic party, dominated generally by Southerners, polled a plurality of the popular vote in 8 of the 10 Presidential elections for which figures are available. Even in 1860 the combined vote of the two branches of the Democratic party exceeded that of the Republican candidate, Abraham Lincoln, by a margin of over 350,000. The war and the events that followed reversed the whole picture. A new class of ambitious, self-made men, composed in part of the free farmers of the West and in part of industrial capitalists in the Eastern cities, now captured the reins of power. The Southern aristocrats were saddled with disabilities, crippled economically, and deprived of all vestiges of political authority. During the turbulent aftermath of the war, bold enterprisers in the North took advantage of a rich harvest of opportunities in land speculation, railroad building, and exploitation of mineral resources. They also made the most of their political power to strengthen their hold upon the government and to use it to enhance their economic interests.

The upheaval wrought by the Civil War

The most obvious cause of the frightful conflict between North and South that raged from 1861 to 1865 was slavery. The first Negro slaves had been brought to Virginia from Africa in 1619. For nearly two centuries thereafter the number increased slowly, and the problem of slavery did not assume serious proportions. By the end of the eighteenth century many Southerners themselves had come to look upon human bondage as undesirable and longed for its early extinction. Increasing numbers of them provided in their wills for the liberation of their slaves and contributed money to various projects for returning the Negroes to Africa. But in 1793 the tables were completely turned by the invention of the cotton gin. The production of cotton was changed overnight from a depressed activity with a doubtful future into a tremendously profitable enterprise. The total output grew from 4000 bales in 1790 to 175,000 in 1810 and 4,000,000 in 1860. In a very real sense Cotton was made King, and the plantation system with its accompaniment of slavery was firmly fixed in the South.

Causes of the Civil War: (1) slavery

Yet it would be a mistake to suppose that the war grew out of an attempt by the North to coerce the South into abandoning slavery. Until virtually the eve of the struggle sentiment among Northerners was far from unanimous in support of abolition. Abolitionists were commonly regarded as fanatics and disturbers of the peace and were

(2) the increasing inequality of North and South

279

sometimes brutally mistreated for their activities. In 1835 an infuriated crowd attacked William Lloyd Garrison, tied a rope around his
neck, and dragged him through the streets of Boston. Two years
later a frenzied mob in Illinois lynched the Abolitionist editor,
Elijah P. Lovejoy. What most Northerners were chiefly concerned
about was the extension of slavery into the territories. They were
willing to tolerate its continued existence in the South, but they resented its intrusion into the Louisiana Purchase or into the regions
of the Southwest conquered from Mexico in 1848. Such areas they
hoped to organize into free states to be settled by land-hungry
migrants from New England and the Middle Atlantic region. Perhaps the South would have tolerated such hopes had the two sections remained substantially equal in power and influence. But such
was far from the case. Although North and South each had the same
number of states as late as 1840, they differed widely in population.
The inhabitants of the North numbered 9,728,000 and those of the
South 7,344,000. This gave to the North a total of 135 seats in the
House of Representatives compared with only 87 for the South.
John C. Calhoun complained that on account of this disparity in
numbers, the North would have a perpetual majority in the Electoral College and could therefore prevent a Southerner from ever
being chosen President.

As the tides of history moved closer to armed conflict, sectional
antagonism loomed ever larger as the real cause of the Civil War.
The South was agricultural, the North increasingly industrial. As a
producer of raw materials for export, the former opposed protective tariffs since they would increase the costs of imports. The latter
saw in protectionism an indispensable device to enable its new industries to maintain themselves against foreign competition. From
the viewpoint of the North a strong central government was necessary to provide internal improvements and to maintain the order
and stability essential to the growth of prosperity. Northern statesmen therefore contended that secession and nullification were
illegal, that the central government derived its authority from the
whole body of the people, and that the Union was older than the
states. Deeply conscious of the unique character of their institutions, Southern leaders hoped to keep the activities of the central
government down to a minimum. They insisted that sovereignty
rested with the separate states, that the states had created the Union,
and that the federal government was merely their agent. Since each
state had entered the Union of its own volition, it was free to withdraw therefrom whenever it saw fit. It was free also to nullify any
act of the central government which conflicted with its own interests. With the passage of time issues of sectionalism and states' rights
became more and more closely linked with the issue of slavery. It
seemed to Southerners that the only way they could defend the interests of their section was to insist upon the right to carry slavery

(3) sectional
antagonisms

280

into all the new territories in the hope that they might organize at least some of them as slave states and thereby redress the balance be- tween North and South. Acceptance of this issue by Northerners as fundamental was exemplified by the organization of the Free Soil party in 1848 with its cardinal objective of excluding slavery from the territories. It was exemplified also by a bloody war in Kansas in 1854–1856 between antislavery immigrants from New England and proslavery partisans who had crossed over from Missouri.

In 1857 the South rejoiced in what seemed a great victory for its contention that slavery could not be outlawed in territories subject to the federal government. On March 6 of that year the Supreme (4) the Dred Court, speaking through Chief Justice Taney, issued its decision in Scott decision the famous case of Scott v. Sandford. Dred Scott was a slave owned by a surgeon in the United States Army. His master had taken him from Missouri to Illinois, thence to Minnesota Territory, where slavery had been forbidden by the Missouri Compromise, and finally back to Missouri. There he sued for his freedom on the basis of having twice been a resident on free soil. The Supreme Court rejected his plea on the ground that the Missouri Compromise was unconstitutional. Congress had no right to prohibit slavery in the territories, for this would deprive Southerners who might wish to go there of their property without due process. The Chief Justice also declared that no Negro, whether bond or free, had a right to sue in the federal courts. Negroes were not citizens of the United States, and no law of Congress or act of a state legislature could give them that status. When the Constitution was adopted, they were considered as subordinate and inferior beings. It was never the intention of the framers of that instrument that they should enjoy an equality of rights and privileges with members of the Caucasian race. The Chief Justice seems to have been actuated by noble motives. He hoped that a definitive answer from the Supreme Court would settle the question of slavery in the territories, once and for all, and thereby avert civil war. Northerners, however, almost to a man condemned the decision. They admitted the possibility that it might be good constitutional law, but they declared that there was a higher law than the Constitution, and many of them stood ready to uphold that law by force. Instead of averting a civil war, the Dred Scott decision did almost as much as any other factor to make such a war inevitable.

The immediate cause of the outbreak of armed conflict was the election of Abraham Lincoln to the Presidency in 1860. Lincoln was the candidate of the Republican party, founded six years earlier for (5) the election of the express purpose of opposing the extension of slavery. In 1856 it Lincoln had nominated John C. Frémont for President and campaigned on the slogan "Free soil, free speech, and Frémont." Four years later it adopted a broad platform designed to appeal to almost everybody in the North but the radical Abolitionists. It promised internal improvements, high tariffs for the benefit of industry, and a quarter-section of free public land for settlers in the Western territories. On the slavery question it took the clear-cut position of no interference with the institution in the Southern states but absolute exclusion from the territories. Despite the moderation of its platform on the slavery issue, the triumph of the Republican party in the election of 1860 was regarded by the South as almost the equivalent of a declaration of war. The candidate of the party was no Abolitionist; indeed, he had gone so far as to declare himself in favor of a Constitutional amendment protecting slavery in the South. But he had also asserted, just two years before his election, that the nation could not endure "half slave and half free," and he continued his denunciation of the Dred Scott decision, which the South regarded as offering almost the only hope of restoring the balance between the two sections. Without such a balance it would be forever impossible to prevent the North from imposing its costly system of tariffs and internal improvements upon an agrarian South which had no desire for such things.

As soon as it was certain that Lincoln had been elected, South Carolina seceded from the Union. The movement spread like a madness, and more and more states announced their withdrawal. On February 8, 1861, delegates from seven seceded states met at Montgomery, Alabama, and established the Confederate States of America. Jefferson Davis was chosen President and Alexander H. Stephens Vice-President. A month later a new constitution was adopted; it resembled the Constitution of the United States with a few notable exceptions. The Confederate Constitution limited the President to a single term of six years. It expressly recognized and protected Negro slavery. It gave to Congress the power to appropriate money only upon the specific request of the President. It authorized the President to veto separate items in appropriation bills. It granted to members of the Cabinet the privilege of holding seats in Congress and participating in the discussions. In throwing off their allegiance to the United States and establishing a new government, Southern statesmen contended that they were doing nothing more than exercising the right vouchsafed in the Declaration of Independence to "alter or abolish" a form of government whenever it becomes destructive of "life, liberty, and the pursuit of happiness." To this the North replied, through President Lincoln, that the right of revolution referred to in the Declaration of Independence applied only to tyrannical governments. There could be no right to destroy the freest and most democratic government on earth.

The Civil War followed its tragic course through four horrible years. It began with the attack on Fort Sumter on April 12, 1861, and ended with Robert E. Lee's surrender at Appomattox Court House on April 9, 1865. From the outset the North had decided advantages, with a population of 22,000,000 compared with only

Establishment of the Confederacy

The military history of the war

282

9,000,000 for the Confederacy, and vastly greater financial resources. The North also had a navy, which the South lacked, and a
much more diversified and highly developed economic structure.
Nearly all the manufacturing establishments were concentrated in
the North, while the South was not even self-sufficient in food supplies. On the other hand, the Confederacy had a military tradition, a
coast line so long that it almost precluded a blockade, and the even
more positive advantage of fighting on its own territory. Its leaders
could easily persuade the people that all they needed to do was to
hold on until the North became weary and abandoned the struggle.
During the first two years the prospects of the South seemed bright.
Its armies managed to win or at least to stave off defeat in most of
the battles, and possibilities of foreign aid were particularly encouraging. But a turning point came in 1862. In September of that
year General Lee, hopeful of capturing the railroad bridge at Har-
risburg and cutting the Union in two, marched a powerful army
across the Potomac. General George B. McClellan, with a Union
force twice as large, advanced to meet him. The two armies clashed
at Antietam Creek in Maryland. Although not decisively beaten,
Lee's troops were sufficiently exhausted that they withdrew across
the Potomac. Had they succeeded in attaining their objective, they
might well have gone on to capture Philadelphia and probably New
York. Lee made one further attempt to invade the North in July
1863, but was again forced to retreat after being checked by the
forces of General Meade at Gettysburg. After Antietam the fortunes of the Confederacy steadily waned. The prospects of Foreign
assistance faded into oblivion, and Lincoln took advantage of the
more favorable turn of events to proclaim the liberation of the
slaves in all states and portions of states still in rebellion against the

*Lincoln and Staff Officers of General McClellan on the Eve of the Battle of
Antietam, 1862.* From a photograph by Mathew Brady in the National Archives, Washington, D.C.

Union. The Emancipation Proclamation transformed the Civil War into a crusade, and the crusading fervor helped to guarantee victory for the North.

The results of the Civil War can only be described as climactic. More than 200,000 men were killed in battle or died of wounds, and 413,000 others died of disease, accidents, and other causes. Many Abolitionists doubtless considered this holocaust of lives justifiable, for slavery was permanently destroyed by the addition of the Thirteenth Amendment to the Constitution just before the war ended. Later the Fourteenth Amendment conferred citizenship upon the liberated Negroes, and the Fifteenth forbade the denial of suffrage to them on account of their race, color, or previous condition of servitude. But the Civil War also had other effects. It left the South prostrate and hagridden by fears and prejudices and incapable for years of taking any part in the democratic evolution of the country. Southerners who had participated in the rebellion were deprived by Congress of the privilege of voting or of holding office, with the result that several of the former Confederate states passed under the control of illiterate Negroes and "carpetbag" politicians who had come down from the North. The Fourteenth Amendment not only bestowed citizenship upon the former slaves, but it contained a provision of tremendous significance for the economic development of the country. The provision referred to forbade any state to "deprive any person of life, liberty, or property without due process of law." Representatives of big business contended that the word "person" in this provision included *corporations* as well as individuals. By 1886 the Supreme Court had come to accept this contention. The result was to give an enormous stimulus to the growth and expansion of corporations, for it made them virtually immune from regulation for several decades. Almost any act of a state legislature prescribing maximum hours or minimum wages could be attacked as depriving corporations of their property without due process. Scarcely anything did more to further the economic revolution in the United States that stemmed from the Civil War.

3. THE RETURN TO REFORM

The Civil War and the antecedent controversy over slavery and states' rights sealed the doom of the Jacksonian Revolution. After 1840 democratic progress and even interest in democracy were relatively slight. Although often acclaimed as a struggle for freedom and equality, the Civil War ushered in a period of frenzied dollar-chasing and crude exploitation which Mark Twain aptly called the Gilded Age. Until about 1890 the popular attitude was to look upon the natural wealth of America as a Great Barbecue to be shared by everyone with ambition enough to elbow his way to the front. The prevailing economic philosophy was that of laissez faire and free competition, or what later came to be known as rugged individualism. Poverty was considered a badge of shiftlessness and wealth a sure sign of virtue. Economic competition was regarded as the counterpart of the struggle for existence and survival of the fittest in the biological sphere. The more ruthless the competition the better, in order to ensure the prompt weeding out of the weak and incompetent. That the prevalence of such doctrines was not favorable to movements for the benefit of the unprivileged masses should be readily apparent.

Nevertheless, such movements did eventually get under way, and by the 1890's several had attained a vigorous growth. Though all had their beginnings as vehicles of class discontent, most of them came in time to be worthy successors of Jeffersonian and Jacksonian Democracy. Their leaders fought for what they considered the birthright of the great mass of citizens. The first of the post-Civil War movements of consequence was the Greenback movement of the 1870's and 1880's. Primarily an expression of the discontent of debt-ridden farmers, it also had the support of the economist Henry C. Carey and the industrialist Peter Cooper, who became the candidate of the Independent National (Greenback) party for President in 1876. The cardinal aim of the movement was to establish what is now called a managed currency. That is, the government by issuing greenbacks would expand the supply of currency to keep pace with the growth of population and the economic development of the country. Much was made of the claim that money in circulation had shrunk from $58 per capita in 1865 to $17 in 1876. This shrinkage, it was argued, had meant severe hardship for debtors and for farmers especially, who had borrowed money to buy land at inflated prices during or soon after the Civil War. What they needed was an increase in the volume of money in circulation, which would produce a rise in prices of the things they had to sell and thereby enable them to pay off their mortgages. But the Greenbackers also had other objectives. They advocated income taxes and the restriction of sales of public lands to actual settlers. In 1888, hoping to win the support of organized labor, they extended their platform to include demands for government ownership of railroads and telegraphs, woman suffrage, and the direct election of United States Senators.

A broader and more virile movement than Greenbackism was the Populist movement of the 1890's. Again the most substantial support came from the farmers. Better prices for agricultural commodities in the late 1880's had allayed the demand for inflation of the currency, but it flared up again in the 1890's as depression reared its ugly head. This time it took the form of agitation for the coinage of silver in the ratio of 16 for silver to 1 of gold. The purpose would be the same: to increase prices of food and raw commodities, which had sunk to abnormal levels, and thereby enable producers to pay their debts. The coinage of silver would also have the advantage of appealing to Western miners as well as to the farmers of the West and South. In the campaign of 1892 the Populists nominated James B. Weaver of Iowa for President, on a platform which advocated a graduated income tax, postal savings banks, government ownership of railroads and telegraph and telephone lines, direct election of United States Senators, and a single term for the President. General Weaver polled a popular vote of over 1,000,000 and the electoral votes of four states. Four years later the Populists repeated their platform, with a few minor additions. In the meantime, free silverites had captured control of the Democratic party and had nominated for President a facile young orator from Nebraska, William J. Bryan, whose speech denouncing attempts to "crucify mankind upon a cross of gold" had swept the convention off its feet. Since the Democratic convention wrote into its platform nearly everything that the Populists stood for, the latter had no alternative but to endorse Bryan as their candidate. The campaign that followed was one of the most exciting in American history. The Populists were denounced as atheists and communists and Bryan as a dangerous demagogue who was nothing but their instrument. The election resulted in a victory for the Republican candidate, William McKinley, with 7,100,000 votes to 6,500,000 for Bryan.

The decline of
Populism and rise
of Progressivism

The election of 1896 marked the high tide of the Populist movement. The party nominated candidates in 1900, but the old fire and fervor were gone. Several factors were responsible. Failure of the wheat crop in India in 1896 was followed by a short European crop in 1897. American farmers who had grain to export benefited from the higher prices. More important were the discovery of rich gold resources in the Klondike and in South Africa and the development of the cyanide process for extracting gold from low-content ores. As a result, the world production of the yellow metal more than doubled in a few years. Prosperity returned, and the silver advocates could no longer make the valid claim that the supply of gold was insufficient to provide for the currency needs of the country. Yet it was too much to expect that the idealism generated by the Greenback and Populist movements would completely die out. In the early years of the twentieth century it rose phoenix-like from the ashes of defeat and gained sufficient momentum to make it by 1914 one of the most vitalizing forces in the history of the Republic. Crystallizing into the Progressive movement, it differed from its earlier examples in having a broader intellectual and urban appeal and in being concerned with a wider variety of issues. Its leaders included not simply orators and statesmen from the prairies, but philosophers like John Dewey, civic reformers like Tom L. Johnson and Lincoln Steffens, educators like Charles Van Hise of Wisconsin and David Starr Jordan of Stanford, and publicists like Walter Lippmann and Herbert Croly.

286

The earliest formulations of Progressive doctrine seem to have been the Wisconsin Idea and the Oregon System. The former, the work of Charles Van Hise and Robert M. LaFollette, called for the direct primary, tax reform, the regulation of railroads, and especially the use of the facilities of the state university in advancing government by the people. The Oregon System was a collection of proposals for reform which were eventually adopted widely. They included the Australian or secret ballot, registration of voters, the initiative and referendum, the direct primary, the recall, and corrupt practices acts restricting campaign contributions and expenditures with a view to clipping the wings of machine politicians. As time went on, the movement embraced nearly all of the Populist doctrines except the currency proposals. Many of its leaders also endorsed the short ballot and proportional representation. The former is a plan for restricting popular election to the principal legislative and executive officials, who would be held strictly accountable for their policies and actions. All other officials would be appointed, for the most part under civil-service regulations. The purpose of the short ballot is to relieve the burden of choice on the voter and thereby enable him to express his preferences more intelligently. As indicated earlier, proportional representation is a scheme for giving representation to political parties in direct proportion to their voting strength. It guarantees seats in the legislative body not merely to the party that has captured a majority of the votes but to each of the minority parties as well.

The Progressive movement reached the climax of its power between 1910 and 1916. The first of these years witnessed the famous Insurgents' Revolt. A band of Progressive Republican members of the House of Representatives, led by George W. Norris of Nebraska, joined with the Democrats in rebellion against the exercise of autocratic powers by Speaker Joseph G. Cannon. They succeeded in debarring the Speaker from membership on the Committee of Rules and in making it and all other committees elective by the House. Proud and confident as a result of this victory, the Insurgents cast about for new triumphs. In January 1911, they organized the National Progressive Republican League in combination with such senators as LaFollette of Wisconsin and Jonathan Bourne of Oregon. They adopted a platform combining the chief elements of the Wisconsin Idea and the Oregon System and gave serious consideration to urging the nomination of LaFollette as Republican candidate for President. Some Progressives, however, favored the nomination of Theodore Roosevelt, who had ended his term in the White House in 1909 and had lately returned from a hunting expedition in Africa. It seemed to his admirers that as a popular idol, he would have a much better chance of winning the election than would LaFollette. Their attitude was summed up in this doggerel:

Quick and hair-triggerous,
   Joyous and vigorous,
Home from the niggerous.
   African shore,
Bringing a zoo with him,
Zebra and gnu with him,
What shall we do with him—
   Our Theodore?

  .   .   .   .   .

No sweet manorial,
   Grave professorial,
Staid senatorial
   Honors will do.
Give him the Stick again,
Freedom to kick again,
Raise the Old Nick again!
   "Whoop!" and "Hurroo!" [5]

The crusade of
1912

When Roosevelt failed to win the Republican nomination in 1912, he and his followers bolted the party. Soon afterward they held their own convention and launched the Progressive party with Roosevelt as its candidate. Enthusiasm knew no bounds. The delegates paraded around the hall singing "Onward Christian Soldiers." The nominee himself declared, "We stand at Armageddon, and we battle for the Lord." In the campaign that followed, Roosevelt labeled his program the "New Nationalism." This title was meant to convey the idea of a strong national government exercising positive functions to protect the people against greedy interests. Such functions would include strict regulation of business by a federal commission, prohibition of child labor and of injunctions in labor disputes, a minimum wage for women, an eight-hour day for women and children, workmen's compensation, the establishment of a Department of Labor in the Cabinet, and insurance against sickness, unemployment, and old age. To the familiar proposals for universal suffrage, direct election of United States Senators, and the initiative, referendum, and recall, Roosevelt added a demand for the recall of judicial decisions. By far the most radical of his doctrines, this proposal would have given the people the right to overturn the decision of any state court declaring an act of the legislature unconstitutional.

The election of
Wilson

Although Roosevelt was defeated for President in 1912, the outcome of the election was nevertheless a Progressive victory. For the candidate who did win was a Progressive in everything but name. The victor in the election was Woodrow Wilson, nominee of the Democratic party. As soon as it became evident that the Republicans would split, a triumph for the Democrats was assured, provided only that they could agree upon a progressive candidate. This con-

[5] Arthur Guiterman, "His Future," *Collier's*, June 18, 1910.

The Progressive Movement, 1912. Theodore Roosevelt, candidate for President on the Progressive, or Bull Moose, ticket, addressing a gathering at Morrisville, Vermont.

dition was not easily fulfilled. Champ Clark of Missouri, favorite of the conservatives, had managed to corral the largest number of delegates. Fortunately for the progressives, Bryan was determined to prevent the selection of a candidate backed by either the New York bankers or by Tammany Hall. On the forty-sixth ballot Wilson received the nomination. Governor of New Jersey and erstwhile President of Princeton, Woodrow Wilson was one of the most unusual of American statesmen. In no sense a politician, he had won distinction chiefly as a scholar and an educational leader. He had become Governor of New Jersey in 1910 mainly because the Democrats needed a "respectable" candidate if they hoped to win against their powerful rivals. Once in office he had proceeded to repudiate the bosses and to push through the legislature a series of impressive reforms. His program as candidate for President duplicated many of the Roosevelt proposals. However, he did take a stronger position against the trusts; he demanded lower tariffs; and he declined to advocate the recall of judicial decisions.

Wilson was inaugurated President on March 4, 1913. For three years thereafter he dedicated almost all his efforts to realization of his progressive program. In large measure he was successful. He fought the tariff lobbyists to a standstill and forced Congress to reduce the duties on over 900 articles. He established the Federal Reserve system designed to provide better regulation of banking and more flexible currency and credit arrangements. He procured the enactment of the Clayton Anti-Trust Act prohibiting interlocking directorates and price discrimination to prevent competition. He established the Federal Trade Commission with power to issue "cease and desist" orders against corporations found to be engaged in unfair business practices. Among his other achievements were an eight-hour law for interstate railways, a child-labor act to prevent the shipment in interstate commerce of products of child labor, and a Federal Farm Loan system to provide for the farmers easier credit than they could obtain from commercial banks. The entire program he proudly named the New Freedom. It came to an untimely end, however, as threats of a war with Germany darkened the skies.

The New Freedom

289

After 1916 Wilson's attention was so completely absorbed in problems of international conflict that he had no time or energy left for domestic reform. As a result, Progressivism passed into history in much the same way as did the Jeffersonian and Jacksonian movements of the preceding century. Each was arrested by the outbreak of war—the first by the War of 1812, the second by the Mexican War of 1846–1848 and the Civil War of 1861–1865, and the third by World War I.

4. THE UNITED STATES AND THE WORLD

The seeds of
isolationism

No view, perhaps, is more widely held than the theory that the United States, during most of its history, adhered to an isolationist policy. Isolationism was certainly a dream of thousands of Americans. Their ancestors came to this continent in the first place with a determination to shake the dust of Europe off their feet. The oppression many of them had suffered in the Old World and the hardships of their voyage across the Atlantic made America seem like the Promised Land. Europe, by contrast, appeared corrupt and degenerate, perpetually involved in dynastic wars and struggles over the balance of power. On the very eve of our independence, Thomas Paine warned in *Common Sense* that it was the "true interest of America to steer clear of European Contentions." Similar feeling prompted President Washington to counsel the nation in his Farewell Address against "interweaving our destiny with that of any part of Europe." But the classic statement of American isolationism was a slogan often attributed to Washington but actually formulated by Jefferson. In his First Inaugural the third President admonished his countrymen to have "peace, commerce, and honest friendship, with all nations—entangling alliances with none."

The Monroe
Doctrine

Isolationist doctrine continued to be preached throughout the nineteenth and into the twentieth century. Undoubtedly its most noted formulation was the Monroe Doctrine in 1823. This was an expression of America's fear that the reactionary powers of Europe (Austria, Russia, Prussia, and France) might use their combined power to force the republics of the Western Hemisphere which had proclaimed their independence of Spain back under the Spanish yoke. There was concern, also, that having done this, the Alliance might turn upon the United States in order to wipe out the real hot-bed of revolutionary ideas. The Doctrine declared that any attempt by European powers to extend their system to the New World would be regarded by the United States as "dangerous to her peace and safety." It also contained the self-denying clause that the United States would refrain from taking part in any of the wars of European powers, "in matters relating to themselves," and would not interfere in the internal concerns of any of these powers. The Monroe Doctrine remained the principal guiding star of United States foreign policy for more than a century. It was used in 1867 to oust the

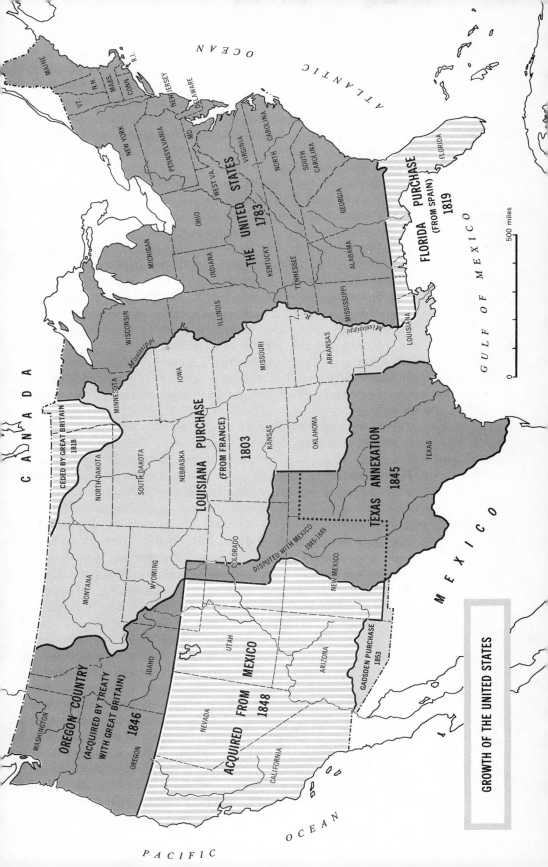

GROWTH OF THE UNITED STATES

French from Mexico after Napoleon III had taken advantage of the American Civil War to establish a puppet empire south of the Rio Grande. It was invoked against the British in 1895 to compel them to accept United States intervention in a boundary dispute between Venezuela and British Guiana. Fear of its being applied in 1903 induced Germany to abandon a blockade of the coast of Venezuela, upon which she had embarked to compel that unfortunate country to acknowledge the claims of some German investors.

Unfortunately, the Monroe Doctrine was also used occasionally as an instrument for the advancement of the "manifest destiny" of the United States. As early as 1820 ardent expansionists like Henry Clay had proclaimed it to be the destiny of the United States to add to its domain the entire North American continent, including the islands off the coast. In 1845 Texas was annexed, soon afterward the Oregon Territory, and in 1848 most of the land now constituting the states of New Mexico, Arizona, and California was taken from Mexico. By the eve of the Civil War there was agitation in the South for the acquisition of Cuba, which the North matched during the war with demands for the annexation of Canada. In 1895 President Cleveland's Secretary of State, Richard Olney, declared that the United States was "practically sovereign on this continent," and that its fiat was law "upon the subjects to which it confines its interposition."

The Monroe
Doctrine and
Manifest Destiny

The most important uses or misuses of the Monroe Doctrine, in the twentieth century at least, concerned the Panama Canal and internal disorder in the Central American and West Indian republics. In 1901 the United States government obtained the consent of Great Britain to abrogation of the Clayton-Bulwer Treaty of 1850, which had given the British joint rights in any canal that might be constructed on the Isthmus of Panama. But another obstacle stood in the way. The Isthmus of Panama belonged to the republic of Colombia, whose government was not inclined to dispose of its rights on the isthmus short of a stiff indemnity. When the United States offer of $10,000,000 in cash and an annuity of $250,000 was rejected, Panamanian leaders organized a revolt, having received the impression that the United States would give them protection and virtually ensure the success of their enterprise. The revolt was timed to begin on the day when a United States cruiser would arrive in the harbor of Colón. Everything proceeded like clockwork. The revolutionists arrested the Colombian officials on the isthmus and proclaimed the independence of the Republic of Panama. United States marines prevented all effective efforts of the Colombian government to suppress the revolution, and four days later the Department of State in Washington recognized the rebel government as the sovereign authority in Panama. The Colombians nursed their wounded feelings until 1921, when the United States Senate, desirous of obtaining access to Colombian oil, ratified a treaty awarding the Colombian government an indemnity of $25,000,000.

Acquisition of the
Canal Zone

Acquisition of the Canal Zone made the existence of stable governments in the surrounding republics all the more important to the United States. In addition, many of these states were rapidly becoming economic colonies of the Colossus of the North. United States bankers, and some European investors also, had lent large sums of money to Central American and West Indian governments. When these governments defaulted on their debts, the specter of European intervention was likely to loom on the horizon. In 1904 this danger confronted the Dominican Republic, which had passed through an orgy of strife and bloodshed. The situation gave President Theodore Roosevelt an excuse for issuing what has since come to be known as the Roosevelt Corollary to the Monroe Doctrine. In it the wielder of the Big Stick announced that "chronic wrong-doing or impotence" in any of the independent states of the Western Hemisphere might force the United States, "however reluctantly," to exercise an international police power. Since, under the Monroe Doctrine, European governments were forbidden to intervene, it would be the duty of the government in Washington to go down into the disorderly republics, clean up the messes, and compel the payment of debts. In pursuance of this policy armed intervention was carried out, not only by Theodore Roosevelt in the Dominican Republic, but also by Wilson in Haiti and the Dominican Republic and by Taft and Coolidge in Nicaragua. The Roosevelt Corollary remained in effect until 1930, when it was repudiated by the Clark Memorandum, issued by J. Reuben Clark, Under-Secretary of State in the Hoover administration.

The history of the foreign policy of the United States can be appropriately divided into two periods, with the year 1898 as the point of division. During the first period the United States did not commonly intervene in the affairs of the Old World or play for the stakes of international power. To be sure, there were apparent exceptions. Jefferson sent naval vessels to the Mediterranean to wipe out the nests of Barbary pirates, and the United States as a nation participated on a limited scale in the Wars of the French Revolution and much more extensively in the Napoleonic Wars. But the purpose of all these activities was essentially the pursuit of domestic interests. They did not involve efforts to conquer distant colonies or to play any part in the power rivalries of foreign empires.

Beginning with 1898 the United States embarked on a new course with respect to foreign policy. No longer were her interests confined to the Western Hemisphere. The maintenance of a balance of power in Europe and the Asiatic intrigues and rivalries of the great empires were also matters of concern. In the summer of 1898 the government of the United States, acting at the behest of a little group of imperialists, took one of the most fateful steps in its history. This was the destruction of the Spanish fleet in the harbor of Manila, which paved the way for the annexation of the Philippine Islands. The pretext was the fact that the United States was then at war with Spain, but the actual purpose was far different. The men responsible for the venture—Theodore Roosevelt, Assistant Secretary of the Navy; Henry Cabot Lodge, Senator from Massachusetts; Albert J. Beveridge, Senator from Indiana; and Alfred T. Mahan, Admiral in the United States Navy—believed that the Philippines would have economic and strategic value in themselves, but that most of all they would provide a precious entering wedge to exploitation of the China trade. None of these expectations was really fulfilled. Instead, possession of the Philippines served mainly to involve the United States in the power politics of the Far East. Every in-

Building the Panama Canal. The Pedro Miguel Lock.

crease in the might of Japan or of Russia, every enlargement of the German or French sphere of influence in China seemed a threat to the interests of the United States.

Between 1898 and 1914 the government of the United States intervened both openly and secretly a number of times in Old World politics. In 1899, when it had become evident that predatory powers, notably Germany, France, Russia, and Japan, were about to carve the whole Chinese Empire into spheres of influence, Secretary of State John Hay, with secret prompting from the British, issued the Open Door Policy. Contrary to popular belief, it did not establish commercial equality in China, but provided merely that the several powers must not discriminate, within their spheres of influence, in favor of their own citizens with regard to commercial privileges. Even in this limited form it failed to receive the definite approval of any of the great powers except Britain. In 1905 President Theodore Roosevelt intervened in the Russo-Japanese War to induce the belligerents to lay down their arms and to sign the Treaty of Portsmouth. Although both contestants were nearly exhausted, United

States intervention came at a juncture favorable to Japan. Roosevelt was pro-Japanese and regarded Russia as the primary menace to a balance of power in the Far East. In the same year, with Germany and France at loggerheads over Morocco, Roosevelt took steps to get the two countries to compose their differences at an international conference. The conference met at Algeciras, Spain, in 1906. Two representatives of the United States participated, and Roosevelt, who was strongly pro-French, boasted, with more braggadocio than accuracy, that he stood the Kaiser on his head "with great decision." In succeeding years the same American President authorized agreements with Japan, giving her a free hand in Korea and receiving in return Japanese recognition of the United States title to the Philippines and pious pledges on the independence of China.

SELECTED READINGS

· *Items so designated are available in paperbound editions.*

· Adams, R. G., *The Political Ideas of the American Revolution*, New York, 1958 (University Paperbacks).

· Beard, C. A., *Economic Origins of Jeffersonian Democracy*, New York, 1915 (Free Press).

———, and M. R., *The Rise of American Civilization*, New York, 1933. A brilliant analysis from the standpoint of economic determinism.

· Becker, C. L., *The Declaration of Independence*, New York, 1942 (Vintage).

———, *The United States: an Experiment in Democracy*, New York, 1920.

Bowers, C. G., *Jefferson and Hamilton; the Struggle for Democracy in America*, Boston, 1925.

Burns, E. M., *The American Idea of Mission*, New Brunswick, N.J., 1957.

· Carleton, W. G., *The Revolution in American Foreign Policy: Its Global Range*, New York, 1963 (Random House).

· Current, R. N., *Lincoln and the First Shot*, Philadelphia, 1963 (Lippincott).

· Dangerfield, George, *The Awakening of American Nationalism, 1815–1828*, New York, 1965 (Torchbook).

Dorfman, Joseph, *The Economic Mind in American Civilization*, New York, 1949, 3 vols. The best of the economic histories.

Faulkner, H. U., *The Quest for Social Justice, 1898–1914*, New York, 1931.

· Filler, Louis, *Crusaders for American Liberalism*, New York, 1939 (Collier).

Gabriel, R. H., *The Course of American Democratic Thought*, New York, 1956. A thoughtful analysis based on the theme of a higher law.

· Hofstadter, Richard, *The American Political Tradition and the Men Who Made It*, New York, 1948 (Vintage). Brilliant studies of famous American leaders.

· ———, *The Age of Reform: From Bryan to F. D. R.*, New York, 1955 (Vintage). A provocative interpretation.

· Jameson, J. F., *The American Revolution Considered as a Social Movement*, Boston, 1956 (Beacon). A study of the revolution behind the Revolution.

Kelly, Alfred H., and Harbison, W. A., *The American Constitution*, 3rd edn., New York, 1963. A good analytical summary.

Lacy, Dan, *The Meaning of the American Revolution*, New York, 1964.

Latané, J. H., *America as a World Power, 1897–1907*, New York, 1907.

Link, A. S., *Wilson: The New Freedom*, Princeton, 1957.

Miller, H. H., *The Case for Liberty*, Chapel Hill, N.C., 1965. Recounts the distinctively American origins of the Bill of Rights.

· Miller, J. C., *Origins of the American Revolution*, Boston, 1943 (Stanford University Press). Excellent for the study of background.

· Morgan, H. W., *America's Road to Empire: The War with Spain and Overseas Expansion*, New York, 1965 (Wiley).

Myers, Gustavus, *The History of American Idealism*, New York, 1925.

Nettels, C. P., *The Roots of American Civilization*, New York, 1938.

· Neumann, W. L., *America Encounters Japan; From Perry to MacArthur*, Baltimore, 1963 (Colophon Book).

Noble, D. W., *The Paradox of Progressive Thought*, Minneapolis, 1958.

· North, Douglass C., *The Economic Growth of the United States, 1790–1860*, Englewood Cliffs, 1961 (Norton Library).

· Parrington, V. L., *Main Currents in American Thought*, 1-vol. edition, New York, 1930 (Harvest). Stimulating but dogmatic.

· Perkins, Dexter, *Hands Off; a History of the Monroe Doctrine*, Boston, 1941. The standard work on the subject. Revised edition also available in paperback under the title *The Monroe Doctrine* (Little, Brown & Co.).

· Pollack, Norman, *The Populist Response to Industrial America*, Cambridge, 1962 (Norton Library).

Pratt, J. W., *America's Colonial Experiment*, New York, 1950. An interesting study of American imperialism.

Randall, J. G., *The Civil War and Reconstruction*, Boston, 1937.

· Rutland, R. A., *The Birth of the Bill of Rights*, Chapel Hill, 1955 (Collier).

Savelle, Max, *The Foundations of American Civilization*, New York, 1942.

· ———, *Seeds of Liberty; the Genesis of the American Mind*, New York, 1948 (University of Washington Press).

Schlesinger, A. M., *New Viewpoints in American History*, New York, 1937.

· Schlesinger, A. M., Jr., *The Age of Jackson*, Boston, 1945 (Mentor).

· Turner, F. J., *The Frontier in American History*, New York, 1921 (Holt, Rinehart & Winston). A provocative interpretation based on the theme that frontier influences have been all-important in determining the character of American democracy.

· ———, *The United States, 1830–1850*, New York, (Norton Library).

Wecter, Dixon, *The Saga of America; a Record of Social Aspiration, 1607–1937*, New York, 1937.

· Weinberg, A. K., *Manifest Destiny; a Study of Nationalist Expansionism in American History*, Baltimore, 1935 (Quadrangle).

Wish, Harvey, *Society and Thought in Early America*, New York, 1950.

SOURCE MATERIALS

· Commager, H. S., *Documents of American History*, New York, 1949 (Appleton).

Hacker, L. M., and Zahler, H. S., *The Shaping of the American Tradition*, New York, 1943.

Hamilton, Jay, and Madison, *The Federalist*, especially Nos. 10, 16, 39, 47, 48, 62, 69, 78, 84.

· Heffner, R. D., *A Documentary History of the United States*, New York, 1950 (Mentor).

Padover, S. K., ed., *The Complete Jefferson*, especially pp. 270, 282–93, 1064–69, 1076–85.

· Tocqueville, Alexis de, *Democracy in America*, New York, 1965 (Vintage, 2 vols. and others).

CHAPTER 10

The Emergence of Latin America

What free nation, ancient or modern, has not suffered dissension? Can you point to a history more turbulent than that of Athens—factions more sanguinary than those of Rome—civil wars of greater violence than those of England—or disturbances more dangerous than those of the United States of North America? Nevertheless, these are the nations that honor mankind most by their virtues, their liberty, and their glory. In citing the tragic and startling examples that these nations afford us, I should like to lessen the shame of our own internal cleavage.
—Simón Bolívar, *Selected Writings*, Vol. I

By far the oldest civilization in the Western Hemisphere is that of Latin America. Here the first settlements were made by the Spanish and Portuguese explorers and conquerors who followed in the path of Columbus. But centuries before any white men set foot on American soil, Indians in Guatemala, Mexico, and the Andean Highland had developed superior cultures which bore almost all the characteristics of civilizations. Had they not been conquered, they might well have provided the basis for a native cultural growth in Central and South America equal to that of any of the other continents. The reasons for this superiority appear to lie almost exclusively in geographic conditions favorable to the progress of agriculture. The lush fertility and benign climate of the valleys of Central America and the northwest portion of South America made possible the production of surplus food. As a result, population increased rapidly, a diversification of trade and industry occurred, cities and towns multiplied, and a priestly class came into existence devoted to the cultivation of sacred lore. Such developments facilitated the growth of science and other branches of learning and the invention of new crafts and skills. By contrast, the Indians of the greater part of the United States and Canada were forced to continue their existence as nomads and hunters. Their homelands were either so densely forested or so arid as to make agriculture discouraging and profitless.

Native civilizations of Latin America

EMERGENCE
OF LATIN
AMERICA

Civilized Indians
in Latin America:
(1) the Aztecs

I. CONQUISTADORES AND COLONISTS

The principal discoverers of Latin America—Christopher Columbus, Amerigo Vespucci, Juan de Solis, and Vasco de Balboa—were
quickly followed by a horde of conquerors. Best-known among
them were Hernando Cortés and Francisco Pizarro. Restless,
greedy, and zealous for adventure, they endured incredible hardships, dragging their men through jungles and swamps and over
snow-capped mountains in quest of plunder. The former won fame
of a sort as the subjugator of Mexico and the latter as the conqueror
of Peru. At the time they made their conquests both countries were
occupied by various peoples in advanced stages of cultural development. Mexico was inhabited by the Aztecs and Mayas, while Peru
was the home of the Incas. The Aztecs were relative newcomers on

Detail of an Aztec Pyramid in Central Mexico. The serpent was an object of
worship for the Aztecs.

the scene of civilization. They established themselves in central
Mexico about the thirteenth century A.D. and founded their capital,
Tenochtitlán (Mexico City), a short time later. Their achievements
included a system of pictographic writing, some knowledge of astronomy and engineering, an elaborate architecture, and the building of roads and aqueducts. Their capital city had a population of
some 200,000. Its streets were paved with stone and were kept
scrupulously clean by an efficient public-works department. The
ruler of the country was an hereditary monarch whose powers were
limited to those of commander of the army and chief justice. Aztec
religion can only be described as a maze of superstitions and cruel

Mayan Pyramid at Chichén Itzá. Unlike the Egyptian pyramids, the Mayan pyramids were not tombs but substructures for temples or altars.

practices. Its distinguishing feature was the sacrifice of war captives and, on occasions, of Aztecs themselves on the altars of the gods. Pouring out the blood of human beings was believed to be especially effective in winning the divine favor.

Representing higher stages of cultural achievement were the Mayas and Incas. The former originated in Guatemala and Honduras and reached the climax of their progress in the eighth and ninth centuries A.D. About 1000 A.D. most of them migrated to Yucatán and were concentrated there when conquered by the Spaniards. Mayan culture seems to have been developed primarily by a leisure class of nobles and priests. It revealed a high level of progress in many fields. A system of writing, in which some of the symbols apparently had phonetic value, was extensively used for religious purposes. Writing materials included stone, deer skin, and a kind of paper made from the maguey plant. A calendar, with a year of 365 days, enabled the priests to determine lucky and unlucky days and the appropriate periods for planting and harvesting crops. Mathematical calculations were refined to the extent of having a vigesimal system (with twenty instead of ten as the basic unit) and a conception of zero as a device for giving different values to the same number. Notable also was progress in the arts. The Mayas excelled in making gold and silver ornaments and in the erection of truncated pyramids with temples on top. Tastes in personal adornment included the curious practice of filing and chipping teeth to give them sharp points and sometimes inlaying them with precious stones. Beards were removed by a scorching process instead of by shaving. Religion was no more highly developed than that of the Aztecs and included the same barbarities of human sacrifice.

Of more recent origin than the culture of the Mayas was that of the Incas, who were at the zenith of their progress when conquered

(2) the Mayas

by the Spaniards. Extending into Ecuador, Bolivia, northern Chile, and northwestern Argentina, the Inca empire had its center in southeastern Peru. It was organized on the basis of collectivist paternalism. All the land belonged to the emperor, to the priests, or to the tribe, and was cultivated by males of the common classes between the ages of twenty-five and fifty. In good years the surplus production was stored by the emperor to provide for his subjects in time of famine. From the produce on its lands the tribe took care of the young and the aged, the disabled and the sick. It was a paradise of security but with little freedom. In intellectual achievements the Incas did not equal the Mayas. They had no system of writing but used knotted strings of many colors to record numbers and sets of facts. On the other hand, they had an extensive knowledge of medicine and surgery and built excellent roads and suspension bridges. They understood also the principles of fertilization and irrigation and knew how to terrace hillsides to prevent erosion.

During the sixteenth and seventeenth centuries the entire area of Mexico and Central and South America passed under the domination of Spain and Portugal. Three-fifths of it was taken by Spain, and the remainder probably would have been also, had not the Pope intervened in an attempt to give equal recognition to the claims of both countries. In 1493 he issued a Bull of Demarcation drawing a line from north to south 100 leagues west of the Azores. All territory that might be discovered east of the line was to belong to Portugal, and everything west of the line to Spain. In 1494 the two countries signed a treaty relocating the line 370 leagues west of the Cape Verde Islands. Portugal thereby acquired a foothold on the eastern bulge of South America, which was later expanded into Brazil.

The methods of colonization and colonial administration followed by both Spain and Portugal were of such a character as to influence

Machu Picchu. The "Lost City of the Incas" is located in the Andes Mountains, Peru.

profoundly the entire history of Latin America. This was particularly true of Spain, which also set the pattern for her neighboring state since both were united under a common sovereign between 1580 and 1640. The cardinal elements in Spanish colonial policy were despotism and paternalism. The highest authorities in the empire were the viceroys, who ruled as the personal representatives of the Spanish king. At first there were two, one in New Spain including Mexico and Central America, and the other in Peru. In the eighteenth century two additional viceroyalties were created: New Granada (Panama, Colombia, Venezuela, Ecuador) and La Plata, or Buenos Aires. The viceroys were paid magnificent salaries, amounting at one time to the equivalent of $200,000 a year. The purpose behind such generosity was to prevent corruption, an objective by no means universally attained. At the same time their royal master took precautions to prevent the viceroys from becoming too powerful. The authority they exercised was to be that of the Spanish crown, not their own. For this reason they had to tolerate the existence of an advisory council, or *audiencia*, which also served as a court of appeal against their decisions. Members of the *audiencia* had the right to communicate with the king regarding the acts of the viceroy without the latter's knowledge. At the end of his term, and occasionally during it, the viceroy must submit to a searching inquiry or investigation in which a royal judge heard the complaints of all and sundry as to official misconduct.

As an adjunct to despotic rule in the colonies, the Spanish kings made use of the Church. The priests gave valuable help in teaching the population to obey the king and his agents and in opposing new ideas and expressions of discontent. In almost any emergency the hierarchy could be counted upon to give loyal support to the government. By the middle of the sixteenth century the Inquisition had been extended to Latin America as an instrument for maintaining absolute rule. Headquarters were established in Mexico City and Lima from which inquisitors were sent out to all parts of the continent to discover and punish unorthodox belief. Public executions were occasionally staged in the principal cities to provide object lessons of the fearful punishment in store for any who might waver in the faith. To such exhibitions the public was regularly invited in the hope that the deterrent effect would be complete. That the penalties of the Inquisition were sometimes invoked for political and personal reasons goes almost without saying.

The keynote of economic administration in the colonies was paternalism. Actually, nothing else could have been expected, since, according to the theory, the land of the Americas was the personal possession of the king. It was his private estate which he could dispose of as he saw fit. But economic administration in the Spanish colonies was also shaped to a large extent by the theory of mercantilism, which was beginning to dominate the thinking of all Western

Brazilian Colonial Church in the Portuguese Baroque Style. Baroque workmanship in colonial Latin America is thought by some authorities to be finer than that in Spain and Portugal.

nations. Mercantilism demanded that colonies should exist for the benefit of the mother country; they should bring bullion into her treasury and contribute in every way possible toward making her rich and powerful. It followed that the government of the mother country had the right to regulate and control the economic activities of the colonies in her own interest—to dictate what they should produce and from whom they should buy and to whom they should sell. In substance this meant a monopoly of colonial trade for the merchants of the mother country and a strict prohibition of manufactures.

The economic policies described had unfortunate effects upon both the Spanish colonies and the homeland. The resources of the former were poorly developed, and some lay unused or undiscovered for centuries. With attention focused upon gold and silver and with manufacturing prohibited, there was little incentive to exploit the deposits of copper, manganese, and other minerals which might well have supported a considerable industry. Some branches of agriculture were also discouraged in order that the colonies might produce vast quantities of sugar, cotton, and tobacco which would help the mother country in maintaining a favorable balance of trade, since these products would not have to be purchased for gold outside the empire. The whole system of restrictive policies was stupid and vicious and retarded the development not only of the colonies but of the country that owned them. As late as the end of the sixteenth century Spain was an economically backward nation, with a large portion of her wealth concentrated in cattle and sheep, with no powerful commercial or industrial class, and with manual labor frowned upon as unworthy of a good Spaniard.

Early in the eighteenth century the Hapsburg dynasty in Spain was supplanted by Bourbon rulers. Recognizing the corruptions and

Effects of economic policies

302

inefficiency of the system of colonial administration, the Bourbon kings initiated reforms. They were no more interested in the welfare of the colonies than their predecessors had been, but they did perceive the danger that a disgruntled colonial population might become a prey to foreign conquest. They hoped, moreover, to increase the flow of revenue into the royal treasury. With these ends in view they modified trade restrictions, encouraged industry and a more varied agriculture, and even granted commercial concessions to foreigners. The most noted of these was the *asiento* of 1701, which conferred upon France the privilege of supplying the Spanish colonies with Negro slaves. In 1713, at the end of the War of the Spanish Succession, it was transferred to Britain. By the close of the eighteenth century the Spanish-American trade as a whole was the richest in the world, and had more than tripled in fifty years.

2. REVOLUTIONS FOR INDEPENDENCE

Between 1808 and 1826 Latin America was engulfed by a tidal wave of revolutions. The underlying causes did not differ greatly from the factors which had produced the North American Revolution of 1775. Pre-eminent among them was dissatisfaction with the mercantilist policies of the home government. Despite the reforms of the Bourbons, many relics of oppression and discrimination survived. A rigid censorship was imposed. Books of European and North American radicals could be obtained only by smuggling. As late as 1773 a Colombian scientist was condemned for giving lectures on the Copernican system. Taxes were numerous and excessive, and monopoly and favoritism flourished. Prosperous Creoles, or colonial whites, resented their exclusion from the highest and most lucrative positions in the government and the Church, which were reserved

Causes of the revolutions for independence

Spanish Colonial Patio. Examples of the cultural heritage of old Spain have been adapted by the wealthier citizens of Latin America.

CANADA
(British)

UNITED STATES
OF AMERICA

ATLANTIC

OCEAN

NEW

GULF OF
MEXICO

Mexico
City

SPAIN

BR.
HONDURAS

CUBA
(Spain)

SAINT DOMINGUE (France)

JAMAICA
(British)

SANTO DOMINGO (Spain)

CARIBBEAN SEA

Orinoco R.

(British after 1803)

FRENCH GUIANA

PACIFIC

Bogotá

NEW
GRANADA

DUTCH
GUIANA

Equator

GALAPAGOS IS.

Amazon R.

OCEAN

B R A Z I L

Lima

P E R U

A N D E S

M O U N T A I N S

BUENOS
AIRES
OR
LA PLATA

Rio de Janeiro

Santiago

Buenos Aires

Montevideo

La Plata R.

P A T A G O N I A

FALKLAND
ISLANDS

CAPE HORN

0   1000   2000 miles

LATIN AMERICA
ON THE EVE OF INDEPENDENCE ca. 1800

Spanish

Portuguese

British

for Spanish-born aristocrats. The former were not starving, any more than were the members of the bourgeoisie in France on the eve of that country's revolution. What rankled in their breasts was being deprived of privileges that they believed should rightly belong to them on the basis of their wealth and intelligence.

It is possible that the discontent of Spain's colonies would never have reached revolutionary proportions had it not been for the examples already set by the revolutions in France and in North America. The colonists' grievances had abated rather than increased and probably would have lessened still further. But revolutions are contagious. An outbreak in one country is almost certain to spread to other countries where similar conditions exist even if in much smaller degree. This is especially true when a philosophy of discontent is propagated on an international scale. During the latter half of the eighteenth century hundreds of Creoles had imbibed revolutionary doctrines from the writings of Voltaire, Rousseau, Jefferson, and Paine. Some had been educated or had traveled in Europe or in the United States. The discovery that intellectual leaders in other countries were boldly attacking despotic government and superstitious religion made a profound impression and led Spanish colonials to ask themselves why such things should be tolerated in their own lands.

Just as in North America a period of indifference and "salutary neglect" by the British government fostered a spirit of independence in the colonies, so in Latin America a similar period weakened the ties between Spain and her possessions. Between 1803 and 1808 Spain as a satellite of France took part in the wars of Napoleon to make himself master of Europe. In 1805 the British defeated Napoleon's fleet at Trafalgar and virtually destroyed the sea power of France and her allies. Spain, in particular, experienced great difficulty in maintaining communications with her empire. As a result her colonies in Latin America acquired habits of self-reliance. More and more they depended upon their own efforts in solving political and economic problems. So great was their isolation from Spain that they cultivated a profitable trade with the British. For the mother country to have forced them back under the yoke of mercantilist restrictions would have been difficult indeed.

The spark that ignited colonial unrest into actual revolution burst forth in 1808. A quarrel had developed between the weak Bourbon king of Spain, Charles IV, and his son Ferdinand. Napoleon forced both to abdicate and gave the Spanish crown to his brother Joseph. When news of these highhanded proceedings reached the colonies, there was general indignation. At first the colonies vented their wrath against the French, but gradually they came to realize that here was an opportunity to get rid of all foreign oppressors. Agitation took an anti-Spanish turn and was ultimately followed by declarations of independence and revolutionary wars. Wealthy

Creoles took the lead, especially in Caracas, Buenos Aires, Quito, Bogotá, and Santiago.

The first of the larger Spanish colonies to proclaim its independence was Venezuela. Here a revolutionary pattern had been developing for a number of years. In 1806 the impetuous Creole, Francisco de Miranda, attempted with the help of foreigners to land filibustering expeditions in his native country and wrest control of it from Spain. He obtained aid from English and American sources but failed to gain more than a temporary foothold on the territory of Venezuela. Five years later representatives from a number of provinces met in a revolutionary assembly and declared Venezuela an independent republic. Learning of the revolutionists' activities, Miranda sailed from England to enlist in the cause. Appointed commander-in-chief of the patriot armies, he launched a campaign to conquer the remainder of the country. Misfortune stalked his efforts. Reverses suffered by his armies were turned into disaster when an earthquake shook the provinces controlled by the revolutionists and snuffed out the lives of 20,000. Equal to the occasion, the Spanish government sent priests with instructions to tell the people that the catastrophe was a divine punishment for their sin of rebellion. The patriot armies disintegrated, and their commander was seized and thrown into a dungeon.

With the defeat of Miranda, the revolution in Venezuela was left to be completed by his erstwhile friend, Simón Bolívar. A wealthy Creole rancher, Bolívar had finally turned against Miranda, accusing him of deserting the revolution, and had been partly responsible for his capture by the Spaniards. Concluding thereafter that the revolutionary cause in Venezuela was hopeless, he went to Colombia and

Equestrian Statue of Simón Bolívar (1783-1830), Soldier, Statesman, and Revolutionary Leader. On Plaza Bolívar, Caracas, Venezuela.

joined the patriot forces there. He returned to Venezuela in 1813
and captured Caracas. In January 1814, the Second Venezuelan Republic was proclaimed with Bolívar as its head with the title of
"Liberator." In six months the new government had been crushed
by the Spaniards, and its founder fled to Jamaica. He did not return
for three years. In 1817 he began the rebuilding of a stronger patriot
force in Venezuela, and two years later, with the help of 4000 soldiers of fortune from Great Britain, completed a spectacular foray
into Colombia. Inflicting a decisive defeat upon the Spaniards and
their collaborators, he proclaimed the Republic of Colombia on
August 10, 1819. Three months later a constitution was issued for
the United States of Colombia, including Venezuela, with Bolívar as
President. Thereafter the great Liberator devoted his efforts to freeing the remainder of the northern portion of the continent from
Spanish rule. By 1821 he had liquidated the royalist forces in
Venezuela. Meanwhile, his able lieutenant Antonio José de Sucre,
had begun the liberation of Ecuador, and in 1822 won a brilliant victory against the Spaniards, which assured the independence of the
country. Soon afterward Bolívar arrived in Quito and persuaded the
Ecuadorean revolutionists to unite with Colombia and Venezuela in
a republic of Gran Colombia.

Concurrently with these events in the northern areas, an independence movement was growing apace in the south. As early as 1790
business men in the port of Buenos Aires had developed a profitable
trade with Spain and an even more profitable one with Great Britain. They longed for relief of these ventures from monopolistic restrictions imposed by the Spanish government. During the Napoleonic Wars their demands were encouraged by the British government. In 1810 a band of Creoles in Buenos Aires overthrew the viceregal government of Joseph Bonaparte and appointed a supreme
governing council to rule in the name of Ferdinand VII. While the
urban Creoles were debating how far they should go in the direction of complete independence, and what form of government
would best suit their needs, delegates from the outlying provinces
assembled at Tucumán in 1816 and declared absolute independence
from the mother country. Thenceforth for some time rivalry between the capital and the rural provinces impeded the progress of
the revolution.

At least one native of Argentina perceived that internal squabbles
would lead to nothing but ultimate defeat. This man was José San
Martín, who had served in the Spanish army from the age of eleven
and had fought the French invaders in the Peninsular campaign.
With Spain under the heel of Napoleon, he had returned to his
native country. Ignoring local quarrels, he determined to give positive direction to the Argentine revolution by attacking the royalists
in Peru, their principal stronghold on the continent. He obtained an
appointment as governor of the province of Cuyo, on the eastern

slope of the Andes, where he planned to organize and equip an army for an incursion into Chile, which would then be used as a base for operations against Peru. In his preparations he was assisted by Bernardo O'Higgins, a Chilean revolutionary of Irish descent. By 1817 everything was ready for the daring expedition. Scrambling over the rocky slopes of the continental divide, the invaders came down into Chile, fell upon the royalists near Santiago, and won a spectacular triumph. The grateful Chileans offered San Martín a dictatorship, which he declined, insisting that it be conferred upon his Chilean collaborator, O'Higgins. San Martín then turned his attention to completing plans for the attack on Peru. The expedition got under way in September 1820. Less than a year later the redoubtable patriot entered Lima, issued a declaration of independence from Spain, and was vested with the title of "Protector" of the new Peruvian government. Although a dictator in theory, he exercised little power. He seemed to feel that his mission as a revolutionist was now fulfilled. Moreover, he was unable to agree with Bolívar as to the form of government to be established when the time should come to unite the countries they had liberated from Spanish rule. In 1822 he left Peru, sojourned briefly in Chile and Argentina, and then left for France, where he died in 1850.

The struggle for independence in Brazil followed a less violent course than that in most other South American countries. Revolutionary feeling was not strong, perhaps for the reason that Brazil was more backward than most of her neighbors. Two-thirds of her population were slaves. There was no large middle class and there were no cities worthy of the name. Schools were few, and scarcely more than a tenth of the people could read and write. Even more than in the Spanish colonies, the impetus for revolution in Brazil came from the Napoleonic Wars. When Napoleon's troops drove the Portuguese rulers from Lisbon in 1807, they sailed to Brazil, arriving in Rio de Janeiro in March 1808. The Regent, Prince John, was chagrined to find his colony so backward and launched an immediate program of reform and improvement. He established schools, a bank, hospitals, and a library. He reorganized the administration of the colony, sponsored new methods of agriculture, and abolished the restrictions on colonial manufacturing. He raised the status of the colony to that of a kingdom on a par with Portugal itself. But upon becoming king of both countries after the death of his deranged mother in 1816, he surrounded himself with a royal court in Brazil and gave a virtual monopoly of high offices in Church and state to his Portuguese favorites. The effect was to antagonize many of his Creole subjects. Although the majority confined the expression of their discontent to grumbling, a group in the north attempted unsuccessfully to establish an independent republic (1817).

In 1820 a liberal revolution broke out in Portugal. King John

sailed for Lisbon and left his young son Pedro as Regent in Brazil.
Scarcely had the new government gained power in Portugal than it
turned to a reactionary policy, particularly with regard to the empire. Brazil was reduced once more to a mere colony, and Pedro was
ordered to return to Portugal to "complete his political education."
The Brazilians implored him to remain as their ruler, and he agreed
to do so. When all attempts to compromise with the Portuguese
failed, a revolt broke out in Brazil. In 1822 Pedro was raised to the
status of emperor, and within a year the Portuguese troops had been
driven from the country.

By 1826 all the South American countries had thrown off the
yoke of European rule. Uruguay remained a province of Brazil,
however, until 1828, and Argentina was unable to solve the problem
of unity between Buenos Aires and her rural provinces until 1861.
Meanwhile another section of Latin America was striving for the
goal of independence. This was the viceroyalty of New Spain,
which included Mexico, Central America, portions of the West
Indies, and the Spanish territory within the present limits of the
United States. The island of Haiti was the first to raise the standard
of revolt. During the eighteenth century it had become a colony of
France—her most lucrative, by the way. It was a seething volcano
of discontent, however. Its population had a three-class structure.
At the top were a few thousand whites, mostly French planters and
officials. At the bottom were 500,000 miserably exploited Negro
slaves. A middle layer comprised the mulattoes, torn into mutually
hostile factions and despised by both blacks and whites. In 1791
Toussaint L'Ouverture, a slave but the grandson of an African king,
emerged as the leader of the Negroes. Under the influence of the
French Revolutionary policy of abolishing slavery in the colonies,
he led the Negroes in a prolonged revolt against their masters. With
some accuracy he can be regarded as a forerunner of twentieth-
century guerrilla leaders. His followers were a straggling force of
irregulars, poorly armed and equipped, who followed a tactic of
strike and run. In ten years they gained control of the entire island.
Toussaint issued a constitution and assumed dictatorial powers.

When Napoleon had established himself as master of France, he
resolved to put an end to the rule of the upstart rebel. Avowing that
he would never "leave an epaulette on the shoulder of a Negro," he
sent a huge expedition under the command of his brother-in-law,
General Le Clerc, to overthrow Toussaint's government. Nearly
two years and an act of treachery were required to accomplish the
task. Informing Toussaint that he would "not find a more sincere
friend than myself," he invited the Negro to his quarters for negotiations. He then seized him and shipped him off in chains to a
prison in France. Angered by this treachery, the slaves again rose in
rebellion and with new and equally capable leaders soon forced the
French to withdraw. In 1803 Haiti was proclaimed an independent **309**

kingdom. Curiously, the precedent set by the Haitians seemed to exert little influence upon the other principal islands of the West Indies. Cuba and Puerto Rico, for example, remained under Spanish rule until 1898.

Scarcely anywhere in Latin America did the revolution present a more discouraging aspect than in Mexico. Here the Creoles did not constitute so powerful a middle class as in some parts of South America. Moreover, the antagonism of the Indians and the poorer *mestizos*, or half-breeds, against the whites hindered combined action to oust the Spaniards. A revolt was finally launched in 1810, however, in the rural provinces. Its leader was a Creole priest, Father Hidalgo. The son of a poor farmer, he had obtained a good education and had become rector of the Colegio de San Nicolàs. But he was an ardent admirer of Rousseau and was reputed to have questioned the Virgin Birth and the authority of the Pope. His original plan was to lead the Indians in a rebellion against the Spanish-born aristocrats, but when his scheme was exposed he turned upon the government itself. He captured the important towns of Guana-juato and Guadalajara and then advanced with 80,000 men upon Mexico City. Ultimately defeated, he was captured, condemned by the Inquisition, and shot. One of his followers, José Morelos, continued the revolution for four more years and attempted to set up an independent government. But like Hidalgo, he eventually fell into the hands of the royalists and was condemned to death. The destinies of the revolution then passed into the hands of a crafty adventurer, Agustín de Iturbide. A soldier by profession, who had hitherto fought on the side of the royalists, Iturbide saw a chance to further his ambitions by joining the patriots. Openly espousing independence and racial equality, he attracted formidable support and in September 1821, entered Mexico City in triumph. The following year he proclaimed himself Emperor of an independent Mexican empire. But since the basic economic and social problems remained unsolved, the future of the nation continued to be fraught with anxiety and turmoil.

The first Mexican revolutions

3. PROBLEMS OF GROWTH AND DEVELOPMENT

Following their achievement of independence, the Latin American states went through a long struggle for national maturity. It could scarcely be said that many of them attained this goal before the end of the nineteenth century. A score of difficulties beset them on every hand. To begin with, the population was heterogeneous. The former Spanish colonies were composed of 45 per cent Indians, 30 per cent *mestizos*, or half-breeds, 20 per cent whites, and 5 per cent Negroes. In Brazil half the people were Negroes, a fourth were whites, and the remainder Indians and half-breeds. Over the continent as a whole the nonwhites outnumbered the Caucasians 4 to 1;

Obstacles to national maturity: (1) heterogeneous population yet the latter fought tooth and nail to maintain a dominant position. The success achieved in this struggle was purchased at the price of class hatred and the perpetuation of social and economic backwardness.

A second obstacle, related to the first, was the wide disparity of economic condition among the classes. At the top was a tiny minority of rich Spaniards and prosperous Creoles. At the bottom was a vast multitude of half-starved peasants, eking out a precarious livelihood on lands no one wanted or compelled to become laborers on the estates of the rich. The inevitable consequence was periodic revolts of the masses to force a redistribution of the land. Since land comprised the bulk of the wealth, capital accumulated slowly. In the main, the deficiency was made up by foreign investors, who frequently demanded political concessions and were eager to fish in troubled waters for their own advantage. Few causes contributed more toward encouraging unscrupulous adventurers to overturn governments at the behest of their foreign sponsors.

(2) the gulf between rich and poor

Still a third difficulty was the political inexperience of the Latin American peoples. More than 90 per cent, of course, were uneducated, and consequently both ignorant and indifferent with respect to political problems. But even many of the educated ones were ill prepared to assume the tasks of governing. Their knowledge of politics came not from experience but from reading the books of theorists. Enthusiasm for this or that form of government burned with white-hot intensity, and factions vied with each other to put their ideas into effect overnight, frequently by revolutionary action. Worse yet, as a result of the long and sanguinary struggles for independence, a military tradition was firmly implanted in most of the states, and swaggering generals overshadowed civilian leaders.

(3) political inexperience

Although Latin Americans are often reproached with their failure to achieve political maturity and stability as soon as did the English-speaking inhabitants of North America, such comparisons have little validity. They leave out of reckoning the fact that the United States went through a long period of sectional conflict, culminating in civil war, before its people could decide whether they were one nation or a confederation of nations. But aside from this, the circumstances affecting Latin America were so different from those obtaining in Canada and the United States that any conception of the two regions as parallel entities is bound to be inaccurate.

Contrasts between North America and Latin America

Perhaps the most important difference resided in the fact that Canada and the United States comprised millions of acres of practically unoccupied land. The native peoples were so few in numbers and so widely scattered that they could easily be pushed aside or exterminated. In Latin America the Indians were more numerous, in many cases more highly civilized, and therefore more successful in resisting the encroachments of the whites. The policy of the Spaniards, moreover, was to convert the natives to Christianity, not to

Contrasting conditions of Indian populations

exterminate them. It did not seem inconsistent with this that they should also be exploited and oppressed. As a consequence, there quickly developed a class system based upon race, with a prosperous minority of Spaniards and Creoles monopolizing the good things of life and a subject population composed of Indians and half-breeds living in squalor and toiling for the barest subsistence.

Differences
between the
founding empires

As a second difference, the Spanish colonies were founded by one of the most unprogressive nations in Europe. The economic system of Spain was outmoded. Her government was despotic and corrupt. Spanish Catholicism reeked with intolerance and superstition. The Church was used by the government as an instrument of repression, and the fanaticism of the Spanish Inquisition was notorious. On the eve of the discovery of America the most enterprising of Spain's inhabitants—the Moors and the Jews—had been driven from the country. England had the advantage of not beginning her colonization of the New World until the seventeenth century. By that time the power of her middle class was well-consolidated and able to set up obstacles to despotic government. Instead of one church having a monopoly of religious authority, the Christians of England were divided into competing sects, and no one of them was strong enough to impose its will upon the others. The country, moreover, had been a haven of refuge for persecuted religionists from other nations, for the Huguenots in particular. Many of these were enterprising merchants and artisans who brought their initiative and skills with them, adding no small amount to the intellectual wealth of England. Long before the end of the seventeenth century, the "tight little island" was the most progressive nation in Europe. And while the Spanish colonists brought with them the customs and institutions of the Middle Ages, those who went out from England carried the ideas of the modern world. They believed in education, in equality of opportunity, and in the application of ambition and intelligence to the solution of human problems. These viewpoints helped immensely in promoting a free and dynamic society in North America in contrast with the static, semifeudal society of Central and South America.

Growth and
development
during the 19th
century

The last three quarters of the nineteenth century unfolded a record of developments in Latin America similar in some respects to that in the United States. There was the same feverish activity in railroad building and in the construction of telegraph and telephone lines. There was the same rapid growth of population, owing largely to the influx of immigrants from Europe. The population of Argentina, for example, grew from 2 million in 1870 to about 4 million in 1900; and more than half of this increase was the result of immigration from Italy, Spain, France, Germany, and the British Isles. In Latin America as in the United States there were bitter struggles over centralization versus states' rights. There was sharp rivalry also between liberals and conservatives over extension of the suffrage and over economic reform for the benefit of the lower classes.

But the differences were quite as significant. Nearly every country of Latin America was torn by revolutions, many of them resulting in the enthronement of military dictators. The history of Colombia was almost unique in that only twice during the century following independence was her government overthrown by violence. In neighboring Venezuela revolutions occurred with such frequency as to reduce economic development virtually to a standstill. Only the accession in 1909 of a man on horseback, Juan Vicente Gómez, who ruled for twenty-six years, brought a semblance of stability to the country. In many states of both Central and South America, religion complicated the struggle between factions. The conservatives, made up of the landholding and aristocratic elements, invariably supported the Church. The liberals, who drew their following mainly from the business classes, were anticlerical. On occasions the latter allied themselves with the landless peasants in attacks upon the extensive holdings of the clergy.

The major difference, however, consists in the numerous wars fought by the Latin American states against each other. The longest was the struggle between Uruguay and Argentina, which lasted for fourteen years (1838–1852). The most famous was the War of the Pacific (1879–1883), in which Chile, Peru, and Bolivia fought over the desert region of Atacama. The bloodiest was the war of 1865–1870, in which the dictator of Paraguay (Francisco López) resisted the combined onslaughts of Brazil, Uruguay, and Argentina for five years. The Paraguayans fought almost literally to the last man. Only a handful of adult males survived, and more than half of the total population was wiped out. The only element of justice in the outcome was the fact that López himself was numbered among those killed. It was this dictator's imperialist ambitions which had precipitated the conflict in the first place.

Two states of Latin America went through experiences during the nineteenth century in a number of respects distinctive. One was Brazil and the other was Mexico. The former was almost unique in her political stability and in her capacity for gradual and orderly change. The reasons lay not in the different character of the Brazilian people but in their stronger national consciousness and in the fact that they gained their independence quickly and easily. In the absence of a protracted military struggle, no clique of generals and colonels emerged to overawe the civil authorities, and no professional revolutionaries threw apples of discord among the masses. As the years passed Brazil made a gradual transition from an absolute to a constitutional monarchy and eventually to a republic.

Soon after Pedro I became Emperor of the new independent state of Brazil, he summoned a constituent assembly. The assembly met in April 1823. It was dissolved six months later, however, when disagreements developed between its leaders and the Emperor. Pedro thereupon appointed a commission of ten to complete the work of drafting a constitution under his own supervision. The constitution was submitted to local governments throughout the country and was proclaimed in effect on March 25, 1824. It was a moderately liberal document. It guaranteed freedom of speech, of the press, and of religion and provided for a legislative assembly, with an appointive Senate and an elected Chamber of Deputies. At the same time it left the Emperor above the law and exempt from responsibility for the acts of his ministers. He not only appointed the members of the Senate, but he had power to dissolve the Chamber of Deputies.

Pedro II and the downfall of the Empire

The constitution of 1824 remained in effect for sixty-five years. It covered the reigns of two emperors, Pedro I and Pedro II. By 1831 Pedro I had suffered a loss of popularity, partly because of his scandalous personal life but also because of military reverses and his practice of bullying the assembly. He gave up the throne in favor of his young son, who became Emperor as Pedro II. The latter ruled until 1889 when he too experienced a decline of prestige and was forced to abdicate. He was accused of favoring the Free Masons against the Catholic Church and of disregarding the rights of high army officers. But the factor which really led to his downfall was the abolition of slavery. In 1887 he sailed for a vacation in Europe leaving his impetuous daughter Isabella in charge of the government. In 1888 she signed a bill emancipating all the slaves without compensation to their owners. This action deprived the empire of its remaining supporters and opened the way for revolution. An armed uprising led by General Deodoro da Fonseca forced the Emperor to abdicate. A republic was proclaimed under a provisional government headed by the victorious general.

The Republic of Brazil

In 1890 a committee of lawyers drafted a constitution for the Republic of Brazil, which went into effect the following year. It provided for a government almost identical with that of the United States. Significantly, it included a bill of rights guaranteeing freedom of religion and the separation of church and state. Executive power was vested in a President elected for a four-year term, and legislative power in a congress comprising a Senate and a Chamber of Deputies. The members of the former represented the states, but both the senators and the deputies were chosen by direct popular vote. The government was reorganized as a federal system with reserved powers left to the states and enumerated powers granted to the central authority. However, the central government was given powers of intervention which could easily be interpreted in such a way as to restrict the freedom of the states. With few changes the Constitution of 1891 continued in effect until the suspension of constitutional government by the Vargas dictatorship in 1930.

The history of Mexico in the nineteenth century resembled the history of Brazil in that both countries wavered between monarchy and republicanism and had similar conflicts over church and state. **314** But Mexico was one of the few Latin American countries in which the *mestizos* and Indians (the former especially) played an active part in determining the course of political developments. Her first ruler after independence, Iturbide, who became Emperor Agustín I, was of mixed white and Indian parentage. As a statesman, though, he was a failure and in little more than a year was driven from the throne and forced into exile. In 1824 a republic was set up with a constitution similar to that of the United States, except that the Roman Catholic faith was made the established religion. Between 1833 and 1855 Mexico was ruled most of the time by the redoubtable Antonio Lopez de Santa Anna, famous as the opponent of the United States in the dispute over Texas and in the war that followed. Although holding the title of President, he governed as a dictator with the support of a clerico-military oligarchy. Cruel, treacherous, and greedy for power, he exemplified that *personalismo* which has been the curse of so many Latin-American countries. His downfall was achieved by a coalition of radicals and liberals led by two full-blooded Indians, Juan Álvarez and Benito Juárez, and a Creole, Ignacio Comonfort. Although Comonfort became President, the real leader of the coalition was Juárez. He and his followers inaugurated a program aimed at the destruction of clerical and military privilege, the suppression of the Church, and the distribution of Church lands to the people. These reforms were eventually incorporated in a new constitution adopted in 1857.

The clericals and conservatives did not take kindly to the Constitution of 1857. The consequence was civil war, the so-called War of the Reform, from 1858 to 1861. It ended in a complete victory for Juárez and his followers, with the result that more drastic anticlerical laws were enacted to supplement the provisions of the constitution. Religious orders were suppressed, Church property was nationalized, and civil marriage was established. But the triumph of the liberals did not obliterate the nation's troubles. The government was so desperate for money that it sold some of the confiscated Church lands to secular landlords. The peasants were merely transferred from one exploiter to another. The war disrupted economic conditions to such an extent that payments on foreign debts were suspended. This gave the wily Napoleon III an excuse to intervene. In 1862 he sent a French army to Vera Cruz, which finally battered its way to Mexico City and took possession of the government. Meanwhile an assembly of Mexican conservatives went through the sham of "offering" the Mexican throne to Archduke Maximilian of Austria, who had already been selected by Napoleon III as his puppet ruler.

As Emperor of Mexico, Maximilian was worse than a failure. Although he was kindly, idealistic, and sympathetic with the plight of most of his new subjects, he was amateurish and dominated by an overly ambitious wife. Moreover, he antagonized the conservatives by his acid criticisms of corruption and indifference in the Church

Maximilian, Emperor of Mexico.
When, in 1862, Napoleon III intervened in Mexico, he chose Archduke Maximilian of Austria, brother
of Emperor Franz Josef I, as puppet
ruler of the Mexican people. In 1867
he was overthrown and executed
by revolutionaries led by Benito
Juárez.

The empire of the
French puppet
Maximilian

and in the army. The followers of Juárez had distrusted him from
the beginning. The primary cause of his downfall, however, was a
shift in the power struggle in Europe. The Austro-Prussian War of
1866 put Napoleon in a position where he could no longer afford to
give military support to Maximilian. As a result of her victory in
that war Prussia now loomed as a dangerous rival of France. Soon
afterward, therefore, the French Emperor withdrew his troops. He
was impelled to take this action partly, of course, by vigorous protests from the government of the United States against French violation of the Monroe Doctrine. But even without these protests, his
decision could not have been long delayed.

The return of
Juárez

In the absence of French military support, Maximilian's empire in
Mexico speedily collapsed. The liberal forces of Juárez closed in
upon him, and he was captured, court-martialed, and executed by a
firing squad. Juárez was quickly elected President and re-elected in
1871, but death overtook him the following year. He had time to
accomplish only a few of his aims for making Mexico a modern,
progressive state. He drastically reduced the size of the army, eliminated waste and extravagance in the government, and initiated steps
for a wide extension of public education. But the troubles of the nation were far from ended. It was impossible to repair overnight the
damage caused by twenty years of civil strife. The national debt
continued to increase, economic activity had shrunk, and the country seemed almost on the verge of exhaustion. In 1877 the government of Juárez's successor was overthrown, and a dictatorship was
established that was destined to remain in power for more than
thirty years. The new ruler was Porfirio Díaz, the son of a Creole
father and an Indian mother. Originally a pupil and follower of
Juárez, he repudiated his master when the latter was re-elected President in 1871. Thereafter he pursued his own ambitions and strove
with an iron will to mold his country in accordance with his cher-
316 ished schemes.

The regime of Díaz brought Mexico prosperity but nothing that resembled democracy. For the most part he ruled benevolently but always with an eye to the perpetuation of his own power. He soon controlled the electoral machinery and used government funds to buy off potential opponents. Those who couldn't be bought he dealt with in more summary fashion. For disposing of suspected revolutionaries his general order to the army and the public was: "When caught in the act, kill in cold blood." Yet under his rule the nation made rapid progress, and the business classes at least luxuriated in dividends and profits. Foreign trade multiplied six times over, and railroad mileage increased from 400 to 16,000. Mines were brought up to unprecedented levels of production, smuggling was eliminated, the national budget was balanced, and interstate tariffs were abolished to the substantial benefit of industry and commerce. Many of these improvements were made possible, however, by the importation of foreign capital. The suppliers of these funds frequently drove unscrupulous bargains as part of the terms of the investment. They exacted concessions to buy land at ridiculous prices, including full title to all minerals beneath the surface. Prosperity at the price of so large a part of the nation's heritage eventually proved to be too much for the middle classes to endure. By 1900 the reputation of Díaz had lost its luster. By 1911 when his government collapsed and the aged dictator sailed for France, the Mexican republic was ripe for revolution to undo the evils of three decades.

4. THE TWENTIETH-CENTURY REVOLUTIONARY ERA

It would scarcely be an exaggeration to say that Latin America witnessed more social and political changes from 1900 to 1968 than in the previous four centuries of her history. Two significant developments distinguish the record of the twentieth century thus far. The first is a phenomenal increase in population. Around 1800, Central and South America had a population of about 17 million; by 1900 this had grown to about 70 million and by 1965 to 165 million. For some countries the rate of increase was even greater than for Latin America as a whole. The population of Brazil more than trebled between 1900 and 1960. Argentina surpassed even this ratio, with a growth in numbers from 4,200,000 in 1900 to 20 million sixty years later. Whether this growth was a milestone of progress may well be questioned. Nearly everywhere population was beginning to exert terrific pressure upon available resources. Most countries did not have enough arable land to support a rapid growth of inhabitants. The expansion of industry and commerce was still too limited to absorb very much of the excess.

The second outstanding development was marked progress toward the solution of the age-old problems of poverty and ignorance among the masses. At the turn of the century 90 per cent of Latin

CANADA

UNITED STATES
OF AMERICA

40°

LATIN AMERICA TODAY

Dates indicate year
of independence

ATLANTIC

OCEAN

*GULF OF
MEXICO*

20°

MEXICO
(1821)

Mexico City ★

Nassau
BAHAMAS
(Brit.)

Havana

HAITI (1804)

CUBA
(1898)

DOMINICAN REP. (1844)

San Juan

JAMAICA
(1962)

Port au Prince

Santo
Domingo

PUERTO RICO (U.S.)

BARBADOS (1967)

TRINIDAD AND
TOBAGO (1962)

SEE INSET
BELOW

CARIBBEAN SEA

Caracas

Port of Spain

VENEZUELA
(1811)

Georgetown

Paramaribo

FRENCH GUIANA

Orinoco R.

GUYANA

SURINAM
(Du.)

Cayenne

Bogotá

COLOMBIA
(1821)

R.

PACIFIC

0°   Equator

GALAPAGOS IS.
(Ecuador)

Quito
ECUADOR (1822)

Amazon

0°

OCEAN

PERU
(1821)

Lima ★

ANDES MTS.

BRAZIL   (1822)

★ Brasília

BOLIVIA
(1825)

La Paz ★

Sucre ★

PARAGUAY
(1811)

0   1000   2000 miles

20°

CHILE
(1818)

Asunción ★

Río de Janeiro

ANDES

URUGUAY (1828)

Santiago ★

Buenos Aires ★

★ Montevideo

La Plata R.

MOUNTAINS

ARGENTINA
(1816)

40°

FALKLAND ISLANDS
(Br.)

CAPE HORN

60°

CENTRAL AMERICA

JAMAICA
(1962)

Kingston

★ Belize
BRITISH HONDURAS

GUATEMALA
(1821)

HONDURAS (1821)

Tegucigalpa ★

*CARIBBEAN

SEA*

Guatemala ★

Salvador ★
EL SALVADOR
(1821)

NICARAGUA
(1821)

Managua ★

PANAMA
CANAL

San José ★

COSTA RICA
(1821)

PANAMA (1903)

Panama ★

PACIFIC OCEAN

120°

100°

80°

60°

40°

20°

Americans lived a hand-to-mouth existence of squalor and wretchedness. Most of them were peons, or laborers on large estates, doomed to a kind of slavery by debts they could never repay. Their families were crowded together in one-room shacks with no stove or fireplace, no running water, and no sanitary facilities. Wages received for a day's toil scarcely equaled the hourly pay for comparable work in the United States. Most of the fertile lands were owned by a few wealthy families, who ruled their great estates, or *haciendas*, in semifeudal fashion. Though less than 10 per cent of the population, this powerful landlord class monopolized the professions, government positions, and the officer ranks in the army. Its members sent their sons to the universities, which produced excellent lawyers, historians, poets, and essayists but neglected the sciences and engineering. The masses, of course, remained illiterate and steeped in ignorance and superstition.

The country which made the most spectacular progress in solving its land problem and in conquering illiteracy was Mexico. We have seen that, as late as 1911, the so-called Republic of Mexico was still under the rule of the suave but sometimes ruthless dictator, Porfirio Díaz. In that year he was forced by open revolt to step down from his exalted position and take refuge in France. His successor as President was Francisco Madero, the intellectual leader of the anti-Díaz forces. A nervous man with a high-pitched voice, a vegetarian and a spiritualist, Madero was ill-equipped for leadership of a country in the throes of a revolution. When he failed to carry out land reform speedily enough, some of his most powerful allies withdrew their support. He seemed helpless in the face of corruption on the part of relatives and subordinates. Denouncing him as a visionary and a lunatic, the United States Ambassador schemed to bring about his overthrow. In February 1913, he was deposed by his chief rival, Victoriano Huerta, and soon afterward was murdered.

Through the next four years chaos reigned supreme in Mexico. Huerta ruled as provisional president until July 1914, when, under pressure from President Woodrow Wilson, he resigned and fled to Europe. Then ensued a long conflict between rival generals contending for power. Venustiano Carranza, although recognized as the lawful President by the United States, did not receive the universal support of his own people. Pancho Villa kept the northern part of the country in turmoil, while in the south General Zapata marshaled the landless Indians in a crusade for economic reform. In 1916 the United States government sent an expeditionary force across the border to capture Villa "dead or alive" as a punishment for his raid on Columbus, New Mexico. He managed to elude his pursuers, but he was finally revealed as little more than a daring bandit, with no large following or substantial military force. Meanwhile, President Carranza, with arms furnished by the United States, was able to solidify his own position and to improve the stability of his government. He was eventually persuaded by his liberal followers to summon a constitutional convention. The convention met early in 1917 and drafted a constitution which was put into effect in May of that year.

The Mexican
Constitution of
1917

The Constitution of 1917 had several objectives in line with the revolutionary ideals of those who had been struggling to remake the country ever since the end of the Díaz regime: (1) to democratize the government; (2) to reduce the influence of the Church; and (3) to give to the nation control over its economic resources and to provide for the masses a more equitable share of the wealth they produced. In pursuance of the first, the Constitution bestowed the suffrage upon all male citizens twenty-one years of age and over and subjected the powers of the President to a measure of control by Congress. In keeping with the second, freedom of religion was guaranteed, the Church was forbidden to conduct primary schools, and the state legislatures were empowered to limit the number of priests in each district. But the most significant provisions of the Constitution were probably those dealing with economic reform. Peonage was abolished. An eight-hour day with one day's rest in seven was proclaimed the standard for industrial workers. The right to strike was recognized, and the government was given the authority to provide for social insurance. Mineral resources were declared to be the property of the nation. No foreigners were to be granted concessions to develop them unless they agreed to be treated as Mexican citizens. Private property of any kind might be expropriated by the government after the payment of just compensation.

Though apparently promising much, the economic provisions of the new Constitution had little immediate effect. Carranza, who was still President, was not a convinced liberal and had no enthusiasm

Library of the National University of Mexico, Mexico City. The decorations exemplify the revival of interest in the art of the Aztecs. *(Below)*

for carrying them out. Realizing this, dissatisfied elements rallied around General Álvaro Obregón, organized a revolt, and drove Carranza from the capital. Obregón became President in December 1920. During his term and those of his successors, especially Plutarco Calles and Lázaro Cárdenas, completion of the revolutionary aims of the Constitution was vigorously pushed. Millions of acres of land were expropriated and distributed to the peasants. Teacher-training programs were instituted and new schools were built. Primary education was made free and compulsory up to the age of fifteen. Legislation was enacted guaranteeing old-age pensions and providing insurance for illness, accidents, and unemployment. The petroleum industry was nationalized, with compensation to the former owners. Under more recent Presidents the government has taken a somewhat more conservative turn. In 1965 President Díaz Ordaz pronounced a five-year development plan based on the preservation of private initiative.

Progress in achieving reforms in some other countries of Latin America was more retarded. Brazil, for example, made no advance toward effective democracy in government until 1934. A Constitution which went into effect in that year forbade the re-election of the President and provided for the secret ballot and for the enfranchisement of both men and women, though a literacy qualification debarred many from voting. It provided also for an eight-hour day, prohibited child labor, and recognized the right of collective bargaining. But this Constitution continued in effect for only three years, and possibly was never intended as more than a polite gesture. Economic depression and the growth of communism gave an excuse to the President, Dr. Getulio Vargas, to make himself a dictator. He issued a new constitution which greatly enlarged the executive powers and gave him practically absolute authority to deal with national problems at his own discretion. Though his rule was comparatively mild, the rights and liberties of the people were virtually at his mercy until he was forced to resign by a bloodless revolution in 1945. His successor, General Eurico Gaspar Dutra, made a pretense of returning to constitutional government. A new fundamental law issued in 1946 lengthened the President's tenure to five years but declared him ineligible for consecutive terms. Freedom of speech and press were granted subject to a number of restrictions. The teaching of subversive doctrines and the dissemination of race and class prejudices were prohibited. Forbidden also were movements advocating a one-party system or questioning the right of private property. The Constitution also contained economic provisions pointing in the direction of autarchy and of government promotion of social improvement.

Through most of its history Brazil has relied upon one or two export crops as the principal source of national income. Coffee has been the great staple. Efforts to produce cotton, sugar, and choco-

Coffee Production in Brazil. Though a native of Arabia, coffee is now produced mainly in Latin America. Because of inadequate production control, plantation owners and workers have frequently been at the mercy of wildly fluctuating markets.

The economic problems of Brazil

late have been moderately successful, though production of most of these commodities can be accomplished more cheaply in other countries. An attempt by Henry Ford in the 1930's and 1940's to develop large-scale rubber production ended in failure. In recent years Brazil has been striving to build a more diversified economy. A large steel mill was projected in 1941, and by 1945 an aluminum plant, capable of supplying the normal peacetime demand, was in full production. The country has an ample variety of mineral deposits, including high-grade iron, manganese, nickel, chromium, tungsten, bauxite, and diamonds. However, the quality of her coal is poor. Even greater handicaps are lack of capital and the technological skill to make the best use of her industrial resources. In large sections of the country, schools, especially of higher grade, do not exist. Except in the coastal area the great majority of the inhabitants are still illiterate, though notable progress has been made in recent years in raising the educational level. Finally, the Vargas policy, continued by most of his successors, of government spending has resulted in serious inflation. Extravagant appropriations have been made for numerous projects, notably for the construction of a resplendent new capital, Brasilia.

Later political developments

In 1950 Dr. Vargas was again elected President, but his rule was so unsuccessful that in August 1954, he was forced by military leaders to turn over his office to the Vice President, João Cafe. A few hours later Vargas committed suicide. For years after that a bitter struggle raged between Vargas's followers and their opponents. The former included the conservative Social Democratic party, dominated by the Governors he had elevated to power during his dictatorship, and the Brazilian Labor party, based on the unions he had fostered. The anti-Vargas forces, organized mainly in the National Democratic Union, included the more enlightened members of the military and the business classes, who distrusted both the labor unions and the professional politicians. In 1955 the pro-Vargas elements triumphed. Five years later the anti-Vargas parties succeeded in turning the tables. They elected Janio Quadros, with the largest majority ever obtained by a Presidential candidate. But in August 1961, Quadros resigned, alleging a plot against him by "reactionary forces." He was succeeded by the Vice President, João Goulart, leader of the Labor party. The anti-Vargas leaders acquiesced in Goulart's accession since they had managed to amend the Constitution transferring most of the executive powers from the President to a Premier chosen by Congress. Early in 1963 a popular referendum sanctioned a return to Presidential government. Conflict and confusion, however, continued to plague the country. In 1964 President Goulart was ousted on account of too strong a Leftist bias, and General Castelo Branco was elected to succeed him. The new government decreed that henceforth executives should be chosen by legislative bodies instead of by direct vote of the people. In 1966 Arthur Costa e Silva, a staunch anti-Communist, was elected President by Congress.

The richest and most highly industrialized of Latin American countries has one of the poorest records as an exemplar of political and economic democracy. Although Argentina adopted universal manhood suffrage, the secret ballot, and minority representation in 1912, most of these provisions have had little meaning, especially in recent years. Voting has often been manipulated by powerful cliques for their own advantage, and authoritarian government has been the rule rather than the exception. The reasons for this lack of democratic progress require careful analysis. It can be traced in part to the rapid industrialization and to the fierce antagonism between urban and rural classes. More than 50 per cent of the population is employed in industry, and a wide gulf separates the interests and attitudes of Buenos Aires from those of the outlying provinces. Industrialization and urbanization proceeded so rapidly after World War I that a precarious stability has characterized the economic system ever since. The country has been especially vulnerable to worldwide depressions. A second cause has been the ebullient nationalism of the Argentine people. Unlike most other Latin American countries, Argentina is a "white" nation. Her Indian population has always been small, and a liberal immigration policy has given her a predominantly European population. This uniqueness has imbued her citizens with an intense national pride. They believe that their country should be the leader of Latin America and particularly resent interference by the United States in the affairs of the southern continent. Devotion to the trappings of national glory has a tendency to foster autocratic government.

Obstacles
to democracy
in Argentina

A Slum on the Outskirts of Rio de Janeiro. The wretchedness depicted here contrasts sharply with the wealth and luxury suggested by the scene on the opposite page.

CONTRASTS IN LATIN AMERICA

Bethlehem Steel Corporation Ore Loading Operation in Venezuela.

Aerial View of Brasilia, Entirely New Capital of Brazil. Planned for completion as a unit, it is designed to accommodate 500,000 inhabitants.

El Teniente Copper Mine, Chile. El Teniente Mining Company is jointly owned by Kennecott Copper Corporation (U.S.) and the Chilean government. Chile ranks third in world copper production, after the United States and Zambia.

Tin Miners in Bolivia. Bolivia produces more than 15% of the world's output of tin. The mines were developed largely by North American capital, but the leading companies were nationalized in 1952.

Modern Freeways near Caracas, Venezuela. As a result of income from oil, Caracas is one of the wealthiest cities in Latin America.

The inauguration of Juan D. Perón as President of Argentina, June 4, 1946. Left is the President pro tempore of the Senate, who administered the oath. On the right is Vice President Quijano.

Irigoyen

Much of Argentine political history in the twentieth century has revolved around a small number of dominating personalities. As early as 1905 a middle-class leader, Hipólito Irigoyen, organized a plot to seize the city of Buenos Aires. The scheme was thwarted, but Irigoyen remained to plague the conservatives and landowning classes for twenty-five years. Reserved, modest, and lacking in oratorical ability, he nevertheless inspired fanatical loyalty among his followers. In 1916 he was elected President for a six-year term and was elected again in 1928. His popularity stemmed partly from the fact that he managed, against powerful opposition, to keep Argentina neutral during World War I and to gain for her later a place of recognition in world affairs. But he ruled as an autocrat, enforcing a vicious antistrike policy against labor, and, during his second term, permitting widespread corruption. He was overthrown by a bloodless revolution in 1930 engineered by conservatives and high-ranking officers of the armed forces.

The road to fascism

Irigoyen was succeeded by José F. Uriburu, a former inspector-general of the army. He promised to govern in accordance with the Constitution, but he immediately dissolved the Congress and filled the administrative offices with his own henchmen. When the date for the next election rolled around, Uriburu dictated the choice of his successor by declaring the opposition candidates ineligible. A period followed when conservatives and bourgeois liberals alternated in the possession of power. With the outbreak of World War II a sinister fascist movement began to develop in Argentina. Sympathy with the Axis, based in part upon fear of communism, was widely prevalent. Large numbers of the business classes were of German or Italian extraction, and many army officers were German trained. The nation was already in the throes of economic crisis. The government was almost bankrupt, and inflation and overcrowding in the cities inflicted cruel hardships on people with meager resources. Besides, the official policy of paying low wages as a means

326

of boosting exports created a surly, rebellious class of workers ready to follow any demagogue who promised to better their condition. The first of such mountebanks to appear on the scene was Juan D. Perón. Leader of a movement to force the resignation of President Ramírez in 1943, he ran for President himself in 1946. By promising wage increases, rent controls, and partitioning of great estates, he won enough support among the masses in addition to that of the military and business elements to ensure his election. Three years after his inauguration he changed the Constitution to make himself eligible for re-election. His methods of governing resembled closely the familiar pattern of fascist dictatorship—censorship, saber-rattling, militarism, antiforeignism, imperialism, and economic nationalism.

By June 1955, the Argentine people had had enough of Perón. He antagonized the Catholics by legalizing divorce and by attempting the separation of Church and state. He incurred the enmity of the middle class by the expensive benefits he conferred upon his followers in the General Confederation of Labor and by his expansion of the national debt. Though a revolt which broke out in June was suppressed, it smoldered and flared up again in September. The rebels won the support of the navy and finally threatened to bombard the city of Buenos Aires if Perón did not surrender. A military junta persuaded him to relinquish his power and to go into exile. He fled to Paraguay and later found refuge in Nicaragua. Following the overthrow of Perón, General Eduardo Lonardi became provisional president under a promise to hold free elections. Two months later he was deposed by a new military junta, which accused him of "fascist" inclinations. The junta then chose General Pedro Aramburu to succeed him. The Aramburu regime maintained some elements, at least, of constitutional government. In May 1956, the Constitution of 1853 was restored. The rights of the individual were reaffirmed, and the great liberal newspaper, *La Prensa*, was given back to its rightful owners.

The overthrow of Perón

The restoration of constitutional government did not end the threat to democracy in Argentina. It was impossible to eradicate overnight the influence of two million *peronistas* who longed for a revival of the dictatorship that had conferred so many favors upon the working classes. It was impossible also to suppress the ambitions of the generals and colonels, who demanded strong government until Peronism and communism should be completely eliminated as effective instruments of class legislation. Although free elections were held in 1958, Arturo Frondizi, the successful candidate, survived as President for only four years. He was ousted by the military, who distrusted him since it was widely known that he owed his victory in the election to the votes of the *peronistas*. The new President, accepted by the military, was José Maria Guido. In order that the nation might continue to receive financial benefits from the

The persistence of the Peronist heritage

United States, amounting to over $300,000,000 annually, he preserved a façade of democracy. But the economic ills dating from the Perón regime and from the depression of the 1930's and 1940's remained—the trade deficit with foreign countries, the chronic unemployment, the mountain of public debt, and the steadily advancing cost of living. In July 1963, Dr. Arturo Illia, a country physician, was chosen to succeed Guido as President of the harassed republic. Illia's rule endured but three years. Accusing him of Leftist sympathies, a military junta overthrew him and established a new dictatorship headed by General Carlos Ongania.

The evolutionary
policies of Chile

The recent history of Chile bears several resemblances to that of Argentina. There have been similar problems of impoverishment of the masses, declining exports, galloping urbanization, and inflation. Chile had its "man on horseback" in the person of Carlos Ibañez, President from 1927 to 1931 and again from 1952 to 1958. Ibañez did not make his appeal, however, to the *descamisados,* or "shirtless ones," as Perón had done, nor was he as ruthless a dictator. He ruled most of the time on behalf of the chief landowners and foreign investors, despite the fact that 60 per cent of his people lived in cities, and that a quarter of the citizens were so poor that they existed on a hand-to-mouth basis almost entirely outside the money economy. Yet Chilean politics tended to follow a moderate course. A radical coalition known as the Popular Action Front attempted to ride into power with the support of the peasants and industrial workers, who constituted 70 per cent of the population, but uncertainty and fear of communism led to its defeat. In 1964 Eduardo Frei, a lawyer of German extraction, was chosen President. His party, the Christian Democrats, took a middle position between socialism and capitalism. Its philosophy derives from the encyclicals of liberal Popes and the teachings of contemporary Catholic thinkers. It promises higher income taxes, higher import duties, more support for education, and rigid control of foreign investments. Much advancement has already been made in redistribution of land, improvement of public health, population control, and advancement of education. In 1966 Chile became the first South American nation to have free, compulsory schooling through the eighth grade. Instead of expropriating foreign owners of natural resources, President Frei has followed a policy of "Chileanization"; that is, he has required the big American copper companies to sell to the Chilean government a share in their ownership and management.

Political and social
progress in
Uruguay

It is an interesting fact that some of the most progressive countries of Latin America are several of those least impressive from the standpoint of size and power. The best example is Uruguay. Inhabited by only two million people and with no great abundance of natural resources, this smallest of South American republics can lay claim to a better record of educational and political progress than many of her

neighbors. She ranks next to Canada and the United States as the most literate nation in the Western Hemisphere. Since 1903 she has had only one revolution, and that a peaceful one. Her constitution, modeled upon that of Switzerland, provides for equal suffrage, the secret ballot, minority representation, and the subordination of the President to a National Council. Among the reforms initiated by her Presidents, especially by José Batlle y Ordóñez, her greatest states-man, are disestablishment of the Church, abolition of capital punishment, provision for the eight-hour day and for minimum wages, old-age pensions, and social insurance. Uruguay also has an extensive program of public ownership, applying to banking, insurance, tourist hotels, electric light and power, and the importation and sale of alcohol, petroleum and cement. By the 1960's, however, the valiant little republic was in danger of sinking under a burden of troubles. The market for wool, the principal export, had declined with the development of synthetic fabrics. Inflation resulted when the peso shrank to a fifth of its former value. In 1967 the nation switched from the supremacy of a nine-member National Council to a single-executive presidency. The new President, Oscar Diego Gestido, instituted wage and price controls, distributed the burden of taxation, and centralized the administration of the welfare state. His major objective was to curb inflation.

Obviously, not all of the small Latin American states exemplify progressive and orderly democracy. Many of the banana and sugar republics of Central America and the West Indies have been notable exceptions. Guatemala, for instance, has gone through the gamut of radical dictatorship, counterrevolution, assassination, and a conser- vative Presidency supported by the United States. Despite acceptable constitutions, the Dominican and Haitian republics passed under personal dictatorships tempered by assassination or the threat thereof. The Dominican Republic suffered under the misrule of General Rafael L. Trujillo for nearly thirty years until he was blotted out by assassins' bullets in 1961. Graft, nepotism, and police terrorism had been the instruments of his power. Elections held in 1962 resulted in the choice of Juan Bosch, a liberal intellectual, as President. After less than a year he was overthrown, and a military clique assumed power. In 1965 Bosch and his followers, including some Communists, launched a counter-revolt. Bloody strife ensued followed by prompt United States intervention. President Johnson professed an obligation to protect American lives and to save the island from communism. Eventually, upon pleas from Washington, the Organization of American States sent a joint expedition to maintain order in the Dominican Republic. In 1966 Joaquín Balaguer became President as the result of a new election.

Similar troubles beset the republic of Haiti. Beginning in 1945 a series of revolutions alternating with chaos culminated in 1957 in the dictatorship of François Duvalier. Though he rules with the title of President, his power rests upon the armed forces. In 1964 he was made President for life. Even if his methods are less harsh than were those of General Trujillo, he must face the constant possibility of revolution. For Haiti is poorer and culturally more backward than the Dominican Republic. It has the highest rate of illiteracy, the deepest poverty, and the most primitive economic development of all the countries of Latin America. Nevertheless, its government has one advantage over the governments of some neighboring states. It enjoys the support of Washington. The State Department evidently considers Duvalier the least of a number of possible evils.

The tragedy of
Cuba

Of the smaller Latin American nations the one with the most tragic recent development has probably been Cuba. Freed from Spanish rule by the United States in 1898, Cuba became an independent republic four years later. But political inexperience combined with the weakness of the two-crop economy left the country a prey to disorder and the breakdown of civilian rule. Events reached a crisis during the world depression of the 1930's. In 1933 the government of Gerardo Machado was overthrown. His successor, Grau San Martin, was considered too radical by the United States and was forced out of office. In 1936 a ruthless army sergeant, Fulgencio Batista, with aid from the United States and the support of the army, gained control of the government. In 1940 he was elected President. With the titular as well as the actual authority in his hands, he maintained a dictatorial rule until 1959. In that year he was overthrown by a coterie of young revolutionists under the leadership of Fidel Castro. Castro's program was essentially a patch-work and his followers a motley assortment. Some were anti-Communists, some were democratic socialists, and several had definite commitments to communism. Calling their movement the Twenty-sixth of July Movement because it had been launched on July 26, 1953, Castro and his comrades eventually demanded a complete revolution in Cuba. They would obliterate all traces of United States imperialism, expropriating American owners of banks, industries, and hotels. They would nationalize these properties and some others in order to provide jobs for the unemployed. They proposed also an extensive land reform for the benefit of the peasants. As the movement extended its power over the country and gained full control in 1959, it took on a more radical character. In 1961 Castro announced himself "a Marxist-Leninist." He proceeded also to align his country more and more closely with the Communist bloc.

The Communist
orientation of the
Castro regime

The pro-Communist orientation of the Castro regime aroused antagonism in the United States. In April 1961 the United States government encouraged and assisted an invasion of Cuba by embittered exiles who had been driven from the country. An attempted landing at the Bay of Pigs was a total failure. In October 1962 the government in Washington obtained evidence of large-scale Soviet military assistance to the Castro regime. Missile bases had been established and considerable numbers of Soviet bombers had been stationed in Cuba. President Kennedy responded to these findings by ordering a naval blockade of the island republic. He informed the Soviets that the blockade would continue until the missiles and bombers were removed from Cuban soil. Premier Khrushchev took alarm at the threat of nuclear war and promised to withdraw, within a few days, both missiles and bombers. Kennedy had gambled on the chance that Khrushchev would not consider Cuba worth a war, and had won. As Secretary of State Dean Rusk is alleged to have expressed it, "We were eyeball to eyeball, and I think the other fellow just blinked."

Cuba. Fidel Castro at the commemoration of the foundation of the "Committee for Defense of Revolution," an organization of vigilance against counter revolutionary activities, which he founded.

But the victory over communism was perhaps more apparent than real. Even if the Castro regime were overthrown, the problems of discontent in Latin America would not be solved. The difficulty arises from the fact that in so many countries population expands too rapidly, the economy is badly balanced, and the gulf between rich and poor yawns too wide. In Latin America as a whole, as late as 1950, about 90 per cent of the land belonged to 10 per cent of the owners. Nearly 65 per cent was in farms of more than 2500 acres. In Venezuela the proportion was 74 per cent. Half the farm land of Brazil was in the possession of 1.6 per cent of the owners, while in Chile 2 ½ per cent held 75 per cent. The majority of farms were too small to provide the farm family with anything approaching a decent living. For the most part, the situation in Cuba was an aggravation of that to be found throughout the continent. Three-quarters of the land was owned or controlled by the sugar plantations. Much of this total was withheld from cultivation, since sugar was in oversupply. Only through government action could land be made available to impoverished peasants. But before the Castro revolution the Cuban government was usually dominated by large landowners and wealthy investors. To the opponents of these classes, both inside and outside Cuba, Castro loomed as a hero. He will doubtless remain such as long as per capita incomes are less than $300 per year, as long as unemployment leaves millions struggling to buy bread, and as long as children sleep on the sidewalks in the shadow of plush hotels.

The deeply rooted problems of Latin America

SELECTED READINGS

· *Items so designated are available in paperbound editions.*

Alexander, R. J., *The Perón Era*, New York, 1951.

———, *Communism in Latin America*, New Brunswick, N.J., 1957.

———, *Prophets of the Revolution: Profiles of Latin American Leaders*, New York, 1962.

American Assembly, *The United States and Latin America*, New York, 1959. Topical studies by journalists and scholars.

Arciniegas, Germán, *Latin America: A Cultural History*, New York, 1967.

Bernstein, Harry, *Modern and Contemporary Latin America*, Philadelphia, 1952.

· Cline, H. F., *The United States and Mexico*, Cambridge, Mass., 1953 (Atheneum).

Crawford, W. Rex, *A Century of Latin American Thought*, Cambridge, Mass., 1944.

Cumberland, C. C., *Mexican Revolution, Genesis under Madero*, Austin, Texas, 1952.

· ——— *The Meaning of the Mexican Revolution*, New York, 1967 (Heath).

Ellsworth, P. T., *Chile, an Economy in Transition*, New York, 1945.

Gordon, W. C., *The Economy of Latin America*, New York, 1950.

Harris, Seymour E., *Economic Problems of Latin America*, New York, 1945.

Hirschman, A. O., ed., *Latin-American Issues*, New York, 1961. An objective study emphasizing economic problems.

Jones, Tom B., and Beatty, W. D., *An Introduction to Hispanic American History*, New York, 1950.

Munro, Dana G., *The Latin American Republics, a History*, New York, 1943.

Rennie, Y. F., *The Argentine Republic*, New York, 1945.

Rippy, J. F., *Latin America and World Politics*, New York, 1938.

Skidmore, J. E., *Politics in Brazil*, New York, 1967.

Smith, T. Lynn, *Brazil: People and Institutions*, Baton Rouge, La., 1946.

Stuart, G. H., *Latin America and the United States*, New York, 1943.

Thomas, A. B., *Latin America: A History*, New York, 1956.

Waddell, D. A.G., *The West Indies and the Guianas*, Englewood Cliffs, N.J., 1967 (Spectrum).

Whitaker, A. P., and Jordan, D. C., *Nationalism in Contemporary Latin America*, New York, 1966.

White, John W., *Argentina, the Life Story of a Nation*, New York, 1942.

Wilgus, A. C., ed., *South American Dictators during the First Century of Independence*, Washington, 1937.

Williams, M. W., *The People and Politics of Latin America*, Boston, 1945.

Wythe, George, *Industry in Latin America*, New York, 1945.

CHAPTER 11

China and Japan under the Impact
of the West (1800-1914)

The virtue and prestige of the Celestial Dynasty having spread far and wide, the kings of the myriad nations come by land and sea with all sorts of precious things. Consequently there is nothing we lack, as your principal envoy and others have themselves observed. We have never set much store on strange or ingenious objects, nor do we need any more of your country's manufactures.
—Edict of the Manchu Emperor Ch'ien Lung to King George III of England, 1793

During the nineteenth century, for the first time in history, the most advanced Western states, through the dynamic effects of the Industrial Revolution, became strong enough to alter the destinies of Far Eastern nations by direct intervention. Consequently, the chief problems affecting the Eastern nations in this period revolved around the readjustments necessitated by Western expansion. Cultural phenomena were subordinated to political objectives, and international relations became of crucial importance. Because China and Japan responded quite differently to the changing world conditions which confronted them, the contrasts between these two countries became greater than ever before.

I. IMPERIALISM AND REVOLUTION IN CHINA

The nineteenth century, which witnessed tremendous economic, political, and intellectual progress in the Western world, was a period of trouble for China. The central factor in China's distress was the decadence of the Manchu Dynasty and the incompetence of its administration, but all her problems were aggravated by the pressure that Western powers were now exerting in the Far East. As in

The misfortunes of China under the impact of imperialism

333

the case of India the objectives of the Westerners at the outset were almost exclusively commercial, and in China as in India the British played the leading role. Although China escaped complete subjugation, her institutions were greatly altered under the Western impact; she suffered the humiliation of seeing her territory and sovereignty infringed upon by Europeans; and for the first time in history Japan displaced China as the leading Asiatic state.

It was unfortunate that increasing interest in the China trade on the part of the Western nations came at a time when the imperial government was almost moribund, undermined by corruption, and lacking in intelligent leadership. During many earlier periods of their history the Chinese had shown themselves not only enterprising traders but also capable of profiting from the stimulation offered by contacts with the outside world. By the nineteenth century the eyes of officials were closed to the desirability of any change and to the danger of having unwelcome changes forced upon them. Both the Manchu aristocracy and the Chinese class of scholar-officials which supported it were schooled in the tradition that trade was a contemptible business, unworthy of a gentleman's attention. The Westerners who came to China specifically for purposes of trade were looked down upon as a low order of humanity, and the power which they were able to exert in enforcing their demands was slow to be recognized. The policy of the Manchu government was to avoid contamination from the Western hucksters by keeping them at a safe distance and requiring them to have relations only with Chinese merchants, not with government officials. At the same time the government expected to derive profit from levying taxes on whatever trade was permitted, and members of the bureaucracy from top to bottom also exacted commissions for extending privileges to merchants.

At the opening of the nineteenth century, although Western trade had reached fairly large proportions, it was still carried on under cumbersome restrictions which in many ways were disadvantageous to the Chinese as well as to foreigners. Aside from the Portuguese settlement at Macao, the only authorized port of exchange was Canton (by an imperial edict of 1757), at the opposite extremity of the empire from Peking, the seat of government. Silk and tea, the leading Chinese exports, had to be carried overland a distance of at least 500 miles to Canton; their transportation by boat along the coast was not permitted for fear that payment of the excise tax might be evaded. The trade at Canton was under the general supervision of a Manchu official known to foreigners as the "Hoppo" and was handled through a guild of Chinese merchants called the Cohong. While the Co-hong merchants enjoyed a monopoly of foreign trade, they were taxed and "squeezed" by numerous officials and also were held personally responsible for the conduct of the foreigners with whom they dealt. Beginning about the middle of the

Chinese Silk Factory, ca. 1800. (Illustration from a French treatise on the silk industry.)

eighteenth century a system of "security merchants" had been instituted, whereby every incoming foreign vessel was assigned to the supervision of a particular member of the Chinese guild during its entire stay in port. Foreign merchants were permitted to come to Canton only during the designated trading season (the winter months) and their acitvities were highly circumscribed. They were forbidden to bring their women or families with them, to ride in sedan chairs, or to employ Chinese servants. They were, theoretically at least, confined to the special area set aside for the "factories," and they could make no request to a government officer except through a Co-hong merchant as intermediary.

That the Canton trade was profitable both to the Chinese and to the foreigners is evidenced by the fact that it continued to grow in spite of the annoying regulations surrounding it and in spite of fluctuations in the assessments upon it. Foreigners were often kept in ignorance of the schedule of duties fixed by the Peking government. The Co-hong merchants—under pressure from the Hoppo, who in turn had to satisfy various other greedy bureaucrats and recover the expenses he had incurred in getting himself appointed to office— were inclined to charge what the traffic would bear. The foreign traders, if fleeced unduly, could of course threaten to break off intercourse altogether. Actually, remarkably stable relations were established between Chinese and foreign merchants at Canton. Large transactions were handled, sometimes on a credit basis, with only oral agreements between the two parties, and by communication through a vernacular known as "pidgin English." [1]

Methods of trade

[1] Some large fortunes were accumulated in the process. In 1834, one member of the Co-hong estimated his personal estate at $26,000,000. H. B. Morse and H. F. MacNair, *Far Eastern International Relations*, p. 68.

As the volume of Western trade increased, however, friction was bound to arise. Two fundamentally different civilizations were coming into contact with each other. There were wide gaps between the Western and the Chinese concepts of justice and legal procedure. Westerners regarded as barbarous the Chinese view of group, rather than individual, responsibility for misbehavior and the use of torture in obtaining confessions. Consequently, misunderstandings occurred over the apprehension and punishment of criminals. Perhaps even more serious was the fact that the character of the trade began to change in a direction which was disadvantageous to China. In early days Chinese exports—tea, silk, and cotton cloth in lesser quantities—had far exceeded the value of imports into China; and the difference was made up in silver payments to Chinese merchants. Western traders would have preferred to make the exchange in goods, but they had difficulty in discovering any appreciable Chinese demand for commodities which they could supply. The Chinese attitude, as expressed by the Emperor Ch'ien Lung to the British in 1793, was: "The Celestial Empire possesses all things in prolific abundance and lacks no product within its borders. There is therefore no need to import the manufactures of outside barbarians in exchange for our own products." [2]

Eventually, a means of altering the balance of trade was supplied by the increase of opium consumption in China. Opium had long been used in China as a medicine and as a drug, and the practice of smoking it was introduced along with tobacco-smoking in the seventeenth century. In spite of imperial edicts against it, traffic in the drug grew steadily, with the bulk of the shipments coming from India. So ineffective was an imperial order of 1800 prohibiting this trade that by 1839 more than 4 million pounds of opium were being shipped in annually. Thoroughly aroused to the gravity of the situation, the imperial government resolved to take stronger measures, both for moral and for economic reasons. The traffic was draining specie out of China and, because it was illegal, it brought no revenue to the state while lining the pockets of smugglers and conniving officials.

Although traders of various nationalities, including Americans, participated in the China trade, the greater share had been in the hands of the British East India Company. When, in 1834, the company was divested entirely of its trading functions and the traffic was thrown open to all comers, the situation in China became more critical than ever. As British mercantile interests in the Far East continued to expand, the demand arose in England for the establishment of regular diplomatic relations with the Chinese government. In 1834 Lord Napier was sent as chief superintendent for British trade, under instructions to announce his arrival directly to the viceroy, the highest Chinese functionary at Canton. Napier was unable to

[2] C. P. Fitzgerald, *China, a Short Cultural History*, 3rd ed., pp. 557-58.

carry out his instructions because the viceroy refused to see him on the ground that the "barbarian headman" must conduct his business through the Co-hong merchants, in keeping with law and custom. According to the viceroy: "The petty affairs of commerce are to be directed by the merchants themselves. The officials are not concerned with such matters. . . . To sum up the whole matter: the nation has its laws; it is so everywhere. Even England has its laws; how much more the Celestial Empire!" [3]

The vigorous attempts of a special Chinese commissioner to enforce the prohibitions against the opium traffic created a series of incidents which culminated in the Anglo-Chinese War of 1839–1842. This conflict, which was confined to the coastal regions near Canton and the lower Yangtze ports, is known as the Opium War because of the dispute that precipitated it. Actually the British objectives were broader and more ambitious than this title suggests. The real importance of the war is that it served as an entering wedge for the expansion of commercial intercourse and marked the beginning of the subjection of China to conditions imposed by the Western powers. By the treaty of Nanking in 1842 (supplemented the following year) the Chinese government ceded the island of Hong Kong to the British, promised an indemnity and compensation for the opium chests which had been confiscated, and agreed to treat Britain as a most favored nation in any future concessions which might be made. Four ports besides Canton were opened to trade, the Co-hong monopoly was abolished, and the right of residence was granted to foreigners in the treaty ports. Other nations, which had followed the course of the war with interest, were quick to follow the example of Britain in demanding similar privileges, confirmed in separate treaties. A significant feature of the treaty negotiated by the American minister, Caleb Cushing, was that it specifically included the principle of extraterritoriality, which conceded to foreigners accused of crime the right to be tried in their own national courts rather than by Chinese tribunals. These initial treaties omitted reference to the opium traffic but provided that the Chinese tariff on exports and imports should be "uniform and moderate," a phrase interpreted as denying the Chinese government the right to raise the tariff without consent of the Western commercial powers. Thus by 1844 China was saddled with "unequal treaties," depriving her of control over her tariffs and limiting the powers of her courts over foreigners.

The results of the first Anglo-Chinese war were to intensify friction instead of removing it. Much of the fault lay with the foreigners, who took advantage of the weakness and corruption in the Chinese administration to enlarge their own interests. The privilege of extraterritoriality was abused, being extended to cover Chinese servants in the employ of foreigners, and inadequate punishment was

[3] H. M. Vinacke, *A History of the Far East in Modern Times*, 5th ed., p. 40.

given by the foreign powers to their own nationals who were convicted of crime. Portuguese vessels, and some others, engaged in "convoying," nominally to protect coastal shipping against piracy but actually to extort tribute from legitimate traders. Another reprehensible practice, carried on by Europeans and Americans during the middle of the century, was the recruiting of Chinese contract labor for export to plantations in the New World under conditions reminiscent of the old African slave trade. On the other hand, Westerners complained that the Chinese were evading both the spirit and the letter of the treaties. The attempt to establish foreign settlements at Canton led to rioting, because the Cantonese interpreted the treaties as granting foreigners the right of residence only outside the city walls. Less trouble was encountered in the new trading ports, where local sentiment was eager to attract commerce away from Canton now that Canton's monopoly had been broken. In Shanghai, the influx of foreigners resulted in the creating of an "International Settlement"—controlled jointly by British and Americans—and a separate French Settlement in the same city.

The war of
1858–1860

In all disputes with China the Western powers had the advantage of superior force, which they did not hesitate to use upon occasion. For a time, pressure was applied only locally, in the particular district where an untoward incident had occurred. In 1858, however, the British and French co-operated in large-scale hostilities against the Peking government. After negotiations at Tientsin (the port of Peking), a misunderstanding arose as to the route for the foreign representatives to follow en route to Peking, whereupon the British and French forced their way up the river to the capital, drove the emperor in flight into Manchuria, and burned the beautiful summer palace of the Manchus. This war of 1858–1860 opened China more widely than ever before to Western penetration. The treaties of Tientsin and Peking added eleven ports to the list of authorized trading centers, legalized and imposed a tax upon the opium traffic, granted foreigners the right to travel in all parts of China, and promised that diplomatic representatives of the Western nations would be received in Peking. Largely because of the interest of the French in missionary activity, the Chinese government, compelled to acknowledge that "the Christian religion inculcates the practice of virtue," undertook to protect missionaries and their property.

Short-sighted
policies of the
Chinese government

Although by 1860 the ineffectiveness of China as a sovereign state had been clearly demonstrated, the Manchu government showed no inclination to take a realistic view of the situation or to profit from its own mistakes. The heavily staffed bureaucracy numbered some men of genuine ability among its ranks, but it was practically paralyzed by its own inertia. Local officials had acquired the habit of minimizing or concealing problems rather than attacking them, and the top authorities provided no incentive for the drastic renovation that was needed to make the country strong enough to stop the in-

trusion of European powers. Unwilling to contemplate the necessity
or the desirability of change, they tended to regard the Western
pressure as a temporary affliction that would disappear in the course
of time, as had other calamities in the past. Unable any longer to
repel the ocean-borne "barbarians," the government nevertheless
indulged in annoying and dilatory tactics, exhausting the patience of
Westerners (not a very difficult task) without gaining any real advantage in reurn. Quite unnecessary was the vexatious and humiliating treatment accorded diplomatic representatives, who came to
Peking armed with credentials from their respective governments
but found it almost impossible to gain admittance to the emperor's
presence. The Manchu rulers were reluctant to give up the illusion
that foreign emissaries were merely tribute-bearers from vassal
states who should perform the *kowtow* (ceremonial prostration)
before the throne. In spite of the pledges given in 1860, no imperial
audience was granted to the foreign diplomatic corps at Peking before 1873, and not until twenty years later was it conducted in a
manner acceptable to the Western ministers. Oddly enough, while
the Manchu rulers persisted in an attitude of irresponsible and
haughty superiority toward the Western nations, they were coming
to rely upon these nations to carry out some of the normal functions
of government within the Chinese Empire and even to protect their
regime when it was menaced by rebellion.

While the Western powers were tightening their grip on China's
commerce and installing their agents in her coastal cities, internal
upheavals created havoc and threatened to overthrow the dynasty.
The most famous example, although actually only one of a number
of contemporary revolts, was the movement known as the Taiping
Rebellion, which began in 1851 and was not suppressed until more
than a decade later. Its originator and leader, Hung Hsiu-ch'üan,
was a native of the region near Canton in Kwangtung province who
had shown promise as a scholar but had thrice failed in the provincial civil-service examinations. Frustrated in office-seeking, he nourished a bitter grudge against the Manchu government (which, with
some justice, was suspected of discriminating against southern Chinese), and gradually his resentment became fused with a conviction
that he had a divine mission to perform. He had received instruction
for a short period from a Baptist missionary in Canton and, after an
illness and a series of visions which he interpreted as revelations
from God Almighty, he undertook to win his countrymen to the
true faith. Hung's religion was largely Christian in ideology but
with peculiar variations. He recognized God the Father as supreme
deity, revered Christ as Elder Brother, and described himself as
"Heavenly King and Younger Brother of Jesus." He also identified
God with the ancient deity Shang Ti whom the Chinese had worshiped in pre-Chou times, and therefore believed that in propagating
his version of Christianity he was actually urging the Chinese to re-

turn to their own original faith. Taoism, Buddhism, and ancestor worship he regarded as idolatry, and his followers first attracted the attention of authorities by their zeal in desecrating temples. Eventually Hung conceived his destiny to be to lead the "Association for Worshiping God" in a movement to overthrow the Manchus and inaugurate the "Heavenly Kingdom of Great Peace." Thus the Taiping Rebellion was both an antidynastic revolt and a religious crusade.

Originating in the extreme south, the rebellion spread northward and in 1853 the Taiping leaders captured Nanking, which they retained as their capital for eleven years, entirely cutting off the rich Yangtze valley from the control of the Peking government. Fighting occurred in fourteen out of China's eighteen provinces, and in 1853 rebel troops came within twelve miles of Tientsin. That the Taiping regime ultimately collapsed in spite of the inability of the Manchus to suppress it was due partly to inherent limitations in the movement and partly to the attitude of the great powers. Fundamentally a peasant uprising, the rebellion failed to win the support of the Chinese intelligentsia and actually antagonized this class by repudiating not only popular religions but the whole Confucian tradition as well. In addition, the Chinese gentry realized that the Taipings would institute radical economic changes, jeopardizing private property rights. Some foreign residents, especially Protestants, were at first inclined to view the revolt with sympathy because of its association with Christian teaching, but they soon became aware that a triumph of the Taipings would not serve the interests of Christian missionaries. Hung evidently believed that all Christians in China should accept his authority because his revelations were more recent than any described in the Bible, and the rebel leaders became increasingly fanatical. Undoubtedly also, a factor influencing the decision of the Western powers not to support the Taiping movement was that these powers had already successfully pressed demands upon the imperial government and preferred a weak but compliant regime to an aggressive one founded upon revolution.

Without formal intervention in the Taiping wars, the Western powers assisted the Manchus in suppressing the rebellion—even while the British and French were conducting their own war against the Peking authorities in 1858–1860. In view of the confused state of Chinese affairs, perhaps it is not strange that one of the military heroes in the imperial service was Frederick T. Ward, a sea captain from Salem, Massachusetts, who raised a volunteer corps for the protection of Shanghai contrary to the wishes of his own government and over the protest of British naval authorities. General Ward adopted Chinese citizenship, and, in gratitude for the exploits of his "Ever-Victorious Army," the emperor commanded that altars should be erected and perpetual sacrifices offered to his spirit.

Reasons for the
failure of the
Taiping Rebellion

Ward's most distinguished successor was an Englishman, Major Charles ("Chinese") Gordon. Meanwhile several able Chinese, from the civilian gentry rather than from the professional military clique, had come to the rescue of the hapless Manchus and earned the major credit for suppressing the rebellion. In 1864, the combined Chinese, French, and British forces captured Nanking, the last Taiping stronghold.

The liquidation of Hung's "Heavenly Peace" movement, however, did not bring peace even of an earthly variety to China. Moslem rebellions in the southwest and the northwest remained unsubdued until considerably later. During the thirteen years of Taiping intransigence two-thirds of the provinces had been devastated, the whole country impoverished, and probably no less than twenty million people killed by battle, massacre, and famine. The Manchu Dynasty had been saved only through the efforts of its Chinese subjects and by grace of the foreign powers. Furthermore, the injury to China's intellectual heritage through the destruction of libraries and academies in the Yangtze valley was incalculable. In reaction against Taiping fanaticism the bureaucracy became more uncompromisingly conservative than ever.

The story of China from 1860 to 1911 is the depressing tale of a discredited dynasty clinging to its prerogatives while its people were oppressed and the nation's independence was being gradually whittled away. A little color was added by the career of the famous Empress Dowager, T'zu Hsi, a Manchu woman of great cunning and strong will, who dominated the Peking administration through her control of puppet emperors during much of the period between 1861 and her death in 1908. The "old Buddha," as she was nicknamed, in spite of her irregular and unscrupulous methods, somewhat recouped the prestige of the ruling house, but she neither understood nor contributed to the solution of China's basic problems. Out of the chaos of the Taiping era came a reorganization and centralization of the Chinese maritime customs service. A temporary arrangement, whereby foreigners had collected tariff duties at Shanghai while the authority of the Peking government was paralyzed, was perpetuated and extended to all the treaty ports. The higher personnel of the customs service was composed of foreigners, nominated by their consuls but appointed by Peking, with the understanding that so long as the English predominated in China's foreign trade the inspector general would always be a British subject. Thus the customs administration, while foreign-staffed, was an agency of the Chinese government, maintained its headquarters at Peking, and operated as a unit regardless of provincial divisions. The fact that the foreign inspectorate functioned efficiently emphasized all the more glaringly the general decrepitude of the Manchu administration.

In the last quarter of the nineteenth century China's weakness was

further revealed in the loss of some of her outlying possessions. By
1860 she had renounced to Russia all claims to territory beyond the
Amur and the Ussuri rivers, thus allowing Russia to surround Manchuria and to control the entire Asiatic seacoast north of Korea.
Through a combination of diplomatic and military pressure, culminating in a small-scale war (1884–1885), France acquired a protectorate over virtually all of Indochina except the independent state
of Siam. The murder of a British explorer in China's southwestern
province of Yunnan led the British to demand, and China to yield,
sovereignty over Upper Burma (1886). The Japanese government
enforced a claim to suzerainty over the Ryukyu Islands (1881). Not
to be outdone, the Portuguese, who had occupied Macao for 300
years, obtained its formal cession in 1887. The full measure of
China's humiliation, however, followed the Sino-Japanese War of
1894–1895. Japan, only recently emerged from feudalism and isolation, gave the world a startling demonstration of China's impotence
by defeating the Celestial Empire in the short space of eight months.
Shortly afterward five great powers—Russia, Great Britain, France,
Germany, and Japan—participated in a "battle for concessions,"
through which the major part of China proper was partitioned into
"spheres of interest." The spheres of interest, somewhat vaguely
defined and usually radiating from a leased port, theoretically did
not impair China's sovereignty; but the concessions as a whole made
her an economic dependency of the great powers.

Before the close of the nineteenth century, conditions in China
provoked a growing spirit of resentment against both the incompetence of the government and the foreign elements that had taken
advantage of it. A group of educated Chinese who were sincerely
interested in their country's welfare and also appreciative of Western institutions began to agitate for reform. As might be expected,
the reformers were mostly from southern China, especially Kwangtung province. Their first outstanding leader was K'ang Yu-wei,
who had been influenced by the Han Learning scholars and wished
to utilize Confucian principles in reconstructing the government. On
social questions K'ang adopted some decidedly radical views, even
contemplating the abolition of the family; but he was not impetuous
and set as his immediate goal the attainment of constitutional monarchy for China. For a brief period, known as the "Hundred Days
of Reform" (June to September 1898), it looked as if the ideas of
K'ang would bear fruit as the young emperor, under K'ang's guidance, issued a series of edicts that indicated a break with the past.
The movement came to an unhappy end, however, when the Empress Dowager T'zu Hsi executed a *coup d'état* and forced the
emperor into retirement. K'ang Yu-wei escaped arrest and decapita-
tion by fleeing the country.

Having rebuffed the liberal reformers, the Manchu court next
gave its blessing to extreme reactionaries. The Empress Dowager

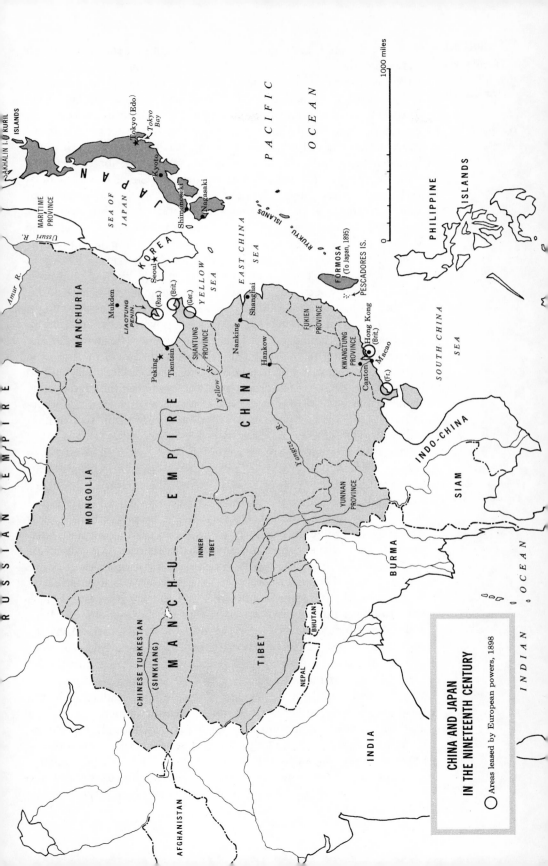

CHINA AND JAPAN
IN THE NINETEENTH CENTURY

○ Areas leased by European powers, 1898

shrewdly directed the fulminations of various secret societies—which were potentially a threat to the dynasty—into the channel of anti-foreignism. The climax came in 1900 when the so-called Boxers ("Society of Harmonious Fists") unleashed a violent attack upon Christians and foreigners in Shantung and the adjacent northeastern provinces. In view of the fact that the movement was secretly encouraged by the Empress Dowager and was based on extreme anti-Western fanaticism, the number of lives lost was not tremendous even in the critical areas. In other parts of China the provincial authorities, disregarding T'zu Hsi's instructions, generally tried to maintain order and protect the resident foreigners. Thus the Boxer movement was neither a revolution nor an actual war against the West; but the Western powers co-operated to stifle it with promptness and vigor, allowing their troops to indulge in wanton looting in Tientsin and in Peking, where far more damage was inflicted after the allied forces occupied the capital than while it had been held by the Boxers. Instead of abolishing the Manchu Dynasty as they might easily have done, however, the Western governments decided to shore it up, extracting certain guaranties of good behavior for the future. By the terms of settlement (the Boxer Protocol of 1901) the imperial government was required to pay heavy indemnities and to mete out punishments to certain of its own officials; the civil-service examinations and the importation of arms were suspended temporarily; and the Western powers were granted permission to maintain military units in the Peking area.

In a final attempt to save the dynasty and partly in response to foreign pressure, the Manchu rulers during the period 1901–1911 projected a series of reforms, which emphasized railroad construction, modernization of the military services, public education, and liberalization of the political structure. These measures, beneficial as they appeared to be, were poorly planned and carried out only half-heartedly, and the reform program actually speeded the coming of revolution. In 1905 the ancient civil-service examinations were formally abolished, preparatory to erecting a modern educational system. But the initiative in implementing the program was left to the provincial governors, most of whom did little about it. Many ambitious Chinese youths went abroad to study, particularly to Japan, where instruction of a very superficial character was supplied to meet the sudden desire for "Western learning." A youth movement began to manifest itself in China, characterized by impatience with the old order but inadequately prepared for leadership in the creation of anything better. The government announced plans for a gradual transition to a constitutional regime with an elected parliament and, as a first step in this direction, established provincial assemblies in 1909. Although these assemblies were not democratically elected and were intended to be only debating societies, they vociferated so loudly that the government deemed it expedient to summon a National Assembly the following year. The National Assembly of 1910 was devised as a bulwark of conservatism, with half its members directly appointed by the emperor. Nevertheless, it proceeded to criticize the government and pressed the demand for more rapid reform.

Meanwhile resentment was mounting against the policy of the government in regard to railroad construction. The original plan had been to build a unified network of roads by letting the provincial authorities assume responsibility for specific sections, raising the necessary funds by stock subscriptions among the wealthy citizens of each province. It was hoped thus to stimulate national interest in the project and also to avoid recourse to foreign loans. In 1909, however, the Peking government took the whole program into its own hands, partly because it feared that decentralization was dangerous to the imperial authority and partly because mismanagement and graft in the provinces were eating up the funds. The government's decision made it necessary to borrow from foreign capitalists and offended provincial interests. Investors were angered when they learned that their stock would not be redeemed at face value, and in the fall of 1911 outbreaks of violence occurred. The railroad controversy was only one among many factors which brought anti-dynastic feeling to the point of open rebellion. A bomb explosion in Hankow, on October 10, touched off a general uprising in the Yangtze valley cities, during which Li Yüan-hung, commander of a rebellious imperial garrison, cast in his lot with the revolutionaries.

The revolutionary elements in China, which moved into the foreground with the impromptu insurrections of 1911, were by no means in agreement as to program or tactics. A number of liberal leaders, headed by K'ang Yu-wei, clung to the ideal of a limited monarchy. They would accept the continuation of the dynasty if it was willing to renounce absolutism and promote progress. A more radical group wished to abolish the monarchy altogether and convert China into a republic. The prime figure among the radicals was Dr. Sun Yat-sen (1866–1925), born of a peasant family near Canton, in the province which had produced the leader of the Taipings and countless other opponents of the Manchu regime. At the invitation and expense of an elder brother, Sun had gone to Hawaii to obtain a Western education and had been converted to Christianity. After returning to China he studied medicine, chiefly with Protestant missionary physicians, and received a medical diploma at Hong Kong. He participated in an abortive revolt against the government in 1895, from which he barely escaped with his life. Thereafter Dr. Sun traveled widely, residing in the United States and visiting both England and Continental Europe. During these years he had studied Western institutions, which he became convinced could be successfully adopted in China, and dedicated his energies to stirring up opposition to the Manchus among Chinese at home and

"Father of the Chinese Republic." Dr. Sun Yat-sen and his second wife, Soong Ching-ling (sister of Mme. Chiang Kai-shek). The widowed Mme. Sun is now a vice-chairman of the People's Republic of China.

abroad. In China his work was carried forward by a secret "Alliance Society," which attracted various disaffected elements in the period preceding the 1911 outbreak.

Establishment of a republic

Lack of co-ordination among reformist and revolutionary groups, the distracted and impoverished state of the country, and the persistence of strong sectional loyalties made it impossible for the revolution to follow a clear-cut pattern. Events of the next few years were confused and somewhat paradoxical. Yüan Shih-k'ai, a conservative bureaucrat who had reorganized the army in northern China, was ordered by the Manchu court to suppress the rebellion. Probably because he realized that the dynasty's days were numbered, he avoided decisive engagements with the southern insurgents, even though his army was superior to theirs. The National Assembly at Peking, while demanding immediate constitutional reforms and amnesty for the rebels, at the same time nominated Yüan Shih-k'ai—the Manchu's last hope—as prime minister. There was even more confusion in the south than in the north, although a united front was presented against the imperial government by an assembly at Nanking in which central Chinese and Cantonese co-operated. The Nanking assembly elected as president Dr. Sun, who had only recently arrived in China, and declared for a republic. Instead of puncturing this radical trial balloon with one stroke, Yüan arranged with the representatives of Nanking a settlement which embodied a compromise between the northern and southern groups. As a concession to the southern (and radical) factions, China was to be designated a republic with Li Yüan-hung as vice-president and with Nanking as the capital. But to promote harmony, Dr. Sun stepped out of the limelight and recommended that Yüan Shih-k'ai, who was supported by the northern armies, be made provisional president of the republic. Although the Manchu emperor was required to abdicate, Yüan secured an extremely generous settlement for the royal family.

Thus, with comparatively little bloodshed or social upheaval and without interference by the great powers, both the Manchu Dynasty and the institution of monarchy had been overthrown. However, these events proved to be only the beginning of China's revolution; and they were a prelude to one of the most severe periods of distress in China's long history. Obviously, any regime that succeeded the Manchus was confronted with the staggering problems of administrative corruption, economic stagnation, and general demoralization which were the fruits of Manchu misrule. Furthermore, the unequal treaties and foreign spheres of interest that had been imposed upon the country made the attainment of a unified modern state doubly difficult. Progress was bound to be slow at best, but the men who attained power during this stage of the revolution seemed more bent on advancing their own interests than those of the country. Yüan Shih-k'ai, who had not the least sympathy with republican principles, maneuvered himself into the position of a dictator. He refused to transfer the seat of government to the south, and when a parliament met at Peking in 1913 to draw up a constitution he intimidated, tricked, and bribed the delegates. Dr. Sun's Alliance Society had reorganized as the Kuomintang ("Chinese Nationalist Party"), and Kuomintang elements were dominant in the parliament which was attempting to prepare a frame of government. The constitution as drafted placed limits on the executive power; but so successful was Yüan in corrupting the members of parliament that they elected him to the presidency. Yüan then contemptuously dissolved the assembly, outlawed the Kuomintang, and promulgated a "Constitutional Compact" of his own devising, retaining himself as president. From 1914 until his death two years later Yüan Shih-k'ai ruled as a military dictator, backed by the northern army which he had organized for the imperial service. The Western governments, whose attitude toward the Chinese revolution had been remarkably apathetic, were on the whole favorably disposed toward Yüan and extended loans to him through an international banking group. The powers were willing to support a "strong man" in China—so long as China herself remained weak. Russian intrigue combined with Mongol nationalist sentiment to secure autonomy for Outer Mongolia; rebellion in Tibet enabled the British to extend their influence in that dependency; and the Japanese were beginning to cast covetous eyes on the Shantung Peninsula.

Although reactionary, Yüan Shih-k'ai's dictatorship at least demonstrated the fact that monarchy was thoroughly discredited in

China. When Yüan committed the mistake of trying to perpetuate the power of his family by ascending the Dragon Throne as the founder of a new dynasty, he met with unexpected opposition. The great powers, particularly Japan, disapproved of his scheme, and fresh rebellions broke out in the southern provinces. The sudden death of the frustrated dictator in the summer of 1916 theoretically restored the republic under its "permanent" constitution. But a clique at Peking carried on Yüan's highhanded methods, while various provincial governors and military commanders were rendering themselves independent of any central authority. China, it seemed, had gotten rid of the Manchus only to fall prey to greedy and unprincipled war lords.

The death of
Yüan Shih-k'ai
and the rise of
the war lords

2. THE TRANSFORMATION OF JAPAN INTO A MODERN STATE

The end of
Japanese isolation

Japan's policy of isolation, carefully maintained since the early seventeenth century by the Tokugawa Shoguns, was bound to give way when Western nations expanded their trading activities in the Far East. Before the middle of the nineteenth century several attempts, all unsuccessful, had been made by European powers to open Japan to trade. That the United States government finally took the initiative in forcing the issue was due partly to the fact that the British were busily engaged in China. It was also an indication that America's Far Eastern commerce had attained considerable proportions. Since about 1800, United States whaling and clipper ships had passed through Japanese waterways en route to China, and with the rise of steam navigation the need for stations where ships could be refueled and provisioned became more imperative.

Commodore Perry
and Townsend
Harris

When Commodore Perry's "black ships" steamed into Tokyo Bay in July 1853, Perry was under instructions from Washington to secure from the Japanese government the promise of protection for shipwrecked United States seamen, permission for merchant ships to obtain repairs and fuel, and the right to trade. Perry's gunboats were sufficiently impressive to induce the Shogun to give a favorable reply when the Commodore returned to Edo early the following year. However, the significance of the change in Japan's position was not apparent until a United States consul-general, Townsend Harris, after many vicissitudes negotiated a commercial treaty with the Shogun in 1858. Harris had no gunboats to back his arguments, but he skillfully used the object lesson of European aggression in China to convince the Japanese that they would be better off to yield peaceably to American demands. The Harris Treaty provided for the opening of several ports to traders and for the establishment of diplomatic intercourse, placed limitations on the Japanese tariff, and recognized the principle of extraterritoriality. Following the United States lead, other Western powers secured treaties granting

Commodore Perry's Landing at the Village of ·Kurihama in Tokyo Bay, July 14, 1853. The Japanese had erected a special building (with conical roofs) to receive the foreigners but also arranged an impressive display of troops (in the background). Perry disembarked with 110 marines (shown flanking the shore), two bands, sailors, and naval officers, while his two frigates kept their guns trained on the beach. The boats in the foreground contain Japanese officers. From a sketch drawn at Perry's request by W. Heine, an artist who accompanied the expedition.

them similar privileges, and it seemed that the pattern which was unfolding in China might be duplicated in Japan. But, as events turned out, Japan's reaction to the Western impact produced results which were almost the opposite of contemporary developments in China. The reason for this contrast is that the Japanese, after recovering from their initial shock, turned enthusiastically to the task of assimilating Western culture and techniques for the purpose of strengthening their state and winning equal recognition among other nations.

The first important effect of the opening of Japan was that it led to the abolition of the Shogunate, making possible a reorganization of the government along modern lines. As will be recalled, the "outer *daimyo*"—especially the heads of the great "western clans" (Choshu, Satsuma, Hizen, and Tosa)—had long been awaiting an opportunity to displace the Tokugawa family from its dominant position. The action of the Shogun in yielding to the Western powers provided just such an opportunity. Before signing the treaties the Shogun had taken the unprecedented step of going to Kyoto to consult the emperor. The clan leaders subsequently demanded that the emperor should be restored to his rightful position as ruler, denounced the Shogun for his weakness in submitting to the foreigners, and raised the cry that the "barbarians" must be expelled. The antiforeignism of the western clan leaders was broken

The abolition of the Shogunate

349

by direct action on the part of the "barbarians." In 1863, after an Englishman had been slain by people of the Satsuma *Daimyo*, British vessels bombarded the Satsuma capital. Duly impressed, the Satsuma leaders immediately voiced the desire to acquire a navy like that of Britain. The feudal lords of Choshu were similarly chastened and reoriented in their thinking in 1864 when British, French, Dutch and United States men-of-war unleashed a joint action upon Shimonoseki. In a remarkably short time the key men of the great feudal estates dropped their attitude of uncompromising hostility to the foreigners, meanwhile becoming more determined than ever to end the outmoded dual system of government.

The Meiji
Restoration
(1867–1868)

In 1867 the Shogun was prevailed upon to surrender his prerogatives to the emperor. He had expected to be retained as generalissimo, and when he was ordered to lay down his military command also, he resisted. However, the principal clans, acting in concert and in the name of the emperor, quickly defeated the ex-Shogun's forces and relegated the Tokugawa family not to obscurity but to private station. Upon the abolition of the Shogunate, which had existed for almost 700 years, the imperial residence was moved from Kyoto to Edo, renamed Tokyo ("Eastern Capital"), and the old castle of the Shogun was converted into an imperial palace. This series of events constituted what is known as the Meiji Restoration.

The emergence
of Japan as a
modern state

It so happened that the Emperor Mutsuhito, a lad of fifteen at the time of the Restoration, proved to be an extremely capable person who helped materially in the task of reorganizing Japanese institutions. The years of his reign, known as the Meiji or "Enlightened" era (1867–1912), witnessed the emergence of Japan as a modern and powerful state. Nevertheless, it would be a mistake to attribute Japan's transformation to the initiative of the emperor. As in previous periods of the country's history, effective leadership was supplied by less exalted figures, who used the throne as a symbol to promote a sentiment of national solidarity and to give the sanction of authority to their program. Quite understandably, the leaders in the political field were recruited chiefly from the ranks of feudal society, although they included some members of the old court nobility. In spite of their aristocratic backgrounds, however, the leaders were quick to perceive the necessity of breaking with the past if genuine progress along Western lines was to be achieved. Some of the western clans voluntarily liquidated feudal institutions within their own jurisdiction, urging others to follow their example, and in 1871 the emperor formally abolished the whole feudal system. The hereditary fiefs reverted to the state and by authority of the emperor were divided into prefectures for administrative purposes; the peasants were made, in theory, free landowners, paying taxes instead of feudal rents. The *daimyo* and their *samurai* retainers were granted pensions (later converted into lump-sum payments) amounting to less than the revenues they had formerly claimed.

It may seem strange that a feudal nobility would so readily surrender its privileges. The explanation lies partly in the genuine desire of forward-looking members of the aristocracy to strengthen Japan and partly in the fact that feudal institutions were no longer very profitable and had been largely undermined by the growth of a mercantile economy. Furthermore, able members of the *samurai* class, who had been the real managers of great domains in Tokugawa times, saw the advantages in establishing a regime in which their talents could be more fully utilized and more adequately recognized. This class did in fact supply many of the leading statesmen during Japan's period of transition. Nevertheless, the abolition of feudalism exacted a real sacrifice of the *samurai* as a whole. The *daimyo* received a fairly generous financial settlement and were assigned ranks in a newly created order of nobility. But the *samurai* found themselves deprived of their incomes while, at the same time, the government forbade them to wear any longer the traditional two swords and ordered them to merge into the ranks of the commonalty. Smoldering discontent among the *samurai* broke out into open revolt in 1877, presenting the government with a test of strength which it met with complete success. The newly organized conscript army, composed of peasants with modern weapons, quickly defeated the proud *samurai*, and the rebellion of 1877 proved to be "the last gasp of a fast dying feudal society."

The sweeping political, social, economic, and intellectual changes which took place in Japan during the Meiji era were sufficient to constitute a revolution. However, they were not the result of a mass movement or of any tumultuous upheaval from the bottom of society. The revolution was one directed and carefully controlled from above. The fact that the Tokugawa regime had already unified the country and through its discipline had instilled habits of docility in the population facilitated the work of the Restoration leaders. The majority of the population played only a passive role in the transformation, even though they were profoundly affected by it.

In carrying out their carefully channeled revolution, Japan's leaders made a painstaking study of the institutions of all the major Western nations and copied, with adaptations, what seemed to be the best features of each. In the political sphere, they reached the conclusion that the principles of constitutional monarchy should be introduced. A bold but somewhat ambiguous statement of policy, known as the Emperor's Charter Oath (1868), had hinted at the establishment of a deliberative assembly; but when plans for the drafting of a constitution were announced, it was made clear that any concessions would be in the nature of a gift from the throne rather than in recognition of inherent popular rights. A hand-picked commission drafted a constitution which, promulgated by the emperor in 1889, was patterned somewhat after the model of the German Imperial Constitution of 1871. It provided for a bicameral parlia-

THE TRANS-
FORMATION OF
JAPAN INTO A
MODERN STATE

The last gasp
of feudalism

The revolution
from above

The Constitution
of 1889

ment or Diet, with a House of Peers (including some representatives of the wealthy taxpayers) and a House of Representatives chosen by an electorate of property owners. The Diet was assigned the normal legislative powers, except that its control over finance was limited, and the Constitution included a Bill of Rights. In spite of some liberal features, the conservative character of the new government was unmistakable. So high was the property qualification for voting that only about 1 per cent of the population was enfranchised. The position of the emperor was declared to be inviolable; he retained supreme command of the army and navy, directed foreign affairs, and could veto bills passed by the Diet. Notably lacking was the principle of parliamentary control over the executive; ministers were responsible not to the Diet but to the emperor. Furthermore, although there was a Cabinet of Ministers as well as a Privy Council, both these bodies were created *before* the Constitution went into effect. A peculiarity of the Japanese Cabinet (aside from the fact that it was not responsible to the Diet) was that the Army and Navy ministers could consult with the emperor directly, without the mediation of the Premier.

The persistence of ancient traditions

While the Japanese Constitution incorporated several important features and much of the nomenclature of Western political institutions, the government remained close to Japanese traditions in its spirit and functioning. These traditions (which had more in common with Confucianism than with Western political concepts) included such fundamental ideas as that men are by nature unequal and the inferior person should be subject to the superior, that society is more important than the individual, that government by man is better than government by law, and that the patriarchal family is the ideal pattern for the state.[4] Political reforms were considered

[4] For an illuminating discussion of these concepts, see R. K. Reischauer, *Japan: Government-Politics*, Chapter I.

The Opening of the First Japanese Parliament, in November, 1890. From a Japanese engraving. Note the Western-style Diet chamber, lighting, decor, and costumes.

only a means to an end, which was not necessarily to produce the greatest happiness of the greatest number but to promote the efficiency, strength, and prestige of the state. The men who, in consultation with the emperor, introduced the Constitution of 1889 had no notion of relinquishing their command at the instigation of parliamentary cliques or under the pressure of public opinion. The guiding personalities were a fairly large group, numbering perhaps a hundred men, chiefly ex-*daimyo* and ex-*samurai*, who together composed a sort of oligarchy. Young men at the time of the Restoration, they retained their influence throughout the Meiji period and beyond, and eventually were referred to as the "elder statesmen" (*Genro*). Acting quietly behind the scenes, they frequently made important decisions of policy. Fortunately for Japan, these "elder statesmen" were as a whole realistic in outlook, moderate in judgment, and highminded.

In spite of the absence of democratic traditions and in spite of the authoritarian character of the Restoration government, the granting of a constitution led, almost from the outset, to a desire for further **Political parties** political reforms. Members of the Diet at least had the right to criticize the ministers, and voices were raised in favor of the extension of parliamentary control over the ministry. Political parties were organized, leading to a struggle in the Diet between the defenders of bureaucratic government and the advocates of the cabinet system. The germination of political parties actually antedated the Constitution. The "Liberal" party, which appeared in 1881, was primarily an outgrowth of an "association for the study of political science" founded several years earlier by Itagaki, a *samurai* of the Tosa clan. In 1882, Count Okuma of the Hizen clan launched his "Progressive" party. These two "radical" aristocrats were doubtless motivated partly by resentment against the fact that their own clans had secured relatively few posts in the bureaucracy, most of which were filled by Choshu or Satsuma men. Nevertheless, the introduction of political parties helped to strengthen the movement for the establishment of representative government.

After the Constitution went into effect, the character and the activities of political parties in Japan were peculiar and not entirely healthy. Emphasizing personalities rather than specific programs, **Significance of** parties came and went, fusing into one another, or changing their **political parties** names in a bewildering fashion. Their effectiveness was lessened by their lack of a broad popular base, by the government's censorship of press and speech, and by the fact that when party spokesmen became too troublesome they could usually be quieted by offering them patronage or admitting them to the lower ranks of the bureaucracy. But, with all their faults, the parties provided opportunities for acquiring political experience and also forced the bureaucrats to explain and defend their policies to the public. The campaign to achieve party government—that is, to make the Cabinet responsible **353**

Militarism and the
abolition of
foreign privileges

The growth of
capitalism

to the Diet—gained considerable headway on the eve of World War I and was resumed vigorously during the 1920's.

Experiments with constitutional government were only one aspect of Japan's political transformation. A modern and efficient military establishment was a prime objective that was rapidly attained, with a navy modeled after Great Britain's and an army copied from that of Germany (largely because the superiority of the latter had been strikingly demonstrated in the Franco-Prussian War). The principle of universal military service, introduced in 1873, was not a Japanese invention (although conscript peasant armies had been known to both China and Japan in ancient times and had played a part in Japan's feudal wars of the sixteenth century), but was based upon the example of modern European states. The administrative system was revised, and new judiciary and legal codes were adopted which compared favorably with those of Western countries and enabled the Japanese to claim successfully that they were not behind the West in the administration of justice. In 1894 Great Britain voluntarily surrendered her extraterritorial rights in Japan, and by 1899 all the other powers had taken the same step. The abrogation of external control over the customs duties required a longer period of negotiation, but tariff autonomy was achieved in 1911. Henceforth Japan was entirely free from the humiliation of "unequal treaties."

The economic changes of the Meiji era were perhaps even more significant than the political. In Tokugawa feudal days Japan was far from being a purely agrarian nation, and before the Restoration of 1867 an urban economy, chiefly mercantile and capitalistic, had come into being. When the new regime undertook to strengthen the state and secure the benefits of Westernization, it launched an ambitious program for the development of industry and a modern system of communications. Because private capital was not available in sufficient quantities to do the job quickly and because of the fear that extensive borrowing from foreign investors would endanger Japan's economic independence, the government assumed the initiative in constructing railroads, telegraph and telephone lines, docks, shipyards, and even manufacturing plants, while it also aided private industry by loans and subsidies. There was no tradition of laissez faire in Japan to stand in the way of government participation in the economic sphere, and public officials were anxious to move ahead as rapidly as possible. However, many enterprises which had been fostered by the state were eventually transferred to private hands, although the state retained control of railways and communications for strategic and security reasons. Hence, in Japan, economic progress led to the growth of a capitalist class, but one which did not correspond exactly with similar classes in the Western industrial nations. The members of the new capitalist class, like the prominent political figures, were drawn largely from the old aristocracy, while

354

not excluding men of bourgeois origin—money-lenders and rice merchants of the Tokugawa era. *Daimyo* now found a profitable field of investment for the funds they had received upon surrendering their feudal privileges, and the more nimble-witted of the *samurai* also participated in industrial development.

The history of the famous house of Mitsui, which grew to be the largest combination of mercantile, financial, and industrial interests in Japan, illustrates the remarkable success of a *samurai* family that was shrewd enough to anticipate future developments. In early Tokugawa times the Mitsui, defying the prejudices of their class, had abandoned fighting in favor of the solider rewards of commerce. They opened a store in Kyoto and in its management apparently anticipated the techniques of modern scientific salesmanship, displaying advertising posters and on rainy days giving away to customers paper umbrellas printed with the Mitsui trademark. Before the close of the seventeenth century, the family had established a banking house in Edo. The Mitsui heartily welcomed the opening of Japan to foreign trade, and so confident were they of the success of the Restoration that they lent large sums of money to the emperor and his entourage while the new government was in the process of formation. The Mitsui family also formed a connection with the great Choshu clan, whose members filled important government posts, and thus were enabled to participate in various aspects of the economic program.[5] The Mitsubishi group of interests, which was the greatest rival of the Mitsui and, like them, developed under *samurai* leadership, effected a similar connection with the

[5] O. D. Russell, *The House of Mitsui.*

Modern View of Mitsubishi Shipyards. A Greek tanker is under construction.

A Pulp Mill. Mount Fuji is in the background.

Satsuma clan. In spite of the rapid industrialization of Japan, capitalists were relatively few, and they were generally affiliated with clan bureaucrats who dominated the government.

Peculiarities of Japanese capitalism Industrial developments in Japan in the late nineteenth and early twentieth centuries differed in several respects from the typical pattern of economic change in the West. In the first place, they were so rapid that in one generation the country was producing a surplus of manufactured goods, and foreign markets had become essential to the national economy. Second, the Industrial Revolution was transported to Japan after it had already reached an advanced stage in the Western nations, and consequently characteristics of the First and Second Industrial Revolutions were intermingled. The employment of women in industry at low wages, the lack of organization among the laborers or of legal safeguards to protect them, and the working conditions in factories and mines were parallel to the early stages of the Industrial Revolution in the West. On the other hand, the projection of the government into the business sphere and the appearance of finance capitalism were phenomena that were only beginning to manifest themselves in Western Europe and the United States. To a considerable extent in Japan, finance capitalism preceded industrial capitalism, because there had not been time for financial reserves to accumulate from the savings effected by a gradual mechanization of industry. The wealth of the aristocracy and of merchant and banking houses—essentially unproductive classes—was drawn upon to expedite industrial progress, and the fortunate members of these groups were in a position to dominate the productive enterprises of mining, manufacturing, and distribution as these grew to maturity.

Another peculiarity of Japan's industrial development was the fact that, while total production increased rapidly and some large plants were built for heavy industries, the majority of the factories remained small. Even in the 1930's, when Japan's industrial laborers numbered six million, almost three-fourths of them worked in small establishments employing fewer than a hundred workers and about one-half of them toiled in plants employing not more than five. The small factories, however, were usually not independent but were controlled by the great financial houses, which resembled trusts in their structure and obtained monopolies of whole fields of production. Workers in the cotton and silk textile mills, for example, might be likened to workers under the domestic system in early modern Europe, even though they tended machines instead of using hand tools. The supplying of raw materials and the distribution and sale of finished products—especially in the export trades—were handled by a few centralized organizations from which a network of controls extended over hundreds of tiny workshops scattered throughout the country. Naturally this system placed the worker at a great disadvantage, and his bargaining position was further weakened by the prevalence of an oversupply of cheap labor. In spite of the growth of huge cities, the larger part of the population remained on the land, which was insufficient in resources to support the peasant families. Hence these families were glad to supplement a meager income by letting some of their members, especially daughters, work in the shops for such wages as they could get. Between the depressed class of small farmers and laborers and the wealthy capitalists, the gulf was as great as that which had separated the upper and lower strata of the old feudal hierarchy.

Extensive social and cultural changes also accompanied the transformation of Japan's economic and political institutions. Some of these changes were brought about deliberately by government action; others were unintended or even unwelcome. To carry out a program of Westernization a system of public education was clearly necessary. A Ministry of Education was established in 1871, careful studies were made of the procedures of Western countries, and schools were built rapidly at state expense. Japan was the first Asian nation to introduce compulsory education and did it so successfully that illiteracy almost disappeared, even among the poorest

The Japanese
trusts

The Japanese
workers

Social and cultural
changes

A Japanese Dancing School. Learning the classic dance is still a social duty for many girls of the upper classes.

classes of society. There was also notable progress in instructional facilities at the higher level, providing boys with opportunities for technical and professional as well as academic training, and offering separate and more limited instruction for girls. The program was extremely ambitious and the curricula of the middle and higher schools were exacting. The study of Chinese classics and Confucian philosophy was retained, and to these were added—besides Japanese language, literature, and history—Western scientific and technical subjects as well as foreign languages. Notably lacking, however, was the encouragement of original thought. The system was devised to serve the ends of the government and aimed to produce a nation of loyal, efficient, and disciplined conformists. To that end, all students were required to take so-called "morals classes," which stressed patriotism. Western science and technology were appropriated without the liberal and humanistic traditions which had engendered them; and investigation of the social sciences was almost entirely neglected. Thus, the emphasis was not upon the fullest development of the individual but upon enabling him to fit into a firmly fixed pattern of society without questioning it. The Ministry of Education exercised strict surveillance over teachers and texts, making the schools a powerful agency for indoctrination.

Literary
production

The creation of a wide reading public, however, stimulated literary production, some of which was intended for mass circulation. Although Japanese writers were greatly influenced by contemporary Western literature, as reflected in their tendency toward realism, they were by no means mere imitators and produced literary work of great merit. Journalism became a flourishing occupation, and some newspapers of high caliber appeared. The Japanese press, however, labored under disadvantages, the most serious being the arbitrary and often erratic governmental censorship. Editors who dared to criticize officials, or who were merely unlucky enough to publish news which officials desired to keep from the public, were likely to be fined and imprisoned or to have their offices closed. It is significant that a considerable number of journalists, in spite of the risks involved, persisted in giving expression to independent and critical opinion.

New social
problems

In passing successfully through the difficult years of the Restoration period, the Japanese gave abundant evidence of vitality, courage, and versatility. In many fields they had come abreast of the Western nations, while they had also retained their own distinctive cultural heritage. At the same time, the accomplishments were not an unmixed good, and social problems had arisen which could not be easily solved. The most dubious aspect of Japan's condition, in spite of her mounting industrial strength, was in the economic sphere. Scientific knowledge, improved sanitation and medical facilities, and especially the impact of the Industrial Revolution induced

a terrific increase in a population that had remained almost stationary for over a century. Between 1867 and 1913, the population
grew from about 30 million to more than 50 million, and from this
time on the rate of growth was still more rapid. There was hardly
enough arable land in Japan to produce food for such large numbers, even under the most efficient methods of cultivation. While a
brisk foreign trade could correct the deficiency, not only was a
sufficient volume of trade difficult to maintain but the profits from
manufacturing and commerce were concentrated in the hands of a
small group. The standard of living of the farmers—the great
majority of the population—remained almost at a standstill while
the total national income was rising. With the abolition of feudalism, the peasants had become free landed proprietors, but their
economic condition was not greatly improved thereby. Taxation
bore far too heavily upon them; they had to compete in a cash
market dominated by large landlords and industrialists; and their
individual holdings were often insufficient to support a family.
Many farmers had to supplement their small plots by renting additional holdings. Tenant farming in place of independent proprietor-
ship became a striking characteristic of Japanese agriculture. The
urban laborers were even worse off than the poor farmers; and
Japan lacked a strong middle class to redress the balance of society.
The revolutions of the Meiji era, unlike their counterparts in the
Western world, were not essentially middle-class movements and
had not broken the ascendancy of leaders whose ideals and outlook
had been shaped in a feudal atmosphere.

The fundamental attitudes and loyalties of the old Japan passed
into the new, even though they wore a somewhat different guise
and were associated with more effective implements. It was not
difficult for the creed of unswerving loyalty to a feudal superior to
be converted into an intense patriotism, for which the emperor
served as a symbol of national unity and object of common devo-

Factors
contributing to an
authoritarian
trend

Japanese Agriculture.
Transplanting rice in the
paddy field early in June.

Japanese Agriculture. Harvesting rice in a farm village. In the background is Mount Fuji with its eternal snow.

tion. Ancient legends and the Shinto cults were refurbished to stimulate patriotic sentiments and to inspire confidence in Japan's unique destiny. As already suggested, an efficient and in many ways progressive educational system was utilized for this same end. The army, also, became an educational agency of a very potent kind. It was made up largely of literate but unsophisticated peasants, who found membership in the military establishment more rewarding financially and more gratifying to the ego than a life of grubbing on a tiny farm. The provincialism, prejudices, and legitimate resentments of the peasant rendered him susceptible to indoctrination by fanatics who preached the superiority of Japan over other nations, the infallibility of the divine emperor, and the subordination of civilians to the military. However, the influences promoting an authoritarian or militaristic regime were never unopposed. Continuous and broadening contacts with the outside world and a gradual reaction to the disturbing consequences of rapid economic change introduced a train of liberal thought, which threatened to collide with the forces of conservatism.

Japanese Religious Festival. The participants are dressed in gorgeous costumes of different epochs.

Pink and Green, Edgar Degas (1834–1917). Degas was an impressionist to the extent of his interest in fleeting motion. But as an admirer of the classicist, Ingres, he emphasized line and careful composition. (MMA)

Etretat, Claude Monet (1840–1926). Monet loved this part of the Normandy coast for its rugged cliffs and the shimmering light of the sun on rocks and waves. He called some of his paintings *Impressions*, and the name soon came to designate a school. (MMA)

The Japanese Divan, Henri de Toulouse-Lautrec (1864–1901). Toulouse-Lautrec found his chief source of inspiration in the night life of Paris. *Divan Japonais* was a noted Paris café. (MMA)

Balzac, Auguste Rodin (1840–1917). Rodin was the great realist of XIX-cent. sculpture. He concentrated most of his attention upon facial detail, no matter how unflattering the result might be. (MMA)

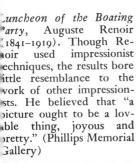

Luncheon of the Boating Party, Auguste Renoir (1841–1919). Though Renoir used impressionist techniques, the results bore little resemblance to the work of other impressionists. He believed that "a picture ought to be a lovable thing, joyous and pretty." (Phillips Memorial Gallery)

Montagne Sainte-Victoire with Aqueduct, Paul Cézanne (1839–1906). This landscape has been a source of inspiration for many of the tendencies of so-called "modern" art. The composition is as structurally balanced and proportioned as a Greek temple. (MMA)

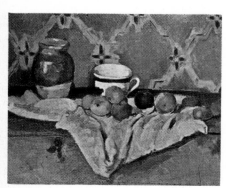

Still Life, Cézanne. It has been said that when the impressionists painted a haystack, there was light, but there was no haystack. When Cézanne painted an apple, there was the play of light; there was also the apple. (MMA)

The Card Players, Cézanne. Here are exemplified Cézanne's skill in composition, his discriminating sense of color, and the sculptured qualities of solidity and depth he gave to his figures. (Stephen C. Clark)

A Gate of the Toshogu Shrine, Nikko National Park. Although the Japanese have adopted Western architectural styles for their public buildings, for religious edifices they retain the native style with its curved roofs and lavish ornamentation.

Japan's external relations during the Meiji era were directly related to, and appreciably affected by, her internal development. It is not strange that Japan, in the process of becoming a modern state, adopted a policy of imperialism, in view of her agility in assimilating the techniques of Western nations and also in view of the stresses created by the industrialization of the country. As time went on, however, differences of opinion appeared among Japanese statesmen, business and financial leaders, and intellectuals as to the proper course to pursue in advancing the interests of the state. Some bureaucrats were conservative or even reactionary, generally unsympathetic to parliamentary institutions, and inclined to favor an aggressive foreign policy. Others were primarily interested in building up Japan's economic and financial strength, securing foreign markets by peaceful penetration, and creating a prosperous and stable society at home. While not genuinely democratic, they at least accepted the implications of constitutional government and were anxious to win an honorable position for their country within the family of nations. Fortunately for Japan, the moderate expansionists were fairly successful during this period in holding the militant faction in check, although not without making some concessions to them.

Japanese expansion in Eastern Asia would almost inevitably be at the expense of the decadent Chinese Empire. In 1876, the Japanese government took direct steps to end the isolation of Korea, a "hermit nation" which had been as tightly sealed against outside influences as Japan under the Tokugawa Shogunate. Copying a page from the Western book, the Japanese negotiated a treaty with the

Moderates vs. extremists

Adventures in imperialism

361

Seoul government which accorded them extraterritoriality and other rights, as well as opening Korea to commercial intercourse. The treaty also recognized Korea as an independent state, in total disregard of the fact that the Peking government considered the peninsula a tributary dependency of the Manchu Empire. Actually the Manchu officials had neglected to enforce their claims, and their belated attempt to recover their position by counterintrigue against the Japanese was almost certain to provoke a clash with Japan. Korea, at this time, was an ideal breeding ground for war. In spite of brilliant episodes in its past, the kingdom had degenerated

The Heian Jingu Shrine, Kyoto.

into one of the most backward regions of Asia. The administration was corrupt and predatory, the peasants ignorant and wretched, and conditions in general thoroughly belied the country's poetic name—Chosen ("Land of the Morning Calm"). Japan's interest in Korea was both economic and strategic, the latter because Russia had acquired the Maritime Province on the Pacific coast directly north of the Korean border and had already attempted to intervene in Korea's troubled affairs. After a local rebellion had furnished the excuse for both China and Japan to rush troops into Korea, the Sino-Japanese war was precipitated.

It could be—and has been—argued that, beginning with her swift victory over China in 1895, Japan's policy in Asia was one of territorial aggression. In the treaty of Shimonoseki, Japan required from China not only recognition of Korean independence and the payment of an indemnity but also the cession of Formosa, the Pescadores Islands, and the southern projection of Manchuria—the Liaotung Peninsula. Japan joined in the scramble for concessions in China, acquiring a sphere of interest in Fukien province opposite Formosa. When harassed by the advance of Russian imperialism in Korea, Japan attacked Russia in 1904 and, after defeating her on

**Wars with China
and Russia**

land and sea, annexed the southern half of Sakhalin Island and obtained economic concessions in Manchuria. These facts, however, are only part of the story, which in its entirety indicates that the Japanese were adept in mastering the object lessons of European diplomacy and power politics. Following the Sino-Japanese war, under pressure from Russia, France, and Germany, Japan had been forced to relinquish her claim to the Liaotung Peninsula, on the ground that occupation of this region by a foreign power would threaten the safety of the Peking government. Almost immediately afterward, Russia, by a treaty of alliance with China, secured control of the very region she had denied to Japan and converted practically all Manchuria into a Russian sphere of interest. Several attempts on the part of the Japanese government to reach an accommodation with Russia in regard to Korea and Manchuria were frustrated by the recklessness and duplicity of the Tsar's agents. Nevertheless, some influential Japanese considered war with Russia too dangerous an undertaking, and the government would probably not have dared to attack Russia except for the fact that the Anglo-Japanese Alliance of 1902 assured Japan of the friendly backing of the world's greatest naval power. The British welcomed Japan's accession to a position of strength as a means of checking Russian expansion in the Far East. During the Russo-Japanese war, sentiment in both Great Britain and the United States was prevailingly in favor of Japan, largely because of the devious and bullying tactics that the Russians had been pursuing. President Theodore Roosevelt's sympathy for Japan helped in terminating the hostilities, and the peace treaty was negotiated at Portsmouth, New Hampshire.

CURRENT HISTORY IN CARICATURE.

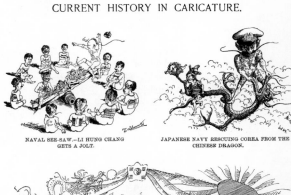

NAVAL SEE-SAW.—LI HUNG CHANG
GETS A JOLT.

JAPANESE NAVY RESCUING COREA FROM THE
CHINESE DRAGON.

The Sino-Japanese Struggle over Korea, as seen by a Japanese Cartoonist (1894).

CHINA AND JAPAN WRESTLING OVER THE MAP OF COREA.

A PAGE OF CARTOONS BY A JAPANESE ARTIST.

CHINA AND
JAPAN UNDER
THE IMPACT
OF THE WEST

A temporary
balance of power
in East Asia

Japan's victory over Russia seemed for a time to restore a balance of power in the Far East. Russia, shaken by her Revolution of 1905, and Japan, her financial reserves drained by the war, quickly agreed on apportioning their respective spheres in Manchuria—publicly affirming, of course, that they had no intention of violating China's territorial integrity. But the balance of power proved to be unstable. The outbreak of the European war in 1914, necessitating a "retreat of the West" from Asia, provided Japan with a golden opportunity to consolidate and extend her position.

SELECTED READINGS—GENERAL

· *Items so designated are available in paperbound editions.*

Allen, G. C., and Donnithorne, A. G., *Western Enterprise in Far Eastern Economic Development*, New York, 1954.

Clyde, P. H., and Beers, B. F., *The Far East*, 4th ed., Englewood Cliffs, N.J., 1966.

Fairbank, J. K., Reischauer, E. O., and Craig, A. M., *East Asia: The Modern Transformation* (*A History of East Asian Civilization*, Vol. II), Boston, 1965. A well balanced, readable text; illustrated.

· Griswold, A. W., *The Far Eastern Policy of the United States*, New York, 1938 (Yale).

King, F. H., *Farmers of Forty Centuries, or Permanent Agriculture in China, Korea and Japan*, Emmaus, Penn., 1948. A classic description of the East Asian agrarian economy.

Linebarger, P. M. A., Djang Chu, and Burks, A. W., *Far Eastern Governments and Politics: China and Japan*, 2nd ed., Princeton, 1956.

MacNair, H. F., and Lach, D. F., *Modern Far Eastern International Relations*, 2nd ed., New York, 1955.

Michael, F. H., and Taylor, G. E., *The Far East in the Modern World*, New York, 1956.

Peffer, Nathaniel, *The Far East: A Modern History*, Ann Arbor, 1958.

Romein, Jan, *The Asian Century: A History of Modern Nationalism in Asia*, Berkeley, 1962.

Vinacke, H. M., *A History of the Far East in Modern Times*, 6th ed., New York, 1959.

—CHINA (*See also Readings for
Chapter 3*)

Bland, J. O. P., and Backhouse, E. T., *China under the Empress Dowager*, Philadelphia, 1910.

Boardman, E. P., *Christian Influence upon the Ideology of the Taiping Rebellion, 1851–1864*, Madison, Wis., 1952.

Chai Ch'u and Chai Winberg, *The Changing Society of China*, New York, 1962 (Mentor). Sympathetic, readable, but not free from errors.

Chan, W. T., *Religious Trends in Modern China*, New York, 1953.

Chang Chung-li, *The Chinese Gentry*, Seattle, 1955.

——, *The Income of the Chinese Gentry*, Seattle, 1962.

Ch'ên, Jerome, *Yuan Shih-k'ai, 1859–1916: Brutus Assumes the Purple*, Stanford, 1961. Illuminating, although strongly biased by adulation of Dr. Sun Yat-sen.

Cohen, Paul, *China and Christianity, 1860–1870*, Cambridge, Mass., 1963.

Collis, Maurice, *Foreign Mud*, London, 1964. An account of life among the English merchants at Canton.

· Fairbank, J. K., *The United States and China*, rev. ed., Cambridge, Mass., 1958 (Compass). Brief but perceptive.

Fleming, Peter, *The Siege at Peking*, New York, 1959. The Boxer uprising and its suppression.

Hail, W. J., *Tseng Kuo-fan and the Taiping Rebellion*, New Haven, 1927.

Hodous, Lewis, *Folkways in China*, London, 1929.

Hummel, A. W., ed., *Eminent Chinese of the Ch'ing Period*, 2 vols., Washington, 1943–1944.

· Levenson, J. R., *Liang Ch'i-ch'ao and the Mind of Modern China*, Cambridge, Mass., 1953 (California).

Tan, C. C., *The Boxer Catastrophe*, New York, 1955.

Wright, A. F., *Buddhism in Chinese History*, Stanford, 1959.

—JAPAN (*See also Readings for Chapter 3*)

Allen, G. C., *Modern Japan and Its Problems*, New York, 1927.

———, *A Short Economic History of Modern Japan*, London, 1946.

Asakawa, Kanichi, *The Russo-Japanese Conflict*, New York, 1904.

Beckmann, G. M., *The Making of the Meiji Constitution: The Oligarchs and the Constitutional Development of Japan, 1868–1891*, Lawrence, Kan., 1957.

Borton, Hugh, *Japan's Modern Century*, New York, 1955.

Craig, A. M., *Chōshū in the Meiji Restoration*, Cambridge, Mass., 1961.

Dennett, Tyler, *Roosevelt and the Russo-Japanese War*, Garden City, N.Y., 1925.

Ike, Nobutaka, *The Beginnings of Political Democracy in Japan*, Baltimore, 1950.

Jansen, M. B., *Sakamoto Ryōma and the Meiji Restoration*, Princeton, 1961. A penetrating study of the conflict and confusion in Japanese politics at the end of the Tokugawa period.

Lederer, Emil, and Lederer-Seidler, Emy, *Japan in Transition*, New Haven, 1938.

· Lockwood, W. W., *The Economic Development of Japan, 1868–1938*, Princeton, 1954 (Princeton University Press).

Norman, E. H., *Japan's Emergence as a Modern State*, New York, 1940.

Quigley, H. S., *Japanese Government and Politics*, New York, 1932.

Reischauer, E. O., *Japan Past and Present*, rev. ed., New York, 1953.

Reischauer, R. K., *Japan: Government-Politics*, New York, 1939.

Russell, O. D., *The House of Mitsui*, Boston, 1939.

Scalapino, R. A., *Democracy and the Party Movement in Prewar Japan*, Berkeley, 1953.

Smith, T. C., *Political Change and Industrial Development in Japan*, Stanford, 1955.

· Storry, Richard, *A History of Modern Japan*, Baltimore, 1960 (Penguin).

Walworth, Arthur, *Black Ships off Japan*, New York, 1946.

· Webb, H., *An Introduction to Japan*, New York, 1957 (Columbia).

White, J. A., *The Diplomacy of the Russo-Japanese War*, Princeton, 1964. An able analysis of the diplomatic backgrounds of the war and of the Portsmouth peace negotiations.

Yanaga, Chitoshi, *Japan Since Perry*, New York, 1949.

SOURCE MATERIALS

- de Bary, W. T., ed., *Sources of Chinese Tradition,* Chaps. XXIV, XXV, XXVI (Columbia).
- ———, ed., *Sources of Japanese Tradition,* Chaps. XXIV, XXV (Columbia).

Emerson, Joyce, tr., *The Lotus Pool.* Autobiographical account of struggle against restrictions of the patriarchal family.

- Teng Ssu-yü, and Fairbank, J. K., *China's Response to the West: A Documentary Survey,* 2 vols. (Atheneum).

The Complete Journal of Townsend Harris.

Waley, Arthur, tr., *The Opium War through Chinese Eyes.*

CHAPTER 12

Intellectual and Artistic Progress during the Age of Democracy and Nationalism

---

> If a single cell, under appropriate conditions, becomes a man in the space of a few years, there can surely be no difficulty in understanding how, under appropriate conditions, a cell may, in the course of untold millions of years, give origin to the human race.
> —Herbert Spencer, *Principles of Biology*

Reference is commonly made to the advancement of learning in the seventeenth and eighteenth centuries as *the* Intellectual Revolution. It would be just as accurate to apply this term to the intellectual progress between 1830 and 1914. Never before in so short a time had the mind of man yielded discoveries and provocative ideas in such profusion. And certainly a large proportion of these were quite as revolutionary in their effects as any that had come down from the past. But in several respects the intellectual revolution from 1830 to 1914 was different from that of the seventeenth and eighteenth centuries. The deductive or rationalist tradition was now almost entirely dead, and the decay of rationalism was reflected in a marked decline in the relative importance of philosophy. Indeed, in the new age philosophy was often little more than an echo of science. It was not that the problems of the universe had finally been solved, or that men had lost the ability to think, but rather that the sciences had come to be accepted as the only worthwhile sources of knowledge. To be sure, there were some seekers of wisdom who rebelled against the new tendency; but there were few who had the hardihood to advocate a revival of pure deduction or the viewpoint of the mystic in discovering truth. In other words, the victory of empiricism, or

The character of the new intellectual revolution

367

that philosophy which derives its truths from concrete experience rather than from abstract reasoning, was almost complete.

1. THE HEYDAY OF SCIENCE

Compared with all preceding epochs, the period from 1830 to 1914 marked the zenith of scientific progress. The attainments of this period were not only more numerous, but they probed more deeply into the hidden mysteries of things and revealed the nature of the world and of man in a hitherto unsuspected light. Each of the older branches of science was greatly developed, and a dozen or more new ones were added to the list. The phenomenal scientific progress of this era was the result of various factors. It was due in some measure to the stimulus of the Industrial Revolution, to the rising standard of living, and to the desire for comfort and pleasure. But to think of modern science as essentially a species of practical knowledge is to misunderstand its import. The contemporary pure physicist or chemist is no more concerned with problems of the workaday world than was St. Thomas Aquinas or Albert the Great. In fact, pure science occupies a position in the modern age somewhat similar to that of Scholasticism in the thirteenth century. It is at once a substitute for logic as a discipline for the mind and an expression of an insatiable desire for the conquest of all knowledge, for an intellectual mastery of the universe.

Although none of the sciences was neglected between 1830 and 1914, it was the biological sciences and medicine which underwent the greatest development. The outstanding achievement in biology was the development of new explanations of the theory of organic evolution. We have seen that this theory was at least as old as Anaximander in the sixth century B.C., and that it was accepted by many of the great minds of antiquity. We have learned also that it was revived in the eighteenth century by the scientists Buffon and Linnaeus. But neither of these men offered much proof or explained how the process of evolution works. The first to develop a systematic hypothesis of organic evolution was the French biologist, Jean Lamarck (1744–1829). The essential principle in Lamarck's hypothesis, published in 1809, is the inheritance of acquired characteristics. He maintained that an animal, subjected to a change in environment, acquires new habits, which in turn are reflected in structural changes. These acquired characteristics of body structure, he believed, are transmissible to the offspring, with the result that after a series of generations a new species of animal is eventually produced. Lamarck's successors found little evidence to confirm this hypothesis, but it dominated biological thought for upwards of fifty years. Though still not absolutely discredited, it is admitted to have no more than a partial validity.

A much more scientific hypothesis of organic evolution was that of Charles Darwin, published in 1859. Darwin was born in 1809, the son of a small-town physician. Though he lived to be seventy-three, he was of frail constitution, and during most of his adult life he seems never to have enjoyed a day of the health of ordinary men. In accordance with his father's wish, he began the study of medicine at Edinburgh, but soon withdrew and entered Cambridge to prepare for the ministry. Here he gave most of his time to natural history and was graduated only tenth in his class among those not seeking honors. In 1831 he obtained an appointment as naturalist without pay on H.M.S. *Beagle*, which had been chartered for a scientific expedition around the world. The voyage lasted nearly five years and

Charles Darwin (1809–1882). More than anyone else, Charles Darwin, shown here in his later years, personified the scientific revolution of the nineteenth century.

gave Darwin an unparalleled opportunity to become acquainted at first hand with the manifold variations of animal life. He noted the differences between animals inhabiting islands and related species on nearby continents and observed the resemblances between living animals and the fossilized remains of extinct species in the same locality. It was a magnificent preparation for his life's work. Upon returning from the voyage he happened to read Malthus' *Essay on Population* and was struck by the author's contention that throughout the world of nature many more individuals are born than can ever survive, and that consequently the weaker ones must perish in the struggle for food. Finally, after twenty more years of careful and extensive research he issued his *Origin of Species*, which has probably done as much to influence modern thinking as any other single book ever written.

Darwin's hypothesis as contained in his *Origin of Species* (1859) is known as the hypothesis of natural selection. This involves the idea that it is nature, or the environment, which selects those variants among the offspring that are to survive and reproduce. Darwin **369** pointed out, first of all, that the parents of every species beget more offspring than can possibly survive. He maintained that, consequently, a struggle takes place among these offspring for food, shelter, warmth, and other conditions necessary for life. In this struggle certain individuals have the advantage because of the factor of *variation*, which means that no two of the offspring are exactly alike. Some are born strong, others weak; some have longer horns or sharper claws than their brothers and sisters or perhaps a body coloration which enables them better to blend with their surroundings and thus to elude their enemies. It is these favored members of the species that win out in the struggle for existence; the others are eliminated generally before they have lived long enough to reproduce. While Darwin assumed, like Lamarck, that acquired characteristics could be inherited, he did not consider them of fundamental importance in evolution. He regarded variation and natural selection as the primary factors in the origin of new species. In other words, he taught that individuals with favorable characteristics would transmit their inherited qualities to their descendants through countless generations, and that successive eliminations of the least fit would eventually produce a new species. Finally, it should be noted that Darwin applied his concept of evolution not only to plant and animal species but also to man. In his second great work, *The Descent of Man* (1871), he attempted to show that the human race originally sprang from some apelike ancestor, long since extinct, but probably a common forebear of the existing anthropoid apes and man.

The Darwinian hypothesis was elaborated and improved by several later biologists. About 1890 the German August Weismann (1834–1914) flatly rejected the idea that acquired characteristics could be inherited. He conducted experiments to show that body cells and reproductive cells are entirely distinct, and that there is no way in which changes in the former can affect the latter. He concluded, therefore, that the only qualities transmissible to the offspring are those which have always been present in the germ plasm of the parents.[1] In 1901 the Dutch botanist, Hugo De Vries (1848–1935), published his celebrated mutation hypothesis, based in large part upon laws of heredity discovered by the Austrian monk, Gregor Mendel (1822–1884). De Vries asserted that evolution results not from minor variations, as Darwin had assumed, but from radical differences or mutations, which appear in more or less definite ratio among the offspring. When any of these mutations are favorable to survival in a given environment, the individuals possess-

---

[1] The teachings of Weismann, while generally accepted by scientists of the present day, are taken with certain reservations. It has been shown that germ cells are not entirely insulated from the rest of the body as Weismann taught. It is admitted also that they are not absolutely stable but appear to be subject, under certain conditions, to parallel modifications at the same time that other parts of the body are affected.

ing them naturally emerge triumphant in the struggle for existence. Not only do their descendants inherit these qualities, but from time to time new mutants appear, some of which are even better adapted for survival than their parents. Thus in a limited number of generations a new species may be brought into existence. The mutation theory of De Vries corrected one of the chief weaknesses in the Darwinian hypothesis. The variations which Darwin assumed to be the source of evolutionary changes are so small that an incredibly long time would be necessary to produce a new species. De Vries made it possible to conceive of evolution as proceeding by sudden leaps.[2]

Next to the exposition and proof of organic evolution, the most important biological achievement was probably the development of the cell theory. The cellular structure of plants had already been described by Robert Hooke in the seventeenth century, but it was left for the German biologist, Theodor Schwann (1810–1882), to draw the full implications from Hooke's discovery. Schwann pointed out about 1835 that not only plants but animals also are composed of cells, and that all but the simplest of living things grow and mature by the division and multiplication of these tiny structural units. A few years later it was discovered that all cells are composed of essentially the same combination of matter, to which Hugo von Mohl (1805–1872) gave the name *protoplasm*. Another of the important biological achievements of this period was the development of embryology. The father of the modern science of embryology was the German-Russian Karl Ernst von Baer (1792–1876), who, about 1830, set forth his celebrated law of recapitulation. This law, which was subsequently elaborated by Ernst Haeckel (1834–1919), states that during the embryonic period each individual recapitulates or reproduces the various important stages in the life history of the species to which it belongs.

Embryology was not the only subdivision of biology to be developed during the nineteenth century. The work of Schwann, von Mohl, and others led to the founding of cytology, or the scientific study of cells. About 1865 Louis Pasteur (1822–1895) laid the basis for the science of bacteriology by his epochal attack upon the theory of spontaneous generation. Hitherto it had been commonly supposed that bacteria and other microscopic organisms originated spontaneously from water or from decaying vegetable and animal matter. Pasteur succeeded in convincing the scientific world that all existing forms of life, no matter how small, are reproduced only by living beings. This was his famous law of biogenesis (all known forms of life come from pre-existing life).

Even more spectacular than the achievements in biology was the progress in medicine. Following the discovery of vaccination for

---

[2] It must be understood that the hypothesis of De Vries is not complete in itself, but is based upon Darwin's main principle of natural selection.

smallpox by Jenner in 1796, the next great landmark in the development of modern medicine was the introduction of ether as a general anaesthetic. Credit for this achievement was formerly given to William T. G. Morton, a Boston dentist, but it is now known that a Georgia physician, Crawford W. Long, performed the earliest operation with the use of ether in 1842. This discovery not only diminished the anguish of the patient, but enabled the surgeon to take his time and thereby increased the number of successful operations. But still many people died as a consequence of the bungling practice of physicians. Mortality was especially high in obstetrical cases, until methods were discovered of controlling the possibilities of infection. In 1847 the Hungarian physician Ignaz Semmelweiss found out that by washing his hands in antiseptic solutions he could reduce the death rate in obstetrical operations by more than four-fifths. This discovery was extended to the whole field of surgical practice about 1865 by the Englishman Joseph Lister (1827–1912), who is considered the father of antiseptic surgery. Lister achieved sensational results in preventing infection by cleansing wounds and surgical instruments with carbolic acid and by introducing carbolized catgut for surgical sewings. He was rewarded by the British government with a baronetcy in 1883 and was elevated to the peerage in 1897.

The most significant milestone of medical progress during the second half of the nineteenth century was undoubtedly the germ theory of disease. Probably no other single accomplishment has contributed so much to the conquest of the most deadly maladies which afflict mankind. The germ theory of disease was mainly the work of Louis Pasteur and Robert Koch. Pasteur had been practically certain of the germinal origin of disease ever since he had established his biogenetic law, but he was unable to convince the medical profession. Because he was a chemist, physicians were inclined to be scornful of his work, holding that he could know nothing of the sacred precincts of medicine. They admitted the existence of germs, but they regarded them as more probably the results of disease than the cause. The opportunity to prove the validity of the theory came with the spread of an epidemic of anthrax, a disease which was carrying off hundreds of thousands of cattle and sheep in Germany and in France. About 1875 Robert Koch (1843–1910), an obscure country physician of East Prussia, began a series of experiments to prove that anthrax was the result of the tiny rodlike organisms found in the blood of the diseased animals. He inoculated mice with this contaminated blood and noticed that they soon sickened and died. He made cultures of the germs, breeding them on potatoes, and found that the germs alone, when introduced into the bodies of animals, were just as deadly as the blood. Meanwhile Pasteur had also been engaged in researches on anthrax. In 1881 he was challenged by his medical opponents to make a public test on cattle. He divided the animals into two groups. Half of them he inoculated with weakened germs of anthrax, and the remainder he left untreated. A few days later he injected malignant germs into all of the cattle. To the discomfiture of his opponents, every one of the animals that had not been inoculated died, while all of the others survived. The theory that germs were the cause of the disease could no longer be disputed.

Once the germ theory was positively established, achievements in medicine multiplied rapidly. The talents of Pasteur and Koch were still by no means exhausted. The former in 1885 evolved a method of treating persons afflicted with hydrophobia, one of the most horrible diseases known to humanity. As a result of this accomplishment, the death rate from a malady hitherto almost always fatal was reduced to less than 1 per cent. In 1882–1883 Koch discovered the bacilli of tuberculosis and of Asiatic cholera. Within a few years the germs of yet other diseases were isolated—of diphtheria, of the bubonic plague, of lockjaw, and of sleeping-sickness. For the prevention and treatment of several of these diseases, antitoxins or serums were developed, the first being the diphtheria antitoxin produced in 1892 by Emil von Behring. About the end of the century effective means of combating malaria and yellow fever were made possible by the discovery that both are spread by particular varieties of mosquitoes. Much advancement was made also in the treatment of syphilis. After the germ had been identified in 1905, August von Wassermann (1866–1925) devised a test for revealing its presence in the human body. In 1910 Paul Ehrlich developed a new drug, known as salvarsan, which proved to be an efficient specific for the disease in its primary and secondary stages. Still later the Austrian pathologist Julius Wagner von Jauregg (1857–1940) found out that a fever temperature induced by malaria or by other means has remarkable effects in alleviating advanced stages of the disease, such as syphilis of the brain or paresis.

The conquest of diseases produced by germs

Finally, it should be noted that by the outbreak of World War I a beginning had been made in the study of the ductless glands and in the discovery of the vitamins. The first step toward an understanding of the ductless or endocrine glands was taken in 1901 when the Japanese scientist Takamine isolated adrenalin, secreted by the suprarenal glands, and showed that it was useful in regulating the action of the heart. About 1912 it was revealed that the pituitary gland yields a substance vitally necessary for regulating the other glands of the body. These discoveries paved the way for a considerable development of glandular therapy in more recent years, including methods of curing certain forms of idiocy by supplementing the hormone secretion of the thyroid gland. On the eve of World War I it was demonstrated by a British biochemist that a healthful diet requires not merely starches, fats, sugars, and proteins but "accessory factors" found only in particular foods. These fac-

The discovery of hormones and vitamins

tors were soon named vitamins, and research was begun to determine their character. In 1915 an American scientist at Johns Hopkins, E. V. McCollum, proved that there are at least two vitamins: Vitamin A, contained in butter, egg yolks, and fish-liver oils; and Vitamin B, which is found most abundantly in yeast, lean meats, whole cereals, and green vegetables. Later investigations have disclosed the existence of at least twenty of these mysterious substances, all of them essential to growth or repair or to the prevention of disease. The discovery of the vitamins has been especially significant in the conquest of illnesses of malnutrition, such as beriberi, scurvy, and rickets.

Achievements in
the physical
sciences

The record of attainment in the physical sciences is somewhat less impressive until practically the final quarter of the nineteenth century. Nevertheless, three achievements stand out in the earlier period. About 1810 the English Quaker schoolmaster, John Dalton, revived the atomic theory of matter and defended it so assiduously that it was soon adopted as a basic premise of scientific thought. In 1847 Hermann von Helmholtz formulated the principle of the conservation of energy, or the first law of thermodynamics. This law states that the total energy in the universe is constant, that it can be changed from one form into another but can neither be created nor destroyed. In 1851 came the second law of thermodynamics, or the law of the dissipation of energy. Explained systematically for the first time by William Thomson (Lord Kelvin), this law maintains that, while the total energy of the universe remains constant, the amount of *useful* energy is being steadily diminished. Few discoveries have been more fruitful in influencing the conclusions of astronomers and also of certain philosophers.

Revolutionary
discoveries in
regard to light,
electricity, and
other forms of
energy

Probably it would be safe to say that the period from about 1870 to 1914 surpassed all others since the age of Copernicus in the number of revolutionary developments in the physical sciences. Indeed, it may be doubted whether there was ever a period when so many time-honored scientific conceptions were seriously challenged or overthrown. First of all, there were some extensive revisions of older theories of light, electricity, and energy. About 1865 Clerk Maxwell (1831–1879) showed that light appears to behave in much the same way as electromagnetic waves. In 1887 the German physicist Heinrich Hertz proved the existence of high-frequency electric waves spreading through space with the velocity and other characteristics of light. The discovery of the X-ray by Wilhelm von Röntgen in 1895 led scientists to wonder whether similar rays might not be given off spontaneously in nature. This suspicion was confirmed by the discovery of uranium in 1896 and of the much more active element, radium, by Madame Curie two years later. About 1903 the British physicists, Ernest Rutherford and Frederick Soddy, developed their disintegration theory, explaining how various radioactive elements break down to form less complex elements, giving off at the same time emanations of electrical energy. The net result of these several discoveries was the conclusion that light, electricity, the X-ray, and all other forms of energy are essentially the same.

From this conclusion it was a comparatively easy step to fundamental revisions of the conception of matter. As early as 1892 Hendrik Lorentz advanced the contention that matter is not composed of solid, indivisible atoms as the Greeks and John Dalton had assumed, but that the atom itself is made up of smaller units of an electrical nature. About 1910 Ernest Rutherford and the Danish scientist Niels Bohr presented a picture of the atom as a kind of miniature solar system, composed of a nucleus containing one or more positively charged *protons* around which revolve a number of negatively charged *electrons*. As we shall see, this conception has been modified in more recent years, but its main implication still stands— that electricity is the fundamental constituent of matter.

Revisions of the conception of matter

The years from 1830 to 1914 were characterized also by an extensive development of the social sciences. Most of these subjects are of comparatively recent origin. Before the nineteenth century nearly all of man's efforts to analyze his social environment were restricted to history, economics, and philosophy. The first of the new social sciences to be developed was sociology, originated by Auguste Comte (1798–1857) and elaborated by Herbert Spencer (1820–1903). Next came the founding of anthropology. Though sometimes defined very broadly as "the science of man," anthropology is more commonly restricted to such matters as man's physical evolution, the study of existing human types, and the investigation of prehistoric cultures and of primitive institutions and customs. About 1870 psychology was broken off from philosophy and cultivated as a separate science. Following its origin in Germany under the guidance of Wilhelm Wundt (1832–1920) and Ernst Weber (1795–1878), it was given a new orientation in the 1890's by the work of the Russian Ivan Pavlov (1849–1936). By experiments with animals Pavlov discovered what is known as the conditioned reflex, a form of behavior in which natural reactions are produced by an artificial stimulus. He showed that if dogs were fed immediately following the ringing of a bell, they would eventually respond to the sound of the bell alone and secrete saliva exactly as if confronted by the sight and smell of the food. This discovery suggested the conclusion that the conditioned reflex is an important element in human behavior and encouraged psychologists to center their attention upon physiological experiment as a key to understanding the mind.

The founding of new social sciences

After the opening of the twentieth century, psychologists divided into a number of conflicting schools. A group of disciples of Pavlov inaugurated a type of physiological psychology known as behaviorism. Behaviorism is an attempt to study the human being as a purely physiological organism—to reduce all human behavior to a series of

New types of psychology: (1) behaviorism

physical responses. Such concepts as *mind* and *consciousness* are relegated to the scrap heap as vague and meaningless terms. For the behaviorist nothing is important except the reactions of muscles, nerves, glands, and visceral organs. There is no such thing as an independent psychic behavior; all that man does is physical. Thinking is essentially a form of talking to oneself. Every complex emotion and idea is simply a group of physiological responses produced by some stimulus in the environment. Such was the extremely mechanistic interpretation of human actions offered by followers of Pavlov.

Sigmund Freud (1856-1939).

Subject to a number of modifications, it remains the dominant approach for those who believe that psychology should be as objective a science as physics or chemistry.

The other most important school of psychology to make its appearance after the turn of the century was psychoanalysis, founded by Sigmund Freud (1856–1939), an Austrian physician. Psychoanalysis interprets human behavior mainly in terms of the subconscious or unconscious mind. Freud admitted the existence of the conscious mind, but he avowed that the subconscious is much more important in determining the actions of the individual. He considered man as exclusively an egoistic creature propelled by basic urges of power, self-preservation, and sex. These urges are much too strong to be overcome; but inasmuch as society has branded their unrestrained fulfillment as sinful, they are commonly driven into the subconscious, where they linger indefinitely as suppressed de-

(2) psychoanalysis

sires. Yet they are seldom completely submerged; they rise to the surface in dreams, or they manifest themselves in lapses of memory, in fears and obsessions, and in various forms of abnormal behavior. Freud believed that most cases of mental and nervous disorders result from violent conflicts between natural instincts and the restraints imposed by an unfortunate environment. His investigations and the theories he evolved from them revolutionized the treatment of mental ailments and exerted a profound influence upon literature and the arts.

2. NEW PHILOSOPHIC TENDENCIES

Most of the philosophic movements in the later decades of the nineteenth century and in the early years of the twentieth were deeply influenced by the progress of science. Characteristic examples are to be found in the evolutionary philosophies of Spencer, Huxley, and Haeckel. The first of this trio, Herbert Spencer (1820–1903), was one of the most influential figures of modern times. Born into a family of English Methodists and Quakers of modest means, he refused the offer of relatives to send him to Cambridge and determined to educate himself and live his own life. He worked for a time as a civil engineer on the London and Birmingham railway. Later he became an assistant editor of the *Economist*, but resigned that position upon inheriting $2500 from an uncle. Despite his humble background, he cared little for wealth or power. Moreover, he was inclined to be indolent, reading but haphazardly and neglecting serious books that failed to arouse his interest. For years his life was ill-planned and his ambitions erratic. He spawned ideas for inventions at every turn and cluttered his notebooks with plans for candle-extinguishers, patent saltcellars, wheel chairs, and other ingenious contraptions. His earliest writings were on political and social problems, the most important of them being his *Social Statics*, published in 1850. Not until he was about forty did he develop a serious interest in philosophy. He completed his three-volume work, *Synthetic Philosophy*, at the age of seventy-six. Herbert Spencer

The keynote of Spencer's philosophy is his idea of evolution as a universal law. He was deeply impressed by Darwin's *Origin of Species* and enriched the hypothesis of natural selection with a phrase that has clung to it ever since—"the survival of the fittest." He contended that not only species and individuals are subject to evolutionary change, but also planets, solar systems, customs, institutions, and religious and ethical ideas. Everything in the universe completes a cycle of origin, development, decay, and extinction. When the end of the cycle has been reached, the process begins once more and is repeated eternally. Strange as it may seem, Spencer was not a mechanist. He argued that back of the evolutionary process there must be some kind of supernatural Power, and he gen- Spencer's evolutionary philosophy erally assumed that in the long run evolution is synonymous with progress. But he referred to this Power as the Unknowable and declared that it should be dismissed from scientific consideration. Man's capacity for knowledge is limited to matter and motion, to the facts of sensory experience; these alone should constitute the field of his speculation. As a political philosopher, Spencer was a vigorous champion of individualism. He condemned collectivism as a relic of primitive society, as a feature of the earliest stage of social evolution when individuals had not yet been separated from the undifferentiated mass. He held the state in such great abhorrence that he delivered his manuscripts to his publisher in person rather than entrust them to any such agency of tyranny as the post office.

The other two philosophers of the evolutionist tradition, Huxley and Haeckel, accepted a great many of the fundamental suppositions

of Spencer's theory. Thomas Henry Huxley (1825–1895) defended the doctrine of evolution, not only with logical arguments but with a convincing array of scientific facts; for he was a brilliant biologist as well as a philosopher. A "square-jawed man, greedy of controversy," he gloried in the title, "Darwin's bulldog." His celebrated book, *Man's Place in Nature*, was almost as influential in converting the world to evolutionary principles as the *Origin of Species*. But Huxley had broader interests than merely defending organic evolution. Like Spencer, he proposed to extend the evolutionary concept to all of the great problems that trouble man's dreams. He argued that social institutions and moral ideals, instead of being divinely ordained, are simply products of a biological heritage. "The actions we call sinful are part and parcel of the struggle for existence." [3] While he did not reject the possibility of a supernatural power, he averred that "there is no evidence of the existence of such a being as the God of the theologians." [4] He pronounced Christianity to be "a compound of some of the best and some of the worst elements of Paganism and Judaism, moulded in practice by the innate character of certain people of the Western world." [5] A large part of his philosophy is embraced in his famous doctrine of *agnosticism*, a word which he invented to express his contempt for the attitude of dogmatic certainty symbolized by the beliefs of the ancient Gnostics.[6] As propounded by Huxley, agnosticism is the doctrine that neither the existence nor the nature of God nor the ultimate character of the universe is knowable. It is not atheism, but simply an affirmation that man does not know and never can know whether a God exists and whether the universe is governed by purpose or is merely a blind machine.

The most uncompromising of the evolutionist philosophers was

---

[3] Leonard Huxley, *The Life and Letters of Thomas Henry Huxley*, II, 282.
[4] *Ibid.*, II, 162.
[5] T. H. Huxley, *Collected Essays*, V, 142.
[6] See p. 95, Volume I

Ernst Heinrich Haeckel (1834–1919). Originally a physician in Berlin, he became disgusted with crotchety patients and soon turned to the more congenial occupation of a professor of zoology. He was the first outstanding scientist on the Continent of Europe to subscribe wholeheartedly to Darwinism. At the age of sixty-five he summarized his conclusions in a book which he entitled *The Riddle of the Universe*. The philosophy of Haeckel comprises three main doctrines: atheism, materialism, and mechanism. He would have nothing to do with Huxley's agnosticism or with Spencer's assumption of an Unknowable Power; on the contrary, he dogmatically affirmed that nothing spiritual exists. The universe, he maintained, is composed of matter alone in a process of constant change from one form into another. This process is as automatic as the ebb and flow of the tides. There is no fundamental difference between living and nonliving matter, except that the former is more complex. The first life originated from the spontaneous combination of the essential elements of protoplasm. From these earliest forms of protoplasm all the complex species of the present have gradually evolved through the process of natural selection. Haeckel regarded the mind of man as just as much a product of evolution as his body. The human mind differs only in degree from the minds of the lower animals. Memory, imagination, perception, and thinking are mere functions of matter; psychology should be considered a branch of physiology. Such was the compact philosophy of materialism and determinism which appeared to Haeckel and his followers to be a logical deduction from the new biology.

The writings of another German—Friedrich Nietzsche—also reveal a decided influence of the idea of evolution. Nietzsche was not a scientist, nor was he interested in the nature of matter or in the problem of truth. He was essentially a romantic poet glorifying the struggle for existence to compensate for his own life of weakness and misery. Born in 1844, the son of a Lutheran minister, he was educated in the classics at Leipzig and Bonn and at the age of twenty-five was made a professor of philology at the University of Basel. Ten years later he was forced to retire on account of ill health. He spent the next decade of his life in agony, wandering from one resort to another in a fruitless quest for relief. If we can believe his own statement, each year was made up of 200 days of pain. In 1888 he lapsed into hopeless insanity, which continued until his death in 1900.

Nietzsche's philosophy is contained in such works as *Thus Spake Zarathustra*, *A Genealogy of Morals*, and *The Will to Power*. His cardinal idea is the notion that natural selection should be permitted to operate unhindered in the case of human beings as it does with plants and animals. He believed that such a constant weeding out of the unfit would eventually produce a race of supermen—not merely a race of physical giants but men distinguished above all for their moral courage, for their strength of character. Those who should be allowed to perish in the struggle are the moral weaklings, the ineffective and craven ones, who have neither the strength nor the courage to battle nobly for a place in the sun. Before any such process of natural selection could operate, however, religious obstacles would have to be removed. Nietzsche therefore demanded that the moral supremacy of Christianity and Judaism should be overthrown. Both of these religions, he alleged, are Oriental cults glorifying the virtues of slaves and of other downtrodden folk. They exalt into virtues qualities which ought to be considered vices—humility, nonresistance, mortification of the flesh, and pity for the weak and incompetent. The enthronement of these qualities prevents the elimination of the unfit and preserves them to pour their degenerate blood into the veins of the race. Nietzsche admired the ancient Germanic virtues of bravery, strength, loyalty, honor, and cunning. He defined *good* as "all that heightens in man the feeling of power, the desire for power, power itself." *Bad* he characterized as "all that comes from weakness." [7]

Toward the end of the period we are considering, philosophy began to reflect the uncertainties and confusion of the sciences. The revolution in physics accomplished by the discoveries regarding the structure of matter caused a number of thinkers to lose confidence in the optimism of Spencer and in the mechanistic universe of Haeckel. Some renounced mechanism and materialism entirely; others embraced attitudes of skepticism and hopelessness or sought refuge in the worship of beauty. Symptomatic of the new trend was a popular American philosophy known as Pragmatism. Founded by Charles Peirce (1839–1914), it was developed in comprehensive form by William James (1842–1910) and John Dewey (1859–1952). Pragmatism takes its name from its central teaching that any idea which meets the pragmatic test—that is, gives practical results—must be accepted as true, provided, of course, it does not conflict with experience. In other words, if a belief in a personal God—or in a multitude of gods—gives mental peace or spiritual satisfaction to any individual, that belief is true for him. The Pragmatists scoffed at all efforts to discover absolute truth or to determine the ultimate nature of reality. They abandoned metaphysics as futile and taught that knowledge should be sought after, not as an end in itself, but as an *instrument* for improving conditions on earth. It should be mentioned also that the Pragmatists rejected all forms of determinism, whether conceived in spiritual or materialistic terms. They denounced interpretations of the universe that reduced man to a slave of some rigid principle or placed him at the mercy of an all-powerful fate.

The reaction
against mechanism
and materialism:
the doctrines of
the Pragmatists

[7] Quoted by E. A. Singer, *Modern Thinkers and Present Problems*, p. 204.

A much more determined protest against the mechanism and materialism of the nineteenth century came from the New Idealists. Among the leaders of this school were the Italian Benedetto Croce (1866–1952), the Englishman F. H. Bradley (1846–1924), and the American Josiah Royce (1855–1916). The New Idealism was essentially a compound of the doctrines of Hegel and of Kant. From the former came the tendency to glorify the state and to subordinate the individual to the group; from the latter was derived the idea of parallel truths in religion and science which never conflict because they belong in two separate realms. The New Idealists admitted that the universe revealed by science is a gigantic machine which grinds on relentlessly, and that man is a helpless atom. But this revelation did not trouble them, for they contended that it is only part of the picture. Science is but a feeble instrument which enables us merely to see as in a glass darkly. We have other methods of knowing which enable us to perceive not merely surface appearances but reality. If we make up our minds to follow the deepest convictions of our being, we shall see the universe as a star-domed city of God, ruled by benevolent purpose and replete with hope for bewildered man. Truths such as these gained by intuition are more valid than any discovered by the telescope of the scientist. Thus did the New Idealists manage to preserve their faith in religion and in ultimate perfection against the onslaughts of skeptics and materialists.

Certain other philosophers drew far different conclusions. A group known as the New Realists despised the tendency to seek refuge in faith or in any other form of retreat from reason. They conceded that the evidence from science may not be the complete or final truth; but they argued that it is the only truth substantial enough to be taken as a guide for living. They felt that the divorce of philosophy from science was an unmitigated disaster, and that a large proportion of the world's woes could be traced to the growth of mysticism. Though recognizing that science confronts man with a cold and alien universe, they saw in this no need for clinging to the skirts of faith. Even if man is no more than a bundle of atoms, whose gift of immortality is merely to mingle with the dust of centuries, this does not prevent him from living nobly and from waging a good fight to overcome such evils as are within his power. He can at least preserve his self-respect by striving to direct the forces of nature to the good of himself and his fellows, by avoiding any action which may be the cause of suffering to others, and by cherishing "the lofty thoughts that ennoble his little day; disdaining the coward terrors of the slave of Fate, to worship at the shrine that his own hands have built." [8] Such in particular was the philosophy of

[8] Bertrand Russell, "A Free Man's Worship," *Mysticism and Logic*, p. 57. **381**

the Englishman Bertrand Russell (1872–   ), one of the most prominent of the New Realists and a leading philosophical writer of the twentieth century.

3. THE AGE OF REALISM IN LITERATURE

The dominant literary trend in the Western world from about 1830 to 1914 was *realism*. Classicism was now practically defunct.

The decline of
classicism and
the emergence of
realism

Romanticism continued as a secondary trend, and even enjoyed a revival of popularity toward the end of the nineteenth century. In truth, realism and romanticism had elements in common. Both believed in the affirmation of human freedom, though the realists emphasized much more than the romanticists the obstacles standing in the way of that freedom. Both were idealistic, striving for a better world, however they might differ as to the means of attaining their goals. Literary realism before World War I was distinguished by a number of extraordinary qualities. First, it was a protest against sentimentality and emotional extravagance. The realists sought to portray life in accordance with the hard facts revealed by science and philosophy. Second, realism was distinguished by an absorbing interest in psychological and social problems—in analyzing in detail the conflicting tendencies of human behavior and in depicting the struggles of individuals to overcome the frustrations of their environment. Finally, it should be noted that realists were quite generally governed by one or another of the popular scientific or philosophic conceptions of their time. Perhaps the majority were determinists, holding to the view that mortals are the irresponsible victims of heredity and environment. Others were guided by the evolutionary concept, interpreting man's nature as made up very largely of bestial qualities inherited from his animal ancestors. Still others were swayed by the fervor for social reform and pictured the inequities of the human scene against a sordid background so as to point the need for abolishing poverty, for eliminating war, or for treating those who had broken the laws of society more justly.

Realism as a distinct literary movement made its initial appearance in France. Its leading exponents were four great novelists who exerted an influence far beyond the confines of their native land. First

in order of time, and possibly also of merit, was Honoré de Balzac (1799–1850). In his stupendous *Human Comedy*, Balzac uncovered with brutal frankness the stupidity, greed, and baseness of men and women, chiefly of the bourgeoisie. He delighted in laying bare the hidden springs of human action and in revealing the rottenness behind the polished exterior of respectable society. An even more precise expression of the realist tradition is to be found in the work of Gustave Flaubert (1821–1880). His foremost novel, *Madame Bovary*, is a cool analysis of human degeneration. It is a study of the tragic conflict between romantic dreams and the dreary realities of ordinary existence. Though the book was condemned as salacious, and its author prosecuted for publishing an immoral work, it has been acclaimed by some critics as one of the greatest novels in modern literature.

Realistic writing of a somewhat different brand flowed from the pen of Émile Zola (1840–1902). Indeed, Zola is sometimes classified as a naturalist rather than a realist, to convey the idea that he was interested in an exact, scientific presentation of the facts of nature without any coloring of personal philosophy. But in actual truth Zola did have a definite philosophic viewpoint. His years of wretched poverty in early life imbued him with a deep sympathy for the common man and with a passion for social justice. Though he portrayed human nature as weak and prone to vice and crime, he was not without hope that a decided improvement might come from the creation of a better society. Many of his novels dealt with such social problems as alcoholism, bad heredity, poverty, and disease. He was an aggressive champion of the Third Republic and toward the end of his life took an active part in exposing the monstrous hypocrisy of the Dreyfus affair. The fourth of the great figures in French realism before World War I was Anatole France (1844–1924), who preached a gospel of wise and tolerant cynicism. Though he satirized human folly, he seldom gave vent to righteous wrath. His goddess was Irony, a gentle and kindly deity who "teaches us to laugh at rogues and fools whom, but for her, we might be so weak as to despise and hate." [9] Yet his tolerance of evil was by no means unlimited. He joined with Zola in a vigorous attack upon the persecutors of Dreyfus and lent his support to many other unpopular causes. In his later years he became so firmly convinced of the injustice of modern society that he allied himself with the socialists. His works included a varied collection of skeptical essays, mischievous short stories, and pungent satires on religion and politics. Among them are *Penguin Island*, *The Revolt of the Angels*, and *The Garden of Epicurus*.

Realist literature in England included the writings of the vast majority of the Victorian novelists and dramatists.[10] Among the first of the novelists to employ the methods of realism were William Makepeace Thackeray (1811–1863) and Charles Dickens (1812–1870). Thackeray was the novelist of the elegant world of the aristocracy, though he was far from admiring all of its qualities. He delighted in exposing the scandals of people in high places and in ridiculing their foibles. Like most of the early Victorians, he was inclined toward a self-satisfied moralizing on the evils of mankind. As Thackeray was the representative of the upper class, so Dickens was the spokesman for the lower. In such novels as *Oliver Twist*,

[9] Alfred Allinson (trans.), *The Garden of Epicurus*, p. 94.
[10] The Victorian period is named, of course, from the reign of Queen Victoria (1837–1901).

Nicholas Nickleby, Dombey and Son, and *David Copperfield* he wrote with poignant sympathy of the bitter lot of the poor. He denounced the horrors of the workhouses and scathingly portrayed the delays in the courts and the inhuman treatment of prisoners for debt. Though he was often swept into excesses of sentimentality, his books exerted considerable influence in hastening the progress of social reform.

The writings of Thackeray and Dickens were forerunners of the realism expressed by English novelists toward the end of the Victorian Age. The most renowned of late Victorian realists was undoubtedly Thomas Hardy (1840–1928). In such well-known narratives as *The Return of the Native, Jude the Obscure,* and *Tess of the D'Urbervilles* he expressed his conception that men are the playthings of inexorable fate. The universe is beautiful, he thought, but in no sense friendly, and the struggle of individuals with nature is a pitiable battle against almost impossible odds. If any such being as God exists, He simply watches with indifference while the helpless denizens of the human ant-heap crawl toward suffering and death. It is to be noted that Hardy's attitude was essentially one of pity for his fellow creatures. He regarded man not as a depraved animal but as an atom of dust caught in the wheels of a cosmic machine.

With the beginning of the twentieth century, realism in English literature took a decidedly different turn. The period from 1900 to 1914 was an era of great progress in social reform and of magnificent dreams for the future. It was natural that this spirit of confidence and hope should be reflected in the leading writings. The first literary genius to sound the clarion call of the new age was George Bernard Shaw (1856–1950). Born in Dublin of Anglo-Irish parents, Shaw betook himself to London at the age of twenty, where he earned his living as a journalist-critic of art and the drama. He soon became interested in socialism and emerged as a leader of the Fabian Society dedicated to the advancement of a modified Marxism. He combined his enthusiasm for socialism with a devotion to materialistic philosophy, an abiding faith in the value of science, and an acid contempt for the artificialities of bourgeois society. By 1900 he had found his true place in literature as the author of realistic dramas. From then on he wrote an amazing number of plays, on subjects ranging from prostitution to socialism and from the Salvation Army to creative evolution. For the most part, his works were not dramas at all in the conventional sense. They were vehicles for the expression of his ideas, in which the plot was completely overshadowed by witty and incisive dialogue. Likewise didactic in tone was the realism of H. G. Wells (1866–1946). The son of a professional cricket player, Wells devoted his early career to teaching science in a private school. As in the case of Shaw, it was a mixture of socialism and faith in the beneficence of science that provided the inspiration for his work as a writer. Most of the novels he published before 1914

depicted scientific utopias, in which toil and poverty would be eliminated by marvelous improvements in technology, while superstition
and war would be banished by proper education. His conception of
the tragedy of life was not that of a hopeless struggle against nature
but the slavery of individuals to outworn institutions and perverted
ideals. Among the best-known of his earlier novels are *Tono
Bungay, Anne Veronica*, and *The History of Mr. Polly*.

Realism was also a virile movement in many other countries. In
Germany it was exemplified in the dramas of Gerhart Hauptmann
(1862–1946) and in the first great novel of Thomas Mann (1875–
1955). Hauptmann was a social dramatist who chose his main
themes from the age-long struggle of the working classes against
poverty and ill treatment at the hands of their masters. He also
wrote satires and symbolical plays of psychological conflict. The
first great novel of Thomas Mann was published in 1903. Entitled
Buddenbrooks, it relates the story of the rise and decline of a great
merchant family of Lübeck. The narrative is presented with the
same lingering fondness for significant detail that distinguishes the
author's later works.

Doubtless the most eminent of all the realists of Teutonic nationality was Henrik Ibsen (1828–1906). Though born in Norway,
Ibsen was descended from ancestors who were mainly Danish and
German. Years of poverty and drudgery in his early life produced a
lasting impression upon his mind and left him resentful and bitter.
Until the age of twenty-two nearly all of his education had been
acquired by assiduous reading. His early dramas were not very
favorably received, and while still a young man he decided to abandon his native country. Residing first in Italy and then in Germany,
he did not return permanently to Norway until 1891. His writings
were characterized most of all by bitter rebellion against the
tyranny and ignorance of society. In such plays as *The Wild Duck,
Hedda Gabbler*, and *An Enemy of the People* he mercilessly
satirized the conventions and institutions of respectable life. Along
with this scorn for hypocrisy and social tyranny went a profound
distrust of majority rule. He despised democracy as the enthronement of unprincipled leaders who would do anything for the sake of
votes to perpetuate themselves in power. He makes one of his characters in *An Enemy of the People* say: "A minority may be right—a
majority is always wrong."

Notwithstanding the strength of the Puritan tradition in the
United States, realism as a literary movement was far from unimportant in that country. Traces of it were to be found as early as the
middle of the nineteenth century in the novels of Herman Melville
(1819–1891). His masterpiece, *Moby Dick*, combined marvelous
descriptions of the wonders and terrors of nature with a profound
searching into the mysteries of the universe and of man. But realism
scarcely became a dominant force until many years later. Toward

the end of the nineteenth century a group of young novelists began writing frankly of political and social abuses, often in such manner as to awaken a desire for reform. Stephen Crane described some of the less romantic aspects of war in his *Red Badge of Courage*. Mark Twain pilloried sham and hypocrisy in a series of novels, the most famous of which was *Adventures of Huckleberry Finn*. The cutthroat speculation of high financiers furnished the theme for Frank Norris's *Octopus*. But the most typical of the realists before 1914 was Theodore Dreiser (1871–1945). His first novel, *Sister Carrie*, was issued in London in 1901 and in New York in 1907, after considerable trouble with timid publishers. It was followed a few years later by two others of similar type—*Jennie Gerhardt* and *The Genius*. Dreiser's novels were characterized by a rigid determinism that recognized neither purpose in the universe nor meaning in life. But he suffused his writings with a quality of sympathy for his puny figures in their hopeless struggles against the forces of disaster.

Another of the great literatures which came into its own during the age of realism was that of the Russians. However, the boundaries separating particular movements in Russian literature are far from distinct. Several of the great novelists combined their realism with attitudes essentially romantic, others were incorrigible idealists. Among the names that stand out are Ivan Turgeniev (1818–1883), Feodor Dostoievski (1821–1881), and Leo Tolstoi (1828–1910). Turgeniev, who spent much of his life in France, was the first of the Russian novelists to become known to western Europe. His chief work, *Fathers and Sons*, describes in brooding and delicate gloom the struggle between the older and younger generations. The hero is a nihilist (a term first used by Turgeniev), who is convinced that the whole social order has nothing in it worth preserving. Dostoievski was almost as tragic a figure as any he projected in his novels. Condemned at the age of twenty-eight on a charge of revolutionary activity, he was exiled to Siberia, where he endured four horrible years. His later life was harrowed by poverty, by family troubles, and by epileptic fits. As a novelist, he chose to write of the seamy side, exploring the anguish of miserable creatures driven to shameful deeds by their raw, animal emotions and by the intolerable meanness of their lives. He was a master of psychological analysis, probing into the motives of distorted minds with an intensity that was almost morbid. At the same time he filled his novels with a broad sympathy and with a mystic conviction that the soul of man can be purified only through suffering. His best-known works are *Crime and Punishment* and *The Brothers Karamazov*.

It is generally conceded that the honor of being Russia's greatest novelist must be divided between Dostoievski and Tolstoi. As a communistic anarchist and an earnest champion of the simple life of the peasant, Tolstoi was somewhat less deterministic than the author of *Crime and Punishment*. Yet in his *War and Peace*, a majestic epic

of Russian conditions during the period of the Napoleonic invasion,
he expounds the theme that individuals are at the mercy of Fate
when powerful elemental forces are unleashed. His other most celebrated novel, *Anna Karenina,* is a study of the tragedy which lurks
in the pursuit of selfish desire. The hero, Levin, is really Tolstoi
himself, who eventually finds refuge from doubt and from the vani-
ties of worldly existence in a mystic love of humanity. As Tolstoi
grew older he became more and more an evangelist preaching a social gospel. In such novels as *The Kreutzer Sonata* and *Resurrection*
he condemned most of the institutions of civilized society and called
upon men to renounce selfishness and greed, to earn their living by
manual toil, and to cultivate the virtues of poverty, meekness, and
nonresistance. He set the example by deeding his property to his
wife and by adopting the dress and humble fare of the peasant. His
last years were devoted mainly to attacks upon such evils as war and
capital punishment and to the defense of victims of persecution.

Realism was by no means the only movement to hold the allegiance of the literary world between 1830 and 1914. Romanticism
continued to be exceedingly popular, especially in the realm of
poetry. Notable among the poets of this age whose attitudes were
essentially romantic were Robert Browning (1812–1889) and Alfred Tennyson (1809–1892). Browning is noted for his sense of the
dramatic and for his penetrating studies of human character; but,
like a true Victorian, he conceived of man as a moral being and the
universe as governed by benevolent purpose. His optimism stands
out in bold contrast to the fatalism and pessimism of so many of the
realists. He understood the baseness of human passions, but he never
lost faith in the ultimate triumph of goodness and truth. A poet of
much greater fame in his own lifetime was Alfred Tennyson. In
1850 he was made poet laureate, and in 1884 he became Lord
Tennyson. His merit, however, consists primarily in his wizardry
with words. The majority of his poems are distinguished for their
pictures and music rather than for the expression of ideas. His mastery of color and rhythm enabled him to invest the most commonplace thoughts with a power and brilliance that seemed to endow
them with lofty and original meaning. Though he tried hard to be a
thinker, he seldom did more than reiterate some of the popular ideas
of the Victorian Age. He sang the praises of virtue and of patriotism
and delved into medieval legends to revive the glories of King
Arthur's court. His nearest approach to profundity is *In Memoriam,*
written after the death of a beloved friend. It is a series of lyrics in
which the author passes from moods of doubt and despair to a final
confident hope in "one far-off divine event, To which the whole
creation moves."

Three other English authors may also be considered as representatives of the romantic tradition. The first two, Thomas Carlyle
(1795–1881) and John Ruskin (1819–1900), were essayists and

INTELLECTUAL
AND ARTISTIC
PROGRESS

The romanticism
of Carlyle, Ruskin,
and Kipling

critics; the other, Rudyard Kipling (1865–1936), was a poet and a writer of popular stories. Thomas Carlyle is perhaps best known for his theory that heroic individuals are the makers of history and for his trenchant criticisms of nineteenth-century culture. Industrialism, democracy, materialism, science, and utilitarianism were the objects of his special fury. A victim of chronic dyspepsia, he often appeared to be crabbed and unreasonable. Yet he was not a mere pessimist and faultfinder. He had a keen perception of the real weaknesses of many modern institutions, and he anticipated some contemporary European ideas of the right of the strong to rule. Carlyle and Ruskin had several attributes in common. Both had a tendency to look back to the Middle Ages. Neither had much use for democracy. Ruskin as much as Carlyle detested the factory regime and abhorred the crude materialism of nineteenth-century science. But Ruskin's philosophy was more nearly that of the aesthete and social reformer. He was repelled not only by the poverty and degradation of the industrial system but also by its ugliness. He condemned the ferocious capitalist struggle for profits and urged that workers be treated as partners in industry, entitled to a more generous share of what they produced. The romanticism of Rudyard Kipling was of an altogether different sort. He had no interest in either the social or the artistic implications of the industrial regime. In his poetry he trumpeted the glories of British imperialism, representing the subjugation of Hindus and Africans as a glamorous missionary enterprise to rescue the heathen from darkness. His prose narratives are mainly stories of adventure, rich in sentimental fondness for the enchantments of India but not very significant from the standpoint of ideas.

4. THE BIRTH OF MODERN ART

From 1830 to about 1860 the leading trend in painting was undoubtedly romanticism. Its most significant expressions were to be found in the work of the Pre-Raphaelites and of Jean François Millet (1814–1875). The chief figure in the Pre-Raphaelite movement was Dante Gabriel Rossetti (1828–1882), an Englishman of Italian ancestry who is better known as a poet than as a painter. Rossetti and his followers aimed to restore painting to the simplicity, directness, and naturalism which they believed it to have possessed in the Middle Ages and in the early Renaissance. All of the artificial and decorative tendencies that had appeared since the time of Raphael they deeply deplored. Repudiating the ideal of pure beauty, they insisted that art, in order to be worthy of the name, must be directly related to life; it must be useful, either in ministering to the needs of man or in conveying intellectual meaning.

A much greater painter than any of the members of the Pre-Raphaelite group was Jean François Millet. Though associated with the

Barbizon school,[11] Millet did not always follow the Barbizon tradition of romantic landscape painting. His paramount interest was in depicting the struggles of humble toilers against poverty and the cruel whims of nature. In *The Man with the Hoe* and *The Sower* he interpreted the bitter life of the peasant in a manner worthy of his realist successors, but in *The Angelus* and in *The Path through the Wheat* he betrayed the romantic fondness for sentimental piety and for intensity of color.

Millet

The development of realism in nineteenth-century painting is generally associated with the work of Gustave Courbet (1819–1877) and Honoré Daumier (1808–1879). Both were concerned with presenting the facts of life as they saw them, often in a coarse or satirical fashion. They were rebellious against classical and romantic traditions and intensely conscious of the social significance of art. Profoundly sympathetic toward the lower classes, especially the poor of the cities, they delighted in portraying scenes of squalor and misery and in pillorying the vices and foibles of the comfortable bourgeoisie. Daumier, in particular, was a powerful satirist of social and political evils. He ridiculed the corruption of petty officials, the pompous blundering of lawyers and judges, and the hypocritical piety of the rich. Courbet won great popularity by scornfully refusing the cross of the Legion of Honor offered to him by Napoleon III. Both Courbet and Daumier were zealous champions of the victims of oppression and exploitation, performing a function in art somewhat similar to that of Dickens and Zola in literature. Of course, not all of their painting took the form of social indictment. Much of it was mild and sympathetic portrayal of homely scenes from the lives of the poor. Whatever the subject, they strove to present it without the sentimental embellishments of the romantic schools.

The realist
painters, Courbet
and Daumier

The first completely original movement in nineteenth-century painting was *impressionism*. In a sense, the impressionist was a realist, for he was determined to paint only what he saw, and he was vitally interested in the scientific interpretation of nature. But his technique was different from that of the older realists. He did not depict scenes from the world around him as they would appear after careful study or thoughtful analysis. On the contrary, he sought to present the immediate impressions of his senses, leaving it to the mind of the observer to fill in additional details. This often resulted in a type of work appearing at first glance to be nonnaturalistic. Figures were commonly distorted; a few significant details were made to represent an entire object; and dabs of primary color were placed side by side without a trace of blending. Convinced that light is the principal factor in determining the appearance of objects, the impressionists fled from the studio to the woods and fields in an at-

Impressionism

[11] See p. 184.

tempt to capture the fleeting alterations of a natural scene with each transitory shift of sunlight and shadow. From science they had learned that light is composed of a fusion of primary colors visible in the spectrum. Accordingly, they decided to use these colors almost exclusively. They chose, for example, to achieve the effect of the green in nature by placing daubs of pure blue and yellow side by side, allowing the eye to mix them. Some of their paintings appear at close view to be nothing but splotches of color, but if studied from across the room, they gradually reduce themselves to a natural design, in which mountains, trees, houses, and the like are more or less clearly discernible.

Like so many of the other artistic movements of modern times, impressionism originated in France. It was founded about 1870 by Édouard Manet (1832–1883), who had been deeply affected by a study of the old Spanish masters, especially Velásquez. Probably the greatest of the impressionists were Claude Monet (1840–1926) and Auguste Renoir (1841–1919). Monet was perhaps the leading exponent of the new mode of interpreting landscapes. His paintings have no structure or design in the conventional sense; they do not depict, but subtly suggest, the outlines of cliffs, trees, mountains, and fields. Intensely interested in the problem of light, he would go out at sunrise with an armful of canvases in order to paint the same subject in a dozen momentary appearances. It has been said of one of his masterpieces that "light is the only important person in the picture." The work of Renoir exhibited a greater variety than that of any of his compeers. His subjects include not only landscapes but portraits and scenes from contemporary life. He is famous most of all for his pink and ivory nudes, done in a manner reminiscent of Titian or Rubens. Renoir made use of the familiar device of spots of sunlight for the purpose of bringing certain parts of a picture into high relief, but he presented his subjects with much more solidity of form than did the other members of his group. To this day he is the most popular of the impressionists.

For upwards of twenty years impressionism flourished as the dominant style of painting in nearly all countries of the Western world. But in the 1890's it yielded its popularity to a new movement, which is called for want of a better name *postimpressionism*. The postimpressionists criticized the formlessness and lack of volume of their predecessors. They contended that the figures of the painter's art should be as solidly and completely molded as statues. They objected also to the impressionist's preoccupation with the casual and momentary aspects of nature, and they deplored his indifference to ideas. The expression of meaning, they argued, should be the fundamental purpose of art; form and method are not ends in themselves but are important only insofar as they contribute to the expression of meaning. Postimpressionism was not only a reaction against impressionism, but in its ultimate tendencies, at least, it was a revolt

The impressionist painters

See color plates at pages 200, 360

Postimpressionism

against all of the hidebound formulas of the past. It was an expression of the chaos and increasing complexity of the machine age. It
symbolized the restlessness and bewilderment that accompanied the
emergence of a new society during the closing years of the nineteenth century. It was the beginning of nearly all that we now understand by *modern* art.

The artist who laid the foundations of postimpressionism was Paul
Cézanne (1839–1906), now recognized as one of the greatest
painters who ever lived. A native of southern France, Cézanne wan- Cézanne
dered through the world of art as in a dream. Ever hopeful of reaching some higher goal of achievement, he cared little for the works
he had finished. His son cut out the windows of some of his masterpieces for amusement, and his servant used others to clean the stove.
Cézanne viewed these disasters quite calmly, for he was convinced
that he would produce much better work in the future. His aim as a *See color plates*
painter was to represent nature in such a way that objects on a flat *at pages 361, 410*
canvas would appear to have the roundness and depth of sculpture.
To accomplish this he practiced mild distortion, applied paint in
thick layers, and modeled his figures with meticulous care. So well
did he succeed that it has been said that since Cézanne there is no
longer any excuse for sculpture.

The influence of Cézanne was reinforced and extended by two
other great artists of the postimpressionist manner. One was the half-
Peruvian Frenchman, Paul Gauguin (1848–1903), and the other Gauguin and
was the Dutchman, Vincent Van Gogh (1853–1890). Both were Van Gogh
revolutionary in their methods. Gauguin threw off all the restraints
of conventional painting. Declaring that the artist should not be the
slave either of nature or of the past, he introduced into his work an
exotic symbolism and the most startling adaptations of color. His
cardinal purpose was to emotionalize nature, to portray the world in
accordance with his own subjective feelings. Gauguin is important
also as a symbol of the disillusionment which spread through intellectual and artistic circles toward the end of the nineteenth century.
Dismayed by the complexity and artificiality of civilization, he fled
to the South Sea islands and spent the last decade of his life painting
the hot and luscious colors of an unspoiled, primitive society. He
was the forerunner of an extensive primitivist movement in twentieth-century art. For a time Gauguin was a friend of the Netherlands painter Van Gogh, but the friendship abruptly ceased when he
awoke one night to find the Dutchman advancing upon him with a
knife. Van Gogh was unquestionably demented; he cut off one of his
ears and carried it to a woman who had offended him, and he finally
took his own life. Yet there can be no denying his genius. The vibrant energy and turbulent emotionalism of his paintings have probably never been equaled. In order to express the intensity of his feelings, he worked with feverish haste, applying directly to his canvas
little worms of violent color which he squeezed from his tubes of **391**

Marcel Duchamp, *Nude Descending a Staircase*. Painting in the cubist-surrealist manner exemplifying the artist's revolt against the traditional premises and values of art. 1912.

paint. Van Gogh has been the chief inspiration for nearly all those modern painters who see in the expression of subjective ideas the exclusive function of art.

In the years between 1900 and World War I modern art underwent still further revolutionary development. First, Henri Matisse (1869–1954) greatly extended Cézanne's use of distortion and gradually evolved a type of painting that definitely repudiated fixed ideas of aesthetic merit. This tendency was carried much farther by Pablo Picasso (1881–   ), a Catalan Spaniard who came to Paris in 1903 and developed *cubism*, a style that takes its name from the attempt to resolve each figure or object into its underlying geometric elements. It is based upon a doctrine once casually enunciated by Cézanne that the fundamental ideas of form could best be expressed through such shapes as cubes, cones, and cylinders. Picasso took this doctrine literally. But cubism is much more than this. It involves not only distortion but in some cases actual dismemberment. The artist may separate the various parts of a figure and rearrange them in other than their natural pattern. The purpose is partly to symbolize the chaos of modern life but also to express defiance of traditional notions of form—to repudiate the conception of art as mere prettiness. It is for this latter purpose also that some of the extreme cubists generally avoided the use of color. In the opinion of leading auhorities cubism represented the real break with nineteenth-

Cubism

See color plates at page 411

392

Portrait of the Artist, van Gogh. This self-portrait shows a deep seriousness and intense concentration. (V. W. van Gogh)

Ia Orana Maria, Paul Gauguin (1848–1903). Gauguin revolted not only against the complexity and artificiality of European life, but against civilization itself. He finally fled to Tahiti to paint the lush, colorful life of an uncorrupted society. (MMA)

Sunflowers in a Vase, van Gogh. The feverish technique seems to have endowed the flowers with rhythmic motion. (V. W. van Gogh)

The Starry Night, Vincent van Gogh (1853–1890). This painting gives vivid expression to van Gogh's bold conceptions. The landscape is peaceful, but the heavens sputter and churn with vibrant energy. The cypress trees in the foreground are symbols of death. (Mus. Mod. Art)

Portrait of Gertrude Stein, Pablo
Picasso (1881–). Picasso seems
to have given this portrait of the
great experimenter in poetry some
elements of the distortion of form
characteristic of the work of both.
(MMA)

The Piano Lesson, Henri Matisse (1869–1954). Matisse con-
veyed a freshness of approach and a vitality of line and color.
(Mus. Mod. Art)

Three Musicians, Pablo Picasso. This painting, regarded by many as
the masterpiece of cubism, sums up the final stage of the movement.
(Mus. Mod. Art)

century art, having little in common with romanticism, impressionism, or even realism. Its influence extended beyond painting to sculpture, literature, and music.

Another of the main offshoots of postimpressionism that made its appearance before World War I was *futurism*. The spiritual father of futurism was a poet, F. T. Marinetti, who later took an active part in launching Italian Fascism. In 1910 Marinetti and a group of disciples issued a stirring manifesto calling for relentless war against the aesthetic ideals of the past. They condemned the worship of old masters, the slavish devotion to Roman ruins and to the art of the Renaissance, "the erotic obsession," "purism," sentimentality, quietism, and nature-worship. As painters the futurists aspired to glorify the machine and the achievements of modern science. They regarded it as imbecilic that an artist surrounded by the wonders of the modern scientific age should spend his time mooning over pastoral landscapes or attempting to recapture the beauty of classical mythology. Taking their cue from the discovery in physics that the ultimate fact of nature is energy, they insisted that *movement* should be the principal theme of art. Accordingly, they proceeded to break up form in such a manner as to produce the illusion of shimmering and vibration. They loved to depict the motion of a racing animal, the speed of an automobile, or the power and beauty of some complicated machine in a factory. Futurism has exerted a decided influence, especially upon the interior decoration of modern skyscrapers, railroad stations, and government buildings.

Futurism

Although sculpture flourished in abundance during the age of democracy and nationalism, there was comparatively little that could be considered significant. Most of it was an imitation of the baroque—grandiose, heavy, and exuberantly decorative. It was developed largely for patriotic purposes, to embellish monuments celebrating national greatness. But in the later years of the nineteenth century there was at least one sculptor whose work stands out as original. He was the Frenchman Auguste Rodin (1840–1917), and his achievements have been compared not unfavorably to those of Michelangelo, by whom he was strongly influenced. Rodin was preeminently a realist, but he also reflected the currents of romanticism and impressionism. He was interested in psychological analysis and in man's animal origins and his struggle against the forces of nature. His most elaborate work was *The Gate of Hell*, inspired by Dante's *Inferno*. It is a tragedy depicting the sufferings of the great mass of mankind, damned by the passions of their animal natures. Rodin is perhaps even better known for his statue, *The Thinker*, which suggests the evolution of man from lower species. Soon after the dawn of the twentieth century, sculpture began to exemplify certain traits of postimpressionist painting. It grew more and more abstract and distorted, indicating the strength of the revolt against prettiness and sentimentality.

Sculpture in the age of democracy and nationalism

See color plates at page 361

As in sculpture, so in architecture the influence of the past was exceedingly strong. Until nearly the end of the nineteenth century the builder's art continued to be governed by classical and medieval principles. In general, it was the classical that predominated, exemplified especially by the survival of the ponderous and ornate baroque. Monuments of this style included the National Opera (1864–1871) in Paris and the Reichstag building (1882–1894) and Protestant cathedral (1888–1895) in Berlin. Accompanying this development of the baroque, there was a vigorous revival of the Gothic. The renewal of interest in Gothic architecture was a product of the romantic tendency to glorify everything medieval. Just as old legends of knights in armor had been refurbished by poets, so there had to be a return to the building style of the thirteenth century. Consequently Gothic was adopted on a generous scale for churches, universities, and even for some parliament and office buildings.

Between 1880 and 1890 certain architects in Europe and America awoke to the fact that the prevailing styles of building construction were far out of harmony with the facts of modern civilization. The result was the launching of a new architectural movement known as *functionalism.* Its chief pioneers were Otto Wagner (1841–1918) in Germany and Louis Sullivan (1856–1924) and Frank Lloyd Wright (1869–1959) in the United States. The basic principle of functionalism is the idea that the appearance of a building shall proclaim its actual use and purpose. There must be no addition of friezes, columns, tracery, or battlements merely because some people consider such ornaments beautiful. True beauty consists in sincerity, in an honest adaptation of materials to the purpose they are

Auguste Rodin, *The Thinker.* An example of realism in sculpture apparently suggesting that man's intellectual faculties are inseparable from his animal heritage. The first copy was destroyed by students of conservative sculptors, but the statue was recast by Rodin.

Taliesin East by Frank Lloyd Wright (1911–1925). A famous example of functional style with the pattern of the house conforming to the natural surroundings.

intended to serve. Functionalism also includes the idea that architecture shall express either directly or symbolically the distinguishing features of contemporary culture. Ornamentation must therefore be restricted to such elements as will reflect the age of science and the machine. Modern man does not believe in the Greek ideas of harmony, balance, and restraint or in the medieval virtues of piety and chivalry, but in power, efficiency, speed, and comfort. These are the ideals which should find a place in his art.

There would seem to be little doubt that the functional style of building construction is one of the most significant architectural developments since the Renaissance. Among all of the styles which have been adopted during the last 300 years, it is the only one that is really original. Known also as *modern* architecture or the *international* style, it is the best approach that has yet been made to an efficient use of the tremendous mechanical and scientific resources of the contemporary world. It permits an honest application of new materials—chromium, glass, steel, concrete—and tempts the builder's ingenuity in devising others. Though many people dislike its stark simplicity and its angular, cubist lines, functional architecture has undoubtedly won an established place for the future. It has been adopted for countless new apartment houses, hotels, office buildings, stores, and factories not only in the United States but also in nearly every other civilized nation of the world.

The significance of functional architecture

395

5.   MUSIC IN THE AGE OF DEMOCRACY AND NATIONALISM

Romanticism did not die out in music nearly so early as it did in literature and in the other arts. It was at its height during the middle of the nineteenth century, and it has continued as an important tendency far into the twentieth. Many of the changes in musical expression and ideals in the later nineteenth century are comparable to the trends in literature and the fine arts, but exact parallels can be drawn only with difficulty. For example, although realism asserted itself, it could not be pushed to extremes in an art which is essentially neither descriptive nor pictorial. So productive was this period that space will permit discussion of only its most salient features and its most eminent composers.

Romanticism was emphasized in the work of the two contemporary German composers and friends, Robert Schumann (1810–1856) and Felix Mendelssohn (1809–1847). Schumann excelled in songs and in chamber and piano music, though he also composed symphonies. While he was one of the most romantic of composers, he was at the same time one of the most intellectual. As an editor and writer he urged the development of musical scholarship and an appreciation of the history of musical achievement. Among his services was the publicizing of the neglected wealth in the songs of Schubert. The insanity which darkened the last two years of Schumann's life was particularly tragic in view of the fineness of his character and influence. Felix Mendelssohn was the grandson of the Jewish philosopher, Moses Mendelssohn. Not the least among his gifts, as in the case of Schumann, were those of his personality. Mendelssohn was at home in all forms of music except opera, and all of it is informed by a classicist elegance and remarkable knowledge of the craft of composition. Mendelssohn's piano music, found too sentimental a generation or two ago, has regained a measure of esteem. His chamber music is the best of the age between Schubert and Brahms. Two of his symphonies and the violin concerto are played everywhere, as is his fine oratorio *Elijah*. The incidental music composed to Shakespeare's *A Midsummer Night's Dream* is unique in that literature.

Franz Liszt (1811–1886) spent his long life moving his place of residence from Paris, to Weimar, to Budapest, to Rome, the model of the modern international musical personality. He early distinguished himself as a concert pianist, and is commonly regarded as the greatest performer upon that instrument who ever lived. Later he turned intensively to composition, with results which were dazzling if not often of lasting import. Schumann and Mendelssohn had cultivated romanticism with restraint; Chopin brought it to the border of sentimentality; Liszt was the first of the romantic realists whose music could be bombastic and sensational but was always highly original.

His flair for exotic effects is most successfully revealed in his treatment of native Hungarian themes. Liszt was acquainted with many French literary figures and showed considerable interest in the revolutionary currents of his day. His chief influence derives from his piano playing and teaching, orchestral conducting, and philanthropic activities on behalf of needy musicians. His kindly assistance to Wagner when the latter was being hounded out of Germany was an incalculable service.

Richard Wagner (1813–1883), the outstanding musical figure of the later nineteenth century, was a thoroughgoing revolutionary in the world of art. His initial interest was in the drama, and when he turned to music it was primarily for its dramatic possibilities. His musical training came comparatively late and was largely self-administered, but was nonetheless remarkable. In his operas—which he preferred to call music-dramas—he applied a technique of blending together action, words, music, and scenic effects; his ideal was really a fusion of all the arts into an integrated whole. The result was something different from the conventional opera. Wagner dispensed with the arbitrary division of acts into scenes and discarded all artificial trappings; he took wide liberties with harmony and departed from stereotyped melodic patterns. He sought for a continuous flow of music, not subject to the tyranny of form but sensitive to every demand of expression. In several ways his operas, especially the later ones, which include the famous *Ring* cycle, sometimes seem to be glorifying a cult of brutality and egoism. (The philosopher Nietzsche was for a time an ardent admirer of Wagner.) There is no other instance in the history of music where a man's political and aesthetic ideas as well as his music exerted such pervasive influence on generations of musicians. Wagner's operatic ideals became binding—even in France—his harmonies and his magical orchestra enslaved practically every musician, and it was with difficulty that composers were able to liberate themselves from his overwhelming personality even in the earlier part of our century.

Such a pervasive force as nationalism could not help making its imprint upon music. In most European countries and even in the United States, folk music came under the scrutiny of scholars or found its way into the compositions of the learned. Many composers were fervent patriots. The early operas of Verdi (d. 1901), dedicated to the cause of Italian liberation, were sufficiently inflammatory to arouse the ire of the Austrian authorities. But Verdi, who lifted the opera to new artistic heights, was no narrow patriot. He drew his mature inspiration from a wide variety of sources, including the plays of Shakespeare. Nationalism is typified in the Bohemians Smetana (d. 1884) and Dvořák (d. 1904) and in the Norwegian Grieg (d. 1907). However, most of the devotees of national music did not deviate widely from accepted idioms of expression, but added their bit to the common European store. César Franck (d.

1890), a Belgian by birth and the founder of a modern French school of composers, is distinguished by a quality of otherworldly mysticism. The Finn, Jean Sibelius (1865–1957), although celebrating national sentiments in his tone poem *Finlandia*, displays in his seven symphonies capacities too universal to classify him as a mere nationalist.

One of the most remarkable of the national schools of music to appear was the Russian. Throughout the greater part of the nineteenth century Russian musicians had been content to follow the lead of the Italians, French, and Germans. Even such a brilliant composer as Tchaikovsky (1840–1893) introduced no real innovations. However, fresh paths were opened up by Borodin, Moussorgsky, and Rimsky-Korsakov, the last of whom lived into the twentieth century. With the exception of Tchaikovsky, none of them was trained as a professional musician, a fact which makes their achievement all the more impressive. While they did not throw overboard the familiar European scales and harmony, they brought to composition a fresh point of view, an indifference to orthodoxy, and an enthusiastic appreciation of Slavic folk songs and dances. These qualities have won a place for Russia in the very front rank of modern music.

Before the close of the period under consideration, several divergent tendencies were asserting themselves, indicative of the dissatisfaction with old forms which characterized all the arts. Some of these trends constituted new departures and others a return to the ideals of the past. The flowering of romanticism did not mean that the classical tradition had withered away. A classicist line runs through the romantic age to the end of the century, its most distinguished representative being Jóhannes Brahms (1833–1897). Though palpably a romantic, Brahms shows a discipline of mind and an understanding for the principles that actuated the old masters. These qualities, as well as his devotion to the symphonic style, made him the successor of Beethoven. Although Richard Strauss (1864–1949) began as a Wagnerian, his fondness for experiment soon became evident and was given free rein, first in his skillfully orchestrated symphonic poems and then in his music-dramas. The latter, in spite of resemblances, are essentially different from the operas of Wagner. While Wagner was romanticism incarnate, Strauss was a realist who summoned all the resources of the modern orchestra to convert music into a pictorial medium capable of evoking concrete and often commonplace images in the listener. Not content with stimulating intangible emotions, as the romanticists had done, he undertook to paint meticulous pictures, asserting that it should be quite possible to depict even a teaspoon by means of musical sounds. The content of his determined realism ranges all the way from the bleating of sheep and the whirring of windmills in *Don Quixote* to

The Russian
school

The classicism of
Brahms and
Richard Strauss

abstract philosophic ideas in *Thus Spake Zarathustra* (based on a text of Nietzsche's).

Another manifestation, perhaps of more enduring significance than Strauss's realism, was impressionism, created by the French composer, Claude Debussy (1862–1918). Like the impressionist painters, Debussy abandoned rigidity of design and intellectuality in the attempt to translate into tone the ecstasy or pathos of a particular mood or moment. Also like the impressionists of the brush he moved freely from one tone color to another without blending. Debussy was probably at his best when he applied his sensitive imagination directly to evoking the imagery implicit in the expanse of the sea, the play of moonlight, or the amorous reverie of a faun on a midsummer afternoon. Rejecting precise form and abstract beauty as artistic imperatives, he sought satisfaction not in the realism of life but in a fantastic world of dreams and shadows.

The impressionism of Debussy

SELECTED READINGS

· *Items so designated are available in paperbound editions.*

PHILOSOPHY

· Barzun, Jacques, *Darwin, Marx, Wagner*, Boston, 1941 (Anchor). Thoughtful and stimulating.
· Brinton, Crane, *English Political Thought in the Nineteenth Century*, Cambridge, Mass., 1949 (Torchbook).
———, *Ideas and Men*, Englewood Cliffs, N.J., 1950.
Burns, E. M., *Ideas in Conflict*, New York, 1960.
Cushman, H. E., *A Beginner's History of Philosophy*, New York, 1918, Vol. II.
· Hayes, C. J. H., *A Generation of Materialism*, New York, 1941 (Torchbook).
· Hofstadter, Richard, *Social Darwinism in American Thought*, Philadelphia, 1949 (Beacon). The standard work on the subject.
Joad, C. E. M., *A Guide to Modern Thought*, New York, 1933.
Marvin, F. S., *The Century of Hope*, New York, 1919.
Mosse, G. L., *The Culture of Western Europe: The Nineteenth and Twentieth Centuries*, Chicago, 1961.
· Perry, R. B., *The Thought and Character of William James*, Cambridge, Mass., 1948 (Torchbook, briefer version).
Randall, J. H., Jr., *The Making of the Modern Mind*, New York, 1926, Chs. XVIII–XXI. A lively summary.
· Reichenbach, Hans, *The Rise of Scientific Philosophy*, Berkeley, 1951 (University of California Press). A book for the student with some knowledge of philosophy.
· Russell, Bertrand, *History of Western Philosophy*, New York, 1945 (Simon & Shuster). Good for both summary and interpretation.
Sabine, G. H., *A History of Political Theory*, New York, 1961. Good for the first half of the nineteenth century.

SCIENCE

Agar, W. M., *The Dilemma of Science*, London, 1941.

· Butterfield, H. B., *The Origins of Modern Science*, Glencoe, Ill., 1957 (Free Press).

Conant, J. B., *On Understanding Science: An Historical Approach*, New Haven, 1947.

· De Kruif, Paul, *Microbe Hunters*, New York, 1926 (Pocket Book).

· Eddington, A. S., *The Nature of the Physical World*, New York, 1946 (Ann Arbor).

Farber, Eduard, *The Evolution of Chemistry*, New York, 1952.

· Jones, Ernest, *The Life and Work of Freud*, New York, 1953 (Anchor, abr.). The best biography of the founder of psychoanalysis.

McKenzie, A. E. E., *The Major Achievements of Science*, New York, 1960.

Pillsbury, W. B., *History of Psychology*, New York, 1929.

Robinson, Victor, *The Story of Medicine*, New York, 1936.

· Russell, Bertrand, *The A B C of Relativity*, New York, 1925 (Mentor).

Sears, Paul, *Charles Darwin: The Naturalist as a Cultural Force*, New York, 1950.

Singer, Charles, *A History of Biology*, New York, 1950.

———, and Underwood, A. E., *A Short History of Medicine*, 2d ed., New York, 1962.

LITERATURE

Brandes, Georg, *Main Currents in Nineteenth Century Literature*, New York, 1901–06.

Lalou, René, *Contemporary French Literature*, New York, 1924.

Olgin, M. J., *A Guide to Russian Literature*, New York, 1920.

· Young, G. M., *Victorian England: Portrait of an Age*, Garden City, N.Y., 1954 (Oxford).

· Wilson, Edmund, *Axel's Castle: A Study in the Imaginative Literature of 1870–1930*, New York, 1931 (Scribner Library).

ART

Faure, Elie, *History of Art*, New York, 1937, Vol. IV. A lucid and instructive account.

Gardner, Helen, *Art Through the Ages*, New York, 1926.

Hitchcock, H. R., *Modern Architecture*, New York, 1929.

Wright, W. H., *Modern Painting*, New York, 1927. An excellent interpretation of the leading movements.

MUSIC

Abraham, Gerald, *A Hundred Years of Music*, New York, 1938.

Einstein, Alfred, *Music in the Romantic Era*, New York, 1947.

Lang, Paul, *Music in Western Civilization*, New York, 1941.

Machlis, Joseph, *The Enjoyment of Music*, rev. ed., New York, 1963.

Newman, Ernest, *The Life of Richard Wagner*, New York, 1937.

Thompson, Oscar, *Debussy, Man and Artist*, New York, 1937.

SOURCE MATERIALS

Baumer, F. L. V., *Main Currents of Western Thought*, New York, 1952.
· Darwin, Charles, *The Origin of Species*, especially Chs. IV, XV, Cambridge, 1964 (Collier and others).
———, *The Descent of Man*, especially Ch. XXI.
Dewey, John, *Human Nature and Conduct*, New York, 1930.
· ———, *Reconstruction in Philosophy* (Beacon, 1957).
· Freud, Sigmund, *An Outline of Psychoanalysis*, New York (Norton Library).
· Huxley, T. H., *Man's Place in Nature*, Ann Arbor, 1959 (Ann Arbor).
James, William, *The Philosophy of William James*, New York, 1925.
· ———, *The Will to Believe*, Gloucester, Mass. (Dover).
· Mill, J. S., *Autobiography; Utilitarianism*, Urbana, Ill., 1961 (Library of Liberal Arts and others).
Spencer, Herbert, *Man versus the State*, London, 1892.
———, *Social Statics*, New York, 1954.

CHAPTER 13

The Second Industrial Revolution, 1860-1914

It may not be true, in spite of *Punch* cartoons, that coal-miners drank champagne in 1871-1873; but certainly many wage-earners were getting more cake as well as tea, cocoa, meat, sugar, rice, and fats. They might return home a little earlier for the evening meal, as trade union pressure was chipping the working week from sixty (or more) hours down toward fifty-five, with a Saturday half-holiday. If they lived in Britain the public health service was beginning to make their living environment a bit better. . . . Parliament had given them a vote in 1867, and in 1870 it finally insisted that the children it had shut out of the factories must go to school. Things had moved since the Hungry Forties.

—Herbert Heaton, "Economic Change and Growth,"
The New Cambridge Modern History, X

About 1860 the industrialization of the modern world entered a new phase so different from what had gone before that historians are disposed to call it the Second Industrial Revolution. It was marked by radical changes in the structure of capitalism, by the decline of the free market, the revival of monopolies and of government intervention to promote prosperity, the rise of the money barons, and the development of new methods of production based in some cases on the substitution of new basic materials for those heretofore considered standard. The events that ushered in this new industrial revolution were mainly three in number: the development of the Bessemer process of making steel in 1856; the perfection of the dynamo about 1873; and the invention of the internal combustion engine in 1876. In general, the features that served to distinguish the Second Industrial Revolution from the First may be stated as follows: (1) the substitution of steel in place of iron as the basic industrial material; (2) the partial replacement of coal by gas and oil as principal

Nature of the Second Industrial Revolution

403

sources of power; (3) the development of electricity as a major
form of industrial energy; (4) spectacular innovations in transportation and communication; (5) the rise of new forms of capitalist organization; and (6) the spread of industrialization to central and
eastern Europe and even to the Far East. A few words must be said
about each of these major developments.

1. DEVELOPMENTS IN THE SECOND INDUSTRIAL REVOLUTION

The discovery
of new processes
of making steel

Methods of making steel had been known for centuries. As early
as the year 1000 the Saracens were producing excellent steel swords
at Damascus. Beginning with the later Middle Ages, Europeans had
also known how to manufacture the desirable material. But the
methods were slow and difficult and the product expensive. In 1856
Sir Henry Bessemer discovered that the introduction of a jet of air
into the molten iron in a blast furnace would eliminate all but the
tiniest percentage of carbon and thereby convert the iron into steel.
The result was to reduce the price of steel to less than a seventh of
its former cost. By 1878 a method was discovered whereby even
low-grade iron with a heavy content of phosphorus could also be
converted into steel. The consequences of this advance were astounding. Not only was the phosphoric iron of England brought
into production, but enormous deposits in Lorraine, in Belgium, and
in the United States now became immensely valuable. Between 1880
and 1914 the output of steel in Great Britain rose from 2,000,000
tons to 7,000,000, in Germany from 1,000,000 to 15,000,000, and in
the United States from 1,600,000 to 28,000,000. Steel almost entirely
supplanted iron for railroad rails, for the framework of large buildings, for bridges, and for other purposes where a cheap metal with a
high degree of tensile strength was desired.

The invention
of the dynamo

The partial displacement of coal as a basic source of power resulted, first of all, from the invention of the dynamo, a machine for
converting mechanical energy into electrical energy. Although the
principle of the dynamo was formulated by Michael Faraday in
1831, no machine of this kind capable of practical use was available
until 1873. From that time on the harnessing of electrical energy to
the mechanism of industry went rapidly ahead. The steam engine
came to be relegated gradually to the background, to be used primarily for driving dynamos. The electric energy thus generated is
converted by electric motors into mechanical energy. In some areas,
especially where coal is scarce, the steam engine for driving dynamos has been superseded by water power. By 1914 electricity provided more than half of the power required by industry in Great
Britain and an even larger proportion in Germany.[1] The German

[1] Herbert Heaton, *Economic History of Europe*, p. 518.

A.E.G. (Allgemeine Elektrizitäts Gesellschaft), manufacturing motors, generators, and other electrical equipment, had evolved into the largest industrial unit in Europe.

A second revolutionary development making available new sources of power was the utilization of petroleum products to add to the supply of energy. The existence of petroleum had been known for some time before its value was discovered. Until the middle of the nineteenth century it was regarded as a curiosity. Labeled as Indian Oil or Seneca Oil, it was sold in the United States for its alleged medicinal properties. Even after its value for lubricating purposes was revealed, its use was limited by scarcity. In 1859 Edwin L. Drake solved the problem of an inadequate supply by drilling the first oil well near Titusville, Pennsylvania. New uses for the product were gradually found, although for many years most of it went into the manufacture of kerosene for lamps. In 1876, however, Nikolaus Otto invented the first successful internal-combustion engine. This was the starting point of a series of developments which heralded the dawn of a motorized age. A few years afterward Gottlieb Daimler adapted the internal-combustion engine to the use of gasoline instead of natural gas, and Karl Benz equipped it with an electric spark to ignite the fuel. The perfection of the carburetor about 1890 by another German, Wilhelm Maybach, also contributed much to the potentialities of gasoline power. Finally, in 1897, Rudolf Diesel invented an internal-combustion engine using as fuel neither gas nor gasoline but crude oil. More recently, Diesel engines have come into extensive use in ocean liners, locomotives, trucks, and buses. In Europe some motor cars are Diesel-powered.

Among the most typical features of the Second Industrial Revolution were the introduction of automatic machinery, an enormous increase in mass production, and a division of the tasks of labor into minute segments of the manufacturing process. All three of these things date from the years just preceding World War I. A charac-

The Bessemer Process of Manufacturing Steel. This process involved the introduction of a jet of air into the molten iron to reduce its impure elements and thereby toughen it for the production of steel.

An Early Assembly Line of the Ford Motor Co., 1913. Bodies were slid down the ramp and attached to the chassis as they passed through the line below. Production amounted to 1000 cars a day.

teristic example of the development of automatic machinery was the invention of the photoelectric cell, or the "electric eye," which could be used to throw switches, to open doors, to sort eggs, to inspect tin cans, to count sheets of paper and measure their thickness, and even to eliminate counterfeit bills. Machines were invented to direct and operate other machines and to complete whole series of manufacturing processes which formerly required much human labor. Not only did automatic machinery result in a marked increase in mass production, but the volume of goods turned out by industry was also greatly expanded by the adoption of the endless conveyor belt. The idea for this was copied originally by Henry Ford about 1908 from the Chicago packers, who used an overhead trolley to move carcasses of beef along a line of butchers. Ford gradually improved the device to a point where he could assemble a complete chassis of his famous Model T in an hour and thirty-three minutes. The principle of the conveyor belt and the assembly line, which requires each worker to toil all day at a simple, monotonous task, was subsequently adopted in every automobile factory in the United States and in many other industries as well. It provided the world with a staggering abundance of goods and reduced the prices of some articles which were formerly luxuries for the rich, but no one was then able to foresee how serious might be its effects upon the minds and morale of the workers.

Radical changes in methods of production came not only from
406 the invention of intricate machines but also from a growing domina-

tion of industry by science. As a matter of fact, the significant discoveries of the Second Industrial Revolution emanated more often from the laboratory of the physicist or chemist than from the brain of the individual inventor. The supremacy of science in the realm of industry was originally foreshadowed in 1856 when William Henry Perkin produced the first aniline or coal-tar dyes. This was the beginning of a marvelous development of synthetic chemistry. From this same coal tar it was discovered that literally hundreds of dyes could be derived, together with an infinite variety of other products, such as aspirin, oil of wintergreen, essence of orange blossoms, saccharine, carbolic acid, and vanilla. As the years passed, many additional subtances were added to the list of synthetic products. Methods were devised for manufacturing nitric acid out of the nitrogen in the air, for making glucose from corn, and for producing textile fibers from wood and from minerals. Chemists likewise came to the aid of many of the older industries, discovering methods of utilizing hitherto worthless by-products or of increasing the yield from available supplies of raw materials. For example, cotton seeds were turned into celluloid, cosmetics, smokeless powder, and salad oil, and the cracking process of refining gasoline greatly increased the yield from a given quantity of petroleum.

The second stage of the Industrial Revolution saw perhaps an even greater revolution in transportation and communication than did the first. The years after 1860 were marked by feverish activity in railroad building. Before that date there were hardly more than 30,000 miles of railroad in the entire world. By 1890 there were 20,000 miles in Great Britain alone, 26,000 in Germany, and 167,000 in the United States. The service itself was greatly improved by the invention of the air brake in 1868 and by the introduction of the sleeping car, the dining car, and the automatic block-signal system soon afterward. As the years passed, however, the railroads began to suffer under competition from newer forms of transportation, especially from the automobile and the commercial airplane.

It is impossible to assign credit for invention of the automobile to any one person, though various individuals have claimed it. Both Daimler and Benz made gasoline vehicles in Germany as early as the 1880's, but their original inventions were little more than motorized tricycles. The first man to apply the principle of the internal-combustion engine to a carriage seems to have been the Frenchman Émile Levassor. About 1890 he designed a vehicle with the engine in front and with the power transmitted to the rear wheels by means of a clutch, a shaft, and reduction and differential gears. So far as the evidence shows, this was the first true automobile in history. Obviously, many other inventions were necessary in order to ensure the success of the motorcar as a comfortable and efficient means of travel. Not the least of these were the pneumatic tire developed by J. B. Dunlop in 1888 and the electric self-starter perfected by Charles Kettering about 1910. But the automobile might have remained indefinitely a toy for the rich had it not been for the determination of Henry Ford to produce a car that could be bought by persons of moderate incomes. In 1908 he began the manufacture of his Model T on the basis of the theory that he could make more money by selling a great quantity of cheap cars on a small margin of profit than by turning out an expensive product for the wealthy few. Other companies followed his example, with the result that eventually the automobile industry grew into the largest single branch of manufacturing in the United States.

Developments in
aviation

No more than the perfection of the automobile can the invention of the airplane be credited to any one person. The idea that some day man might be able to fly is an old one indeed. Not only was it suggested by Roger Bacon in the thirteenth century, but it was actually embodied in some definite plans for flying machines conceived by the fertile mind of Leonardo da Vinci. Nevertheless, the birth of aviation as a mechanical possibility really dates from the 1890's. It was about that time that Otto Lilienthal, Samuel P. Langley, and others began their experiments with heavier-than-air machines. The work of Langley was carried forward by the Wright brothers, who, in 1903, made the first successful flight in a motor-driven plane. From that point on advancement was rapid. In 1908 the Wright brothers flew nearly 100 miles. The following year Louis Bleriot crossed the English Channel in the monoplane he had recently invented. During World War I each of the belligerent nations made strenuous efforts to utilize the possibilities of the airplane as a weapon of slaughter. As a consequence, improvements in design and in efficiency came thick and fast. However, it should be remembered that, even without the war, progress would still have been rapid; for, once an invention has been successfully launched, improvements follow in a kind of geometric ratio.

The First Successful Airplane Flight. The Wright brothers' motor-driven craft takes to the air at Kitty Hawk, North Carolina, on December 17, 1903.

The early Industrial Revolution, or the age of coal and iron, resulted in but one important advance in communication. This, as we have seen, was the invention of the telegraph, which was already in extensive use by 1860. The age of electricity and the internal-combustion engine were accompanied by the perfection of a number of devices that went far toward annihilating both time and distance in the dissemination of news and in communicating with far-off places. First came the telephone, for which the credit is commonly given to Alexander Graham Bell, though only a few hours after Bell had applied for a patent in Washington on February 15, 1876, Elisha Gray appeared with practically the same idea.[2] Next came the invention of the wireless telegraph by Guglielmo Marconi, on the basis of discoveries by Heinrich Hertz and others relative to the transmission of electromagnetic waves through the ether. In 1899 Marconi dispatched a wireless message across the English Channel and two years later across the Atlantic. The invention of wireless telegraphy paved the way for the development of radio, the wireless telephone, and television.

The foregoing list of inventions by no means exhausts the record of mechanical progress during the Second Industrial Revolution. Particular reference should be made to the invention of the electric light, which has probably contributed as much to the well-being of the human race as any other invention in history. Not only has it enhanced the comfort and safety of contemporary living, it has been a boon to miners, and many of the difficult operations of modern surgery would be impossible without it. The electric light was first conceived by Sir Humphrey Davy about 1820, but it did not become a commercial success until 1879 when Thomas A. Edison invented the incandescent-filament lamp. Even after that a great many improvements were necessary before it could be widely used. Not until George Westinghouse and Nikola Tesla completed their experiments with the alternating current in 1893 was it possible to provide for the efficient transmission of light and power over long distances. Among other significant mechanical achievements of the period since 1860 were the invention of type-bar casting (the linotype machine) by Ottmar Mergenthaler, the perfection of artificial refrigeration by J. J. Coleman and others, the invention of the typewriter by Christopher Sholes and Carlos Glidden, and the development of motion-picture photography, originated mainly by Edison.

2. THE NEW CAPITALISM

The Second Industrial Revolution was distinguished from the First not merely by technological advances, but even more strikingly by the development of new forms of capitalist organization.

[2] Clive Day, *Economic Development in Modern Europe*, p. 26.

The age of coal and iron was also, generally speaking, the age of small enterprise. Until the middle of the nineteenth century, at least, the partnership was still the dominant form of business organization. To be sure, many of these partnerships did business on a considerable scale, but they were hardly to be compared with the giant corporations of more recent years. Their capital came mainly from profits plowed back into the business, and their owners generally took an active part in the work of management. Many joint-stock companies had also been formed, but, except for their attributes of permanence and limited liability, they differed little from the partnerships. All of these types of business organization, insofar as they were concerned with manufacturing, mining, or transportation, may be designated as forms of *industrial capitalism*. During the Second Industrial Revolution, especially after 1890, industrial capitalism was largely superseded by *finance capitalism*, one of the most crucial developments of the modern age. Finance capitalism has four outstanding characteristics: (1) the domination of industry by investment banks and insurance companies; (2) the formation of huge aggregations of capital; (3) the separation of ownership from management; and (4) the growth of holding companies. Several of these require brief explanation.

The domination of
industry by invest-
ment institutions

One of the earliest examples of the domination of industry by investment bankers was the formation of the United States Steel Corporation in 1901 with the aid of J. P. Morgan and Company. Thenceforth financial institutions gained control over an increasing number of corporations. Of course they did not own all of the stock, or any considerable fraction of it. Many corporations had tens of thousands of stockholders. But these people were chiefly absentee owners; they had little to do with influencing corporate policy, and some of their shares did not even carry voting privileges. Banks and insurance companies wielded control in some cases through ownership of a majority of the *voting stock* and in others through floating loans under terms which provided the lenders with extensive powers or with representation on boards of directors.

Another element in finance capitalism was the separation of ownership from management. The real owners of industrial enterprises were the thousands of men and women who had invested their savings in shares of stock; management was in the hands of a group of officers and directors, chosen by a minority of shareholders who had monopolized the voting stock or collected the proxies of absentee owners. In some cases the officers were little more than salaried employees, owning but a tiny percentage of the company's capital. Indeed, it was not unknown that some of them preferred to invest their surplus earnings in sounder enterprises than the ones over which they presided.

Lastly, finance capitalism included the growth of the holding company as a basic form of capitalistic organization. The holding company is a device whereby a number of producing units are united under the control of a company that owns their stock. The holding company does not engage in production but receives its income from management fees and from dividends paid by the producing units. Though sometimes justified on the ground that it promotes integration of industry and facilitates business expansion, it is really a symbol of the triumph of the financier over the old-fashioned type of productive capitalist.

In addition to the foregoing changes in the structure and organization of capitalism, the fundamental character of the system underwent a transformation with the advent of the Second Industrial Revolution. The 100-year period from 1770 to about 1870 was the heyday of the free market economy. Free trade, free competition, and freedom of contract were the golden calves that the business establishments in nearly all countries theoretically worshiped. Monopolies, tariffs, and other special privileges conferred by governments were gradually abolished. Every manufacturer and merchant was supposed to compete on equal terms with his rivals. If success did not crown his efforts, he had nothing but the laws of bankruptcy to save him from complete disaster. The rule that he who does not work shall not eat was ruthlessly applied to the working classes. Strikes and collective bargaining were almost universally condemned. Labor unions were few and rudimentary in character. Nothing resembling the welfare state was tolerated lest a premium be given to indolence and improvidence. The success of the free market economy depended, in theory at least, upon the use of a uniform monetary standard. In 1821 Great Britain put into operation the gold standard, a device whereby the value of all other commodities was measured in terms of gold. The other leading countries gradually adopted it, and most of them clung to it until the Great Depression of the 1930's. The financial classes preferred it because it placed obstacles in the path of government manipulation of currencies and served as a convenient means of balancing accounts between nations.

Changes in the
fundamental char-
acter of capitalism

Such was the ideal economic system which is often thought of as a golden age of economic liberalism when Britain led the world in the development of industry and finance. Some authorities, however, maintain that it never really existed, except as a British utopia. There was perhaps never a time when all of its features reigned unchallenged. Great Britain herself did not adopt free trade until 1846. Prussia instituted protectionism in 1818 and laid the foundations for a customs union, or Zollverein, for all of Germany in 1834. United States tariff policy became definitely protectionist in 1816. The fact may be noted, in addition, that most of the railroads in Continental European countries were established under government ownership. Nevertheless, these modifications were pygmy deviations compared with those that were to follow after 1870. Increasing attention was now given to government subsidy and sponsorship. In France, for example, the tobacco and match industries became government monopolies. In practically all countries except Great Britain tariffs for the protection of domestic manufactures were boosted sky-high. Labor unions waxed in power, and the right of collective bargaining was increasingly recognized. Most important of all, perhaps, a trend toward the welfare state made definite progress. In the 1880's Bismarck inaugurated his program of social insurance, and other governments, including even that of Great Britain, gradually followed suit. Even in the early 1900's some leaders, notably Louis D. Brandeis, later Associate Justice of the United States Supreme Court, were boldly proclaiming the need of a guaranteed annual income. In many quarters it was coming to be recognized that poverty is not always the fruit of laziness and improvidence, but may often be the product of conditions beyond the individual's control. These it may be the duty of the state to mitigate or correct.

Of course, the working classes were not the only ones to benefit from the changed outlook on economic policy. Trusts, mergers, and **Trusts, Mergers, and Cartels** cartels, controlled generally by limited numbers of financiers, attained respectability. Trusts are combinations of all or nearly all of the producers of certain articles in order to control their price and production. Mergers are combinations of companies producing the same or related articles. They differ from trusts in the fact that their constituent units generally lose their identity and are "merged" into a controlling corporation. Cartels may be defined as loose associations of independent companies for the primary purpose of restricting competition in the sale of their products. They differ from both trusts and mergers in not being corporate entities. They may function on either a domestic or an international scale.

Finally, it should be noted that the Second Industrial Revolution spread with fair rapidity to nearly every country in the civilized world. During the age of coal and iron, mechanized production was restricted primarily to Great Britain, France, Belgium, and the United States; and Great Britain was far in advance of the others.

After 1860 industrialization spread until every one of the major powers had reaped a full harvest of its benefits and evils. The adoption of the new methods was especially conspicuous in Germany. Before 1860 the German states had been predominantly agrarian, with at least 60 per cent of their people obtaining their living from the soil. By 1914 the empire of the Kaisers was the greatest industrial nation in Europe, producing more steel than Great Britain and leading the world in the manufacture of chemicals, aniline dyes, and electrical and scientific equipment. For such remarkable expansion there were several main explanations. In the first place, Germany had no tradition of laissez faire. Her economists had been preaching for years that the state should intervene in every way possible to promote the economic strength of the nation. As a consequence it was easy for the government to bolster up feeble industries, to nationalize the railroads and operate them for the benefit of business, and even to encourage the growth of trusts. As a second reason may be mentioned the German emphasis upon applied science in the schools, resulting in an abundant supply of technicians who could be hired by industrial corporations for a low wage. The famous Krupp munitions works at Essen employed a larger staff of trained scientists than any university in the world. Last, but by no means of least importance, was the fact that Germany acquired, as a result of her victory over France in 1870, the rich iron deposits of Lorraine, which ultimately supplied her with three-fourths of the ore for her basic industry of steel manufacture.

Industrialization did not spread into eastern Europe quite so soon as it did into Germany, nor did it proceed as far. Nevertheless, by 1890 a considerable development of the factory system and of mechanized transportation had begun in Russia. The Industrial Revolution in Russia, like that in Germany, was in part the result of governmental encouragement. Through the influence of Count Serge Witte, distinguished minister under Alexander III and Nicho-

Industrialization in Germany. The Krupp munitions works at Essen in 1876.

Inside a French Locomotive Factory, 1900.

las II, the government of the Tsars levied prohibitive tariffs and borrowed money from France to subsidize railroads and numerous industrial enterprises. These and other efforts bore some amazing fruit. By 1914 Russia was producing more iron than France, her coal production had more than doubled, and in textiles she ranked fourth in the world. No fewer than 3,000,000 people were engaged directly in manufacturing, while some of her industrial establishments employed as many as 10,000 workers.[3] The Industrial Revolution in Italy and Japan was also advanced very largely by state intervention, at least in its earlier stages. In both countries the movement began about 1880 and had completed a cycle of definite progress by the outbreak of World War I. In Italy the government extended the railway system and fostered the growth of silk and cotton manufactures in such measure that Italian exports increased nearly 300 per cent between 1895 and 1914. The achievements of Japan were even more remarkable. By 1914 the little island empire had 6000 miles of railroad, almost entirely owned by the state. Her textile industry almost equaled that of Great Britain, while her foreign commerce had risen in value from virtually nothing to nearly $700,000,000.

3. SOCIETY IN THE AGE OF THE MACHINE

The phenomenal growth of population

In later chapters there will be occasion to observe some of the political effects of the two industrial revolutions of the late eighteenth, nineteenth, and early twentieth centuries. For the present it is sufficient to take note of the social results. There is no doubt that most of the important social developments of the nineteenth and early

414   [3] Clive Day, *op. cit.*, p. 388.

twentieth centuries have sprung from the great economic changes of that period. Perhaps the most obvious and yet one of the most crucial of these developments was an enormous increase in population. Between the French Revolution and World War I the population of nearly every civilized country grew at an unprecedented rate. Some evidences of this phenomenon were noticeable as early as 1800, especially in England, where the increase was about 50 per cent in the second half of the eighteenth century. But in the main the spectacular growth came later. Between the Battle of Waterloo and the outbreak of World War I the population of England and Wales nearly quadrupled. That of Germany rose from about 25,000,000 in 1815 to almost 70,000,000 a hundred years later. The number of inhabitants in France almost doubled between the overthrow of Napoleon and the Franco-Prussian War, and the total of Russians more than doubled in the fifty years preceding 1914. In spite of such adverse factors as famine in Ireland and Russia, emigration to America, and disease resulting from congestion in cities, the population of Europe as a whole mounted from an estimated 190,000,000 in 1800 to 460,000,000 in 1914. During the same period the population of the United States increased from 5,000,000 to almost 100,000,000.

To discover the reasons for this unprecedented growth in numbers we must look to several factors. First, it was due in some measure to the effects of the Commercial Revolution in improving the vigor of peoples by providing a more abundant and a more varied diet. Second, it was a consequence of the establishment of infant and maternity hospitals and of advancements in medical science and sanitation, which led to the practical elimination of smallpox, scurvy, and cholera, at least from western Europe and America. Possibly a third cause was the influence of nationalism, of the growth of racial pride and patriotic obsession. Peoples with a solid conviction of their own superiority and buoyant with hopes of victory in future struggles are almost certain to reproduce very rapidly. These were the qualities that characterized most of the nations in the nineteenth century. But apparently the most important cause, in Europe at least, was the influence of the industrial revolutions in making it possible for limited areas to support large numbers of people. This increase in population came about not only because the mechanization of agriculture increased the yield from the land, but also because the factory system enlarged the opportunities for earning a living away from the soil. Thus it became possible for countries rich in industrial resources to support several times as many people as ever could be done on an agrarian basis.

Closely related to growth of population as an effect of the industrial revolutions was an increasing urbanization of Western society. By 1914 the artificial conditions of city life had come to be the accepted norm for a large percentage of the inhabitants of industrialized nations. Growth in urbanization was particularly striking in

Urban Poverty: A "Sweatshop" on the Lower East Side, New York City, in 1910. Conditions similar to those depicted in this garment-maker's workshop were endured by thousands of immigrant workers and their families.

such countries as Germany and England. In the former as late as 1840 there were only two cities of 100,000 inhabitants or more; in 1910 there were forty-eight. In England during the last thirty years of the nineteenth century, approximately one-third of the agricultural population withdrew permanently from the land. The English census of 1901 revealed that the number of persons engaged in farming was only about 20 per cent of the number employed in industrial pursuits. In the United States, despite its wealth of agricultural resources, there was a similar movement away from the land, albeit at a slower pace. By 1915 the proportion of Americans living in urban areas had risen to about 40 per cent. The causes of this drift to the cities and towns were the increasing attractions of urban life and the steady decline in need for agricultural labor as a result of mechanized farming. The effects were a mixture of good and evil. Escape from the soil freed large numbers of men and women from the isolation of rural life, from the tyranny of the weather, from the idiocies of primitive folkways, and from a humdrum existence of lonely toil on stubborn acres. But at the same time it transformed many of them into pawns or tools of their employers. It made some of them robots, who performed their tasks automatically with little sense of responsibility or comprehension of their place in the economic scheme, and with nothing to inspire their efforts but the hope of a living wage. If it rescued them from the hazards of blight and drought, it plunged them into new dangers of loss of employment from overproduction and forced them to live pell-mell like rats in wretched slums.

416   A third great result of the industrial revolutions was the creation of two new classes: an industrial bourgeoisie and a proletariat. The industrial bourgeoisie, composed of the owners of factories, mines, and railroads, cast in its lot with the old middle class of merchants, bankers, and lawyers. Thus strengthened in numbers and in influence, the combined bourgeoisie soon ceased to be merely a middle class and became for all practical purposes the ruling element in society. In some cases this rise to power was accomplished by pushing the old landed aristocracy into the background; in others, by joining with it. But no sooner had the capitalists and entrepreneurs gained the ascendancy than they began to divide among themselves. The great bankers and magnates of industry and commerce came to constitute an upper bourgeoisie with ambitions somewhat distinct from those of the lower bourgeoisie, made up of small merchants, small industrialists, and professional men. The tendency was for the upper bourgeoisie to become more and more deeply absorbed in finance capitalism. Its members were interested in stock-jobbing operations, in launching new ventures for an immediate profit, and in reorganizing businesses already in existence for purposes of monopolistic or speculative control. To the leaders of this class most forms of government intervention, except protective tariffs, were anathema; they insisted that free enterprise was absolutely essential to vigorous economic growth. On the other hand, the lower bourgeoisie began to show signs of a vital concern with stability and security. In many countries the members of this class were to be found advocating measures to curb speculation, to ensure the stability of prices, to eliminate chain stores and monopolies, and even to provide for state ownership of public utilities. It was this group which furnished some of the strongest support for Mussolini and Hitler in the early stages of their rise to power.

The emergence of the industrial bourgeoisie

The industrial revolutions also brought into existence a proletariat, which ultimately attained sufficient strength to challenge the supremacy of the bourgeoisie. In a sense the proletariat has existed since the dawn of civilization, for the term includes all persons who are dependent for their living upon a wage. The free workers in ancient Greece and Rome were proletarians, and so were the journeymen and the crofters and cotters in the Middle Ages. But prior to the First Industrial Revolution the wage earners were a small proportion of the working class, since the majority of those who toiled for a living were engaged in agriculture, originally as serfs and later as tenant farmers and sharecroppers. Furthermore, the few proletarians who did exist were scarcely conscious of their identity as a class. The industrial revolutions, by concentrating large numbers of workers in the cities and by subjecting them to common abuses, infused into wage earners a degree of solidarity and imbued them with common aspirations. Nevertheless, their power as an economic class was limited for many years by stringent legislation. The right to strike, for instance, was not granted by any Western nation until

The rise of the proletariat

after 1850. And not until late in the nineteenth century were the organized workers able to exert much influence upon the policies of governments.

That the industrial revolutions bestowed great material benefits upon the inhabitants of Western nations is a conclusion which even the most bilious of critics would hardly deny. Without question they supplied modern man with tremendous quantities of goods and with an astounding number of appliances to minister to his comfort and convenience. But whether the various classes participated in these benefits in anything like an equitable ratio is a different question. There seems little doubt that real wages, or wages in terms of purchasing power, rose quite rapidly during the nineteenth century. A leading economist, Sir Josiah Stamp, estimated that the ordinary Englishman in 1913 was four times as well off, in relation to the amount his income would buy, as were his ancestors in 1801. Evidences of improvement in standards of living were indicated by substantial increases in the consumption of quality foods, notably meat and milk. The per capita consumption of meat in Germany, for example, advanced from 38 pounds in 1816 to 115 pounds in 1912.

On the other hand, it is at least open to doubt that the mechanization of industry contributed as much to the well-being of the laboring classes as is commonly supposed. During the First Revolution, at least, the introduction of machines often meant that able-bodied men were thrown out of employment by the cheap labor of women and children. Moreover, some of the factories, especially those devoted to making textiles, were viler than prisons. Windows were small and were generally kept closed to preserve the moisture desirable for cotton manufacture. In addition, the new industrial towns grew so rapidly and in such haphazard fashion that housing conditions for the poor remained abominable for some time. In Manchester as late as 1840 one-eighth of the working-class families lived in cellars. Others drifted into wretched tenements with as many as a dozen people to a room. Many British factory employees were scarcely any better off than the slaves on American plantations. But against these evils must be reckoned the fact that the industrial revolutions did facilitate the organization of workers, thus enabling them to use the power of collective action to improve their condition. Besides, the common people undoubtedly benefited from lower prices made possible by mass production.

SELECTED READINGS

THE SECOND INDUSTRIAL REVOLUTION

Items so designated are available in paperbound editions.

418   Barnes, H. E., *An Economic History of the Western World*, New York, 1937.

Bonbright, J.C., and Means, G.C., *The Holding Company, Its Public Significance and Its Regulation*, New York, 1932.
· Briggs, A., *The Age of Improvement*, London, 1960 (Torchbook).
Carr-Saunders, A.M., *World Population*, New York, 1936.
Edwards, G.W., *The Evolution of Finance Capitalism*, New York, 1938.
· Feis, Herbert, *Europe, the World's Banker, 1870–1914*, New Haven, 1930 (Norton Library).
Giedion, S., *Mechanization Takes Command*, New York, 1948.
Hobson, J.A., *The Evolution of Modern Capitalism*, New York, 1926.
Levy, H., *The New Industrial System*, London, 1936.
Polakov, W.N., *The Power Age*, New York, 1930.
· Rostow, W.W., *The Stages of Economic Growth*, New York, 1960 (Cambridge University Press).
Sombart, Werner, *The Quintessence of Capitalism*, New York, 1915.
Tarbell, I.M., *The Nationalizing of Business, 1878–1898*, New York, 1936.
Thompson, W.S., *Population Problems*, New York, 1930.

PART THREE

The Contemporary World, 1914-

From the beginning of the Renaissance to the outbreak of World War I in 1914, European culture and technology set the standards for the majority of nations in both East and West, except for the more isolated ones like China and Japan. Near the end of the nineteenth century a struggle ensued among Western European Powers for control of the outside world. But they did not have the field to themselves. They were soon confronted with formidable competition from the United States, Japan, and eventually Russia. Indeed, the history of the twentieth century thus far has been occupied largely by contentions for mastery over the hundreds of millions of people in Asia, Africa, and the islands of the Pacific. The great question has been, who shall rule the world? Before 1914 a varied collection of candidates vied for the honor—Britain, France, the Netherlands, Germany, Russia, Japan, and the United States. Between 1918 and 1933 the list was narrowed principally to Germany, Russia, the United States, and Japan. The defeat of 1945 eliminated, for the time being at least, Germany and Japan, leaving the world a bipolar structure with the Soviet Union and the United States competing for the right to rule it. After 1949 the collision course followed by these two giants was modified by the emergence of a new colossus, Communist China, with claims to inherit the remains of European empires.

A Chronological Table

	INTERNATIONAL	THE AMERICAS

Triple Alliance, 1882–1914
Diplomatic Revolution, 1890–1907
Berlin-to-Baghdad Railway, 1890–1914

1900

Entente Cordiale, 1904–1923
Triple Entente, 1907–1917
Bosnian Crisis, 1908
Balkan Wars, 1912–1913
Assassination of Archduke Francis Ferdinand, 1914
World War I, 1914–1918
U.S. enters World War I, 1917

New constitution in Mexico, 1917

1919

Treaty of Versailles, 1919

League of Nations, 1920–1946

John Dewey, *Reconstruction in Philosophy*, 1920
Eugene O'Neill, *Strange Interlude*, 1920
Renaissance of painting in Mexico, *ca.* 1921
Discovery of insulin, 1922

French invasion of Ruhr Valley, 1923

Locarno Agreements, 1925

Pact of Paris, 1928

1929

Great Depression 1929–1934

Regionalism in art, U.S., ca. 1930

Japan invades Manchuria, 1931

Cancellation of German reparations, 1932

World Economic Conference, 1933

Anglo-German naval pact, 1935
Franco-Soviet alliance, 1935
Italy conquers Ethiopia, 1935–1936
Hitler remilitarizes Rhineland, 1936
Rome-Berlin Axis, 1936
Germany absorbs Austria (*Anschluss*), 1938
Appeasement at Munich, 1938

U.S. abandons gold standard, 1933
Good Neighbor policy, 1933
NRA, 1933–1935
New Deal 1933–1939

INDIA, AFRICA, THE MIDDLE AND FAR EAST	BRITAIN AND WESTERN EUROPE	CENTRAL AND EASTERN EUROPE	
		Pan-Slavism, 1890–1914 Expressionism in art, 1893 Pan-Germanism, 1895–1914 Greater Serbia movement, 1900–1914 Industrial supremacy of Germany, 1900–1914	1900
Dictatorship of Yüan Shih-k'ai, 1914–1916 Era of war lords in China, 1916–1928	A. N. Whitehead, *The Organization of Thought*, 1916		
	Impressionism in music, 1918 Surrealism, 1918	Overthrow of Tsar, 1917 Bolshevik Revolution, 1917 Expressionism in music, 1918 Revolution in Germany, 1918 O. Spengler, *Decline of the West*, 1918	
Amritsar Massacre (India), 1919 Intensification of Indian nationalism, 1919–1947		First Communist regime in Hungary, 1919 Weimar Republic, 1919–1933	1919
		NEP in Russia 1921–1929	
		Fascist Revolution in Italy, 1922 Runaway inflation in Germany, 1923	
	First Labour Government, 1924	Death of Lenin, 1924 Thomas Mann, *The Magic Mountain*, 1924 Dictatorship of Stalin, 1924–1953	
Nationalist regime in China (Chiang Kai-shek), 1928–1949	General strike, 1926		
	Second Labour Government, 1929–1931 Discovery of penicillin, 1930	First Five-year Plan in Russia, 1929–1933	1929
Japanese invasion of Manchuria, 1931	Overthrow of monarchy in Spain, 1931		
	Abandonment of gold standard, 1931 Discovery of neutrons, 1932 Abandonment of free trade, 1932	Nazi Revolution in Germany, 1933	
	Development of sulfa drugs, 1935		
Triumph of militarists in Japan, 1936 Japan invades China, 1937	Popular Front in France, 1936–1938 Civil War in Spain, 1936–1939 Existentialism, *ca.* 1938		

	INTERNATIONAL	THE AMERICAS

1939

INTERNATIONAL	THE AMERICAS
Nazi-Soviet Pact, 1939	Discovery of streptomycin, *ca.* 1940
World War II, 1939–1945	
Atlantic Charter, 1941	
Attack on Pearl Harbor, 1941	
Cairo Conference, 1943	
Teheran Conference, 1943	
Establishment of United Nations, 1945	Fair Deal in the U.S., 1945–1953
Atomic bombs dropped on Japan, 1945	
Yalta Conference, 1945	
Potsdam Conference, 1945	
Cold War of East and West, 1946–	Perón regime in Argentina, 1946–1955
Truman Doctrine, 1947	
European Recovery Program (Marshall Plan), 1948	Discovery of cortisone, 1948

1949

INTERNATIONAL	THE AMERICAS
NATO, 1949	
Korean War, 1950–1953	
Schuman Plan, 1952	Hydrogen bomb, 1952
	Return of Republicans to power in U.S., 1953–1961
Summit Conference, Geneva, 1955	Overthrow of Perón regime in Argentina, 1955
	Establishment of Castro regime in Cuba, 1959
	Election of John F. Kennedy, Democrat, as President of U.S., 1960
	The New Frontier, 1961–1963
	Cuban missile crisis, 1962
	Assasination of President Kennedy and the beginning of the presidency of Lyndon B. Johnson, 1963
Vietnamese War, 1964–	The Great Society, 1963–
	U. S. escalates Vietnam War, 1964
	Leftist regime of Eduardo Frei in Chile, 1964
	Revolt of youth, 1964–
	Black revolt in U. S., 1965–
	First walk in space, 1966
	Assassination of M. L. King, black nonviolent leader, 1968

INDIA, AFRICA, THE MIDDLE AND FAR EAST	BRITAIN AND WESTERN EUROPE	CENTRAL AND EASTERN EUROPE	
	Franco regime in Spain, 1939–	Atomic fission, 1939 Neo-Orthodoxy, *ca.* 1940	1939
Japanese conquest of Southeast Asia and South Pacific, 1941–1942			
	Third Labour Government, 1945–1950		
	Fourth Republic in France, 1946–1959		
Vietnam war: French phase, 1947–1954	Dissolution of Empire in India, 1947	Communist coup in Hungary, 1947	
Dead Sea Scrolls found, 1947		Communist coup in Czechoslovakia, 1948	
India and Pakistan achieve independence, 1947		Division of Germany into East and West zones, 1948	
State of Israel proclaimed, 1948		Establishment of German Federal Republic and German Democratic Republic, 1949	1949
Establishment of Communist regime in China, 1949	Return of Conservatives to power, 1950		
Japan peace treaty, 1952			
Egypt becomes republic, 1952–1953		Death of Stalin, 1953	
SEATO, 1954		Russia develops hydrogen bomb, 1953	
Suez crisis, 1956			
War in Middle East, 1956			
U. N. Emergency Force in Middle East, 1956		Dictatorship of Khrushchev, 1958–1964	
Military coup under General Ayub Khan in Pakistan, 1958	Fifth Republic in France, 1959–		
Sino-Soviet rift, 1960–			
Revolt in The Congo, 1960–1965			
	Fourth Labour Government, 1963–		
		Breszhnev-Kosygin regime, 1964–	
Military junta seizes power in Indonesia, 1965			
Great Proletarian Cultural Revolution in China, 1966–	Revolt of youth, 1966–		
Arab-Israeli conflict, 1967–1968			
Communist China explodes a hydrogen bomb, 1967			
First successful heart transplant, South Africa, 1967			
Civil War in Nigeria, 1967–		Communist Occupation of Czechoslovakia, 1968	

CHAPTER 14

World War I

After the attempts to come to an understanding with the Entente powers have been answered by the latter with the announcement of an intensified continuation of the war, the Imperial Government—in order to serve the welfare of mankind in a higher sense and not to wrong its own people—is now compelled to continue the fight for existence, again forced upon it, with the full employment of all the weapons which are at its disposal.
—Count Johann von Bernstorff, German Ambassador to U.S., Message to U.S. Sec. of State, Jan. 31, 1917

The war that broke out in 1914 was one of the most extraordinary in history. Though it was not really the "first world war," since such conflicts as the Seven Years' War and the Napoleonic Wars had also been global in extent, it had an impact far exceeding either of these. It quickly became a "people's war" in which civilians as well as soldiers in the trenches participated in violent demands for extermination of the enemy. It bore fruit in an epidemic of revolutions and sowed the dragon's teeth of new and even more venomous conflicts in the future. In such ways it set the pattern for an age of violence that continued through the greater part of the twentieth century. Even more extraordinary was the fact that World War I marked the close of a long era of peace. For almost a century after the end of the Napoleonic Wars in 1815, Europe experienced no major conflicts. True, there were the Crimean War in 1854–1856, the Franco-Prussian War in 1870–1871, and the Russo-Turkish War in 1877–1878, but these were minor affrays compared with those that were to follow. That no more serious conflicts occurred until 1914 must be attributed chiefly to the celebrated balance of power, established by Great Britain about 1818 with the cooperation of Austria, Prussia, and France. Essentially it was a *Pax Britannica*, since it rested upon British economic supremacy and the power of the British navy. When war threatened or broke out in Europe, Britain

End of the Hundred Years' Peace

427

generally threw her weight into the scales on the side of the weaker country, thereby restoring or redressing the balance.

I. UNDERLYING CAUSES OF THE WAR

The European Balance of Power

But the balance of power was never in perfect adjustment. It was threatened by Napoleon III in mid-century, by Bismarck in 1870, and by Russia in 1878. Much more serious threats came after 1900. By that date Germany had emerged as the most powerful state on the European Continent. France was no longer a match for her, and even Russia could not hold a candle to her in military might and efficiency. The Germans cultivated grandiose schemes for enlarging their power in world affairs. Under Kaiser William II, who came to the throne in 1888, they developed ambitions for control of North Africa, for economic imperialism in Turkey, and for the building of a navy able to throw down a challenge to that of Great Britain. That they might speedily attain these goals was evidenced by their phenomenal economic growth after 1871. By 1914 Germany was producing more iron and steel than Britain and France combined. In chemicals, in aniline dyes, and in the manufacture of scientific equipment she led the world. Even in the production of articles, such as cutlery, for which other nations had been famous for centuries, she managed to achieve a leading position. She threw down a challenge to the supremacy of Britain in the carrying trade and produced some of the largest and fastest ships on the Seven Seas. Bursting with pride in these accomplishments, she was impatient with the refusal of other nations to accord her a dominant position on the European Continent. Indeed, many historians have drawn the conclusion that it was Germany's threat to the European balance of power that constituted the real and primary cause of the two world wars of the twentieth century.

The qualities of power politics

The balance of power was not an ideal of philosophers or political dreamers. Instead, it was an appurtenance of the system of power politics that dates back to the very beginnings of the modern state system. Power politics refers to the pursuit of power by sovereign states as an end in itself or a means to the attainment of other ends. Each state is assumed to be a law unto itself with complete freedom to follow its own devices in enlarging and maintaining its power. The methods employed have traditionally included nearly every form of deceit, trickery, and barbarity invented by the wit of man. Nations in a formal relationship of peace spy upon each other, issue threats and counterthreats, form alliances and counteralliances, and attempt to bluff and hornswoggle each other. Finally, when fear and greed gain the upper hand, they resort to war. Though the crudities are frequently glossed over by embassy teas and striped-pants diplomacy, the fundamental rule of power politics is the law of the jungle. Had the balance of power operated successfully, it might well have superseded the law of the jungle; but it was so obviously linked with the aims of power politics that it was bound to be challenged by some powerful and ambitious nations.

Threats to the balance of power were implicit in the aims of a number of principal states. By 1900 six great powers in Europe—Germany, France, Russia, Italy, Austria-Hungary and Great Britain—were competing for power, security, and economic advantage. Each had specific objectives, the fulfillment of which it regarded as essential to its national interest. Germany built her ambitions around eastward expansion. After 1890 German capitalists and imperialists dreamed of a *Drang nach Osten* (Drive to the East) and planned the construction of a railway from Berlin to Baghdad to facilitate economic control of the Ottoman Empire. Austria also looked to the east, but to the Balkans rather than to any part of western Asia. Her hold on Trieste and other portions of the Adriatic coast was precarious, since much of this territory was inhabited by Italians. If she could carve a highroad through the Balkans to the Aegean, her access to the sea would be more secure. As time passed, Austria and Germany became more dependent upon each other, the former because of trouble with the Slavs both inside and outside her borders, and the latter because of a growing fear of encirclement. In 1879 Bismarck entered into an alliance with Austria, which was renewed and strengthened in subsequent years. It was an alliance with a corpse, but the Germans clung to it more and more desperately as international tensions deepened.

Aims of the great powers: Germany and Austria-Hungary

To a large degree the objectives of France were dictated by a desire to curb or counterbalance the growing might of Germany. France hoped to recover Alsace and Lorraine, which had suddenly become very valuable as the result of a discovery by Sidney Thomas and P. C. Gilchrist in 1878 of a method of converting low-grade iron ore into steel. But recovery of the lost provinces was not the only French objective. The French were determined to add Morocco to their African empire regardless of the interests of other powers in that sadly misgoverned country. The motives of the Paris statesmen were both economic and political. Morocco contained rich mineral deposits, but it would be valuable also for strategic reasons and as a reservoir from which troops might be drawn to offset the manpower shortage at home.

Ambitions of France

A paramount ambition of Russia was to gain control of the Bosporus and the Dardanelles. She had regarded this as her "historic mission" since early in the nineteenth century. Achievement of this mission would prevent her fleet from being bottled up in the Black Sea in the event of war with some naval power or powers. Besides, it would give her unquestioned access to the Mediterranean and probably possession of Constantinople. Turkey would be eliminated from Europe, and Russia would fall heir to the Balkans. In addition, if the Tsar's agents could get to Constantinople before the Germans,

Ambitions of Russia

they could turn the Berlin-to-Baghdad railway into an empty dream. But Imperial Russia had other ambitions. She coveted access to the Persian Gulf and Indian Ocean and tried for years to make Persia a Russian protectorate. She strove also for better outlets to the Pacific and attempted to extend her control over Manchuria. Finally, through Pan-Slavism she aspired to play the role of guide and protector of all the Slavic peoples of eastern Europe, including those who were under the rule of Austria-Hungary. That each of these ambitions constituted a threat to the status quo scarcely needs emphasis.

The power policies of Great Britain and Italy were somewhat less closely related to the specific actions of other countries. The policy of Britain, in fact, was directed against almost everyone. She was no less suspicious of the Russian ambitions at Constantinople than she was of the German. Until after the beginning of the twentieth century she distrusted France. Her cardinal aims were (1) to maintain the life lines of her empire, (2) to keep open the sea lanes to her sources of imports and her foreign markets, and (3) to preserve a balance among the nations on the European Continent so that no one of them would ever become strong enough to attack her. If the actions of any other country threatened to interfere with these cardinal aims (as they often did), the hostility of Britain would instantly be aroused. She would seek to put the offending nation in its place by diplomatic pressure, forming an alliance against it, or by going to war, as she finally did against Germany in 1914. The ambitions of Italy before 1914 were almost entirely territorial. She had no great empire to defend, nor was her security threatened from any external source. But she did covet Tripoli in northern Africa, which she expected to take from Turkey, and *Italia irredenta*, the "unredeemed Italy," including Trieste and the South Tyrol, which was still in the possession of Austria.

Shortly before 1900 the empire of Japan began to participate actively in power politics. During the second half of the nineteenth century the island kingdom emerged from its Oriental seclusion and went through a transformation that astonished the world. Feudalism was abolished, and a highly centralized state with a constitution modeled after that of Imperial Germany was established. Science, industrialism, universal education, and conscription were imported from the West. Every large city had its streetcars, skyscrapers, and electric lights, although, in the opinion of many authorities, these were nothing but Western trappings on the surface of a culture still fundamentally Oriental. In 1895, as has been mentioned, Japan inflicted a decisive defeat upon China, taking from her the island of Formosa and acquiring a free hand in Korea. In 1904–1905 the Mikado's generals and admirals surprised the world even more by defeating Russia. These victories gave Japan a virtually unquestioned place among the Great Powers. Western diplomats courted

Great Britain and Italy

Japan becomes a great power

her favor and bowed and scraped in the presence of her rulers.

One of the clearest expressions of the realities of power politics before 1914 was the growth of militarism. Since the nations of the world were living in a condition of international anarchy, it was almost inevitable that their fears and suspicions should lead to competition in armaments. Europe in particular became an armed camp. After 1870 every one of its chief powers, with the exception of Great Britain, adopted conscription and universal military training. Not only that, but they adopted the belief that national security depended almost entirely upon the extent of military and naval preparedness. After every war scare the size of armies and navies increased until, by 1914, all of the important countries, and many of the smaller ones also, were staggering under a burden which, in a saner world, would have been regarded as intolerable. There were, of course, men of humanity and wisdom who recognized the danger and did all in their power to ward it off. But there were far too many others who not only denied that any danger existed but stoutly maintained that militarism was a positive benefit. Theodore Roosevelt argued that training for war was necessary to preserve the "manly and adventurous qualities" in a nation. Field Marshal von Moltke and Heinrich von Treitschke saw in military conflict one of the divine elements of the universe and a "terrible medicine" for the human race. The French philosopher, Ernest Renan, justified war as a condition of progress, "the sting which prevents a country from going to sleep." Although the propagation of such doctrines was not the chief cause of militarism, it undoubtedly strengthened the position of those who believed in armaments and war as the best methods of solving a nation's problems.

Power politics and the failure of the balance of power may be regarded as perhaps the paramount underlying causes of World War I. Prominent also among these causes was nationalism. This factor, as previously explained, had roots extending at least as far back as the French Revolution. By the early twentieth century, however, nationalism had come to assume a variety of particularly dangerous forms. Foremost among them were the Greater Serbia scheme, the Pan-Slav movement in Russia, the revenge movement in France, and the Pan-German movement. The first two were closely related. Since the beginning of the twentieth century at least, little Serbia had dreamed of extending her jurisdiction over all the peoples alleged to be similar to her own citizens in race and in culture. Some of these peoples inhabited what were then the two Turkish provinces of Bosnia and Herzegovina. Others included Croatians and Slovenes in the southern provinces of Austria-Hungary. After 1908 when Austria suddenly annexed Bosnia and Herzegovina, the Greater Serbia scheme was directed exclusively against the Hapsburg Empire. It took the form of agitation to provoke discontent among the Slav subjects of Austria, in the hope of drawing them away and uniting the territories they inhabited with Serbia. It resulted in a series of dangerous plots against the peace and integrity of the Dual Monarchy. And the fateful climax of these plots was the murder of the heir to the Austrian throne on June 28, 1914.

In many of their activities the Serbian nationalists were aided and abetted by the Pan-Slavists in Russia. The Pan-Slav movement was founded upon the theory that all of the Slavs of eastern Europe constituted one great family. Therefore, it was argued that Russia as the most powerful Slavic state should act as the guide and protector of her little brother nations of the Balkans. The latter were to be encouraged to look to Russia whenever their interests were endangered. Serbs, Bulgarians, and Montenegrins, in their struggles with Austria or with Turkey, were to be made to understand that they always had a powerful and sympathetic friend on the other side of the Carpathians. Pan-Slavism was not merely the wishful sentiment of a few ardent nationalists, but was really a part of the official policy of the Russian government. It goes far toward explaining Russia's aggressive stand in every quarrel that arose between Serbia and Austria.

Another of the malignant forms of nationalism contributing to the war of 1914 was the *revanche* (revenge) movement in France. Ever since 1870 fire-eating patriots in France had looked forward to the time when the defeat in the Franco-Prussian War might be avenged. It is almost impossible for non-Europeans to form any adequate notion of the hold which this idea had taken upon the minds of millions of Frenchmen. It was carefully cultivated by sensation-mongering newspapers, and it was fed to the children in the schools as a regular part of their intellectual fare. The noted politician, Raymond Poincaré, declared that he could see no reason for his generation to go on living except to recover the two lost provinces of Alsace and Lorraine. It must be understood, however, that the idea was probably never the opinion of more than a minority of the French people. By 1914 it was strongly opposed by socialists and by many liberal leaders.

The influence of Pan-Germanism as a species of nationalism before 1914 is difficult to assess. The name of the movement is generally taken to refer to the ideas of the Pan-German League, founded about 1895. Specifically, the League advocated the expansion of Germany to incorporate all of the Teutonic peoples of central Europe. The boundaries of the Empire should be extended to take in Denmark, the Netherlands, Luxemburg, Switzerland, Austria, and Poland as far east as Warsaw. A few of the leaders were not even satisfied with this but demanded a large colonial empire and a vast expansion into the Balkans and western Asia. They insisted that such peoples as the Bulgars and the Turks should at least become satellites of the German Reich. Although the Pan-German League made a great deal of noise, it could scarcely claim to represent the entire

Pan-Slavism

The *revanche* movement in France

The Pan-German movement

German nation. As late as 1912 it had a membership of only 17,000, and its violent criticism of the government was widely resented. Nevertheless, a large number of its doctrines had been latent in German thinking for upwards of a century. The philosopher Fichte had taught that the Germans, because of their spiritual superiority, had a mission to impose peace upon the rest of Europe. Ideas of Aryanism and of Nordic supremacy also contributed to the notion that the Germans had a divine destiny to persuade or compel "inferior races" to accept their culture. Finally, the efforts of philosophers like Heinrich von Treitschke to deify the great state and to glorify power as the instrument of national policy helped to impregnate the minds of many Germans of the middle and upper classes with an intolerance of other nations and a belief in the right of Germany to dominate her weaker neighbors.

Nationalism of the types described would have been almost sufficient in itself to have plunged a considerable number of European nations into the maelstrom of war. But the conflict might well have remained limited in character had it not been for the system of entangling alliances. It was this system which transformed a local squabble between Austria and Serbia into a general war. When Russia intervened on behalf of Serbia, Germany felt obliged to come to the defense of Austria. France had close ties to Russia, and Great Britain was drawn in at least partly on account of her commitments to France. Moreover, the system of alliances was a source of suspicion and fear. It was impossible to expect that Europe would continue indefinitely to be divided into opposing camps of substantially equal strength. Conditions were bound to change with the passage of time. Motives which had originally impelled certain nations to enter into partnership with others lost their importance, and the basis for the alliance disappeared. Thus we shall see that Italy practically abandoned her alliance with Germany and Austria, which at first she had been so eager to join. The result was to bind her former partners more closely together and to magnify their obsession of encirclement by a ring of hostile powers.

The effects of the system of entangling alliances

The evolution of the system of entangling alliances goes back to the 1870's, and its original architect was Bismarck. In the main his purposes were peaceful. Prussia and her German allies had emerged victorious in their war with France, and the newly created German empire was the most powerful state on the Continent. Bismarck was anxious, above all, to preserve the fruits of this victory; there is nothing to indicate that he planned any further conquests. However, he was disturbed by fears that the French might start a war of revenge. There was little prospect that they would attempt such a thing singlehanded, but they might with the help of some other power. Therefore Bismarck determined to isolate France by attaching all of her potential friends to Germany. In 1873 he managed to form an alliance with both Austria and Russia, the so-called League of the

The evolution of the system of alliances

433

Three Emperors. But this combination was of a precarious nature and soon went on the rocks. With the League of the Three Emperors defunct, Bismarck cemented a new and much stronger alliance with Austria. In 1882 this partnership was expanded into the celebrated Triple Alliance when Italy was added as a member. The Italians did not join out of love for either Germany or Austria but from motives of anger and fear. They resented the French occupation of Tunisia (1881), a territory which they regarded as properly theirs. Moreover, the Italian politicians were still at odds with the Church, and they feared that the clericals in France might gain the upper hand and send a French army to defend the Pope. In the meantime, the Three Emperors' League had been revived. Though it lasted for only six years (1881–1887), Germany managed to hold the friendship of Russia until 1890.

The diplomatic revolution of 1890–1907

Thus after little more than a decade of diplomatic maneuvering, the Iron Chancellor had achieved his ambition. By 1882 France was cut off from nearly every possibility of obtaining aid from powerful friends. Austria and Italy were united with Germany in the Triple Alliance, and Russia after a three-year lapse was back once more in the Bismarckian camp. The only conceivable quarter from which help might come was Great Britain; but, with respect to Continental affairs, the British had returned to their traditional policy of "splendid isolation." Therefore, so far as the danger of a war of revenge was concerned, Germany had little to fear. But if either Bismarck or anyone else imagined that this security would be permanent, he was headed for disillusionment. Between 1890 and 1907, Europe went through a diplomatic revolution which practically annihilated Bismarck's work. To be sure, the Germans had Austria still on their side; but they had lost the friendship of both Russia and Italy, and Britain had abandoned her isolation to enter into agreements with Russia and France. This shift in the balance of power had fateful results. It convinced the Germans that they were surrounded by a ring of enemies, and that consequently they must do everything in their power to retain the loyalty of Austria—even to the extent of supporting her reckless foreign adventures.

Causes of the diplomatic revolution

The causes of this diplomatic revolution are not hard to discover. First, disagreements between Bismarck and the new Kaiser, William II, led to the great Chancellor's retirement in 1890. Second, the growth of Pan-Slavism in Russia brought the empire of the Tsars into conflict with Austria. Germany, faced with a choice between Russia and Austria, quite naturally chose the latter. Third, the establishment of financial ties between Russia and France inevitably paved the way for a political alliance. In 1888–1889 arrangements had been made for floating Russian loans to the amount of nearly $500,000,000 on the Paris Bourse. Offered at an attractive price, the bonds were eagerly bought by French investors. From then on large

434 numbers of influential citizens of France had a direct interest in the political fortunes of Russia. A fourth cause was the abandonment of UNDERLYING CAUSES isolation by Great Britain. The reasons for this change were several. One was apprehension over the growing economic power of Germany. Another was the discovery by the British and the French about 1900 of a basis for cooperation in the partitioning of northern Africa. A final cause of the diplomatic revolution was the shift in Italy's attitude toward the Triple Alliance. By 1900 the republicans were firmly in the saddle in France, with the result that Italy no longer had anything to fear from monarchist-clerical intervention on behalf of the Pope. Besides, the Italians had largely resigned themselves to the loss of Tunisia and were turning their attention to the recovery of territories from Austria and to winning the support of France for the conquest of Tripoli. For these reasons Italy lost interest in preserving her loyalty to the Triple Alliance.

The first of the major results of the diplomatic revolution was the formation of the Triple Entente. This came about through a series of stages. In 1890 Russia and France began a political flirtation which gradually ripened into a binding alliance. The secret military convention signed by the two countries in 1894 provided that each should come to the aid of the other in case of an attack by Germany, or by Austria or Italy supported by Germany. This Dual Alliance of Russia and France was followed by the *Entente Cordiale* between France and Great Britain. During the last two decades of the nineteenth century the British and the French had frequently been involved in sharp altercations over colonies and trade. The two nations almost came to blows in 1898 at Fashoda in the Egyptian Sudan. But suddenly the French withdrew all of their claims to that portion of Africa and opened negotiations for a broad compromise of other disputes. The result was the conclusion in 1904 of the *Entente Cordiale*. It was not a formal alliance but a friendly agreement, covering a variety of subjects. The final step in the formation of the Triple Entente was the conclusion of a mutual understanding between Great Britain and Russia. Again there was no formal alliance. The two powers simply came to an agreement in 1907 concerning their ambitions in Asia. The core of it provided for the division of Persia into spheres of influence. To Russia was assigned the northern portion and to Great Britain the southern. A middle section was to be preserved, temporarily at least, as a neutral area under its legitimate ruler, the Shah.

Results of the diplomatic revolution; formation of the Triple Entente

Thus by 1907 the great powers of Europe had come to be arrayed in two opposing combinations, the Triple Alliance and the Triple Entente. Had these combinations remained stable and more or less evenly matched, they might well have promoted the cause of peace. But no such condition prevailed. Each grew weaker and less stable with the passage of time. The Triple Alliance declined in strength because of a growing coolness between Italy and Austria. Moreover, Italian nationalists coveted territory in North Africa, notably Trip-

Instability of the two alliances

oli, which they believed they could obtain only by supporting French ambitions in Morocco. Meanwhile, the Triple Entente was threatened by discord between Britain and Russia. Because their life-line to the East might be imperiled, the British could not view with equanimity the cardinal aim of Russia to "open the Straits" and gain control of Constantinople. Disharmony in the Triple Entente also increased when Britain and France refused to support Russia in her dispute with Austria over the latter's annexation of Bosnia and Her-zegovina. In short, conflicts were so numerous that the members of neither alliance could be quite sure where their opposite numbers might stand in case of a real threat of a European war.

Between 1905 and 1913 five serious international crises endan-gered the peace of Europe. In a sense they were not so much causes as they were symptoms of international animosity. Yet each of them left a heritage of suspicion and bitterness that made war all the more probable. In some cases hostilities were averted only because one of the parties was too weak at the time to offer resistance. The result was a sense of humiliation, a smoldering resentment that was almost bound to burst into flame in the future. Three of the crises were generated by disputes over Morocco. Both Germany and France yearned for control of that unhappy country, mainly because of the mineral wealth and trading opportunities it was supposed to contain. In 1905, 1908, and 1911 the two powers stood on the brink of war. Each time the dispute was smoothed over but not without the usual legacy of suspicion and resentment.

In addition to the clash over Morocco, two crises occurred in the Near East. The first was the Bosnian crisis of 1908. At the Congress of Berlin in 1878 the two Turkish provinces of Bosnia and Herzego-vina had been placed under the administrative control of Austria, though actual possession was still to be vested in the Ottoman Em-pire. Serbia also coveted the territories, since they would double her kingdom and place her within striking distance of the Adriatic. Sud-denly, in October, 1908, Austria annexed the two provinces, in flat violation of the Treaty of Berlin. The Serbs were furious and ap-pealed to Russia. The Tsar's government threatened war, until Ger-many addressed a sharp note to St. Petersburg announcing her firm intention to back Austria. Since Russia had not yet fully recovered from her war with Japan and was plagued by internal troubles, she finally informed the Serbs that they would have to wait until a more favorable time.

Still more bad blood between the nations of Eastern Europe was created by the Balkan Wars. In 1912 Serbia, Bulgaria, Montenegro, and Greece, with encouragement from Russia, joined in a Balkan al-liance for the conquest of the Turkish province of Macedonia. The war was started in October, 1912, and in less than two months the resistance of the Turks was shattered. Then came the problem of dividing the spoils. In secret treaties negotiated before hostilities be-

The series of international crises: the clash over Morocco

The Near Eastern Crises: 1) the annexa-tion of Bosnia and Herze-govina

2) the Balkan Wars

gan, Serbia had been promised Albania, in addition to a generous slice of Macedonia. But now Austria, fearful as always of any increase in Serbian power, intervened at the peace conference and obtained the establishment of Albania as an independent state. For the Serbs this was the last straw. It seemed that at every turn their path to western expansion was certain to be blocked by the Hapsburg government. From this time on, anti-Austrian agitation in Serbia and in the neighboring province of Bosnia became ever more venomous.

2. THE ROAD TO ARMAGEDDON

It is generally held that the immediate cause of World War I was the assassination of Archduke Francis Ferdinand on June 28, 1914. This was the match thrown into the powder-keg of accumulated suspicion and hate. Nevertheless, it was not quite so trivial an event as many people think. Francis Ferdinand was not simply a useless member of the Austrian nobility; he was soon to become Emperor. The reigning monarch, Francis Joseph, had reached his eighty-fourth year, and his death was expected momentarily. The murder of the heir to the throne was therefore considered as in a very real sense an attack upon the state.

The assassination of Francis Ferdinand

The actual murderer of Francis Ferdinand was a Bosnian student by the name of Princip. But this does not tell half of the story. Princip was merely the tool of Serbian nationalists. The murder, though committed in Sarajevo, the capital of Bosnia, was the result of a plot hatched in Belgrade. The conspirators were members of a secret society officially known as Union or Death but commonly called the Black Hand. What were the motives of the conspirators? If there is any one answer, it would seem to lie in the plan which Francis Ferdinand was known to be developing for the reorganization of the Hapsburg Empire. This plan, designated as *trialism*, involved a proposal for changing the Dual Monarchy into a triple monarchy. In addition to German Austria and Magyar Hungary, already practically autonomous, there was to be a third semi-independent unit

Motives of the assassins

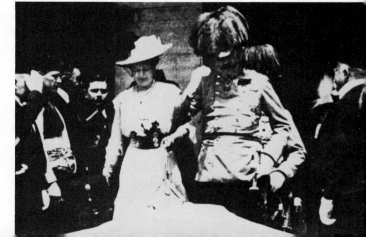

The Archduke Francis Ferdinand. He and his wife are leaving the Senate House in Sarajevo shortly before the assassination, June 28, 1914.

composed of the Slavs. This was exactly what the Serb nationalists did not want. They feared that if it were put into effect their Slovene and Croatian kinsmen would be content to remain under Hapsburg rule. Therefore they determined to get Francis Ferdinand out of the way before he could become Emperor of Austria-Hungary.

In the weeks immediately following the tragedy, Austrian officials conducted an investigation which confirmed their suspicions that the plot was of Serbian origin. Consequently, on July 23, they dispatched to the Serbian government a severe ultimatum consisting of eleven demands. Among other things Serbia was to suppress anti-Austrian newspapers, to crush the secret patriotic societies, to eliminate from the government and from the army all persons guilty of anti-Austrian propaganda, and to accept the collaboration of Austrian officials in stamping out the subversive movement against the Hapsburg Empire. On July 25, in accordance with the time limit of forty-eight hours, the Serbian government transmitted its reply. Of the total of eleven demands, only one was emphatically refused, and five were accepted without reservations. The German Chancellor regarded it as almost a complete capitulation, and the Kaiser declared that now all reason for war had fallen to the ground. The Austrians, however, pronounced it unsatisfactory, severed diplomatic relations, and mobilized part of their army. The Serbs themselves had been under no illusions about pleasing Austria, since, three hours before transmitting their reply, they had issued an order to mobilize the troops.

At this point the attitude of other nations becomes important. In fact for some time before this, several of the rulers of the great powers had assumed very positive attitudes. As early as July 18 Sazonov, the Russian Foreign Minister, warned Austria that Russia would not tolerate any effort to humiliate Serbia. On July 24 Sazonov exclaimed to the German ambassador: "I do not hate Austria; I despise her. Austria is seeking a pretext to gobble up Serbia; but in that case Russia will make war on Austria." [1] In the adoption of this belligerent attitude, Russia had the support of France. About the twentieth of July, Raymond Poincaré, who was now President of the French Republic, paid a visit to St. Petersburg. He kept urging Sazonov to "be firm" and to avoid any compromise which might result in a loss of prestige for the Triple Entente. He warned the Austrian ambassador that "Serbia has very warm friends in the Russian people. And Russia has an ally, France." [2]

The attitude of Germany in these critical days was ambiguous. Although the Kaiser was shocked and infuriated by the assassination, his government did not make any threats until after the actions of Russia gave cause for alarm. Unfortunately, both the Kaiser and the Chancellor, von Bethmann-Hollweg, adopted the premise that

The Austrian ultimatum to Serbia

Russia and France assume a belligerent attitude

The attitude of Germany

---

[1] S. B. Fay, *The Origins of the World War*, II, 300.
[2] *Ibid.*, II, 281.

stern punishment must be meted out to Serbia without delay. They hoped in this way to confront the other powers with an accomplished fact. The Kaiser declared on June 30: "Now or never! Matters must be cleared up with the Serbs, *and that soon.*" On July 6 Bethmann-Hollweg gave to the Austrian Foreign Minister, Count Berchtold, a commitment which was interpreted by the latter as a blank check. The Austrian government was informed that the Kaiser would "stand true by Austria's side in accordance with his treaty obligations and old friendship." In giving this pledge Bethmann and his imperial master were gambling on the hope that Russia would not intervene for the protection of Serbia, and that therefore the quarrel would remain a mere local squabble.

Austria declared war against Serbia on July 28, 1914. For a fleeting, anxious moment there was a possibility that the conflict might be localized. But it was quickly transformed into a war of larger scope by the action of Russia. On July 29 Sazonov and the military clique persuaded the Tsar to issue an order to mobilize all of the troops, not only against Austria but against Germany as well. Their argument was a logical one. Such a vast country as Russia would require considerable time to get her military machine into operation. But before the order could be put into effect, Nicholas changed his mind, having just received an urgent appeal from the Kaiser to help in preserving peace. On July 30 Sazonov and General Tatistchev, the Chief of Staff, went to work to induce the Tsar to change his mind again. For more than an hour they sought to convince the reluctant autocrat that the entire military system should be set in motion. Finally, General Tatistchev remarked: "Yes, it is hard to decide." Nicholas retorted with a show of irritation: "I will decide," and signed an order for immediate mobilization. Sazonov hurried to the telephone to communicate the news to the Chief of Staff. The next morning in a remote Siberian village an English traveler was awakened by a commotion outside his window, followed by the query of an excited peasant: "Have you heard the news? There is war." [3]

There was now no drawing back from the abyss. The Germans were alarmed over Russian preparations for war. The latest action of the Tsar's government made the situation far more critical, since in German military circles, and also in French and Russian, general mobilization meant war. Upon learning that the Tsar's decree had gone into effect, the Kaiser's government sent an ultimatum to St. Petersburg demanding that mobilization cease within twelve hours. On the afternoon of August 1 the German ambassador requested an interview with the Russian Foreign Minister. He appealed to Sazonov for a favorable answer to the German ultimatum. Sazonov replied that mobilization could not be halted, but that Russia was willing to continue negotiations. The ambassador repeated his question a second and a third time, emphasizing the terrible consequences of a

Russian mobilization

The German ultimatums to Russia and France

[3] *Ibid.*, II, 472–73.

August 1, 1914. A German officer reading the declaration of war in the streets of Berlin.

negative answer. Sazanov finally replied: "I have no other answer to give you." The ambassador then handed the Foreign Minister a declaration of war and, bursting into tears, left the room.[4] In the meantime, the Kaiser's ministers had also dispatched an ultimatum to France demanding that she make known her intentions. Premier Viviani replied on August 1 that France would act "in accordance with her interests," and immediately ordered a general mobilization of the army. On August 3 Germany declared war upon France.

The attitude of Britain

All eyes now turned in the direction of Britain. What would she do, now that the other two members of the Triple Entente had rushed headlong into war? For some time after the situation on the Continent had become critical, Britain vacillated. Both the cabinet and the nation were divided. Sir Edward Grey and Winston Churchill advocated a positive stand on the side of France and Russia with an appeal to arms if Britain's interests should be threatened. But some of their colleagues were much less enthusiastic about intervention in Continental quarrels. Throughout the country there was likewise considerable opposition to mixing in squabbles which were not believed to be of vital concern to England's welfare. Although Grey had on several occasions encouraged the Russians and the French to count upon British aid, it was not until after he received pledges of support from the leaders of the Conservative party that he made any formal commitments.

Britain enters the war

It is difficult to believe that Britain would have long remained out of the war, even if the neutrality of Belgium had never been violated. In fact, as early as July 29, Sir Edward Grey had given the German ambassador in London a "friendly and private" warning

[4] G. P. Gooch, *Before the War: Studies in Diplomacy,* II, 368.

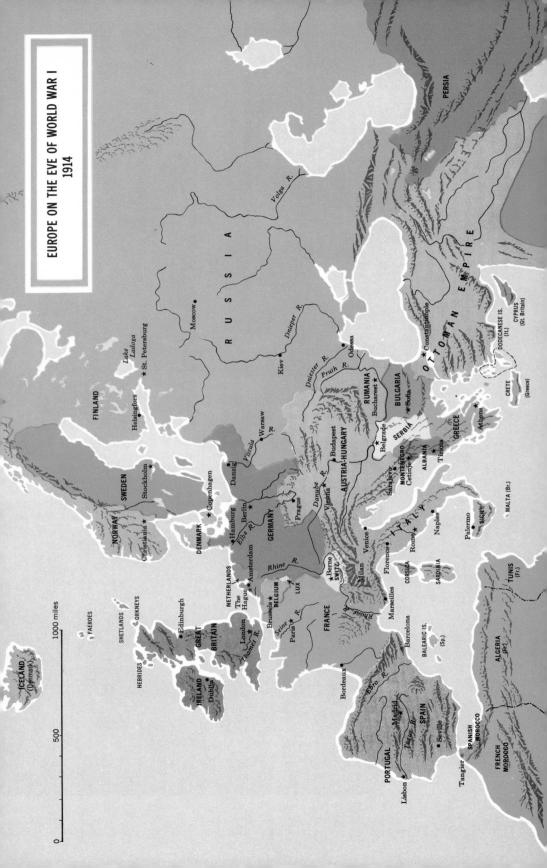

EUROPE ON THE EVE OF WORLD WAR I
1914

I and the Village, Marc Chagall (1889–   ). The subject refers to the artist's childhood and youth in Vitebsk, Russia. The profile on the right is probably that of the artist himself. (Mus. Mod. Art)

The Table, Georges Braque (1881–   An example of later cubism showing predominance of curvilinear form and l instead of geometric structure. (Mus. M Art)

Around the Fish, Paul Klee (1879–1940). Klee is recognized as the most su humorist of XX-cent. art. The central motif of a fish on a platter suggest banquet, but many of the surrounding objects appear to be products of fanta (Mus. Mod. Art)

that if France were drawn into the war, Great Britain would enter also.[5] Nevertheless, it was the invasion of Belgian territory which provided the immediate cause of Britain's unsheathing the sword. In 1839, along with the other great powers, she had signed a treaty guaranteeing the neutrality of Belgium. Moreover, it had been British policy for a century or more to try to prevent domination of the Low Countries, lying directly across the Channel, by any powerful Continental nation. But the famous Schlieffen Plan of the Germans provided for attacking France through Belgium. Accordingly, they demanded of the Belgian government permission to send troops across its territory, promising to respect the independence of the nation and to pay for any damage to property. When Belgium refused, the Kaiser's gray-coated legions began pouring across her frontier. The British Foreign Secretary immediately went before Parliament and presented the idea that his country should rally to the defense of international law and to the protection of small nations. He argued that peace under the circumstances would be a moral crime, and declared that if Britain should fail to uphold her obligations of honor in this matter she would forfeit the respect of the civilized world. The next day, August 4, the cabinet decided to send an ultimatum to Berlin demanding that Germany respect Belgian neutrality, and that she give a satisfactory reply by midnight. The Kaiser's ministers offered no answer save military necessity, arguing that it was a matter of life and death for Germany that her soldiers should reach France by the quickest and easiest way. As the clock struck twelve, Great Britain and Germany were at war.

Other nations were quickly drawn into the terrible vortex. On August 7 the Montenegrins joined with their kinsmen, the Serbs, in fighting Austria. Two weeks later the Japanese declared war upon Germany, partly because of their alliance with Great Britain, but mainly for the purpose of conquering the German possessions in the Far East. On August 1 Turkey negotiated an alliance with Germany and in October began the bombardment of Russian ports in the Black Sea. Thus most of the nations definitely bound by alliances entered the conflict in its early stages on one side or the other. Italy, however, though still technically a member of the Triple Alliance, proclaimed her neutrality. The Italians insisted that Germany was not fighting a defensive war, and that consequently they were not bound to go to her aid. Italy maintained her neutrality until May, 1915, when she was bribed by secret promises of Austrian and Turkish territory to engage in the war on the side of the Triple Entente.

The tumult and excitement that accompanied the beginning of the great holocaust of 1914 have long since died away. But the questions of how and why the conflagration occurred are still vital ones.

The conflagration spreads

The question of war guilt

[5] B. E. Schmitt, "July, 1914: Thirty Years After," *Journal of Modern History*, XVI (1944), 193.

Historians who have studied the evidence are generally of the opinion that no one nation was solely responsible. Perhaps none of the great powers really wanted war; they would have preferred to achieve their aims by other means. But in pursuing these aims they followed policies that made war virtually inevitable. The most dangerous of national objectives were probably those of Germany. This was true not because they were more selfish than those of Russia or Austria but because they posed a more serious threat to the balance of power in Europe. Germany was attempting to achieve on the Continent of Europe objectives that Britain and France succeeded in attaining in Asia and Africa. Fritz Fischer has shown that, from the beginning of the war, some of Germany's rulers were thinking in terms of a vastly enlarged German empire that would include as satellite states, Poland, Belgium, Holland, the Balkans, and Turkey. Thus would be established a great sphere of influence comparable to that of the United States in the Western Hemisphere and of Russia in the heartland of Eurasia. How many of these territories would be annexed was not made clear; in any event they would constitute a gigantic *Mitteleuropa* dominated by Germany.[6] Fears of what this German scheme would do to the European balance of power produced nightmares in the chancelleries of London and Paris.

The guilt of individuals

During the war and for years afterward there was a tendency among many historians to blame the conflict on the stupidity or criminality of rulers. The villain most commonly singled out was Kaiser Wilhelm II. Count Berchtold, Foreign Minister of Austria, and Alexander Sazonov, Foreign Minister of Russia, were also frequently named. It is doubtful, however, that any of these individuals acted with malevolent intent. For the most part, they did what they felt they had to do. They responded to pressure from various groups within their own countries—industrialists and financiers eager for new economic opportunities, and organizations of expansionists and chauvinists such as the Pan-German League and the Navy League in the Hohenzollern Empire. In some cases they feared revolution if they did not follow a bellicose foreign policy. Like numerous politicians throughout history they sensed the efficacy of a belligerent stand against foreign enemies as the best means of allaying dissension at home. Doubtless the motive that prompted most of them, though, was conformism with the prevailing system of power politics. This system involved suspicion and fear of neighboring countries. The world of nations was assumed to be a jungle, and the only way of preserving peace in that jungle was to curb the predations of warlike states with a balance of power. Whenever that

[6] *Germany's Aims in the First World War*, pp. 348–349. Prof. Fischer is concerned primarily with German war aims formulated after the beginning of the war. He pays little regard to the fact that the objectives of a nation at war are almost invariably expanded *during* the conflict. Evidence for this can readily be found in the statement of Allied war aims contained in the notorious Secret Treaties, 1915–1917.

balance was disturbed, it was taken for granted that the rulers of
threatened nations must always be ready to throw down the gage of
battle. No potential aggressor must be allowed to gain an advantage
by springing a surprise of any kind. In some military circles it was
argued that to preclude such a possibility launching a preventive
war would be justified.

3. THE ORDEAL OF BATTLE

The holy war
of the principal
powers

In the prophetic gospel known as Revelation it is related that the
forces of good and evil shall be gathered together on "the great day
of God" to do battle at Armageddon. The unknown author might
almost have been thinking of the titanic conflict which engulfed the
nations of Europe in 1914. For World War I was seldom admitted
to be a struggle between rival imperialist powers or a product of nationalist jealousy. Instead, it was represented by spokesmen for both
sides as a crusade against the forces of evil. No sooner had the war
begun than social and political leaders in England and France pronounced it a gallant effort to safeguard the rights of the weak and to
preserve the supremacy of international law and morality. Prime
Minister Asquith on August 6, 1914, declared that Britain had entered the conflict to vindicate "the principle that smaller nationalities are not to be crushed by the arbitrary will of a strong and over-
mastering Power." Across the Channel, President Poincaré was
pompously assuring his countrymen that France had no other purpose than to stand "before the universe for Liberty, Justice and
Reason." Later, as a consequence of the inspiring preaching of such
eloquent writers and orators as H. G. Wells, Gilbert Murray, and
Woodrow Wilson, the crusade of the Entente powers became a war
"to end all wars," to "make the world safe for democracy," and to
redeem mankind from the curse of militarism. In the opposing camp
the subordinates of the Kaiser were doing all in their power to justify Germany's military efforts. The struggle against the Allies was
represented to the German people as a crusade on behalf of a superior *Kultur* and as a battle to protect the Fatherland against the
wicked encirclement policy of the Entente nations.[7]

World War I was unique in several respects. Not only were
scores of new weapons introduced, but methods of fighting differed
quite radically from those in most earlier conflicts. Open warfare
disappeared from the Western Front almost at the beginning. After
the first few weeks the opposing armies settled down in a vast network of trenches, from which attacks to dislodge the enemy were
launched usually in the murky hours just before dawn. For the most
part, the struggle was an endurance contest, in which victory depended mainly upon natural resources and upon the ability of the

[7] The quotations in this paragraph are taken from J. S. Ewart, *The Roots
and Causes of the Wars*, I, 16, 104. See also I. C. Willis, *England's Holy War*.

Trench Warfare. After the first few battles, World War I on the Western Front settled into static or position warfare. During the four-year period veritable cities of mud, stone, and timber sprang up behind the trenches.

Entente nations to obtain almost unlimited supplies of money, food, and munitions from across the sea. Probably it is safe to say that World War I was fought with greater savagery than any preceding military engagement of modern times. The use of poison gas, of the machine gun, of liquid fire, and of explosive bullets took a toll in lives and in ghastly wounds unprecedented even in the much longer campaigns of Napoleon. It is an interesting sidelight on this savagery that the number of civilians killed in air raids, in massacres, in famines, and in epidemics exceeded the number of soldiers killed in battle. Finally, the war was unique in the tremendous size of its armies. Altogether about 65,000,000 men fought for longer or shorter periods under the flags of the various belligerents. This was the climax of the steady trend toward mass warfare that had had its beginning during the French Revolution.

As the conflict dragged on through four appalling years, more and more nations threw down the gage of battle on one side or the other. We have seen that Italy postponed her entrance until the spring of 1915. Bulgaria joined the Central Powers in September, 1915, and Rumania entered on the opposite side about a year later. But the event which finally tipped the scales in favor of an Entente victory was the declaration of war against Germany by the United States on April 6, 1917. The United States entered the war for a variety of reasons. All sorts of moral arguments were avowed by President Wilson and other high officials of the government—to "make

Widening of the conflict; entrance of the United States

the world safe for democracy," to banish autocracy and militarism, and to establish a league or society of nations in place of the old diplomatic maneuvering. Undoubtedly, the primary reason, though, was the concern of the American government over maintenance of the balance of power in Europe. For years it had been a cardinal doctrine in the State Department and among military and naval officers that the security of the United States depended upon a balance of forces in the Old World. No one power must be allowed to establish its supremacy over all of Europe. So long as Great Britain was strong enough to prevent that supremacy, the United States was safe. Some authorities believe that American officials had grown so accustomed to thinking of the British Navy as the shield and buckler of American security that they could hardly tolerate the thought of any different situation. Germany, however, presented not merely a challenge to British naval supremacy but threatened to starve the British nation into surrender and make herself dominant over all of Europe.

The direct cause of United States participation in World War I was the submarine warfare of the Germans. Some historians regard it as the most important of all the factors, on the ground that without it the United States would not have entered the war at all. When the war began, Germany had only a small fleet of submarines, but she rapidly increased their number. On February 4, 1915, the Kaiser's government announced that neutral vessels headed for British ports would be torpedoed without warning. President Wilson replied to this challenge by declaring that the United States would hold Germany to "a strict accountability" if any harm should come to American lives or property. The warning had little effect. The Germans were convinced that the U-boat was one of their most valuable weapons, and they considered themselves justified in using it as an answer to the British blockade. They violated pledges to respect American rights and continued occasional sinkings of passenger vessels, in some cases causing the deaths of American citizens. When the Kaiser's ministers announced that, on February 1, 1917, they would launch a campaign of unrestricted submarine warfare, Wilson cut off diplomatic relations with the Berlin government. On April 2 he went before a joint session of the two houses of Congress and requested a declaration of war. The declaration was approved four days later with only six negative votes in the Senate and fifty in the House of Representatives.

The submarine warfare of the Germans

While fighting on the several fronts raged through four horrible years, various attempts were made to bring about the negotiation of peace. In the spring of 1917 Dutch and Scandinavian socialists decided to summon an international socialist conference to meet at Stockholm in the hope of drafting plans for ending the fighting which would be acceptable to all the belligerents. The Petrograd Soviet embraced the idea and on May 15 issued an appeal to social-

Peace proposals

ists of all nations to send delegates to the conference and to induce their governments to agree to a peace "without annexations and indemnities, on the basis of the self-determination of peoples." The socialist parties in all the principal countries on both sides of the war accepted this formula and were eager to send delegates to the conference; but when the British and French governments refused to permit any of their subjects to attend, the project was abandoned. That the rulers of the Entente states were not afraid of these proposals merely because they emanated from socialists is indicated by the fact that a similar formula suggested by the Pope was just as emphatically rejected. On August 1 of this same year Pope Benedict XV appealed to the various governments to agree to the renunciation of claims for indemnities, to the future settlement of international disputes by arbitration, to a reduction of armaments, to the restoration of all occupied areas, and to the holding of plebiscites to determine what should be done with such territories as Alsace-Lorraine, Poland, and the Trentino. Nowhere was there a disposition to take these proposals seriously. Woodrow Wilson, as spokesman for the Allies, declared that negotiation of peace *under any conditions* was impossible so long as Germany was ruled by the Kaiser. The Central Powers professed to regard with favor the general import of the papal suggestions, but they refused to commit themselves on indemnities and restorations especially the restoration of Belgium.

Wilson's Fourteen Points

The most famous of all the peace proposals was President Wilson's program of Fourteen Points, which he incorporated in an address to Congress on January 8, 1918. Summarized as briefly as possible, this program included: (1) "open covenants openly arrived at," or the abolition of secret diplomacy; (2) freedom of the seas; (3) removal of economic barriers between nations; (4) reduction of national armaments "to the lowest point consistent with safety"; (5) impartial adjustment of colonial claims, with consideration for the interests of the peoples involved; (6) evacuation of Russia; (7) restoration of the independence of Belgium; (8) restoration of Alsace and Lorraine to France; (9) a readjustment of Italian frontiers "along clearly recognizable lines of nationality", (10) autonomous development for the peoples of Austria-Hungary; (11) restoration of Rumania, Serbia, and Montenegro, with access to the sea for Serbia; (12) autonomous development for the peoples of Turkey, with the Straits from the Black Sea to the Mediterranean "permanently opened"; (13) an independent Poland, "inhabited by indisputably Polish populations," and with access to the sea; (14) a League of Nations. On several other occasions throughout 1918 Wilson reiterated in public addresses that this program would be the basis of the peace for which he would labor. Thousands of copies of the Fourteen Points were scattered by Allied planes over the German trenches and behind the lines in an effort to convince both soldiers and people that the Entente nations were striving for a just and durable peace.

By the close of the summer of 1918 the long nightmare of carnage was approaching its end. A great offensive launched by the British, French, and United States forces in July dealt one shattering blow after another to the German battalions and forced them back almost to the Belgian frontier. By the end of September the cause of the Central Powers was hopeless. Bulgaria withdrew from the war on September 30. Early in October the new Chancellor of Germany, the liberal Prince Max of Baden, appealed to President Wilson for a negotiated peace on the basis of the Fourteen Points. But the fighting went on, for Wilson had returned to his original demand that Germany must drop the Kaiser. Soon afterward Germany's remaining allies were tottering on the verge of collapse. Turkey surrendered at the end of October. The Hapsburg Empire was being cracked wide open by the revolts of the Slavs. Moreover, an Austrian offensive against Italy had not only failed but had incited the Italians to a counteroffensive, with the consequent loss to Austria of the city of Trieste and 300,000 prisoners. On November 3 the Emperor Charles, who had succeeded Francis Joseph in 1916, signed an armistice which took Austria out of the war.

Germany was now left with the impossible task of carrying on the struggle alone. The morale of her troops was rapidly breaking. The blockade was causing such a shortage of food that her people were in danger of starving. The revolutionary tremors that had been felt for some time swelled into a mighty earthquake. On November 8 a republic was proclaimed in Bavaria. The next day nearly all of Germany was in the throes of revolution. A decree was published in Berlin announcing the Kaiser's abdication, and early the next morning the neurotic old gentleman was hustled across the frontier into Holland. In the meantime, the government of the nation had passed into the hands of a provisional council headed by Friedrich Ebert, leader of the socialists in the Reichstag. Ebert and his colleagues immediately took steps to conclude negotiations for an armistice. The terms as now laid down by the Allies provided for acceptance of the Fourteen Points with three amendments. First, the item on freedom of the seas was to be stricken (in accordance with the request of the British). Second, restoration of invaded areas was to be interpreted in such a way as to include *reparations*. Third, the demand for autonomy for the subject peoples of Austria-Hungary was to be changed to a demand for *independence*. In addition, troops of the Entente nations were to occupy cities in the Rhine valley; the blockade was to be continued in force; and Germany was to hand over 5000 locomotives, 150,000 railway cars, and 5000 motor trucks, all in good condition. There was nothing that the Germans could do but accept these terms. At five o'clock in the morning of November 11, two delegates of the defeated nation met with Marshal Foch in the dark Compiègne forest and signed the papers officially ending the war. Six hours later the order, "cease fire," was given to the troops. That night thousands of people danced through the streets of London, Paris, and Rome in the same delirium of excitement with which they had greeted the declarations of war.

Victory had been won at last, but what a grim tragedy it turned out to be. Of a total of over 42,000,000 men mobilized by the Entente allies, at least 7,000,000 had been slaughtered. Five million of these had been killed in action or had died of wounds; the remainder had been reported "missing" after the battles were over. More than 3,000,000 others had been totally disabled. Thus it will be seen that almost one out of every four of the soldiers enlisted in the Allied armies suffered a major casualty. This would have been a terrific price even if all the results which were supposed to flow from an Entente victory had really been achieved. But few indeed were the permanent gains. The war which was to "end all wars" sowed the seeds of a new and more terrible conflict in the future. The autocracy of the Kaiser was indeed destroyed, but the ground was prepared for new despotisms which made the empire of William II look like a haven of liberty. In addition, World War I did nothing to abate either militarism or nationalism. Twenty years after the fighting had ended, there were nearly twice as many men under arms as in 1913; and national rivalries and racial hatreds were as deeply ingrained as ever.

The price of victory

4. THE VICTORS' PEACE

Character of the Allied peace settlement

The peace concluded at the various conferences in 1919 and 1920 resembled more closely a sentence from a court than a negotiated settlement. The explanation may be found primarily in the fact that the war became a peoples' war rather than a war of governments. Mob passions raged during the conflict and inhibited rational judgments. Politicians pandered to these passions and, in some instances, cultivated them zealously. Thus David Lloyd George campaigned during the election of 1918 on the slogan, "Hang the Kaiser!", while one of his partisans demanded "Squeeze the German lemon until the pips squeak!". In all the Allied countries nationalism and democracy combined to make compromise impossible and to interpret the war as a crusade of Good against Evil. The peace settlement drafted by the victors inevitably reflected these feelings.

The Treaties of Brest-Litovsk and Bucharest

Had the Central Powers emerged victorious in the war, the world might well have seen an even harsher peace. The major examples leading to such a conclusion are the treaties of Brest-Litovsk and Bucharest. The former was concluded by Germany with Russia in March 1918. Its terms required the Russians to surrender control over Estonia, Latvia, Lithuania, and Russian Poland, to recognize the independence of Finland and the Ukraine, and to pay an indemnity of $1,500,000,000. The treaty of Bucharest, imposed upon Rumania in February 1918, provided for the cession of territory to Bulgaria and Hungary and gave to the Central Powers such extensive control over the Danube and over the railways and oilfields that Rumania would have been placed in a condition of economic vassalage for years to come. The final defeat of Germany and her allies resulted in the abrogation of both of these treaties, though most of the territories taken from Russia were not restored to her because of antagonism in Western countries toward the new Soviet rulers.

The conference convoked in Paris [8] to draft a peace with Germany was technically in session from January until June of 1919, but only six plenary meetings were ever held. Most of the delegates

The Big Four in Paris, 1919. From left to right: Prime Minister Lloyd George, Premier Orlando, Premier Clemenceau, and President Wilson.

might just as well have stayed at home. All of the important business of the conference was transacted by small committees. At first there was the Council of Ten, made up of the President and Secretary of State of the United States, and the premiers and foreign ministers of Great Britain, France, Italy, and Japan. By the middle of March this body had been found too unwieldy and was reduced to the Council of Four, consisting of the American President and the English, Italian, and French premiers. A month later the Council of Four became the Council of Three when Premier Orlando withdrew from the conference in a huff because Wilson refused to give Italy all she demanded.

The final character of the Treaty of Versailles was determined almost entirely by the so-called Big Three—Wilson, Lloyd George, and Clemenceau. These men were about as different in personality

[8] The conference did most of its work in Paris. The treaty of peace with Germany, however, takes its name from Versailles, the suburb of Paris in which it was signed.

as any three rulers who could ever have been brought together for a common purpose. Wilson was an inflexible idealist, accustomed to dictating to subordinates and convinced that the hosts of righteousness were on his side. When confronted with unpleasant realities, such as the secret treaties among the Entente governments for division of the spoils, he had a habit of dismissing them as unimportant and eventually forgetting that he had ever heard of them. Though he knew little of the devious trickeries of European diplomacy, his unbending temperament made it difficult for him to take advice or to adjust his views to those of his colleagues. David Lloyd George was a canny little Welsh attorney who had succeeded Asquith as Prime Minister of Britain in 1916. His cleverness and his Celtic humor enabled him to succeed, on occasions, where Wilson failed; but he was above all a politician—shifty, ignorant of European conditions, and unconcerned about even his most critical mistakes. Clemenceau said of him: "I suppose that man can read, but I doubt that he ever does."

The third member of the great triumvirate was the aged and cynical French Premier, Georges Clemenceau. Born when the nineteenth century was still young, Clemenceau had been a journalist in the United States just after the Civil War. Later he had won his nickname of "the Tiger" as a relentless foe of clericals and monarchists. He had fought for the French Republic during the stormy days of the Boulangist episode, the Dreyfus affair, and the struggle for separation of church and state. Twice in his lifetime he had seen France invaded and her existence gravely imperiled. Now the tables were turned, and the French, he believed, should take full advantage of their opportunity. Only by keeping a strict control over a prostrate Germany could the security of France be preserved.

From the beginning a number of embarrassing problems confronted the chief architects of the Versailles Treaty. The most important was what to do about the Fourteen Points. There could be no doubt that they had been the basis of the German surrender on November 11. It was beyond question also that Wilson had represented them as the Entente program for a permanent peace. Consequently there was every reason for the peoples of the world to expect that the Fourteen Points would be the model for the Versailles settlement—subject only to the three amendments made before the armistice was signed. But what was the result? Not a soul among the highest dignitaries at the conference, with the exception of Wilson himself, gave more than lip service to the Fourteen Points. In the end, the American President was able to salvage, in unmodified form, only four of the parts of his famous program: point seven, requiring the restoration of Belgium; point eight, demanding the return of Alsace and Lorraine to France; point ten, providing for independence for the peoples of Austria-Hungary; and the final provision calling for a League of Nations. The others were ignored or

Clemenceau

Emasculating the Fourteen Points

450

Germany Receives Her Sentence. Premier Clemenceau, in the Hall of Mirrors at Versailles, inviting the Germans to affix their signatures to the Versailles Treaty.

modified to such an extent as to change their original meaning.

Germany sentenced

By the end of April 1919 the terms of the Versailles Treaty were ready for submission to the enemy, and Germany was ordered to send delegates to receive them. On April 29, a delegation, headed by Count von Brockdorff-Rantzau, Foreign Minister of the provisional republic, arrived in Versailles. A week later the members of the delegation were commanded to appear before the Allied representatives to receive the sentence of their nation. When Brockdorff-Rantzau protested that the terms were too harsh, he was informed by Clemenceau that Germany would have exactly three weeks in which to make up her mind whether to sign or not to sign. Eventually the time had to be extended, for the heads of the German government resigned their positions rather than accept the treaty. Their attitude was summed up by Chancellor Philip Scheidemann in the pointed statement: "What hand would not wither that sought to lay itself and us in those chains?" The Big Three now made a few minor adjustments, mainly at the instance of Lloyd George, and Germany was notified that seven o'clock on the evening of June 23 would bring either acceptance or invasion. Shortly after five a new government of the provisional republic announced that it would yield to "overwhelming force" and accede to the victors' terms. On June 28, the fifth anniversary of the murder of the Austrian Archduke, representatives of the German and Allied governments assem-

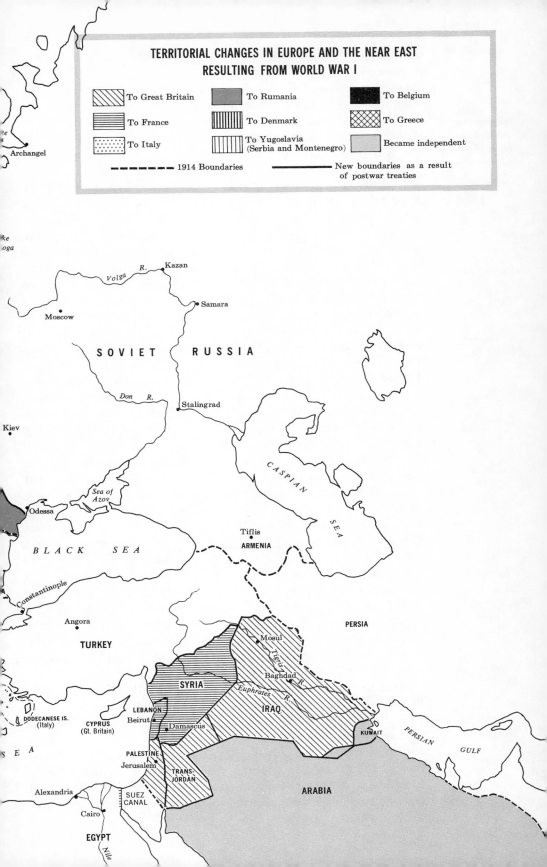

TERRITORIAL CHANGES IN EUROPE AND THE NEAR EAST RESULTING FROM WORLD WAR I

To Great Britain	To Rumania	To Belgium
To France	To Denmark	To Greece
To Italy	To Yugoslavia (Serbia and Montenegro)	Became independent

- - - - - - 1914 Boundaries   ———— New boundaries as a result of postwar treaties

Archangel

ke oga

Moscow

Volga R.   Kazan

Samara

SOVIET RUSSIA

Don R.

Stalingrad

Kiev

Sea of Azov

Odessa

CASPIAN SEA

Tiflis
ARMENIA

BLACK SEA

Constantinople

Angora

TURKEY

Mosul

PERSIA

Tigris R.

Baghdad

SYRIA

Euphrates R.

IRAQ

LEBANON
Beirut

DODECANESE IS. (Italy)

CYPRUS (Gt. Britain)

Damascus

KUWAIT

PERSIAN GULF

SEA

PALESTINE
Jerusalem

TRANS-JORDAN

ARABIA

Alexandria

SUEZ CANAL

Cairo

EGYPT

Nile

bled in the Hall of Mirrors at Versailles and affixed their signatures to the treaty.

The provisions of the Treaty of Versailles can be outlined briefly. Germany was required to surrender Alsace and Lorraine to France, Eupen and Malmedy to Belgium, northern Schleswig to Denmark, and most of Posen and West Prussia to Poland. The coal mines of the Saar Basin were to be ceded to France, to be exploited by her for fifteen years. At the end of this time the German government would have the privilege of buying them back. The Saar territory itself was to be administered by the League of Nations until 1935 when a plebiscite would be held to determine whether it should remain under the League, be returned to Germany, or be awarded to France. Germany's province of East Prussia was cut off from the rest of her territory, and her port of Danzig, almost wholly German, was subjected to the political control of the League of Nations and to the economic domination of Poland. Germany was, of course, disarmed. She gave up all of her submarines and her navy of surface vessels, with the exception of six small battleships, six light cruisers, six destroyers, and twelve torpedo boats. She was forbidden to have any airplanes, either military or naval, and her army was limited to 100,000 officers and men, to be recruited by voluntary enlistment. To make sure that she would not launch any new attack upon France or Belgium, she was forbidden to keep soldiers or maintain fortifications in the Rhine valley. Lastly, Germany and her allies were held responsible for all the loss and damage suffered by the Entente governments and their citizens, "as a consequence of the war imposed upon them by the aggression of Germany and her allies." This was the so-called war-guilt provision of the treaty (Article 231), but it was also the basis for German reparations. The exact amount that Germany should pay was left to a Reparations Commission. In 1921 the total was set at $33,000,000,000.

For the most part, the Treaty of Versailles applied only to Germany. Separate pacts were drawn up to settle accounts with Germany's allies—Austria, Hungary, Bulgaria, and Turkey. The final form of these minor treaties was determined primarily by a Council of Five, composed of Clemenceau as chairman and one delegate each from the United States, Great Britain, France, and Italy. The settlement with Austria, completed in September, 1919, is known as the Treaty of St. Germain. Austria was required to recognize the independence of Hungary, Czechoslovakia, Yugoslavia, and Poland and to cede to them large portions of her territory. In addition, she was compelled to surrender Trieste, the south Tyrol, and the Istrian peninsula to Italy. Altogether the Austrian portion of the Dual Monarchy was deprived of three-fourths of its area and three-fourths of its people. In several of the territories surrendered the inhabitants were largely German-speaking—for example, the Tyrol, and the region of the Sudeten Mountains awarded to Czechoslo-

The main provisions of the Treaty of Versailles

The Treaty of St. Germain

454

vakia. The Austrian nation itself was reduced to a small, land-locked state, with nearly one-third of its population concentrated in the city of Vienna.

The second of the minor treaties was that of Neuilly with Bulgaria, which was signed in November 1919. Bulgaria was forced to give up nearly all of the territory she had gained since the First Balkan War. The Dobrudja went back to Rumania, western Macedonia to the new kingdom of Yugoslavia, and western Thrace to Greece. All of these regions were inhabited by large Bulgarian minorities. Since Hungary was now an independent state, it was necessary that a separate treaty be imposed upon her. This was the Treaty of the Trianon Palace, signed in June 1920. It required that Slovakia should be ceded to the Republic of Czechoslovakia, Transylvania to Rumania, and Croatia-Slavonia to Yugoslavia. In few cases was the principle of self-determination of peoples more flagrantly violated. Numerous sections of Transylvania had a population that was more than half Hungarian. Included in the region of Slovakia were not only Slovaks but almost a million Magyars and about 500,000 Ruthenians. As a consequence, a fanatical irredentist movement flourished in Hungary after the war, directed toward the recovery of these lost provinces. It may be pertinent to add that the Treaty of the Trianon Palace slashed the area of Hungary from 125,000 square miles to 35,000, and her population from 22,000,000 to 8,000,000.

The settlement with Turkey was a product of unusual circumstances. The secret treaties had contemplated the transfer of Constantinople and Armenia to Russia and the division of most of the remainder of Turkey between Britain and France. But Russia's withdrawal from the war after the Bolshevik revolution, together with insistence by Italy and Greece upon fulfillment of promises made to them, necessitated considerable revision of the original scheme. Finally, in August 1920, a treaty was signed at Sèvres, near Paris, and submitted to the government of the Sultan. It provided that Armenia be organized as a Christian republic, that most of Turkey in Europe be given to Greece, that Palestine and Mesopotamia become British mandates, that Syria become a mandate of France, and that southern Anatolia be set apart as a sphere of influence for Italy. About all that would be left of the Ottoman Empire would be the city of Constantinople and the northern and central portions of Asia Minor. The decrepit government of the Sultan, overawed by Allied military forces, agreed to accept this treaty. But a revolutionary government of Turkish nationalists, which had been organized at Ankara under the leadership of Mustapha Kemal (later called Ataturk), determined to prevent the settlement of Sèvres from being put into effect. The forces of Kemal obliterated the republic of Armenia, frightened the Italians into withdrawing from Anatolia, and conquered most of the territory in Europe which had been **455** given to Greece. At last, in November 1922, they occupied Constantinople, deposed the Sultan, and proclaimed Turkey a republic. The Allies now consented to a revision of the peace. A new treaty was concluded at Lausanne in Switzerland in 1923, which permitted the Turks to retain practically all of the territory they had conquered. Though much reduced in size compared with the old Ottoman Empire, the Turkish republic still had an area of about 300,000 square miles and a population of 13,000,000.

Incorporated in each of the five treaties which liquidated the war with the Central Powers was the Covenant of the League of Nations. The establishment of a League in which the states of the world, both great and small, would cooperate for the preservation of peace had long been the cherished dream of President Wilson. Indeed, that had been one of his chief reasons for taking the United States into the war. He believed that the defeat of Germany would mean the deathblow of militarism, and that the road would thenceforth be clear for setting up the control of international relations by a *community* of power instead of by the cumbersome and ineffective balance of power. But in order to get the League accepted at all, he felt himself compelled to make numerous compromises. He permitted his original idea of providing for a reduction of armaments "to the lowest point consistent with domestic safety" to be changed into the altogether different phrasing of "consistent with *national* safety." To induce the Japanese to accept the League he allowed them to keep the former German concessions in China. To please the French he sanctioned the exclusion of both Germany and Russia from his proposed federation, despite his long insistence that it should be a combination of *all* the nations. These handicaps were serious enough. But the League received an even more deadly blow when it was repudiated by the very nation whose President had fathered it.

Established under such unfavorable auspices, the League was never a brilliant success in achieving the aims of its founder. In only a few cases did it succeed in allaying the specter of war, and in each of these the parties to the dispute were small nations. But in every dispute involving one or more major powers, the League failed. It did nothing about the seizure of Vilna by Poland in 1920, because Lithuania, the victimized nation, was friendless, while Poland had the powerful backing of France. When, in 1923, war threatened between Italy and Greece, the Italians refused to submit to the intervention of the League, and the dispute had to be settled by direct mediation of Great Britain and France. Thereafter, in every great crisis the League was either defied or ignored. Its authority was flouted by Japan in seizing Manchuria in 1931 and by Italy in conquering Ethiopia in 1936. By September 1938, when the Czechoslovakian crisis arose, the prestige of the League had sunk so low that scarcely anyone thought of appealing to it. On the other hand,

The League of
Nations

Successes and
failures of the
League

the point must be made that Wilson's great project justified its existence in other, less spectacular, ways. It checked the international opium traffic and aided poor and backward countries in controlling the spread of disease. Its agencies collected invaluable statistics on labor and business conditions throughout the world. It conducted plebiscites in disputed areas, supervised the administration of internationalized cities, helped in finding homes for racial and political refugees, and made a notable beginning in codifying international law. Such achievements may well be regarded as providing a substantial groundwork for a later effort at international organization, the United Nations, formed after World War II.

SELECTED READINGS

· *Items so designated are available in paperbound editions.*

WORLD WAR I

Albertini, Luigi, *Origins of the War of 1914,* New York, 1952–1962, 3 vols.

Chambers, Frank, *The War behind the War, 1914–1918: A History of the Political and Civilian Fronts,* London, 1939. A graphic portrayal of civilian attitudes and political and economic problems.

· Dehio, Ludwig, *Germany and World Politics in the Twentieth Century,* London, 1959 (Norton Library).

Dickinson, G. L., *The International Anarchy,* New York, 1926.

Earle, E. M., *Turkey, the Great Powers and the Bagdad Railway,* New York, 1924.

· Fay, S. B., *The Origins of the World War,* New York, (Free Press). 2 vols.

· Feis, Herbert, *Europe: The World's Banker, 1870–1914,* New Haven, 1930 (Norton Library).

Fischer, Fritz, *Germany's Aims in the First World War,* New York, 1967.

Gooch, G. P., *Before the War,* London, 1936–38, 2 vols.

· Lafore, Laurence, *The Long Fuse: An Interpretation of the Origins of World War I,* Philadelphia, 1965 (Lippincott). A discriminating account.

Langer, W. L., *The Diplomacy of Imperialism, 1890–1902,* New York, 1951.

· Lee, D. E., *The First World War—Who Was Responsible?,* New York, 1963 (Heath, rev. ed.).

· Liddell Hart, B. H., *The Real War, 1914–1918,* Boston, 1930 (Atlantic-Little Brown).

Link, A. S., *Wilson: The Struggle for Neutrality,* Princeton, 1961. A well-balanced, scholarly account.

Lutz, Hermann, *Lord Grey and the World War,* New York, 1928.

Millis, Walter, *The Road to War: America 1914–1917,* New York, 1935. A popular account.

Morgenthau, Hans, *Politics among Nations,* New York, 1954.

Ponsonby, A., *Falsehood in War Time,* New York, 1928. A good study of propaganda.

Read, J. M., *Atrocity Propaganda, 1914–1919,* New Haven, 1941.

Remak, Joachim, *Sarajevo,* New York, 1959. Fascinating and scholarly.

Renouvin, Pierre, *The Immediate Origins of the War (28th June–4th August, 1914),* New Haven, 1928. The crisis of 1914 through the eyes of a French historian.

Seymour, Charles, *American Diplomacy during the World War*, Baltimore, 1942.

Sontag, Raymond, *European Diplomatic History, 1871–1932*, New York, 1933. An' excellent summary.

Tansill, C. C., *America Goes to War*, Boston, 1938. A scholarly and very critical account.

Taylor, A. J. P., *The Struggle for Mastery in Europe, 1848–1918*, New York, 1954. A well-balanced account.

Thomson, G. M., *Twelve Days, 24 July–4 August*, London, 1964. Thorough and scholarly.

Vagts, Alfred, *A History of Militarism*, New York, 1937.

Willis, I. C., *England's Holy War*, New York, 1928.

THE PEACE OF 1919–1920

· Bailey, T. A., *Woodrow Wilson and the Lost Peace*, New York, 1944 (Quadrangle).

Baker, Ray Stannard, *Woodrow Wilson and the World Settlement*, New York, 1922.

Birdsall, Paul, *Versailles Twenty Years After*, New York, 1941.

Dillon, E. J., *The Inside Story of the Peace Conference*, New York, 1920.

Keynes, John Maynard, *The Economic Consequences of the Peace*, New York, 1920.

Nicolson, Harold, *Peacemaking, 1919*, New York, 1946.

SOURCE MATERIALS

Baker, Ray Stannard, ed., *The Life and Letters of Woodrow Wilson*, New York, 1931, 2 vols.

———, and Dodd, W. E., eds., *The Public Papers of Woodrow Wilson*, 6 vols.

Bethmann-Hollweg, T. von, *Reflections on the World War*.

Carnegie Endowment for International Peace, *The Treaties of Peace, 1919–1923*, 2 vols.

Gooch, G. P., and Temperley, H., eds., *British Documents on the Origins of the War, 1898–1914*.

Grey of Fallodon, Edward Grey, 1st viscount, *Twenty-five Years*, New York, 1937, 2 vols.

Hendrick, B. J., ed., *The Life and Letters of Walter Hines Page*, 2 vols.

Lichnowsky, Karl Max, Furst von, *Heading for the Abyss*, New York, 1928.

Seymour, Charles, ed., *The Intimate Papers of Colonel House*, New York, 1926–28, 4 vols.

CHAPTER 15

Dictatorship and Democracy

between Two Wars

Fascism does not, generally speaking, believe in the possibility or utility of perpetual peace. It therefore discards pacifism as a cloak for cowardly supine renunciation in contra-distinction to self-sacrifice. War alone keys up all human energies to their maximum tension and sets the seal of nobility on those peoples who have the courage to face it. . . . Therefore all doctrines which postulate peace at all costs are incompatible to fascism.
—Benito Mussolini, *Fascism: Doctrine and Institutions*

Conspicuous among the consequences of World War I was a decline of liberal and democratic ideals. For a time it appeared that the reverse would be true. Not only was militarism destroyed in the defeated countries, but the list of republics in Europe was enlarged by the addition of Germany, Austria, Poland, Finland, Turkey, and Czechoslovakia. Yet in most of these countries democracy was more of a superficial phenomenon than an underlying reality. Neither democracy nor liberalism was grounded upon firm tradition in very many parts of Continental Europe. The real issue in most of them was whether control of the government should continue in the possession of feudal aristocrats, industrialists and financiers, or a combination of all. None of these elements had gone very far in providing the masses with an equality of rights and privileges. It was perhaps inevitable, therefore, that the war, in many countries, should have taken on the character of a war within a war, that the masses should have seen in the emergency an opportunity to dethrone their oppressors. In some cases, the opportunity was not firmly grasped until after the international conflict had ended. But in Russia bourgeois liberals overturned the autocracy in March 1917, and were themselves overturned by the Bolsheviks later in the

The challenge to the old ruling classes

459

same year. Socialists in Germany overthrew the Kaiser in early November 1918. The French and British governments had serious trouble with striking workmen during the war, and Britain passed under the control of the Labour party a few years after the conflict ended. Nearly everywhere the right of the old ruling classes to govern became a major issue. Except in Russia, the gravest challenge to that right was thrown down in Italy and Germany. Brutal and perverted though their fascist regimes were, they had many of the characteristics of mass movements.

1. THE FASCIST REVOLUTION IN ITALY

Causes of the
Fascist
revolution:
(1) frustrated
nationalism

The first of the nations of western Europe to repudiate the practices of the old ruling classes was Italy. This may seem strange in view of the fact that the Italians fought in the war on the winning side. But the point must be kept in mind that Italy had been the victim of frustrated nationalism for many years. Time after time her aspirations for power and for empire had been shattered. In 1881 her hope of acquiring Tunisia had been brought suddenly to an end by the French occupation of that country. Her effort to conquer Abyssinia in the 1890's had been terminated by a crushing defeat at the hands of uncivilized natives in the Battle of Adowa. The effect of these reverses was to produce a sense of humiliation and shame, especially in the minds of the younger generation, and to foster an attitude of contempt for the existing political regime. Blame for Italy's failures was placed not so much upon foreign nations as upon her own governing class. Members of this class were held up to the scorn of the people as degenerate old men—cynical, vacillating, defeatist, and corrupt. Even before World War I there was talk of revolution, of the need for a drastic housecleaning that would deliver the country from its incompetent rulers.

(2) the demoralizing and humiliating effects
of the war

But the establishment of a Fascist dictatorship in Italy would never have been possible without the demoralizing and humiliating effects of World War I. The chief business of the Italian armies had been to keep the Austrians occupied on the Southern Front while the British, French, and Americans hammered Germany into submission along the battle lines in Flanders. To accomplish her purpose Italy had to mobilize more than 5,500,000 men, and of these nearly 700,000 were killed. The direct financial cost of her participation in the struggle was over $15,000,000,000. These sacrifices, of course, were no greater than those made by the British and the French; but Italy was a poor country. Moreover, in the division of the spoils after the fighting was over, the Italians got less than they expected. While Italy did receive most of the Austrian territories promised her in the secret treaties, she maintained that these were inadequate rewards for her sacrifices and for her valuable contribution to an Entente victory. At first the nationalists vented their spleen for the "humiliation of Versailles" upon President Wilson, but after a short time they returned to their old habit of castigating Italy's rulers. They alleged that such men as Premier Orlando had been so cravenly weak and inept that they had allowed their own country to be cheated.

The war contributed to the revolution in a multitude of other ways. It resulted in inflation of the currency, with consequent high prices, speculation, and profiteering. Normally wages would have risen also, but the labor market was glutted on account of the return to civilian life of millions of soldiers. Furthermore, business was demoralized, owing to extensive and frequent strikes and to the closing of foreign markets. Perhaps the most serious consequence of the war, to the upper and middle classes at least, was the growth of economic radicalism. As hardship and chaos increased, the socialists embraced a philosophy akin to Bolshevism. In 1918 they voted as a party to join the Moscow International. In the elections of November 1919, they won about a third of the seats in the Chamber of Deputies. During the following winter socialist workers took over about a hundred factories and attempted to run them for the benefit of the proletariat. Radicalism also spread through the rural areas, where the so-called Red Leagues were organized to break up large estates and to force landlords to reduce their rents. But by 1921 the danger that Italy would go Bolshevik was practically over. Nevertheless, the owning classes had been badly frightened and were therefore ready to accept Fascism as a less dangerous form of radicalism that might save at least part of their property from confiscation.

(3) inflation, radicalism, and economic chaos

How much the Fascist movement depended for its success upon the leadership of Mussolini is impossible to say. Undoubtedly his fiery eloquence, his Napoleonic poses, and his Machiavellian ruthlessness proved potent attractions to weaklings in mind and body who had been nurtured on romantic worship of Julius Caesar and Garibaldi. Benito Mussolini was born in 1883, the son of a socialist blacksmith. His mother was a schoolteacher, and in deference to her wishes he entered a normal school and eventually became a teacher. But he was restless and dissatisfied and soon left Italy for further study in Switzerland. Here he gave part of his time to his books and the rest of it to begging his bread and writing articles for socialist newspapers. He was finally expelled from the country for fomenting strikes in factories. Upon returning to Italy he took up journalism as a definite career and eventually became editor of *Avanti*, the leading socialist daily. His ideas at this time were a mixture of contradictory forms of radicalism. He professed to be a Marxian socialist, but he mingled his socialism with doctrines taken from the syndicalists. In fact, the great syndicalist leader Sorel once referred to him as his most promising disciple.

The career of Mussolini

Rather than a thinker or a sincere believer, Mussolini was essen-

Mussolini. Addressing a crowd of his followers from the balcony of the Palazzo Venezia in Rome.

Mussolini's
contradictory
ideas

tially a rebel against the status quo. No man with a definite philosophy could have reversed himself so often. He not only condemned the imperialism which he later practiced so zealously, but at one time or another before the war he defamed the Church, vilified the king, and called the Italian flag "a rag to be planted on a dung hill." [1] When World War I broke out in August 1914, Mussolini insisted that Italy should remain neutral. But he had scarcely adopted this position when he began urging participation on the Entente side. As early as October 1914, he had gone over bag and baggage to the interventionist camp. Deprived of his position as editor of *Avanti*, he founded a new paper, *Il Popolo d'Italia*, and dedicated its columns to whipping up enthusiasm for war. The decision of the government the following spring to go in on the side of the Entente allies he regarded as a personal victory. He entered the army as a private in September 1915, and eventually rose to be a corporal. In February 1917, he was wounded by the explosion of a trench mortar and was allowed to return to his position as editor of *Il Popolo* in the hope that he might stimulate the flagging enthusiasm of the Italian people. From then he worked zealously for a Fascist revolution.

The word Fascism had a dual origin. It derives in part from the Latin *fasces*, the ax surrounded by a bundle of rods representing the authority of the Roman state; it comes also from the Italian *fascio*, meaning group or band. *Fasci* were organized as early as October 1914, as units of agitation to swing Italy over to the Entente cause. Their membership was made up of young idealists, futurists, fanati-

The evolution
of Fascism

[1] For these and other contradictions between his earlier and later teachings, see Gaudens Megaro, *Mussolini in the Making*.

cal nationalists, bored white-collar workers, and misfits of every description. The original platform of the Fascist movement was prepared by Mussolini in 1919. It was a surprisingly radical document, which demanded, among other things, universal suffrage; abolition of the Senate; the establishment by law of an eight-hour day; a heavy capital levy; a heavy tax on inheritances; confiscation of 85 per cent of war profits; acceptance of the League of Nations; "opposition to all imperialisms"; and annexation of Fiume and Dalmatia. This platform was accepted more or less officially until May 1920, when it was supplanted by another of a much more conservative character. Indeed, the new program omitted all reference to economic reform and consisted of nothing but condemnation of "politicians' socialism" and some vague assertions about "revindicating" the principles for which the war had been fought. On neither of these platforms did the Fascists achieve much political success. Even after the elections of 1921 they had only thirty-five representatives in the Chamber of Deputies.

The Fascists made up for their lack of numbers by disciplined aggressiveness and strong determination. And when the old regime became so decrepit that it practically abdicated its functions, they prepared to take over the government. In September 1922, Mussolini began to talk openly of revolution and raised the cry, "On to Rome." On October 28 an army of about 50,000 Fascist militia occupied the capital. The Premier resigned, and the following day Victor Emmanuel III invited Mussolini to form a cabinet. Thus without firing a shot the blackshirted legions had gained control of the Italian government. The explanation is to be found, not in the strength of Fascism, but in the chaos created by the war and in the weakness and lack of resolution of the old ruling classes. By the end of the next three years Mussolini's revolution was virtually complete. He had abolished the cabinet system, made the political system a one-party system, and reduced the functions of the parliament to ratifying decrees.

The march on Rome

The political and economic system in Fascist Italy was officially known as the corporate state. This meant, first of all, that the government rested upon an economic basis. The people were represented in the government, not as citizens inhabiting definite districts, but in their capacity of producers. But the corporate state also included the idea that individual and class interests must be subordinated to the interests of the state. In case of a conflict between workers and employers, the state had the final authority to intervene and impose a settlement. The corporate principle also involved the complete repudiation of laissez faire. Though private ownership was still largely preserved and though the capitalists were recognized as "a socially productive class," the time-honored principles of classical economics were thrown on the scrap heap. Every economic activity of the citizen was subject to regulation, and any industrial

The corporate state

or commercial enterprise might be taken over by the government if the interests of the nation required it. The state had acquired by 1939 a controlling interest in 25 per cent of Italian industry.

The idea of the corporate state was an exceedingly important element in Fascist theory, but it was by no means the only one. The other leading doctrines may be summarized as follows:

Other major
doctrines of
Fascism

(1) Totalitarianism. The state incorporates every interest and every loyalty of its members. There must be "nothing above the state, nothing outside the state, nothing against the state."

(2) Nationalism. The nation is the highest form of society ever evolved by the human race. It has a life and a soul of its own apart from the lives and souls of the individuals who compose it. There can never be a real harmony of interests between two or more distinct peoples. Internationalism is therefore a gross perversion of human progress.

(3) Romanticism. Reason can never be an adequate instrument for the solution of great national problems. Intellect needs to be supplemented by mystic faith, by self-sacrifice, and by worship of heroism and strength. "The Fascist spirit is will, not intellect."

(4) Authoritarianism. The sovereignty of the state is absolute. The citizen has no rights but simply duties. What nations need is not liberty, but work, order, prosperity. Liberty is "a putrefying corpse," an outworn dogma of the French Revolution. The state should be governed by an *élite*, which has demonstrated its right to rule by its strength and by its superior understanding of the national ideals.

(5) Militarism. Strife is the origin of all things. Nations which do not expand eventually wither and die. War exalts and ennobles man and regenerates sluggish and decadent peoples.

Achievements
of the Fascist
regime

No unprejudiced person would deny that the Fascist regime in Italy had a few achievements to its credit. By June 1940, when Italy entered World War II, the government had reduced illiteracy, effected what appeared to be a satisfactory settlement of the old quarrel with the papacy,[2] and obliterated the Mafia, or Black Hand organizations, in Sicily. It had succeeded also in making a number of improvements in the economic sphere. By instructing the peasants in scientific farming, it had increased the productivity of the soil by about 20 per cent. Subsidies and protective tariffs had greatly expanded industrial production, particularly of such commodities as silk, rayon, and automobiles. Between 1923 and 1933 Italy almost doubled her hydroelectric power resources.

But the ledger had also a debit side. The attempt to make Italy self-sufficient had resulted in much higher prices for certain com-

[2] By a treaty with Pius XI in 1929 the Fascist government abrogated the 1871 Law of Papal Guaranties (see p. 231) and recognized the complete independence of the Vatican City. The agreement also provided that Roman Catholicism should be the official religion of the state, that religious instruction should be given in the schools, and that the laws of the Church should be enforced by the government.

modities. While business and employment conditions were undoubtedly more stable than in the years just after World War I, there was no evidence that the lot of the workers had materially improved. Wage rates had indeed gone up, but on account of the advances in prices and the movement to spread the work, it was open to serious doubt that there had been any actual increase in real wages. Furthermore, the Italians had been compelled to purchase their stability and order at the price of a deadly uniformity of thought and action—a condition which Mussolini himself described in 1914 as "boredom and imbecility." [3] It should be mentioned also that Fascist rule had involved two costly ventures into foreign war: the conquest of Ethiopia in 1935–1936 and intervention in the Spanish Civil War in 1936–1939. There was little to indicate that the Italian people benefited from either of these ventures despite the enthusiasm displayed for them in the beginning.

2. THE NAZI TRIUMPH IN GERMANY

Germany succumbed to fascism much later than Italy, mainly for the reason that the forces of nationalism and militarism were temporarily discredited as a result of her defeat in World War I. From 1918 to 1933 Germany was a republic. The revolution which overthrew the Kaiser in November 1918, brought into power a coalition of Socialists, Centrists, and Democrats. In 1919 the leaders of these parties drafted the Weimar Constitution, an instrument of government remarkable for its numerous progressive features. It provided for universal suffrage; the cabinet system of government; and for a bill of rights, guaranteeing not only the traditional civil liberties but the right of the citizen to employment, to an education, and to protection against the hazards of an industrial society. But the republic set up under this constitution was beset with troubles from the start. Reactionaries and other extremists plotted against it. Moreover, the German people had had little experience with democratic government. The Weimar Republic did not spring from the desires of a majority of the nation. It was born of a revolution forced upon Germany in her hour of defeat.

The era of the
republic in
Germany

The factors which led to the eventual triumph of German fascism were many and various. First was the sense of humiliation arising from defeat in the war. Between 1871 and 1914 Germany had risen to lofty heights of political and cultural prestige. Until 1900, at least, she was the leading power on the European Continent. Her universities, her science, her philosophy, and her music were known and admired all over the world. She had likewise attained a fabulous prosperity, and by 1914 she had surpassed even Britain and the United States in several fields of industrial production. Then came the crushing blow of 1918. She was toppled from her pinnacle and

Causes of the
triumph of German fascism:
(1) defeat in
the war

[3] Gaudens Megaro, *Mussolini in the Making*, p. 329.

left at the mercy of her powerful enemies. It was too much for the German people to understand. They could not believe that their invincible armies had really been worsted in battle. Quickly the legend grew that the nation had been "stabbed in the back" by Socialists and Jews in the government. There was, of course, little truth in this charge, but it helped to salve the wounded pride of German patriots.

A few other causes of the rise and growth of National Socialism may also be mentioned. There was the fact that Germany had always been a military state, imbued with traditions of discipline and order. To many of the people the army was the symbol not merely of security but of national greatness. The qualities of obedience and regimentation, which the military life represented, were virtues most dear to the German heart. As a consequence, many patriotic citizens were seriously disturbed by the laxity and irresponsibility that appeared to distinguish the republican regime. It was alleged that Berlin had displaced Paris as the most frivolous and immoral city of Europe. Another cause of more than minor importance was the fear of Bolshevism. The followers of this philosophy in Germany originally called themselves Spartacists. Subsequently they changed their name to Communists. In the Presidential election of 1932 the Communist party polled about 6,000,000 votes, or over one-seventh of the total. As had happened in Italy, a number of capitalists and property owners took alarm at what they regarded as a growing danger of Bolshevik revolution and secretly gave their support to the triumph of fascism as the lesser of two evils.

The foregoing factors had major importance in generating the Nazi movement and fostering its gradual evolution, but the influence that gave it the proportions of an avalanche and made possible its ultimate triumph was the Great Depression. This conclusion is supported by the fact that the party was never able to win more than 32 seats (barely $\frac{1}{20}$) in the Reichstag prior to the election of 1930. In the early days the movement had drawn its converts chiefly from dissatisfied and uprooted members of the lower middle class and from former army officers unable to adjust to civilian life. After 1929 it received much broader support from a large segment of the German people who felt themselves disinherited and at odds with the ruling elements. Some were farmers angered by the collapse of agricultural prices and by their crushing burdens of debt and taxes. Others were university students who saw little prospect of gaining a place in the overcrowded professions. Undoubtedly the most numerous of all were the unemployed, whose ranks had swelled to 6,000,000 by 1932. Members of all these classes were groping in bewilderment and terror. By no means all of them were Nazis, but their despair was so great as to induce them to accept almost any demagogue who promised to deliver them from confusion and fear. Never in the history of the nation had the future appeared so dark.

(2) militarism and fear of Bolshevism

(3) Influence of the Great Depression

Apparently, another sizable proportion of the German nation did not really believe in the promises of the Nazis, but *acquiesced* in their assumption of power on the premise that almost any change would be a change for the better. To such people the loss of political and intellectual liberty mattered little, for they had never had any firm conviction of the value of liberal doctrines.

The origins of German fascism go back to 1919 when a little group of seven men met in a beer hall in Munich and founded the National Socialist German Workers' party.[4] Presently the most obscure of the seven emerged as their leader. His name was Adolf Hitler, born in 1889, the son of a petty customs official in the Austrian civil service. His early life was unhappy and maladjusted. Rebellious and undisciplined from childhood, he seems always to have been burdened with a sense of frustration. He wasted his time at school drawing pictures and finally decided that he would become an artist. With this purpose in view he went to Vienna in 1909, hoping to enter the Academy. But he failed the required examinations, and for the next four years he was compelled to eke out a dismal existence as a casual laborer and a painter of little sketches and watercolors which he sometimes managed to sell to the humbler art shops. Meanwhile he developed some violent political prejudices. He became an ardent admirer of certain Jew-baiting politicians in Vienna; and since he associated Judaism with Marxism, he hated that philosophy also. He likewise became a convert to extreme Nordicism, doting on the qualities of the proud German nation and despising Austria-Hungary for its lack of racial unity. When World War I broke out, Hitler was living in Munich, and though an Austrian citizen, he immediately enlisted in the Bavarian army. He served through the four years of fighting with enough distinction to be awarded the Iron Cross and a promotion as corporal. He was wounded and gassed at least twice; and it was while recuperating in a hospital just before the armistice that he resolved to become a politician.

The Nazi revolution began in what appeared to be a quite harmless fashion. During the summer of 1932 the parliamentary system broke down. No Chancellor could retain a majority in the Reichstag; for the Nazis declined to support any cabinet not headed by Hitler, and the Communists refused to collaborate with the Socialists. In January 1933, a group of reactionaries—industrialists, bankers, and Junkers—prevailed upon President von Hindenburg to designate Hitler as Chancellor, evidently in the belief that they could control him. It was arranged that there should be only three Nazis in the cabinet, and that Franz von Papen, a Catholic aristocrat, should hold the position of Vice Chancellor. But the sponsors of this plan failed to appreciate the tremendous resurgence of mass feeling back of the Nazi movement. Hitler was not slow in making the most

[4] The name of the party was soon abbreviated in popular usage to Nazi. **467**

of his new opportunity. He persuaded von Hindenburg to dissolve the Reichstag and to order a new election on March 5. The voting took place in the midst of intense excitement. Just a few days before, the Reichstag chamber was gutted by a fire, which Hitler contended was of Communist origin. But in spite of this attempt to frighten the nation by conjuring up the specter of Bolshevism, the Nazis won less than a majority of the popular vote and only 288 seats out of the total of 647 in the Reichstag. Nevertheless, with the fifty-two members chosen by their allies, the Nationalists, they did have a slight majority. When the new Reichstag assembled on March 21, it voted to confer upon Hitler practically unlimited

Hitler in 1936. Germany at this time was rapidly rearming and had remilitarized the Rhineland, the first steps toward her objective of European domination.

powers. Soon afterward the flag of the Weimar Republic was hauled down and replaced by the swastika banner of National Socialism. The new Germany was proclaimed to be the Third Reich, the successor of the Hohenstaufen Empire of the Middle Ages and of the Hohenzollern Empire of the Kaisers.

Of course, these events marked only the initial stage of the Nazi revolution. Within a very few months, other and more sweeping changes were added. Germany was converted into a highly centralized state with the destruction of the federal principle. All political parties except the Nazi party were declared illegal. Totalitarian control was extended over the press, over education, the theater, the cinema, radio, and many branches of production and trade. Drastic penalties were imposed upon the Jews: they were eliminated from government positions, deprived of citizenship, and practically ex-

Consolidation of Nazi rule

cluded from the universities. With the passing of the years, the entire regime seemed to shift more and more in a radical direction. The new tendency approached its climax in 1938 with the extension of party control over the army, with the elimination of Hjalmar Schacht (a banker of somewhat conservative views) from his position as economic dictator, and with the institution of a fanatical crusade against the Jews to expel them from the Reich or to annihilate them entirely.

So far as its ideology was concerned, German fascism resembled in a great many of its essentials the Italian variety. Both were collectivistic, authoritarian, nationalistic, militaristic, and romantic (in the sense of being anti-intellectual). Yet there were some outstanding differences. Italian Fascism never had a racial basis. True, after the formation of the Rome-Berlin Axis, Mussolini issued some anti-Jewish decrees; but most of them appear not to have been enforced very strictly. By contrast, National Socialism made the factor of race a central pillar of its theory. The Nazis argued that the so-called Aryan race, which was supposed to include the Nordics as its most perfect specimens, was the only one ever to have made any notable contributions to human progress. They contended further that the accomplishments and mental qualities of a people were actually determined by blood. Thus the achievements of the Jew forever remained Jewish, or Oriental, no matter how long he might live in a Western country. It followed that no Jewish science or Jewish literature or Jewish music could ever truly represent the German nation. Obviously, most of this racial doctrine was mere rationalization. The real reason why the Nazis persecuted the Jews seems to have been that they needed a scapegoat upon whom they could place the blame for the nation's troubles. Before this extremism had run its course millions of Jews had been exterminated in concentration camps.

German fascism compared with the Italian variety: racism

There were also other differences, both in theory and in practice. Despite the fact that Germany was one of the most highly industrialized countries in the world, National Socialism had a peculiar peasant flavor which Italian Fascism did not possess. The key to Nazi theory was contained in the phrase *Blut und Boden* (blood and soil). The word *soil* typified not only a deep reverence for the beautiful homeland but an abiding affection for the peasants, who were considered to embody the finest qualities of the German race. No class of the population was more generously treated by the Nazi government. This high regard for country folk came partly no doubt from the circumstance that they were the most prolific of the nation's citizens and therefore the most valuable for military reasons. It was explainable also by the reaction of the Nazi leaders against everything that the city stood for—not only intellectualism and radicalism but high finance and the complicated problems of industrial society. As upstarts of obscure origin, the Nazis strove to compen-

Blood and soil; the state and the economy

sate for their sense of inferiority by glorifying the simple life. Still another difference between the German and Italian varieties of fascism was the fact that under the former the corporate state was not fully developed. To be sure, both involved the complete subjection of economic activities to political control; but in Germany there was no direct representation of economic interests in the government. Members of the Reichstag continued to be chosen from geographic districts, and the state retained its exclusively political character. Finally, it may be said that National Socialism was more frenzied and fanatical than Italian Fascism. It was comparable to a new religion, not only in its dogmatism and its ritual, but in its fierce intolerance and its zeal for expansion.

The significance of fascism, whether German or Italian, is still a subject of controversy among students of modern history. Some argue that it was simply the enthronement of force by big capitalists in an effort to save their dying system from destruction. But this does not square with all of the facts. Neither Italian Fascism nor National Socialism showed any inclination in the beginning to protect the interests of monopolies or of speculative finance. Indeed, if we can judge from their original platforms, their purpose was just the opposite. It is true, however, that the success of both movements in gaining control of the government depended in some measure upon support from great landowners and captains of industry. A second interpretation of fascism would explain it as a reaction of debtors against creditors, of farmers against bankers and manufacturers, and of small businessmen against high finance and monopolistic practices. Still other students of the movement interpret it as a revolt against communism, a reversion to primitivism, a result of the despair of the masses, a protest against the weaknesses of democracy, or a supreme manifestation of chauvinism. Undoubtedly fascism was all of these things combined and a great many others besides. An increasingly popular view in recent years holds that fascism was simply an extreme expression of tendencies prevalent in all industrialized countries. Certainly France had its militant exponents of violence and hatred, notably the Cagoulards, or Hooded Ones. In Britain the Black Shirt movement led by Oswald Mosely was smaller but no less militant. Even in the United States counterparts of these movements could also be found: witness the followers of Fritz Kuhn and his German-American Bund and Gerald L. K. Smith. Though most of these groups were minority aggregations, they nevertheless exerted a wide influence. Indeed, official policies in most Western countries in the 1930's took on more and more of a fascist semblance—a tightly controlled economy, limitation of production to maintain prices, and expansion of armaments to promote prosperity. In brief, nearly all nations in that period were beset with similar problems. Had it not been for the expansionist dynamics of the German Reich and its threat to the balance of power, perhaps

The complex significance of fascism

470

little opposition would have developed, in the outside world, to Nazi policies.

3. THE COMMUNIST REGIME IN RUSSIA

Although Russia fought in World War I on the side of the powers that eventually triumphed, she was the first of the belligerent nations to be engulfed by revolution. The reasons for the initial explosion, at least, seem fairly obvious. The Russian government's conduct of the war was not distinguished for brilliance. The weak-willed Tsar came more and more under the influence of the superstitious Tsarina, who was putty in the hands of an infamous "holy man," Gregory Rasputin. In some instances soldiers were sent to the front without rifles and were inadequately supplied with suitable clothing. There were seldom enough surgeons or hospital facilities to take care of the wounded. The Russian railway system broke down, producing a shortage of food not only in the army but in the congested cities as well. Added to these troubles was a series of crushing defeats by the Germans. Though Russia mobilized 15,000,-000 men, she was unable to hold up her end of the fight on the Eastern Front. By the end of 1916 her power of resistance had practically collapsed.

Effects of the war
in causing the
initial outbreak
of revolution

The revolution in Russia followed a succession of stages somewhat similar to those of the great French Revolution of 1789. The first of these stages began in March 1917 with the forced abdication of the Tsar. For this the principal cause was disgust with the conduct of the war. But there were also many other factors—the inflation and consequent high prices, the scarcity of food and of coal in urban areas, the influx of peasants who overcrowded the cities, the preaching of radicals, and the legacy of bitterness left by the revolt of 1905. With the overthrow of the Tsar, the authority of the government passed into the hands of a provisional ministry organized by leaders in the Duma in conjunction with representatives of the Petrograd workers. The most important members of the new cabinet were the Foreign Minister, Paul Milyukov, and the Minister of Justice, Alexander Kerensky. With the exception of Kerensky, who was a Social Revolutionary, nearly all of the ministers were bourgeois liberals. Their conception of the revolution was mainly to transform the autocracy into a constitutional monarchy modeled after that of Great Britain. In accordance with this aim they issued a proclamation of civil liberties, released thousands of prisoners, granted permission for political exiles to return to the country, and made plans for the election of a constituent assembly.

The provisional government proved itself inadequate to the responsibilities thrust upon it. Its leaders did not seem to understand the new conditions created by the war or even some of those arising in the prewar period. Among them were congestion in the cities, the

Beginning of the Russian Revolution, March 1917. Soldiers in Petrograd set up a barricade and distribute arms to striking workers, thus making a revolution possible.

emergence of a proletariat, and the inevitable harshness of the class conflict in the initial stages of industrialization. Further, the heads of this provisional government made the mistake of attempting to continue the war on the old basis of 1914–1917. They were just as imperialistic as the Tsar and his minions. They hoped to get Constantinople and everything else that had been promised in the secret treaties. But the masses of the people were desperately weary of the years of hardship and struggle. What they wanted was peace and a chance to return to a normal life. Consequently, in May, when Milyukov reiterated his pledge of support for the Allies, criticism was so strong that he was forced to resign. A new government was organized which managed to stay in power until September. Its head was Alexander Kerensky, and it consisted primarily of moderate socialists. The ultimate failure of both the Milyukov and Kerensky regimes may be ascribed chiefly to the insignificant role played by the middle class in Russia at that time. In no sense can it be compared as a revolutionary force with the bourgeoisie in France in 1789. It was much smaller in size and lacked the prestige and wealth of the elements that destroyed the absolute monarchy of Louis XVI. Moreover, it had little support from the masses.

The downfall of Kerensky's regime marked the end of the first stage of the Russian revolution. The second began immediately after with the accession of the Bolsheviks to power on November 7, 1917. The Bolsheviks were originally members of the Social Democratic party, but in 1903 this party had split into two factions: a majority or Bolshevik faction of Marxist revolutionists and a minority faction

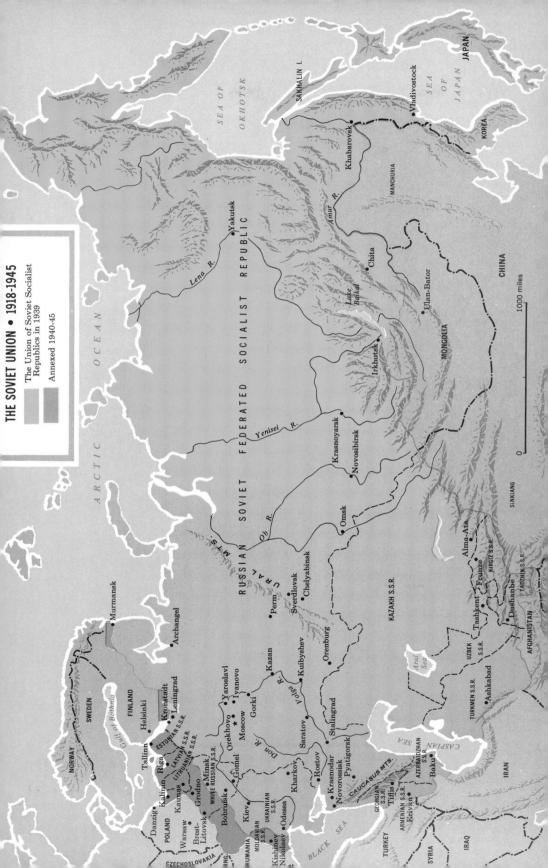

THE SOVIET UNION · 1918-1945

The Union of Soviet Socialist
Republics in 1939

Annexed 1940-45

JAPAN

SAKHALIN I.

SEA OF OKHOTSK

SEA OF JAPAN

Vladivostock

KOREA

Khabarovsk

Amur R.

MANCHURIA

Yakutsk

Chita

CHINA

Lena R.

Lake Baikal

Ulan-Bator

Irkutsk

MONGOLIA

RUSSIAN SOVIET FEDERATED SOCIALIST REPUBLIC

1000 miles

ARCTIC OCEAN

Yenisei R.

Krasnoyarsk

Novosibirsk

SINKIANG

Ob R.

Omsk

Murmansk

Archangel

URALS

KAZAK S.S.R.

Alma-Ata

Perm

Sverdlovsk

Chelyabinsk

Frunze

KIRGIZ S.S.R.

Tashkent

TADZHIK S.S.R.

Orenburg

Dushanbe

NORWAY

SWEDEN

FINLAND

Helsinki

Kronstadt

Leningrad

Kazan

Kama R.

Kuibyshev

UZBEK S.S.R.

AFGHANISTAN

Gulf of Bothnia

Tallinn

ESTONIAN S.S.R.

Yaroslavl

Ivanovo

Gorki

Volga R.

Saratov

TURKMEN S.S.R.

Ashkabad

Riga

LATVIAN S.S.R.

Orekhovo

Moscow

Aral Sea

Danzig

Kalinin

Kaunas

LITHUANIAN S.S.R.

Minsk

WHITE RUSSIAN S.S.R.

Gomel

Stalingrad

Pyatigorsk

CASPIAN SEA

IRAN

POLAND

Warsaw

Brest-Litovsk

Grodno

Bobruisk

Kiev

Don R.

Rostov

Krasnodar

Novorossisk

CAUCASUS MTS.

Baku

AZERBAIDZHAN S.S.R.

RUMANIA

MOLDAVIAN S.S.R.

Kishinev

UKRAINIAN S.S.R.

Nikolaev

Odessa

Kharkov

BLACK SEA

GEORGIAN S.S.R.

Tiflis

ARMENIAN S.S.R.

Erivan

TURKEY

SYRIA

IRAQ

CZECHOSLOVAKIA

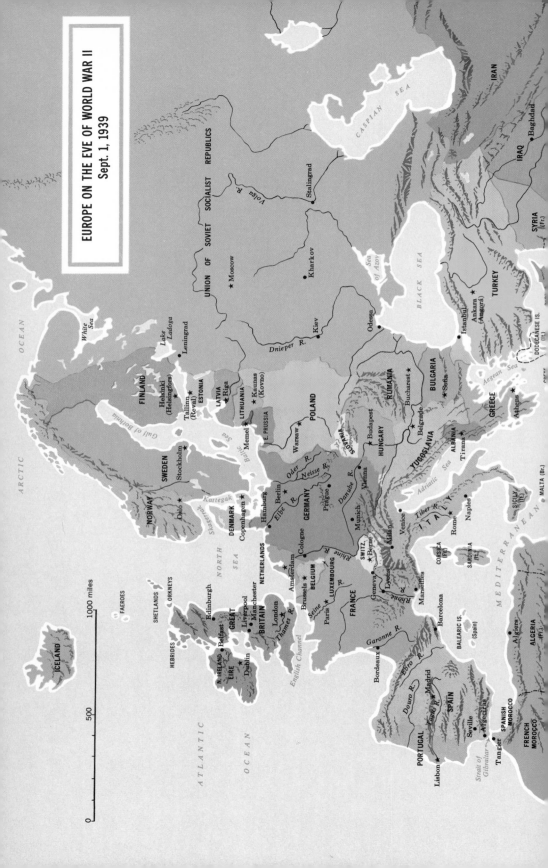

of Mensheviks, who contended that the time for revolution was not yet ripe. Soon after the overthrow of the Tsar the Bolsheviks began laying plans for a socialist revolution. They worked their way into the Petrograd Soviet, or Council of Workers' and Soldiers' Deputies, and eventually wrested control of it from the Mensheviks and Social Revolutionaries. They organized an armed Red Guard and took possession of strategic points throughout the city. By November 7 everything was ready for the grand *coup*. Red Guards occupied nearly all the public buildings and finally arrested the members of the government, though Kerensky himself escaped. Thus the Bolsheviks climbed to power with scarcely a struggle. Their slogan of "Peace, Land, and Bread" made them heroes to the soldiers disgusted with the war, to the peasants hungry for land, and to the poor of the cities suffering from the shortage of food. In addition, their ideas may well have reflected the hopes of a large section of the Russian population.

The chief actor in the Bolshevik drama was Vladimir Lenin, whose real name was Vladimir Ulianov (1870–1924). His father was an inspector of schools and a state counsellor and therefore entitled to rank in the petty nobility. An older son, Alexander, was hanged for participating in a plot to assassinate the Tsar. In the very same year Vladimir was admitted to the University of Kazan. However, he was soon afterward expelled for engaging in radical activity. Later he was admitted to the University of St. Petersburg and in 1891 obtained a degree in law. From then on he devoted his entire life to the cause of socialist revolution. From 1900 to 1917 he lived

Nicholas II, after the Revolution of 1917. The deposed Tsar and his guards in the park of the imperial castle outside Petrograd. From here he and his family were transferred to a village in Siberia and murdered by the Bolsheviks in 1918.

Lenin. Addressing a crowd in Red Square, Moscow, two years after the Revolution.

principally in Germany and England, acting much of the time as editor of the Bolshevik journal *Iskra* (*The Spark*). Like most of the Russian revolutionists, he wrote under a pseudonym, signing his articles N. Lenin.[5] When the revolution broke out in March 1917, he was living in Switzerland. With the aid of the Germans he made his way back to Russia and immediately assumed leadership of the Bolshevik movement. Lenin had all of the qualities necessary for success as a revolutionary figure. He was an able politician and an exceedingly effective orator. Absolutely convinced of the righteousness of his cause, he could strike down his opponents with the zeal and savagery of a Robespierre. On the other hand, he cared nothing for the fleshpots of wealth or of personal glory. He lived in two rooms in the Kremlin and dressed little better than an ordinary workman. His expensive marble mausoleum in Moscow, where his body has been kept in a glass case since his death in 1924, stands out in bold contrast to the simplicity of his life.

The most prominent of Lenin's lieutenants was the brilliant but erratic Leon Trotsky. Originally named Lev Bronstein, he was born in 1879 of middle-class Jewish parents in Ukrainia. He seems to have been the stormy petrel of revolutionary politics during most of his life. Before the revolution he refused to identify himself with any particular faction, preferring to remain an independent Marxist. Though he collaborated with Lenin in editing *The Spark*, he did not become a Bolshevik until 1917. For his part in the revolutionary movement of 1905 he was exiled to Siberia; but he escaped, and then for some years led a roving existence in various European capitals.

Leon Trotsky

[5] The "N." did not stand for anything in particular, though many people have assumed that it was a symbol for Nikolai.

He was expelled from Paris in 1916 for pacifist activity and took refuge in the United States. Upon learning of the overthrow of the Tsar, he attempted to return to Russia. Captured by British agents at Halifax, he was eventually released upon the plea of Kerensky. He arrived in Russia in April and immediately began plotting for the overthrow of the provisional government and later of Kerensky himself. He became Minister of Foreign Affairs in the government headed by Lenin and subsequently Commissar for War.

No sooner had the Bolsheviks come to power than they proceeded to effect some drastic alterations in the political and economic system. They proclaimed their own rule to be the dictatorship of the proletariat, and when elections for a constituent assembly returned a majority of opposition delegates, they dissolved the assembly by force. On November 8 Lenin decreed nationalization of the land and gave the peasants the exclusive right to use it. On November 29 control of the factories was transferred to the workers, and a month later it was announced that all except the smallest industrial establishments would be taken over by the government. Banks also were nationalized soon after the Bolshevik victory. But the problem of greatest urgency was termination of the war. After vain attempts to induce the Allies to consent to a peace without annexations or indemnities, Trotsky signed an armistice with Germany on December 15. This was followed by the peace of Brest-Litovsk in March 1918, which officially ended the war so far as Russia was concerned.

Revolutionary political and economic changes

Scarcely had the Bolsheviks concluded the war with the Central Powers than they were confronted with a desperate civil war at home. Landlords and capitalists did not take kindly to the loss of their property. Besides, the Allies were determined to punish Russia and accordingly sent troops into the country to support the armies of reactionary generals. The result was a prolonged and bloody combat between the Reds, or Bolsheviks, on the one side, and the Whites, or reactionaries, and their foreign allies on the other. Both sides were guilty of horrible brutality. The Whites massacred the inhabitants of captured villages—women and children as well as men. The Reds, in order to exterminate spies and counterrevolutionists, instituted a reign of terror. An extraordinary commission known as the Cheka was set up to arrest and punish suspected persons without a trial. No one knows the exact number of its victims, but authorities agree that there were thousands. At times the Cheka resorted to mass executions, as was done in August 1918, after a Social Revolutionary had attempted to assassinate Lenin. But at length the terror abated. By the end of 1920 the civil war was practically over. The Bolsheviks had driven nearly all of the foreign soldiers from the country and had forced the reactionary generals to abandon the struggle.

The civil war between Whites and Reds

The civil war was accompanied by an appalling economic breakdown. In 1920 the total industrial production was only 13 per cent of what it had been in 1913. To make up for the shortage of goods the government abolished the payment of wages and distributed supplies among the workers in the cities in proportion to their absolute need. All private trade was prohibited, and everything produced by the peasants above what they required to keep from starving was requisitioned by the state. This system was not pure communism, as is often alleged, but was mainly an expedient to crush the bourgeoisie and to obtain as much food as possible for the army in the field. It was soon abandoned after the war had ended. In 1921 it was superseded by the New Economic Policy (NEP), which Lenin described as "one step backward in order to take two steps forward." The NEP authorized private manufacturing and private trade on a small scale, reintroduced the payment of wages, and permitted the peasants to sell their grain in the open market. The new policy continued in force until 1929 when the first of the famous Five-Year Plans was adopted. By 1939 two of these plans had been completed and a third was under way. Their purposes were mainly to complete the process of socialization, to make Russia a great industrial country, and to further the evolution of a classless, communist society.

In the meantime, the death of Lenin in January 1924 precipitated a titanic struggle between two of his lieutenants to inherit his mantle of power. Outside of Russia it was generally assumed that Trotsky would be the man to succeed the fallen leader. But soon it was revealed that the fiery commander of the Red Army had a formidable rival in the shaggy and mysterious Joseph Stalin (1879–1953). The son of a peasant shoemaker in the province of Georgia, Stalin received part of his education in a theological seminary. But he was expelled at the age of seventeen for "lack of religious vocation" and thereafter dedicated his career to revolutionary activity. In 1917 he became Secretary-General of the Communist party, a position through which he was able to build up a party machine. The battle between Stalin and Trotsky was not simply a struggle for personal power; fundamental issues of political policy were also involved. Trotsky maintained that socialism in Russia could never be entirely successful until capitalism was overthrown in surrounding countries. Therefore he insisted upon a continuous crusade for world revolution. Stalin was willing to abandon the program of world revolution, for the time being, in order to concentrate on building socialism in Russia itself. His strategy for the immediate future was essentially nationalist. The outcome of the duel was a complete triumph for Stalin. In 1927 Trotsky was expelled from the Communist party, and two years later he was driven from the country. In 1940 he was murdered in Mexico City by Stalinist agents. It is interesting to note that Lenin did not hold either of the two rivals in lofty esteem. In a "testament" written shortly before his death, he criticized Trotsky for "far-reaching self-confidence" and for being too much preoccupied with administrative detail. But he dealt far less gently with Stalin, condemning him as "too rough" and "capricious" and urging that the comrades "find a way" to remove him from his position at the head of the party.[6]

THE COMMUNIST
REGIME IN
RUSSIA

About 1934 the Bolshevik regime entered a new and in some ways more conservative phase, which should perhaps be considered as the third stage of the Russian revolution. It was characterized by a number of significant developments. First, there was the revival of such capitalist devices as the payment of interest on savings accounts and the issuance of bonds to which premiums were attached. Second, the disparity of wage payments was greatly increased. Some menial workers received as little as 100 rubles a month, while skilled employees in the heavy industries and certain administrative officials were permitted to enjoy monthly salaries as high as 6000 rubles.[7] No longer were members of the Communist party limited to incomes of $1500 per year as was the case when Lenin was in power. Third, the laws of marriage and divorce were made more stringent, and women were urged to bear more children. Fourth, there was a revival of militarism, of nationalism, and of an interest in playing the game of power politics. The army was more than doubled in size

The third stage
of the Russian
revolution

[6] The Testament of Lenin is contained in Leon Trotsky, *The Real Situation in Russia*, Supplement I. The authenticity of the document was implicitly admitted by Stalin in a session of the party Central Committee in October 1927. W. H. Chamberlin, *Soviet Russia: a Living Record and a History*, p. 93n. In an effort to discredit Stalin, Nikita S. Khrushchev distributed the full text of this Testament at the Twentieth Party Conference in February 1956.
[7] The ruble was officially worth about 25 cents.

Trotsky. Soviet War Minister in full regalia, arriving in Petrograd after a tour of various areas.

and was reorganized in accordance with the Western model. Patriotism, which the older strict Marxists despised as a form of capitalist propaganda, was exalted into a Soviet virtue. In like manner, there was a growing tendency to discard the internationalism of Marx, to strive to make Russia self-sufficient, and to play an active part in old-fashioned diplomacy. With Nazism firmly established in Germany, the rulers of the Kremlin seemed to have decided that Russia needed friends. Along with their efforts to build up a great army and to make their own country self-sufficient, they adopted a policy of co-operation with the Western powers. In 1934 they entered the League of Nations, and in 1935 they exchanged ratifications of a military alliance with France. It is apparent, however, that the real purpose of these moves was to drive a wedge between Germany on the one side and Britain and France on the other. At any rate, when the Soviet leaders became suspicious in 1938–1939 that Britain and France were encouraging Hitler to expand eastward, they did not hesitate to conclude a nonaggression pact with the Nazi government.[8]

The original philosophy of Bolshevism, now more popularly known as communism, was developed primarily by Lenin. It was not supposed to be a new body of thought but a strict interpretation of the gospel of Marx. Nevertheless, from the beginning there were various departures from the master's teachings. Whereas Marx had assumed that a capitalist stage must prepare the way for socialism, Lenin denied that this was necessary and insisted that Russia could leap directly from a feudal to a socialist economy. In the second place, Lenin emphasized the revolutionary character of socialism much more than did its original founder. Marx did believe that in most cases revolution would be necessary, but he was inclined to deplore the fact rather than to welcome it. Furthermore, in his Amsterdam speech of 1872 he had stated that "there are certain countries such as England and the United States in which the workers may hope to secure their ends by peaceful means." Last of all, Bolshevism differed from Marxism in its conception of proletarian rule. There is nothing to indicate that Marx ever envisaged a totalitarian workers' state as arbitrary and oppressive in its methods of governing as fascism. True, he did speak of the "dictatorship of the proletariat"; but he meant by this a dictatorship of the whole working class over the remnants of the bourgeoisie. Within the ranks of this class, democratic forms would prevail. Lenin, however, set up the ideal of the dictatorship of an *élite*, a select minority, wielding supremacy not only over the bourgeoisie but over the bulk of the proletarians themselves. In Russia this *élite* is the Communist party, whose membership has varied from 1,500,000 to 12,000,000.

In 1936, eighteen years after coming to power, the rulers of Communist Russia drafted a new constitution for the entire country to

[8] See p. 620.

replace earlier ones that had proved inadequate. It was adopted by popular vote and went into effect January 1, 1938. The official name retained for the state was the Union of Soviet Socialist Republics. It provided for a union of eleven (later fifteen) republics, each supposedly autonomous and free to secede if it chose. The constitution established universal suffrage for all citizens eighteen years of age and over. They were to vote not only for the local soviets but for members of a national parliament. The highest organ of state power was declared to be the Supreme Soviet of the U.S.S.R., composed of two chambers—the Soviet of the Union and the Soviet of Nationalities. The former was to have 600 members elected by the people for four-year terms. The Soviet of Nationalities was to consist of 400 members chosen for similar terms by the governments of the several republics. Both chambers were given equal legislative powers. To represent it between sessions, the Supreme Soviet was to elect a committee of thirty-seven members known as the Presidium. This body also was empowered to issue decrees, to declare war, and to annul the acts of administrative officials which did not conform to law. The highest executive and administrative agency was to be the Council of Ministers, likewise elected by the Supreme Soviet. Each Minister was to be head of a department, such as War, Foreign Affairs, Railways, Heavy Industry, Light Industry, and so forth.[9] Finally, the constitution of 1936 contained a bill of rights. Citizens were guaranteed the right to employment, the right to leisure, the right to maintenance in case of old age or disability, and even the traditional privileges of freedom of speech, of the press, of assemblage, and of religion.

The constitution of 1936 was, and still is, more of a sham than a reality. Its provisions for universal suffrage, for the secret ballot, and for a bill of rights looked good on paper but had little substance. The explanation lies in the fact that the real power in the Soviet Union rests with the Communist party, the only party allowed to exist. The organs of the government are little more than the vocal mechanisms through which the party expresses its will. It is noteworthy that the very period in which the constitution was being put into effect witnessed an eruption of mass arrests and executions of persons alleged to be "Trotskyists, spies, and wreckers." Nearly all the old war-horses who had worked with Lenin to make the revolution a success, with the exception of Stalin, fell victims in the frenzied purges. Altogether at least fifty prominent theoreticians and party leaders were put to death, in most cases with little evidence except the accused's own confessions. In addition, about 9,000,000 other persons were arrested and imprisoned or sent to Siberia.

Perhaps enough has been said already to indicate that the Soviet

---

[9] Before 1946 the Ministers were called Commissars.

Economic and
social results of
the Soviet
upheaval

upheaval was not merely political in character but had profound economic and social results. By 1939 private manufacturing and private trade had been almost entirely abolished. Factories, mines, railroads, and public utilities were exclusively owned by the state. Stores were either government enterprises or producers' and consumers' cooperatives. Agriculture also had been almost completely socialized. State farms included about 10 per cent of the land; collective farms, organized on a cooperative basis, occupied nearly all of the remainder. No less revolutionary were the developments in the social sphere. Religion as a factor in the lives of the people declined to a place of small importance. To be sure, Christianity was still tolerated; but churches were reduced in number, and were not permitted to engage in any charitable or educational activities. Furthermore, members of the Communist party were required to be atheists. Communism not only renounces all belief in the supernatural but attempts to cultivate a new ethics. The primary aim is to create a *positive* morality, based upon duty to society, in place of the old negative morality, founded upon a notion of personal sin. The cardinal virtues in this positive morality are industry, respect for public property, willingness to sacrifice individual interests for the good of society, and loyalty to the Soviet fatherland and to the socialist ideal at all times. Nevertheless, a strong element of bourgeois morality persists. It is exemplified by the emphasis upon diligence as a cardinal virtue and by the ascetic attitude toward drinking, sexual pleasure, and other frivolities.

Accomplishments
of the Bolshevik
regime

By the outbreak of World War II the Soviet regime had undeniable accomplishments to its credit. Among the principal ones may be mentioned the following: (1) the reduction of illiteracy from a proportion of at least 50 per cent to less than 20 per cent; (2) a notable expansion of industrialization; (3) the establishment of a planned economy, which at least operated successfully enough to prevent unemployment; (4) the opening of educational and cultural opportunities to larger numbers of the common people; and (5) the establishment of a system of government assistance for working mothers and their infants and free medical care and hospitalization for most of the citizens.

The price of
revolution

But these accomplishments were purchased at a very high price. The program of socialization and industrialization was pushed at so dizzy a pace that the good of individual citizens was almost overlooked. It must not be forgotten either that the Soviet regime fastened upon Russia a tyranny just as extreme as that of the Tsar. Indeed, the number of its victims sentenced to slave-labor camps probably exceeded the number consigned by the Tsars to exile in Siberia. And it is significant that nearly all the old Bolsheviks who took a leading part in the uprising of November 1917, were subsequently shot or driven into exile.

By 1939 only three of the chief powers—Great Britain, France, and the United States—remained in the list of democratic countries. Among the lesser states democracy survived in Switzerland, the Netherlands, Belgium, the Scandinavian countries, a few republics of Latin America, and the self-governing dominions of the British Commonwealth. Nearly all of the rest of the world had succumbed to despotism of one form or another. Italy, Germany, and Spain were fascist; Russia was communist; Hungary was dominated by a landowning oligarchy; Poland, Turkey, China, and Japan were essentially military dictatorships. For the most part, this cleavage represented a division between the so-called Have and Have-not nations—the former including the democracies, and the latter the dictatorships. Great Britain, France, and the United States were sated countries, comparatively rich in territorial empire and in mineral resources. Italy, Germany, and Japan were "hungry nations," coveting more lands in the belief that greater amounts of soil and other natural resources would solve their economic problems. They were disgruntled also with their power status, considering it inferior to that of other nations with large empires. Evidence is far from convincing that the citizens of the so-called Have-not countries were really worse off than the inhabitants of states with more extensive territory. But politicians greedy for power used this alleged inequality for propaganda purposes. They overlooked the fact that standards of living bear little relation to extent of territory. The people of Sweden and Switzerland were just as prosperous as the citizens of France or Great Britain notwithstanding their total lack of imperial possessions.

It will be impossible to recount the history of all the democracies between the two wars or even to describe minutely internal developments in any one of them. In general, events in the principal states ran closely parallel. Preeminent among them was a struggle between wealthy bankers and industrial monopolists, on the one side, and organized labor and the lower middle class, on the other. In some countries members of the old order were able to hold their supremacy until after the onslaught of the Great Depression in 1929. In the United States and France, for example, there was little difference between the type of rule in the 1920's and that which had prevailed before the war. Great Britain, however, experienced the triumph of a Labour government as early as 1924. Its tenure was brief and its accomplishments few, but two years later the strength of the working class was sufficient to tie the whole national economy in knots by a general strike, which lasted for nine days. During most of the 1920's France was firmly under the thumb of such arch-conservatives as Georges Clemenceau and Raymond Poincaré. The years 1924–

Division of the
world into de-
mocracies and
dictatorships

The struggle of
classes in Britain,
France, and the
U.S.A.

Stock Market Crash, October 24, 1929. Crowds milling outside the New York Stock Exchange on the day of the big crash.

1926, though, witnessed a brief tenure of power by the Radical Socialists under the leadership of Édouard Herriot; better than any other party they represented the interests of small business and the lower middle class. The United States was undoubtedly the most impregnable fortress of conservative power among the democracies. The Presidents elected during the 1920's—Warren G. Harding, Calvin Coolidge, and Herbert Hoover—upheld a social philosophy formulated by the barons of big business in the nineteenth century, and the Supreme Court used its power of judicial review to nullify progressive legislation enacted by state governments and occasionally by Congress.

The depression of 1929

The depression that began in 1929 was one of the most shattering experiences in the economic history of the modern world. It was not limited to any one country, nor can the policies of any one nation be blamed for its origin. Nevertheless, the role of the United States in bringing it on cannot be discounted. At the end of World War I America was the richest nation in the world. While the states of Europe had been mauling each other on the battlefield, Americans had been capturing their markets, penetrating their fields of investment, and expanding their own industry and agriculture enormously. Yet much of the prosperity stimulated by these practices rested upon foundations of sand. It had been fostered in the beginning by the high prices of the war era. Farmers in the mid-West had plunged head over heels into debt to buy land in the arid regions of western Nebraska, eastern Colorado, and western Oklahoma, in the expectation that wheat would always be selling for more than $2.00 a bushel. When the price dropped to 93 cents in 1923, they found themselves stuck with their mortgages. But farmers were not the only ones who had been tempted into overexpansion by fantastic prices; many more coal mines and factories were opened than were necessary to supply the normal demand. A second weakness in American prosperity was the fact that it was based quite largely upon foreign loans. By 1930 American private loans in foreign countries amounted to about $16,000,000,000. Many of these were founded upon inadequate security or mere promises to pay. As a consequence, defaults were widespread. Nor should it be forgotten that United States tariff policy made it difficult for foreign nations to sell their products in American markets and thus to acquire the resources with which to pay their debts. Even as late as 1930 President Hoover, against the advice of more than 1000 economists, signed the Hawley-Smoot bill, which raised the duties on many commodities to the highest levels in the nation's history. Since this was followed by retaliatory tariffs elsewhere, the effect was virtually to strangle international trade.

The results of the depression took varied forms in different countries. In 1931 Great Britain abandoned the gold standard, and the government of the United States followed suit in 1933. This action was the forerunner of a broad program of currency management, which became an important element in a general policy of economic nationalism. By way of illustration, President Franklin D. Roosevelt informed the London Economic Conference of 1933 that "the sound internal economic system of a nation is a greater factor in its well-being than the price of its currency in changing terms of the currencies of other nations." As early as 1932 Great Britain abandoned completely her time-honored policy of free trade. Protective tariffs were raised in some instances as high as 100 per cent. Of the European democracies France went farthest in the direction of a controlled economy, though little change occurred until 1936. In that year the nation came under the rule of the so-called Popular Front, headed by Leon Blum, and composed of Radical Socialists, Socialists, and Communists. The Popular Front nationalized the munitions industry and reorganized the Bank of France so as to deprive the 200 largest stockholders of their monopolistic control over credit. In addition, it decreed a 40-hour week for all urban workers and initiated a program of public works. For the benefit of the farmers it established a Wheat Office to fix the price and regulate the distribution of grain.

Results of the depression

The most spectacular changes in policy after the depression occurred, not in Europe, but in the United States. The explanation was twofold. The United States had clung longer to the economic philosophy of the nineteenth century. Prior to the depression the business classes had adhered firmly to the dogma of freedom of contract and insisted upon their right to form monopolies and to use the

The severity of the depression in the United States

government as their agent in frustrating the demands of both workers and consumers. The depression in the United States was also more severe than in the European democracies. Industrial production shrank by about two-thirds. The structure of agricultural prices and of common stocks collapsed. Thousands of banks were forced to close their doors. Unemployment rose to 15,000,000, or to approximately one-third of the total labor force. Had it not been for widespread feelings of hopelessness and despair, revolution might well have swept the country. Rescue from disaster was finally provided by a program of reform and reconstruction known as the New Deal. The chief architect and motivator of this program was Franklin D. Roosevelt, who succeeded Herbert Hoover in the Presidency on March 4, 1933.

Results of the Roosevelt program

Few historians would deny that the New Deal was one of the most significant events in the history of modern nations. Since its results were mainly in the direction of preserving rather than destroying capitalism, it can scarcely be called a revolution. Nevertheless, it probably did more for the farmer and the wage earner than any of the so-called revolutions in American history. Under the New Deal the incomes of these classes increased nearly 100 per cent compared with their level during the depth of the depression. Perhaps more important, these classes gained a degree of economic security they had never known before. On the other hand, a number of crucial problems remained unsolved. The most serious was unemployment. In 1939, after six years of the New Deal, the United States still had more than 9,000,000 jobless workers—a figure which exceeded the combined unemployment of the rest of the world. Ironically, it seemed that only the outbreak of a new world war, with its wholesale destruction of wealth and consumption of manpower, could provide the full recovery and full employment that the New Deal had failed to assure.

SELECTED READINGS

· *Items so designated are available in paperbound editions.*

FASCIST ITALY

Borgese, G. A., *Goliath: The March of Fascism*, New York, 1927.
Ebenstein, William, *Fascist Italy*, New York, 1939.
Megaro, Gaudens, *Mussolini in the Making*, New York, 1939.
Schneider, H. W., *Making the Fascist State*, New York, 1928. A penetrating analysis.

NAZI GERMANY

· Bullock, A. L. C., *Hitler: A Study in Tyranny*, London, 1952 (Bantam). A good biography.

Carr, E. H., *German-Soviet Relations Between the Two World Wars, 1919–1939*, Baltimore, 1951.

Clark, R. T., *The Fall of the German Republic*, New York, 1935.

de Wilde, J. C., *Building the Third Reich*, New York, 1939.

Ebenstein, William, *The Nazi State*, New York, 1943. A perceptive analysis.

· Halperin, S. W., *Germany Tried Democracy, 1918–1933*, New York, 1946 (Norton Library). A dependable history of the Weimar Republic.

Heiden, Konrad, *Der Fuehrer*, New York, 1944. The best biography of Hitler.

Neumann, Franz, *Behemoth, The Structure and Practice of National Socialism*, New York, 1942.

Roberts, S. H., *The House That Hitler Built*, New York, 1938. An illuminating survey.

Rothfels, H., *The German Opposition to Hitler*, Hinsdale, Ill., 1948.

Scheele, Godfrey, *The Weimar Republic: Overture to the Third Reich*, London, 1946.

Schuman, F. L., *The Nazi Dictatorship; A Study in Social Pathology*, New York, 1935.

Schweitzer, Arthur, *Big Business in the Third Reich*, Bloomington, Ind., 1964. Contends that big business held Nazi regime in check in early days.

· Shirer, W. L., *The Rise and Fall of the Third Reich*, New York, 1960 (Crest). A lengthy, popular account, but it reflects some bias against everything German.

SOVIET RUSSIA

Beloff, Max, *The Foreign Policy of Soviet Russia*, New York, 1952. A scholarly study covering the years 1929–1941.

· Brinton, Crane, *The Anatomy of Revolution*, New York, 1952 (Vintage, rev. ed.). Includes a suggestive comparison of the Russian Revolution with earlier revolutions in Western Europe.

Chamberlin, W. H., *Soviet Russia: A Living Record and a History*, Boston, 1951.

Citrine, Sir Walter, *I Search for Truth in Russia*, New York, 1937.

Crankshaw, Edward, *Cracks in the Kremlin Wall*, New York, 1951.

· Curtiss, J. S., *The Russian Revolution of 1917* (Anvil).

Dallin, D. J., *Soviet Russia's Foreign Policy, 1939–1942*, New Haven, 1942.

——, *Soviet Russia and the Far East*, New Haven, 1948.

· Daniels, R. V., *The Nature of Communism*, New York, 1962 (Vintage). An objective study.

· ——, *Russia*, Englewood Cliffs, N. J., 1964 (Spectrum). Emphasizes period of the U.S.S.R.

· Deutscher, Isaac, *Stalin; A Political Biography*, London, 1949 (Vintage).

Fainsod, Merle, *How Russia Is Ruled*, Cambridge, Mass., 1953. The best governmental study.

Florinsky, M. T., *Toward an Understanding of the U.S.S.R.*, New York, 1939.

· Hunt, R. N. Carew, *The Theory and Practice of Communism*, New York, 1951 (Penguin). A splendid introductory study.

· Maynard, Sir John, *Russia in Flux*, New York, 1948 (Collier). A discussion of continuing influences in Russian history.

· Pares, Sir Bernard, *A History of Russia*, New York, 1953 (Vintage). One of the best short histories.

Randall, F. B., *Stalin's Russia*, New York, 1965.

Seton-Watson, Hugh, *From Lenin to Malenkov*, New York, 1953.

· Shub, David, *Lenin*, New York, 1948 (Mentor, abr.). Perhaps the best biography.

Taracouzio, T. A., *War and Peace in Soviet Diplomacy*, New York, 1940.

· Von Laue, T. W., *Why Lenin? Why Stalin? A Reappraisal of the Russian Revolution, 1900–1930*, Philadelphia, 1964 (Preceptor).

· Wolfe, B. D., *Three Who Made a Revolution*, New York, 1948 (Beacon). A penetrating study of Lenin, Trotsky, and Stalin.

THE DEMOCRACIES

· Allen, F. L., *Only Yesterday*, New York, 1931 (Bantam). A colorful account of the 1920's.

Beard, C. A., and M. R., *America in Midpassage*, New York, 1939.

Brand, C. F., *The British Labour Party: A Short History*, Stanford, 1964.

Brinton, Crane, *The United States and Britain*, Cambridge, Mass., 1945.

Brogan, D. W., *France Under the Third Republic*, New York, 1940.

· Burns, J. M., *Roosevelt: The Lion and the Fox*, New York, 1956 (Harvest). A thoughtful interpretation.

· Feis, Herbert, *The Diplomacy of the Dollar, 1919–1932*, Baltimore, 1950 (Norton Library).

Friedel, Frank, *Franklin D. Roosevelt: The Triumph*, Boston, 1956. A stimulating and scholarly account.

Fusfield, D. R., *The Economic Thought of Franklin D. Roosevelt and the Origins of the New Deal*, New York, 1956.

· Graves, Robert and Hodge, Alan, *The Long Week-end: A Social History of Great Britain, 1918–1939*, London, 1940 (Norton Library).

Guérard, Albert, *France, a Short History*, New York, 1946.

Heaton, Herbert, *The British Way to Recovery*, Minneapolis, 1934.

Hill, Helen D., *The Spirit of Modern France*, New York, 1934.

· Hofstadter, Richard, *The American Political Tradition: and the Men Who Made It*, New York, 1948 (Vintage).

· Keller, Morton, *The New Deal: What Was It?* New York, 1963 (American Problem Studies).

Mitchell, Broadus, *Depression Decade; from New Era through New Deal, 1929 to 1941*, New York, 1947.

Mowat, C. L., *Britain between the Wars, 1918–1940*, Chicago, 1955.

Nevins, Allan, *The United States in a Chaotic World*, New Haven, 1950.

Schlesinger, Jr., A. M., *The Age of Roosevelt: The Crisis of the Old Order, 1919–1933*, Boston, 1957.

Siegfried, André, *France; a Study in Nationality*, New Haven, 1930.

· Spitz, David, *Patterns of Anti-Democratic Thought*, New York, 1949 (Free Press).

Wecter, Dixon, *The Age of the Great Depression, 1929–1941*, New York, 1948.

SOURCE MATERIALS

Columbia University, *Introduction to Contemporary Civilization in the West*, Vol. II, pp. 1062–66, 1077–86, Soviet Constitution of 1936 and Weimar Constitution.

· Hitler, Adolf, *Mein Kampf*, especially Vol. I, Chs. II, IV, XI; Vol. II, Chs. II, XIII, XIV, New York, 1962 (Sentry).

· Lenin, Vladimir, *The State and Revolution* (International Publishers).

Rocco, Alfredo, *The Political Doctrine of Fascism*.

Roosevelt, F. D., *On Our Way*.

———, *Public Papers*.

Stalin, Joseph, *Leninism*, 2 vols.

———, *Problems of Leninism*.

Trotsky, Leon, *History of the Russian Revolution*, Ann Arbor, 1957, 3 vols.

CHAPTER 16

The Commonwealth of Nations

We have, then, if I may sum up, two duties in the West, first to
protect our institutions within the city walls from deterioration
and decay, and then to defend the walls themselves. There is, however, a third and even more important duty: to bring about a
state of affairs in the world where no one will wish to attack us
at all—or we, them; where eventually walls themselves will be as
much of an anachronism as trenches, barbed wire, and forts on
the United States-Canadian border.
—Lester B. Pearson, *Where Do We Go From Here?*

One of the most significant developments in the history of democracy
in the modern world has been the evolution of the Commonwealth
of Nations. Originally called the British Commonwealth of Nations,
it now includes a number of states which repudiate any suggestion of
allegiance to Britain. Officially, its twenty-nine members comprise
two distinct classes. Thirteen of them recognize the British monarch,
represented by a governor-general, as their head of state. They are
the United Kingdom, Australia, Canada, New Zealand, Barbados,
Ceylon, Gambia, Guyana, Jamaica, Malta, Sierra Leone, Antigua,
and Trinidad and Tobago. Sixteen other members have their own
chiefs of state and recognize no allegiance to the British Crown. They
are India, Pakistan, Botswana, Cyprus, Ghana, Kenya, Lesotho,
Malawi, Malaysia, Mauritius, Nigeria, Singapore, South Yemen,
Tanzania, Uganda, and Zambia. Because of the fact that members
may secede and new states may join, the Commonwealth is an
evolving organization. Ireland withdrew in 1949 and South Africa
in 1961. The history of the United Kingdom and of the principal
African members is discussed elsewhere. The purpose of this chapter is to give an account of the two chief Asian republics and of

The Common-
wealth defined

487

the self-governing dominions settled primarily by emigrants from Britain.[1]

The Commonwealth of Nations as an association of independent or virtually independent states has a history of about seven decades. At an Imperial Conference in 1887, attended by prime ministers of the principal British possessions, suggestions were made that the colonies farthest advanced ought to have the right to participate in the government of the Empire. The idea was revived at subsequent Imperial Conferences, in 1897, in 1902, and in 1907. It was not, however, until World War I that the proposal gave much promise of becoming a reality. The free and liberal assistance given to the Mother Country by the dominions in that struggle fortified their claims not only to a direct voice in imperial affairs but to a more definite recognition of their own independence. The Imperial Conference of 1921 agreed that the events of the war had clearly established the right of the self-governing dominions to be considered co-equals with the Mother Country in foreign affairs. The Conference of 1926 adopted a report prepared by Arthur James Balfour, former Prime Minister of Great Britain. The report described the self-governing areas under the British flag (including the United Kingdom) as "autonomous communities within the British Empire, equal in status, in no way subordinate one to another in any aspect of their domestic or external affairs, though united by a common allegiance to the crown, and freely associated as members of the British Commonwealth of Nations." In 1931 the substance of the Balfour Report was enacted by Parliament in a memorable law known as the Statute of Westminster.

Since the enactment of the Statute of Westminster the several states of the Commonwealth of Nations have functioned as practically independent republics. No longer may any law passed by a dominion parliament be disallowed by the Parliament in London or vetoed by the British Cabinet, and no law of the British Parliament may be applied to any dominion unless its government specifically requests that this be done. The prime minister of each dominion has an equal right with the Prime Minister of Britain to "advise" the king directly. The king himself serves as a mere symbol of the unity of the Commonwealth. Although he is represented in each dominion (but not in the Republics) by a governor-general, the latter has no real authority. His primary function is to receive the resignation of an outgoing prime minister and to designate the leader of the opposition party as his successor. This involves no more freedom of choice than is exercised by the monarch himself

[1] The Commonwealth of Nations must be distinguished clearly from the British Empire. The latter consists of two parts: the independent empire and the dependent empire. The independent empire includes those members of the Commonwealth of Nations which still render some tenuous allegiance to Great Britain. The dependent empire comprises more than thirty colonies scattered all over the globe and ruled directly from London.

when the head of the British Cabinet loses the support of the majority in the House of Commons and gives way to the leader of His (Her) Majesty's Loyal Opposition.

The Commonwealth is no longer the boon to Great Britain that it formerly was. Even those members that acknowledge allegiance to the British monarch have shown an increasing spirit of economic independence and indifference to the welfare of the United Kingdom. It has been said that most of the Old-World members are about as beneficial to the former Mother Country as "poor relations on pay day." Though they continue to look for generous contributions of British aid, they show little disposition to confer any benefits in return. Ghana, for example, grants no preference to British goods. While Australian industrial products enter New Zealand duty free, British goods are subject to tariffs. Not only do Air India and Pakistan International Airways compete with BOAC, but they equip their fleets with Boeings and DC-8's purchased from the United States. In 1965 British auto shipments to Australia declined by 38 per cent. During the same year Britain had a total trade deficit with the Commonwealth nations of over 1 billion dollars. Meanwhile, because of squabbles within several of the Commonwealth countries, or threats from neighboring states, Britain must maintain a costly military force that places a heavy burden on her domestic economy.

Deficiencies of the Commonwealth

1. THE DOMINION OF CANADA

The recorded history of Canada dates from 1608 when Samuel Champlain, a French naval officer with an interest in the fur trade, founded a settlement at Quebec. For thirty years thereafter he continued his activities in the St. Lawrence valley, staking claims for the French king as far west as Lake Huron. Later in the seventeenth century the French government granted monopolies to trading companies to colonize and develop "New France." Although the companies ultimately failed, they did establish a few forts and trading posts and brought over a few thousand of their countrymen as permanent settlers. Finally, Jesuit missionaries contributed their part toward opening up the country and enlarging knowledge of its resources and attractions. By the middle of the eighteenth century the population of Canada included about 60,000 Frenchmen.

The founding of Canada

France lost Canada to Great Britain in the French and Indian War. However, for some years thereafter the British continued to assume that their newly acquired possession would remain French. When the British Parliament passed the Quebec Act in 1774 to correct certain defects in the organization of the Empire, Canada was not given a representative assembly, since it was taken for granted that the people could neither understand nor be loyal to

Troubles between French and British Canada

489

British institutions. But after the American War for Independence so many Loyalist refugees from the United States, together with immigrants from Great Britain, settled in Ontario that William Pitt thought it advisable to have Parliament enact a law in 1791 separating Upper Canada (Ontario), which was almost entirely British, from Lower Canada (Quebec), which was overwhelmingly French, and providing for an elective assembly in each of the two provinces. The scheme ended in failure. The French and British distrusted each other, and conflicts soon arose between the elective assemblies and the royal governors sent out from London. In 1837 the antagonism flared into an open rebellion. Although quickly suppressed, it called attention to Canada's grievances and impressed upon the British government the necessity of doing something about them. The result was the appointment of a High Commissioner, Lord Durham, with authority to investigate conditions and to institute reforms. When he proceeded to act in too arbitrary a fashion, the government in London withdrew its support and revoked some of his decrees. Durham resigned in anger and returned to England, but subsequently published a report which was destined to become famous in the history of dominion government.

The beginning
of responsible
government

The Durham Report enunciated two principles, which may be regarded as the cornerstone of the dominion system. First, its author declared that colonies already possessing representative institutions should be granted "responsible government." This meant that they should be permitted to manage their local affairs through cabinets or ministries responsible to their own legislatures. In the second place, Lord Durham urged the principle that similar colonies in the same geographic area should be federated into one large unit. Applying this to Canada, he pleaded for the unification of the British and French portions into a single dominion. In accordance with this recommendation Upper and Lower Canada were presently united. In 1847 Lord Durham's son-in-law, Lord Elgin, became governor of Canada and put into effect the principle of choosing his cabinet from the party which controlled a majority of seats in the assembly. He allowed it to be inferred that the cabinet would remain in office only so long as it received the support of the majority party. In addition he signed bills sponsored by the cabinet, despite the fact that they conflicted with the interests of the Mother Country. By these means he conferred upon Canada for all practical purposes a system of responsible government similar to that of Great Britain.

But the dominion government as we now know it dates only from 1867. In that year the hitherto separate colonies of New Brunswick and Nova Scotia united with Quebec and Ontario to form a confederation under the name of the Dominion of Canada. A frame of government was provided for them by the British

North America Act passed by the London Parliament in the same

year. This Act embodied a constitution which the Canadians themselves had adopted in 1864. It established a federal system with a
division of powers between the central government and the governments of the provinces. All powers not delegated to the governments of the provinces were declared to be reserved to the central
government. This departure from the federal pattern in the United
States was inspired in part by the fact that the claims of the seced-
ing Southern states to full sovereignty had helped to bring on the
American War between the States.

The British North America Act confirmed the principle of responsible government. A Governor-General, appointed technically
by the king, but actually by the British Cabinet, was made the
nominal head of the Dominion. The real power over local affairs
was placed in the hands of a Dominion cabinet, nominally appointed by the Governor-General but actually responsible to the
lower house of the legislature for its official acts and its tenure of
office. Legislative power was vested in a Parliament of two houses,
a Senate appointed by the Governor-General for life, and a House
of Commons elected by the people. Except for the fact that cabinet
responsibility was to be enforced by the House of Commons exclusively and that money bills must originate therein, both houses
were given equal powers. In practice, however, the Senate has retired into a kind of dignified obsolescence, performing no functions
except those of an unambitious revising chamber. The Canadian
constitution also provided for responsible government in the provinces. The nominal head of each province is a Lieutenant-Governor
appointed by the Dominion cabinet. The effective authority is exercised by a cabinet responsible to the provincial legislature. Except
in Quebec the legislative bodies in the provinces have only one
house.

Since 1867 the growth of Canada has roughly paralleled that of
the United States. When the British North America Act was
passed, Canada had a population of 3½ million. By 1966 it had
grown to 20 million. During the same period the population of the
United States increased from 38 million to 196 million. The growth
in area of the Dominion of Canada was equally phenomenal. In 1869
the province of Manitoba was carved out of territory purchased
from the Hudson's Bay Company. In 1871–1873 British Columbia
and Prince Edward Island were added to the Dominion. By 1905
the completion of the Canadian Pacific Railway made possible the
creation of two new prairie provinces, Alberta and Saskatchewan.
But the growth of Canada cannot be measured in terms of area and
population alone. The latter half of the nineteenth century and the
early years of the twentieth witnessed the establishment of a sound
banking and currency system, a civil service, and a protective tariff
for the benefit of Canadian industry. Marked progress occurred
also in the exploitation of mineral and forest resources. Canada

became the chief supplier of nickel, asbestos, cobalt, and wood pulp to the United States.

But the Dominion had not yet attained national maturity. It could not amend its own constitution, which in form was an act of the British Parliament, and it was dependent upon the Mother Country for the conduct of its foreign relations. Perhaps more significant, its population was not being welded into homogeneity. With the opening up of the West, thousands of Ruthenians, Russians, Poles, Scandinavians, and Germans flooded the prairie provinces. Between 1903 and 1914 nearly 2,700,000 such immigrants made their way into Canada. As late as 1941 more than 40 per cent of the population of the prairie provinces was of Central or East European origin. But by far the largest minority population was to be found in Quebec. It comprised the French Canadians, whose settlement in the country went back to the earliest beginnings. At the present time they constitute about 30 per cent of the total population, and with the high birth rate that prevails among them, the percentage is likely to increase. Fearful of domination by the English-speaking majority, they have resisted assimilation and have clung to ancient customs in defiance of innovations. The ideal which many of them strive to uphold seems to be: "In this land of Quebec naught shall die and naught shall suffer change."

For a long time the French Canadians were the chief impediment to the attainment of full independence by the Dominion of Canada. They preferred to perpetuate the ties with Britain, not because of affection for the British but as the lesser of two evils. They looked with disfavor upon full independence lest it give new opportunities to the English-speaking majority for monopolizing control of the country. Their attitude was exemplified dramatically in the defeat of the Reciprocity Agreement between Canada and the United States in 1911. For some time Canadian agricultural and mining interests had longed to expand their markets in the United States. Accordingly, in 1910, the Dominion Prime Minister, Sir Wilfrid Laurier, entered into an agreement with the Taft Administration in Washington providing for reciprocal tariff concessions on a wide list of natural products and a few manufactured articles. The agreement was to be put into effect by concurrent legislation in the two countries. The scheme precipitated a furious controversy in Canada. Manufacturers portrayed it as a Yankee plot to annex the Dominion to the United States. Unfortunately, some weight was given to their denunciations by reckless utterances south of the border. Champ Clark, Speaker of the House of Representatives, proclaimed his desire to see the American flag wave over the whole expanse of territory to the North Pole. It is doubtful, though, that the industrialists would have succeeded had they not been able to enlist the support of ultranationalists in Quebec. To these die-hards among the French minority reciprocity looked like a scheme to destroy the unique way of life of Canada and harness the country to the ambitions of American imperialists.

It is generally asserted that Canada achieved maturity as a nation during World War I. Although interested but little in the tortuous diplomacy leading up to the conflict, the Ottawa government accepted Britain's declaration as an automatic commitment for the whole Empire. The Dominion pledged itself to unlimited support and made sacrifices proportionately equal to those of the Mother Country itself. Out of a population of only 9 million at the time, 600,000 joined the armed forces, and more than 50,000 gave up their lives on the fighting front. Proud of their efforts in what was generally regarded as a noble cause, Canadians lost their sense of colonial inferiority and came forth as leading champions of Western ideals of democracy and peace. After 1917 the Canadian Prime Minister sat in the Imperial War Cabinet as an equal of the Prime Minister of Great Britain in formulating policy. When the war ended, Canada demanded and received a seat at the Peace Conference and subsequently was admitted to the League of Nations. In the years that followed, the Dominion asserted its independence in foreign policy by refusing to accept commitments under the Locarno Agreements and other treaties negotiated by the British without Canadian participation. Nevertheless, when World War II broke out, Canada plunged into the fray with hardly a moment's hesitation. The threat to the survival of Britain was almost universally regarded as a threat to the interests of Canada. Although she might legally have remained neutral, she pledged her wealth and the lives of her youth in the same unstinted measure as had characterized her action in World War I.

Victory for the Allies in World War II did not free Canada from uncertainties and troubles. Many of her old problems remained unsolved. As a nation she was still underpopulated. With an area almost equal to that of Europe, she had fewer inhabitants than New York State. Forty-five per cent of her people dwelt in the St. Lawrence valley in an area covering but 2 per cent of the country. Her Yukon and Northwest territories, equal in size to half of the United States, contained only 14,000 inhabitants. At least 50 per cent of the land of the Dominion remained unsuitable for agriculture or for almost any other occupation except fur trading and mining. Worse still, the population was sharply divided on the basis of sectional and ethnic interests. Ontario was dominated by industrial and financial ambitions, which gave to the province a conservative outlook in economic affairs and at the same time a determination to achieve independence from British and American influences. The prairie provinces, inhabited largely by immigrants from the United States and from Continental European countries, were the stronghold of agrarian collectivism and of radical innovations for currency inflation and cheap credit. French Canada, embraced by the province of Quebec, continued its devotion to the culture and religion of its ancestors and its resistance to domination from Ottawa.

The geographic position of Canada was also a source of uneasiness. She had the misfortune to lie directly athwart the air routes between Russia and the United States. As the Cold War between these two giants waxed in intensity, Canada had reason to fear that the United States might attempt to dictate an increasing number of her military and economic policies. Many Canadian businessmen disliked the influx of capital investment from the United States, the control of branch factories by American head offices, and the excess of American imports over Canadian exports purchased by the United States. So strong was the ill feeling that President Eisenhower paid a visit to Ottawa in 1958 and arranged for the setting up of a joint committee of the Canadian and American governments to promote co-operation and a better understanding between the two countries. Any results the committee may have achieved were nullified by sharp criticism by the United States government, early in 1963, of Canada's unwillingness to equip her armed forces with nuclear weapons from the United States. In the ensuing controversy Prime Minister Diefenbaker lost the support of a majority in the House of Commons. Instead of resigning forthwith he exercised his option of dissolving Parliament and ordering a general election for April 9. The result was the failure of any one party to gain a majority. But since the Liberals emerged with a plurality,

A Lumber Mill in British Columbia. Wood pulp and paper production is a mainstay of the Canadian economy.

Diefenbaker soon announced his resignation in order to make way
for the Liberal leader, Lester B. Pearson, to succeed him as Prime
Minister. The Liberals were returned to power in 1965 with Pearson as their leader. Three years later Pearson resigned on account of
ill health and was succeeded by Pierre Trudeau.

Yet, with full allowance for all of Canada's difficulties, there seems
little doubt that her future is bright with promise. She is one of the
most richly endowed countries in the world in natural resources.
Although her population is only one-tenth that of the United
States, her total foreign trade is almost one-third as large. She leads
the world in the production of asbestos, nickel, platinum, zinc, and
wood pulp. She ranks second in the production of aluminum,
cobalt, and uranium, third in the production of gold and titanium,
and fourth in the production of wheat. Recently, extensive deposits
of iron ore have been discovered in Labrador and oil in the prairie
provinces and in British Columbia. The development of atomic
fission has made the uranium resources in the vicinity of Great
Bear Lake immensely valuable. She is rapidly developing a national
culture and an independent foreign policy. Perhaps the prediction
of Sir Wilfrid Laurier fifty years ago that "the twentieth century
is Canada's" is not mere empty rhetoric.

*Promise for the
future*

2. THE COMMONWEALTH OF AUSTRALIA

The second largest island [2] in the world and the smallest of the
continents, Australia began its recorded history under inauspicious
circumstances. Discovered by the Dutch in the seventeenth century and rediscovered and claimed for England by Captain James
Cook in 1770, it was too remote from the homeland to offer attractions for settlement. When the American Revolution eliminated the thirteen colonies in the Western Hemisphere as dumping
grounds for British convicts, the government in London turned to
Australia. The first convict ship sailed for the island continent in
1787, and Australia remained a penal colony for fifty years. It
should be noted, however, that not all the prisoners transported
were burglars and cutthroats. The criminal laws of England at that
time provided drastic penalties for trivial offenses, such as petty
larceny or hunting partridges on some noble's estate. We can rea-
sonably assume, therefore, that many of the original colonists in
Australia were far from being what we would now call hardened
criminals.[3]

*Australia as a
penal colony*

[2] Australia has an area of 2,967,000 square miles. Antarctica, also an island and
a continent, has an estimated area of 6,000,000 square miles.

[3] It is an interesting fact, however, that among these convicts a kind of *esprit
de corps* developed. To bolster their own pride they began to look down their
noses at the free immigrants. One of them is quoted as saying: "Thank God,
I came out honourable. Some poor fellows are sent out for nothing, but thank
God it was not for nothing I was sent out." R. M. Crawford, *Australia*, p. 94.

Convicts and
settlers

The discovery
of gold

Effects of the
gold rushes

The first settlers were convicts exclusively, except for 200 soldiers sent to guard them. This continued to be the case for some time. Gradually a few adventurous free citizens learned of the possibilities of sheep-raising and filtered into the colony to establish ranches or "stations." Convicts were released to them as shepherds, with the provision that after the expiration of their terms of sentence they would continue to live in Australia. By 1830 the wool industry had become the backbone of the Australian economy. Ten years later the number of free settlers had grown sufficiently large to justify a decision by the British government to abandon the practice of dumping prisoners in most parts of the continent.

In 1848 the trend of Australian development was abruptly changed by the discovery of gold in New South Wales and Victoria. Fortune-hunters and adventurers from all over the world followed the magic lure of the yellow metal. Between 1850 and 1860 the population of the continent almost trebled. Inevitably more people came than could find a livelihood in prospecting and mining. When the excitement died away, and the hills and streams no longer yielded gold in easy abundance, the problem arose of what to do with the surplus population. The logical solution seemed to be to encourage them to become farmers. Efforts to establish themselves in this occupation involved a desperate struggle. Scanty rainfall, inadequate transportation facilities, and refusal of the wool-growers to "unlock" their vast estates dogged the footsteps of all but the most fortunate farmers with disaster. Not until the building of railways to the ports, the perfection of dry-farming techniques, the development of suitable strains of wheat, and the improvement of chemical fertilizers was agriculture in Australia placed on a sound foundation.

A considerable number of the basic political and social policies of Australia as a nation can be traced to the gold rushes of the 1850's and their aftermath. First was the White Australia policy, designed to exclude black, brown, and yellow races from settlement on the continent. This policy was an outgrowth of conflicts between Chinese and Caucasian miners in the gold fields. A second was the attempt to build up a manufacturing industry through the use of protective tariffs. Originally adopted by the colony of Victoria in the 1860's, tariffs were later extended to the Commonwealth as a whole. Their use was motivated in part at least by the need for domestic industry to absorb the surplus miners. A third policy was the adoption of heavy governmental borrowing for the construction of public works. Obviously, the need for public-works construction could be justified for many reasons: to provide irrigation projects for the benefit of farmers in arid regions; to speed up the development of transportation facilities; to furnish employment opportunities for the influx of immigrants brought in by the discovery of gold.

The Australian Commonwealth as an organized state did not come into existence until 1901. Previous to that time the continent was divided into separate colonies, most of which had split off from the original colony of New South Wales. Movements to federate them made slow progress, mainly because the weak feared domination by the strong and prosperous. But such fears did not prevent a rapid growth of local democracy. By 1850 each of the colonies had its legislative council as a check upon the Governor, and had obtained the right to alter its own constitution. Soon afterward the eastern colonies achieved responsible government. Universal manhood suffrage was introduced in South Australia in 1855, in Victoria in 1857, and in New South Wales a year later. About the same time the secret ballot was adopted in Victoria, South Australia, New South Wales, and Queensland. Before 1900 two colonies had begun payment of salaries to members of their legislatures, and several had given women the privilege of voting.

The growth of democracy in the Australian states

The stage was eventually reached where the arguments for federation outweighed the objections. Foremost among them was the need for a common defense against the militant imperialism of the Great Powers. Important also was the growing inconvenience of tariffs levied by the various colonies against each other. The first step for a union of the continent was taken in 1885 with the establishment of the Australasian Federal Council. Possessing only legislative power with no executive or financial authority, this agency was reduced to impotence by the non-cooperation of New South Wales. Its chief significance lay in the renewed impetus it gave to the demand for effective union. In 1897–1898 a series of conferences resulted in the drafting of a plan of federation which in 1901 was approved by the British Parliament and became the Constitution of the Commonwealth of Australia. The Commonwealth was organized as a federal union comprising the six states of New South Wales, Victoria, Queensland, South Australia, Western Australia, and Tasmania. The capital was temporarily established at Melbourne, but the Constitution contained a provision that a permanent capital should be built in the state of New South Wales, not less than 100 miles from Sydney. In the course of a decade the government invited city planners from all over the world to submit blueprints for a garden municipality to be known as Canberra. The award was given to W. B. Griffin of Chicago, an associate of Frank Lloyd Wright. In 1927 the seat of government of the Commonwealth was formally transferred to the new federal city.

Establishment of the Commonwealth of Australia

The government of Australia bears a closer resemblance to that of the United States than does the government of Canada. Such a development was rendered inevitable by the spirit of independence existing within the states of Australia and by their distrust of each other. Consequently, when the division of powers was made by the Constitution, it was logical that the government of the Common-

The government of Australia

wealth should be given only specified powers, and that all powers
not thus delegated should be reserved to the states. In some other
respects also the Australian system resembles, superficially at least,
the American. The Australian Parliament consists of two houses, a
Senate and a House of Representatives. The former is composed of
six members from each state, elected directly by the people for six
years. Membership in the House is proportionate to population. It
seems to have been the intent of the framers of the Constitution to
give to the Senate almost equal authority with the lower house, except for the power to initiate and amend financial legislation. As
events have worked out, however, the Australian Senate has played
no more significant a role than its counterparts in the other Dominions. It does not have the prestige of the United States Senate, and
it initiates few important bills. The cabinet acknowledges no responsibility to it but to the House of Representatives exclusively.
This is dictated in part by the custom in Britain and in Canada, but
also by the fact that the lower house is the guardian of the public
purse. Like several other members of the Commonwealth, Australia
has a Governor-General representing the British Crown, but his
powers are insignificant. As in all countries having responsible government, executive authority as well as the primary control over
legislation is vested in the cabinet headed by the Prime Minister.

One of the most interesting facts of Australian history is the extent to which the country has pursued a policy of social and economic planning. Even during the nineteenth century when the
Mother Country was worshiping the slogans of free competition
and free trade, Australia was steadily enlarging the sphere of governmental action to promote social cohesion and maintain a high
standard of living. The reasons for this policy are numerous and
varied. Geography alone provides a large part of the explanation.
One-third of the continent has an average annual rainfall of less
than 10 inches, and most of the remainder has less than 20. But
even these averages do not reflect the poor distribution of the rain
that does fall. In many areas the precipitation may be concentrated
within a short period of the year, with months or years of subsequent drought. As a result, only about 8 per cent of the total area
can be utilized for farming or orchard purposes. About 40 per cent
is waste, and 50 per cent is used for pasture. Under such conditions, it has been impossible for Australia to develop into a nation
of independent proprietors cultivating small plots as family farms.
In the pasture areas rainfall is so scanty or unreliable that sheep and
cattle must be grazed over thousands of acres. This has necessitated
the development of vast estates or pastoral "stations" established by
owners with considerable capital. They provide employment for
what is essentially an agricultural proletariat: shepherds, shearers,
and "boundary riders," who have no hope of ever becoming proprietors. Conscious of their grievances, they have been drawn since

the later nineteenth century into militant trade unions to struggle for old-age pensions, unemployment insurance, and minimum wages. They have been among the most consistent supporters of government intervention in economic affairs.

A second factor contributing to governmental control and regulation was the gold rushes of the 1850's. As previously noted, these produced a surplus of prospectors and miners who had to be channeled into new occupations. The result was positive action by the colonial governments to promote the development of industry and to extend agriculture into all parts of the limited area where rainfall would permit. The discovery of gold also gave rise to racial problems. In the 1850's thousands of Chinese poured into Victoria and New South Wales and threatened the wage scales and living standards of the white miners. Rapidly the Australians became obsessed with the idea that their country was a "white island in a vast colored ocean." They pointed to the hundreds of millions of dark-skinned inhabitants of India, the Netherlands Indies, China, and Japan as a flood-tide which would overwhelm them unless they built dikes in the form of rigid exclusion laws. Even the tropical regions of northern Australia were to be kept uncontaminated by Oriental labor. Queensland, for example, has taken pride in recent years in the ability of its white inhabitants to cultivate its sugar plantations without being defeated by the moral and physical diseases that have commonly wreaked such havoc upon Caucasians in the tropics.[4] We can say, therefore, that the White Australian policy has been motivated both by feelings of race superiority and by fear of economic competition. Some of its sponsors argue that it is essential to democracy. Racial divisions, they say, would create tensions and conflicts and destroy the spirit of compromise which can exist only in a community of equals. After World War II immigration policy was modified somewhat. Yet as late as 1960 only 5 per cent of Australians were of non-British origin. A few of these were Asians, but most had migrated from European countries other than Britain.

Still another influence promoting intervention by the government for social and economic purposes has been the peculiar nationalism of the Australians. Since the 1880's their statesmen and poets have extolled the nation as the bearer of a grandiose destiny. Its mission was to reclaim a vast continent from savagery. While Britain and other European countries were engrossed in militarism and in the sordid disputes of power politics, Australia was building a humanitarian democracy. Here, if anywhere, men would be equal and free, and no one would suffer want or be left unprotected against the slings and arrows of evil fortune. Whatever gov-

[4] It is an ironical fact, however, that in the nineteenth century thousands of Melanesians and Polynesians were brought in from the Pacific islands and shamelessly exploited. They were deported in 1906.

ernment might do to give such protection would be considered within its province, and no "natural economic laws" or dogmas of individualism would be allowed to stand in the way.

Protectionism

One of the earliest forms of government intervention in Australia was control of international trade. The methods employed have included tariffs, bounties, quotas, and marketing restrictions. From the middle of the nineteenth century the several Australian colonies imposed protective tariffs on intercolonial trade. They did so not merely for the benefit of the business classes but to provide employment and to maintain as high a standard of living as possible for farmers and workers. When the Commonwealth was established in 1901, the tariff policy was continued, and the rates have been steadily increased. Sentiment in favor of protection is almost universal. Labor as well as capital insists upon the importance of controlling economic forces for the general welfare. Neither has any respect for the laissez-faire philosophy or is willing to trust the fate of Australia to the shifting trends of the international market. Although recognizing that import restrictions mean higher prices, the public accepts them readily as the best guaranties of full employment at respectable wages. Besides, they help to maintain the White Australian policy by excluding the competition of cheap Oriental labor.

Government ownership

A second form of government intervention for which Australia has been particularly noted is public ownership of a wide variety of economic enterprises. Ventures brought under government ownership include railways, shipping lines, power plants, hotels, banks, insurance companies, lumber mills, and coal mines. Because of the federal structure of the government, most of such enterprises are conducted by the states rather than by the Commonwealth. Government ownership in Australia is the result in part of the strong influence which labor wields in both state and national politics. Owing to a rigid control of immigration, the supply of labor has

A Mine in Australia. A section of the Mt. Isa lead-zinc-copper mine, 500 miles inland from Townsville, Queensland. Mt. Isa is one of the leading copper producers of the world.

been kept from exceeding the demand. This has fostered the growth of a unionism surpassing in strength that of most other countries. In Australia at the present time about 40 per cent of all wage earners are enrolled in labor unions, compared with little more than 25 per cent in the United States. But organized labor has not been the only force supporting state ownership. The geography of Australia has impelled many capitalists and landowners to look with favor upon government operation of railways and public utilities, at least. Scanty rainfall over most of the continent has limited the growth of cities and towns in the hinterland. But the construction of railroads to bring out the grain, wool, meat, and minerals has been none the less important. With few private corporations bold enough to incur the risks involved, there was no alternative but for governments to shoulder the burden. As a consequence, in these and in some other lines, public ownership of economic ventures has been welcomed as an aid and support of private business.

In social-welfare legislation Australian achievements have been little more distinctive than those of most other democracies. In a number of cases Australia (together with New Zealand) pioneered in this type of regulation. In other cases she merely duplicated the pattern of Great Britain. Old-age pensions, widows' allowances, unemployment and health insurance, slum clearance, and child subsidies stand out as the principal examples. A bonus is paid for every infant born in Australia, and an endowment is provided for every child under 16. A National Health System furnishes free drugs, subsidizes hospital and medical expenses, and provides pensions for the blind and victims of tuberculosis. One other element of Australian collectivism, however, has had no counterpart in the Mother Country. This is a system of compulsory arbitration and wage-fixing, designed to maintain industrial peace and safeguard standards of living for industrial workers. In sharp contrast with the attitude of organized labor in most countries, Australian workers have accepted, and for the most part actually welcomed, compulsory arbitration. They regard it as a means to security and as a source of strength for the labor movement, since it tends to bring more members into the union. Moreover, the political strength of the workers is so great that they look upon the government as an agency they can hope to control. Therefore, they do not fear compulsory arbitration as a device which anti-labor elements might use against them.

Other forms of collectivism

In several respects Australia occupies a position unique among nations. Geographically, she is a part of the East, yet her culture is wholly Western. Nevertheless, she cannot and does not ignore the political problems created by her Eastern location. What happens in Indonesia or in South Vietnam or Laos is of more intimate concern to her than is the threat of Soviet expansion in Europe. Her

Australia's unique position

Sydney, Australia. In the foreground are road and rail approaches to the Harbour Bridge, linking the northern suburbs with the inner city area. Sydney has a population of about 2,500,000 and is the largest city in Australia.

foreign policy, in recent years, has comported more closely with that of the United States than with that of Great Britain. Economically, however, she remains within the British trading area and is a leading member of the Sterling Bloc. In 1960 Great Britain purchased about 27 per cent of her exports and was the source of supply for 36 per cent of her imports. How long this can continue is open to doubt. Since World War II Australia has emphasized industrialization to such an extent that far more people are now employed in factories and commercial establishments than work on the land.

3. THE DOMINION OF NEW ZEALAND

Located about 1100 miles southeast of Australia, New Zealand was also discovered by the Dutch but explored and claimed for the British by Captain James Cook. At the time of discovery (1769) it was inhabited exclusively by Maoris, an intelligent but warlike people of Polynesian stock. For three-quarters of a century thereafter the only white settlers were missionaries, who labored with modest success to convert the Maoris to Christianity. In 1840 the first boatload of British colonists entered the harbor of what is now Wellington. They had been sent out by the New Zealand Company, founded by Edward Gibbon Wakefield, leader of the new British school of systematic colonizers. While completing a prison term for abducting a schoolgirl heiress, Wakefield came to the conclusion that Britain would be engulfed by civil war unless new economic opportunities could be found for the distressed population of her industrial cities. Caught in the maelstrom of depression and unemployment, workers by the thousands were turning to Chartism and sundry varieties of socialism. A conflict with the privileged classes was inevitable. Eventually Wakefield hit upon the idea that colonization would banish the specter of civil war. The

Discovery and settlement

company he founded would transport selected colonists to New Zealand. They would be provided with land at prices sufficiently high to discourage easy accumulation. Only the more prosperous and enterprising colonists would attain the status of owners. The others would have to content themselves for years with jobs as farm laborers. In time they too would buy land, and the proceeds from the sale would be used to finance further immigration.[5]

Wakefield's scheme attracted so much attention that the British government decided to take action. A governor was appointed, and the islands were formally annexed to the British Empire. The announced purpose was to protect the Maoris against unscrupulous white settlers. A week after the first colonists landed at Wellington the newly appointed governor arrived. He proceeded to negotiate a treaty with the native chiefs recognizing the sovereignty of the British Crown over all New Zealand. In return the British guaranteed to the Maoris full possession of their lands, "except as the Crown might wish to purchase them," and granted to the natives the rights and privileges of British subjects. Perhaps it was well that the government acted as it did, for a broadening stream of colonists continued to flow to the islands. By 1856 New Zealand had a white population of 45,000.

In 1852 the British Government endowed New Zealand with a constitution. It conferred the executive power upon a Governor-General representing the King, and acting with the advice of an Executive Council. Legislative authority was vested in a House of Representatives elected by the people and a Legislative Council appointed for life by the Governor-General. In 1891 the term of members of the upper house was shortened to seven years. Thereafter it sank into a harmless desuetude comparable to that of the Canadian Senate. In 1951 it was abolished. A few years after the constitution was issued, the British Government allowed it to become known that objections would not be raised if members of the Executive Council remained in office as long as they possessed the confidence of the legislature, regardless of the attitude of the Governor-General. In 1856 the Executive Council was formally recognized as a cabinet, exercising its functions under the principle of responsible government. Other steps in the direction of political democracy came easily. In 1879 universal manhood suffrage was adopted, and a few years later plural voting was abolished. In 1893 New Zealand led the Commonwealth of Nations in bestowing the suffrage upon women in national elections.

Economic reform followed in the wake of political democracy. When the Liberals came into power in 1891 they dedicated their efforts to making New Zealand a nation of small, independent

[5] The scheme had already been tried in South Australia, but with limited success. Wakefield subsequently turned to New Zealand in the hope that his theories would be vindicated.

farmers and herdsmen. Measures were adopted to break up large holdings, the formation of which had previously been encouraged by the sale of Maori lands to wealthy individuals. To combat the power of the big landowners required the support not only of landless agriculturists but also of workers in the cities. The Liberals therefore espoused a program of combined agrarian and labor reform which won the allegiance of both classes. The agrarian measures took the form primarily of special taxes on land held for speculative purposes and limitation of the size of holdings in the future. For the benefit of the workers the Liberals provided old-age pensions, factory inspection, regulation of working hours, and compulsory arbitration of industrial disputes. The accession of the Labor party to power in 1935 brought an extension of these measures, with increased benefits to the urban workers.

New Zealand has followed policies of collectivization quite similar to those of Australia. The reasons also have been similar. Lacking the capital to take advantage of new inventions, especially the railroad and the telegraph, the Dominion turned to foreign sources. Money proved to be more easily obtainable when the government itself was the borrower. Moreover, there was a deeply rooted fear among the colonists themselves of private monopoly. The beginning of collectivism occurred about 1870, when the Dominion Government entered the London capital market for funds to construct roads, trunk railways, and telegraph lines. About the same time a state life-insurance system was established, and later state fire and accident insurance. A few coal mines also were added to the list of public enterprises, and finally a Bank of New Zealand. Important as a principle of collectivization has been the use of state-owned enterprises for "yardstick" purposes. Government purchase of coal mines, for example, was dictated by the theory that private companies needed the restraint of state competition to keep them from charging excessive prices.

It is not an exaggeration to say that New Zealand enjoys all the advantages for future progress possessed by Australia with none of Australia's disadvantages. The two dominions have homogeneous populations overwhelmingly British in origin. In Australia 99.2 per cent of the people are of European extraction, and 97 per cent of these are of British ancestry. In New Zealand the percentages are 93 and 96, respectively. In both dominions systematic efforts have been made to preserve perpetually the British character of the nation. The early emigrants to New Zealand brought with them not merely the social customs and political institutions but the flowers, trees, birds, and even animal pests of their native England. New Zealand, like Australia, was populated in considerable measure by people of liberal and even radical tendencies. Both dominions received inundations of immigrants attracted thither by the discovery of gold. Coming from the landless and unemployed elements of

Collectivism

Comparison of New Zealand and Australia

Britain, many were infected with Chartism and even traces of socialism. As a consequence, they developed in the colonies institutions of political and economic democracy surpassing those of the
Mother Country.

But with respect to one political and social policy New Zealand
has had an advantage over Australia. She has not been under the
same pressure to embrace an extreme nationalism. Her problem of
providing employment opportunities for displaced gold miners was
not so acute as Australia's, and therefore the necessity of developing industry was not so imperious. More important, New Zealand-
ers exported some 80 per cent of what they produced, and consequently recognized the need of continuing to purchase imports.
Both factors militated against economic nationalism as a dominion
policy. In addition, New Zealand has never been threatened with
incursions of Oriental immigrants to the same extent as Australia.
One reason is the greater distance from the chief centers of Asian
congestion. Another is the fact that she has no vast areas of
sparsely populated territory inviting occupation by impoverished
Orientals. Nevertheless, immigration is not left unrestricted. Barriers have been erected against the influx of laborers allegedly a
menace to the white man's standard of living. Though it has never
been propagated with the emotional fervor behind its Australian
equivalent, a "White New Zealand policy" does exist.

Geographically, also, New Zealand has a wide margin of superiority over Australia. Although a mountainous region, with peaks
that rise to 12,000 feet, extends the entire length of the southern
island, there are no deserts and few areas unsuited to agriculture or
grazing. Almost everywhere rainfall is adequate and permits an intensive use of the land. North Island, which contains over 60 per
cent of the population, has an average of about 50 inches of rain
annually. Throughout the Dominion temperatures fluctuate within
a comparatively narrow range. Extremes of over 100 degrees or
below zero have never been recorded, and in both islands 75 degrees
is considered unpleasantly high and 40 degrees uncomfortably low.
Such favorable geographic conditions have given to New Zealand a
character quite different from that of Australia. For one thing, the
distribution of population is much more even. Instead of a few
large cities along the seacoast and an almost unoccupied hinterland,
there are hundreds of towns of moderate size and not a single city
exceeding 400,000. The mean density of population is slightly over
15 persons per square mile compared with 2 for Australia. Geography, more than anything else, has made New Zealand a democracy
of small, independent agrarians.

New Zealand has remained more closely connected with her
British antecedents than has Australia. For one reason, the British
and New Zealand economies are complementary rather than competitive. New Zealand is predominantly agricultural. Two-thirds

of her land is suitable for farming and grazing. Her only important manufactures are meat and dairy products, fertilizer, pulp and paper. Two-thirds of New Zealand's exports are sold to Great Britain, and half of her imports come from British sources. Unlike Australia, New Zealand has not faced any dangerous threat of Oriental aggression. She has therefore not felt the necessity of developing an independent foreign policy. She has generally been content to walk in the shadow of Great Britain, with occasional glances in the direction of Australia and the United States. However, with the recent British trend toward withdrawal from responsibilities east of Suez, New Zealand ties with Great Britain appear to be loosening.

4. INDIA UNDER COMPANY AND CROWN

Both in the manner of its acquisition and in its character when established, the British rule in India was peculiar, not only in comparison with earlier empires established in India but also in comparison with the general pattern of modern imperialism. First of all, the British had originally been avid to capture the trade of the East Indies and, when bested in that quarter by the Dutch, had somewhat reluctantly turned to the Indian subcontinent as their second choice. Also, in securing outposts in India, the British were motivated solely by an interest in trade and had no intention either of colonizing or of ruling territories. Gradually and quite unsystematically, the trading posts were transformed into centers of political administration. The absorption or conquest of native states, even though it ultimately involved large-scale military operations, was carried out not by the British Government but by the British East India Company—a privately owned joint-stock corporation.

The East India Company had been chartered by the Crown and was increasingly subjected to control by Parliament, with the strange result that the Company ceased to function as a commercial

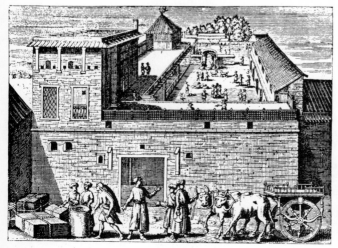

The Modest Beginning of British Rule in India. An early "factory" or trading station, with walled enclosure containing a warehouse, promenade area, and church. From a copper engraving.

organization while it continued to operate as an administrative authority, expanding its jurisdiction over more and more of India and exercising actual sovereignty. When finally (in 1858) the Company was dissolved and the British Government assumed full responsibility for Indian affairs, the administrative and financial system developed by the Company was continued in essential features. Another distinctive aspect of the British position in India was the fact that the country was never conquered in its entirety. The British seized strategic regions until their possessions formed a ring around the whole subcontinent (and included substantial portions of the interior as well), but they left hundreds of native states nominally independent. Nevertheless, although Britain's control over India was acquired piecemeal and indirectly, it became as thorough as if it had been imposed by a conquering horde capable of beating down all resistance.

As the trading posts of the East India Company were expanded, they gradually took on the nature of colonies. This process had begun even before the close of the seventeenth century and increased rapidly during the eighteenth century. The assumption by the Company of sovereign power over various territories created a need for efficient administration, a need which was not met promptly or adequately. In the early days Company agents had been selected without regard to their knowledge of Indian affairs (proficiency in Latin and Greek literature was considered much more important), and most of the agents did not remain in India long enough to become well-acquainted with the country or its people. There was little integration between the administration of the separate British holdings, although the acquisition of the great

Homage to Governor Warren Hastings. Chait Singh, Raja of Benares, was induced to transfer his allegiance from the Mogul's representative to the British East India Company in 1775. (Later Hastings deposed the Raja and transferred his dominions to Chait's nephew at double the previous assessment.)

province of Bengal (by Robert Clive, in 1757) made Calcutta eventually the Company's most important center of administration. Furthermore, the governing body of the Company, the Court of Directors in London, was so far away that its members could not be adequately informed as to what was going on in India. The governors, sent out as servants of the Company, in practice often modified or even formulated its policies. They negotiated treaties with native rulers, fought wars, and annexed territories.

Tipu's Tiger. Wooden model of a tiger mauling a British East India Company Officer. This monstrosity (fitted inside with a bellows and miniature organ pipes to simulate groans) was made for Sultan Tipu, ruler of Mysore. Tipu was defeated and killed by Governor Wellesley's troops in 1799.

Successive reorganizations of the Company had little effect upon the course of events in India, which depended largely on the initiative of the Governor-General at Calcutta. Space does not permit a detailed account, but at one time or another most of the tactics and stratagems of successful conquerors were employed in enlarging the British dominion, often without authorization and sometimes against the express commands of the home authorities. Although sharp criticism was directed against the Company, especially when the renewal of its charter was under consideration, there was little disposition on the part of Parliament to undertake full responsibility. The strongest opposition was expressed not to the Company's political activities or derelictions but to its possession of a commercial monopoly. The Charter Act of 1814 threw open the commerce of India to all British subjects but allowed the Company to retain its monopoly in China and the Far East. By 1834 free-trade sentiment had become so influential in England that the Charter Act of that year deprived the Company of all its trading privileges, in

Changes in the status of the Company

508

China as well as in India. Since it had originally been founded for the purpose of engaging in trade and had now lost that function altogether, the British East India Company might logically have expired in 1834. Instead of doing so, it was permitted to continue administering patronage in the British portions of India, serving as a governmental agency although ultimately subject to parliamentary check. Furthermore, to satisfy the English stockholders, dividends of the Company were fixed by law at 10½ per cent annually, to be derived no longer from the profits of commerce but levied as a permanent charge upon the revenues of India.

British territorial expansion inevitably led to conflicts with states beyond the Indian borders. Two Burmese wars made possible the annexation of Lower Burma (1852) and gave the British control of the Bay of Bengal. Less fortunate in sequel was an intervention in the independent state of Afghanistan in 1838–1839, a project unjustified in the first place and so thoroughly bungled that out of an invading force of 16,000 troops only one man escaped death or capture. The fiasco of the Afghan war, however, was a prelude to one of the boldest strokes in the history of British imperialism—the conquest and annexation of Sind. In violation of a signed treaty, the British, during the Afghan war, marched their troops through this independent and neutral state and used the country as a military base. Shortly afterward the British government sent Sir Charles Napier with an army into Sind to impose new demands upon the ruling princes. Without even a declaration of war Napier razed a fortress, exiled the rulers, and transferred their sovereignty to the Company (1843). Apparently Sir Charles (whose share of the plunder was £70,000) believed that the benefits of British rule outweighed any irregularities in the methods used to establish it. He referred to his own conduct in Sind as "a very advantageous, useful, humane piece of rascality." [6] After two wars against the Sikhs in the Punjab, the Governor-General, acting on his own responsibility, annexed the Punjab in 1849. Thus, by the middle of the century, most of the sovereign units in India capable of offering a serious military threat to the British position had been neutralized or brought under the jurisdiction of the Company.

Expansion and conquest

In 1857 an armed uprising, known as the Great Mutiny, produced a crisis in Anglo-Indian relations and necessitated significant changes in British policy. Although the revolt was technically a mutiny because it originated among the native troops (sepoys) employed by the British, it received some popular support and it reflected the political aspirations both of Moslem and of Hindu elements. The underlying causes of the Mutiny lay in general discontent and in suspicions which British policies had aroused. There were rumors—quite unfounded—that the British planned to proscribe the native religions. More specifically, the vigorous adminis-

The Great Mutiny of 1857

[6] P. E. Roberts, *History of British India*, p. 330.

Bengal Lancers. This cavalry unit formed a picturesque part of the professional Indian army which the British —after the Mutiny of 1857—recruited from the so-called "martial races" of the Northwest and Northeast.

tration of Lord Dalhousie (1848–1856), who annexed seven states by applying a technicality of feudal tenure (the "doctrine of lapse"), seemed to herald a new era of aggression. The immediate cause of the Mutiny can be attributed to carelessness and gross errors of judgment on the part of the military commanders. The British officials were caught quite unprepared for the revolt, which began near Delhi in May 1857, raged intensively for a few months in parts of northern and central India, and was not entirely suppressed until the following year. Many Europeans were slaughtered indiscriminately by the rebel troops, and sickening atrocities were committed on both sides, but the uprising never assumed the character of a mass movement or a genuine revolution. Its leaders were divided in purpose from the beginning. While Moslems dreamed of rehabilitating the Mogul Empire, the Marathas hoped to recover their ascendancy as a powerful Hindu state. The great majority of native princes remained aloof from the rebellion, probably because they recognized the superiority of British military resources.

The most important political result of the Mutiny was the termination of the East India Company and the transfer of full responsibility for the government of India to the British Crown and Parliament.[7] The Government of India Act of 1858 created a Secretary of State for India with an advisory council to assist him and bestowed upon the Governor-General the title of Viceroy. There

Results of the Mutiny: transfer of authority to the Crown

[7] The Company stockholders were still treated with tender consideration. The guaranteed annual dividends of 10½ per cent continued to be paid until 1874, at which time the stock was redeemed by a government purchase in the amount of £12,000,000.

was no immediate change in the details of the administrative system, but a royal proclamation issued by Queen Victoria offered conciliatory assurances in regard to religious toleration, material improvements, and the admission of native Indians to government service.

After 1858, in contrast to the earlier period, the policy of the British government in India was one of caution and conservatism. To minimize the danger of rebellion in the future, the bulk of the people were disarmed and the army was reorganized. The recruited troops were carefully trained, instilled with pride in the service, and grouped in accordance with sectarian, tribal, or local divisions so that there would be little feeling of common interest among the different units. Although Europeans formed a minority of the military personnel, they monopolized the ranks of commissioned officers and retained possession of the heavy artillery. At the same time the government sought to avoid antagonizing any powerful element or prejudice within the population. Notably, the British authorities refrained from further territorial aggression. By treaties with the remaining native princes, the British government guaranteed to these rulers their hereditary rights and possessions but required them to relinquish all control over external affairs. (The government also reserved the right to intervene in cases of flagrant abuse within the states.) Henceforth a clear division was maintained between the five or six hundred native states and the British provinces. The states ranged in size from Hyderabad—with an area almost equal to that of Great Britain—to tiny principalities, and included altogether about 40 per cent of the land area of India. A few of the rulers were more progressive than the British, but most of them were uninspiring survivals from an age of despotism, quite content to enjoy the protection of the "paramount" power, Great Britain.

The government's policy of conservatism and caution

The several changes introduced into the government of British India between 1858 and 1919 were more in form than in substance. Beginning in 1861 the Governor-General (or Viceroy) was provided with a "legislative" as well as an executive council, and the proportion of Indian members in the legislative council was increased from time to time. The members were handpicked rather than elected, however, and they had no powers other than to offer advice. An Indian Councils Act of 1909 added more Indians to the legislative councils of the Viceroy and of the provincial governors; but, while it made some of the native members elective instead of appointive, it incorporated the dubious device of class electorates. Meanwhile, the door was gradually opened for Indian participation in the governmental machinery by the development of the Indian Civil Service. From the 1880's on, Indians were allowed to compete in the examinations for the selection of civil servants, and they eventually came to supply most of the personnel for the lower and

Changes in the government: the Indian Civil Service

intermediate positions. The Indian Civil Service grew to be one of the most remarkable institutions of its kind in the world and a source of great pride to the British because of the integrity, efficiency, and loyalty of its members. It exhibited, however, the typical faults of a bureaucracy—inflexibility, conservatism, and lack of imagination. Because there was always an oversupply of educated Indians seeking government posts, and the lucky ones who obtained appointments found their modest salaries considerably above the average income of their countrymen, the civil servants usually developed an attitude of subservience to their superiors. In spite of its beneficent aspects, the Indian Civil Service became—like the native states—a bulwark of English supremacy and of the *status quo*.

Benefits
of British rule

Widely divergent views have been expressed concerning the over-all effects which British administration had upon India and her people, particularly in the nineteenth century. The British themselves do not agree on this question. Some of the harshest criticisms of British imperialism and its fruits in India have been voiced by Englishmen. Indisputably, a number of material benefits resulted from British rule. English authorities were generally effective in checking the more violent types of crime, suppressing organized bands of marauders, reducing the hazards of travel, and protecting property. They also attempted to eliminate such cruel customs as suttee, which was outlawed in 1829, and infanticide. Under British rule the population of India expanded greatly, rising from 150 million in 1850 to 250 million in 1881. By 1921 it exceeded 300 million, and another 100 million was added by 1945. This impressive increase is attributable largely to the curbing of internal warfare and to improvements in sanitation and medical facilities under British auspices. Irrigation works were constructed sufficient to provide for 30 million acres of land. Modern communications were introduced, including an extensive network of railroads totaling eventually more than 40,000 miles, a figure far in excess of the railroad mileage of any other Asian country.

The darker side
of the picture

Almost all the improvements, however, had their darker side. The rapid increase in population depressed the living conditions of large numbers of the people, and the problem of an adequate food supply was never solved. Severe famines had been known in India long before the British arrived, but some of the worst occurred during the period of British control. Ironically, the proclamation of Queen Victoria as Empress of India in 1877 coincided with the greatest famine in India's history, which took a toll of 5 million lives. It is estimated that between 1877 and 1900 no fewer than 15 million people died of famine.[8] A basic cause of these disasters was the fact that a majority of the population lived close to the starvation level even in normal times and had no savings and no reserves of physical stamina to carry them through an emergency.

[8] Romesh Dutt, *The Economic History of India under Early British Rule,* p. vi.

Although British rule did not introduce poverty into India, it did little to alleviate it and in some areas intensified it. The taxation system contributed heavily to the poverty of India's population. One of the "reforms" introduced in the province of Bengal was the so-called Permanent Settlement of the land revenues in 1793. The settlement was made with the native tax collectors (*zamindars*) and bound them to pay a fixed sum each year to the Company (which was actually the government), regardless of how much they collected from the peasants. In effect this act transformed the *zamindars* from revenue officers into feudal proprietors, who profited enormously as rental values in the province increased. Even where a system of assessment directly upon the peasants was employed, the tax rate was revised periodically, almost always in an upward direction. The principle generally followed by the government was to demand *one-half* the rental value of the land. British officials pointed to the fact that the tax schedules were somewhat less extortionate than those of earlier autocratic regimes. An important difference, however, was that the British assessments were not theoretical; they were actually collected. Also, in contrast to the situation under earlier empires, much of the revenue raised was drained out of India—in salaries to the higher administrative officials and to European army officers, in dividends to the East India Company stockholders, and in interest on the public debt, most of which was held by Englishmen. Not only did taxation bear too heavily upon the poorest classes but only a small fraction of the government's budget was allotted to relief, social welfare, or education. The major portion was expended on the police, the courts, and especially the Indian army, a professional body which was sometimes used in imperial wars outside of India—in Afghanistan, Burma, or China. In spite of the introduction of sanitation measures, the Indian death rate remained appallingly high, augmented by such diseases as cholera, malaria, and bubonic plague, which can be controlled by modern medical science and have been almost eliminated in Western countries.

Probably the aspect of British rule in India most open to criticism was its economic policy. In the early days of the East India Company there had been a great demand for Indian handmade goods of superior quality, especially silks, cottons, and muslins, which were generally paid for in specie. With the coming of the Industrial Revolution in England, the character of Far Eastern commerce changed. The British became interested in India as a source of raw materials and, even more, as a market for manufactured goods. The Indians were forced to accept "free trade" as applied to British manufactures but were effectively denied the right to export their own manufactures either to England or other countries. An inevitable result of this policy was the decline of village handicrafts which had for centuries constituted a vital element in the whole Indian economy. During the period of British rule, in spite of the growth of some large cities, the proportion of India's population dependent on the land for sustenance actually increased, until by the opening of the twentieth century it constituted more than 80 per cent of the total. Excessive ruralization, small tenant holdings, oppressive taxes, and the unchecked extortions of money-lenders go far to explain why India remained a land of poverty and famine. The introduction of factory industries in the late nineteenth century offered a new source of employment, but only for a tiny fraction of the population. An oversupply of labor kept wages extremely low, and the sordid conditions of English mill towns during the early Industrial Revolution were repeated and far exceeded in India.

Somewhat more difficult to assess are the effects of the British occupation upon Indian society, culture, and mentality. Quite early the English rulers recognized an obligation to promote educational facilities. Several European scholars became intensely interested in the study of Sanskrit and the related ancient languages and advocated the promotion of a fuller knowledge of India's intellectual heritage. The printing press, introduced by missionaries, was utilized for works in the vernacular. The first newspaper, published in the Bengali dialect, appeared in 1818. However, a fundamental change in English educational policy in India came in 1833 with the decision to devote all educational funds henceforth to instruction solely in the English language. Lord Macaulay, the famous essayist and historian, who was a member of the Governor's council at this time and was primarily responsible for the decision, regarded Hindu literature as nothing but "false history, false astronomy, false metaphysics, false religion." [9] As a matter of fact, the government did very little to carry out the educational plans which had been announced, and it is probable that, with the economic and political decline of the formerly autonomous villages, instructional facilities in India actually deteriorated. Some village schools were still flourishing in the early nineteenth century, but with the decay of village life education gradually fell into neglect and illiteracy increased accordingly. Nevertheless, the official emphasis upon Western studies familiarized Indian intellectuals with nineteenth-century liberal traditions and in the long run intensified their desire for self-government.

Toward the close of the nineteenth century the growth of an Indian nationalist sentiment manifested itself in various ways. The event of greatest import for the future was the formation of the Indian National Congress in 1885 under the initiative of educated Hindus and English sympathizers. The objectives of the organization were ambitious if somewhat vague, and embodied the hope that it would "form the germ of a Native Parliament and . . .

Social and cultural effects of British rule

The growth of Indian nationalism: The Indian National Congress

514 [9] H. G. Rawlinson, *India, a Short Cultural History*, p. 409 .

INDIAN AND BURMESE ART OF THE EIGHTEENTH AND NINETEENTH CENTURIES

Royal Chair of Ranjit Singh(1780–1839), Able Sikh Maharaja of the Punjab. The chair is of wood and lacquer, overlaid with gold.

Burmese Royal Headdress (Nineteenth Century). Of gold openwork on a cloth base, ornamented with gold, beetles' wings, and precious stones.

Cotton Tapestry. Embroidered with colored silks and silver (eighteenth century), it illustrates scenes from the *Mahabharata*. It was executed for the Raja of Chamba.

constitute in a few years an unanswerable reply to the assertion
that India is still wholly unfit for any form of representative institutions." [10] The Congress was never exclusively a Hindu body. It
attracted a number of Moslems, and during the first thirty years of
its existence five Englishmen were elected to its presidency. The
most influential nationalist leader at this time was G. K. Gokhale, a
splendid orator, who had held government office both in Bombay
province and in the Viceroy's Council. A student and admirer of
British civilization, Gokhale depicted India's goal as self-government
within the British Empire, together with the enactment of comprehensive social and educational reforms.

Factors
accounting for the
growth of Indian
nationalism

Government officials had at first looked upon the Indian National
Congress with benevolence, regarding it as a harmless debating society or as a safety valve for upper-class discontent. However, as
the Congress—which met every December in a different Indian
city—pressed more insistently for reform measures, the official attitude became cool or hostile. The result was that the nationalist
movement entered a more radical phase about the turn of the century. A contributing factor to this trend was the shattering of the
myth of European invincibility by the Italian defeat in Ethiopia in
1896, by the difficulty which Britain encountered in subduing the
small Boer states of South Africa, and by Japan's dramatic victory
over the great Russian empire in 1905. Incensed by the dictatorial
policy of the Viceroy, Lord Curzon, some Indian patriots began to
demand *swaraj* (independence) and also launched a *swadeshi* campaign, which was an attempt to injure Britain economically by
boycotting the sale of British goods and reviving native industries.
Outbreaks of violence in western Bengal and in the Punjab merely
strengthened the determination of the government to stand firm.
The vernacular press was muzzled; agitators were arrested and
some of them were deported.

The conflicts be-
tween moderates
and extremists and
the rise of the
Moslem League

The growth of a militant opposition to British rule led to dissension within the Indian National Congress and to a cleavage between
the moderates and the extremists. The 1907 meeting of the Indian
Congress was disrupted by rioting, but the moderate faction succeeded in retaining control of the organization. The nationalist
movement, hampered by disagreement among the Hindu leaders,
was also weakened somewhat by the establishment of a Moslem organization which stood in rivalry to the Indian National Congress.
The Moslem League, founded in 1905, was inspired partly by the
fear of the Moslem minority that they might be subjected to
Hindu domination if popular government was established in
India—a fear heightened by the truculence and the appeal to religious prejudice which some radical Hindu nationalists had displayed. The League also reflected an attempt to reawaken interest
in the whole community of Islam, which seemed to be jeopardized

[10] Quoted in T. W. Wallbank, *India in the New Era*, p. 80.

by the decline of the Ottoman Empire. In contrast to the Indian
Congress the Moslem League was a communal (sectarian) organization; further, it was founded under conservative rather than liberal
auspices. In the years immediately preceding World War I, however, India was relatively quiet. The moderate element in the Indian Congress, led by Gokhale, sought to prevent either sectarian
strife or open conflict with the authorities, looking forward to
gradual reform and the attainment of representative government
through co-operation with the British.

Following World War I Indian nationalism became a powerful
movement, with increasingly definite aims and capable and articu-
late leadership. Many of Britain's critics had asserted that in the *The nationalists*
event of a major war, involving the Empire, her subject peoples *and World War I*
would revolt and she would be unable to retain control of India.
Contrary to this prediction, only minor disturbances occurred in
India during the war. Representatives of all important organizations
expressed their sympathy for the British cause and offered assistance. Indian contributions in behalf of Britain and her allies were
tremendous. Indian troops fought on the Western front, in East
Africa, in the Middle East, and in the Far East; and the country
furnished vast supplies of raw materials, foodstuffs, and even
manufactures, as cotton, jute and steel production was intensified.

The co-operative attitude of the Indian people during the war
was to a large extent induced by the belief that a victory for Britain and her allies would bring benefits to the world's colonial areas. *Hope of reward*
Woodrow Wilson's utterances on war aims and peace objectives *from a grateful*
aroused enthusiasm in India as elsewhere, and from the beginning *Britain*
of the war British spokesmen had intimated that generous reforms
would be forthcoming in recognition of Indian loyalty. In 1917, a
semiofficial pledge was given by the British government when
Edwin Montagu, Secretary of State for India, announced in the
House of Commons that England's policy toward India was: "the
increasing association of Indians in every branch of the administration and the gradual development of self-governing institutions
with a view to . . . responsible government as an integral part of
the British Empire."

Although the close of the war found India in a state of high ex-
pectancy, the prevailing mood quickly changed to disappointment
for several reasons. First, the period was one of widespread suffer- *The bitter fruit of*
ing, caused by inflated prices, a severe famine, and the ravages of *disillusionment*
disease, including an influenza epidemic which wiped out 13 million
people in 1918–1919. Second, the political reforms embodied in the
Government of India Act of 1919 fell far short of responsible government. The Act was undeniably a step forward. It introduced to
a limited degree the principle of ministerial responsibility in the
British provinces by giving provincial legislatures certain "transferred" powers (over such fields as education, health, and sanita-

tion). But through their "reserved" powers, provincial governors retained control over the police, prisons, and courts, as well as over other important areas. Moreover, the governor could, if he considered it necessary, override the legislature even in its "transferred" powers, and his budget was independent of legislative enactment. Dyarchy—as the scheme of divided authority in the provinces was called—did not apply at all to the central government over which the Governor-General (Viceroy) was still supreme, although he was to be assisted by a bicameral legislature, the majority of whose members were elected. The Act of 1919 did enlarge the Indian electorate, but the franchise was still restricted to a tiny minority of property owners numbering about 3 per cent of the population of British India. In addition, the electorate was split up into communal groups, with separate constituencies for Hindus, Moslems, Sikhs, landholders, and other special interests. To Indian nationalists, the constitution of 1919 appeared to be a breach of promise on England's part.

British repression; the Amritsar massacre

Probably an even greater factor than the Act of 1919 in arousing resentment was the repressive policy which the British Government of India adopted at the close of the war. Punitive measures against rioting led to angry protests and to open violence, climaxed by one of the most shocking affairs in the annals of British rule in India—the Amritsar massacre of 1919. To check a series of outrages in the Punjab, the government had sent troops into the province under the command of Brigadier-General Dyer. At Amritsar on April 13, learning that a large crowd of people was assembling for a public demonstration, General Dyer took a detachment of soldiers to the meeting place and immediately ordered his men to open fire. The crowd, which was listening to speeches and was unarmed, had gathered in an enclosed space, of which Dyer blocked the exit. After ten minutes of steady rifle fire, almost 400 people were killed and more than a thousand wounded. News of this cold-blooded butchery—perpetrated in the name of upholding the "rule of law"—inflamed public indignation throughout India and elsewhere. A commission appointed by the British government to investigate the affair eventually pronounced a mild censure of Dyer, finding him guilty of a "grave error"—apparently in firing too long and in making no provision for the wounded.[11] General Dyer was deprived of his commission but received no other punishment, and English admirers raised a purse in his behalf. The Amritsar massacre, and the indulgent attitude of the government toward those responsible for it, antagonized many Indian leaders who had previously been consistent defenders of Britain. The great poet and educator, Rabindranath Tagore, returned the commission of knighthood with which he had been honored. Another Hindu and friend

[11] Dyer's comment was, "I was ready to help them if they applied." Louis Fischer, *The Life of Mahatma Gandhi*, pp. 182–83.

Leaders of Indian Nationalism—Nehru and Ghandi. Ghandi was assassinated in 1948. Nehru served as Prime Minister of India from 1947 to his death in 1964.

of Tagore who now became the enemy of British rule and threw himself into the nationalist cause was Mohandas K. Gandhi.

The man who was destined to make the greatest single contribution to the movement for Indian independence gave little evidence in his early life that such would be his role. Gandhi was born in 1869 in a small native state on the western coast of India. He came from a middle-class family which had supplied prime ministers to the prince, and his mother, a pious Hindu, endeavored to instill in him fidelity to the traditions of their caste. His family sent him to England to study law, and after his return home he was offered a position with an Indian firm in South Africa, where he spent some twenty years and had a successful legal practice. His chief interest in South Africa, however, became a deep concern for the unfair treatment to which his countrymen were subjected in that color-conscious region. At the risk of his life and in disregard of insults and humiliation, he campaigned continually against economic and social discrimination, encouraging the timid Indian laborers to organize and calling upon the government to remove flagrant injustices. In this campaign he eventually met with considerable success, but even more important to his later career was his discovery of a technique of mass action that could be effectively employed in defending a moral principle against superior physical force. Gandhi called this technique *satyagraha*, which is loosely translated as "nonviolent resistance" but which means literally "soul force" or "the power of truth." With a keen sensitivity to social injustice, he also became convinced that social and political evils could never be eliminated through violence. He believed these evils should be fought against, but with such weapons as refusal to co-operate with oppressors, no matter what the price; attempting to change the evil-

The emergence of Gandhi

519

doer by force of example; and, above all, developing in oneself the attitudes and the disciplines which are essential to an improved social order. While arriving at these ideas by the route of religion, Gandhi also applied them to the political sphere.

Returning to India in 1914, Gandhi warmly endorsed the cause of Britain in the war against the Central Powers, even putting aside his pacifist principles to urge people to enlist, so confident was he that the struggle was against autocracy and militarism. But disillusioned by the government's behavior and shocked by the Amritsar massacre, he repudiated the new Indian Constitution of 1919 and persuaded the Indian National Congress to adopt a program of noncooperation with the government. In 1922, he launched his first mass campaign of nonviolent resistance or "civil disobedience," but suspended the movement after a few weeks when he found that it was being used by terrorists to injure life and property. The program of the Indian National Congress and of the associated Gandhian movement, however, was already significant because it had begun to attract wide support and cut across sectarian lines. The Moslem League was behind it for a while, partly because Gandhi had endorsed the so-called Khilafat (Caliphate) movement—a protest of Indian Moslems against the imminent dismemberment of Turkey, which they regarded as a threat to the head of Islam (the Sultan-Caliph). This particular issue was short-lived, but Gandhi was unswerving in his insistence upon Hindu-Moslem cooperation.

During the 1920's, as the nationalist movement acquired momentum, a number of new personalities came to the fore, of whom the most prominent was Jawaharlal Nehru. The Nehrus were a distinguished Brahman family, wealthy and influential. They had everything to lose, from the purely material standpoint, by casting their lot with a revolutionary movement; but such was the choice they made. Both father and son (and other members of the family) became admirers of Gandhi and joined the National Congress. The father adhered generally to the moderate faction, while his son, who was elected president of the Congress several times, became a leader of the militant and radical wing. The son, Jawaharlal (1889–1964), was educated at the best English schools, taking a B.A. degree at Cambridge University, and became thoroughly Westernized in his tastes and personal interests. Unlike Gandhi, he was by temperament rational and scientific and approached India's problems from a secular standpoint, welcoming industrial development and material progress. While he revered India's cultural heritage, he was emancipated from the dogmas and taboos of traditional Hinduism and—like most of the educated nationalist reformers—opposed the institution of caste. Nehru also became intensely concerned with the need for social reform. He did not embrace Marxism, but he advocated government intervention to alleviate poverty, rehabilitate the peasants, and protect industrial workers. Under Nehru's influence a substantial segment of the National Congress adopted as its two major objectives the winning of complete independence for India and the establishment of a democratic and moderately socialistic regime.

The Indian National Congress at its 1928 session had adopted a resolution demanding that Britain grant Dominion status within one year. At a lively and unusually large conclave of the Congress in December 1929, the dynamic triumvirate of Gandhi and the two Nehrus persuaded members to take the pledge of *Purna Swaraj* ("Complete Independence"). They announced that January 26 would be celebrated as "Independence Day," reinforced by the threat of civil disobedience. Accordingly, Gandhi's second mass campaign of civil disobedience was launched in the spring of 1930. Indians resigned from public office, stopped buying foreign goods, picketed shops and courts, and even refused to pay taxes. The most dramatic event was Gandhi's famous "march to the sea," in which he led a large body of followers on foot through village after village until they reached the coast. There they filled pans with sea water and let it evaporate to make salt, breaking the law by evading the salt tax and defying a government monopoly. In the salt episode as in the boycotting of state liquor shops, Gandhi shrewdly combined a political issue with a moral principle, thus putting his opponents in an embarrassing position. Widespread arrests accompanied the disobedience campaign. Gandhi was imprisoned in May, and the total number of Congress members jailed at this time has been estimated as high as 60,000.

Modifying his strategy but not his objectives, Gandhi next attempted to reach an understanding with the British authorities. He had been released from prison early in 1931 and obtained a series of interviews with the Viceroy, Lord Irwin (much to the disgust of Winston Churchill, who was "nauseated" at the thought of "a seditious fakir striding half-naked up the steps of the Viceregal Palace").[12] Gandhi agreed to suspend the civil-disobedience campaign and to participate in the second Round Table Conference in London. Nothing substantial came from the conference, however, except evidence of the divergence between Indian and British views and also of the serious differences among the various Indian elements. At the London Round Table, Gandhi, as the Indian Congress representative, probably pressed unwarrantably his claim to speak for the whole of India, but at the time his chief concern was the problem of the "Untouchables" (outcastes). In disagreement with the representative of the "Untouchables" (Dr. Ambedkar), Gandhi firmly opposed the proposal to place them in a special electorate, so convinced was he that these depressed classes should be treated as an integral part of the Hindu community and freed from all discrimination.

Gandhi's crusade
on behalf of the
"Untouchables"

[12] Quoted in T. W. Wallbank, *India in the New Era*, p. 128.

Gandhi's
temporary re-
tirement from
politics

At the close of the civil-disobedience campaign of 1931–1934, Gandhi retired temporarily from politics. He had proved to be the most powerful political figure in the Congress; he was a factor to reckon with at Whitehall and Westminster as well as at Delhi, and he had thousands of followers who would carry out his will almost blindly. Furthermore, he had developed, in the technique of non-violent resistance, an instrument of mass action of immeasurable potency. In stepping out of the political arena Gandhi was not unaware of the effectiveness of the political weapons he had forged. He recognized, however, the dangers in any form of mass action, and he believed that the Indian people, including himself, needed to perfect their self-control. He said openly that he would prefer for India to remain subject to Britain than for her to attain freedom through a violent revolution. At the opposite pole from Machiavelli, Lenin, and many others, Gandhi denied that the end justifies the means. He believed instead that the means largely determine what the end will be.

The religious
motivation of
Gandhi's phi-
losophy

Another factor which influenced Gandhi to disassociate himself from the Congress temporarily was that he did not consider politics to be the most important activity and did not consider himself as primarily a political leader. Already he had come to be known to his followers as the Mahatma ("Great Soul"). He disavowed the title and strenuously discouraged the tendency of ignorant admirers to deify him. Still, he was essentially a religious figure in his personal convictions and in his world view. His beliefs were derived partly from the *Bhagavad-Gita* (which he first read in London in an English translation), partly from the writings of Tolstoi and Ruskin, and partly from the New Testament. He considered himself a Hindu and retained many traditional notions, but he embraced much of the spirit of Christianity, and his real interest lay in the development of religious and ethical values in human society. He had no faith in any political or economic formula and believed that the only real hope for India—or for the world—lay in the cultivation of spiritual resources.

Gandhi's
economic and
social views

Finally, Gandhi wished to devote the remaining years of his life to helping the downtrodden peasants. He established his *ashram* (hermitage) in one of the poorest regions of Central India and attempted to educate the villagers in better methods of cultivation and sanitation and in the use of subsidiary industries, especially home spinning and weaving, to improve their living standards. He gave impetus to a widespread movement to rehabilitate the ancient village economy which had long been in decay. At one time he repudiated the entire Industrial Revolution and even Western science. However, he came to recognize that industrialization was inevitable; and under Nehru's influence he was converted, not to socialism, but to the necessity of government intervention to promote land reform and a more equitable distribution of wealth. He became the particular champion of the "Untouchables," declaring that if the stigma of untouchability did not disappear, then Hindu- ism would have to disappear. He named his weekly newspaper *Harijan*, which was the term he coined for the "Untouchables" and which means "Children of God."

The new constitution embodied in the Government of India Act of 1935 was very disappointing to Indian nationalists, both radicals and moderates. It introduced the principle of dyarchy into the cen- tral government by giving the legislature jurisdiction over certain subjects, but it left the Governor-General with power to interfere at any point. Seemingly a great advance was made in the provincial governments because here the dyarchy was abolished and the assemblies were permitted to discuss and act upon any matter not reserved to the central authority, and the provincial ministries were made responsible to the elected assemblies. However, the provincial governor retained "special responsibilities" and "discretionary powers," which raised doubts as to whether the new system would be much different from the old. The franchise was considerably extended to include about 30 million voters, roughly one-fourth of the adult population of British India, but the device of communal electorates was carried to an excess. Not only religious groups but also special economic classes were given separate representation, and the constitution seemed to be weighted in favor of religious minorities and the propertied interests. The Act also provided for letting the native states enter a federation with the central government under terms which would have given the states (most of which were autocracies) an excessive representation.

The Indian National Congress strongly condemned the new constitution, which Nehru pronounced a "new charter of slavery." The Congress decided, however, to run candidates in elections, first with the intention of obstructing the processes of government, and later, as the Congress party gained sweeping victories at the polls, with the idea of forming ministries and enacting legislation. By 1937, the Indian Congress had working majorities in seven of the eleven provinces of British India, and during the next two years these provinces enjoyed a taste of responsible parliamentary government. The ministries gave a good account of themselves and sponsored substantial reforms in the fields of education and social welfare. Most remarkable was the novel sight of English civil servants dutifully executing the policies of Indian ministers.

In spite of the good omen of Anglo-Indian cooperation, there were signs of trouble in the offing. A cleavage was growing between the moderate and radical wings of the National Congress, and even more serious was the increased friction between the Congress and the Moslem League. The Hindu-Moslem tension was caused partly by occasional outbreaks of violence incited by religious fanatics; partly by a fear among Moslems that if India became self-governing, as now seemed possible, they would be at a disadvantage as a minority group; and partly by the fact that the Moslem League had come under the aggressive leadership of Mohammed Ali Jinnah. After a period of relative quiescence and impotence the League had begun to revive as a definite political force.

That M. A. Jinnah (1876–1948) should become the guiding figure of a militant sectarian organization was somewhat ironic.

Jinnah, a successful lawyer, had received a Western education and was decidedly secular in temperament. He did not observe the code of pious Moslems, and he had married a Parsee. Jinnah joined the Indian National Congress, in which he took an active part, but he resigned when Gandhi began to come into ascendancy. After withdrawing from political activity for a while, Jinnah undertook to vitalize the Moslem League and succeeded in making it, for the first time, the mouthpiece of the majority of Indian Moslems and a political party which would have to be bargained with in the future. Jinnah insisted that special guaranties were necessary to protect the Moslem minority, and finally (by 1940) went so far as to claim that the Indian Moslems were not merely a minority or a religious community but a distinct nation. The claim was dubious. Most Moslems in India were the descendants of natives who had been converted to Islam (Jinnah's family belonged to a group of recent converts) and were as truly Indian as the Hindus. If religious affiliation were to be made the basis of nationhood, then India would have to be split into many fragments and a united state would be impossible. The championing by the Moslem League of the interests of the Islamic community finally culminated in the demand for a separate state—Pakistan—an idea not original with Jinnah but which he at last adopted.

The outbreak of World War II brought matters to a critical juncture in India. The Congress took the blunt position that India would fight only as a free nation and demanded self-government

with permission to draw up a new constitution. The Viceroy could only promise that the 1935 Constitution would be reconsidered after the war and that, for the time being, he would welcome greater "consultation" with representative groups. In October 1940, the Congress authorized the Mahatma to inaugurate a nonviolent civil-disobedience campaign, which began at once. It was not a mass movement, though, and took the form of having individuals make speeches against the war. In each instance the authorities were duly notified in advance, the speaker was arrested quietly, and the jails began to swell again. There was no active interference with the civil or military administration. Actually, Indian contributions to the war against the Axis were enormous—far greater than in World War I—because Indian manufactures had now become important. Two million men were recruited for the Indian army

and many Indian officers were commissioned.

With the Japanese invasion of Malaya and Burma, the British government determined on a new effort to rally Indian public opinion to its support and sent Sir Stafford Cripps to India in March 1942 to present a proposal. The "Cripps Offer" was in many ways a generous one, promising (after the war) full Dominion status for India under a constitution drafted by Indians, including representatives of the native states. Practically all the articulate Indian groups rejected the proposal for several reasons. First, although Cripps was looked upon as a sincere friend of India, there was hesitancy in accepting at face value an offer from the Churchill government. Churchill had previously declared that the Atlantic Charter did not apply to Britain's colonial areas and he was remembered for strong denunciations of the Congress leaders. Second, the plan gave permission for any province to refuse to join the proposed federation and retain a separate connection with Britain, a provision which the nationalists feared might lead to the "Balkanization" of the Indian subcontinent. Finally, the Indian demand for immediate transfer of responsibility to Indians in the Viceroy's Council was rejected.

The failure of the Cripps Offer of 1942 revealed that Indian nationalist sentiment had reached such a degree of agitation that it could no longer be easily smoothed over. The National Congress passed a resolution calling upon England to "Quit India." Congress leaders, who had been released during the Cripps mission, were reimprisoned, and rioting broke out in some regions. However, as the war neared its close, it became evident that the British government would renew or even go beyond the Cripps proposal. Events moved rapidly when the Churchill government was replaced by a Labour cabinet under Clement Attlee. In March 1946 Attlee announced that the choice of a new constitution would be India's alone and that, while he hoped the Indian people would remain within the Commonwealth, this must be by their own free will. A Cabinet Mission accordingly was sent to India to work with Indian leaders in arranging the transfer of authority.

The Labor government's offer of self-rule to India

Now that the British government was prepared to grant independence, the chief stumbling block was found to lie in the Hindu-Moslem controversy, which had grown to large proportions as a political issue only during the preceding decade. For a while it looked as if the partition of India could be avoided. The Cabinet Mission drafted a scheme for a federal union with safeguards to protect minorities and with provisions for considerable regional autonomy. Both the Congress and the League at first accepted this general plan, but in July (1946) Jinnah, reversing his earlier position, rejected the Mission proposal, demanded a separate Moslem state, and summoned his followers to engage in "direct action." The consequence was bloody communal rioting in which about 12,000 lives were lost. When a Constituent Assembly met in December 1946 to draft a constitution, the Moslem League sent no

The Hindu-Moslem controversy and the decision for partition

representatives, nor could it be persuaded to do so. Although Jinnah's intransigence was evident, some of the blame must rest with Congress members, who made it clear that they would not be bound by any pledges emanating from the British Cabinet Mission. So much ill will had been aroused on both sides that compromise was very difficult. A few extreme Hindu nationalists viewed the prospect of partition with indifference, rashly assuming that a separate Moslem state would sooner or later have to seek reunion with India on India's terms. The British government's determination to

Moslem Immigrants to Pakistan. They are leaving Amritsar in the Punjab, one of the provinces which was split by the Partition agreement. Some 10 million refugees fled across the borders from both directions before the end of 1947, and many of the survivors have not yet found permanent homes.

**The end of
British Raj**

relinquish its responsibilities as quickly as possible—in striking contrast to the cautious and dilatory policy of the preceding 90 years—doubtless also lessened the chances of resolving the deadlock between the Hindu and Moslem communities. Attlee had served notice that England would leave India by June of 1948. Seeing no other alternative, the new Viceroy (Lord Mountbatten) prepared to transfer British authority to two governments instead of one, a delicate and difficult operation. Not only were the Hindu and Moslem provinces separated, but three provinces—Bengal, the Punjab, and Assam—had to be split in order to prevent large Hindu minorities from being assigned to Pakistan. Although Pakistan did not include all the areas demanded by the Moslem League, the division was accepted by both sides in the controversy. Indian independence was formally granted by act of Parliament in July 1947, and in August all authority was surrendered to the two new Dominions.

5. INDEPENDENT INDIA AND PAKISTAN

It was a tragic circumstance that the Indian struggle for independence, characterized more by patience than by slaughter, should conclude with the country divided and in an atmosphere of hostility. The partition of India, from the standpoints of geography and economics, was highly artificial. Pakistan consists of two separate regions 1000 miles apart. They include the areas producing jute, cotton, and rice. India, with an insufficient food supply, has the factories needed to process Pakistan's raw materials. Important canals and river systems are bisected by the political boundaries. Nor did partition solve the minority problem. Approximately 15 per cent of Pakistan's inhabitants are non-Moslems, chiefly Hindus. The Republic of India has a Moselm minority of approximately 10 per cent. Even before partition was completed, refugees began to stream across the borders—Hindus and Sikhs fleeing from Moslem domination and Moslems fearing Hindu persecution. More than 10 million people were involved in the mass exodus during the latter part of 1947, and their suffering was indescribable. The governments of India and Pakistan tried to assist and protect the refugees but could not prevent the outrages committed by frenzied fanatics on both sides. It was in connection with this religious strife that Gandhi, a frail old man in his late seventies, performed his last service to India. By appealing to the Hindus and by threatening to fast, he stopped riots in Calcutta that had seemed to be unquenchable. Early in 1948 he went to Delhi, where violence had also occurred, and began a fast which ended when the key spokesmen for the Congress and the Hindu community pledged protection for the lives and property of Moslems. On January 30, on his way to evening prayers, Gandhi was shot to death by a member of a chauvinistic Hindu society. He was mourned all over India and in Pakistan, and the shock of his assassination had at least a temporarily sobering effect upon the public temper.

A prime source of controversy between India and Pakistan was the disposition of the native states. Since the states were no longer protected by the British Raj, it was assumed that they would voluntarily join either India or Pakistan. Most of them did so, the greater number of course going to India, but in a few instances there was trouble. Hyderabad in the Deccan, the largest state in India, had a Hindu population ruled over by a Moslem prince, the Nizam. The Indian government refused to let the Nizam remain independent, as he apparently planned to do. It dispatched an army into Hyderabad and quickly took over the administration (September 1948). In this instance the Indian government claimed to be acting on behalf of the Nizam's Hindu subjects, but it had already taken a somewhat different position in the Kashmir dispute. In this northern state a Hindu prince ruled over subjects who were pre-

The tragic division
of India; the
assassination
of Gandhi

527

dominantly Moslems. In 1947 the New Delhi government announced that Kashmir had acceded to the Indian Union at the request of the Maharaja, who, it was argued, had the legal right to
transfer his sovereignty. The Maharaja, faced with an invasion of
Moslem tribesmen, had appealed to India for military support, and
the Indian government had insisted upon the accession of Kashmir
to India as a prior condition to granting his request. Fighting between Indian and Pakistani troops was halted in 1949 by a cease-fire
agreement arranged through a United Nations commission. The
cease-fire, however, proved to be only a truce and left Kashmir
divided into two parts, occupied respectively by Pakistan and
India, with the larger portion under Indian control.

The Kashmir controversy has remained the most stubborn and
serious source of friction between India and Pakistan. Both states

**Failure to resolve
the conflict**

accepted in principle the U.N. Security Council's proposal for a
plebiscite which would allow the Kashmiris to determine their own
political destiny; but they could not agree upon the conditions for
implementing this proposal. Indian leaders would have welcomed
the. acquisition of Kashmir by plebiscite because such a victory, in
a region overwhelmingly Moslem, would strengthen their claim
that India was a nonsectarian state. However, they were doubtful
of securing a favorable vote, especially with Pakistani troops stationed in the country. Although some facts are disputable, New
Delhi's attitude in the Kashmir affair has been both unyielding and
contradictory. The government at first insisted that the future of
Kashmir should be determined by referendum held under international auspices. In 1953 the prime ministers of India and Pakistan
jointly called for the appointment of a Plebiscite Administrator. In
that same year, however, Indian authorities abruptly deposed and
held in prison without trial Sheikh Abdullah, the first Premier of
Kashmir, who had played a leading part in its accession to India but
later advocated independence. In January 1957 New Delhi announced the formal annexation of Kashmir to India, but the very
next month Nehru affirmed: "We cannot stay in Kashmir for a
moment without the consent of the Kashmiris. It is not our
property." [13] Subsequently Nehru took the position that Kashmir
was a domestic issue not subject to mediation by any outside
agency.

India retained the status of a Dominion only until 1950, when a
new constitution made it an independent republic, replacing the

**The Republic
of India**

Governor-General by an elected President and severing all ties
with the British crown. Nevertheless, India voluntarily remained
within the Commonwealth of Nations (with the term "British"
deleted) and thus became the first completely independent republic
to hold membership in the association. India has an independent

[13] Sheikh M. Abdullah, "Kashmir, India and Pakistan," *Foreign Affairs*, April
1965, p. 532.

judiciary and a President chosen by an electoral college, but follows the English system of parliamentary government, with the chief power vested in a Prime Minister responsible to the lower house of the central legislature. The subordinate states, with unicameral legislatures, have the same type of ministerial government. Both the state and national legislative bodies are elected by universal adult suffrage for five-year terms. The Constitution includes a comprehensive Bill of Rights, outlawing untouchability and discrimination based on caste, and providing for legal equality of the sexes. Although federal in structure, the government has been handicapped by a distribution of power between the center and the states which is both rigid and ambiguous. The Constitution gives the President power to suspend a state government in an emergency, but some very critical areas of jurisdiction are reposed in the states, including education, agriculture, and taxes on land.

Many difficulties confronted the Republic of India from the very beginning. The absorption of more than 500 princely states into the new political structure, a formidable task in itself, was handled with relative dispatch. Some of the dethroned rajas were retained as governors for a time, but by 1957 all of them were removed from office, having been compensated for their loss of power by the award of perhaps overly generous pensions. Other problems proved more obstinate, revealing dangerous sectional and social cleavages. One of them had to do with linguistic rivalries. In the interest of promoting national unity, the government announced that Hindi, the principal tongue of northern India but spoken by only about one-third of the total population, was to become the official language of the country by 1965. Resistance on the part of other regional linguistic groups proved so strong, however, that on the date when the change was to go into effect, in January 1965, bloody riots broke out in the south, two cabinet ministers resigned, and the government felt constrained to announce that English would remain an "associate official language" as long as non-Hindi-speaking Indians desired.

While possessing the framework of democratic institutions, India during her first two decades of independence operated under what was in effect a one-party system. The Congress party dominated all branches of the government, and Jawaharlal Nehru served continuously as Prime Minister until his death in May 1964. This long tenure of power was not an unmixed blessing either for the party or for the country. Once the focal point of an indomitable struggle for freedom, the Congress developed into a kind of Establishment, entrenched behind its monopoly of patronage and the Administrative Services (vastly larger than the old British Indian Civil Service), and its vigor, idealism, and integrity became corroded. Even the luster of Nehru—generally revered as a revolutionary hero and Gandhi's "heir"—dimmed in later years. Endowed with qualities of

529

mind and heart that entitled him to high rank among the popular leaders of this century, Nehru was not entirely successful as a statesman. He refused to take the initiative in any serious attempt to settle the Kashmir dispute. As an avowed enemy of colonialism, in 1961 he authorized the forcible occupation of Goa, Diu, and Damão, the last remnants of Portugal's empire on the subcontinent; but he grossly miscalculated in dealing with India's powerful northern neighbor, Communist China. When a boundary dispute with China erupted into a small-scale war along the southern slopes of the Himalayas in the fall of 1962, the Indian government was caught unprepared and its forces offered feeble resistance. Fighting stopped when the Chinese unilaterally declared a cease-fire, after they had occupied positions claimed by the Indians as rightfully theirs. The humiliation of this debacle and the shattering of his faith in the solidarity of the two great Asian republics were a blow from which Nehru never recovered.

Nehru's death left the party with no leader of sufficient stature to hold its dissident factions together; rivalries broke out into the open, while India's internal condition deteriorated. As a compromise choice, the premiership fell to frail, mild-mannered L. B. Shastri, who described himself as "mediocre" but who gave a creditable performance in office until his death of a heart attack in January 1966. To succeed him as Prime Minister the party chiefs picked Nehru's daughter, Mrs. Indira Gandhi. Although her assets included considerable personal charm as well as the prestige of the family name, she was unable to solve critical problems or restore public confidence. Disenchantment with the administration was amply demonstrated in India's fourth general election (February 1967), the first one to be marred by tumult and violence. Although the Congress party retained a slim majority in the central parliament, it lost control in half of the state governments, and several members of its top echelon were defeated for re-election in their own districts. While the challenge to Congress's long monopoly of power was potentially salutary, the opposition did not constitute a united group with a coherent program but merely an assortment of various parties, many of them representing purely sectional interests. Considering the seemingly golden opportunity presented by the widespread poverty of India, it is remarkable that the Communists have not been more effective. Although strong in some localities they have had little success on a national scale, and the party split into rival factions over the Sino-Soviet dispute. The Socialists also have been relatively impotent politically. The largest gains in the 1967 election were scored by parties of the Right, including the Jan Sangh, a militant Hindu organization that had demanded legislation to prohibit cow slaughter and adamantly opposed reconciliation with Pakistan.

530   The independent states of India and Pakistan were bequeathed

many things of value by the British: the rudiments of parliamentary government, trained civil servants, an excellent network of railroads, the nuclei of effective military forces, and an educated elite versed in Western institutions and practices. The new states also inherited the unsolved problems of the era of colonial rule, chief of which is the backwardness and crushing poverty of most of the population. Steady and substantial economic progress is necessary if India and Pakistan are to make their way as successful modern states—or even to survive as political entities. The Indian government, committed to material progress, created a Planning Commission and launched a series of Five-Year Plans, beginning in

Economic problems; the Five-Year Plans

531

1951. In many fields impressive results were achieved. During the First Plan grain production rose by 20 per cent, 26 million acres of new land were brought under cultivation, while the manufacture of cement and electric power potential were nearly doubled. However, even in the vital area of agriculture, improvements were insufficient to offset an inexorable increase in the numbers of people. With population expanding at the rate of more than a million each month, India seems to be in the desperate position of having to run at top speed in order merely to stand still. Despite an extensive government campaign to encourage the practice of birth control, the rate of increase during the 1950's rose to 2.3 per cent annually. It is estimated that the total population figure, which stood at about 510 million in 1967, will climb to 775 million by 1986.

Deficiencies in
the Plans

The later Plans have fallen far short of their objectives, partly because they made the mistake of attempting to develop heavy industry before elementary consumer needs had been met. Even more serious was the failure to create a tax structure capable of providing capital for an ambitious development program. The logical source of untapped capital reserves would be the upper strata of relatively wealthy peasants, who have almost entirely escaped taxation. It is estimated that not more than 1 per cent of the gross agricultural output is available to the government through tax revenues.[14] The government has been unable or unwilling to take drastic steps to avert food crises, which have been intensified by the refusal of states with grain surpluses to relieve the stricken areas. Although the 1965 grain harvest set a record—67 per cent above the 1951 yield—6.5 million tons had to be imported from abroad. The 1966 season was threatened by the worst drought of the century, and Mrs. Gandhi announced in June that India's economy was in its most critical state since independence.

The need for
further progress

While the government and the Congress party are not to blame for natural calamities or for inability to perform miracles, they can be justly criticized for ineffectiveness, inertia, and seeming indifference to the people's welfare. Nature has not condemned India to be a land of poverty forever. The country has great potential resources—notably rich reserves of iron ore—and probably could well support an industrialized, educated society. But impatience at the slow rate of change may bring irresistible pressures for drastic action under more aggressive and less scrupulous leadership. To their credit Nehru and his associates tried to adhere to democratic principles, but they did little to solve basic economic and social problems. The per-acre yield of wheat, rice, corn, peanuts, and cotton is the lowest in the world. Although India's electrical capacity has more than tripled since 1947, only 2½ per cent of her small towns and villages enjoy the advantages of electricity. Her population is 75 per cent illiterate, and she has only one doctor for every

[14] S. S. Harrison, *India: The Most Dangerous Decades*, p. 301.

6000 inhabitants. Poor peasants and farm laborers are not yet emancipated from the grip of moneylenders; farm co-operatives are mostly controlled by a small minority of larger landowners, who also wield disproportionate influence over the state legislatures. Regardless of the principles enunciated in the Constitution, the influence of caste is still potent. It intensifies linguistic jealousies and class competition; it has entered the arena of politics, especially at the state level, and it is exploited by political parties.

Under Nehru's guidance India's foreign policy initially was one of "neutralism" or nonalignment, stemming from a distaste for military alliances and from a desire to cultivate a spirit of friendship and co-operation with other Asian countries, including the Communist. However, Sino-Indian relations, which had been marked by expressions of cordiality on both sides, suffered a rude shock following China's provocative action in Tibet and in the disputed border area between India and Tibet. The New Delhi government gave asylum to the Dalai Lama, who escaped from his country while Chinese troops were suppressing the Tibetan rebellion in 1959. When the border clash with China in 1962 revealed India's vulnerability, the government appealed to the great powers for help and obtained agreements for limited military assistance both from the United States and from the Soviet Union. Following Nehru's death, friction between India and Pakistan over the Kashmir issue increased, and it culminated in open warfare during the summer and fall of 1965. The only victor in this senseless conflict was the Soviet Union, which scored a diplomatic triumph when Premier Kosygin persuaded President Ayub Khan and Prime Minister Shastri to meet with him at Tashkent in January 1966 and agree to a mutual withdrawal of forces, the repatriation of pris-

Indian foreign policy: from non-alignment to "bi-alignment"

Indian Troops on Their Way to Defend a Himalayan Pass in the Northeast against the Chinese Communists, November 1962. (Later this pass fell to the Communists.)

oners, and the re-establishment of diplomatic relations. India's confrontation with China and her belligerence towards Pakistan has involved her more and more deeply in the meshes of power politics. In the early days Nehru had hoped that his country could remain outside the power blocs and perhaps assume the role of peacemaker between them. Lately she has become more like a client of two superstates—the United States and the U.S.S.R.—drawn from a position of nonalignment to one of "bi-alignment." [15]

The problems confronting Pakistan have been similar to India's and just as acute. An exodus of Hindus at the time of Partition deprived Pakistan of middle-class businessmen and financiers, and the migration of Sikhs from the Punjab left that rich agricultural region temporarily disorganized. The new state was an artificial body from its inception. The West and East wings—separated geographically by 1000 miles—are perhaps even farther apart in terms of economics, language, and cultural traditions, with only religion (and the Pakistan International Airlines) serving as a common bond. East Pakistan (eastern Bengal but excluding the great port of Calcutta), with only one-sixth of the area, holds more than half of Pakistan's 100 million people, but, until recently, received inadequate attention from the national government. Separatist movements within a state which is itself the fruit of separatism have threatened to pull it apart. A controversy over the language question was settled by a reasonable compromise which designated two official languages—Urdu (actually the native speech of a minority even in West Pakistan) and Bengali. Meanwhile, as in India, English continues to be an essential medium of communication.

Political democracy has been almost nonexistent in Pakistan, where the creation of any kind of viable government proved an arduous task. The attempt to reconcile the concept of an Islamic community (theoretically guided by the Koran and the body of sacred law) with the modern ideal of a national state presented a stumbling block, and some unscrupulous politicians exploited religious sentiments for their own ends and usually in support of reactionary policies. Against a background of dissension and without effective leadership (M. A. Jinnah died in 1948 and the Moslem League gradually disintegrated) two successive constituent assemblies struggled with the drafting of a constitution, which was declared in effect in March 1956. Pakistan, while remaining a member of the Commonwealth, was defined as an "Islamic Republic" under a President who was required to be a Moslem. Elections were never held under this constitution. The ensuing period was one of unbridled political bickering, racketeering, and corruption, terminated only when General (later Field Marshal) M. Ayub Khan in October 1958 seized control of the government and imposed martial

[15] S. S. Harrison, "Troubled India and Her Neighbors," *Foreign Affairs,* January 1965, p. 326.

law. Although Ayub had acted at the instigation of the President, he soon removed him from office along with other prominent party officials, offering them a choice between jail sentences or retirement from politics (most of them chose the latter). Ayub's avowed purpose was to "clean up the mess," and in this he largely succeeded, by direct and peremptory measures but without terror and brutality.

Not a stereotype of the military dictator but a "strong man" reminiscent in some ways of Turkey's Kemal Ataturk, Ayub Khan has won considerable respect among his own countrymen and among foreign observers. His regime (operated by civilians subject to military supervision) brought some improvement over the conditions prevalent during the politicians' paradise of the preceding decade. Inflation was halted, a few modest reforms were enacted, a new capital was built at Rawalpindi near the Northwest Frontier, and industrialization in West Pakistan was extended.

Pakistan received a new constitution in March 1962, after a report by an appointed constitutional commission but bearing the stamp of Ayub Khan, who had by this time assumed the office of President. The new government incorporates the principle of "Basic Democracy." Some 80,000 "councillors"—representatives of local units—constitute a series of electoral colleges for electing the two provincial assemblies, the National Assembly, and even the President. The voters have no direct representation in the legislatures, and effective power is concentrated in the hands of the President. Ayub publicly defended the adoption of a "Presidential system" on the ground that it was the only alternative to instability—"a luxury that a developing country like ours cannot afford." Declaring that the parliamentary experiment had failed, he warned: "Don't let us kid ourselves and cling to clichés and assume that we are ready to work such a refined system knowing the failure of earlier attempts." [16] Obviously the 1962 Constitution is authoritarian rather than democratic, even though it is hoped that it will stimulate initiative and participation in local affairs among the villagers. Political parties have been permitted to reappear, including two separate versions of the Moslem League, but no effective opposition has developed. The strength of Ayub's position was demonstrated in 1965, when the 80,000-member electoral colleges chose him President for a five-year term by a substantial majority. The rival candidate was no less a figure than Fatima Jinnah, daughter of Pakistan's revered founder. Although support could be found for Miss Jinnah's allegation that democracy in Pakistan is "a joke," Ayub Khan has committed himself to the "ultimate aim" of restoring democracy.

In the face of internal dissension and, as in India, the onus of an alarming birth rate, Pakistan has made considerable economic prog-

[16] From a radio address, quoted in Hugh Tinker, *India and Pakistan*, p. 90.

A Fertilizer Factory in East Pakistan Built by Japanese Contractors. The central figure in the inspection group is President Mohammed Ayub Khan of Pakistan. The factory, which is based on natural gas, will produce annually over 1,000,000 tons of high-powered fertilizer effective for rice, jute, and tea.

Economic progress

ress. An agricultural assistance program brought about a partial redistribution of lands for the benefit of small cultivators, and farm income has risen by more than 30 per cent since 1958. With almost no manufactures at the outset, Pakistan has attained a high rate of industrial growth. A Third Five-Year Plan, begun in 1965, aims to increase national income by 37 per cent and also to redress the imbalance between the two sections of the country. Nevertheless, disaffection in East Pakistan has not been entirely allayed.

Divergent views on foreign policy have contributed to animosity between India and Pakistan. Pakistan became a member both of

Foreign relations of India and Pakistan

SEATO and of CENTO, thus identifying herself with the Western alliance system. Under a military aid pact of 1954, the United States agreed to provide supersonic aircraft and other modern weapons and in turn received permission to use Pakistan territory for strategic intelligence activities. The Kashmir stalemate and especially the outbreak of war with India created doubt as to the value of Pakistan's alliances. The Pakistani resented United States military assistance to India, and the Indians charged that American weapons were being used against them. While India quietly abandoned her policy of nonalignment, Pakistan endeavored to extricate herself from the bonds tying her to the Western bloc; the Rawalpindi government declined to participate in the 1967 SEATO military exercises. In spite of mutual suspicion and a heritage of controversy, the strained relations between India and Pakistan are by no means irreparable. Both states are members of the United Nations and of the Commonwealth. Each is a natural market area for the other, and they have amicably settled a number of issues. An outstanding achievement was the agreement for division of the

536 Indus valley waters signed by Nehru and Ayub Khan in 1960. The agreement cleared the way for a multiple-purpose development project in the area, with capital supplied jointly by the World Bank, India and Pakistan, and several other countries, including the United States.

SELECTED READINGS—THE BRITISH
COMMONWEALTH

· *Items so designated are available in paperbound editions.*

Belshaw, Horace, *New Zealand*, United Nations Series, Berkeley, 1947.

Brady, Alexander, *Democracy in the Dominions*, Toronto, 1958.

Clokie, H. McD., *Canadian Government and Politics*, New York, 1945.

Creighton, Donald G., *Dominion of the North, A History of Canada*, Boston, 1944.

Dawson, R. M., *The Government of Canada*, Toronto, 1963.

Fitzpatrick, Brian, *The Australian People, 1788–1945*, Melbourne, 1946. An analytical and revealing account.

Grattan, C. H., *Australia*, Berkeley, 1947.

———, *Introducing Australia*, New York, 1942.

Lipson, Leslie, *The Politics of Equality; New Zealand's Adventures in Democracy*, Chicago, 1948.

MacInnes, Colin, *Australia and New Zealand*, New York, 1966.

McInnis, E. W., *Canada; a Political and Social History*, New York, 1959.

Nash, Walter, *New Zealand, a Democracy That Works*, New York, 1943.

Rawson, Geoffrey, *Australia*, London, 1948.

Shaw, A. G. L., *Convicts and the Colonies*, New York, 1966.

· Siegfried, André, *The Race Question in Canada*, New York, 1907 (McClelland & Stuart). A perceptive study.

Wade, Mason, *The French Canadians*, New York, 1955.

Wheare, K. C., *The Statute of Westminster and Dominion Status*, New York, 1938.

—INDIA AND PAKISTAN (*See also* Readings for Chapter 4)

Anstey, Vera, *The Economic Development of India*, rev. ed., London, 1952.

Azad, M. A. K., *India Wins Freedom: An Autobiographical Narrative*, New York, 1960. By a Moslem statesman within the Congress party.

Bauer, P. T., *Indian Economic Policy and Development*, New York, 1961.

Binder, Leonard, *Religion and Politics in Pakistan*, Berkeley, 1961. Deals with the period of constitution making, 1949–1954.

· Bondurant, Joan, *Conquest of Violence; The Gandhian Philosophy of Conflict*, rev. ed., Berkeley, 1965 (California).

Bowles, Chester, *Ambassador's Report*, New York, 1954. A sympathetic interpretation of independent India by a respected diplomat.

Brecher, Michael, *Nehru: A Political Biography*, New York, 1959. Especially good account of events since 1920.

· Brown, D. M., *The Nationalist Movement: Indian Political Thought from Ranade to Bhave*, Berkeley, 1961 (California).

Brown, W. N., *The United States and India and Pakistan*, rev. ed., Cambridge, Mass., 1963.

· Fischer, Louis, *The Life of Mahatma Gandhi*, New York, 1950 (Collier). An admirable biography.

Gadgil, ·D. R., *Planning and Economic Policy in India*, New York, 1961. A highly critical analysis by an Indian economist associated with the Indian Planning Commission.

Gopal, Ram, *Indian Muslims: A Political History (1858–1947)*, New York, 1959. Throws light on the factors leading to Partition.

Griffiths, Percival, *Modern India*, 4th ed., London, 1965.

Harrison, S. S., *India: The Most Dangerous Decades*, Princeton, 1960. A vigorous study of the disruptive elements in Indian society and politics.

Heimsath, C. H., *Indian Nationalism and Hindu Social Reform*, Princeton, 1964.

Hutchins, F. G., *The Illusion of Permanence; British Imperialism in India*, Princeton, 1967.

Ikram, S., and Spear, P., eds., *The Cultural Heritage of Pakistan*, London, 1956.

Jain, G., *Panchsheela and After: Sino-Indian Relations in the Context of the Tibetan Insurrection*, New York, 1960.

Malik, Hafeez, *Moslem Nationalism in India and Pakistan*, Washington, 1963.

Masani, R. P.; *Britain in India: An Account of British Rule in the Indian Subcontinent*, New York, 1960.

Mehrotra, S. R., *India and the Commonwealth, 1885–1929*, New York, 1965. Illuminating study by an Indian scholar.

Menon, V. P., *The Transfer of Power in India*, Princeton, 1957. Informative account covering the period 1939–1947.

Misra, B. B., *The Indian Middle Classes: Their Growth in Modern Times*, New York, 1961.

Moon, Penderel, *Divide and Quit*, Berkeley, 1962. Sees Partition as the consequence of blunders on all sides.

Moraes, Frank, *India Today*, New York, 1960. A critical examination of political trends by the editor of a leading Indian newspaper.

————, *Jawaharlal Nehru*, New York, 1956.

· Morris-Jones, W. H., *The Government and Politics of India*, London, 1964 (Anchor).

Mosley, Leonard, *The Last Days of the British Raj*, New York, 1962. A vivid account, especially in portrayal of the personalities involved.

· Nehru, Jawaharlal, *The Discovery of India*, New York, 1946 (Anchor).

Norman, Dorothy, ed., *Nehru, the First Sixty Years*, 2 vols., New York, 1965. Traces the development of Nehru's political thought, largely through selections from his own writings.

· Palmer, N. D., *The Indian Political System*, Boston, 1961 (Houghton Mifflin).

Reed, Stanley, *The India I Knew, 1897–1947*, London, 1952. Especially informative on the Indian Civil Service.

Roberts, P. E., *History of British India under the Company and the Crown*, 3rd ed., New York, 1952. An excellent political text.

Sheean, Vincent, *Nehru: The Years of Power*, New York, 1960. Sympathetic in treatment.

Symonds, Richard, *The Making of Pakistan*, 2nd ed., London, 1951.

Thompson, E. J., and Garratt, G. T., *The Rise and Fulfilment of British Rule in India*, London, 1934.

· Tinker, Hugh, *India and Pakistan: A Political Analysis*, New York, 1962 (Praeger). By a former member of the Indian Civil Service.

· Wallbank, T. W., *India in the New Era*, Chicago, 1951 (Mentor).

Weekes, R. V., *Pakistan; Birth and Growth of a Muslim Nation*, Princeton, 1964.

· Woodruff, Philip, *The Men Who Ruled India*, 2 vols., New York, 1954 (Shocken).

Birla, G. D., *In the Shadow of the Mahatma: A Personal Memoir.* Selections from Gandhi's correspondence, interviews and conversations.

Chakravarty, A., ed., *A Tagore Reader.*

· Gandhi, M. K., *The Story of My Experiments with Truth* (Beacon). Autobiography.

· Jack, H. A., ed., *The Gandhi Reader: A Source Book of His Life and Writings* (Evergreen).

· Nehru, Jawaharlal, *Toward Freedom* (Beacon). Autobiography.

———, *Independence and After* (Speeches, 1946–1949).

———, *Jawaharlal Nehru's Speeches, 1949–1953.*

Russell, W. H., *My India Mutiny Diary* (contemporary account by the London *Times* correspondent).

Tagore, Rabindranath, *My Reminiscences.*

CHAPTER 17

The Middle East and Africa

(1800-1968)

Africa is once more true to her reputation for novelty. May she also yet find the formula of understanding and co-operation between white and black! The young nations of the world have their own contribution to make to the human causes, and they can best begin to do so by setting their house in order and pledging themselves afresh to the great human principles on which our Western civilisation rests.

—J. C. Smuts, *Freedom*

Civilization is based more on the village and on God's earth than on the town, however attractive certain features of our town life may be. It is in the quiet nooks and corners of the village that the language, the poetry and literature of a country are enriched. The stability of the country does not depend so much on the towns as on the rural population. The more numerous and the more settled the latter, the wider and more solid is the basis of the state. . . .

—Chaim Weizmann, *Trial and Error*

I. THE MIDDLE EAST

The term "Middle East" first came into general usage during World War II. British and United States military authorities employed it to designate all the territory of Southwestern Asia and Northeastern Africa from the western border of India to the western border of Egypt. Heretofore this region had often been called the Near East. But for Allied military purposes this term was unsatisfactory, since Near East generally included the Balkans, which were then under Axis domination. Although the Middle East contains the cradle of civilization and nourished a larger number of superior cultures than any other part of the globe, in the modern era it has been barren and unprogressive. It affords a glaring example of the consequences of greed, war, and the neglect and misuse of a priceless heritage of fertile land.

Few areas of the earth have witnessed more turbulence and rapidity of change than have the countries of the Middle East in recent times. The pattern of their history has been much the same. Before World War I most of them stagnated and slumbered under the rule of the Ottoman Turks. With the breakup of the Ottoman Empire they saw visions of independence and a chance to throw off all traces of foreign domination. Nationalist movements, in some cases as fanatical as that of the Nazis, sprang up to prod governments into vigorous action. In many instances they gained control of governments, often in defiance of the religious authorities. They proceeded then with attempts to launch programs of modernization, for building highways, railroads, and schools, subsidizing industries, and sponsoring scientific agriculture and land reform. The problems they encountered, however, in the form of ignorance, corruption, vested interests, and foreign meddling were often too great to be overcome. To this day illiteracy, disease, and high death rates persist in many parts of the Middle East, and poverty is all but universal.

A survey of the Middle East may properly begin with Turkey, since it ranks first in population and since nearly the whole region at one time was subject to Turkish rule. We have already seen that the dismemberment of the Turkish Empire began as early as 1829 when the Sultan's government was forced to acknowledge the independence of Greece. Thenceforth one after another of the European provinces broke away. By 1914 Turkey in Europe had been reduced to nothing but Constantinople and a corner of eastern Thrace. But Turkey in Asia still included a vast area from the western border of Persia to the Mediterranean Sea. At the end of World War I, the Turkish government, which had fought on the losing side, accepted a treaty depriving the Empire of virtually everything except Constantinople and the northern and central portions of Asia Minor. But before this treaty could be put into effect a group of nationalists, under the leadership of Mustapha Kemal, reconquered much of the lost territory. In 1922 they marched on Constantinople, deposed the Sultan, and in 1923 proclaimed Turkey a republic. The Allies, in the meantime, consented to the making of a new treaty at Lausanne, Switzerland, which permitted the Turks to retain practically all the lands they had reconquered. The new state included Anatolia, Armenia, and eastern Thrace, but none of the outlying territories of Mesopotamia, Arabia, Palestine, or Syria.

For two decades the history of the Turkish republic was almost synonymous with the personal history of Mustapha Kemal. It was his imagination and determination that made the country over from a corrupt and somnolent Oriental despotism into a modern, progressive state with most of the forms if not the substance of democratic government. He began by abolishing the Caliphate and secularizing the state. Under the Sultan religion and the state were intertwined. The Sultan himself was the Caliph, or "Successor of the Prophet," and therefore the spiritual ruler of all Moslems. The law was religious law, and the only officially recognized schools were those attached to the mosques. Kemal's decree abolishing the Caliphate declared that the antiquated religious courts and codes must be replaced by "modern scientific civil codes," and that the schools of the mosques must give way to government schools, which all children between the ages of six and sixteen would be required to attend. But before much progress could be made in educational reform, it was necessary to take one further step, and that was to adopt a new system of writing. The Turkish language was still written in Arabic script, which Kemal regarded as an impossible medium for the expression of Western ideas. Accordingly, he shut himself up in his house near Ankara and began the study of the Latin alphabet. When he had taught himself, he proceeded to teach others, traveling throughout the country with his blackboard, lecturing audiences on how the new characters should be formed. In five months it was considered expedient to issue a decree forbidding the holding of public office by anyone who was not adept in the new writing.

The achievements of Kemal also included a social and economic revolution. He issued decrees abolishing the fez, discouraging polygamy, and encouraging women to appear unveiled and both sexes to wear Western clothes. He established schools for girls and made women eligible for business careers and for the professions. In 1929 he gave women the suffrage in local elections and five years later in national elections. Equally significant were his economic reforms. He endowed agricultural colleges, established model farms, and founded banks to lend money to farmers. He freed the peasant from the tithe and set up agencies to distribute seed and farm machinery to almost anyone who could offer a guaranty to use them effectively. Although he undoubtedly had the power to do so, he refrained from instituting measures of forced collectivization such as those of the Russians. He chose rather to adhere to the tradition of Mohammed in encouraging small holdings, in helping the farmer to buy his land, and in teaching him to work it profitably. At the same time he recognized the importance of promoting industrialization. Agriculture alone could not provide the people with a high standard of living or enable the country to make the best use of all its resources. He therefore built thousands of miles of railways and established state monopolies for the manufacture of tobacco, matches, munitions, salt, alcohol, and sugar. Despite the fact that Turkey has abundant resources of coal, iron, copper, and petroleum, and is the world's largest producer of chrome, three-fourths of the 31 million inhabitants still derive their living from agriculture.

Social and economic reforms

Mustapha Kemal Ataturk.
Photographed at the window
of his special train.

Mustapha Kemal (later called Kemal Ataturk) ruled over Turkey from 1922 until his death in 1938. His successors have continued his policies. Whether he was simply another twentieth-century
dictator, somewhat more benevolent than his compeers, is a question for debate. Legally, his position was that of an elective President, chosen by the Assembly for a four-year term and indefinitely
re-eligible. But he himself was president of the Assembly, and,
except for a brief period in 1930, he permitted no opposition party
to exist. On the other hand, he always described his regime as
temporary and transitional. After ten years he still maintained that
the people were not yet ready for self-government. He must continue to rule for another decade or so until the citizens grew in
wisdom and a sense of responsibility and liberated themselves from
the habits and prejudices of the past. To his credit it can be said
that he did not involve his country in war and that he never sought
the extermination of racial minorities. Although he suppressed a
revolt of the Kurds in 1930 with merciless severity, executing
twenty-nine of the leaders, he never maintained a Gestapo or
Cheka or any similar agency of irresponsible tyranny.

Under Kemal Ataturk's successors, Ismet Inonu and Celal Bayar,
Turkey took steps toward supplanting her benevolent dictatorship
with a democratic republic. But after World War II, severe economic difficulties, resulting mainly from inflation, led the government of Premier Adnan Menderes to impose restrictions. Freedom of
the press was abolished, and members of Parliament opposing the
government were arrested. Successive student demonstrations
against these repressive measures triggered a revolt in 1960 by army
officers, who seized control of the government. Lieutenant-General
Cemal Gursel established a provisional government. In 1961 a new
constitution was adopted proclaiming the Second Turkish Republic. It provided for a President elected by Parliament for a seven-

The benevolent
despotism of
Mustapha Kemal

Turkey in more
recent years

544

year term and ineligible for re-election. It included also guaranties of human rights and safeguards against abuses of executive power. How much these would mean in practice may be deduced from the fact that leading members of the deposed government and of the opposition party were arrested and held for trial. In 1961 former Premier Menderes was executed. Perhaps the real reason was that he continued to be idolized by peasants and other conservatives who opposed the program of the new government for industrialization and Westernization. About a month after Menderes' execution elections were held. No party gained a majority. A group of political leaders formed a coalition government and summoned the aged Ismet Inonu to take the office of Premier. Economic chaos continued and kept the new regime on shaky foundations.

Second in population among nations of the Middle East is Egypt, or, as it is now officially called, the United Arab Republic. Although technically a part of the Ottoman Empire until 1914, Egypt was for all practical purposes a dependency of Great Britain after 1882. The British kept up the pretense of acknowledging the sovereignty of the Khedive and his overlord the Sultan, but when Turkey joined the Central Powers in 1914 the London government issued a proclamation that Egypt would henceforth constitute a protectorate of the British Empire. The new arrangement did not work entirely to the satisfaction of the Egyptian people. Though shopkeepers and hotel proprietors in Cairo and Alexandria grew rich, many of the common people felt themselves exploited. The British conscripted peasants for forced labor and commandeered their grain, cotton, and livestock. When the war ended, the London authorities refused to allow Egypt to send a delegation to Paris to lay her case before the peace conference. It was argued that Egypt was not a belligerent, although other small countries that had taken no active part in the fighting were allowed to be represented. The upshot was the emergence of an Egyptian nationalist movement known as the *Wafd*. The name means literally "delegation," and the movement had been organized originally to present Egypt's demands and grievances at the peace conference. When the British attempted suppression and deported its leader to Malta, the *Wafd* came forth with an insistence upon nothing less than complete independence.

The beginning of nationalism in Egypt; the rise of the Wafd

Following a campaign of sabotage and terrorism waged by the *Wafd*, the British decided to abolish the protectorate and in 1922 proclaimed Egypt an independent and sovereign state. But "independence" was made subject to four reservations, to be left absolutely to the discretion of the British pending adjustment by mutual agreement. The first was the protection of the Suez Canal and other vital links in the lifeline of the British Empire. The second was the defense of Egypt itself against foreign encroachments or interference. The third was the protection of foreign interests

Abolition of the British protectorate

545

and minorities in Egypt. The fourth was the maintenance of the dependent status of the Sudan under the joint rule of Britain and Egypt. For the next three decades the history of Egypt was largely occupied by controversy and conflict over these four points or reservations.

The Anglo-
Egyptian
Agreement of
1936

In the elections of 1924 the *Wafd* captured over 80 per cent of the seats in the Egyptian parliament. Swollen with self-conceit, it changed its character from a people's party to a ruthless political machine. It did not hesitate to employ secret agents and terrorist methods and to perpetrate assassinations. It finally brought so much discredit upon itself that it was repudiated by King Fouad I, who established a dictatorship of his own. The party continued to survive, however, becoming more and more fascist in character, and the nationalism for which it stood lost none of its fire or urgency. The majority of the Egyptians resented the attempts of the British to keep their country in a state of vassalage. But all efforts to work out an agreement for terminating the relationship failed until after Mussolini invaded Ethiopia in 1935. The Egyptians now began to wonder if they were not in greater danger from the Italians than they were from the British. The result was the conclusion of an Anglo-Egyptian Treaty of Friendship and Alliance in 1936. Britain agreed to remove her troops from Cairo and Alexandria in return for Egyptian recognition of Britain's right to defend the Suez Canal. Egypt agreed to co-ordinate her foreign policy with that of Britain in exchange for British assistance in gaining admission to the League of Nations. The British consented to the abolition of the hated Capitulations under which British citizens in Egypt had extraterritorial rights. In return, Egypt accepted the *status quo* in the Sudan.

The revival of
nationalism after
World War II

Before all the terms of the Anglo-Egyptian Treaty could be put into effect, World War II broke out. The British were reluctant to take any steps which might threaten their communications with the East, and the Egyptians did not press the issue. But when the war ended, the flames of nationalist aspirations were kindled anew. The Egyptians now demanded that the British withdraw entirely from both the Suez Canal area and the Sudan. In spite of mob attacks upon her citizens and soldiers, Britain insisted that the Suez link between East and West was of vital concern to all the democracies, and that it was therefore essential that the Canal be protected by a country capable of defending it. With respect to the Sudan the British took the position that neither Britain nor Egypt should have rights of exclusive dominion. At the same time they pointed out that they had rescued the area from the misrule of fanatics in the 1890's, and they contended that they deserved credit for the social and economic progress subsequently achieved in the territory. None of these arguments made much of an impression upon the
Egyptians. They resented the presence of foreign soldiers on

Egyptian soil in the Canal area, and they insisted that the very life
of their country depended upon control of the Sudan, since the
headwaters of the Nile are located there. In 1951 the Egyptian
government announced that it was abrogating the Anglo-Egyptian
Treaty of 1936 and also the condominium or joint rule in the
Sudan. In July 1954 Britain acceded to Egyptian demands for the
withdrawal of all British troops from Egyptian territory.

In July 1952, Major General Mohammed Naguib seized control
of the Egyptian government and the army. The pleasure-loving
King Farouk I, alleged to be subservient to the British, was deposed. The constitution was suspended, political parties were abolished, and a provisional government was brought into existence. A
year later Egypt was proclaimed a republic, with General Naguib
as its first President and Premier. The new ruler announced a program of sweeping economic and social reforms. Compulsory education was ordered for all children between the ages of seven and
twelve. Provisions for land reform were also enacted. Holdings
were limited to 200 acres, and large estates were to be broken up
and redistributed. They were to be made available to landless
peasants on a plan of 30-year payments. But before these reforms
could be fully effected, conflict developed within the military junta
which had overthrown the monarchy. Naguib was temporarily deposed in February 1954. Though he was restored to the Presidency
a few days later, the Premiership was retained by his rival, Lieutenant-Colonel Gamal Abdel Nasser. But still Nasser was not satisfied. In June 1956, by a carefully managed election, in which he
was the only candidate, he was chosen President. He received 99.9
per cent of the votes cast, thereby proving that his state was even
more "monolithic" than those of Hitler and Stalin. Ironically, in
the same election the Egyptian voters adopted a new constitution
proclaiming the country an Islamic-Arab state with a democratic
form of government.

Nasser resolved to continue and enlarge the program of economic and social reform. In particular, he was determined to relieve the condition of the impoverished masses. He proceeded with
plans to distribute 750,000 acres of land, giving farms to 250,000
landless peasants. He soon realized, however, that on account of
Egypt's rapid growth in population, more productive land must be
made available. To accomplish this purpose he decided upon the
construction of the Aswan High Dam, a gigantic reservoir to back
up the waters of the Upper Nile and provide irrigation for 2 million acres of arable land. Since the cost ($1.3 billion) would be more
than Egypt could stand, he hoped to borrow large sums of money
from the World Bank and from the United States and British governments. Alarmed by the Egyptian purchases of arms from Czechoslovakia (a Communist source), the United States suddenly withdrew its offer of a loan to Nasser, and great Britain did likewise soon

The Suez Canal after Nationalization. An Egyptian tugboat tows an oil rig down the famous waterway which is now operated by the Egyptian government.

after. Nasser retaliated by expropriating the owners of the Suez Canal, who were chiefly British and French, and declared that he would use the revenues of the Canal to build the dam. After months of fruitless negotiation, the British and French encouraged an invasion of Egyptian territory by the Republic of Israel. The Israelis had plenty of grievances, since they had been the victims of border raids from the Sinai Peninsula for many years. The invasion began on October 29, 1956, and the British and French intervened soon afterward. The affair precipitated a crisis which threatened for a time to engulf the world. The Soviet rulers warned Israel that its very existence was in danger and darkly hinted their intention of joining forces with Egypt. The United Nations finally arranged a cease-fire, and in March 1957 the Nasser government reopened the Canal, under its own terms of national ownership, to all users except Israel. Soon afterward Nasser resumed his program of reform. He nationalized about 90 per cent of Egyptian industry and reduced maximum land holdings to 100 acres. In 1958 he established the United Arab Republic with Syria as the Northern Region, Egypt as the Southern Region, and Yemen as a federated member. Three years later Syria seceded.

The most barren and backward of the countries formerly included in the Ottoman Empire is that which now goes under the name of Saudi Arabia. Covering an area more than one-fourth that of the United States, Arabia is almost 100 per cent desert. Not a single river or lake exists to relieve the monotonous aridity. Inhabited to this day by only 8½ million people, the country did not become a united state until 1927. Previous to that time it was divided into the two main areas of the Hejaz and Nejd. The king of the

The formation of Saudi Arabia

Hejaz was Sherif Hussein, Protector of the Holy Cities of Mecca and Medina and, after 1924, self-appointed Caliph of Islam. Nejd and a number of surrounding areas acknowledged the rule of Ibn Saud (1880–1953), who was supported by the Wahhabi, a puritanical sect of Moslems opposed to smoking, drinking, and the wearing of silk or gold. The two men had been bitter rivals for many years. When Hussein assumed the Caliphate, Ibn Saud needed no further excuse for making war. In less than two years he had driven Hussein from his kingdom, and in January 1926 he was himself proclaimed King of the Hejaz in the Great Mosque of Mecca. Soon afterward he united his two kingdoms of Hejaz and Nejd into a theocratic state which he named Saudi Arabia.

Ibn Saud, the Arab League, and Aramco

Such progress as has occurred in Saudi Arabia can be credited in part to the shrewdness of Ibn Saud. He realized that the Moslem world could not hold its own against Western encroachments without adopting Western improvements. Accordingly, he allowed a few railways to be built and imported motor vehicles for his own court and for the transportation of pilgrims to the Holy Cities. He instituted plans for free education for the children of his subjects and made provision, on paper at least, for free medical attention. But by far the greater proportion of Saudi Arabian advancement has been the result of capitalist enterprise from the United States. About 1932 it was discovered that eastern Arabia contained undreamed-of riches in the form of petroleum deposits. In 1933 and in later years Ibn Saud granted concessions for the exploitation of this wealth to the Arabian-American Oil Company (Aramco), owned jointly by Texaco and the Standard Oil Company of California. Royalties paid by Aramco have provided the funds for electrification of cities and the construction of highways, railroads, and airports, to say nothing of aid to agriculture, education, and public health. They also enabled Ibn Saud (and his son and successor King Saud) to make generous contributions for the support of the Arab League, established in 1945 and composed of Egypt, Iraq,

Kuwait, an Arab Sheikdom on the Persian Gulf. Oil resources, exploited by the Kuwait Oil Company, jointly owned by Gulf Oil and Anglo-Iranian Oil, give Kuwait one of the highest per capita incomes in the world.

Jordan, Syria, Lebanon, Yemen, and Saudi Arabia. Later, Kuwait, Libya, the Sudan, Tunisia, Algeria, and Morocco were admitted to membership. The announced purpose of the League was to promote the solidarity of the Arab world. In addition, it took as one of its specific objectives resistance to the expansion of the Zionist movement in Palestine. But after the accession of Nasser as ruler of Egypt, the League tended to grow weaker. Nasser's ambition to dominate the Arab world aroused the antagonism of other member states, especially of Iraq. The Iraqi Premier, Abdul Karim Kassem, accused Nasser of fomenting revolts against him. The two dictators were rivals also for the domination of Syria. The League was weakened further by a tendency of its members to align themselves in conservative and progressive blocs. The former, under the leadership of Saudi Arabia and Jordan, strove to preserve the old culture and to pursue relentlessly the struggle against Israel. They are fundamentalists in religion and oppose the socialism and anti-imperialism of the progressive bloc. The progressives, dominated by Nasser and his Syrian allies, believe in a secularized state, a nationalized or socialized economy, and staunch opposition to the imperialism of the West. No less anti-Israeli than the conservatives, they look to the Soviet Union for economic assistance and moral support. They received a modicum of such support during and after the Arab-Israeli Wars of 1967–1968.

Several provinces of the Ottoman Empire did not obtain immediate independence at the end of World War I, but were organized

as Class A mandates of the League of Nations. Theoretically, this meant that they were to be prepared for independence under the guardianship of a great power acting under the supervision of the League. Actually, the mandates were awarded in suspicious conformity to the secret plans of the Allied governments for distribution of the spoils of victory at the end of the war. Thus, Iraq (Mesopotamia) and Palestine became mandates of Great Britain, while Syria-Lebanon became a mandate of France.

Of these mandates, the one whose history bears the greatest significance for the Western world is Palestine. In 1918 Palestine had

a population about 70 per cent Arab and the remainder Christian and Jewish. For many years nationalistic Jews had longed to possess it as a national home for their persecuted kinsmen all over the world. The idea, known as Zionism, was first conceived by Theodor Herzl during the Dreyfus Affair of the 1890's. During World War I, British Zionists worked zealously on behalf of the British Government. Their leader was Dr. Chaim Weizmann, a distinguished chemist, who perfected a method of converting wood into alcohol, when that commodity, so essential for making munitions, could not be obtained in sufficient quantities from other sources. In gratitude for the efforts of Weizmann and other Zionists, the British government issued, in November 1917, the famous Balfour

Declaration: "His Majesty's Government view with favour the establishment in Palestine of a National Home for the Jewish people, and will use their best endeavours to facilitate the achievement of that object, it being understood that nothing shall be done that may prejudice the rights of existing non-Jewish communities in Palestine, or the rights and political status enjoyed by Jews in any other country."

On the basis of the Balfour Declaration, as well as the secret wartime bargains with her Allies, Britain accepted the mandate for Palestine. She promised as she did so not merely to establish a Jewish National Home, but "to secure the preservation of an Arab National Home and to apprentice the people of Palestine as a whole in the art of self-government." It was an optimistic ambition, but at the time optimism seemed justified. In fact, for a period of ten years there was every reason to expect that the undertaking would be successful. Palestine prospered as never before in its history. Factories were built, land was reclaimed, irrigation works were constructed, the Jordan River was harnessed for electric power, and unemployment disappeared from the face of the land. Except for rioting in Jaffa in 1921, no incident of violence occurred to disturb the general tranquillity. The aspect of the country was so peaceful that in 1926 the British reduced their armed forces to a single RAF squadron and two companies with armored cars.

By 1929, however, evidences of disharmony had begun to appear in the land that was holy to three great religions. The Jews were too prosperous and well-educated and were arousing the envy and fears of the Arabs by their high standard of living and their more strenuous competition. Their purchases of land, in many cases from absentee owners, had resulted in the displacement of thousands of Arab cultivators and had thrown them into the cities at a time when the Great Depression was beginning to make unemployment a serious problem. But the major cause of Arab foreboding was the steady increase in the Jewish population. The opportunity to emigrate to Palestine had offered a greater temptation than the Arabs had expected. As a consequence, some of them foresaw a relentless advance and expansion of Europeans and Americans, backed by foreign capital and flaunting a culture that was alien to the ways of the Arab majority. In 1929, 1930, and 1931 armed attacks were waged upon Jewish settlements followed by terrorist murders.

But these episodes paled into insignificance when compared with the bloody violence that followed. When the mandate was established, no one could have foreseen the desperate plight that was to overtake the European Jews with the accession of the Nazis to power in Germany. As news of the persecutions spread, it was inevitable that pressure should be brought upon the British government to relax the barriers against immigration into Palestine. During the period 1933–1935 the admission of more than 130,000

Jewish immigrants was authorized, and uncounted thousands more came in illicitly. From this time on Palestine was a seething caldron of violence and warfare. The Arabs rose in open rebellion against the mandate. Organized terrorism swept the country. Guerrilla attacks in the rural areas and looting, burning, and sabotage in the towns and cities kept the whole population in turmoil. By 1938 Britain had 20,000 troops in Palestine, and even these were unable to maintain order.

Renewal of the conflict after World War II

The early years of World War II were characterized by relative quiet in Palestine. Both sides were subdued in some measure by fears that the war would spread, but the primary reason was the White Paper of 1939, which the British government issued a few months before the conflict began. In this document Britain envisioned the "establishment within ten years of an independent Palestine State," with protection for the "essential interests" of both Jews and Arabs, and a government in which both peoples would share. Meanwhile, land purchases from Arabs were to be restricted, and the number of Jews admitted to Palestine was to be limited to 75,000. Though the plan was unfavorably received by the Mandates Commission of the League of Nations, it seemed to allay the fears of the Arabs and to give them a ray of hope that their interests would be protected. But trouble broke out anew when a conference of American Zionists at the Biltmore Hotel in New York, in May 1942, adopted the so-called Biltmore Program, repudiating the White Paper of 1939 and demanding the establishment of a Jewish state and a Jewish army in Palestine. Soon afterward both Jews and Arabs prepared for war to the hilt. Fanatical Zionists, as well as Arabs, resorted to the use of terrorist methods. Illegal military

Israeli Schoolchildren Celebrating the First Anniversary of Israel's Independence near Tel Aviv. The Israeli Minister of Education addressed the gathering.

organizations sprang up on both sides and devoted their energies to raiding, burning, and assassination.

In April 1947 the British government referred the Palestine problem to the United Nations and announced that a year later it would terminate the mandate and withdraw all its troops from the country. On May 15, 1948, the British mandate came to an end, and on the same day a Jewish provisional government proclaimed the establishment of an independent State of Israel. Elections were held for a Constituent Assembly, which met in February of the following year and adopted a temporary constitution for a democratic republic. Its chief features were a weak president, a strong cabinet, and a powerful parliament. It was clearly intended that the last two agencies should really govern the country. The cabinet was vested with general direction of the legislative process as well as with executive authority. But the parliament, or Knesset, would exercise independent legislative power, and could overturn cabinets which no longer enjoyed its confidence. The constitution also provided for proportional representation, a unicameral parliament, and universal suffrage for Jews and Arabs alike. A unique element in the system was the close association of religion with the state. Marriage and divorce were placed under the exclusive jurisdiction of religious courts—Jewish, Christian, or Moslem as the affiliation of the parties might require.

Termination of the
mandate and
establishment of
the State of Israel

Meanwhile, from the day of proclaimed independence until the spring of 1949, Israel and its Arab neighbor countries were at war. United Nations efforts brought about truces several times, but nothing lasting was achieved until Israel and Egypt signed a general armistice agreement in February 1949; Jordan and Syria also signed armistices in April. The United Nations peace effort was at first under the direction of Count Folke Bernadotte of Sweden; when he was assassinated in September 1948, by Israeli extremists in Jerusalem, it was continued by Dr. Ralph Bunche of the United States. The status at the cease-fire was regarded as a victory for Israel and a defeat for the Arab powers; neither, however, accepted it as final. Violent incidents continued to occur, including retaliatory massacres. In 1956 and again in 1967–1968 warfare between Israel and one or more of the Arab states broke out, for the third time since the founding of the Israeli state.

Despite her troubles with the Arabs, Israel strengthened her economy and stabilized her domestic life. Except for property values, inflation was held within bounds, and many new industries were created. Large sums of money flowed into the country as a result of West German restitution for the outrages of Nazism. Agriculture advanced to a stage sufficient to supply the needs of the home market while export crops such as melons and citrus fruits were rapidly developed. Politically, the voters tended to bestow their support on the center, or middle-of-the-road, parties. Of these,

553

David Ben-Gurion's Mapai, or Labor, party maintained a representation of more than a third of the seats in the Knesset. Ranking next to Mapai were the Liberal and Herut (Freedom) parties, each with about 14 per cent of the seats. They differed from Mapai chiefly in demanding a restriction of government in business. In foreign policy the Liberals advocated neutrality while Herut was strongly irredentist, urging the conquest of Palestinian territory still held by Arab states.

British and Russian imperialism in Persia

The only country of the Middle East which was not under the rule of Turkey at one time or another before 1918 was Persia. But this did not mean freedom from foreign domination. Remote, steeped in languor, and rich in resources, Persia was a constant temptation to ambitious imperialists. In 1907 Great Britain and Russia signed an agreement providing for the division of the country into spheres of influence. The northern sphere was assigned to Russia and the southern to Great Britain. A middle zone was to be left, temporarily at least, under the control of the native Shah. The overthrow of the Tsar in 1917 filled the minds of British imperialists with hopes that all Persia might be theirs. By 1919 Lord Curzon had extorted from the Shah an agreement transferring to Great Britain political and military control of the entire country.

The rise of Iranian nationalism

But the plans of the British were not destined for easy fulfillment. In 1921 there appeared in Teheran a young army officer who essayed for himself a role somewhat similar to that of Mustapha Kemal in Turkey. His name was Riza Khan (1877–1944). With no more than 3000 troops at his back he forced the Shah to appoint him Minister of War and commander-in-chief of the army. In 1923 he became Premier and two years later Shah with the title Riza Pahlevi. He took steps to reduce foreign influences, and forbade his own officials to associate with Europeans. In 1932 he canceled the concession of the powerful Anglo-Persian Oil Company and obtained a new contract with terms more advantageous to his own government. In 1935 he changed the name of his country from Persia to the more grandiose name of Iran, or land of the Aryans.

Iran's increasing troubles after World War II

World War II brought almost as much turmoil and anguish to Iran as if she had been one of the belligerents. Riza Shah abdicated in 1941 and was succeeded by his son Mohammed Riza Pahlevi. Because of its strategic importance, Iran's territory was occupied by the British, Russians, and Americans under pledges to respect her sovereignty and independence and to render economic assistance during and after the war. Despite these pledges, unrest and inflation plagued the country. Communism flourished under the aegis of the Tudeh (Masses) party, and conflicts developed between the Shah and political leaders. In 1951 antiforeign extremists in the Iranian Parliament voted to nationalize the oil industry, and the Premier, Dr. Mohammed Mossadegh, rejected all proposals for arbitration. The result was the closing down of the Anglo-Iranian oil refinery

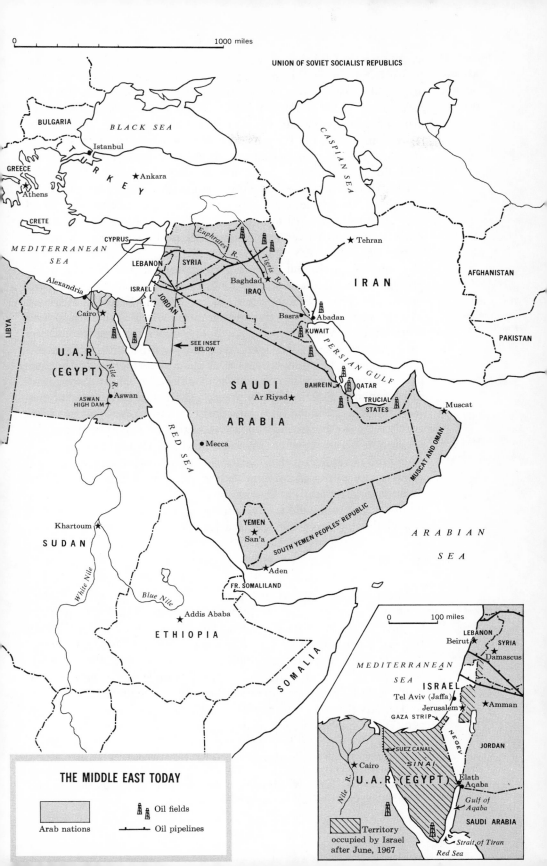

0   1000 miles

UNION OF SOVIET SOCIALIST REPUBLICS

BULGARIA

BLACK SEA

GREECE

★Ankara

TURKEY

Istanbul

CASPIAN SEA

Athens

CRETE

CYPRUS

MEDITERRANEAN
SEA

LEBANON   SYRIA

Euphrates R.

Tigris R.

★ Tehran

IRAN

AFGHANISTAN

Alexandria

ISRAEL

JORDAN

Baghdad ★
IRAQ

Cairo ★

Basra
Abadan

KUWAIT

PAKISTAN

LIBYA

U.A.R
(EGYPT)

SEE INSET
BELOW

Nile R.

ASWAN
HIGH DAM ★ Aswan

SAUDI

Ar Riyad ★

BAHREIN ★ QATAR

PERSIAN GULF

TRUCIAL
STATES

Muscat ★

ARABIA

RED SEA

● Mecca

MUSCAT AND OMAN

Khartoum ★

SUDAN

White Nile

Blue Nile

YEMEN
★
San'a

SOUTH YEMEN PEOPLES' REPUBLIC

ARABIAN

SEA

★ Addis Ababa

★ Aden

FR. SOMALILAND

ETHIOPIA

SOMALIA

0   100 miles

LEBANON

Beirut ★   SYRIA

Damascus

MEDITERRANEAN

SEA

ISRAEL

Tel Aviv (Jaffa) ●

★ Amman

Jerusalem ★

GAZA STRIP

NEGEV

JORDAN

THE MIDDLE EAST TODAY

SUEZ CANAL

SINAI

Cairo ★

Arab nations

Oil fields

U.A.R. (EGYPT)

Elath
Aqaba

Oil pipelines

Nile R.

Gulf
of
Aqaba

SAUDI ARABIA

Territory
occupied by Israel
after June, 1967

Strait of Tiran

Red Sea

at Abadan, the largest in the world, which employed over 55,000 persons at an annual wage total of $67,000,000. Since the company also paid over $38,000,000 in taxes, the shutdown meant virtual bankruptcy for the Iranian government. Nevertheless, the fanaticism of Mossadegh and his followers prolonged the dispute for more than a year. No signs of a possible compromise appeared until after the Premier was seized and imprisoned by supporters of the Shah during a civilian and military uprising in August 1953. A year later his successor signed an agreement with a consortium of eight foreign oil companies which provided that the consortium should extract, refine, and market the products of Iran's nationalized oil industry and turn over to the government approximately one-half of the net profits.

The critical
nature of the
Middle East

Though partial solutions have been found for a number of its problems, the Middle East will doubtless remain a troubled area for some time. For one thing, it is the crossroads between East and West, and therefore of strategic interest to both the great power blocs of the Western world. In addition, its teeming population struggling to gain a livelihood from barren wastes makes it an inevitable center of discontent. One of the last strongholds of oil imperialism and European colonialism, it cultivates a fiery nationalism as a weapon against foreign oppression. Its backwardness, combined with the wide gulf which separates the poverty of the masses from the luxury of sheiks and monarchs, makes it a natural focus for revolutionary movements. But most of all, its riches in oil keep it a center of intrigue for rival alliances. Without access to its vast oil reserves, Europe, and to some extent the United States, would be badly handicapped. The Soviets know this, and realize that they would reap a tremendous advantage from gaining control of even a few vital segments of this crucial area.

2. THE REPUBLIC OF SOUTH AFRICA

Geographic
handicaps

The most unfortunate member of the Commonwealth of Nations, with the possible exceptions of Pakistan and India, was the Union of South Africa.[1] From the beginning of her history tragedy dogged her footsteps like a cruel Nemesis. Not the least of her handicaps were those which arise from geography. To begin with, rainfall is inadequate and unevenly distributed. The Union as a whole has a mean precipitation of only 19 inches a year, and in some years the total fall may be as little as 15 per cent of this average. When rain does come it usually descends in torrents and flows quickly to the sea. The fertile top soil, pulverized by months of drought, is easily washed away. Probably no other country in the

[1] In 1961 South Africa withdrew from the Commonwealth of Nations and became an independent republic. See p. 487.

world lives under such imminent risk of national disaster from soil erosion. Only about 13 million of the 300 million acres can be cultivated, and more than 80 per cent of the country is never likely to be used for other than pastoral purposes.

Second only to geographic handicaps is the racial problem. The white men who came to South Africa found the country inhabited by scattered Bushmen and Hottentots who offered little resistance. But this happy condition did not last. Instead, the would-be conquerors soon found themselves confronted by prolific and warlike Bantus and Zulus who came down from the north and fought tooth and nail to drive out the Europeans. The latter soon came to conceive of themselves as Children of Israel battling the Canaanites and Philistines. Through the eighteenth and much of the nineteenth century bitter native wars recurred, and to this day one of the chief national observances commemorates a victory over savage tribes. But nothing approaching extermination resulted. At the present time the native population is larger than ever, and constitutes over two-thirds of the total. Although their standard of living is higher than that of most other African natives, the Negroes of South Africa live under conditions of exploitation. When outside the reserves on which many of them are required to reside, they must carry identification cards or passes, and failure to produce one on request is a criminal offense. All males must pay an annual head tax of 20 shillings, which in some cases amounts to a month's wages. In urban areas they are subject to a curfew and are forbidden to strike under penalty of long imprisonment. To the privileged class of Europeans they constitute a danger as great perhaps as that of the helots to the ancient Spartans.

The political history of South Africa has been punctuated with defeats and frustrations. Founded by the Dutch in 1652, it was captured by the British during the Napoleonic Wars. At that time its European inhabitants numbered about 10,000 Dutch farmers, or Boers. Strong-willed, bigoted, and conservative, the Boers soon came to detest their conquerors. And with good reason, for the latter showed little tact in governing. They enforced the use of English exclusively in the law courts and replaced public officials with their own appointees. But the most flagrant of all their offenses, in the eyes of the Boers, was the emancipation of the slaves in 1833 at a price to their owners of half their alleged value. This was a severe blow to the Dutch farmers, for their economic system was founded on slave labor. From the beginning of their settlement they had looked upon the black-skinned natives as inferior people, fit only to be the servants of white masters. The bloody wars to conquer them had intensified this feeling, and the Dutch Reformed Church had lent the support of Calvinist interpretation of the Old Testament to prove that slavery was just. Negroes were the descendants of Ham, whom Noah had cursed and

The Great Trek
and the founding
of the Boer
republics

consigned to the fate of a "servant of servants." For the proud
Boers to be deprived of their property and to be told that the benighted natives were really their equals was galling indeed.

Nursing their grievances, the Dutch farmers determined to abandon their original colony and found new homes for themselves in
lands to the north. Between 1834 and 1840 about 10,000 Boers and
their families trekked into the wilderness beyond the Orange River
and established what later became the Orange Free State. Others
crossed the Vaal River and founded a republic known as the
Transvaal. Still a third group moved northeastward into Natal
where the British already had a coastal settlement. For twenty
years the Boers tended their flocks and herds in their little republics undisturbed except by sporadic skirmishes with the natives. But
in 1870 diamonds were discovered at Kimberley, and fifteen years
later the fabulous gold fields of the Witwatersrand became a mecca
for prospectors and adventurers from all over the world. Between
1872 and 1902 the white population of South Africa quadrupled.
Congested cities such as Johannesburg and Bloemfontein mush-
roomed on the veldt. The simple pastoral economy of the old-
fashioned Boers had come to an end.

The discovery of diamonds and gold multiplied the political
difficulties of the Boer republics. Britishers and other foreigners
swarmed in in such numbers that they threatened to overwhelm
the Dutch settlers. The latter retaliated by branding the immigrants
as outlanders and denying them political privileges except under
the most rigorous conditions. The suffrage was refused, the press
censored, and public meetings practically forbidden. In desperation
the British organized a conspiracy to overthrow the most obstinate
of the Boer governments, that of Paul Kruger, President of the
Transvaal. Ammunition was collected, with the connivance of

THE RHODES COLOSSUS
STRIDING FROM CAPE TOWN TO CAIRO.

*Cartoon Satirizing the Grandi-
ose Scheme of Cecil Rhodes for
a British Colonial Empire extending from Capetown to
Cairo.*

Cecil Rhodes, Prime Minister of the Cape Colony; and on December 29, 1895, 600 Britons and their armed retainers, under the leadership of Rhodes's friend, Dr. Leander Jameson, raided the Transvaal. The invaders were quickly surrounded and captured, but their act greatly magnified the tension between British and Boers. The Dutch governments increased the restrictions against foreigners and accumulated arms in preparation for a showdown. In October 1899, war broke out between the Boer republics and the colonies predominantly British.

The Boer War dragged its length through three bloody years. Not until Britain sent huge reinforcements under the leadership of her best generals was she able to snatch victory from the jaws of defeat. Finally, outnumbered seven to one, the Boers yielded and signed the Treaty of Vereeniging. In return for submitting to British rule, they were exempted from indemnities, promised representative institutions at an early date, and permitted to retain their own language in the courts and schools. The British government provided $15,000,000 to accelerate the process of reconstruction. It was one of the most generous peace settlements in history.

In 1909 Cape Colony, Natal, the Orange Free State, and the Transvaal were merged into the Union of South Africa. The National Convention that drafted the Constitution provided for a unitary instead of a federal state. The reasons were several. The need for railway construction and for solving the problems of a large native population seemed to demand unification. More important was the fact that the two white nationalities did not occupy separate provinces as in Canada. In most states the rural population was Afrikaner or Boer, the urban population British. In some additional respects also the government of South Africa differed from that of the other dominions. The Cabinet did not stand or fall as a unit, but, theoretically at least, disagreements were permitted among the members. Its control over the upper house of Parliament was more effective. In case of a conflict between the Cabinet and the Assembly, or lower house, both houses might be dissolved and their members compelled to stand for re-election. South Africa had a much more illiberal attitude toward the suffrage than did the other dominions. Universal manhood suffrage for whites was not adopted until 1930. Woman suffrage was also adopted in the same year, but in the face of stiff opposition. The Minister of Justice, for example, declared that the female franchise conflicted "with the intentions that the Creator had for women." As for the natives, who constitute more than 75 per cent of the population, all were disfranchised except in the southernmost Cape Province, where Negro and Asian citizens vote under limited conditions.

The sharpest controversies in South African politics since the formation of the Union have been those relating to nationality and race. Although the British made repeated efforts at reconciliation following the Boer War, the old hatreds died hard. In 1912 a faction of extremist Boers broke away from their kinsmen and formed the Nationalist party. Under the leadership of General Hertzog, they strove to preserve the cultural independence of the Afrikaners and to tolerate no fusion with the British. They resented British aggressiveness and regarded it as synonymous with an imperialism which threatened to obliterate the customs and institutions of their revered ancestors. They eventually came to advocate the severance of all ties with the British and the transformation of the Dominion into an Afrikaner republic. Anti-Semitism also emerged as a cardinal policy in the minds of the most fanatical. The finance capitalists who controlled the gold and diamond mines of the Rand[2] were alleged to be mostly Jews who were lightly taxed by the British-dominated government. By 1938 the Nationalists seemed almost as greatly disturbed by the "Jewish Menace" as they were by the "Black Peril" and were demanding the exclusion of all Jewish immigrants.

The two world wars of 1914 and 1939 contributed to the strength of the Nationalist movement. The followers of General Hertzog were determined that South Africa should not be dragged into war at the behest of the London government. The right to remain neutral they considered an indispensable badge of their nation's sovereignty. In 1914 some of them organized a rebellion as an armed protest against enslavement to British objectives. But the policy of their opponent, General Jan Christiaan Smuts, prevailed, and South Africa contributed its share toward winning the war. Eight years after the Armistice the Nationalists, supported by Labour, gained control of the government, but with a watered-down program that did not demand complete independence. When Brit-

[2] The Rand, or Witwatersrand, is a 60-mile ridge which constitutes a watershed between the Vaal and Limpopo Rivers.

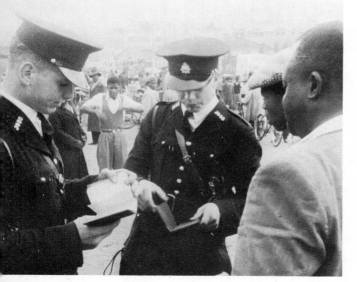

Apartheid in South Africa. Among the restrictions imposed upon the black natives is the requirement that they carry passports. Here a policeman and an interpreter check the papers of a native bound for Johannesburg to work in the mines.

ain again went to war in 1939, the South African government split. Six Cabinet ministers supported the war, five opposed. In the Assembly the vote was 80 in favor of the war to 67 against. It was obvious that the termination of hostilities would leave the country torn asunder and that the difficulties and tensions growing out of the war would widen the cleavage still further. Military production brought thousands of natives into the towns and created fears of Communist uprisings or some other form of social revolution. As a party of the extreme right, the Nationalists played upon these fears and gained control of Parliament in 1948. They not only espoused the idea of a republic but demanded a policy of *apartheid*, or strict separation of races. Raising the cry of "a white civilization in peril," they clamored for curtailment of the natives' privileges and denounced the citizens of British extraction for fostering the amalgamation of races through the promotion of industrialism.[3] Indeed, the program of the new Nationalists was almost as anti-British as it was anti-Negro. They longed for a republic completely purged of British influence. Its children would learn but one language, Afrikaans, a colloquial form of Dutch, and venerate the life of their grandfathers on the lonely veldt. It would be a republic founded upon the ideals of Paul Kruger, not upon those of Cecil Rhodes.

In 1961 Prime Minister Hendrik Verwoerd took steps toward implementing these ideals when he ordered the withdrawal of South Africa from the Commonwealth of Nations and proclaimed the country an independent republic. For the time being there would be two capitals, Cape Town and Pretoria, and two languages, English and Afrikaans. It was clear, however, that the ultimate objective was an Afrikaner nation thoroughly purged of British influences. In 1960 the attempted assassination of Verwoerd had already led to severe restrictions on the Negro population. They were forced to live in "reserved" areas, subjected to a rigid curfew, and deprived of all rights to freedom of assemblage, speech, and press. In 1967 a severe Terrorism Act was passed presuming the guilt of everyone accused of terrorism until he could prove himself innocent.

In common with Australia and New Zealand, South Africa has embraced an extensive policy of government control over economic affairs. The reasons have been partly geographic. The severe droughts, the frequent visitations of locusts, the perennial struggle to keep the topsoil from being washed into the sea—all make farming a desperate gamble against odds that are often too great for an individual to withstand. But in South Africa the additional objective of protecting the white man against the competition of the natives has fostered economic collectivism. Agrarian leaders have be-

Apartheid

Toward an Afrikaner republic

Factors contributing to economic collectivism

[3] It should be emphasized that *apartheid* is merely an extreme form of the racial philosophy accepted almost universally by South Africans of European extraction. Only a negligible minority believes that Negroes can be given political and social equality with whites in the foreseeable future.

561

Diamond Mining in Southwest Africa. To make the diamond-bearing gravels accessible, vast quantities of sand must be removed. Diamonds are sometimes buried 70 feet beneath the surface.

lieved for some time that nothing short of tariffs, bounties, and subsidies will enable the Caucasian farmer to stay on the land and save him from becoming a "poor white." Only with the help of such forms of government intervention can he maintain his standard of living and not be driven into bankruptcy by low-cost production.

Forms
of collectivism

Collectivism in South Africa has assumed an even greater variety of forms than in most other countries. A Land and Agricultural Bank, deriving its capital from the government, lends money to farmers to buy land, to prevent foreclosures, and for such special purposes as the construction of fences and silos. Imports of wheat have been prohibited at times for the purpose of promoting self-sufficiency. Sugar production is carefully fostered by tariffs, price controls, and crop limitation. But the policy of collectivism is not restricted to agriculture. Public utilities and railroads are government-owned. More unusual is the South African Iron and Steel Industrial Corporation, established by the government in 1928 because of a belief that private companies were unable to raise sufficient capital to expand their capacity. The government corporation currently supplies about half of the country's steel requirements. Finally, it should be noted that South Africa has an extensive program of welfare and labor legislation for the white population. It includes old-age pensions, unemployment insurance, maximum-hour and minimum-wage laws, and compulsory arbitration of industrial disputes.

3. THE NEW INDEPENDENT STATES OF NORTHERN AND CENTRAL AFRICA

The 1950's and 1960's witnessed a groundswell of colonial revolts in northern and central Africa. For the most part, they were directed against Great Britain and France, though Belgium, Italy, and

Portugal were also involved. The first of the former colonies to gain independence was Libya. Taken by Italy from Turkey in 1912, Libya passed under the control of the United Nations at the end of World War II. In 1949 the U.N. recognized the Libyan demand for freedom, and two years later independence was formally proclaimed.

If any one country could be considered the leader of the African colonial revolt, it was Ghana, formerly called the Gold Coast, a colony of Great Britain. In 1954 Britain granted self-government and in 1957 independence. In 1960 Ghana became a republic. As such she remains a member of the Commonwealth of Nations but recognizes Queen Elizabeth II only as head of the Commonwealth, not as sovereign. Leadership of the Ghana independence movement was supplied by Kwame Nkrumah. The son of an illiterate goldsmith, he was educated at Lincoln University in Pennsylvania. Subsequently he studied at the University of Pennsylvania and at the London School of Economics. He returned to his homeland in 1948 and became a nationalist agitator. For his activities he was arrested by the British and sentenced to a year's imprisonment. He continued his agitation from behind the bars, using sheets of toilet paper to write editorials for his newspaper. While he was still in prison, his party won control of the Legislative Assembly. He was soon afterward released and, in 1951, was chosen Prime Minister. His political philosophy was puzzling and contradictory. He classified himself as a Marxian Socialist and an undenominational Christian. He denied that he was a Communist, but he admired Lenin. He was a neutralist in foreign policy and he professed admiration for Gandhi; yet his regime contained numerous elements of totalitarianism, and in international controversies he tended to support the Communist bloc more often than he did the Western powers. Apparently the key to most of his thinking was opposition to imperialism. He thought it abhorrent that the Negroes of Central Africa, with their proud traditions of an ancient culture, should be ruled

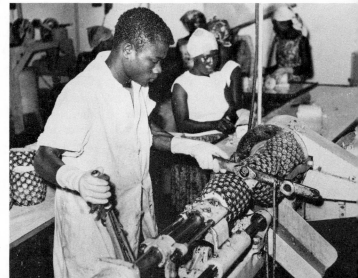

A Pineapple Processing Plant in Ghana. The new African states, rich in natural resources, are now attempting to meet the challenge of industrialization.

by Europeans. He strove to imbue his followers with pride in their race and, to this end, regaled them with stories of a Golden Age in Africa when great civilizations flourished before the beginning of the slave trade. He boasted of a glorious University of Timbuctoo, where eminent scholars translated their works into Hebrew and Greek and exchanged professorships with the University of Cordova in Spain. In 1966 Nkrumah as a ruler fell into disfavor. Accused of extravagance and corruption, he was deposed by a cabal of army and police officers. Absent on a trip to Peking and North Vietnam, he never returned to his homeland. He found refuge in Guinea and was made titular President of that country, theoretically as a co-equal of Sékou Touré.

The most violent of the colonial revolts in northern and central Africa occurred in Algeria and the Belgian Congo. Algeria had

The war in Algeria been a part of the French Empire since the middle years of the nineteenth century. The French poured millions of dollars of capital into their colony, and thousands of French nationals came there to settle. Many people of other nationalities, especially Spaniards, also emigrated to Algeria, with the result that by 1960 the European inhabitants numbered about 1 million in a total population of 10,300,000. These Europeans, inaccurately referred to as the "French" population, monopolized not only the government positions but also the best economic opportunities in industry, agriculture, trade, and finance. The Arab and Berber inhabitants were chiefly peasants and laborers, though some, of course, maintained their own shops in the *casbah*, or native quarter, of each of the large cities. In 1954 Arab and Berber (Moslem) nationalists rose in revolt when their demand for equal status with the European population was denied by the French government. The revolt continued its bloody course for seven years. It was complicated by the fact that many of the European settlers (*colons*) hated the government in Paris almost as much as they did the Algerian nationalists. They were determined to keep Algeria "French" and feared a sell-out by President Charles de Gaulle that would make the former colony independent and subject the *colons* to the rule of the Arab and Berber majority. In April 1961, the announcement of a plan by de Gaulle to negotiate a settlement in Algeria that would pave the way for eventual independence led to a revolt in the territory by four French generals. They seized government buildings, arrested loyal French officials, and threatened to invade France. De Gaulle proclaimed a state of emergency and ordered a total blockade of Algeria. In the face of such determined opposition the revolt collapsed. The war of the nationalists, however, continued for another year. On a promise of immediate self-government and eventual independence the nationalists laid down their arms in March 1962. Three months later Algeria entered the ranks of independent states and was admitted to the United Nations. The war had cost the lives of about 40,000 soldiers and civilians and had left a heritage of bitterness that would probably linger for years.

As in many other colonial territories, revolt in the Belgian Congo had smoldered for some time before the climactic outbreak. In January 1959, disturbances in Leopoldville prompted the Belgian government to announce a plan for establishing "democracy" in her colony. In little more than a year independence was proclaimed. Baudouin I, King of the Belgians, attended the ceremonies in Leopoldville. It was perhaps symptomatic of events to come that, during the ceremonies, a native seized the monarch's sword and ran off with it.

Scarcely had an independent Republic of the Congo been established than civil war broke out. In July 1960, the southeastern province of Katanga seceded and organized a separate republic. Here are located rich copper resources controlled by Belgian capitalists. The latter were in no mood to surrender control of their wealth to native nationalists. They had long been accustomed to exercising power through puppet governments in the Congo, and they were determined to continue doing so in its most crucial province. Faced with a disastrous civil conflict, Premier Patrice Lumumba of the Republic of the Congo appealed to the United Nations. Secretary-General Dag Hammarskjöld interpreted the war in the Congo as a threat to the peace of the world and sent a U.N. military force to compel Katanga to accept the authority of the Republic of the Congo. After a delay of more than a year, punctuated by bloody battles and assassinations, Moise Tshombe, President of the Katanga Republic, went to Leopoldville, in December 1961, and signed an agreement with Cyrille Adoula, the Congolese Premier, recognizing the unity of the Congo. But this agreement was not implemented, and it did not mark the end of the violence. Sporadic outbreaks continued to occur among discontented elements. As late as December 1962, Secretary-General U Thant, who had succeeded Dag Hammarskjöld after the death of the latter in a plane accident in September 1961, requested Katanga's principal copper and cobalt customers to impose a boycott as a means of forcing Moise Tshombe to end his secession movement. When he refused, even larger military forces were sent by the U.N. He surrendered finally in January 1963, and was sent into exile. His followers renewed the struggle on occasions thereafter but were defeated in 1967. The people of Katanga were readmitted, under a general amnesty, into the Republic of the Congo.

Not all of the northern and central African states achieved independence by wading through slaughter. Several made a peaceful transition, through a number of stages, under moderate and conciliatory leaders, from colonies or protectorates to independent republics or kingdoms. These included Morocco, Tunisia, and Nigeria. France gave up her protectorate over French Morocco in

Civil war

1955. The following year Spain recognized Moroccan sovereignty over what had been Spanish Morocco on the northern coast. In 1960 Tangier, which for many years had had the status of an international city, was integrated into the Kingdom of Morocco. Soon after the French granted self-government to Morocco they also renounced their protectorate over Tunisia, although they retained a naval and air base at Bizerte. The Tunisian President, Habib Bourguiba, demanded that this base be vacated, and imposed a siege. After a brief interval of fighting the issue was taken to the United Nations. In July 1961, the U.N. requested the French to withdraw from the Bizerte base.

The most populous and most influential of the former colonies to achieve independence by gradual and peaceful stages was Nigeria, a possession of Great Britain. In 1947, 1951, and 1958 the British granted constitutional changes, with increases in local autonomy. A new government chosen in 1959 advanced the former colony toward independence. For several years after gaining independence, Nigeria followed a stable course under the dominance of the Northern Region and its Western allies. Her valuable exports of petroleum, columbium (a steel alloy), cocoa, and tobacco assured a measure of prosperity to the productive areas. In 1966 junior army officers from the Eastern Region staged a military coup resulting in the assassination of the Prime Minister. The main object of dispute was income from oil concessions, 60 per cent of which were in the Eastern Region. In 1967 this region seceded and proclaimed itself the Republic of Biafra. The result was civil war of uncertain consequences.

By 1967 thirty-eight states in Africa had gained full independence, all but ten of them in the 1960's. But advancement to this stage had not solved the problems of all of them. Guinea was a dictatorship under the despotic rule of Sékou Touré. Touré's government is a one-party affair, and its methods include forced labor and the ruthless suppression of opposition. The condition of some other independent countries is even more unhappy, especially in such areas as the Congo, where inadequate preparations were made by the former rulers to train native administrators for their new role of governing. Nor were the territories that remained colonies enjoying contentment and prosperity. In the Portuguese colonies of Angola and Mozambique the natives lacked both political and civil rights, and repeated complaints were made to the United Nations of the persistence of slavery. The former British possession of Kenya on the Indian Ocean was the scene of tribal warfare and of the deadly attacks of the Mau Mau upon white settlers. The situation was equally explosive in the Rhodesias. In 1953 the British government merged Northern Rhodesia, Southern Rhodesia, and Nyasaland into the Federation of Rhodesia and Nyasaland. The merger aroused little enthusiasm. It was supported by the majority

of the white settlers under the leadership of Sir Roy Welensky.
But a "hard-core" Caucasian minority in Southern Rhodesia determined to perpetuate white supremacy. In 1964 Nyasaland became independent as the Republic of Malawi and Northern Rhodesia as the Republic of Zambia. When, two years later, Southern Rhodesia proclaimed its independence, Great Britain refused to grant it unless the white government agreed to a constitution extending voting privileges to native Africans. Southern Rhodesia continued to resist despite an economic blockade imposed by Britain with the endorsement of the United Nations.

SELECTED READINGS—THE MIDDLE EAST

· *Items so designated are available in paperbound editions.*

Ahmed, J. M., *The Intellectual Origins of Egyptian Nationalism*, New York, 1960. Informative and well-documented account by a Sudanese scholar and diplomat.

Banani, Amin, *The Modernization of Iran, 1921–1941*, Stanford, 1961.

Fisher, S. N., ed., *Social Forces in the Middle East*, Ithaca, 1955.

Frye, R. N., *The Near East and the Great Powers*, Cambridge, Mass., 1951.

Halpern, Manfred, *The Politics of Social Change in the Middle East and North Africa*, Princeton, 1967.

Harris, C. P., *Nationalism and Revolution in Egypt*, Stanford, 1967.

· Hitti, Philip K., *History of the Arabs*, New York, 1940 (St. Martin's). A classic work.

Hoskins, H. L., *The Middle East*, New York, 1954. A careful, judicious study.

Hurewitz, J. C., *The Struggle for Palestine*, New York, 1950.

Issawi, Charles P., *Egypt: an Economic and Social Analysis*, New York, 1947.

Karpat, Kemal, *Turkey's Politics: the Transition to a Multi-Party System*, Princeton, 1959. Sophisticated account by a Turkish political scientist of liberal views.

Khadduri, Majid, *Independent Iraq, 1932–1958: A Study in Iraqi Politics*, New York, 1960.

· Kirk, George E., *A Short History of the Middle East*, London, 1948 (Praeger).

Lenczowski, George, *The Middle East in World Affairs*, 3rd ed., Ithaca, 1962.

———, *Oil and State in the Middle East*, Ithaca, 1960.

Lewis, Bernard, *The Emergence of Modern Turkey*, New York, 1961. Optimistic as to the prospects of democratic development.

Lowdermilk, W. C., *Palestine, Land of Promise*, New York, 1949.

Nolte, R. H., *The Modern Middle East*, New York, 1963.

Shwadran, Benjamin, *The Middle East, Oil and the Great Powers*, New York, 1955.

Smith, Elaine, *Turkey: Origins of the Kemalist Movement and the Government of the Grand National Assembly (1919–1923)*, Washington, 1959.

Speiser, E. A., *The United States and the Near East*, Cambridge, Mass., 1950.

Twitchell, K. S., *Saudi Arabia*, Princeton, 1958.

Warriner, Doreen, *Land and Poverty in the Middle East*, New York, 1948.

Webster, Donald E., *The Turkey of Ataturk*, Philadelphia, 1939.

Wilber, D. N., *Iran, Past and Present*, Princeton, 1948.

Bartlett, Vernon, *Struggle for Africa*, New York, 1953.

Carter, G. M., *The Politics of Inequality*, New York 1958. A penetrating study of South Africa.

Clark, M. K., *Algeria in Turmoil*, New York, 1959.

· Macmillan, W. M., *Africa Emergent*, 1949 (Penguin).

· Marquard, L., *The Peoples and Policies of South Africa*, New York, 1952 (Oxford).

· Oliver, Roland, and Atmore, Anthony, *Africa since 1800*, New York, 1967 (Cambridge).

Pannikkar, K. M., *The Afro-Asian States and Their Problems*, New York, 1959. Brief but discerning.

CHAPTER 18

Eruption in the Far East

How can a government be made all-powerful? Once the government is all-powerful, how can it be made responsive to the will of the people?

—Dr. Sun Yat-sen

The democratic system is to be carried out within the ranks of the people, giving them freedom of speech, assembly, and association. The right to vote is given only to the people and not to the reactionaries. These two aspects, namely democracy among the people and dictatorship over the reactionaries, combine to form the people's democratic dictatorship.

—Chairman Mao Tse-tung

The contemporary era of the Far Eastern countries began under the stimulation provided by the impact of Western explorers and merchants. By the middle of the twentieth century profound changes had taken place not only within the Eastern countries but also in their relationship to the West. No longer merely peripheral to the main fields of interest of the Western nations, they had become in some measure the pivotal center of world affairs. Japan seized upon a large empire in Asia and the Pacific, which she retained until defeated in a long struggle against the most powerful of the Western states. China, after almost disintegrating and after passing through a cycle of revolution, emerged with radically altered institutions but, once again, as one of the strongest states of Asia. Moreover, China for the first time in her history was in a position to assume a major role in world politics.

I. NATIONALISM AND COMMUNISM IN CHINA

The overthrow of the Manchu Dynasty, accomplished with comparatively little effort in 1911, marked the beginning in China of a long period of instability and disorder that has witnessed a wide displacement of China's traditional institutions and culture. **569**

Perhaps never before in the country's history has there occurred such a transformation as during her modern revolutionary era. The Chinese Revolution falls roughly into four overlapping stages: (1) the pseudo-republic of Yüan Shih-k'ai, 1912–1916; (2) the rule of war lords and the weakening of the central government, 1916–1928; (3) the Nationalist revolution, 1923–1949; and (4) the Communist revolution, which gained momentum in the 1930's and triumphed in 1949. The second period, almost purely negative, was the natural result of the decadence that had preceded the downfall of the Manchu Dynasty. The third and fourth stages had some objectives in common and were combined for a time, although they finally came to be directly opposed to each other.

Yüan Shih-k'ai, the first President of the Republic, who tried unsuccessfully to restore the monarchy, maintained at least a semblance of unity in the state. After his death in 1916, much of China passed under the rule of independent military commanders, although a group at Peking preserved the fiction of a republican government. Some of these militarists had been officials under the Manchus; others were ex-soldiers or ex-bandits who had collected an army and taken over the administration of one or more provinces. Most of them were extortionate, and the common people of China suffered deplorably from their tyranny. Realignments in the Peking administration usually reflected a new combination among the war lords of the northern area. China's participation in World War I at a time when the central government was unable even to put its own house in order was a factor contributing to internal confusion. At the urging of the Allied powers, the Peking government declared war on Germany in 1917, hoping to gain advantages at the peace settlement. During the war, however, Japan seized the opportunity to "assist" her weak ally, selling war materials and extending loans to China and securing economic concessions within the country. At the Paris Peace Conference the requests of the Chinese delegation were almost completely disregarded, and Japan refused to restore the Shantung Peninsula, which she had taken over from Germany.

The third stage of the Revolution is associated with the personality and program of Sun Yat-sen. Dr. Sun's part in the inauguration of the Republic in 1912 had been a brief one, but after returning to Canton, where his following was strongest, he directed a barrage of criticism against the Peking military government. The rise of war lords was not confined to the north, and Sun actually was dependent for support upon militarists in control of the Kwangtung-Kwangsi area. His party, the Kuomintang, was a small faction, and its professed principles of parliamentary democracy seemed utterly unrealistic in a "phantom Republic" ravaged by irresponsible military bands. But with remarkable swiftness the Kuomintang changed into a dynamic organization capable of making a bid for control of the state. The initiative and organizing skill for accomplishing this transformation were largely supplied from outside China, by agents of the revolutionary Communist regime in Russia.

Understandably, the Bolshevik leaders, faced with the task of consolidating their power in Russia and confronted by the hostility of the Great Powers, were eager to win support in revolutionary China. Rebuffed by the Peking government, they turned to Dr. Sun in Canton. The Third (Communist) International had organized a Far Eastern division and established at Moscow a university named after Sun Yat-sen to train Chinese revolutionaries, some of whom joined the Communist party. Although Dr. Sun rejected communism, he had hoped for the support of Western nations and welcomed the offer of Russian co-operation. In 1923 Sun and the Russian emissaries arrived at a working agreement which provided for Russian assistance and for the admission of Chinese Communists to the Kuomintang but left Sun the undisputed head of the Kuomintang party. Acknowledging that China's immediate task was to achieve national unity and free herself from the yoke of foreign imperialism, the Russians promised to support these objectives, while recognizing the fact that conditions in China were not suitable for establishing communism. Accordingly the Soviet government sent military and political advisers to Canton.

During the Moscow-Canton entente of 1923–1927, the Chinese nationalist movement acquired a disciplined leadership, clear-cut objectives, and considerable popular support. A general dissatisfaction with the dreary and corrupt rule of the military cliques, the humiliation of China at the Paris Peace Conference, and the entrenched position of the Great Powers in their spheres of interest all helped to intensify nationalist sentiment. Disillusionment following the war stimulated a spirit of revolt among young intellectuals and among the lower classes, as evidenced by the growth of labor unions in the Yangtze valley industrial cities, peasant movements, youth movements, and movements for the emancipation of women. The various dissident elements needed only effective leadership to be enlisted in a campaign for the regeneration and strengthening of China under a truly national government. Soviet advisers taught Sun Yat-sen and his associates how to supply this leadership. Under the direction of Michael Borodin, a seasoned revolutionary who had worked as an agitator in Turkey and Mexico, the Kuomintang was revamped on the model of the Russian Communist party. On the propaganda front, posters, pictures, and slogans dramatized the Kuomintang program, which was to unseat the war lords, introduce honest and democratic government, stamp out the opium habit, and promote other reforms.

By 1925 Canton had become the center of a small but effective government, which collected taxes, regulated commerce, and was developing its own "new model" army, officered by men trained at the Whampoa Academy (near Canton) under supervision of European military experts, and indoctrinated with loyalty to Sun Yat-sen and to his party. This Canton government was actually a Soviet regime without being Communist. Controlled neither by war lords nor by democratically elected representatives but by the high command of the Kuomintang, it provided the first example of a party dictatorship in China. Although the Canton government showed vigor, it was not recognized by foreign powers, not even by Soviet Russia. Russia maintained correct relations with the Peking government (and restored some Russian concessions to its jurisdiction) after Peking recognized the Soviet Union in 1924. At the same time, Russian agents were assisting Sun Yat-sen's group in preparations to overthrow the Peking regime.

Dr. Sun did not live to see the phenomenal success of the organization which he had founded, but he left a body of doctrines as a heritage of the Kuomintang party. His most important writings were put together rather hastily during the period of Communist-Kuomintang collaboration and partly at the urging of Borodin, who recognized their value for propaganda purposes. The gist of Sun's program and political philosophy is contained in the famous *San Min Chu I* ("Three Principles of the People"), which became a sort of Bible for the Kuomintang. The Three Principles, usually translated as "Nationalism," "Democracy," and "Livelihood," have been likened to Abraham Lincoln's "government of the people, by the people, and for the people"; but there is considerable difference between the American and the Chinese interpretations of the terms. By *nationalism* Sun meant, first, the freeing of China from foreign interference and, second, the development of loyalty among the people to the state instead of to the family or the province. The Chinese, he felt, had achieved a cultural unity but had never taken sufficient interest in the political structure, thus making it easy for stronger states to impose upon them. His concept of nationalism was tinged with racial theories (he asserted that the Chinese were the only nation and China the only state coinciding with a distinct race), but these were more naïve than truculent. In his second Principle, Sun was concerned with popular sovereignty and the ideal of representative government. Recognizing that people are unequal in capacity, he believed that the chief political problem (in both China and the West) was to discover how popular sovereignty could be combined with direction by experts. Those "who see and perceive first" should be allowed to guide the others until they have reached a point of understanding and participation. The Principle of Livelihood referred to the necessity for material progress and also to social reform, rejecting Marxism but failing to outline any specific program. Sun's ideas as a whole were neither very original nor very radical nor even very clear. Democracy appeared in his conception as a rather remote goal, to be attained at the end of the revolutionary struggle. The three stages of revolution, according to Sun, would be: (1) the military stage, necessary to establish order, (2) the "tutelage" stage, devoted to training the people and with power restricted to the revolutionary leaders (the Kuomintang party), and (3) the constitutional stage, embodying representative popular government.

In view of Dr. Sun's limitations both as a leader and as a thinker, it is remarkable that he came to be revered as the "father of the Revolution." His life ended, characteristically, on a note of futility. He had gone north in the latter part of 1924 to arrange an alliance with two of the war lords against a third, but arrived in Peking to find that a settlement had been made without his knowledge. Already in poor health, he died the following March. But when finally removed from the scene, Sun became a legendary figure to his followers, and "Sunyatsenism" proved to be a far more potent force than Dr. Sun had ever been. He left behind him a legacy of hope, and he had stirred the imagination of Chinese all over the world with the vision of a strong and free China under a republican constitution which would combine the best thought of ancient sages with modern scientific techniques. By the Kuomintang his writings and speeches were treasured as unalloyed wisdom, while their vagueness made it possible to invoke the master's authority for contradictory policies.

By 1926, when the Canton government had become strong enough to challenge the northern militarists, the Nationalist revolution entered its active phase. Kuomintang forces under command of the young general Chiang Kai-shek swept rapidly northward into the Yangtze valley and in less than six months overran half the provinces of China. The success of this "punitive expedition,"

Dr. Sun Yat-sen (seated) with Chiang Kai-shek.

however, brought to the surface a dissension which had been stirring for some time within the party. A conservative faction distrusted the Communist connection and wanted to oust Communists entirely. The radical wing, hoping to base the organization upon the support of the peasant and working classes, stressed the desirability of a concrete reform program and of continued association with the Russian advisers. Temporarily the radicals seemed to have won. Chiang Kai-shek, whose sympathies were conservative and who had suppressed radical demonstrations at Shanghai and executed Communists and suspected Communists when Kuomintang troops occupied this important city, was temporarily deprived of his command. But by midsummer of 1927 the picture had completely changed. Borodin and the other Russian advisers were dismissed; trade unionists and radicals were disciplined or driven out of the party, and some party members went into voluntary exile in Russia (including the widow of Sun Yat-sen).

The temporary
defeat of the
Communists

Although the reversal of direction in 1927 was startling and decisive, actually there had been little likelihood that the radicals could maintain their ascendancy. The Chinese Communists at this time numbered only about 50,000. While there were plenty of discontented peasants and a Chinese Federation of Labor claimed two and a half million members, these groups were not capable of carrying to successful conclusion the fight against the northern militarists. And the Kuomintang army was far from being a radical body. Kuomintang leaders had welcomed and benefited from Russian assistance, but now that they felt strong enough to stand alone they had no desire to serve the interests of a foreign power. There were grounds for suspecting that the Russians intended to convert the Chinese revolution into an outpost of Soviet Communism, and the discovery of a Soviet plot at Peking prompted the northern government to break off relations with Russia. In supporting the Moscow-Canton entente of 1923-1927, the Soviet leaders, hoping for the speedy coming of world revolution, had gambled and lost—or so it seemed. But they had provided the spark without which the Kuomintang might never have been fired into action.

Capture of Peking
(Pei-p'ing) by
Kuomintang forces

After the purge of the radical wing, the Kuomintang leaders proceeded rapidly with their plan to extend their authority throughout the country. From this time forward the dominant figure of the party was Chiang Kai-shek, whose return to a position of influence was automatic with the triumph of the conservatives. In addition to his ability as a military commander, Chiang enjoyed the prestige of belonging to the "ruling family" of the Revolution, through his marriage to the American-educated Soong Mei-ling, a sister of Madame Sun Yat-sen. Kuomintang forces pushed on, without too much difficulty, through the territories of discredited military governors, and occupied Peking in 1928. The Nationalists renamed the city *Pei-p'ing* ("Northern Peace") and moved their capital to Nanking, in keeping with pledges made in the early period of the Revolution.

The task of national reconstruction confronting the Kuomintang leaders was a far more difficult undertaking than the seizure of power had been. Even the maintenance of power was not easy, as remnants of the war-lord regimes lingered on in various parts of China. These, however, did not seriously challenge the Nanking government, and Chiang defeated a coalition of two powerful rivals in 1930. Although Kuomintang supremacy still depended upon military support, the party claimed that it had completed the first, or military, stage of Dr. Sun's formula of revolution and had inaugurated the second stage—that of political "tutelage." In spite of its anti-Communist orientation, the structure both of the Kuomintang and of the government which it set up at Nanking followed closely the Soviet pattern. The party was a hierarchy, reaching from the smallest units, or cells, through district and provincial bodies up to the Central Executive Committee at the top. Theoretically, ultimate authority rested with the National Party Congress, a general session of party members representing the local divisions. Actually, the Party Congress was seldom convoked, and effective control remained with the Central Executive Committee, of which the key member was Chiang Kai-shek. The President of the National Government and the members of his Council of State were selected by the Central Executive Committee of the Kuomintang. At the central, provincial, and local levels the government embodied, not democracy, but a party dictatorship.

Chiang Kai-shek's Nationalist regime at Nanking

A number of important accomplishments can be credited to the Nationalist regime at Nanking. The portions of China which were brought under its jurisdiction became more unified than at any time since the eighteenth century, and China's prestige in the eyes of the world was enhanced. The Nationalists promptly secured diplomatic recognition and financial assistance from abroad, and they made progress, although slowly, toward revision of the unequal treaties. Following the lead of the United States, the Great Powers agreed to relinquish their control over customs duties, granting tariff autonomy to China by 1929. Nationalist forces had occupied foreign concessions in several of the Yangtze valley cities, and a few of the ports which had been leased to foreign powers were voluntarily returned to China soon after the Nanking government was established. It was more difficult to persuade the Great Powers to surrender their privileges of extraterritoriality, a step not taken by the United States and Great Britain until 1943.

Accomplishments of the Nationalist regime

Internal developments, also, indicated that China was throwing off the lethargy that she had displayed through most of the nineteenth century. There was considerable industrial growth, although it by no means equaled that of Japan. Cotton manufacture increased so greatly between 1900 and 1930 that by the latter date **575** cotton cloth was contributing about 10 per cent of China's exports. While the factory system was expanding, the number of laborers which it affected was relatively very small. The bulk of production was still carried on by the domestic system; labor organizations were weak, and the ancient guilds had largely been transformed into employers' organizations.

While progress undeniably occurred during the era of Nationalist rule, the defects of the regime became more and more serious. Radical elements had been expelled before the triumph of the Kuomintang, and even moderate liberals were given scant encouragement. Originating as a party of revolution, the Kuomintang when in power neglected to carry out the social reforms which were necessary to relieve the suffering and win the allegiance of the common people. Very little was done to improve the condition of poor tenants and farm laborers, even though Sun Yat-sen had specified that assistance to these classes was a primary object of the "Principle of Livelihood." In command of a one-party government and eager to perpetuate its own authority, the Kuomintang employed coercive measures against those who opposed it. It maintained secret police, disguised under the title of "Bureau of Investigation and Statistics." To indoctrinate potential party members it organized a tightly disciplined Youth Corps (ironically named the *San Min Chu I* after Sun's "Three Principles"). One group within the party formed a terrorist organization known as the "Blue Shirts," which showed more than a superficial resemblance to fascist groups in Western Europe. The Kuomintang dictatorship was never complete, nor was it a one-man affair, and divergences appeared among various factions within the party. Nevertheless, the Nationalist regime seemed to be preparing the Chinese people less for constitutional democracy than for a permanent condition of "tutelage."

The downfall of the Kuomintang in China after a rule of twenty years was caused by three factors: (1) failure of the Kuomintang regime to solve the problems of Chinese society, (2) unrelenting opposition from the Chinese Communists, who ultimately set up a rival government, and (3) the long war beginning with the Japanese invasion of 1937, which drained the country's resources, demoralized the people, and promoted the chaotic conditions so favorable to the spread of communism. The struggle against the Communists began almost as soon as the Kuomintang had established its government at Nanking and was a continuous process even during the most successful years of the Nationalist period. Following the rupture with the Kuomintang in 1927, the Communist party had been driven underground but extended its activities in both rural and urban areas of central and southern China, and in Kiangsi province it organized a rival government in the form of a Soviet Republic. Almost annihilated by Kuomintang forces in a series of military campaigns, the Communist leaders turned the desperate struggle to their advantage by inciting revolutionary aspirations among the depressed peasantry and by developing the technique of guerrilla warfare into a fine art. Mao Tse-tung (b. 1893) was the key personality behind both of these policies.

The son of a relatively well-to-do peasant, Mao Tse-tung as a youth had rebelled against landlordism and the tyranny of parental authority. One of a dozen men who founded the Chinese Communist Party in 1921, he became a deputy member of the Central Executive Committee of the Kuomintang and was entrusted by the Communists with the task of peasant organization. A report prepared for the Chinese Communist Party in 1927 on peasant revolutionary activity in Hunan (south central China) provides the clue to Mao's strategy of revolution and is prophetic of his ultimate program for China. Already he was instigating direct action among the lowliest tenants: (1) forming village co-operative associations, (2) smashing temples and burning the wooden idols for fuel, (3) intimidating and assaulting "bad gentry." "A revolution is not the same as inviting people to dinner," he wrote. "A rural revolution is a revolution by which the peasantry overthrows the authority of the feudal landlord class." "In a very short time . . . several hundred million peasants will rise like a tornado or tempest, a force so extraordinarily swift and violent that no power, however great, will be able to suppress it." In sharp disagreement with both the Chinese and Russian party leaders, Mao was convinced that whoever won the peasants would win China.

For the time being, however, threatened with extinction by Chiang's superior troops, Mao Tse-tung conceived and executed the famous "Long March" of October 1934 to October 1935—a mass migration across 6,000 miles of difficult terrain and one of the most amazing exploits in military history. Of the 90,000 men who slipped through Chiang's lines in southwestern China, not more than 20,000 reached Yenan (in northern Shensi Province), which was to be the Communists' headquarters until their final victory in the civil war. Shattering as the experience had been, it served to weld the survivors into a solid group of tested loyalty and toughness, relying upon their own ingenuity rather than upon directives from Moscow, and it established Mao Tse-tung as undisputed leader of the Party. He had demonstrated his tactics of "retreat in order to advance" and his ability to sustain and renew his forces directly from the countryside while the cities and economic apparatus of the state were in the hands of his enemies. Gradually the Communist region of the northwest acquired the attributes of a separate state, with a fluid political structure and well-organized military units. In expanding the area of their influence, the Communists' chief asset was their introduction of reforms which the Nanking government had promised but never fulfilled. They tackled the

Mao Tse-tung's strategy of revolution

The "Long March" to Yenan

land problem directly, breaking up great estates, forcing rent re-
ductions, establishing land banks and co-operative societies, building irrigation works, and educating ignorant peasants in better
methods of cultivation and crop control. Their immediate and
practical assistance to farmers who had been oppressed by high
rents and high taxes and their success in eliminating graft in the
region under their administration enabled them to compete successfully with the Kuomintang regime for popular favor. The Communists also strengthened their position by calling for national resistance against Japanese aggression, to which Chiang Kai-shek,
intent upon crushing Communism, had offered only half-hearted
opposition.

When, in line with the Soviet strategy of fostering antifascist
"popular fronts," the Chinese Communists appeared co-operative,
pressure within the Kuomintang induced Chiang Kai-shek to enter
into an alliance with them to halt the common enemy, Japan. But
this had the unfortunate effect of encouraging the Japanese militarists to make war. Faced with the prospect of a united China, they
goaded their government into launching an attack in the Peiping
area (July 7, 1937). This was the beginning of a fateful conflict
which soon expanded into World War II.

The course of the war revealed that China was a far stronger nation than she had been forty years earlier. Even though the mighty
Japanese military machine eventually occupied the coastal cities
and almost all of eastern China and forced the Nationalist government to move its capital far inland to Chungking, it was never able
to conquer the entire country. In spite of staggering military reverses, the Nationalists even made progress toward laying the basis
for a sounder economy. They organized both rural and industrial
co-operatives and improved agricultural methods to increase farm
production. They announced a program of land purchase to provide additional holdings for small farmers and outlined a scheme
for democratizing local government. These forward-looking movements, however, were vitiated by inefficiency and corruption
within the Chungking administration and the Kuomintang party.
Hoarding, profiteering, and a runaway inflation added to the impoverishment of the very groups which were most in need of help.
Even more ominous for the future was the underlying hostility between the Nationalists at Chungking and the "Border Region" government of the Communists at Yenan in the north. Each group
accused the other of failure to observe the terms of their common
alliance against Japan, and during the war the Nationalists diverted
an army of 500,000 men to police the frontier of the Communist
Border Region. Through skillful guerrilla tactics the Communists
extended their control in northern China. At the close of the war
when, with the aid of an American airlift, the Nationalists occupied
the principal cities of Manchuria, Communist forces penetrated the

President of the "Other China."
Generalissimo Chiang Kai-shek
reviewing cadets of the Chinese
Army military academy in Taiwan (Formosa).

countryside, and they seized stores of Japanese arms and ammunition which the Russian troops withdrawing from Manchuria had
conveniently left behind. After the Japanese surrender, China's international war gradually turned into a civil war.

Before the close of World War II the Nationalists had formulated plans for replacing the "tutelage" stage of party dictatorship
with representative constitutional government. As early as 1938 a
People's Political Council was organized, which contained representatives of non-Kuomintang elements, including the Communists. A
National Constituent Assembly (boycotted by the Communists)
convened in November 1946 and drafted a constitution of a democratic character, providing for an elective bicameral national parliament and for popularly elected local assemblies as well. The new
constitution was promulgated on January 1, 1947; elections were
duly held, and the National Assembly, which met the following
March, named Chiang Kai-shek as President of the Republic. But
while the Nationalists were inaugurating a democratic constitution
for China, they were rapidly being dispossessed from the country
by the advance of Communist armies. In 1949 the southerly retreat
of the Nationalist forces turned into a rout which ended with all
the mainland in the hands of the Communists. By 1950 the jurisdiction of President Chiang's government was confined to the island
of Taiwan (Formosa). After an eight-year war against a foreign
enemy the score for the Nationalists could be reckoned as the recovery of one island from Japan and the loss of half a continent to
Chinese rivals.

Although the conquest of China by the Communists represented
a military victory, it was greatly facilitated by the failure of the
Nationalists to win the confidence of any substantial segment of **579**

The constitution
of 1947; the
triumph of
Communism

the Chinese population. The promise of democratic constitutionalism was too little and too late, and the long anticipated social and economic reforms were not forthcoming at all. Not only did the Nanking government fail to take any significant steps in this direction but in the years following the war it seemed to be more bureaucratic and more honeycombed with corruption than ever. The impression spread rapidly that many of the Kuomintang leaders were primarily interested in feathering their own nests and were no better than the old war lords of the 1920's. So low had the prestige of the party fallen that it could summon very little assistance in its hour of peril. From the purely military standpoint, the Nationalists committed the grave mistake of attempting to recover the north and even to drive the Communists out of Manchuria before the Nanking government had consolidated its hold upon central and southern China. By extending their lines too far they weakened their position and made its collapse the more catastrophic.

After their victory over the Nationalists, the Communist leaders moved rapidly to secure their hold upon the vast territory of China. In October 1949 they proclaimed "The People's Republic of China," with its capital in Peking. An Organic Law, promulgated as a temporary frame of government, was replaced by a formal constitution in 1954. The Constitution of The People's Republic, like that of Soviet Russia, combines the language and forms of parliamentary democracy with the principle of domination by the Communist party (which, with some 17 million members, is the largest such party in the world). Nominally, supreme authority is vested in an All-China People's Congress, which meets annually and which, in addition to enacting laws, elects the major officials, including the President (Chairman of the Republic). The Constitution contains a Bill of Rights which covers the whole field of individual liberties, recognizes equality of the sexes, declares all persons over 18 years of age eligible to vote and to hold office, and even guarantees the ownership of private property. However, it leaves the application of these rights very tentative by giving the government power to punish "traitors, counterrevolutionaries, and bureaucratic capitalists."

The Communist regime in China is defined officially not as a dictatorship of the proletariat but as a "People's Democratic Dictatorship." Allegedly it came into existence as the result of a coalition of classes, namely peasants, workers, petty bourgeoisie, and "national bourgeoisie." The inclusion of the last two classes marked a departure from orthodox Marxism and an attempt to win the support of financial and industrial elements whose co-operation was essential to bolstering the national economy. Businessmen who qualified as "Communist" or "national" capitalists by being willing to work with the new government were allowed to retain their properties temporarily, but found their affairs subjected to rigid control, and in 1956 the national bourgeoisie were formally expropriated. In spite of the monolithic tendencies of Communism, Chinese society—in theory at least—has retained some flexibility. Mao admitted that contradictions could exist even in a socialist society (though he distinguished between "antagonistic" and "nonantagonistic" contradictions), advocated "democratic methods of discussion," and stressed the necessity of continuous struggle for improvement and "purification." In practice, the Central Committee of the Communist party or Chairman Mao himself has determined public policies, the permissible limits of debate, and the operation of organs of government.

The economic transformation of China since 1949 is one of the most impressive aspects of the revolutionary regime. As in India and most other developing nations, industrialization was given high priority, and—in contrast to India—the government possessed sufficient coercive power to effect rapid change. Although available statistics cannot be accepted uncritically, there is ample evidence of progress, all the more remarkable when viewed against the retarded condition of China earlier. Geological surveys have revealed mineral resources far in excess of previous estimates: gigantic deposits of iron ore and coal, the indispensable ingredients of heavy industrial growth; oil reserves of more than 2 billion tons; and adequate supplies of manganese, tungsten, antimony, tin, copper, and aluminum. By 1960 China's furnaces were producing almost as much steel as was made in France; her pig iron production (partly low grade) exceeded West Germany's as well as Great Britain's. Also by 1960 the output of electric power had been increased ten times, even though many hydro-electric projects were still in the planning stage. The acreage of irrigated land more than doubled between 1949 and 1960, and the same period witnessed an extensive forestation program highly significant for soil and water conservation. A complex system of dams and reservoirs in the Yellow River valley may eventually end the danger of flood in the region which has so often been the scene of "China's sorrow" and promises a bigger and surer crop yield—of rice as well as wheat. These ambitious projects have not been entirely completed, and it was reported in 1965 that only 40 per cent of the large conservation installations were functioning properly. Railroad mileage has doubled but is still far from adequate, especially since the objective is a wide dispersion of industry hitherto concentrated in Manchuria and the eastern seaboard. With Soviet technical assistance the Chinese trained their own engineers capable of designing precision tools. Their manufactures include such items as cars, trucks, and jet planes; also electronic, surgical, and scientific instruments. Grim and dramatic evidence that scientific technology had reached a high level of sophistication came in October 1964 with the detonation of China's first nuclear device. Less than three years later, in June 1967, the

Chinese exploded a hydrogen bomb, and they had begun to manu-facture nuclear-tipped missiles.

The agrarian
revolution and
the "Great Leap
Forward"

More profound than the changes in the scope and tempo of industrialization has been the agrarian revolution. First inaugurated among the peasants, Mao's brand of Communism—in contrast to that of the Soviet Union—has remained largely peasant-based down to the present day. However, the character of agriculture and of the society engaged in it has been altered radically, through successive stages. The first phase of land reform was simply expropriation of the landlords, many of whom were killed. Then, the newly created peasant proprietors were urged to form co-operatives, pooling the resources of one or more villages. The next step was a drive for collective farms, communally owned and directed by party members or supporters. This was accomplished with remarkable swiftness, between 1955 and 1957, by which time more than 90 per cent of the family holdings had been collectivized. Although Chinese farmers undoubtedly "volunteered" to join co-operatives because they were given little choice, the government relied primarily upon psychological and social pressure, employing what Mao has described as "persuasive reasoning," and there was no liquidation of resisting peasants. But without waiting for the collectives to prove themselves, the party leaders in 1958 announced a third stage of the Communist agrarian pattern. It called for the merging of rural co-operatives and collective farms into large communes, which, it was claimed, embodied the principle of ownership by the whole people rather than by a single community. The purpose of the communes was to provide a mobile labor force to implement an overly ambitious program of rapid industrialization advertised as the "Great Leap Forward" and to increase food production. For a variety of reasons—including the callousness and ineptitude of local directors and a prolonged drought in the Yellow River valley that brought poor harvests in 1959 and 1960—the Great Leap Forward turned out to be a disaster. Food shortages necessitated the importation of grain; the demoralization of labor and the drainage of capital resources caused a severe industrial depression; and the Second Five-Year Plan, scheduled for the period 1958–1962, had to be abandoned. Forced to revise its tactics drastically, the government in 1962 announced its intention to give agriculture top priority for the immediate future. While the communes were retained (and their number increased from 24,000 to 74,000), they were reduced in size, a degree of ownership and management was restored to local production teams, and farmers were permitted to cultivate small private plots and sell on the open market. By 1965 the danger of famine seemed to have passed, and a Third Five-Year Plan, emphasizing both the expansion of heavy industry and the development and modernization of agriculture, was launched in 1966.

NATIONALISM
AND
COMMUNISM
IN CHINA

Changes in
society and living
conditions

It is still difficult to assess the character of Chinese society and culture under the Communist regime. At the least it can be said that tremendous energies have been set in motion and channeled toward concrete goals. Probably never before in history have so many people been changed so much in so short a time. A significant aspect of social change is the demise of the centuries-old patriarchal family structure, which had already begun to decay. A marriage law of 1950 gave women equal rights with men in respect to choice of spouse, conjugal privileges and obligations, and divorce. Legal equality between the sexes led not to unbridled promiscuity or the disappearance of the family as an institution but to enhanced status for the single-unit monogamous family. Intensive efforts to expand medical facilities, to improve standards of hygiene and sanitation in the cities and villages, and to stamp out opium addiction and eliminate prostitution have raised the level of public health. While China is still poor in comparison with Western countries, there is no doubt that the bulk of her people are better off in regard to basic material necessities than they have been for many centuries. At the same time, a steady growth in population, increasing at an annual rate of 2 per cent, intensifies the problem of fulfilling these needs more abundantly. Now about 750 million, the population figure may reach one billion in little more than a decade. While the party scoffs at Malthusian theories and hails the human increment as proof of the vitality of a socialist society, it has nevertheless publicized and actively encouraged the practice of contraception. The government undertook to expand and refashion education, establishing not only full-time day schools but also "half-study, half-work" schools, evening and correspondence schools, factory schools, and others. A program of language reform includes the unification of pronunciation, the simplification of written characters, and even the goal of eventually replacing the characters with more easily learned phonetic symbols.

Of course there is a darker side to the picture of China's changing social scene, and a high price has been paid for rapid material progress. The party chiefs used ruthless means to seize power and to keep it. No one knows how many enemies and "counterrevolutionaries" were killed in the process, but sober estimates run into the hundreds of thousands. Still, in view of China's long tradition of civil strife and brutal dictatorship, it is noteworthy that violence and terror have not been the typical weapons either of party discipline or of popular coercion. There has been no mass liquidation of "kulaks" or of bourgeoisie. There has been no party purge equal to those of the Stalin era in Russia. On the other hand, psychological pressure, "thought control," and "reform through labor" have been employed extensively in the effort to remold recalcitrants. Political indoctrination is effected through the mass communication media, entirely controlled by the government, and is a primary aim of

CONTRASTS IN MODERN CHINA

Blast Furnaces at Anshan. The major steel producing center in southern Manchuria, it is a testament to China's growing industrial strength.

The Cultural Revolution at the Grass Roots. Agricultural workers have erected red painted signs with quotations from Chairman Mao and carry copies of his "Quotations" into the fields with them.

A Reservoir and Irrigation Project in Chekiang Province, eastern China. Labor saving machinery is still in short supply.

education. In conformity with the slogan, "Let politics take command," the schools must base their curricula on "the thought of Mao Tse-tung." Individual freedom, especially freedom of the mind, has been dealt a severe blow; but there is no reason to believe that the Chinese have been turned into soulless robots. Foreign observers report manifestations of popular enthusiasm, puritanical zeal, and an almost priggish morality. But while an avowed objective of the Communist revolution was to eliminate class distinctions, the growth of a huge body of governmental and party functionaries has already tended to create new classes. Not only do the state and party agents—generally referred to as cadres—constitute an elite, set apart from the ordinary citizens, but they have also developed into a complex hierarchy, marked by wide variations in prestige, privileges, and salary scales.[1] Thus the drift toward bureaucracy, perhaps essential to implement far-reaching economic and social programs, militates against the Communist egalitarian ideal. Sensing this dilemma, the party leaders have attempted to circumvent it by subjecting the cadres to corrective discipline—requiring them to attend study sessions and "struggle meetings," periodically assessing their performance and fitness, and, through a program of "downward transfer," assigning them to work as manual laborers at the lowliest tasks.

Chinese Communist ideology, while indebted to the Russian model, has evolved some distinctive characteristics of its own. Mao's disciples have acclaimed him as the greatest living exponent of Marxism-Leninism, and they affirm that the Chinese Communist revolution—stemming from the peasants and gaining momentum through guerrilla warfare—is the exemplar to be followed by other peoples of Asia and Africa. Like most Marxists, Chinese Communists defend their program as the logical culmination of historic forces. Mao Tse-tung's interpretation of Chinese history is vivid and pointed, though boldly oversimplified. A period of some 3000 years, reaching to the middle of the nineteenth century, he designates as "feudal," referring to the dominance of the scholar-gentry elite. He identifies the class struggle with recurring though unsuccessful peasant uprisings, including the nineteenth-century Taiping rebellion. There is a strong flavor of nationalism in Mao's ideology. He invokes reverence for China's "splendid historical heritage" and "glorious revolutionary tradition," and pays tribute to some pre-Communist reformers. Sun Yat-sen (whose widow—Chiang Kai-shek's sister-in-law—holds one of the two vice chairmanships of the

Ideology; Mao's interpretation of history

[1] One curious aspect of this phenomenon is that the most highly placed and highly paid cadres are subject to the most rigid surveillance. They live in collectivized government quarters with practically no personal life of their own. A. Doak Barnett, "Social Stratification and Aspects of Personnel Management in the Chinese Communist Bureaucracy," *The China Quarterly*, Oct.–Dec., 1966, pp. 8–39. Barnett observes that only the common people at the bottom of the bureaucratic pyramid are "free"—in the sense of enjoying some privacy (a situation reminiscent of the condition of the "proles" in Orwell's *1984*).

People's Republic) is especially honored for his "clear-cut stand as a Chinese revolutionary democrat." Another distinctive feature of Mao's teaching is his rejection of the historical determinism implicit in orthodox Marxism. While admitting the influence of objective social forces, he stresses the importance of ideas and of human will and resolution in shaping events, holding that these nonmaterial factors can themselves become an objective force in history.[2]

The rapid unification of China under a totalitarian regime has drastically altered the power relationships in Asia and the Far East.

China's foreign relations

With a powerful army at their disposal, the Communists reestablished Chinese jurisdiction over important areas that had been lost during the decline of the Manchu Dynasty. They took possession of Manchuria, retained Sinkiang in the far west, and installed their forces in Tibet. And while augmenting China's national prestige they posed as the champions of Asian peoples against Western imperialism, assisting revolutionary movements against the British in Malaya and against the French in Indochina.

A basic principle of Communist China's foreign policy during the first decade was cordiality toward the Soviet Union. In 1950

The Sino-Soviet rift and its significance

representatives of the two states signed a thirty-year treaty of "friendship, alliance, and mutual assistance," which invalidated the 1945 treaty between the U.S.S.R. and the Chinese Nationalists. The preamble of China's 1954 Constitution reaffirms "indestructible friendship" with the Soviet Union. China relied heavily upon Russia for technical assistance in economic development. Between 1950 and 1955 China's exchange with the Soviet-bloc countries increased from 26 per cent to 75 per cent of her total foreign trade. By the late 1950's, however, there was evidence of disaffection between the two Communist giants. Differences flared into the open at the Moscow international conference of Communist parties in 1960 and led swiftly to deterioration in both diplomatic and economic relations. By 1962, 61 per cent of China's foreign trade had shifted to countries outside the Communist bloc. The Sino-Soviet rift is attributable to a number of causes. The Chinese resented the Russians' failure to fulfill their aid agreements, including the promise of help in developing atomic weapons. Other factors were the inevitable rivalries of great-power politics and conflicting national territorial ambitions. The Chinese hinted at the eventual rectification of their frontiers at Russia's expense, and both China and the Soviet Union deployed large numbers of troops along their common border from Central Asia to Manchuria. Probably the greatest source of disagreement, however, was ideological. Peking accused the Russians of abandoning the cause of world revolution against imperialism, condemned Khrushchev's policy of peaceful coexistence

[2] H. L. Boorman, "Mao Tse-tung as Historian," *The China Quarterly*, Oct.–Dec., 1966, pp. 82–105.

and the test ban treaty of 1963, claimed that Moscow had joined a counterrevolutionary "Holy Alliance" with the United States, India, Yugoslavia, and others to encircle China, and even charged that Soviet leaders were working "hand in glove" with American imperialists in the Vietnam war. The breach between Peking and Moscow (not complete or irreparable) reflects the differences in outlook between the heirs of an old revolution and the directors of one which is still comparatively young. In Mao Tse-tung's view Soviet Russia, now a "have nation," has succumbed to revisionism and is taking the primrose path to accommodation with the capitalist powers for the sake of security and the gratification of consumer demands.

While China's relations with the Soviet Union have fluctuated, her attitude toward the United States has been consistently hostile, partly because the United States replaced Great Britain as the dominant Western power in the Far East and partly because in attempting to regiment and energize the Chinese people the Communists needed the spur of a tangible external enemy. "Hate America" campaigns were useful to stimulate more heroic labor efforts. It must be admitted that American Far Eastern policy has helped to intensify Chinese suspicion and animosity. The United States gave Chiang Kai-shek financial support throughout the war, even after he had stopped fighting the Japanese, and the United States financed his military establishment (600,000 troops) on the island of Taiwan (which the Communists and the Nationalists both regard as an integral part of China). Washington has withheld diplomatic recognition from Peking, blocked its admission to the U.N., discouraged U.S. citizens from visiting Red China, and urged allied nations not to trade with her. American feeling toward China was exacerbated during the Korean War of 1950–1953, but the issue of the Nationalist regime in Taiwan remained the prime obstacle in the way of better relations. In 1955, in 1958, and again in the summer of 1962, the threat of war in the Far East became grave because of the bellicose attitudes of the Nationalist and mainland Chinese armed forces.

Disputes with the United States

The truculence and seeming recklessness of the Peking government should not be given undue weight. Although party spokesmen have denounced Russia's policy of coexistence and declared that they are not afraid of any war that might be launched against them, in practice they have followed a prudent course, avoiding any major conflict and even some minor ones. They negotiated bilateral agreements with several non-Communist states on the periphery of China—Afganistan, Pakistan, Nepal, Burma, and Cambodia. Thus far they have allowed Britain to retain Hong Kong and Portugal to retain Macao (under severe restrictions). Sensing the danger of intervention by Russia and the United States, they failed to seize any advantage from the Indo-Pakistan war of 1965. China's

Signs of restraint in China's foreign policy

unexpectedly rapid development of a thermonuclear capacity was clearly intended to strengthen her hand in the desperate game of international politics. However, at the time of the first Chinese atomic explosion in 1964 the government issued a formal statement declaring that "China will never at any time and under any circumstances be the first to use nuclear weapons," and proposed a summit conference of all countries to discuss the question of the "complete prohibition and thorough destruction" of such weapons.

The "Great Proletarian Cultural Revolution"

The most puzzling series of events in the history of the Chinese Communist regime began in the fall of 1965 with newspaper attacks upon a minor official (the deputy mayor of Peking) who was more noted as a playwright and historian, and erupted the following year into a widely heralded "Great Proletarian Cultural Revolution." Heretofore, the Communist movement in China had been remarkable for the semblance of harmony within the party and the solidarity of its leadership, dominated by Mao Tse-tung but including members who, like him, were veterans of the Long March and had grown old together in the revolutionary cause. Now, an increasingly bitter struggle within the party and state structure revealed the existence of serious cleavages. Under a barrage of charges ranging from "hedonism" to "revisionism," "anti-party activity," and "taking the road to capitalism," scores of officials were demoted, consigned to obscurity, or forced to make public confession of their "crimes." The purge, which shook the party hierarchy severely,

A Red Guard Demonstration in Peking. Middle school students display their solidarity with the Cultural Revolution by waving copies of the book of quotations from Chairman Mao. The slogan painted on the wall proclaims: "We are not only able to destroy the old world, we are able to build a new world instead —Mao Tse-tung."

THE FAR EAST TODAY

Countries aligned with
the United States

Communist countries

Unaligned countries

U. S. S. R.

KURIL ISLANDS

MONGOLIA

Ulan-Bator ★

MANCHURIA

Amur R.

Vladivostok

J A P A N

N. KOREA

Yalu R.

Pyongyang 38°

Peking ★

S. KOREA
★ Seoul
Pusan

Tokyo ★

Osaka

Hiroshima

SHANTUNG PENIN.

Yellow R.

YELLOW SEA

Nagasaki

EAST CHINA SEA

TIBET

C H I N A

Nanking

Shanghai

BHUTAN

Chungking

Yangtze R.

PACIFIC

RYUKYU ISLANDS

OKINAWA

E. PAKISTAN

INDIA

Mandalay

BURMA

Taipei

OCEAN

Calcutta

Canton

TAIWAN

Hong Kong

BAY OF

Rangoon ★

Hanoi ★ Haiphong

Macao

PESCADORES IS.

Vientiane ★

G. of Tonkin

HAINAN

BENGAL

THAILAND

LAOS

N. VIETNAM

17°

Mekong R.

Hue

REPUBLIC

INDIAN

Bangkok ★

CAMBODIA

Da Nang

Qui Nhon

S. VIETNAM

Manila

Quezon City

OF THE

PHILIPPINES

Phnom Penh ★

Saigon ★

Cebu

SOUTH CHINA SEA

Davao

Jesselton

Medan

FEDERATION OF MALAYSIA

SABAH
(N. BORNEO)

OCEAN

MALAYA

★ Kuala Lumpur

BRUNEI

SARAWAK

Equator 0°

Kuching

WEST IRIAN
(NEW GUINEA)

0°

SUMATRA

★ Singapore

KALIMANTAN
(BORNEO)

SULAWESI
(CELEBES)

CERAM

Palembang

Bandjarmasin

R E P U B L I C   O F   I N D O N E S I A

Makassar

Djakarta ★

Bandung

JAVA

Surabaja

TIMOR

0 _____ 1000 miles

AUSTRALIA

numbered among its targets such prominent figures as Liu Shao-ch'i, President of the Republic since 1959 and long regarded as Mao's heir apparent, the Secretary General of the Party, and the Army Chief of Staff. Into the spotlight as Mao's most trusted comrade stepped Marshal Lin Piao, Defense Minister and Commander of the People's Liberation Army, a man noted for his industry and integrity and also for his austere fanaticism. As the stepped-up purification campaign met with stubborn resistance, Mao closed the schools and urged students to organize themselves into units of Red Guards (formally inaugurated at Peking in August 1966) and devote their energies to ferreting out enemies of the revolution. China was treated to the unprecedented spectacle of mobs of teenage youths denouncing their elders, smashing ancient monuments, invading private homes, and noisily demanding unswerving devotion to the thought of Mao Tse-tung. Conflicts between revolutionary zealots and their opponents led to chaos, bordering on civil war, in many parts of China.

Origins of the
Cultural Revolu-
tion: Mao vs. Liu

It is not yet possible to assess the full significance of the Proletarian Cultural Revolution or to predict its consequences. Diverging interpretations include the thesis that Mao Tse-tung was confronted with a formidable opposition determined to unseat him; that he was an egomaniac who demanded nothing short of worship from his followers; or that he had actually become insane. These are unlikely explanations in view of Mao's demonstrated shrewdness and his long record of successful leadership. It is clear that a struggle between rival factions within the party had been in progress ever since the controversy over the Great Leap Forward of 1958 and its subsequent failure. Liu Shao-ch'i, an opponent of radical experimentation, in 1959 replaced Mao as President of the Republic

Chairman Mao Tse-tung. Shown here with his "closest comrade" Marshal Lin Piao (Defense Minister and Vice Chairman of the Republic). Premier Chou En-lai stands behind them.

and worked assiduously during the next six years to restore the country's shaken economy. Meanwhile Mao sought to strengthen his own position by an intensive campaign of political indoctrination carried out among the masses and, with the help of the fanatical Defense Minister Lin Piao, within the Army. The breach between Party Chairman Mao and State Chairman Liu was brought to a climax by Chinese reaction to American expansion of the Vietnam war in 1965. Liu Shao-ch'i, viewing escalation as a prelude to an attack on China, called for united action by Socialist countries, necessarily including the Soviet Union, to intervene in defense of North Vietnam. Mao, backed by Commander Lin Piao, rejected any suggestion of collaboration with Soviet "revisionists." Arguing that a people's "war of liberation" like that in Vietnam must be fought by the people directly involved, he insisted that China should not permit herself to be drawn into the conflict unless attacked and that she should concentrate on her own internal development. He was determined to "bypass the Soviet Union on its way to Communism" and apparently felt that the time was ripe for another "leap forward." By August 1966 the Mao-Lin faction, supported by Premier Chou En-lai, had attained dominance in the Central Committee of the party, although it by no means controlled the entire party hierarchy, the state apparatus, or even all units of the Army.

While Mao's firm hand may have played a significant part in averting a direct military confrontation with a major power, it is probable that his main objective in precipitating the Cultural Revolution was ideological. He feared that the prospect of material success was bringing a relaxation of effort, which China could ill afford in view of her still unrealized potential and her weak military position. Seeing China as "poor and blank," he warned that decades of austerity and sacrifice on the part of her people would be necessary. Mao and his more zealous associates viewed with misgivings the tendency of the bureaucracy to become rigid and complacent, creating its own managerial class more "expert" than "red." They were determined above all to keep the revolution from losing its fervor, and to this end were willing to sacrifice immediate material benefits. Meeting resistance within the bureaucracy and from key party members, Mao turned to the nation's youth, who were exhorted by slogans to undertake their own Long March and to "learn revolution-making by making revolution."

Ideological factors

Mao's desperate crusade undoubtedly brought great travail to the People's Republic of China. The civil strife that erupted in 1966 continued throughout the next two years, and at times seemed to augur the approach of anarchy. Strikes in major industrial centers, disruption of the transport system, and widespread disorders in rural areas placed China's economic gains in jeopardy. At the same time

Unfavorable effects

the Chinese found themselves increasingly isolated diplomatically, even in the Communist world. These setbacks, however, were perhaps neither permanent nor disastrous. In spite of her domestic crisis, China succeeded in producing the hydrogen bomb, far earlier than Western experts had believed possible. The Proletarian Cultural Revolution is unique among revolutions that have witnessed intense convulsions in that it has not destroyed its protagonists—nor its antagonists. Although violence has taken a heavy toll of life and property, at the higher level the struggle has been political, psychological, and ideological rather than lethal. It is remarkable that Liu Shao-ch'i, vilified repeatedly in mass meetings, on wall posters, and by the press, has lost neither his life nor his position as President. In the course of his turbulent career Mao has displayed a fixity of purpose combined with versatility in methods and flexibility in tactics—an advantage not always shared by his opponents either inside or outside China. More dubious is Mao's belief in the possibility of a permanent revolution. China, now about 20 per cent urban, has begun to develop her own bourgeois class, and it is unlikely that a Chinese bourgeoisie will differ fundamentally from its counterpart in other countries.

2. THE CLIMAX OF IMPERIALISM AND THE BEGINNING OF A NEW ERA IN JAPAN

The ascendancy of Japan by 1914

While China was in the throes of revolutionary struggle, Japan was enjoying relative stability and increasing prosperity. The transformations which characterized the Meiji Restoration had been accomplished without seriously disturbing the structure of Japanese society. Before 1914 Japan had won an acknowledged place in the family of nations, had enlarged her territories, and had acquired the basis for a strong industrial economy. Building upon these foundations, the Japanese gained an ascendancy among Asian peoples and finally found themselves in a position to seek hegemony in the Far East.

Results of participation in World War I

Japan's participation in World War I had the curious effect of stimulating both expansionist and liberal tendencies within the country. The Japanese government entered the war against Germany in 1914, nominally out of regard for the Anglo-Japanese alliance but actually from a desire to secure Kiaochow Bay and the German concessions in the Shantung Peninsula. The German sphere of interest was occupied with little difficulty, and during the war the Japanese also seized the German outposts in the Pacific north of the equator—the Marshall, Caroline, and Mariana Islands. Japan showed little interest in the Western phases of the war, but utilized to the utmost the opportunities presented by China's weakness and by the involvement of the Western powers in the titanic struggle in Europe. Japan obtained Peking's permission to extend her economic interests in Manchuria and Inner Mongolia and to provide capital for industrial development in the Yangtze valley, and secured further guaranties of her interests by secret treaties with her Western allies.

The success of Japan's policy of exerting diplomatic and economic pressure was demonstrated at the Peace Conference of 1919. The Chinese delegation naturally demanded the restoration of Shantung, a request entirely consonant with Wilsonian principles. The Japanese, however, refused to comply, and Wilson did not press the matter vigorously, partly because another Japanese objective of a less questionable character had been defeated. The Japanese had asked for a declaration endorsing the principle of "the equality of nations and the just treatment of their nationals." On this issue the Chinese and Japanese stood together, supported also by the representatives of several European states. But the fear that such a declaration would conflict with the policy of limiting Oriental immigration led the Americans and British to oppose it when the matter was put to a vote in the League of Nations Commission. In this instance the Western statesmen had rebuffed Japan when she was supporting a moral issue entirely consistent with the ideals for which the war had been fought. And they yielded to her on the Shantung question where her claims had no moral justification whatever. The North Pacific islands which Japan had taken from Germany she was allowed to retain, in accord with the secret treaties of 1917, although these possessions were to be held as mandates under the League of Nations.

In spite of having plucked the fruits of imperialism, Japan after World War I seemed to be moving in a liberal direction, both in domestic affairs and in her international relations. The antiwar sentiment which became prevalent for a short time in much of the Western world was manifest, to a lesser degree, in Japan and provoked a revulsion against military leadership. Japan had been associated with the foremost Western democracies during the war; she had been one of the "Big Five" at the Paris Peace Conference; and—in contrast to Wilson's own United States—she had signed the Versailles Treaty and joined the League of Nations. Twice before in their history the Japanese had revealed a capacity for adopting what seemed to be the most effective and up-to-date institutions in the world as they knew it, and many of their leaders were persuaded that democracy was essential for progress in the twentieth century. Even purely from the standpoint of strengthening Japan as a state, there was much to be said for the democratic thesis. Japanese statesmen were impressed by the fact that autocratic and militaristic Germany had been defeated (and autocratic Russia had collapsed in revolution), while the apparently weaker democratic nations had been victorious. And, although few of these statesmen were convinced democrats in the full sense of the term, they were at least desirous of retaining the good will of the democratic powers which seemed to be in command of the world's destiny at the moment.

During much of the 1920's Japan's international policy was on the whole conciliatory, amounting to a partial reversal of her earlier aggressiveness. This is illustrated by her part in the Washington Conference of 1921–1922, which produced a Naval Arms Limitation Agreement, a Nine-Power "Open Door" Treaty concerning China, and a Four-Power Pacific Pact. The Conference had been summoned by the United States largely because of American fear that Japan, with the increased industrial and military potential which she had acquired during the war, was endangering the balance of power in the Far East. Obviously the Washington treaties did not succeed in binding Japan permanently to a policy of nonaggression, but the Japanese delegates accepted a limitation of Japan's battleship tonnage to a figure three-fifths that of the United States and of Britain, at a time when naval spokesmen in Japan were loudly demanding parity with the Western sea powers. With considerable reluctance the Japanese agreed (largely at the insistence of the United States and Canada) to terminate their alliance of twenty years' standing with Great Britain. The Four-Power Pact which replaced the alliance was based on nothing more substantial than the promise of friendly consultation on problems of the Pacific and pledges to maintain the *status quo* in regard to fortifications in this area. The Nine-Power Treaty affirmed the principle of the Open Door in China, giving the term a somewhat broader definition than it had had before, and assured China that the signatory powers would seek no further spheres of interest in her dominions. The treaty actually restored nothing to China, but the Japanese delegates, in private conferences with the Chinese, promised that their government would withdraw its troops from Shantung and return the administration of the province to China, leaving Japanese interests represented only in the form of private capital investments. This action was carried out as promised before the close of 1922.

The reasonable attitude displayed by Japan at the Washington Conference, particularly in the attempt to conciliate China on the Shantung question, was based to some extent upon economic considerations. China, only slightly developed industrially, represented an enormous potential market for Japanese goods and a valuable source of raw materials. Many Japanese businessmen were convinced that the cultivation of friendly relations with the sprawling mainland state would pay far bigger dividends than would the seizure of territory by force and at the risk of inviting a boycott of Japanese trade.

At the same time there were elements among the Japanese population genuinely interested in promoting democratic progress for its own sake. The demand for responsible ministries, dependent upon parties in the Diet rather than upon bureaucrats in the Privy Council, was renewed after the emergency of the war had passed. In 1918, for the first time in Japan's history, a commoner had been named premier. He was assassinated by a fanatical nationalist at the time of the Washington Conference; but during the decade following the war most of the cabinets reflected the trend toward party government as opposed to bureaucratic dictation. In 1925 a major step in the direction of political democracy was taken when the government passed a law establishing universal manhood suffrage. While the extension of the franchise did not immediately produce active participation in public affairs on the part of the common people, there was a growing and articulate group of intellectuals, professional men, and white-collar workers in the cities who favored the extension of individual liberties and supported social and economic as well as political reform. Along with this rising middle class, the laboring class was increasing and was beginning to demand better conditions. Strikes, although dealt with severely by the government, were frequent during the 1920's.

The progress toward democracy

Promising as were the liberal-democratic trends in Japan, they did not become vigorous enough to extinguish the deeply entrenched reactionary forces which eventually led the country to disaster. The failure of the liberal elements must be attributed in part to external factors. The disillusionment and cynicism that became general in the postwar years throughout the West had their counterpart in Japan. Contrary to the optimistic predictions of liberal statesmen in Japan and other countries, the trends of international politics did not indicate a substantial gain for democratic processes. The rise of fascism in Europe demonstrated a powerful movement in the opposite direction. Almost everywhere, virulent nationalism seemed to be in the ascendancy, obscuring the hope of a co-operative world order. With democracy on the defensive or in retreat in the countries of the West, where it was indigenous, it could scarcely be expected to triumph easily in such a nation as Japan, where it was a recent innovation with no cultural or institutional roots.

The counter influence of nationalism

Inimical to the growth of a vigorous liberalism was the fact that the sensibilities of the Japanese were irritated by the discrimination which they encountered in the form of tariffs against their goods and immigration laws against their persons. In 1924 the United States Congress passed an Oriental Exclusion law, placing Asians in a category inferior to that of the most backward Europeans. The United States was not alone in such a policy, and many Japanese began to feel that the great white nations were determined never to treat them as equals. The high tariff policies of the United States and other Western powers were another disturbing factor, producing psychological as well as economic repercussions. By

Discriminatory policies of Western nations

1930 the larger share of Japan's foreign trade, both export and import, was with the United States, with a trade balance decidedly favorable to the latter country. Protectionists in the United States alleged that American standards were threatened by competition from "cheap" Japanese labor. Yet the chief Japanese import was raw cotton and Japan's leading export to the United States was raw silk, an item hardly competitive with American industry.

In the last analysis, the defeat of liberal forces was due to deficiencies in the structure of Japanese society and in the economic system. The fundamental problem of creating a stable economy and satisfactory living standards for the majority of the people was never solved, and the problem became steadily more acute as the population continued to increase at the rate of one million a year. In spite of the expansion of commerce and manufacture, Japan's per capita income by 1928 was equal only to about one-eighth of that of the United States. Japan's prosperity, such as it was, depended upon participation in a world market that was subjected to more and more intense competition. Her foreign trade received a severe blow when the price of silk, her leading article of export, declined about 75 per cent between 1925 and 1934. To compensate for the collapse of the silk market, Japanese manufacturers stepped up the production of cotton cloth, but in this field they were bucking old and strongly established competitors. The Great Depression struck Japan just when the country seemed to be pulling out of a slump. Between 1929 and 1931 Japan's foreign commerce fell off by one-half, while rural and industrial indebtedness swelled to a figure in excess of the national income. Viewed superficially, Japanese economy appeared to have made a rapid recovery from the Depression, since by 1935 Japanese exports actually exceeded in value the total for 1925. However, this was accomplished only by drastic price-cutting and by forcing down the wages of Japanese workers, so that the increase in exports did not represent a net gain in national wealth.

The highly inequitable distribution of wealth within Japan made for an artificial stratification of classes and interests that was unfavorable to the development of a democratic society. The middle class was too small and insecure to be a very effective liberal force. The great body of farmers and laborers had been ushered out of the discipline of Tokugawa feudalism into the discipline of an efficient centralized bureaucracy, without ever being emancipated from their traditions of docility and the acceptance of direction from above. Aspects of a feudal mentality persisted within the nation after feudalism had been replaced by a modern capitalist order. Industry, commerce, and finance were concentrated in the hands of a few huge trusts, known collectively as the *Zaibatsu*, each controlled by a closely integrated family group and almost beyond the reach of public supervision. The *Zaibatsu* not only dominated the

Fatal defects in the economic system

The persistence of a feudal mentality

economic picture but also were affiliated with bureaucrats in the government and deeply influenced political parties.

The flimsy foundations of Japanese liberalism are revealed in the history and character of political parties during the 1920's and early 1930's, by which time two competing parties had risen to prominence. About 1900 the *Seiyukai* party had been organized under the auspices of one of the most influential clan bureaucrats. The *Seiyukai* was a descendant of the old Liberal party of Itagaki, but it exemplified a metamorphosis of liberalism into something almost its opposite. Itagaki's party, largely agrarian from the beginning, had passed under the domination of great landlords in place of the small tenants. To this conservative agrarian element was added the leading representative of big business, the house of Mitsui. Thus the *Seiyukai* constituted an alliance of landlords, monopoly capitalists, and bureaucrats, and it had connections also with the armed services. While the party favored constitutional methods, it was extremely conservative on domestic issues and rabidly expansionist on foreign policy, advocating forceful measures to improve Japan's economic position.

In 1927 an opposition party to the *Seiyukai* was formed, incorporating remnants of the old Progressive party of Count Okuma. This new party, the *Minseito*, was backed primarily by industrial rather than agrarian interests, and favored policies conducive to the health of the business community, including social welfare measures to relieve working-class discontent. The *Minseito* frowned on a policy of territorial aggression and deplored the reckless braggadocio of chauvinistic nationalists. But while it was progressive in comparison with the *Seiyukai*, it could hardly be considered truly liberal in composition or principles. It was supported by one of the great *Zaibatsu* houses (the Mitsubishi) and was as intensely nationalistic as the *Seiyukai*, differing from the latter chiefly on the question of which methods would best advance the country's interests.

A hopeful interlude, of brief duration, began when a *Minseito* cabinet came into office in 1929 and attempted to reverse the "strong" policy of the previous ministry, which had thrown troops into Shantung province as the Chinese Nationalist forces advanced toward Peking. The impact of the world depression upon Japan's economy, however, jeopardized the position of the moderate *Minseito* cabinet, and the assassination of the premier by a fanatic not only weakened the cabinet but also gave ominous warning of the length to which intransigent nationalist groups would go in promoting their own cause. Then, in September 1931, the Japanese army stationed in Manchuria took matters into its own hands by attacking Chinese troops. By the following February, Manchuria had become the "independent" state of Manchukuo under Japanese auspices, and in 1933 Japan, branded publicly as an aggressor, defiantly withdrew from the League of Nations.

Throughout the 1930's liberal elements in Japan never entirely abandoned their struggle to hold back the tide of militant nationalism. But when the issues became international, as in the struggle over Manchuria and, later, in the war against China, patriotic sentiments blunted the edge of popular opposition. The only groups strong enough to challenge the militarists were the financial and business interests, and these were easily seduced by the promise of profits in the offing. Most of the business leaders had come to regard expansion as essential to Japan's economy. They hoped it could be carried out peacefully and painlessly, but they had helped to build (and had profited from building) a war machine which would be extremely difficult to hold within bounds.

Of course, the primary center of aggressive truculence lay in the military services themselves, particularly the army. As was previously pointed out, the Japanese army was composed largely of peasants, an unfortunate class, whose legitimate discontents were, under skillful direction, sublimated into an unreasoned and frenzied patriotism. After the Meiji period the army officers also were drawn chiefly from small towns and rural communities, and they lacked the temperate and relatively broad-minded attitude that had distinguished the *samurai* leaders. Gradually a "young officer" group developed an ideology of its own, which began to permeate the rank and file. Idealists in the worst sense of the term, these soldier fanatics preached absolute loyalty to the emperor and affirmed that Japan, of divine origin and superior to other nations, had the right to extend her rule over other parts of the world. At the same time, reflecting their peasant affinities, they demanded agrarian reforms or even nationalization of the land and castigated both capitalists and politicians as selfish and corrupt. Their program, a medley of radical and reactionary principles, aimed to make Japan an invincible state, solidly unified under the imperial will, which they claimed to represent most faithfully. Although it has been likened to fascism, the "Imperial Way" proclaimed by the ultranationalists undoubtedly had more in common with the ancient Japanese concepts of the state as a patriarchal society and of the superiority of government by men to government by law.

While sponsoring an aggressive policy abroad, the military extremists (aided by terroristic secret societies) endeavored to seize control of their own government at home. They intimidated moderate spokesmen, disrupted cabinets, and, when all else failed, resorted to assassination. During the critical years following the Manchurian "incident," the government imposed severe restrictions upon the expression of unpatriotic or unorthodox ideas. Labor leaders, professors, and journalists suspected of radicalism were imprisoned or prosecuted on the ground that every "dangerous thought" must be suppressed. The stifling of liberal opinion made it all the easier for the fanatical nationalists (some of whom harbored decidedly radical ideas) to spread their propaganda with impunity.

That the army was able to defy popular will was illustrated by a
grim incident in February 1936. After a general election had resulted in a victory for the moderates and a defeat of the ultranationalists, a group of young officers revolted, held part of the city
of Tokyo for three days, and murdered three members of the government. Although the army disavowed these actions, it blocked
the appointment of a liberal cabinet through its control of the
strategically placed Minister of War. Finally, the army held a
trump card in the fact that Japanese troops were already stationed
in northern China and at any time could provoke an incident that
would transfer the initiative to the military authorities.

The creation of the puppet state of Manchukuo in 1932 and its
development under Japanese management did not yield the substantial benefits to Japan's economy which had been anticipated. To *The conquest of*
exploit the coal, iron, and oil resources of Manchuria required an *Manchuria as a*
extensive outlay of capital, and Japanese capital was not readily *prelude to war*
forthcoming, partly because of the fear that industry in Man- *against China*
chukuo would compete with Japan's and partly because of the
rigid governmental controls imposed upon capital and industry in
the puppet state. Reflecting the antifree-enterprise bias of the army
nationalists, the government attempted to create in Manchukuo a
type of state-directed economy; and, when the *Zaibatsu* houses
seemed reluctant to participate, an independent group of Japanese
investors was recruited to support the new "capitalism of the people." As plans matured for making Manchuria not simply a source
of raw materials for Japan but a center of heavy industry for Asia,
it became apparent that the assurance of access to a wide market
area was imperative. Hence, Japanese expansionists attempted to
convert China's northeastern provinces into an "autonomous" region, linked economically with Manchukuo. Finally they enlarged
their objectives to encompass the creation of a "Greater East Asia
Co-Prosperity Sphere." Instead of alleviating Japan's economy, her
leaders had saddled it with additional burdens, entailing larger and
larger expenditures for armaments in support of a program that
had no foreseeable limits and was bound to meet with resistance at
every point.

The role of Japan in World War II, into which her conflict with
China was merged, is discussed elsewhere in this volume. Japan's
surrender in 1945 was the prelude to a new phase of her history, in *The defeat of*
many ways different from anything she had experienced in the *Japan in World*
past. Never before had the Japanese nation been defeated in war *War II*
and never before had the country been occupied by a foreign
power. The occupation of a conquered country was also a new experience for the United States. At the very least it can be said that
both the Japanese and the Americans conducted themselves in such
a way as to produce a minimum of friction in relationships which
were necessarily difficult.

For six and a half years the real authority in Japan was nominally **599**

ERUPTION IN
THE FAR EAST

The American
Occupation

The Constitu-
tion of 1946

held by the Far Eastern Commission in Washington and the advisory Allied Council for Japan in Tokyo, with General of the Army Douglas MacArthur as Supreme Commander for the Allied Powers; actually it was held by General MacArthur, under orders from Washington, and by the Japanese government. From beginning to end the Japanese Occupation was an undertaking and a responsibility of the United States. Military rule was indirect, however, and was exercised through the regular Japanese government, which had not disintegrated with Japan's military defeat. The emperor accepted the surrender terms, called upon his subjects to co-operate with the occupying forces, and served as the connecting link between the old order and the new. In spite of the relative unimportance of the emperor politically in modern times, his role was of great value psychologically in providing a symbol of continuity when so much of the past seemed to have been destroyed forever.

One of the first major tasks of the Occupation authorities was to furnish Japan with a new constitution grounded in democratic principles. A draft prepared by a group of Japanese consultants was replaced by an American document, which was approved by the emperor and formally promulgated by him in the Diet in November 1946. It went into effect in May of the following year. The Japanese Constitution of 1946 is one of the most remarkable documents of its kind ever issued. It has been aptly described as "the world's outstanding model of the conveying of political rights by constitutional fiat." [3] Breaking cleanly with tradition and with the Constitution of 1889, it declared that sovereignty lay with the Japanese people and left the emperor with only formal powers like those of the British monarch. (The emperor himself had previously issued a rescript repudiating the myth of his divine origin.) The new Constitution contained an elaborate Bill of Rights, in which to the normal civil liberties were added such benefits as the right to work and to bargain collectively, social equality, and equality of the sexes. Universal adult suffrage was established, with a bicameral Diet, and a cabinet responsible to the House of Representatives. The Constitution also incorporated the American principles of separation of church and state and judicial review of acts of the legislature. Particularly arresting was Article 9, which declared that "the Japanese people forever renounce war as a sovereign right of the nation" and that "land, sea, and air forces, as well as other war potential, will never be maintained." Altogether, the new Constitution had a highly utopian flavor. If its principles could have been carried into active and complete realization, they would have made Japan a more advanced democratic nation than the United States.

While introducing political changes the Occupation authorities projected a reform program which, on the directive level at least,

[3] Linebarger, Djang, and Burks, *Far Eastern Governments and Politics: China and Japan,* p. 479.

was far-reaching. In conformity with the policy of demilitarization, an extensive purge was conducted to remove from office and from teaching positions all persons suspected of ultranationalist proclivities. A direct attack was launched against the *Zaibatsu* groups with the passage of an Antimonopoly Law and the creation of a Fair Trade Commission. General MacArthur, who claimed complete success for the campaign, appeared to be a greater trust buster than even Theodore Roosevelt. Pursuant to the liberal economic provisions of the new Constitution, labor organizations were encouraged. Between 1945 and 1950 membership in labor unions increased from 5000 to more than 6,000,000 and the government enacted a comprehensive labor welfare code. Perhaps most significant among the reforms was that which dealt with the long-neglected problem of land ownership. An agrarian law of 1946 provided for government purchase of tracts from absentee landlords and for the sale of these tracts to tenant farmers at moderate prices. This measure led to a sweeping transformation of agricultural land ownership. Only about 4 per cent of the cultivated area of Japan is now held in tenantry as compared with 46 per cent in 1944. Comprehensive and rigorous as it was, Japan's "New Deal" could not of course remake the whole fabric of society in a few years. All of the reforms were initiated by the Occupation authorities rather than by the Japanese themselves. Furthermore, the experience of the Occupation illustrates how difficult it is to couple reform with coercion, no matter how benevolent the administration. For example, the purge directed against militarists and ultranationalists caught some liberals whose only fault seemed to be their adherence to the ideals which were boldly announced in the new Constitution. Labor was prodded into organizing and collective bargaining, but strikes were restricted by the Occupation government. Also, beginning in 1947, Occupation policy, reflecting the pressures of global power politics, shifted from reform to retrenchment and recovery. The pro-

The Beginning of the Occupation in Japan. American troops entering Tokyo, September 8, 1945. The devastating effects of bombing raids are plainly evident.

gram of decentralizing industry, which perhaps would have proved temporary in any case, halted with the realization that if Japan's industrial strength were preserved it could be an asset to the West in the Cold War with the Communist powers.

A peace treaty between the United States and Japan was negotiated at San Francisco in September 1951, and ratified the following April. It was also signed by 48 other states, not including the Soviet Union, however, which remained technically in a state of war with Japan until 1956. The peace settlement, although it ended the Occupation and restored formal independence to Japan, was very drastic territorially. Depriving the nation of all its empire, the treaty reduced Japan to the same area it had held at the time of Commodore Perry's visit in 1853, although its population was now three times as great. The peace treaty (supplemented by a security treaty) acknowledged Japan's right to arm for "self-defense" and authorized the stationing of foreign troops (meaning American) in Japan for the defense of the country.

Political trends
and parties in
postwar Japan:
the Liberal
Democratic
Party

Democracy has undoubtedly made progress in Japan, but its extent and character are still somewhat ambiguous. The press is free and often criticizes the government sharply and with impunity. Japan's Constitution is one of the most democratic in the world; but, while it operates and is accepted by a majority of the people, it does not seem to have related itself vitally to the currents of social and cultural change. In line with the new democratic machinery the role of parties has become paramount. However, as in prewar Japan, parties have been hampered by the persistent tradition of loyalty to personalities, kinship groups, or local interests, in contrast to association for common objectives on an impersonal basis. A multitude of parties soon appeared (363 participated in the 1946 elections), but nation-wide coalitions have achieved considerable stability. The electorate has shown a consistently conservative bias, as illustrated by the fact that Shigeru Yoshida, a career diplomat of the prewar era, held the premiership five times between 1946 and 1954. Two major parties, successors respectively of the old *Seiyukai* and *Minseito*, merged in 1955 to form the Liberal Democratic party, which has held a preponderant position ever since. In spite of its name the party is conservative, deriving its support from business (big and medium-sized), some old-line bureaucrats, rural constituencies (which are over-represented in the Diet), and—because it has held office so long—officials of the civil service. Its program calls for continued expansion of the economy, an "independent foreign policy" within the framework of the American alliance, the rejection of neutralism but friendly relations with all nations, and the strengthening of Japan's defenses.

The principal, though not very effective, opposition has been supplied by the Socialists, weakened by a wide range of ideological differences and internal disputes. The party attracts some intellectuals, but its main backing comes from the larger of two national labor federations. (The other labor federation supports the Right-wing Democratic Socialist party which split off from the main body in 1960.) The Socialists' avowed objectives include protection of civil liberties, extension of workers' benefits and eventual realization of a socialist economy; and, more emphatically, the abrogation of the security treaty with the United States and the removal of all American military bases from Japan. While some of these points elicit broad popular sympathy, the Socialists have never been able to win more than a third of the vote in national elections, largely because unprecedented material prosperity has come about under a succession of conservative administrations and the average voter is not convinced that he would be better off under different and untried leadership. In the January 1967 elections for the House of Representatives, the Liberal Democrats retained a comfortable majority despite the fact that the government was under attack for flagrant cases of corruption involving high officials. None of the parties has appealed sufficiently to the emerging middle class and none has demonstrated real mass support—least of all the Communists, whose voting strength, after reaching 10 per cent of the total in 1949, declined to almost insignificant proportions. In attempting to attract middle-class support the Liberal Democratic coalition in recent years has expounded a welfare-state philosophy, while the Socialists have tempered the edge of their revolutionary Marxism. In 1962 the Socialist Secretary General envisioned Japan's future as a blend of Soviet welfare measures, the American standard of living, and British parliamentarianism. The extreme Right embraces a number of small parties and the religiously oriented Soka Gakkai (Value Creating Association), which has made rapid headway among unskilled workers and the lower middle class and claims a membership of some 5 million families. Its political arm, the Clean Government Party, by the mid-1960's ranked in third place among the national parties.

The economic difficulties confronting Japan immediately after her surrender seemed practically insurmountable. Before the close of hostilities almost one-third of the homes in Japan's urban areas were destroyed by air attacks, and the direct economic loss caused by the war was staggering. Japan was shorn of her empire, her industrial production had fallen 80 per cent below the 1937 level, her foreign trade stood at zero, and she was dependent upon imports even for foodstuffs. Viewed against this dismal background, Japan's economic recovery and advance have been spectacular. By 1953 the index of production was 50 per cent above the level of the mid-1930's, and it continued upward, with textiles, metal goods, and machinery leading the way. During the past decade Japan's economic growth rate averaged close to 10 per cent annually, and her gross national product rose to the fifth largest in the world. By

The opposition

Japan's spectacular economic recovery and expansion

1957 her shipbuilding industry exceeded that of every other country, including Great Britain; she now holds second place in electronics and third place in the production of crude steel. Tokyo became a boom town with all the symptoms of prosperity. Its population swelled from 3 million to 11 million by the mid-1960's, making
it the world's largest city—also one of the dirtiest, noisiest, and
most hopelessly crowded. Expansion has been evident in practically
every branch of the economy, and the Japanese have won distinction in such specialized fields as optical and scientific instruments.
Through the use of machinery, chemical fertilizers and advanced
scientific methods, agricultural output has increased by 50 per cent
since 1950, and Japan is approaching self-sufficiency in foodstuffs,
even though the labor force devoted to agriculture has declined to
25 per cent of the total.

Recovery and a high level of prosperity do not mean that Japan
has no serious economic problems. She imports 80 per cent of her

**Economic
problems**

raw materials for manufacture and consequently must reach a wide
export market in the face of severe competition. One-third of her foreign trade is with the United States and Canada. A serious disadvantage—reflecting the logic of international politics rather than economics—is the loss of the Chinese mainland market. China absorbed
26 per cent of Japan's exports in 1928; in 1961, .4 of 1 per cent.
Not surprisingly, both major political parties have called for the re-
opening of the China market even though Japan has not granted
diplomatic recognition to Peking. By 1964 trade with mainland
China had risen slightly but still barely exceeded 1 per cent of
Japan's total foreign trade. A rapidly expanding population has
posed another problem, which appears to be approaching solution.
Between 1940 and 1964 the number of inhabitants rose from 73 million to 96.6 million, but meanwhile the birthrate dropped from one
of the highest in the world to one of the lowest (from 33 births
per thousand to fewer than 10 per thousand). Population has been
shifting to the cities, with 40 per cent now living in urban areas

A Section of Downtown Tokyo.
In spite of its strikingly modern
appearance, Tokyo is distressing-
ly overcrowded and dirty and
has one of the world's worst
traffic problems.

and 25 per cent in cities of 100,000 or over. Accumulated wealth is very unevenly distributed and wages have remained relatively low in the small shops and home factories which still employ a majority of the working force. The relentless pressure of rapid industrialization has brought stresses and strains in the economy, evidenced by labor shortages, excessive plant expansion, price inflation, and temporary recessions.

Mass production in contemporary Japan: a camera assembly line. Japan's high quality optical and electronic instruments have found a world wide market.

In spite of flaws in the picture, the zooming prosperity of Japan is one of the impressive facts of the mid-twentieth century. Per capita income—still low by American standards—is twice what it was in 1940; and the government aims at, and probably will succeed in, doubling the economy again by 1970. Already the Japanese standard of living is by far the highest in Asia, and wages are approaching the level of France and West Germany. Even in rural areas 8 families out of 10 own television sets. It is reported that the "three sacred treasures" desired by every Japanese household are no longer the ancient mirror, jewel, and sword but the television set, refrigerator, and washing machine, or, more recently, the hi-fi set, car, and "room cooler." Several factors provide the explanation of this seemingly fantastic success story. First, in spite of devastating losses from the war, the Japanese retained their technical proficiency, labor force, and traditions of hard work. A second factor helping to initiate recovery was American financial aid, not only during the Occupation but also by the purchase of goods and services during the Korean conflict. A third factor was the initiative of the government in stimulating and guiding the growth of an essentially private-enterprise economy. The government encouraged capital investment by incentive tax and loan policies and by generous spending to offset the effects of recessions, and it operates an

Economic Planning Agency which compiles data, predicts market trends and sets production targets. But the most important asset of all was—paradoxically—the defeat and elimination of Japan's military complex, which had systematically drained the country of its resources. Contemporary Japan enjoys the distinction of being the only great industrial nation operating on a peace economy instead of a war economy. Supporting armed forces totaling only 230,000 men, the "Defense Agency" consumes not quite 10 per cent of the annual budget and less than 1½ per cent of the national income.

Improvement in
foreign relations

The Japanese, no less than other nations, have encountered problems in the realm of foreign affairs. Edging her way precariously between two worlds, the new Japan made steady progress toward rehabilitating her relations with other states. The hostility and distrust that were the heritage of Japanese aggression in Southeast Asia have slowly receded. Japan signed reparations agreements with Burma and the Philippines, promising to supply goods, technical assistance, and investments over a long period, and awarded outright grants to Laos and Cambodia. To reach an understanding with the Soviet Union proved more difficult, but in October 1956 Russia and Japan signed a peace declaration, formally ending the state of war between the two countries. The negotiations left undetermined the future of the Kuril Islands—claimed by Japan and held by Russia—but it provided for restoring diplomatic intercourse, repatriating Japanese prisoners of war, and the relinquishing of Russian demands for reparations. Also, because Russia now withdrew her opposition, Japan became a member of the United Nations, in December 1956. Not until the summer of 1965 did Japan resume normal relations with South Korea, and agreement for settling Singapore's claims for World War II damages was reached as late as October 1966. Through the Colombo Plan of assistance to underdeveloped countries in Southeast Asia, Japan has contributed more than $6 billion for projects in Ceylon, India, Pakistan, Indonesia, Thailand, Cambodia, and Vietnam. She is a contributing member of the recently formed Asian Development Bank.

Points of friction
between the
United States
and Japan

The scope and objectives of Japan's foreign policy hinge on the delicate subject of relations with the United States. In spite of economic interdependence, treaty ties, and the profession of similar political ideals, there are several points of friction between the two countries. A persistent source of Japanese resentment arises from the status of the Bonin and Ryukyu Islands, occupied by the United States as security bases under terms which recognized Japan's "residual sovereignty". In June 1968 Japan recovered jurisdiction over the Bonin Islands, but Okinawa, transformed into a major American military outpost with scant regard for the feelings of its 900,000 inhabitants, became for many a symbol of the callousness and ineptitude of foreign military rule. Opposition to renewal of the United States security treaty was behind Tokyo riots that led to the cancelling of President Eisenhower's projected visit to Japan in the early summer of 1960. This crisis produced no measurable political change, and the security treaty, amended to permit termination by either party after ten years, was ratified by the Diet. Within recent years tension between Tokyo and Washington has augmented perceptibly. Beneath discreet official statements and indiscreet popular outbursts there is evident a growing conviction that Japan is ready to assume a more independent role. The factor most responsible for increasing anti-American feeling has been the escalation of the Vietnam war. Japanese opposition to the United States policy of massive military intervention in Indochina stems partly from a feeling of solidarity with other Asians and partly from the fear that escalation may lead to war with China, which could be disastrous for Japan.

SELECTED READINGS—GENERAL (*See also Readings for Chapters 3 and 11*)

· *Items so designated are available in paperbound editions.*

Battistini, L. H., *The United States and Asia*, New York, 1956.

Beckman, George, *The Modernization of China and Japan*, New York, 1962.

Low, Francis, *The Struggle for Asia*, New York, 1956.

Scalapino, R. A., ed., *The Communist Revolution in Asia: Tactics, Goals, and Achievements*, Englewood Cliffs, N. J., 1965. A symposium.

—CHINA

· Barnett, A. Doak, *Communist China and Asia: Challenge to American Policy*, New York, 1960 (Vintage). A reliable and thoughtful summary.

· ——, *Communist China, the Early Years, 1949–1955*, New York, 1964 (Praeger).

· Briere, O. (L. G. Thompson, tr.), *Fifty Years of Chinese Philosophy, 1898–1950*, London, 1956 (Praeger).

· Ch'en, Jerome, *Mao and the Chinese Revolution*, New York, 1965 (Galaxy).

· Clubb, O. E., *Twentieth-Century China*, New York, 1963 (Columbia). One of the best surveys of recent Chinese history.

· Cohen, A. A., *The Communism of Mao Tse-tung*, Chicago, 1964 (Phoenix).

Fei Hsiao-t'ung, *Peasant Life in China*, London, 1962.

· Floyd, David, *Mao Against Khrushchev: A Short History of the Sino-Soviet Conflict*, New York, 1964 (Praeger). A readable account.

· Griffith, W. E., *The Sino-Soviet Rift*, Cambridge, Mass., 1964 (M.I.T.). An analysis with pertinent documents.

· Isaacs, H. R., *The Tragedy of the Chinese Revolution*, Stanford, 1964 (Atheneum).

Leng, S. C., and Palmer, N. D., *Sun Yat-sen and Communism*, New York, 1960. Laudatory of Sun and critical of the West for tending to dismiss him lightly as "impractical" and "disreputable."

Levenson, J. R., *Confucian China and Its Modern Fate: The Problem of Historical Significance*, Berkeley, 1965.

· Lewis, J. W., *Leadership in Communist China*, Ithaca, 1963 (Cornell).

· Lifton, R. J., *Thought Reform and the Psychology of Totalism*, New York, 1961 (Norton). A psychiatrist's analysis.

Lin, Yutang, *My Country and My People*, rev. ed., New York, 1938.

MacFarquar, Roderick, *The Hundred Flowers Campaign and the Chinese Intellectuals*, New York, 1960. A study of Mao Tse-tung's experiment in inviting internal criticism of his regime.

Quigley, H. S., *China's Politics in Perspective*, Minneapolis, 1962.

· Schram, Stuart, *The Political Thought of Mao Tse-tung*, New York, 1963 (Praeger).

Schwartz, B. F., *Chinese Communism and the Rise of Mao*, Cambridge, Mass., 1951.

Sharmon, Lyon, *Sun Yat-sen: His Life and Its Meaning*, New York, 1934. A critical biography.

· Snow, Edgar, *Red Star over China*, New York, 1938 (Black Cat). A classic account of the Communists' early years of struggle.

———, *The Other Side of the River: Red China Today*, New York, 1961. A highly informative book incorporating the results of extensive first-hand observation.

Tang, P. S. H., *Communist China Today*. Vol. I: *Domestic and Foreign Policies*, Washington, 1961.

· Walker, R. L., *China under Communism: The First Five Years*, New Haven, 1955 (Yale).

· Zagoria, D. S., *The Sino-Soviet Conflict, 1956–1961*, Princeton, 1962 (Atheneum). A cautious assessment based largely on an analysis of Russian and Chinese newspapers.

—JAPAN

Allen, G. C., *Japan's Economic Expansion*, New York, 1965. A lucid account of Japan's postwar economic growth.

Beardsley, R. K., Hall, J. W., and Ward, R. E., *Village Japan*, Chicago, 1959.

Benedict, Ruth, *The Chrysanthemum and the Sword*, Boston, 1946. A sympathetic analysis of Japanese character and psychology by an anthropologist.

Bisson, T. A., *Zaibatsu Dissolution in Japan*, Berkeley, 1954.

· Burks, A. W., *The Government of Japan*, New York, 1961 (Crowell). Brief but informative on both government and politics in postwar Japan.

Butow, R. J. C., *Japan's Decision to Surrender*, Stanford, 1954.

———, *Tojo and the Coming of the War*, Princeton, 1961.

Kawai, Kazuo, *Japan's American Interlude*, Chicago, 1960. Outspoken but cautiously optimistic account by an able journalist and political scientist.

Lu, David J., *From the Marco Polo Bridge to Pearl Harbor: Japan's Entry into World War II*, Washington, 1961.

· Maki, J. M., *Government and Politics in Japan: The Road to Democracy*, New York, 1962 (Praeger).

Maxon, Y. C., *Control of Japanese Foreign Policy: A Study of Civil-Military Rivalry, 1930–1945*, Berkeley, 1957.

Mendel, D. H., *The Japanese People and Foreign Policy*, Berkeley, 1961. Examines the controversial aspects of Japanese foreign policy during the 1950's.

Morris, Ivan, *Nationalism and the Right Wing in Japan: A Study of Post-War Trends*, London, 1960. A clear and forceful study of the role of nationalism in present-day Japan, disturbing in its implications.

Quigley, H. S., and Turner, J. E., *The New Japan: Government and Politics*, Minneapolis, 1956.

Reischauer, E. O., *The United States and Japan*, 3rd ed., Cambridge, Mass., 1965.

Scalapino, R. A., and Masumi, J., *Parties and Politics in Contemporary Japan*,
Berkeley, 1962. An illuminating study based on statistical analysis.
· Storry, Richard, *A History of Modern Japan*, Baltimore, 1960 (Penguin).
——, *The Double Patriots*, London, 1957. A study of extremists of the Right.

SOURCE MATERIALS

· Brandt, C., Schwartz, B. F., and Fairbank, J. K., *A Documentary History of Chinese Communism* (Atheneum).
Chiang Kai-shek, *China's Destiny*.
· de Bary, W. T., ed., *Sources of Chinese Tradition*, Chaps. XXVII, XXVIII, XXIX (Columbia).
· ——, ed., *Sources of Japanese Tradition*, Chaps. XXVI, XXVII, XXVIII, XXIX (Columbia).
· Fraser, S., *Chinese Communist Education* (Science Editions). A collection of documents for the period 1944–1960.
Grew, Ambassador Joseph C., *Ten Years in Japan*.

CHAPTER 19

The Origins and Legacy of
World War II

I shall strike and not capitulate. The fate of the Reich depends on
me alone. . . . Every hope of compromise is childish.
                                        —Adolf Hitler, November 23, 1939

The President [Roosevelt] and the Prime Minister [Churchill],
after a complete survey of the world situation, are more than ever
determined that peace can come to the world only by a total
elimination of German and Japanese war power. This involves
the simple formula of placing the objective of this war in terms
of an unconditional surrender by Germany, Italy, and Japan.
                         —Franklin D. Roosevelt, Casablanca, January 24, 1943

In September 1939, Europe plunged again over the rim of the abyss.
The peace of 1919–1920 had turned out to be only an armistice,
and millions of people were now locked in a conflict that surpassed
in frightfulness any that had occurred heretofore. As had happened
in 1914–1918, the new struggle soon became worldwide. Of course,
World War II was not merely a continuation of, or a sequel to,
World War I. Yet the similarity in causes and characteristics was
more than superficial. Both were precipitated by threats to the
balance of power. Both sprang in some measure out of rivalry between the sated and the dynamic nations—the first resolved to keep
what they had already gained, and the others determined to conquer
living space for their burgeoning populations and to gain new
sources for wealth and power. Both were conflicts between peoples,
whole nations, rather than between governments. The lineup of the
two sides, in the beginning, was similar, with Great Britain and
France opposing Germany, and with Italy remaining temporarily
neutral. On the other hand, there were notable differences. Japan
aligned herself with Germany instead of with the Western powers,

A comparison of the two world wars

and Russia did not enter the conflict until two years after it began. The methods of warfare in World War II had little in common with those of the earlier conflict. Trench warfare was largely superseded by aerial bombing and by blitzkrieg attacks with highly mobile armies. It seems safe to say that the distinction between soldiers and civilians was more completely obliterated in the second conflict than it had been in the first.

1. UNDERLYING AND IMMEDIATE CAUSES

The causes of World War II went back a great many years. To some extent they were related to the failure of the peace of 1919–1920. That peace, while perhaps as good as could be expected in view of the passions and hatreds engendered by the war, created almost as many problems as it solved. By yielding to the demands of the victors for annexation of territory and the creation of satellite states, the peacemakers sowed new seeds of bitterness and conflict. Had the League of Nations they set up been better organized, it might have relieved some of the tensions and prevented clashes between nations still unwilling to relinquish their absolute sovereignty. Moreover, it was not a league of all nations. Both Germany and Russia were excluded, thereby pushing them into the role of outcasts.

Although President Wilson and other sponsors of the League acclaimed it as a means of eliminating the balance of power, it did nothing of the sort. It merely substituted a new and more precarious balance for the old. The signatures on the peace treaties had scarcely dried when the victors began the construction of new alliances to maintain their supremacy. A *cordon sanitaire* consisting of the Baltic states, Poland, and Rumania was created as a buffer against Soviet Russia. A Little Entente composed of Czechoslovakia, Yugoslavia, and Rumania was established to prevent a revival of Austrian power. These combinations, together with a Franco-Belgian alliance and a Franco-Polish alliance would also serve to isolate Germany. Thus the old system of power politics was reconstituted along essentially the same lines it had had before World War I. Even the League itself was fundamentally an alliance of the victors against the vanquished. That there would be fears and anxieties over a disturbance of the new power arrangement could hardly be unexpected. The first sign of such a disturbance appeared in 1922 when Germany and Russia negotiated the Treaty of Rapallo. Though disguised as a mere trade agreement, it opened the way for political and, according to some accounts, even military collaboration between the two states. In 1935 the German government under the direction of Hitler tore up the disarmament provisions of the Treaty of Versailles. It announced the revival of conscription and the return to universal military training. By threatening the creation

Defects of the peace of 1919–1920

Threats to the balance of power

League of Nations Buildings, Geneva, Switzerland. Since the dissolution of the League in 1946, its main building has been occupied by the International Labor Office.

of a huge air force Hitler hoodwinked the British into signing a naval agreement permitting Germany to build war vessels up to 35 per cent of the strength of Britain's navy. Finally, in 1936, he flouted the peace settlement by sending troops into the Rhineland to occupy the area of Germany demilitarized by the Treaty of Versailles.

Apostles of peace made various attempts to preserve or restore international amity during the 1920's and 1930's. Some saw in disarmament the most promising means of achieving their purpose. Accordingly, a succession of conferences was called in the hope of limiting at least the competition in armaments. The results were negligible. The Washington Conference of 1921–1922 established a naval ratio of 5:5:3 for the United States, Great Britain, and Japan, but it applied only to capital ships, i.e., battleships and battle cruisers. The London Conference of 1930 and the Geneva Conference of 1932–1934 ended in total failure. Some advocates of peace believed in supplementing the League of Nations by international agreements. In 1925 representatives of the chief European powers met at Locarno and acted on the suggestion of the German Foreign Minister, Gustav Stresemann, that Germany and France pledge themselves to respect the Rhine frontiers as established in the Versailles Treaty. They agreed also that they would never go to war against each other except in "legitimate defense." More widely celebrated than the Locarno Agreements was the Pact of Paris, or Kellogg-Briand Pact, of 1928. Its purpose was to outlaw war as an international crime. Eventually nearly all the nations of the world signed an agreement renouncing war as "an instrument of national policy" and providing that the settlement of international disputes "of whatever nature or of whatever origin" should never be sought "except by peaceful means." Neither the Locarno Agreements nor the Pact of Paris was much more than a pious gesture. The signatory nations adopted them with so many reservations and exceptions in favor of "vital interests" that they could never be effective instruments for preserving peace.

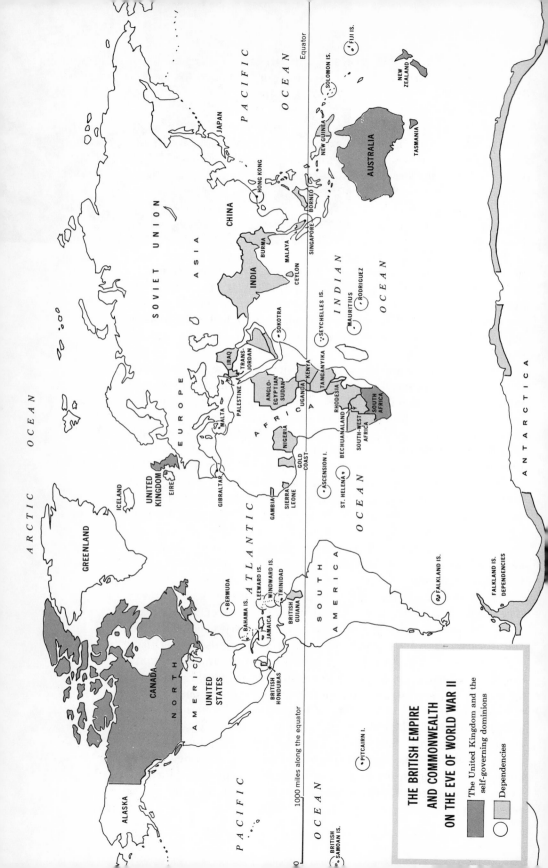

THE BRITISH EMPIRE
AND COMMONWEALTH
ON THE EVE OF WORLD WAR II

The United Kingdom and the
self-governing dominions

Dependencies

As Germany recovered strength during the 1930's, the victorious powers adopted varying attitudes. France, for a time, remained inflexible in her determination to hold Germany down. Her government, however, tolerated Japan's invasion of Manchuria in 1931 and even encouraged Italy's conquest of Ethiopia in 1936. As a trading nation anxious to rebuild her markets in central Europe, Britain favored a policy of leniency toward Germany. Although she had a good legal case for doing so, she refused to take any action against the military occupation of the Rhineland. She was tolerant also toward the Japanese invasion of Manchuria and the Italian conquest of Ethiopia. Like France, she declined to take positive steps to assist the Spanish Republic when Germany and Italy intervened in the Spanish Civil War to guarantee a victory of the Spanish fascists under General Franco. Not until Germany revealed, in 1939, that she had definite ambitions for conquests in Eastern Europe did Britain and France show serious concern over enforcing the balance of power. Their action came too late, for the balance had already been badly upset by the gains Germany and Italy had made through their aggressive policies.

If we look for economic causes of World War II, we can consider, first of all, division of the world into Have and Have-not powers. The former included Great Britain, the United States, France, and Russia. Britain had the smallest homeland, but her empire extended over 13,000,000 square miles, one-fourth of the land area of the earth, and was inhabited by 500,000,000 people, or one-fifth of the population of the globe. France had a total empire of 4,000,000 square miles and 100,000,000 inhabitants. Neither the United States nor Russia owned vast overseas possessions, but both had extensive home areas rich in natural resources. The former ruled over 3,735,000 square miles with a population of 130,000,000. The Union of Soviet Socialist Republics extended over an area of 8,000,000 square miles and was inhabited by no fewer than 170,000,000 people. The position of the Have-not powers—Germany, Italy, and Japan—seemed poor indeed by comparison. The three of them combined had an area of less than 1,500,000 square miles, to accommodate a home population that exceeded the total for Great Britain and the United States. German patriots could point out that the average German citizen had only .004 of a square mile of living space at his disposal, whereas the average Briton could draw upon the wealth and economic opportunities of almost three square miles of imperial territory.

The fallacies in this view of the matter were seldom noticed. It seemed sufficient for the German nationalist to reflect upon the fact that standards of living in Britain were higher than in his own country to prove to him that the existing division of the earth's surface was unjust. He was therefore ready to disrupt the status quo by any means in his power. Perhaps diplomatic cunning would be sufficient, but if not, he would resort to war. Italians and Japanese seemed to have even weightier evidence of the injustice of the existing order, since standards of living in their countries were lower than in Germany. None of them appeared to recognize the fact that living standards in some small European countries, totally or almost completely lacking colonial empires, were just about equal to the average in Britain. But Germany, Italy, and Japan had a sense of grievance for a number of reasons, and presenting themselves before the world as Have-not nations helped to justify their bellicose foreign policies.

Perhaps the most serious economic cause of World War II was the Great Depression. The depression contributed to the coming of the war in several ways. First and foremost, it intensified economic nationalism. Baffled by problems of unemployment and business stagnation, governments resorted to high tariffs in a frenzied attempt to preserve the home market for their own producers. When tariffs proved insufficiently effective, they turned to currency controls, bilateral trade agreements, and outright prohibitions of imports. None of these methods achieved its purposes for more than a brief interval. The ultimate results were indescribable confusion, a partial strangulation of trade, and a deepening of antagonism between nations.

The Great Depression as a cause of the war

The depression also had other effects perhaps more difficult to assay. For one thing, it was responsible for a marked increase in armaments. Armaments expansion, on a large scale, was first undertaken by Germany about 1935. The results in a few years were such as to dazzle the rest of the world. Unemployment disappeared and business boomed. It would have been too much to expect that other dissatisfied nations would not copy the German example. Similarly, the depression resulted in a new wave of militant expansionism directed toward the conquest of neighboring territories as a means of solving economic problems. Japan took the lead in 1931 with the invasion of Manchuria. A primary cause was the decline of Japanese exports of raw silk and cotton cloth. Since the nation as a consequence was unable to pay for needed imports of coal, iron, and other minerals, Japanese militarists were furnished with a convenient pretext for seizing Manchuria, where supplies of these commodities could then be purchased for Japanese currency.

Other effects of the depression

Most important of all, the depression was primarily responsible for the triumph of Nazism in Germany. The Nazi party would probably have remained weak and ineffectual had it not been for the influx of millions of followers from the ranks of the farmers and the unemployed and from frightened members of the white-collar classes. The whirling spiral of economic decline had overwhelmed these people with a sense of despair. Convinced that capitalism, socialism, and democracy had all failed, they were ready to grasp at almost any straw that would save them from sinking deeper into the

The depression primarily responsible for the Nazi revolution quicksands of depression. Some members of the upper classes had also reached the conclusion that the Nazi party was the only party that could save the nation from political and economic breakdown. According to Konrad Heiden, the little group that persuaded President von Hindenburg to appoint Hitler Chancellor believed that the Nazi leader alone had a chance to govern the country with the support of a majority in the Reichstag. They assumed that they could control him, since one of their number, Franz von Papen, was to be Vice Chancellor, and the cabinet was to include only three Nazis out of a total membership of about ten.[1]

It may be well before leaving this subject of underlying causes of the war to look at the matter from the standpoint of a different interpretation. According to an important school of thought, which may be called the power-politics school, only a few of the factors mentioned above deserve more than slight consideration. Doubtless leaders of this school would accept the economic causes, but most of the others they would dismiss as inconsequential. They place nearly all of the emphasis upon power politics. They maintain that power rivalries and power struggles have been the real causes of international wars since the beginning of modern history. Such forces as nationalism, militarism, and imperialism have simply been instruments for achieving the ends of a quest for power. The seventeenth century, they point out, was marked by a great power struggle between France and Austria, in which France was victorious. During the eighteenth century a primary struggle raged between Britain and France and culminated in the Seven Years' War, with a decisive victory for Britain. The French attempted to recover their power during the wars of the Revolution and under Napoleon, but the effort failed, and Britain gradually emerged as the dominant nation on the earth. Toward the end of the nineteenth century, however, Germany rose to challenge British supremacy, and the result was World War I. After the war conflicting ambitions among the victors permitted a revival of Teutonic power, with the consequence that, by 1939, Germany was ready to challenge again the ability of the dominant nations to continue ruling the world. The fact that Germany and her allies had fascist governments had little to do with the case. According to the power-politics theorists, fascism was simply a by-product of an age-old struggle among nations to gain advantages at their neighbors' expense.

Power politics as a cause of wars

That there is much truth in the foregoing hypothesis seems almost indisputable. The existence of the modern state system practically guarantees that nations shall be engaged in either cold or hot wars nearly all of the time. Under it the relation among states is the same as that among individuals in the supposed state of nature, which philosophers like Locke and Rousseau believed to have ex-

Evidence for the power-politics hypothesis

---

[1] *Der Fuehrer*, pp. 531–37.

isted before the formation of political society. In other words, there is no law or order except that which results from agreements between sovereign units. In making these agreements, the units retain their full sovereignty, and therefore may repudiate them whenever they choose. Another element in the hypothesis which is difficult to refute is the contention that ideologies are not fundamental causes of wars. If British politicians had been gravely concerned about the evils of fascism they could never have pursued their policy of appeasement, for they must have known that its effect would be to strengthen Italy and Germany. Indeed, there is evidence that Neville Chamberlain was perfectly willing to collaborate with fascist governments for his own purposes. One of his chief reasons for going to Munich was to bring Germany, Italy, France, and Britain into a four-power alliance to determine the destinies of Europe. It is significant also that Germany and the Soviet Union became allies in 1939, despite the fact that, shortly before, Hitler had described the Bolsheviks as "scum of the earth," while Stalin had referred to the Nazis as "bloody assassins of the workers." The power-politics hypothesis would appear to suffer, not from inaccuracy, but, like most specialized theories, from a failure to give proper recognition to all of the factors. If nationalism and militarism are not originally primary causes of wars, they often become so as international tension increases.

If there was any one immediate cause of World War II, it could doubtless be found in the appeasement policy of Britain and France. Appeasement may be defined as a policy of granting concessions to an aggressive and unscrupulous nation from motives of fear or indolence. Invariably, the concessions are made at the expense of a

The appeasement policy

"Peace in Our Time." On September 30, 1938, Prime Minister Chamberlain returned to London from his conference with Hitler at Munich. To the crowd which had gathered to meet him he waved a copy of the Munich Agreement, proclaiming it a pledge of "peace in our time." The event was the supreme irony of the prewar years.

Czech Reaction When German Troops Entered Prague, April 2, 1939. While Nazi motorized units passed by, some Czechs sang "Where Is My Home" and "Above the Tatra Mountains"; others wept.

weaker country. The appeaser himself sacrifices nothing; in fact, his usual motive is the desire to avoid giving up anything of value. Appeasement should be distinguished clearly from a policy of conciliation. The latter represents an attempt to pacify an enemy by acts of benevolence and justice. Appeasement has nothing to do with either benevolence or justice. Appeasement was used several times during the 1930's. It characterized the policy of Britain with regard to Japan in 1931 when the Japanese invaded Manchuria, technically a part of China. Though China appealed to the League of Nations, the British would allow nothing to be done since they feared retaliation against their own interests in the Far East and hoped to use Japan in the future as a counterweight against Russia.

The classic example of appeasement, however, was the Munich Agreement of 1938. By September of that year Hitler had pushed his drive to the East so far that only one obstacle, Czechoslovakia, stood in his way. Earlier in the year he had annexed Austria, which left Czechoslovakia almost surrounded by German territory. From that point on he exerted relentless pressure against the Slav republic. Convinced of the imminent danger of war, the British Prime Minister, Neville Chamberlain, determined to leave nothing undone to pacify the German dictator. Frantic appeals came also from other sources, including France, Italy, and the United States. Finally, on September 28, the Fuehrer agreed to meet with Chamberlain, Premier Daladier of France, and Mussolini in a four-power conference in Munich. The result was a complete surrender to the violent, browbeating Chancellor. During the next few months Hitler not only annexed the Sudetenland, or western portion of Czechoslovakia (as the Munich Agreement had permitted him to do), but he annihilated the entire Czech republic. Instead of bringing peace to a

The Munich Agreement

619

The Beginning of World War II. A long line of German tanks speeding into Poland.

frightened Europe, this action intensified the crisis. The Soviet government was convinced that the Munich settlement was a diabolical plot by Britain and France to save their own skins by diverting Nazi expansion eastward. In August 1939, Stalin and his colleagues entered into a pact of their own with the Nazi government. Its effect was to give Hitler the green light for an attack on Poland. Apparently, there was an understanding that the two dictators would divide Poland between them. In going to Munich, Britain and France had thought of nothing but their own interests; Russia would now look to hers.

2. THE OUTBREAK OF HOSTILITIES

The beginning
of World
War II

See color map
at page 440

Following the extinction of Czechoslovakia, Hitler turned his aggressive designs against Poland. He demanded the abolition of the Polish Corridor and the return of Danzig to Germany. Convinced finally that the Fuehrer's appetite for power was insatiable, Chamberlain announced that Britain would give Poland armed assistance. Soon afterward he declared that his government would come to the aid of *any* country that felt itself menaced by Hitler's ambitions. In the weeks that followed, both Britain and France gave definite guaranties not only to Poland but to Greece, Rumania, and Turkey. Hitler apparently believed that these pledges were worthless. With the Soviets drawn into his camp, he probably thought that Poland would quickly capitulate, and that the Western allies would back down once more as they had done at Munich. When Poland stood firm, the Fuehrer decided to attack. On September 1, 1939, a long column of German tanks crossed the Polish border. Upon learning of the attack, Britain and France sent a joint warning to Germany that she must cease her aggression. To this there was no reply. September 3 brought a radio announcement by Neville Chamberlain that Britain was at war with Germany. He spoke of the "bitter blow" it was to him that his "long struggle for peace" had failed. He asserted that it was evil the British nation would be fighting against —"brute force, bad faith, injustice, oppression, and persecution." Later the same day France also entered the war.

World War II passed through several stages. The conflict with Poland proved to be a brief encounter. In less than three weeks the Polish armies had been routed, Warsaw had been captured, and the chiefs of the Polish government had fled to Rumania. For some months after that the war resolved itself into a kind of siege, a "phony war" or "sitzkrieg," as it was sometimes called. Such fighting as did occur was largely confined to submarine warfare, aerial raids on naval bases, and occasional battles between naval vessels. In the spring of 1940 the sitzkrieg was suddenly transformed into a blitzkrieg. The Germans struck lightning blows at Norway, Denmark, Belgium, the Netherlands, and France, conquering them one after another. Following these disasters the war entered a new stage, the so-called Battle of Britain. Instead of launching an invasion across the Channel, the Nazis decided to attempt the reduction of Britain to submission by air raids. From August 1940 to June 1941 thousands of planes smashed at British ports, industrial centers, and air defenses throughout the country. Despite the fact that whole sections of cities were laid in ruins and more than 40,000 citizens killed, the British held firm and finally were able to retaliate by even more devastating attacks upon German cities.

Stages of the war

Frustrated in his attempt to subjugate Britain, Hitler turned eastward, on June 22, 1941, with a massive invasion of Russia. Before the end of the year his armies had smashed their way to the very

Development of the war into a global conflict

London During the Blitz. This picture gives a vivid impression of the agony which the British capital suffered during the Battle of Britain, from August 1940, to June 1941. Back of the tumbling ruins brought down by fire bombs is St. Paul's Cathedral.

"The Day That Will Live in Infamy." Damage inflicted upon the United States Navy by Japanese bombers at Pearl Harbor, December 7, 1941.

gates of Moscow but never succeeded in capturing it. Meanwhile, the war was converted into a global war when Japan struck a deadly blow at Pearl Harbor on December 7 of the same year. The Japanese were already involved in a costly war with China. To wage it successfully they needed the oil, rubber, and extensive food resources of the Netherlands Indies, the Malay Peninsula, and Indochina. Before attacking these areas they apparently considered it necessary to lock the back door by crushing American naval and air power on the great base of Pearl Harbor. The next day the United States Congress recognized a state of war with Japan, and on December 11 Germany and her fascist allies declared war upon the United States.

The course of the war was marked by several turning points. The first was the stubborn defense of Moscow by Stalin's armies in November and December, 1941. The second was the defeat of the Germans in North Africa, which opened the way for the Allied invasion of Italy and the overthrow of Mussolini. The third was the Battle of Stalingrad in 1943, when the Germans failed in their attempt to cut northern Russia off from the food-producing region of the Ukraine and from the oil resources north and south of the Caucasus. The turning points in the Pacific war came during the spring of 1942 with the defeat by the United States Navy of Japa-

nese forces in the battles of the Coral Sea and of Midway. These
defeats spelled the doom of Japanese attempts to capture Australia
and the Hawaiian Islands and thereby deprive the United States of
advance bases for a counteroffensive against Japan.

By the winter of 1944–1945 World War II was nearing its end.
On June 6, 1944 (D-Day), American forces had crossed the English
Channel and landed successfully in northern France. On August 25
they liberated Paris. In September advance detachments drove to
the Rhine, and eventually whole armies penetrated to the heart of
Germany. Meantime, Soviet troops were approaching from the east.
On April 21 they hammered their way into the suburbs of Berlin.
During the next ten days a savage battle raged amid the ruins and
heaps of rubble. On May 2 the heart of the city was captured, and
the Soviet red banner flew from the Brandenburg Gate. A few
hours earlier Adolf Hitler killed himself in the bomb-proof shelter
of the Chancellery. On May 7 representatives of the German High
Command signed a document of unconditional surrender. Peace had
come at last to an exhausted Europe after five years and eight
months of slaughter and barbarism.

The end of the war in the Pacific was delayed for another four
months. Victory over the Japanese empire had to be achieved by
savage naval battles and by bloody assaults upon almost impregnable
islands. In June 1945, Okinawa was taken, after eighty-two days of
desperate fighting. The Americans now had footholds less than 500
miles from the Japanese homeland. The government in Tokyo was
nervously anticipating an invasion and calling upon the citizens for
supreme endeavors to meet the crisis. On July 26 the heads of the
United States, British, and Chinese governments issued a joint proclamation calling upon Japan to surrender or be destroyed. In the absence of a reply the highest officials of the United States government
resolved to make use of a new and revolutionary weapon to end the
war quickly. This weapon was the atomic bomb recently developed in great secrecy by American scientists. Though many high mil-
tary and naval officers contended that use of the bomb was not necessary, on the assumption that Japan was already beaten, President
Harry S. Truman decided otherwise. On August 6 a single atomic
bomb was dropped on Hiroshima, completely obliterating about 60
per cent of the city. Three days later a second bomb was dropped,
this time on Nagasaki. That night President Truman warned that
the United States would continue to use the deadly new weapon as
long as might be necessary to bring Japan to her knees. On August
14 Tokyo transmitted to Washington an unconditional acceptance
of the Allied demands. As the news spread through the victorious
nations millions of people danced and cheered and paraded in the
streets amid the screaming of horns and the shrieking of sirens.
Some of the more thoughtful assembled in churches the following
day to give thanks that the terrible ordeal was over.

View of Hiroshima after First Atom Bomb Was Dropped, August 6, 1945. This photo, taken one month later, shows the utter devastation of the city. Only a few steel and concrete buildings remained intact.

3. THE PEACE SETTLEMENT

The Atlantic
Charter and the
United Nations
Declaration

The peace settlement at the end of World War II, if such it can be called, was a fragmentary accomplishment. The first statement of Allied objectives in the event of victory was the Atlantic Charter, issued by President Roosevelt and Prime Minister Winston Churchill on August 14, 1941. Its essential principles were as follows:

(1) No territorial changes that do not accord with the wishes of the people concerned.

(2) The right of all peoples to choose the form of government under which they will live.

(3) All states to enjoy access, on equal terms, to the trade and raw materials of the world.

(4) Freedom to traverse the seas without hindrance.

(5) Disarmament of all nations that threaten aggression.

The Atlantic Charter acquired a broad significance when it was reaffirmed by the United Nations Declaration on January 2, 1942. Twenty-six nations signed this Declaration, including Great Britain, the United States, the Soviet Union, and China. Subsequently about **624** fourteen others added their signatures.

As the war progressed, high officials of the leading United Nations met in various conferences for the purpose of determining the conditions of peace. The first of outstanding importance was the conference that met in Cairo in November 1943, to discuss the fate of the Japanese empire. The participants were President Roosevelt, Prime Minister Churchill, and Generalissimo Chiang Kai-shek. They agreed that all of the territories taken by Japan from China, with the exception of Korea, were to be restored to the Chinese Republic. Korea was to become free and independent. They agreed, further, that Japan was to be stripped of all the islands in the Pacific which she had seized or occupied since 1914, and of "all other territories which she had taken by violence or greed." What disposition was to be made of these islands and territories was not specified.

The second important conference to determine the conditions of peace met in Yalta, in the Crimea, in February 1945. This time the chief participants were Roosevelt, Churchill, and Stalin. A formal report issued at the close of the conference declared that the Big Three had agreed upon plans for the unconditional surrender of Germany, upon methods of controlling Germany and her allies after the war, and upon the establishment of a United Nations Organization to keep the peace. In addition, it was announced that Poland would surrender her eastern provinces to Russia and be compensated by "substantial accessions of territory" in the north and west—to be taken, of course, from Germany. The existing government of Poland, set up under Soviet auspices, was to be reorganized with the inclusion of democratic leaders from among the Poles. The government of Yugoslavia was also to be broadened in similar fashion. Regarding the Far East, it was agreed that Russia should enter the war against Japan and receive as her reward all the territories taken from her by Japan in the war of 1904–1905.

The Yalta Conference, February 1945. Standing directly behind the Big Three are Anthony Eden, British Foreign Secretary; Edward R. Stettinius, United States Secretary of State; and Vyacheslav M. Molotov, Soviet Foreign Minister. The exhaustion of President Roosevelt in the 15 months since the Teheran Conference is clearly evident.

The surrender of Germany on May 8, 1945 seemed to require yet another conference of the victorious powers. On July 17 Joseph Stalin, Winston Churchill, and Harry S. Truman, who had suc-

ceeded Franklin D. Roosevelt as President of the United States on April 12, met in Potsdam, a suburb of Berlin. Before the conference had finished its work, Churchill was replaced by Clement Attlee, the new Labour Prime Minister of Great Britain. The most important provisions of the formal Declaration, issued on August 2, were 1) East Prussia to be divided into two parts, the northern part to go to the Soviet Union, and the southern part to be assigned to Poland; 2) Poland to receive the former free city of Danzig; 3) all German territory east of the Oder and Neisse rivers to be administered by Poland, pending a final settlement; 4) the military power of Germany to be totally destroyed; and 5) Germany to be divided into four occupation zones to be governed, respectively, by the U.S.S.R., Great Britain, the United States, and France.

After the end of the war the victorious states drafted peace treaties with Japan and with Germany's satellites. The treaty with

The "Big Three" at Potsdam, August 1945. Winston Churchill, Harry S. Truman, and Josef Stalin pose before one of their luncheons in the early days of the Potsdam Conference. At this Conference attempts were made to implement the Yalta Agreements and to consolidate the peace of the world.

Japan deprived her of all the territory she had acquired since 1854—in other words, her entire overseas empire. She gave up the southern half of Sakhalin Island and the Kuril Islands to Soviet Russia, and the Bonins and Ryukyus to control by the United States. She also renounced all rights to Formosa, which was left in a status still undefined. She yielded to the United States the right to continue maintaining military installations in Japan until the latter was able to defend herself. The treaty went into effect in April 1952, against the opposition of the Russians, who had hoped that

Japan would be crippled by drastic punishments and thereby left an easy prey to communism.

The treaties with Germany's satellites derive such importance as they have mainly from the fact that they altered the map of Europe. The Italian treaty provided for the cession of small areas to France, Venezia Giulia to Yugoslavia, and the Dodecanese Islands to Greece. Hungary was required to surrender the eastern half of Transylvania to Rumania. Rumania was forced to acquiesce in the loss of Bessarabia and northern Bukovina to the Soviet Union and a portion of southern Dobrudja to Bulgaria. Finland was obliged to hand over the province of Petsamo, with its valuable nickel mines, to the U.S.S.R. All of the treaties provided for demilitarization of the conquered states and for reparations penalties of varying amounts.

As in the case of the Versailles Treaty one of the most significant elements in the World War II settlement was its provision for international organization. The old League of Nations had failed to avert the outbreak of war in 1939, and in April 1946, it was formally dissolved. Allied statesmen had long recognized the need for a new organization. In February 1945, they agreed at Yalta that a conference to implement that need should be convoked for April 25 in San Francisco. Despite the tragic death of President Roosevelt two weeks earlier, the conference met as scheduled. A charter was adopted on June 26, providing for a world organization to be known as the United Nations and to be founded upon the principle of "the sovereign equality of all peace-loving states." Its important agencies were to be 1) a General Assembly composed of representatives of all the member states; 2) a Security Council composed of representatives of the United States, Great Britain, the U.S.S.R., China, and France, with permanent seats, and of six other states chosen by the General Assembly to fill the nonpermanent seats; 3) a Secretariat consisting of a Secretary-General and a staff of subordinates; 4) an Economic and Social Council composed of eighteen members chosen by the General Assembly; 5) a Trusteeship Council; and 6) an International Court of Justice.

By far the most important functions of the new organization were assigned by the Charter to the Security Council. This agency has the "primary responsibility for the maintenance of international peace and security." It has authority to investigate any dispute between nations, to recommend methods for settlement, and, if necessary to preserve the peace, to employ diplomatic or economic measures against an aggressor. If, in its judgment, these have proved, or are likely to prove, inadequate, it may "take such action by air, naval, or land forces" as may be required to maintain or restore international order. The member states are required by the Charter to make available to the Security Council, on its call, armed forces for the maintenance of peace.

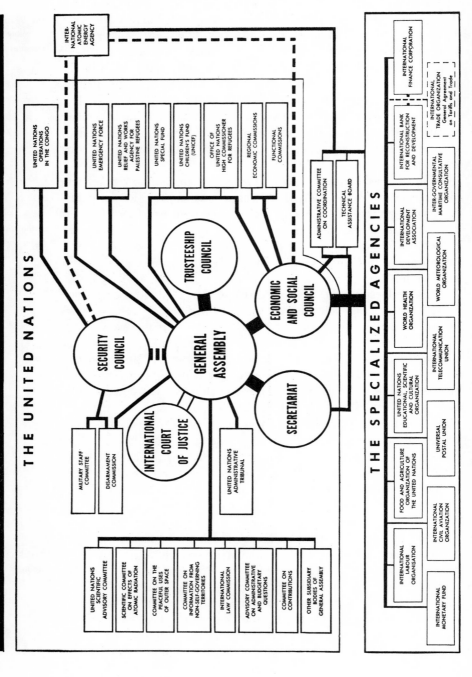

THE UNITED NATIONS AND RELATED AGENCIES

THE UNITED NATIONS

INTER-NATIONAL ATOMIC ENERGY AGENCY

UNITED NATIONS OPERATIONS IN THE CONGO

UNITED NATIONS EMERGENCY FORCE

UNITED NATIONS RELIEF AND WORKS AGENCY FOR PALESTINE REFUGEES

UNITED NATIONS SPECIAL FUND

UNITED NATIONS CHILDREN'S FUND (UNICEF)

OFFICE OF UNITED NATIONS HIGH COMMISSIONER FOR REFUGEES

REGIONAL ECONOMIC COMMISSIONS

FUNCTIONAL COMMISSIONS

TRUSTEESHIP COUNCIL

SECURITY COUNCIL

GENERAL ASSEMBLY

ECONOMIC AND SOCIAL COUNCIL

INTERNATIONAL COURT OF JUSTICE

SECRETARIAT

MILITARY STAFF COMMITTEE

DISARMAMENT COMMISSION

UNITED NATIONS ADMINISTRATIVE TRIBUNAL

ADMINISTRATIVE COMMITTEE ON COORDINATION

TECHNICAL ASSISTANCE BOARD

UNITED NATIONS SCIENTIFIC ADVISORY COMMITTEE

SCIENTIFIC COMMITTEE ON EFFECTS OF ATOMIC RADIATION

COMMITTEE ON THE PEACEFUL USES OF OUTER SPACE

COMMITTEE ON INFORMATION FROM NON-SELF-GOVERNING TERRITORIES

INTERNATIONAL LAW COMMISSION

ADVISORY COMMITTEE ON ADMINISTRATIVE AND BUDGETARY QUESTIONS

COMMITTEE ON CONTRIBUTIONS

OTHER SUBSIDIARY BODIES OF GENERAL ASSEMBLY

THE SPECIALIZED AGENCIES

INTERNATIONAL FINANCE CORPORATION

INTERNATIONAL TRADE ORGANIZATION General Agreement on Tariffs and Trade

INTERNATIONAL BANK FOR RECONSTRUCTION AND DEVELOPMENT

INTER-GOVERNMENTAL MARITIME CONSULTATIVE ORGANIZATION

INTERNATIONAL DEVELOPMENT ASSOCIATION

WORLD METEOROLOGICAL ORGANIZATION

WORLD HEALTH ORGANIZATION

INTERNATIONAL TELECOMMUNICATION UNION

UNITED NATIONS EDUCATIONAL, SCIENTIFIC AND CULTURAL ORGANIZATION

UNIVERSAL POSTAL UNION

FOOD AND AGRICULTURE ORGANIZATION OF THE UNITED NATIONS

INTERNATIONAL CIVIL AVIATION ORGANIZATION

INTERNATIONAL LABOUR ORGANISATION

INTERNATIONAL MONETARY FUND

The Security Council was so organized as to give almost a monopoly of authority to its permanent members. It was the belief of the Big Three who assembled at Yalta, and of President Roosevelt especially, that the peace of the world depended upon harmony among the states primarily responsible for winning the war. Accordingly, they agreed that when the Security Council should be set up, no action of any kind could be taken without the unanimous consent of Great Britain, France, the United States, China, and the Soviet Union, and two other members besides. Even the Charter of the United Nations itself was not to be amended except with the approval of every one of the permanent members. This absolute veto given to each of the principal states had none of the hoped-for effects. Instead of bolstering the peace of the world, its chief result was to cripple the Council and to render it helpless in the face of emergencies. The primary cause was the growth of distrust between Soviet Russia and the West. Each has opposed most of the demands of the other with respect to disarmament, the control of nuclear weapons, and the admission of new states.

Compared to the powers of the Council, the authority of most of the other U.N. agencies is limited. The General Assembly was originally intended to be largely an advisory body. It could initiate studies, make recommendations, and call the attention of the Council to situations likely to endanger peace. It was planned as a place where the little nations could air their grievances while the big powers in the Security Council ran the world. It was not even permitted to make recommendations on any dispute being considered at the time by the Council. In the fall of 1950, however, the General Assembly took steps to remedy this defect. It adopted a series of resolutions providing that if a veto prevents the Security Council from discharging its responsibilities of curbing aggression, the General Assembly may be convened in an emergency session within twenty-four hours, either at the request of seven of the members of the Security Council or by a majority of members of the United Nations. The Assembly then has the power, by a two-thirds vote, to make recommendations for collective action even to the extent of using force.

The remaining agencies of the U.N. were given a wide variety of functions. The Secretariat, composed of a Secretary-General and a numerous staff, is chiefly an administrative authority. Its duties, though, are by no means routine, for the Secretary-General may bring to the attention of the Security Council any matter which, in his opinion, may threaten international peace. The Trusteeship Council exercises supervision over the trust territories, or non-self-governing territories, administered directly by various nations under the authority of the U.N. The functions of the Economic and Social Council are the most varied of all. Composed of eighteen members elected by the General Assembly, it has authority to initi-

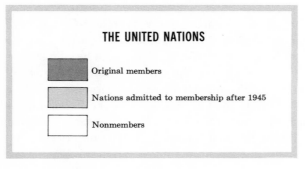

THE UNITED NATIONS

Original members

Nations admitted to membership after 1945

Nonmembers

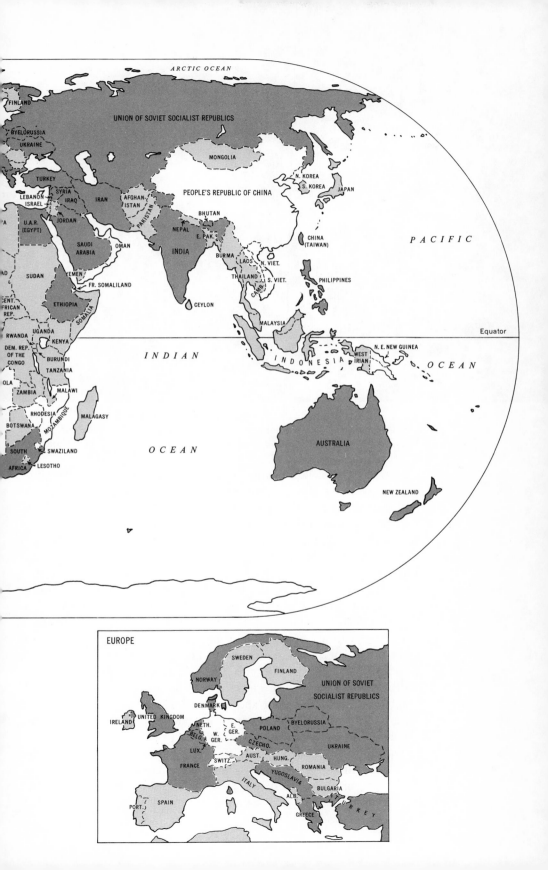

The Security Council of the United Nations. In this beautiful air-conditioned room the Security Council holds its meetings. The spectators in the foreground listen to the proceedings through earphones in the language of their choice.

ate studies and make recommendations with respect to international social, economic, health, educational, cultural, and related matters, and may perform services within such fields at the request of U.N. members. Under its jurisdiction are such specialized agencies as the following: the United Nations Educational, Scientific, and Cultural Organization (UNESCO), whose purpose is to promote international cooperation through education, science, and culture "in order to further respect for justice, for the rule of law, and for the human rights and fundamental freedoms of all"; the World Health Organization (WHO), which works to control epidemics and to assist backward nations in stamping out cholera, typhus, and venereal disease and in raising standards of health and sanitation; and the Food and Agriculture Organization (FAO), which seeks to promote increases in food production by finding remedies for agricultural depressions, for plant and animal diseases and insect pests, and by projecting plans for mechanizing small farms and for the more efficient distribution of food.

Achievements of the U.N.

During the first two decades of its history the achievements of the U.N. constituted a modestly impressive record. It induced Soviet Russia to withdraw her troops from Iran, and Britain and France to take their forces out of Syria and Lebanon. It appointed a commission to investigate the infiltration of foreign Communists into Greece. It terminated a bloody war between Dutch and native forces in Indonesia. It induced the British to agree to the partition of Palestine, and it persuaded the warring Jews and Arabs to conclude a truce. It assisted in arranging a cease-fire agreement between India and Pakistan, which temporarily prevented war from inundating some 400 million people. But against these accomplishments must be recorded several failures. It failed completely in its efforts to establish control of nuclear weapons. Despite the specific requirements of Article 26 of the Charter, it did nothing to provide for a general reduction of armaments. It failed also to curb the increasing friction between the U.S.S.R. and the United States, which was certainly a threat to international peace. It was powerless in the face of Soviet suppression of the Hungarian revolt in 1956. It has been argued, however, that one of the main contributions of the U.N. was the prevention of a direct clash between the U.S. and the U.S.S.R. By providing makeshift solutions as well as a forum for the discussion of grievances, the U.N. helped to keep the two giants from a head-on collision. As a consequence, crises mounted to a crescendo of bitterness without resulting in a holocaust that would destroy the world.

In the light of conditions obtaining after World War II, it was perhaps inevitable that internationalism should assume a number of forms. Some thoughtful observers criticized the United Nations as a mere replica of the old League of Nations. Both, it was said, were leagues of governments, not federations of peoples. Those who felt this way argued for nothing less than a world federal republic similar in structure to the United States, with an actual transfer of sovereign powers to a central government. They believed that the government of this republic should include not merely a court to hear disputes and a world executive with police authority, but, above all, a world parliament representing peoples rather than governments and capable of enacting laws which would apply directly to individuals. It was not argued that the functions of the world state should entirely supersede those of national governments. On the contrary, only such sovereign powers as control over armaments, tariffs, and colonial areas should be transferred to the central authority; the rest would be reserved to the national units.

Other forms of internationalism: (1) the movement for a world republic

Less idealistic statesmen and publicists held to the belief that the U.N. should be supplemented by military and political alliances. Convinced that the U.S.S.R. was bent upon world conquest, they could think only in terms of a combination of force for the "containment" of Soviet power. Such was the opinion of President Truman and his advisers in the United States, and they seem to have converted to similar views most of the governments of the Atlantic region. At any rate, in April 1949, representatives of Canada, Denmark, Portugal, Iceland, Britain, France, Italy, the Netherlands,

(2) NATO

Norway, Belgium, Luxembourg, and the United States signed an agreement providing for the establishment of the North Atlantic Treaty Organization (NATO). Subsequently Greece, Turkey, and West Germany were added as members. The treaty declared that an armed attack against any one of the signatory parties would be regarded as an attack against all, and that they would combine their armed strength to whatever extent necessary to repel the aggressor. At a conference held in Lisbon in February 1952, the NATO members agreed to set up a permanent organization, with a Council and a Secretariat, and a permanent headquarters in Paris. It was decided also that the joint military command, or NATO army established in 1950, should be increased from thirty to fifty divisions in 1953, and that West Germany should be rearmed and invited to contribute twelve of the divisions. It was thereby hoped that NATO would be ready for any emergency that might arise as a consequence of the expansionist policies of Soviet Russia. By 1966, however, the status of the alliance had been compromised by disharmony between France, on the one side, and Great Britain and the United States on the other. Whereas Britain generally supported the policies of the United States, France under de Gaulle aspired to organize Western Europe as an independent entity opposing the threat of communist expansion. He seemed anxious to exclude the United States from a dominant role in European affairs. Western European nations, he believed, were capable of saving themselves and taking care of their own future. To accomplish his aims he was ready for a reconciliation with Germany and practically forced the withdrawal of NATO troops from French soil.

Internationalism may be said to have made some progress also on a more limited geographic scale. About 1950 Robert Schuman, Foreign Minister of France, conceived the idea of bringing the coal, iron, and steel industries of Western Europe under a supranational authority. No tariff barriers or other international restrictions would exist; each industry, regardless of country, would have equal access to markets and to sources of raw materials. The plan would also have the advantage of preventing the industries of the Ruhr from ever being used as a foundation for German militarism. After months of negotiation France, West Germany, Belgium, the Netherlands, Luxembourg, and Italy agreed to the plan, and it went into operation in August 1952. Officially known as the European Coal and Steel Community, it represented a significant step on the long and difficult road toward European federation. So confident were its leaders of the importance of their project that they embarked almost immediately upon the drafting of a constitution for a union of Western Europe.

The most that could be accomplished, however, was the adoption of a plan for bringing Great Britain and West Germany into a close association with the other states of Western Europe. Britain agreed

(3) the coal and steel community

634

to maintain part of her armed forces on the European Continent as long as a majority of her allies considered it necessary. In return for a restoration of sovereignty and full membership in NATO, West Germany promised to refrain from manufacturing atomic, biological, and chemical weapons, guided missiles, warships larger than 3,000 tons, and bomber aircraft. The association—composed of France, Italy, Belgium, the Netherlands, and Luxembourg, together with West Germany and Britain—was given the name Western European Union. In 1957 the six Continental nations took the further step of agreeing to pool their nuclear-energy resources and to introduce gradually, over a period of twelve to seventeen years, a common tariff-free market, or customs union, for all commodities. The union, known as the European Economic Community, or the Common Market, inspired largely by the French statesman Jean Monnet, was formally established in 1959 with headquarters in Strasbourg. Three years after its establishment Great Britain applied for admission. Whether she would actually be admitted remained to be seen. Britain was faced with opposition from the Commonwealth nations, which had long depended upon the mother country as a primary market for their exports. The most formidable obstacle, however, was the attitude of President de Gaulle of France. He regarded Britain as a non-European power and a close ally of the United States. He insisted that management of European affairs should remain in the hands of the Continental powers, with France as their leader.

SELECTED READINGS

· *Items so designated are available in paperbound editions.*

· Ambrose, Stephen E., *Eisenhower and Berlin, 1945: The Decision to Halt at the Elbe*, New York, 1967 (Norton).

Armstrong, H. F., *Chronology of Failure: The Last Days of the French Republic*, New York, 1940.

· Aron, Raymond, *The Century of Total War*, Boston, 1955 (Beacon).

Beard, C. A., *President Roosevelt and the Coming of the War: A Study in Appearances and Realities*, New Haven, 1948. A radical interpretation implicating President Roosevelt in responsibility for Pearl Harbor.

· Carr, E. H., *The Twenty Years' Crisis*, London, 1946 (Torchbook). Stimulating but somewhat dogmatic.

Coox, A. D., *Year of the Tiger*, Tokyo, 1964. A study of the beginning of the Sino-Japanese War in 1937-1938.

Einzig, Paul, *The World Economic Crisis, 1929-1932*, London, 1932. A searching analysis by a distinguished economist.

Eubank, Keith, *Munich*, Norman, Okla., 1963.

· Eyck, F. Gunther, *The Benelux Countries: An Historical Survey*, Princeton, 1959 (Anvil).

· Feis, Herbert, *The Road to Pearl Harbor*, Princeton, 1950 (Atheneum).

· ———, *Churchill-Roosevelt-Stalin: The War They Waged and the Peace They Sought*, Princeton, 1957 (Princeton).

Finer, Herman, *America's Destiny*, New York, 1947.

Fuller, J. F. C., *The Second World War, 1939–1945*, London, 1948. A military history.

Gantenbein, James W., ed., *Documentary Background of World War II, 1931 to 1941*, New York, 1948.

Géraud, André, *The Gravediggers of France*, New York, 1944. A critical and impassioned account.

Haines, C. G., and Hoffman, R. J. S., *The Origins and Background of the Second World War*, New York, 1943.

Heiden, Konrad, *Der Fuehrer*, Boston, 1944.

Henderson, Sir N., *Failure of a Mission*, New York, 1940.

Holborn, Hajo, *The Political Collapse of Europe*, New York, 1951. A penetrating analysis.

· Langer, William L., *Our Vichy Gamble*, New York, 1947 (Norton Library).

· Mayne, Richard, *The Community of Europe*, New York, 1903 (Norton).

McInnes, Edgar, *The War*, New York, 1940–1944, 4 vols. A factual account.

Mitchell, Broadus, *Depression Decade: from New Era through New Deal, 1929 to 1941*, New York, 1947.

Morgenthau, H. J., *Politics among Nations: The Struggle for Power and Peace*, New York, 1948. A provocative analysis from the viewpoint of a realist.

Orton, William, *Twenty Years' Armistice*, New York, 1938. A provocative and rather caustic account by a liberal historian.

· Reves, Emery, *The Anatomy of Peace*, New York, 1945 (Compass). An eloquent plea for a world federal republic.

· Rowse, A. L., *Appeasement: A Study in Political Decline, 1933–39*, New York, 1961 (Norton Library).

Schuman, F. L., *Europe on the Eve*, New York, 1939.

· Trevor-Roper, H. R., *The Last Days of Hitler*, New York, 1947 (Collier).

Viorst, Milton, *Hostile Allies: FDR and Charles de Gaulle*, New York, 1965.

· Wilmot, Chester, *The Struggle for Europe*, New York, 1952 (Colophon Book). A critical account of American leadership in the War by an Australian journalist.

Wittman, Erno, *History: A Guide to Peace*, New York, 1948.

· Wolfers, Arnold, *Britain and France between Two Wars*, New York, 1940 (Norton Library).

SOURCE MATERIALS

· Churchill, W. S., *Blood, Sweat, and Tears*. Also available in paperback under the title *The Years of Greatness* (Capricorn).

· ———, *The Second World War*, New York, 1960, 6 vols. (Bantam, 1962, 6 vols.).

· Eisenhower, D. D., *Crusade in Europe*, New York, 1948 (Dolphin).

Grew, J. C., *Report from Tokyo*, New York, 1942.

Liebling, A. J., ed., *The Republic of Silence*, New York, 1947. A collection of materials on the French Resistance movement.

Lochner, L., ed., *The Goebbels Diaries*, New York, 1948.

Marshall, G. C., Arnold, H. H., and King, E. J., *The War Reports*, New York, 1947.

Maurois, André, *Tragedy in France: An Eyewitness Account*.

U.N. Dept. of Public Information, *Yearbook of the United Nations*.

United States Department of State, *Peace and War, U.S. Foreign Policy, 1931–1941*.

CHAPTER 20

The Revolution of Our Age

. . . a torrent of events is pouring down upon mankind. A social transformation of planetary range is being topped by wars of an unprecedented type in which a score of states crashed, and the contours of new empires are emerging out of a sea of blood. But this fact of demoniac violence is merely superimposed on a swift, silent current of change which swallows up the past without so much as a ripple on the surface. A reasoned analysis of the catastrophe must account both for the tempestuous action and the quiet dissolution.

—Karl Polanyi, *The Great Transformation*

The world that emerged from the crucible of World War II bore little resemblance to the dreams of idealists set forth during the conflict. Over vast areas it was a world of hunger and fear, of ashes and rubble, of misery and violence. The hopes of the masses in all nations that security and peace would automatically result when the carnage was over were badly shattered. The revival of power politics and the fear of a new war, to be fought with nuclear weapons and chemical and bacteriological poisons, made the decade of the 1930's by comparison seem almost serene and orderly. Even as late as the 1960's fear and anxiety had little abated. The peace of the world still rested upon a balance of terror and increasing rivalry between the two chief communist states, the U.S.S.R. and Communist China. The one consolation most people could find in the new era was a rising standard of living. Improvements in productive efficiency turned out a plethora of goods, and the upper and middle classes lived in an "affluent society." Yet it remained a world of uncertainty and confusion. To a host of questions no one knew the answers. How long would prosperity continue? Was it soundly based, or was it an artificial product of armaments expansion? Would the balance of terror postpone indefinitely World War III, or, as more and more countries crashed their way into the "nuclear club," would some reckless dictator precipitate a conflict that would engulf the

Bewilderment and anxiety after World War II

637

globe? Ethics, religion, and the arts were all fraught with similar uncertainties. In these realms, as well as in politics and economics, confusion and anxiety tortured the minds, especially of the young, and
sometimes led to bizarre results.

1. POLITICAL REVOLUTION

The most significant political revolution of the twentieth century
has probably not been the rise of communism or fascism. Rather it
has been the changing character of the international community.
Gordon A. Craig has pointed out that before 1914 only about
twenty states in the entire world "had any serious and continuous
interest in foreign affairs," and "all but two or three of those were
European powers." [1] At its founding in 1920 the League of Nations
had 41 members, 25 of them non-European. But a much more radical expansion of the world community occurred after 1945. When
the United Nations was established in that year, it had 59 members.
By 1966 this total had grown to 121. During the 1960's alone 30 new
states were added to the world roster, nearly all of them in Africa
and Asia.

More fundamental than the increase in number of states has
been the change in their character. Because of the lack of political experience of their leaders, many of the new states are
unstable. Some are states only in name, with actual authority
exercised by chiefs of discordant tribes. Central governments were
often extravagant in the hope of impressing local chieftains and
also the outside world. The very number of new states gave
them an influence out of proportion to their importance. This was
especially true in the Assembly of the United Nations where all
members had equal votes. By the mid-1960's the so-called Afro-Asian
Bloc held virtually the balance of power in the world organization.
This fact was but one of a number of evidences of the decline of
European supremacy. No longer was it possible for a handful of
European powers to dictate policy to the rest of the world. For one
reason, their old homogeneity was gone. During the nineteenth century they had all been characterized by an underlying similarity of
aims and principles. They were all capitalist, parliamentary, and, on
the surface at least, Christian nations. In the years that followed
World War I this fundamental unity disappeared. Socialism, totalitarianism, and paganism spread through Eastern and eventually Central Europe. Meanwhile, racial disunity added to the troubles of the
contemporary world. Before 1914 the only world that counted was
the white man's world. After 1919 a colored world, comprising
three-fifths of the human race, rose to challenge Caucasian supremacy. In the light of this political revolution some observers believe

[1] *On the Diplomatic Revolution of Our Times*, p. 42.

that the remainder of the twentieth century can scarcely be other than a time of continuing war and social conflict. The conditions that made for relative peace and stability in the nineteenth century, they assert, no longer hold sway.

2. ECONOMIC AND SOCIAL REVOLUTION

The economic history of the modern world has been characterized by three industrial revolutions. The First extended from about 1760 to 1860, the Second from 1860 to about 1914, and the Third from 1914 to the present. Each has had distinctive features. The First was the age of coal and iron. The Second was the age of steel, electricity, and the internal combustion engine. The Third has been distinguished by synthetic products, electronics, and automation. The production of synthetics actually began at the end of the First Revolution, when William H. Perkin discovered that coal tar could be converted into an infinite variety of products. The process continued apace during the Second Revolution, but it did not reach its full potential until the past three decades. Today it is probably safe to say that the quantity of goods produced synthetically exceeds those derived from natural materials. Most automobile tires, for example, are made from petrochemicals such as butadiene. Rubies, sapphires, and other gems can be produced so perfectly in factories as to be scarcely distinguishable from the genuine precious stones. Even many foods, such as whipped cream, salad oil, coffee cream, butter substitutes, flavoring, and preservatives consist wholly or partially of synthetic ingredients. A reflective Chinese woman said recently: "When I was a little girl in China, I ate dirt; now that I am a grown-up woman in America, I eat chemicals."

The Third Industrial Revolution: synthetics

The electronics industry has been one of the miracle industries of the Third Industrial Revolution. Electronics derives from that branch of physics which deals with the behavior and effects of electrons, or negative constituents within the atom. Electronic devices have multiplied in staggering profusion since World War II. Among them are devices to measure the trajectory of missiles, to give warnings of approaching missiles or aircraft, to make possible "blind" landings of airplanes, to store and release electrical signals, to amplify and regulate the transmission of light and sound images, and to provide the power for photoelectric cells that open doors and operate various automatic machines. The spacecraft industry, which may some day make possible the full exploration of outer space, including voyages to the moon and the major planets, is closely dependent upon electronics.

Electronics

Scarcely any two developments in modern industry could be more closely related than electronics and automation. Indeed, it was the use of electronic devices for radio reception that led to the initial progress in automation. Automation should not be confused

Automation

with mechanization, though it may be considered the logical extreme of that process. More correctly conceived, automation means a close integration of four elements: (1) a processing system; (2) a mechanical handling system; (3) sensing equipment; and (4) a control system. Though all of these elements are necessary, the last two are the most significant. Sensing equipment performs a function similar to that of the human senses. It observes and measures what is happening and sends the information thus gained to the control unit. It employs such devices as photoelectric cells, infra-red cells, high-frequency devices, and devices making use of X-rays, isotopes, and resonance. It operates without fatigue and much faster and more accurately than do the human senses. Moreover, its observations can be made in places unsafe for, or inaccessible to, human beings. A control system receives information from a sensing element, compares this information with that required by the "program," and then makes the necessary adjustments. This series of operations is continuous, so that a desired state is constantly maintained without any human intervention, except for that initially involved in "programming." Through automation expensive and complicated machines are constantly taking the place of much human labor. Data processing machines and electronic computers are employed to control switching operations in railroad yards, to operate assembly lines, to operate machines that control other machines, and even to maintain blood pressure during critical operations in hospitals.

New materials

The Third Industrial Revolution has gone beyond the Second in the adoption of new materials in the manufacturing process. Foremost among them have been plastics, manufactured from various substances, such as casein, phenol, and coal and petroleum derivatives. Plastic steering wheels, plastic machinery housings, and plastic bottles are only a few of them. To a considerable extent aluminum is taking the place of steel and copper, and in some instances where an even lighter material is required, as in airplane construction, magnesium is being substituted for aluminum. Other new metals have been adopted, not principally as substitutes for older metals, but to give toughness and strength or rust-proof qualities to steel. Notable among these are the ferro-alloys, which include tungsten, manganese, nickel, molybdenum, and chromium. Found largely in such countries as Turkey, Russia, China, India, Canada, and Rhodesia, they are indispensable to modern industry. Together with other widely scattered critical materials, they furnish excellent examples of the economic interdependence of the contemporary world.

The revolution in
transportation and
communication

With respect to transportation and communication the most noteworthy developments of the Third Industrial Revolution have been jet propulsion engines and television. The first jet-propelled airplanes were products of World War II. Their advantages of power and speed were so great that it was inevitable that they would be adapted to peacetime use. The first jetliner passenger service was in-

augurated in 1952 between London and Johannesburg, South
Africa. The distance covered was 6724 miles, and the time required
was less than 24 hours. The first jet plane passenger service across
the Atlantic was opened by British Overseas Airways in October
1958. Later in the same year an American firm, National Airlines,
established the first jet plane service in the United States, with a
flight from New York to Miami. By 1965 jet planes had almost entirely superseded piston-engine planes for long flights. Though
average speeds had mounted in excess of 500 miles per hour, the industry and some of its customers were not satisfied. In Britain, France,
and the United States plans were being drawn for a supersonic
transport plane which would be capable of flying faster than the
speed of sound, perhaps about 2000 miles per hour. In the field of
communication the outstanding achievement was the development
and perfection of television. Invented by a Scotsman, J. L. Baird, in
1926, television was not widely used until after World War II. Only
about 10,000 receiving sets were in operation before Pearl Harbor.
Following the war developments came thick and fast. Transmission
channels were opened in every major city in the United States. In
1952 color television was patented, and its popularity gradually
spread.

That the Third Industrial Revolution would germinate problems
affecting labor was a foregone conclusion. The most obvious was
technological unemployment. Though new industries absorbed
many workers, others were bound to be displaced by automation. In
the mid-1960's no one could be quite sure of the extent of this displacement. Apparently, most of those whose jobs were taken found
new opportunities with the development of new industries. In any
case unemployment, in the United States, had declined by February
1966, to 3.7 per cent of the labor force. But this was a condition of a
war economy. What would happen when peace returned, no one
could say. Moreover, it was a fact that while the demand for skilled
labor remained high, the so-called "entry jobs" as helpers, sweepers,
and miscellaneous unskilled workers were fast disappearing. They
were being eliminated not by computers so much as by fork-lift
trucks and motorized conveyors and sweepers. Mechanization of
agriculture also knocked out thousands of jobs for unskilled and uneducated workers. The mechanical cotton picker in the South and
Southwest and the combine on the great wheat farms of the West
displaced innumerable field hands who fled to the cities to lead lives
of misery and despair in the slums. The problem of the future
seemed to be not so much a repetition of the mass unemployment of
the 1930's as a dearth of jobs at the bottom, and a scarcity of ex-
pertly trained men to meet the demand for skilled employees at the
top.

That the Third Revolution would involve further changes in the
nature of capitalism goes almost without saying. Though holding

Problems affect-
ing labor

TECHNOLOGICAL ADVANCES
IN THE MID TWENTIETH CENTURY

Center: *IBM Computer System 360.* The operator sits at a communications desk feeding in and receiving data. Behind him is the computer console. In the background are the information storage units. To the right, from front to back, a card sorter, a high-speed printer, and a disk-drive and information storage unit.

Top right: *High-speed Train*, built by Pullman under subcontract to United Aircraft and designed to run between Boston and New York. Propelled by gas turbine engines, one in front and one in the rear, it will operate at speeds from 120 to 160 miles per hour.

Center right: *Docking in Outer Space.* The Gemini space vehicle (open hatch in the right foreground) has joined the Agena (left foreground) in an orbit around the earth.

Bottom right: *The Boeing* 747, is the largest airplane designed for commercial aviation. It will carry 350 to 490 passengers. Cruising speed will be 625 miles per hour at an altitude of 45,000 feet.

companies had been largely eliminated in the public utility industry by New Deal legislation in the United States, in other industries they continued and even proliferated. They usually took the form, not of trusts but of mergers, composed of dozens of subsidiaries, more or less closely related, and formerly independent companies. The object usually was to strive for product diversification and thereby guard the parent company against shifting patterns of consumer demand. Thus Olin Mathieson Chemical Corporation, with headquarters in New York, acquired enterprises manufacturing not only chemicals but ethical drugs, aluminum, paper, and guns and ammunition. Eastman Kodak continued to manufacture cameras and photographic materials but also acquired subsidiaries extensively engaged in the production of plastics, chemicals, and synthetic fibers. A trend toward consolidation characterized the railroad industry, merchandising, and even banking. The largest bank in New York City, the Chase Manhattan—itself the result of a merger of two giant banks—acquired 130 branches in the Greater New York area, to say nothing of 33 overseas branches throughout the free world.

Along with this trend toward consolidation has gone, strange as it may seem, a diffusion of ownership. In 1965 it was estimated that 1 out of every 6 of the people of the United States was a shareholder in one or more American corporations. The amount they owned was usually an infinitesimal fraction of the total shares outstanding and therefore precluded any control over the affairs of the companies. The bulk of the stock in large corporations generally came into the possession of investment trusts, insurance companies, and pension funds, colleges and universities, and foundations. Yet another characteristic of ownership in the Third Revolution has been the virtual disappearance of the old "dynastic" capitalism. The DuPont and Ford families are among the few exceptions. The name Rockefeller is no longer synonymous with oil or the name Carnegie with steel. Management has become increasingly separate from ownership. Presidents and board chairmen of modern corporations are not proprietors but financiers and bureaucrats who made their way up as lawyers or bankers or as successful heads of smaller companies. In some cases they have little direct knowledge of the basic operations of the firms over which they preside. It has been said that a recent chairman of the board of one of our largest steel corporations never saw a blast furnace until "after he died."

3. THE POPULATION EXPLOSION

The years after World War II experienced a tremendous increase in population growth in nearly all countries of the world. This increase was all the more striking since it followed a period of declining or relatively static population during the interwar period in many Western nations. In some measure the decline resulted from a curtailment of immigration. This policy, adopted by numerous governments, prevented the filling up of sparsely settled areas and the relief of congestion in older countries. Mainly, however, the decline occurred because of a diminishing birthrate. The conditions of the depression caused a tendency to postpone marriage, and even among those who did marry, a reluctance to have children. In western Europe, on the average, the birthrate was halved during the years between the late 1800's and the 1930's. In England it dropped from 36.3 per thousand in 1876 to 14.8 in 1934. During approximately the same period in Germany the decline was from 40.9 to 17.5, less than enough to maintain even a stationary level. The decline was especially marked in the period between the two wars. The English birthrate fell from 24 in 1914 to 15 in 1939. The German birthrate was 28 in 1914; in 1939 it was 19.

During World War II young people began to marry at earlier ages, and the trend continued after the war. The result was a bumper crop of babies in the past three decades. By 1964 the birthrate in the United States had risen to 21.1 per thousand. In Latin America, Asia, and Africa it rose still higher. The average for these continents remains about 40 per thousand, notwithstanding a decline to about 18 per thousand in Japan. In Mexico, in 1960, it was 45 per thousand, and in Venezuela 49.6, approximately twice the rate for economically advanced nations such as Britain, West Germany, the United States, and Japan. Of course, these high birthrates were not exclusively a consequence of the war. They resulted even more from improvements in the general vitality of the population, advances in sanitation, and reduction of infant mortality. Birthrates increase in a kind of geometric progression, that is, the larger the number of infants surviving to reproductive age, the greater the number of parents to produce more infants, and so on.

Rising birth rates

Rising birthrates were not the only, or even the major, cause of the population explosion. More important was the so-called demographic revolution. By this is meant an overturning of the ancient balance between births and deaths, which formerly kept the population on a stationary or slowly rising level. This balance is a biological condition common to nearly all species. For thousands of years of his history man was no exception. It is estimated, for example, that the total population of the earth at the beginning of the Christian era was about 250 million. More than sixteen centuries passed before another quarter billion had been added to the total. Not until 1860 did the population of the globe approximate 1 billion. From then on the increase was vastly more rapid. The sixth half billion, added about 1960, required scarcely more than ten years.[2] According to United Nations projections, the total population of the world by 1975 will be 4 billion. To add the last half billion will require only seven or eight years.

The demographic revolution

[2] P. M. Hauser (ed.), *The Population Dilemma*, pp. 8-11.

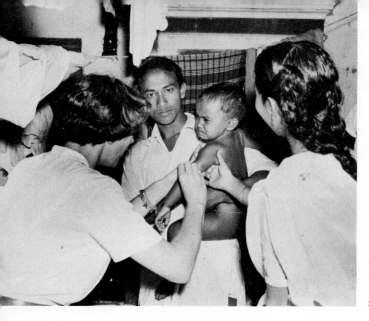

Preventive Medicine on an International Scale. A technician of the United States Foreign Operations Administration inoculates a child against cholera in Pakistan.

What have been the causes of this radical imbalance known as the demographic revolution? Fundamentally, what has happened has been the achievement of a twentieth-century death rate alongside a medieval birthrate. Medicine and the other health sciences have made such rapid strides that the span of life has been substantially lengthened all over the world. Infant mortality rates have markedly declined. Deaths of mothers in childbirth have also diminished. The great plagues, such as cholera, typhus, and tuberculosis, take a much smaller toll than they did in earlier centuries. Wars and famines still number their victims by the millions, yet such factors are insufficient to counteract an uncurbed rate of reproduction. Though the practice of contraception has been approved by the governments of such nations as India, China, and Japan, only in the last have the effects been worthy of notice. In some countries the desire of adults to have numerous offspring to care for them in old age has stood as an obstacle. In others poverty, religion, and abysmal ignorance have made the widespread use of contraceptives impossible.

Of course, the demographic revolution has not affected all countries uniformly. Its incidence has been most conspicuous in the underdeveloped nations of Central and South America, Africa, and Asia. Whereas the population of the world as a whole will double, at present rates of increase, in thirty-five years, that of Central and South America will multiply twofold in only twenty-six years. An outstanding example is that of Brazil. In 1900 its population was estimated to be 17 million. By 1960 this total had grown to 71 million, more than a fourfold increase. Mexico and Venezuela have two of the highest birthrates in the world. The population of Asia (excluding the U.S.S.R. and Japan) grew from 813 million in 1900 to approximately 2 billion in 1960. By way of summary, at midcentury, the population of the underdeveloped portions of the globe was more than twice that of the developed portions. Their total land areas were about equal.

What will be the consequences of the demographic revolution? Some writers maintain that the population explosion is proceeding at so rapid a rate that its effects can be nothing but calamitous. They *Implications of* foresee not only impaired standards of living but famine, wretched- *the demographic* ness, despair, and war. Others contend that natural or artificial ad- *revolution* justments may occur which will bring births and deaths into something akin to their old balance. They believe that industrialization and urbanization will tend to make large families a liability rather than an asset. The real question is whether these adjustments can come soon enough to avert wholesale disaster. Famines are already of common occurrence in India and elsewhere in Asia. With more mouths to be fed, it would seem that such famines will increase in frequency and extent unless vast new resources of food are made available, either by increased production or by gifts from the wealthier nations. Neither prospect appears very good. But hunger and famine are not the only likely consequences. Overcrowding and diminution of economic opportunities may well lead to the destruction of liberty and the subjection of the individual even in some of the advanced countries. Conditions of chronic emergency foster unrest, and threats of revolution encourage the establishment of dictatorships to keep order among the masses. It has been said that the gravest dangers threatening modern man are nuclear energy and sexual energy, and it is not at all certain which of these is the more serious.

4. GALLOPING URBANIZATION

Closely allied to the population explosion has been the rapid growth of urban areas in nearly all countries. Though the highest birthrates are generally found in agricultural nations, the pressure *The increase in* of increased numbers inevitably forces thousands to flee from the *urban living* land to the cities. The core population of several American cities is already made up of refugees from the cotton fields of the South or from the sugar plantations of West Indian islands. The urban explosion has been much more rapid than the population explosion in general. The population of the United States in 1920 was slightly less than 106 million, with only a little more than half of this total living in urban centers. By 1960 the total had grown to 180 million, with 68 per cent living in other than rural communities. Urbanization, of course, was not confined to the United States. During the first half of the twentieth century, as world population increased by 49 per cent, the inhabitants of cities increased by over 200 per cent. Of the total urban world population of 314 million in 1950, Asia had **647**

106 million living in cities of 100,000 or more, while Europe had only 83 million and North America but 48 million living in cities of this size. Even the number of cities of 100,000 and over in Asia was more than twice the number in North America.[3]

In some respects it would be more accurate to speak of galloping "metropolitanization" instead of an urban explosion. Actually, the so-called growth of cities, especially in the United States, has consisted of the growth of large urban areas, each comprising a central city and surrounding suburbs. An almost universal tendency has been for the more prosperous and better educated inhabitants to leave the older sections in the heart of the city and move to the suburbs. The older sections then fill up with migrants from other areas or from foreign countries. The result has often been a deterioration of property values and an increase in corruption and crime. In a few instances the central city and its suburbs sprawl over so large an area that it is difficult to tell where one metropolis ends and another begins. Some observers predict the development, in the United States, of the "megalopolis," a huge aggregation of cities and suburbs formerly maintaining independent existences. One such megalopolis would be an area extending from Boston to Washington, taking in Providence, New Haven, New York, Philadelphia, and Baltimore. A second would be the Milwaukee–Chicago–South Bend area. Still another would stretch all the way from San Francisco to Los Angeles and San Diego.

Rapid urbanization has had a profound impact upon contemporary society. As in past ages, cities have been the principal means of fostering cultural growth. They provide the art museums, centers of learning, scientific institutes, the great libraries, and other cultural and educational facilities. It is almost a commonplace that without cities civilization can neither grow nor flourish. At the same time, it appears also to be true that metropolitan cities pose a threat to the very existence of civilization. In recent times, particularly, they present problems that almost defy solution. Made possible originally by the automobile, such cities today face strangulation by traffic congestion. Overcrowding combined with industrialization results in air and water pollution and in an environment favorable to the spread of disease. Blight and decay in the older areas magnify the problem of finding sufficient revenue to provide for essential services. These must be constantly expanded because of the increasing numbers of indigent, unemployed, and ignorant who populate the widening slums. So grave were these problems that, in the 1960's, national governments were forced to come to the rescue of many cities, helping them to finance urban renewal, slum clearance, specialized education, and relief for the disabled and unemployable.

Metropoli-
tanization

The impact of
urbanization

[3] P. M. Hauser, *Population Perspectives*, p. 94.

5. THE ANTI-IMPERIALIST REVOLT

The late nineteenth and early twentieth centuries were marked by an imperial aggrandizement that led to the carving of most of the underdeveloped areas of the world into colonies or spheres of influence of the great powers. Great Britain led the way with her acquisitions of India, southern Persia, and the lion's share of Africa. France took Indochina, Algeria, Tunisia, Morocco, and the more arid portions of northern and central Africa. Japan, Britain, and Russia shared portions of Chinese territory as colonies or spheres of interest. Even some of the smaller European states took possessions exceeding in area their own homelands. To illustrate, Belgium acquired the Congo, and the Netherlands extended control over what is now known as Indonesia. Germany and Italy entered the scramble late on account of their delayed unification. But eventually even they annexed empires in Africa of no mean extent. The United States confined its imperialism mainly to gobbling up fragments of the decrepit Spanish empire after the war of 1898.

The acquisition of empires

World War I heralded the beginning of the end of the old imperialism. As a defeated nation, Germany was forced to give up her possessions in Africa as well as her bases on the coast of China. Great Britain began to have trouble in India as early as 1919. In 1930 the United States government repudiated the Roosevelt Corollary by which Theodore Roosevelt had proclaimed the right of intervention in Latin American states in cases of "chronic wrongdoing or impotence." True, there had been some earlier reactions on the part of subject peoples. At the turn of the century the Boxer Rebellion had threatened the schemes of the great powers for dividing the Chinese melon, while the Boer War had inflicted a decisive defeat upon the British in South Africa. But it was the exhaustion of most of the great powers in World War I, together with the doctrine of the "self-determination of nations," that produced an upsurge of nationalism which eventually sealed the doom of most of the colonial empires. The peace conferences themselves *encouraged* this upsurge when they granted independence to Slovaks, Czechs, Yugoslavs, and Poles, and a semi-independence to Syria, Palestine, and Iraq as mandates of the League of Nations. All three of these subsequently obtained complete independence.

Decline of the British Empire

The most serious conflicts in the mandated territories arose with respect to Palestine. Britain surrendered her mandate over that ancient land largely in response to Zionist pressure, but also in accordance with a decision of the United Nations General Assembly to partition the country between the Arabs and Jews. In 1948 the Jewish portion of Palestine was organized as the Republic of Israel. Its history thereafter was a record of turmoil and strife. The surrounding Arab states resented its establishment and plagued its existence by repeated raids across its borders. Elsewhere in Asia, Great

Nationalist revolts in Israel and Egypt

649

THE DECLINE OF COLONIALISM AFTER WORLD WAR II

Territories gaining independence during postwar period

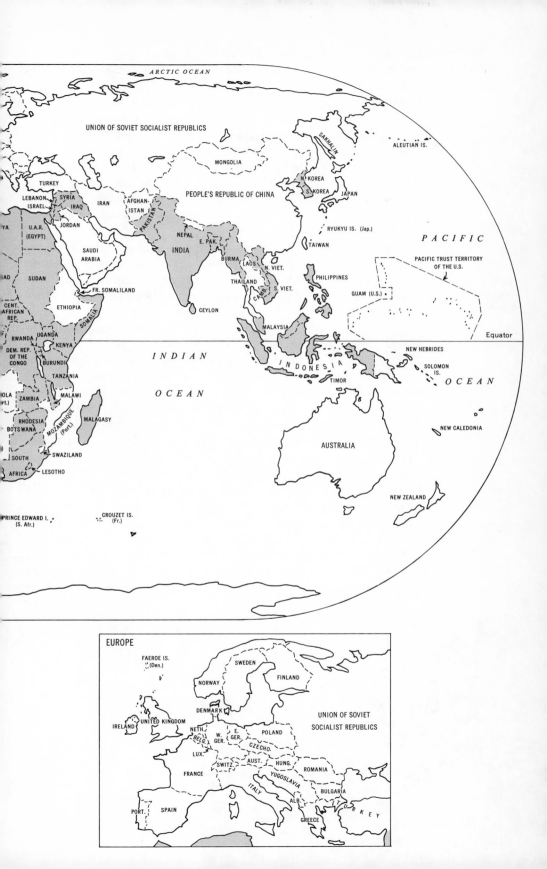

Britain recognized the independence of Ceylon, Malaysia, and Singapore, in most cases with the proviso that they remain members of
the Commonwealth of Nations. Nationalist resurgence in Egypt
forced Britain to abandon her protectorate and to recognize the
country as a sovereign state subject to powers reserved by Britain
over national defense and the security of the lifeline to the East. In
1952 a revolt of young army officers drove the pro-British king,
Farouk I, into exile and proclaimed Egypt an independent republic.
By 1966 little remained of the once mighty British Empire except
Hong Kong, British Honduras, Bermuda, the Bahamas, Gibraltar,
Aden, and Southern Rhodesia—and even the status of the last two
was uncertain.

The British
withdrawal
from India

The liquidation of no part of Britain's empire raised so many
crucial problems as did the departure of the British from India. In
1947 the British Labour Government yielded to pressure from Hindu
and Moslem Nationalists by announcing its intention to withdraw
from India and to partition the country into two dominions. In
August of that year the Hindu provinces were organized as the
Union of India and entered the British Commonwealth of Nations as
a self-governing dominion. In 1950 India became a sovereign republic, remaining a member of the Commonwealth of Nations, but with
the word "British" omitted. Meanwhile, the Moslem provinces had
been organized as the Dominion (later the Republic) of Pakistan.
The division was necessarily an artificial one, since boundary lines
between the two peoples had never been clearly drawn. The results
were persecution and bloodshed. Millions of both Hindus and Moslems fled from territories controlled by their opponents. Frenzied
fanatics fell upon them and slaughtered them by the thousands.
Rioting and persecution continued for more than a year. They were
temporarily halted in January 1948, when Mohandas K. Gandhi, the
saintly Hindu leader who had led the long struggle for Indian independence, was shot and killed by a reactionary chauvinist. The
shocking deed seemed to arrest, at least for a time, outbreaks of violence between the hostile factions. Nevertheless, relations between

The Israeli-Arab Conflict. An
Israeli farmer, constantly under
threat from border raiders,
keeps a rifle within easy reach
as he works his land.

Anti-imperialist Revolt in Algeria, 1960. At Dar-es-Saada, Moslems take furniture from the homes of Europeans and burn it in the streets.

the two states continued strained, especially because of the conflict over Kashmir, where the natives showed little enthusiasm for either Indian or Pakistani rule.

During the postwar period the French and Dutch empires were also in the process of forced liquidation. The bloodiest of all the struggles against France occurred in Algeria. Though its population is predominantly Arab, the French had monopolized the best of the agricultural and mineral resources during more than 100 years of rule. Arab nationalism flared into open rebellion in 1954. The fighting was desperate and continued for seven years. Though the French employed half of their armed forces and sacrificed more than 10,000 soldiers, they were obliged to concede independence. Another sanguinary struggle occurred in Indochina, or Vietnam. Taken by the French during the reign of Napoleon III, it had been neglected and misgoverned for 100 years. A revolt waged chiefly by guerrilla fighters broke out in 1945. The French fought desperately but were finally cut to pieces at Dienbienphu in 1954. An agreement was signed at Geneva that provided for the division of Vietnam into two zones, pending elections to determine the future government for the entire country. The most valuable jewel in the Dutch imperial crown was undoubtedly the Netherlands Indies. Indeed, it is one of the richest countries in the world in natural resources. Controlled by the Dutch since the sixteenth century, it was occupied by Japan during World War II. Toward the end of the war, nationalists, under the leadership of Sukarno, rebelled, and in 1945 proclaimed Indonesia an independent republic. Although the Dutch attempted for four years to regain their sovereignty, the op-

Dissolution of the French and Dutch empires

653

position of the natives proved too formidable. In 1949 the government of the Netherlands recognized the independence of the Indonesian Republic.

The dissolution of the old empires was the result not only of nationalist rebellion, but also of other causes. One was a long record of neglect or abuse by the mother country in some of the colonies. In the Netherlands Indies, for example, 96.8 per cent of the population was illiterate as late as 1930. In 1950 there was only one physician per 60,000 inhabitants and less than one hospital bed per 1000 inhabitants. In most of the African colonies, with the exception of Nigeria, none of the ruling powers made much effort to train administrators or other specialists for the responsibilities of self-government. Small wonder that, once they had gained self-rule, so many of the new states on that continent would be torn by strife and ruled by incompetence. Yet another cause of the rebellion of colonies was the so-called "revolution of rising expectations." After World War I hundreds of bright young men from the colonies went to Britain, France, and the United States to study in the universities. After the second war the number increased to the thousands. Not only did they imbibe the heady wine of nationalism in Western countries, but they learned of standards of living incomparably higher than those in their homelands. The truth was quickly impressed upon them that there was a better way of life than the cycle of famine, poverty, filth, and disease handed down by their ancestors. Finally, we must not overlook the influence of communism. Not a few colonial leaders became convinced that the U.S.S.R. was a better beacon light for their guidance than any of the Western powers. Here was a nation that had lifted itself by its own bootstraps out of the mire of backwardness, ignorance, and poverty. Why could not Indochina, the Netherlands Indies, and Algeria do the same, provided they could throw off the yoke of oppression fastened upon them by their colonial masters?

6. THE END OF IDEOLOGY?

A significant feature of the revolution of our time, in the opinion of some observers, is the decline of ideology. Gone, they say, are the days when Europeans and Americans professed ardent devotion to social, political, and economic ideals that were once the sustaining faiths of millions. Orthodox gospels have almost disappeared from the picture except in Communist China and Albania. Socialists no longer advocate collective ownership of the means of production; they have faded into exponents of the welfare state. It is not uncommon to hear from them slighting references to "baggy-pants Marxism." One notes the existence of militant defenders of capitalism, but few would recognize it if they saw it in full operation. For capitalist economies are no longer free enterprise systems but "mixed" economies, involving government controls of prices and production, to say nothing of forced distribution of profits through rigorously progressive taxation. Even communism, in the U.S.S.R., and especially in Poland and Yugoslavia, has adopted so many elements of production for profit and for the satisfaction of consumer demands that it has traveled far from the orthodox teachings of Marx and Lenin. A Polish wit has distinguished thus between capitalism and communism: "Capitalism is a system wherein man exploits man. And communism—is vice versa." [4]

The factors responsible for the decline of ideology have been several. Many of the architects of utopias were naïve. They believed in the inherent goodness of human nature and assumed that new and better institutions would provide the open sesame to a perfect society. Rising incomes and the increasing availability of luxuries for members of the lower middle class fostered a disinterest in reform movements. Instead, workers and their families began dreaming of houses in the suburbs, luxury automobiles, and expensive vacations. Even in the Soviet Union, according to Nikita Khrushchev, near the end of his regime, what the Russian masses wanted was not more doctrine but "better goulash." The decline of ideology can also be illustrated by the history of the Socialist party in the United States since World War I. In the Presidential election of 1920 the party polled about 1 million votes. By 1928 the vote had dwindled to 267,000. Though this total more than trebled in the depression year of 1932, by 1960 the fortunes of the party were at so low an ebb that it did not even nominate a candidate for President. A final cause of the diminishing importance of ideology was disillusionment with radicalism itself, especially in Western countries. Socialists failed to present a united front against World War I. Though a few remained steadfast in opposing the conflict, most of them were nationalists first and socialists second. Even more disenchanting were the attitudes of Communists in the years that followed. In Germany members of the party collaborated with the Nazis to assist the latter's accession to power. They more or less openly mouthed the slogan, "After Hitler, Our Turn." Communist rulers of the Soviet Union entered into a virtual alliance with Nazi Germany in 1939 which practically assured that Hitler would attack Poland and plunge Europe into World War II. With the outbreak of war most Communists in Western nations turned into embattled supporters of their own governments on the assumption that the destruction of fascism must be given priority over everything else. From apostles of revolution they were converted temporarily, at least, into exponents of reform, exemplified by such nonideological movements as the New Deal.

Causes of the decline of ideology

[4] Daniel Bell, *The End of Ideology*, p. 16.

SELECTED READINGS

· *Items so designated are available in paperbound editions.*

· Almond, G. A., *The Appeals of Communism*, Princeton, 1954 (Princeton University Press).

· Bell, Daniel, *The End of Ideology*, Glencoe, Ill., 1960 (Free Press).

Drucker, P. F., *The End of Economic Man*, New York, 1939. A really profound study of modern man's predicament.

· Hauser, P. M., ed., *The Population Dilemma*, Englewood Cliffs, N.J., 1963 (Spectrum).

———, *Population Perspectives*, New Brunswick, N.J., 1960.

Kahn, A. E., *Great Britain in the World Economy*, New York, 1946.

Laski, H. J., *Reflections on the Revolution of Our Time*, New York, 1943. A discerning analysis not seriously marred by a Marxist viewpoint.

Mannheim, Karl, *Diagnosis of Our Time*, New York, 1944. A thoughtful study.

Monroe, Elizabeth, *Britain's Moment in the Middle East, 1914–1956*, Baltimore, 1963.

Neumann, Sigmund, *The Future in Perspective*, New York, 1943.

Schapiro, J. S., *The World in Crisis*, New York, 1950.

· Ward, Barbara, *The Rich Nations and the Poor Nations*, New York, 1962 (Norton).

· ———, *Nationalism and Ideology*, New York, 1966 (Norton).

———, *The West at Bay*, New York, 1948.

SOURCE MATERIALS

Dolivet, Louis, *Handbook of the United Nations*, Charter of the United Nations.

Proposed Constitution for a World Republic, *Saturday Review of Literature*, Vol. 31 (April 3, 1948).

CHAPTER 21

New Power Relationships

From Stettin in the Baltic to Trieste in the Adriatic, an iron curtain has descended across the Continent.
—Sir Winston Churchill, March 5, 1946

Unconditional war can no longer lead to unconditional victory. It can no longer serve to settle disputes. It can no longer concern the great powers alone. For a nuclear disaster, spread by winds and waters and fear, could well engulf the great and the small, the rich and the poor, the committed and the uncommitted alike. Mankind must put an end to war—or war will put an end to mankind. . . . Let us call a truce to terror. Let us invoke the blessings of peace. And as we build an international capacity to keep peace, let us join in dismantling the national capacity to wage war.
—President John F. Kennedy, September 25, 1961, Address to the General Assembly of the United Nations.

Prior to 1914 the list of world powers included no fewer than eight states. Of these, the six European nations—Great Britain, France, Germany, Austria-Hungary, Russia, and Italy—were generally the real arbiters of world affairs. The United States and Japan were newcomers whose position did not weigh very heavily in the international scale. After World War I the number of great powers shrank to five. Austria-Hungary was eliminated permanently and Germany and Russia for a period of years. On the other hand, the United States and Japan rose to positions much higher than they had previously occupied, while Britain and France sank a bit lower. The effects of World War II upon power relationships were far more upsetting. Germany, Italy, and Japan were defeated so overwhelmingly that they seemed destined to be relegated permanently to the background. They recovered more quickly than expected, however, and regained positions nearly comparable to those they had occupied before the war. Officially, the list of great powers included five

Changing status of the great powers

657

states—the U.S.S.R., the United States, Great Britain, France, and China. These were the famous Big Five who occupied the permanent seats in the Security Council of the United Nations and seemed fated to rule the world. However, China was soon overwhelmed by communist revolution, while Britain and France became increasingly dependent upon the United States. As a consequence, the world of nations took on a bipolar character, with the United States and the U.S.S.R. contesting for supremacy and striving to draw the remaining states into their orbits. But this duality did not continue indefinitely. By 1964 rifts had begun to appear in the communist world. Under Premier Khrushchev and his successors, Kosygin and Breszhnev, Soviet Russia moved into somewhat closer relations with the United States, while Communist China posed as a new champion of Leninist orthodoxy and denounced the Soviet "peaceful coexistence" policy as a surrender to capitalist imperialism.

I.   THE UNITED STATES AS A WORLD POWER

One of the most impressive results of World War II was the emergence of the United States as the most powerful nation in the world. Except for the Soviet Union, there was not a country anywhere on earth that could throw down a challenge to her. For a brief period at the end of the war the United States had the largest army in the world, and her navy was equal to the combined navies of all the other powers. Her tonnage in aircraft carriers alone just about matched the total tonnage of the entire British navy. Though both her land and naval forces were substantially reduced by 1950, she still had impressive strength. From the standpoint of economic power, also, she had far outdistanced the rest of the nations. Since 1939 her people had doubled their national income and quadrupled their savings. Though they constituted only 7 per cent of the world's population, Americans enjoyed over 30 per cent of the world's estimated income. For the first time in her history the United States was in a position to be the arbiter of the destinies of at least half of the earth. Japan was virtually her colony; she controlled both the Atlantic and Pacific Oceans, policed the Mediterranean, and shaped the development of international policy in Western Europe. But it must not be imagined that her people had found for themselves an earthly paradise. The national debt in 1945 stood at $260,000,000,000. More money was required to pay the interest on this debt than had been necessary to defray the entire cost of government before the war. By 1948 the cost of living had risen to 172 per cent of the 1935–1939 average, and one family out of every four was spending in excess of its earnings. Moreover, despite her sacrifice of billions of dollars and 350,000 lives, the United States had not gained security. For years after the war, her citizens lived in as much dread of a new attack as they had felt at almost any time while the war was in progress.

With the end of World War II comparatively little evidence was to be found of a desire on the part of the United States to retreat into the kind of isolationism that had followed the victory in the previous war. At least this was true of the government. In 1945 the United States Senate ratified the Charter of the United Nations almost unanimously. Little clamor was raised in Congress or elsewhere for repayment of the sums advanced by the United States under Lend-Lease. Instead, there was an almost universal disposition to treat those loans as gifts. Eventually about nine-tenths of the amount was written off, and in 1946 a new loan of about $4,000,-000,000 for economic recovery was made to Great Britain, the chief beneficiary under Lend-Lease. Although there was some grumbling by extreme isolationists, Congress appears to have approved these actions in the belief that they would be contributions to world recovery. Hardly anyone believed any longer that the United States could go her own way and prosper and leave the rest of the world to survive or perish.

The decline of isolationism

The most vigorous leadership in inducing the United States to live up to her new obligations of power and responsibility came naturally from the executive branch of the government. In 1947, in an address to Congress, President Truman enunciated the first of a series of important policy statements on foreign affairs. It soon became known as the Truman Doctrine. Pointing to the spread of communism in Eastern Europe, the President declared that the United States must go to the aid of any country whose "freedom and independence" were threatened by aggression from within or without. Referring specifically to Soviet pressure against Greece and Turkey, he avowed that the survival and independence of these countries were essential to preserve the integrity of the Middle East. Accordingly, he requested the appropriation of $400,000,000 to send weapons and economic aid to both nations and to provide them with military and naval advisory commissions from the United States. Two months later a bill appropriating the sum requested was passed by bipartisan majorities in both houses of Congress.

The Truman foreign policy

The second of the policy statements coming from the executive branch was the Marshall Plan, or European Recovery Program. This program was first suggested in a speech at Harvard University, June 5, 1947, by George C. Marshall, Secretary of State. Marshall said that if the states of Europe would come to an agreement on what they needed to cover the costs of reconstruction, the United States would see what it could do to help them. He declared that United States policy was not directed "against any country or doctrine but against hunger, poverty, desperation, and chaos." At the same time, he issued a warning that any government attempting to block recovery to perpetuate human misery for its own profit would receive no help. Secretary Marshall's proposal aroused an enthusiastic re-

The Marshall Plan

sponse from European nations. Even the U.S.S.R. participated in a
preliminary conference of the Big Three to see what could be done.
But this conference ended in deadlock when Molotov demanded
that the United States should give up the idea of a combined program for all of Europe and provide for the needs of each nation in-
dividually. Apparently he feared that a combined plan might be
used as an instrument for organizing Europe under United States
control.

The Marshall
Plan and the
Truman Doctrine

To a considerable extent the Marshall Plan and the Truman Doctrine were related programs. Both were elements in a broad strategy
of "containing" Soviet Russia. In the development of the Truman
Doctrine, open avowals were made of the need to keep Greece and
Turkey in the Anglo-American sphere of influence. Control of
them was held to be necessary to the protection of British and
United States interests in the Middle East. It was argued also that if
either or both should fall under the sway of Communists, Soviet
power would expand into the Mediterranean. In other words, the
two countries were considered almost exclusively from the standpoint of pawns in a gigantic struggle for power. It may be doubted
that the Marshall Plan as originally conceived was intended as a
weapon against the U.S.S.R. The United States was certainly interested in the economic recovery of Europe as a contribution to peace
and also as an aid to maintaining her own prosperity. Nevertheless,
supporters of the Plan occasionally used arguments that created the
impression that the major interest Americans had in assisting European recovery was to prevent the spread of communism. The Soviets, at any rate, tended to interpret both the Truman Doctrine and
the Marshall Plan as maneuvers in a Cold War or war of nerves
against them.

The continuity
of U.S. foreign
policy

Though the United States government underwent a change of political control in 1953, no fundamental revision of foreign policy
was clearly apparent. For a brief period there was talk of "liberating" the Soviet satellites in Eastern Europe and "unleashing" Chiang
Kai-shek for an attack upon the Chinese mainland, but the Republican administration soon reverted to the "containment" policy of its
Democratic predecessor. This became evident especially in 1957
with the issuance of the Eisenhower Doctrine against communist inroads in the Middle East. Though couched in vaguer language, it did
not differ essentially from the Truman Doctrine for Greece and
Turkey in the 1940's. Both were designed to prevent Soviet expansion into areas where the West could claim vital interests. If the
pursuance of either doctrine were to require temporary or permanent occupation of the endangered territories, there was scarcely
any doubt that occupation would be undertaken.

The return of the Democrats to power in 1961 brought a stiffening of the government's attitude toward many issues of foreign
policy. Though President Kennedy, in his inaugural address, de-

The Cuban Quarantine. A U.S. destroyer intercepts a Soviet freighter in the Atlantic to inspect cargo of missiles being withdrawn from Cuba under agreement with Premier Khrushchev. A U.S. Navy patrol plane hovers overhead.

clared that "we must not negotiate through fear, but we must never fear to negotiate," he showed only a limited interest in carrying out the second clause of this statement. In April of that year he approved a plan for the invasion of Cuba to overthrow the allegedly communist regime of Fidel Castro. The plan had been developed during the final months of the Eisenhower administration by the Central Intelligence Agency of the United States government. The invading army, consisting of Cuban exiles and refugees, was trained by American military leaders at bases in Florida and in Guatemala. The attempted execution of the plan ended in disaster. Many of the invaders were captured or killed, and the remainder were put to rout. The prestige of the United States throughout Latin America suffered a serious impairment, despite President Kennedy's Alliance for Progress, a long-range program of foreign aid designed to spur the economic growth of Latin American countries. This prestige was in some measure revived, however, in October 1962, when Kennedy instituted a naval blockade of Cuba in order to prevent the Soviet government from supplying "offensive" weapons to that country. The Soviet rulers took alarm at the threat of a general war and promised to remove their missiles and bombers from Cuban soil. Possibly their military strength was not so great as they had led the world to believe; in any event they were not prepared to risk a war

The stiffening of U.S. attitudes: (1) Cuba

661

so far from Russian soil. The Khrushchev surrender was soon followed by a Kennedy pledge to eliminate United States bases in Turkey.

Though President Kennedy gave no encouragement to the ambitions of Chinese Nationalists to overthrow the communist regime in mainland China, he took an aggressive position against the spread of communism beyond its existing borders. He continued the bipartisan policy, established during the Eisenhower administration, of giving economic assistance to pro-Western regimes in the petty states of Indochina, notably in Laos and South Vietnam. He served notice on the Soviet government that the United States was determined to uphold its rights of access to and occupation of West Berlin, and that its stand with respect to these rights was not "negotiable." Through each of the recurring international crises he took the position that the United States had a responsibility to ensure the survival of the free world. In 1961 he went so far as to announce that "in some circumstances we might have to take the initiative" in using nuclear weapons against our enemies. After Kennedy was assassinated in 1963, his successor, Lyndon B. Johnson, adhered to essentially the same premises. Most of his foreign policy, however, came to be concerned with the war in Vietnam, which will be discussed in a later context.[1]

2. THE U.S.S.R. AS A GREAT POWER

Soviet Russia emerged from World War II as the second strongest power on earth. Though her navy was small, her land army and possibly her air force by 1948 were the largest in the world. Her population was climbing rapidly toward 200,000,000, and this in spite of the loss of 7,000,000 soldiers and about 8,000,000 civilians during the war. In mineral wealth her position compared favorably with that of the richest countries. Her territory contained about 20 per cent of the world's coal deposits and more than 50 per cent of the supply of iron. As a result of the discovery of rich oil reserves in the Urals in 1946, she claimed a large percentage of the world supply of petroleum. On the other hand, there can be no doubt that her industrial machine had been badly crippled by the war. According to estimates of her own statisticians, no fewer than 1700 of her cities and towns had been totally destroyed and about 40,000 miles of railway and 31,000 factories. Stalin declared in 1946 that it would probably require at least six years to repair the damage and rebuild the devastated areas.

It seems reasonable to suppose that many of the peculiar attitudes displayed by the U.S.S.R. in her dealings with other nations were attributable in some measure to the losses she sustained during the war. Resentful of the fact that she had been compelled to make such

[1] See pp. 688–89.

sacrifices, she became obsessed with security as a goal that must be attained regardless of the cost to her neighbors. Fearful that poverty and hardship might make her own people rebellious, her rulers adopted a chip-on-the-shoulder attitude in their foreign policy. Soviet citizens must be led to think that their country was in imminent danger of an attack by capitalist powers. For similar reasons they must be induced to believe that their rulers were entitled to a kind of worship hitherto reserved for divine-right monarchs. On the thirtieth anniversary of the Bolshevik revolution, Stalin was hailed as "the sun of the entire universe." In accordance with a new nationalism designed to bolster the people's courage, the Russians laid claim to a majority of the inventions and scientific discoveries of modern times—from the electric light and wireless telegraphy to penicillin.

The tenseness of Soviet attitudes seemed to relax a bit after the death of Joseph Stalin in March 1953. Stalin was succeeded within twenty-four hours by Georgi M. Malenkov, a dominant figure in the party apparatus. Soon after his elevation to power he declared that there was no dispute or unresolved question between the Soviet Union and any other nation which could not be settled by "mutual agreement of the interested countries." Prospects for better relations between the Soviet Union and the West were further enhanced in 1955 when Malenkov resigned and the supreme power passed into the hands of Nikita S. Khrushchev. Though he did not immediately become Premier, he held the all-important position of Secretary of the Communist party. Khrushchev seemed more anxious than his predecessor to create the impression that the Soviet government was ready to repent of the error of its ways. He denounced Stalin for his paranoid suspicions of everyone around him and for his brutal tyranny. He and his colleagues announced their approval of the doctrine of "more than one road to socialism." They concluded peace with Austria and withdrew their occupying troops. They returned the Porkkala naval base to Finland. In 1955 they agreed to a "conference at the summit" with the chiefs of government of Great Britain, France, the United States, and the U.S.S.R. as the participants. The conference was held in Geneva, and the utmost cordiality prevailed. Repeated pledges of trust and friendship were given by both sides.

Soviet policy under Stalin's successors

This policy of the "Great Thaw," or the "New Look," as it was variously called, was undoubtedly prompted by discontent within the country. The Russian masses had no zest for another war, and they were weary of the restrictions and rigidities imposed by the Stalin regime. They believed that they had endured enough sacrifices in the past, and that the time had come for less emphasis on the production of munitions and capital goods and more on providing the amenities of life. The most genial of Soviet dictators, Khrushchev was disposed to sympathize with these demands. The new

The "Great Thaw" or "New Look" and its partial breakdown

663

policy, however, soon ran into heavy weather. The first sign of change was the suppression of revolts in Poland and Hungary in 1956. The Poles were let off rather lightly when they promised to remain within the Soviet orbit in return for permission to make various modifications in their socialist system. The Hungarians were repressed with bloody violence when they attempted not merely to change the economic system but to break all ties with the Soviet Union. At the beginning of another "summit" conference in Paris in May 1960, Premier Khrushchev erupted violently when he learned that the United States was sending U-2 planes far over Soviet territory to discover the location of bases and other military installations. Though at first Washington officials denied these flights, they later admitted them and sought to justify them as necessary for the

Revolt in Hungary. By 1956 discontent with Soviet domination manifested itself in several of the satellite states. Violent revolt broke out in Poland and Hungary. The photograph indicates the extent of the violence in Budapest. In the center is a gun turret blown off a Red Army tank on the right.

military security of the United States. The summit conference terminated immediately, with nothing but a poisoned atmosphere to mark its effects, despite the subsequent suspension of U-2 flights. Yet Khrushchev was not ready to abandon completely his policy of conciliation. Later in 1960 he enunciated his principle of "peaceful coexistence." Though he did not renounce the ultimate triumph of communism, insisting that "we will bury you," he refused to admit that this triumph must be accomplished by force of arms.

With respect to Germany, the Soviet leaders remained intransigent. They nurtured the fear that Germany might launch a new war, aided and abetted by her capitalist allies. For this reason they staunchly opposed unification of the country and insisted upon recognizing East Germany as one of their satellites. They likewise opposed any change in the status of Berlin that might have the effect of restoring it as the national capital. In 1961 they ordered the East German government to build a high wall separating the two sectors of Berlin, in order to cut off the escape of thousands of East Germans to West Berlin and thence to western Germany. Many did

Intransigent
attitude toward
the problem of
Germany

EUROPE IN 1967

Members of NATO

Members of the Communist Bloc

ICELAND

Reykjavik ★

ATLANTIC OCEAN

SCOTLAND
Edinburgh •

NO. IRELAND
Belfast •

IRELAND
Dublin •

ENGLAND
Birmingham •
London •

WALES

ATLANTIC

OCEAN

NORWAY
Oslo ★

SWEDEN
Stockholm ★

FINLAND
Helsinki ★

BALTIC SEA

Leningrad •

ESTONIAN S.S.R.
LATVIAN S.S.R.
LITHUANIAN S.S.R.

Moscow ★

Smolensk •

UNION OF SOVIET SOCIALIST REPUBLICS

Ural R.

Volga R.

Volgograd ★

WHITE RUSSIAN S.S.R.

Kharkov •

Dnieper R.

Kiev •

UKRAINIAN S.S.R.

Odessa •

BLACK SEA

Yalta ★

DENMARK
Copenhagen •

NORTH SEA

NETHERLANDS
The Hague •
Amsterdam ★
Hamburg •
Bonn ★

BELGIUM
Brussels ★

LUX.

Seine R.

Paris ★

FRANCE

Loire R.

Bordeaux •

Garonne R.

Elbe R.

Berlin ★
EAST GERMANY

WEST GERMANY
Frankfurt ★
Munich •

Rhine R.

Bonn ★

POLAND
Warsaw ★

Oder R.

Vistula R.

Prague ★
CZECHOSLOVAKIA

Vienna ★
AUSTRIA

Berne ★
SWITZ.
Geneva •
Milan •
Po R.

Rhone R.

Marseilles •

Barcelona •

SPAIN
Madrid ★

Tagus R.

PORTUGAL
Lisbon ★

Gibraltar (Br.)

MOROCCO
Rabat ★

Budapest ★
HUNGARY

Zagreb •

YUGOSLAVIA

Belgrade •

Adriatic Sea

ITALY
Florence •
Rome ★

CORSICA

SARDINIA

BALEARIC ISLANDS

MOLDAVIAN S.S.R.

Dniester R.

RUMANIA
Bucharest ★
Danube R.

BULGARIA
Sofia ★

ALBANIA
Tirana ★

GREECE
Athens ★

Aegean Sea

BLACK SEA

Istanbul •
Ankara ★

T U R K E Y

GEORGIAN S.S.R.

AZERBAIDZHAN S.S.R.
ARMENIAN S.S.R.

CASPIAN SEA

IRAN

Tigris R.
Baghdad ★

Euphrates R.

IRAQ

SYRIA
Damascus ★

LEBANON
Beirut ★

CYPRUS

CRETE

Palermo •
SICILY

Tunis ★
TUNISIA

Algiers ★
ALGERIA

M E D I T E R R A N E A N   S E A

500 miles

0

THE MIDDLE EAST AND FAR EAST IN 1967

Members of the Communist Bloc

Members of the Southeast Asia
Treaty Organization

make their escape, but the wall remained as a symbol of Soviet determination to prevent the absorption of East German territory into a united Germany. The development of nuclear weapons fixed in the minds of the Soviet leaders another obsession regarding Germany. They feared that West Germany as a member of NATO might be given a finger on the trigger of some project that could be used to destroy the Soviet Union.

3.   THE COLD WAR AND ITS TORRID INTERLUDES

Scarcely had the hostilities of World War II ended than a so-called Cold War began between the United States and Great Britain, on the one side, and the U.S.S.R. on the other. Indeed, there were some evidences of growing animosity as far back as the spring of 1945. Why the squabbling started is a question difficult to answer. Most authorities agree that it grew out of discord arising from the Yalta Conference. That conference had assigned Rumania, Bulgaria, Yugoslavia, and Poland to the Soviet orbit. Perhaps in making this assignment the Western powers did not intend that the U.S.S.R. should do more than establish "friendly" governments there. The Russians, however, soon gave indications of a desire to dominate these countries and to convert them into communist satellites. They also antagonized the Western powers when they refused to revoke the absorption of Estonia, Latvia, and Lithuania into the Soviet Union, which had been carried out in 1940.

Beginning of the Cold War

However it began, the Cold War raged with increasing fury during the succeeding years. Early in 1946 the U.S.S.R. became embroiled in a dispute with Iran. The Iranian government accused Moscow of refusing to permit troops to be sent from Teheran for the suppression of a revolt in the northern Iranian province of Azerbaijan. The real issue was the claim that the U.S.S.R. was attempting to separate Azerbaijan from Iran and incorporate it in the Soviet Union. The Iranian government appealed to the Security Council of the United Nations, where British and United States representatives vigorously condemned Soviet action. Finally, with world opinion strongly against her, the Soviet Union withdrew the troops she had sent for the protection of the separatist movement in Azerbaijan. Meanwhile, Soviet leaders had been infuriated by the issuance of the Truman Doctrine. Western statesmen were accused of villainous plots to force the U.S.S.R. into war in the hope that they could conquer her with atomic weapons and then divide up the world to suit themselves.

Continuation of the Cold War

A more serious crisis began during the summer and autumn of 1948. In the spring of that year the United States government had initiated plans for consolidating the United States, British, and French zones of Germany into a single West German state. The U.S.S.R. replied to these plans by attempting to force the Western

The struggle for Germany

Air Lift over Berlin. In 1948, as the result of a dispute over Germany, Russian occupation forces began a blockade of Berlin. The United States and Britain broke the blockade by a system of airplane transport of food and vital materials into the city.

powers out of Berlin. The issue was the basic one of who should control Germany. The United States government seemed to be convinced that the economic recovery of Europe could not be successful without the development and use of the resources of the Ruhr and of other areas of western Germany. Moreover, a strong West German state would be a bulwark for the containment of Russia. The Soviets were determined to prevent the organization of a compact state in western Germany under Anglo-American auspices. They feared its attractive power for the eastern zone under their own control. Besides, from their viewpoint, there was always the danger that it might be developed into a base of operations for an attack upon Soviet territory. For both the East and the West, Germany was the key to the control of Europe, and the control of Europe was regarded by each side as another name for security. The Soviet blockade of Berlin was eventually relaxed, but rivalry for control of Germany persisted, and the curtain that separated East from West continued to be tightly drawn.

The objective of Soviet foreign policy, many observers contended, was nothing less than world conquest. They could cite the famous assertion of Lenin that "it is inconceivable that the Soviet republics should continue to exist for a long period side by side with imperialist states." [2] They could also quote Stalin to the effect that the final stage of Socialism in the Soviet Union could not be achieved until workers' regimes had been established in at least several other countries.[3] In addition, they could point to the Russian dictator's statement in 1926 that "the Soviet power (and only the Soviet power) is able to withdraw the army from bourgeois com-

Apparent objectives of Soviet foreign policy

[2] A. Fineberg (ed.), V. I. Lenin, *Selected Works*, Moscow, n.d., VIII, 33; Russian edition, 1932, XXIV, 122.

[3] Stalin, *Problems of Leninism*, p. 64.

mand, and to change it from an instrument for the oppression of the people into an instrument for freeing the people from the yoke of the bourgeoisie at home and abroad." [4]

Confirmation of these views seemed to be provided by the outbreak of war in Korea on June 25, 1950. To most people in the West this appeared to be an obvious extension of the Cold War into The outbreak of war in Korea a hot war. The conflict in Korea began suddenly when troops from the Soviet-dominated northern portion of the country crossed the 38th parallel to attack the noncommunist republic of South Korea. At the instigation of the United States, the Security Council of the United Nations condemned the invasion as "armed aggression" in

War in Korea. On a bleak hillside in Korea, U.S. Marines pour rifle and machine gun fire into a Chinese Communist roadblock.

open defiance of the interest and authority of the United Nations, and called upon the North Koreans to cease hostilities and withdraw their troops. The invaders ignored this demand. Two days after the attack President Truman sent armed assistance to the South Koreans. On July 7 the Security Council authorized the United States to establish a unified command of the United Nations forces in Korea. A short time earlier the first United States troops had gone into action in a vain attempt to check the Red invasion. Weak in numbers and lacking heavy equipment, they were slowly pushed back into a small area surrounding the port of Pusan near the tip of the peninsula. Here they accumulated strength for a counteroffensive. So successful were their efforts that they drove the North Koreans back across the 38th parallel, captured their capital

[4] Stalin, *Leninism*, I, 120–21.

(Pyongyang), and were advancing rapidly toward the Yalu River. Late in October the United Nations commander, General Douglas MacArthur, announced that the war was coming to an end, and that a complete United Nations victory was only a matter of days.

These dreams were rudely shattered when MacArthur's armies found themselves confronted by huge forces from Communist China that had come to the rescue of the North Koreans. Soon the opponents of aggression were once again retreating southward. By the end of 1950 they had lost more than half the territory conquered in their counteroffensive. Thereafter the two sides alternated in retreating and assuming the offensive. But by the spring of 1951 the war had reached a stalemate, with the line of battle almost stabilized just north of the 38th parallel. In June 1951, the Communists aroused hopes for an early termination of the conflict when they proposed negotiation for a truce. Two years later a peace settlement formally divided the peninsula at the 38th parallel. Communist aggression had been halted, and North Korea and South Korea reverted to the same status they had occupied when the war began.

The next major scene of battle in the Cold War was Southeast Asia. Here, after the defeat of Japan in 1945, France had sought to recover her empire in Indochina. She was immediately confronted by a rebellion of Vietnamese nationalists under the leadership of a Moscow-trained Communist, Ho Chi Minh. The rebels resorted to guerrilla warfare and inflicted such costly defeats upon the French that the latter decided to abandon the struggle. An agreement was signed at Geneva in 1954 providing for the division of Vietnam into two zones, pending elections to determine the future government of the entire country. Ho Chi Minh became ruler of North Vietnam and established his capital at Hanoi. His followers, who came to be called Viet Cong, were numerous in both halves of the country. Had elections been held as provided by the Geneva Agreement, Ho Chi Minh would probably have been elected President of all of Vietnam. But the government of South Vietnam, backed by the United States, refused to permit the elections to be held.

From this point on the United States became more and more deeply committed in the Southeast Asian struggle. Presidents Eisenhower and Kennedy pledged economic aid and the assistance of military advisers to the South Vietnam government. In February 1965, President Lyndon B. Johnson sent armed forces to help the South Vietnam military chieftains save their country from being overrun by the Communists. By the end of 1966 nearly 400,000 U.S. soldiers were embattled on Vietnamese soil. Some believed that several more hundred thousand would be required in order to win a military victory. Despite stringent criticism for "escalating" the war, the Johnson Administration insisted that the United States had a solemn obligation to fulfill pledges of support made to South Vietnam at the beginning of the struggle. Besides, it was

The intervention of Communist China

The war in Vietnam

American intervention in the Vietnam war

argued that America had the responsibility under the Truman Doctrine of "containing" communism wherever it might menace the independence of self-governing nations. Communist China, it was held, was threatening to overrun all of Southeast Asia. The defeat of South Vietnam would simply be a prelude to the fall of Thailand, Burma, and perhaps India. China, by giving aid and encouragement to North Vietnam, was considered the real source of aggression. Little account was taken of the fact that the war was in considerable measure a civil war. The Viet Cong in South Vietnam had the obvious support of a large proportion of the population in a struggle against corrupt and dictatorial rulers. Overlooked also was the possibility that China was really following a course parallel to that of

War in Vietnam. U.S. Infantrymen leave their helicopter and head into the jungle near Ben Suo.

the United States. The whole Western Hemisphere had long been regarded by the American government as a United States sphere of influence. Any attempt by overseas powers to gain a foothold in South America, the Caribbean, or Central America was deeply resented by the United States, as evidenced by the Cuban crisis in 1962. To the Chinese U.S. intervention in Vietnam may well have appeared to be an effort to penetrate their own sphere of influence.

4. THE NEUTRAL OR UNALIGNED CAMP

By no means all of the nations of the world in the 1960's were definitely aligned in the Western "democratic" bloc or in the Eastern communist alliance. More than two score considered themselves neutral or non-aligned nations. But this classification does not necessarily mean a total lack of feeling for either side. Perhaps, as a noted Irish statesman said in 1939, with respect to a different power antagonism, it depended "upon whom you are neutral against." The majority of the members of the neutralist camp in the 1960's were

Neutralism
defined

669

probably procommunist, or at least anti-Western, in their sympathies. Yet others, for example Ireland, Sweden, Israel, and Switzerland, seemed clearly to prefer the triumph of the West. What neutralism really meant was the refusal of a nation to give unequivocal support to one or the other great-power combination or to agree that either held the key to the salvation of the world in its own self-righteous hands. It did not mean that a government and the majority of its subjects must be completely neutral in thought and deed between the two rivals for world supremacy.

India and Nehru

The most important of the neutralist nations—up to the mid-1960's, at least—was India. She was commonly regarded as the leader of the nonaligned nations, and both East and West courted her favors. Her wealth of resources, enormous population, and geographic position would have sufficed alone to magnify her influence. In addition, she had the prestige of her Prime Minister, Jawaharlal Nehru, who was widely respected as a statesman, philosopher, and hero of India's struggle for independence. In matters of foreign policy Nehru was not always consistent. Professedly a pacifist and a follower of Gandhi's philosophy of nonviolence, he seemed determined to acquire Kashmir in defiance of the wishes of Pakistan, and to use force if necessary to ensure success. In 1961 he seized Goa, the Portuguese enclave on the west coast of India, by methods that could hardly be described as nonviolent. Far from being completely neutral, he displayed a marked cordiality toward the communist bloc, as evidenced by his endorsement of the Khrushchev principle of "peaceful coexistence," his support of Soviet disarmament proposals, and his deferential attitude toward Communist China—at least before the invasion of Tibet and India's frontier in the Himalaya region. At the same time, he was one of the staunchest opponents of colonialism and one of the most valiant defenders of the United Nations and other instruments of international cooperation. His role as a mediator on the international scene may in time be taken up by his daughter, Indira Gandhi, who was chosen Prime Minister of India in 1965 and reelected in 1967.

Yugoslavia
and Tito

The most baffling of the nations pursuing neutralist policies was probably Yugoslavia. At the end of World War II the country was considered just another satellite of the Soviet Union. The Communist party was in firm control, and its leader, Marshal Tito (Josip Brosz), had studied communist ideology and tactics in Moscow. In 1948, however, the Kremlin denounced the policies of Yugoslavia's Communist party as "heresies." Instead of recanting as erring Communists were supposed to do, Tito condemned the Soviet charges as "unjust fabrications," and defended his own policies as completely in harmony with Marxist-Leninist doctrine. This controversy was followed by a limited flirtation of Yugoslavia with Western nations. Her leaders never repudiated communism, but they entered into a series of trade agreements with Western powers. As a reward their government received a limited amount of military assistance. The accession of Khrushchev as Secretary of the Communist party of the Soviet Union brought conciliatory gestures to Yugoslavia. In 1955 he and Bulganin, the Soviet Premier, visited President Tito and apologized for the mistreatment of his country. They promised "to do anything necessary" to normalize relations between the two nations. The Yugoslavs responded with cordiality, but at the same time they made clear that their government had no thought of joining either power bloc. Instead, it would continue to support "all trends toward peace and the peaceful elimination or blunting of antagonisms between blocs." By the 1960's Tito had come to be regarded as one of the foremost leaders of the neutralist camp.

5. NEW NATIONS AND OLD

The political history of the contemporary world since 1945 has been remarkable in several ways. World War II did less directly than World War I to create new nations. It did, however, inspire colonialist revolts that brought a considerable number of new independent states into existence. We have seen that within a short time after the end of the war native rebellions established sovereign governments in India, Indonesia, Pakistan, and Israel. Meanwhile, and during the period following, colonies of European powers in Africa were asserting and making good their independence.

Revolts against colonialism

If any one country could be considered the leader of the African colonial revolt, it was Ghana, formerly called the Gold Coast, a colony of Great Britain. In 1954 Britain granted self-government, and in 1960 Ghana became a republic. Leadership of the Ghana independence movement was supplied by Kwame Nkrumah. The son of an illiterate goldsmith, he obtained an education in the United States and in England. He returned to his homeland in 1948 and became a nationalist agitator. Though he classified himself as a Marxist, he denied being a Communist. Yet he admired Lenin and generally looked to Moscow for support of his policies rather than to London or Washington. Apparently the key to his thinking was opposition to imperialism. He considered it preposterous that the Negroes of Central Africa, with their proud traditions of an ancient culture, should be ruled by Europeans. He regaled his followers with stories of a Golden Age in Africa, whose cultural center was in Timbuctoo, with a great university manned by distinguished scholars. In February 1966, Nkrumah was deposed while on a visit to Peking by a clique of army officers. They charged him with inefficiency, extravagance, and pro-communist sympathies.

Ghana, the leader of the African revolt

The most violent of the colonial revolts in northern and central Africa occurred in Algeria and the Belgian Congo. The revolt in Algeria has been covered in a preceding chapter. Faced with the danger of a violent outbreak in the Congo, Belgium made the

The revolt in the Congo

former colony an independent republic in 1960. Scarcely had this transpired when civil war broke out. In July 1960, the southeastern province of Katanga seceded and organized a separate republic. Here were located rich copper resources controlled by Belgian capitalists. The latter were in no mood to surrender control of their wealth to native nationalists. The Republic of the Congo obtained help from the United Nations to force the secessionists to abandon their schemes. After a delay of more than a year punctuated by bloody battles and assassinations, they finally surrendered. Disorders, however, continued, and in November 1965, a *coup* staged by the military overturned the last of the civilian governments.

Most of the other emergent states of northern and central Africa have also been rife with disorder. In a two-month period in late 1965 and early 1966 no fewer than six independent governments were overturned by military cliques. The reasons had little to do with communism or any other ideology. In fact, attempts of the Chinese Communists to win followers in Africa accomplished little and were largely abandoned. The causes of strife and discontent were more closely related to primitivism, poverty, and political inexperience than to any form of radicalism. Such states as the Central African Republic and Upper Volta were plunged from a tribal, stone-age society into the twentieth century, and were unable to make the necessary adjustments. The French gave their former colonies independence overnight, with little or no attempt to provide the necessary political training. By contrast, Britain brought her African colonies to independence more gradually. Many of their leaders were educated at the London School of Economics, where they learned ideas suitable for application in advanced economies. Efforts by such men as Nkrumah to implement these ideas in underdeveloped nations like Ghana resulted in inflation, near-bankruptcy, and frustration. Even in Nigeria, where the proportion of British-trained officials was unusually high, the familiar charges of corruption and inefficiency led to the murder of the Premier and the overthrow of the government by military leaders in January 1966.

Political conditions in South Africa in recent years have presented an altogether different picture from those in the northern and central portions. The latter are native states, inhabited and ruled almost exclusively by Negroes. The former has small minorities of white settlers ruling over vast populations of native blacks. Although the Union of South Africa has been self-governing since 1910, its rulers alternated between moderate and extreme policies of dealing with the natives until 1948. In that year an extremist party known as the Nationalists gained control of the government. Their program was both anti-British and anti-Negro. They demanded complete severance of all ties with Great Britain, including withdrawal from the Commonwealth of Nations. In 1961 they proclaimed South Africa an independent republic. They tried to make Afrikaans rather than

MEDITERRANEAN SEA

MOROCCO
TUNISIA
IFNI (Sp.)
SPANISH
SAHARA
ALGERIA
LIBYA
U.A.R.
(EGYPT)
RED SEA

MAURITANIA
NIGER
CHAD
SUDAN
MALI
SENEGAL
GAMBIA
UPPER
VOLTA
GUINEA
PORT. GUINEA
SIERRA LEONE
IVORY
COAST
GHANA
LIBERIA
TOGO
DAHOMEY
NIGERIA
CAMEROON
CENTRAL AFRICAN
REPUBLIC
FR. SOMALILAND
ETHIOPIA
SOMALIA

RÍO MUNI
(Sp.)
GABON
CONGO REPUBLIC
DEMOCRATIC
REPUBLIC
OF THE CONGO
UGANDA
KENYA
RWANDA
BURUNDI
CABINDA
(Port.)
TANZANIA
ZANZIBAR

ATLANTIC

OCEAN

ANGOLA
(Port.)
ZAMBIA
MALAWI
MOZAMBIQUE
(Port.)
MALAGASY
REPUBLIC
SOUTH-WEST
AFRICA
(South
Africa)
BOTSWANA
RHODESIA

Independent before 1945

Independent since 1945

Remaining dependent

SWAZILAND
REPUBLIC
OF
SOUTH AFRICA
LESOTHO

INDIAN

OCEAN

0   1000 miles

THE NEW AFRICA · 1969

English the exclusive language of the country. For the natives they
instituted an extreme policy of *apartheid*, or segregation. Natives
were forced to live in "reserved" areas, subjected to a rigid curfew,
and were deprived of all rights to freedom of assemblage, speech,
and press. Conditions in the other major area of southern Africa,
Rhodesia, were somewhat similar. The Federation of Rhodesia and
Nyasaland, established by the British in 1953, reached the end of its
stormy history ten years later. Northern Rhodesia became independent in 1964 and renamed itself the Republic of Zambia. Nyasa-

Problems in
South Africa

673

Negro Slums in South Africa. In the Republic of South Africa, where blacks outnumber whites by more than 3 to 1, race segregation creates monumental problems. Many blacks live in shanty towns, undrained and unwatered, like the one shown on the outskirts of Johannesburg.

land also became independent the same year, under the name Malawi. Although Southern Rhodesia proclaimed its independence, Britain refused to grant it unless the white minority extended voting rights to include a majority of native Africans. When the Rhodesians ignored these conditions and proceeded with their plan for independence, Great Britain, with the support of the United States, imposed economic sanctions. By 1967 it appeared that the white supremacists of Southern Rhodesia might actually achieve their aim of independence or merge their country with the racist republic of South Africa.

The most successful of the emergent nations in the post-World War II period were undoubtedly Israel and Egypt. In 1948 Great Britain terminated its mandate over Palestine, withdrew its troops, and permitted the establishment of an independent Republic of Israel. A constitution was drawn up providing for a weak President, a strong cabinet, and a powerful parliament. The constitution also provided for proportional representation and universal suffrage for Jews and Arabs alike. Despite these liberal provisions, warfare broke out between Jews and Arabs. Though a truce was signed in 1949, border raids and other acts of violence continued for many years. But they were not sufficiently serious to prevent some remarkable economic progress in Israel. New industries were created. Top-ranking universities and research institutes were established. Irrigation and reforestation projects were carried out. Agriculture advanced to a

The Republic of Israel

674

stage sufficient to supply the needs of the home market, while export crops such as melons, olives, and citrus fruits were rapidly developed. Land under cultivation more than doubled between 1955
and 1967. Israel has had the notable advantage of an inflow of large
sums of money into the country in the form of American contributions and West German restitution for the outrages of Nazism.

Although Britain proclaimed Egypt an independent and sovereign
state in 1922, the British were slow in relinquishing control over the
country. In 1936 they concluded with Egypt a Treaty of Friendship
and Alliance, by which they agreed to remove their troops from
Cairo and Alexandria in return for Egyptian recognition of Britain's
right to defend the Suez Canal. This did not satisfy the Egyptian
nationalists. In 1951 they persuaded their government to abrogate
the Treaty of 1936, and soon afterward they compelled the British
to withdraw all their troops from Egyptian territory. In 1952 a
coterie of nationalist army officers seized control of the government. They deposed the playboy king, Farouk, alleged to be subservient to the British, and proclaimed the state a republic. The
government was headed at first by General Mohammed Naguib,
who was succeeded two years later by Lieutenant-Colonel Gamal
Abdel Nasser. The new leaders inaugurated a program of sweeping
reforms. Compulsory education was ordered for all children between the ages of seven and twelve. Landholdings were limited to
200 acres, and large estates were to be broken up and redistributed.
To make more land available the government decided upon the construction of the Aswan High Dam, a gigantic reservoir to back up
the waters of the Upper Nile and provide irrigation for 2 million
acres of arable land. Various decrees in 1961 nationalized about 90
per cent of industry and further reduced landholdings to 100 acres.
But these and other economic reforms would avail little as long as
the demographic imbalance remained uncorrected. In the mid-1960's
Egypt's birthrate was over 40 per thousand and her death rate about
18 per thousand.

*Israeli Tanks Move Into Jeru-
salem* during second Arab-Israeli war, June 1967.

Partly because of failure to solve internal problems Egypt became one of the most aggressive of the new nations. President Nasser aspired to leadership of all the Arabs of the Middle East. His immediate objectives were mainly two: to eliminate "Western imperialism" from the Middle East and to destroy or seriously cripple the Republic of Israel. In 1956 he nationalized all the British and French banks in his country and seized the Suez Canal. In retaliation the British and French encouraged the Israelis to invade Egypt and followed the invasion with an attack of their own. The fighting ended five days later when the participants accepted a U.N. appeal for a cease-fire in response to pressure from the United States and the Soviet Union.

An even more serious crisis developed in the summer of 1967. Taking advantage of a border conflict between Syria and Israel, Nasser closed the Gulf of Aqaba, Israel's only direct outlet to the Red Sea. The Israelis responded with a lightning war against Egypt and her Arab allies. The Egyptian and Jordanian forces were routed in 84 hours. The Syrians accepted a cease-fire two days later. The ultimate results of these climactic events were uncertain. For the moment all semblance of a balance of forces in the Middle East had vanished. The Arab world was in disarray. High officials in Israel were demanding compensations, especially in Jerusalem, and avowing that their country would never return to the status quo preceding the war. The U.S.S.R., having supported the Arabs, was disgruntled and belligerent. Her government severed relations with Israel and used the United Nations as a forum for vilification of the United States. Wise statesmanship and restraint among all the nations concerned seemed imperative to avert even graver crises in the future.

The new states of Southeast Asia have some apparent advantages over those of Africa. Besides containing great stores of strategic raw materials, they normally produce a surplus of foodstuffs and—in comparison with India, China, and Japan—are underpopulated. However, their progress toward political stability and economic development has been hampered by the fact that they were catapulted from the age of colonialism into that of Cold War rivalries. Billions of dollars' worth of "aid" poured into this region has gone mostly to feed military establishments. The Malay Federation, a successful union of eleven states formerly under British rule, in 1963 expanded into the Federation of Malaysia, which combined Malaya and most of the British-controlled portions of the island of Borneo. Indonesia, with a population in excess of 100 million, is the largest and potentially richest state of Southeast Asia. Under the colorful but erratic leadership of President Sukarno, a hero of the struggle for independence against the Dutch, Indonesia assumed an aggressive role in Asian politics, seizing West Irian (former Dutch New Guinea) in 1962 and carrying on a three-year "Crush

Malaysia" campaign against the British-backed Federation (1963–1966). Sukarno's reckless policies brought both economic disaster and internal discord. An abortive coup on September 30, 1965, attributed to the Communists, led to the imposition of a military regime which gradually stripped Sukarno of all his powers. The Indonesian Communist party—the third largest such party in the world—was shattered, but at the price of a reign of terror lasting several months and a bloodbath that took the lives of at least half a million people.

Indochina, a focal point in the East-West power struggle, has remained the most distressed area in all of Southeast Asia. The Vietnam war—appalling in its brutality—not only foreshadowed the possibility of the total destruction of a country but also threatened to erupt into World War III after the United States sent ground forces to supplement the ineffectual South Vietnamese army and began to bomb North Vietnam. A world holocaust seemed to be held in abeyance by nothing more substantial than disaffection between the two major Communist powers. China, sworn enemy of American "imperialists," was quite willing to see the Vietnam war protracted, so long as it drained American resources without leading to an invasion of China; and Peking gave only moral support to the North Vietnamese. On the other hand, the Soviet government, more inclined toward a rapprochement with the United States and negotiation of the conflict, felt constrained to match American escalation with increased military assistance to North Vietnam. Meanwhile, the war inevitably impinged upon the other states of Indochina. Laos was ruptured by conflict between Right-wing and Left-wing factions, abetted by the great powers, who had pledged themselves to uphold a neutralist regime. Thailand, theoretically a constitutional monarchy and proud of its long history of independence, became in effect a military outpost of the United States.

Indochina and the Vietnam war

Early hopes for the achievement of solidarity among the states of Asia and Africa have remained unfulfilled. The most dramatic attempt to give substance to this ideal was the Asian-African Conference held at Bandung, Indonesia, in 1955, where twenty-nine nations joined in a display of friendship and dedication to humane objectives. While the internationalism envisioned by the Bandung Conference has failed to materialize, some progress has been made toward economic co-operation. The so-called Colombo Plan, originated in 1950, arranges loans and technical assistance for underdeveloped areas. In addition to the Commonwealth countries and the United States, most of the non-Communist states of Asia have participated in the Plan, either as donors or as recipients. An Asian Development Bank, capitalized at $1 billion, was formally inaugurated in August 1966 with headquarters in Manila.

The Bandung Conference; the Colombo Plan

If the Southeast Asian states have failed to establish a common identity, they have resisted being drawn into the power blocs of

CONFRONTATION IN ASIA

Countries aligned with
the United States

Communist countries

Unaligned countries

U.S.S.R.

KURIL ISLANDS

Ulan-Bator ★

MONGOLIA

MANCHURIA

Vladivostok

Amur R.

Yalu R.

N. KOREA

Pyongyang 38°

Peking ★

Seoul
S. KOREA
Pusan

JAPAN

★ Tokyo

Osaka

Hiroshima

Nagasaki

SHANTUNG
PENIN.

YELLOW
SEA

Yellow R.

EAST CHINA

C H I N A

Nanking

SEA

Shanghai

Chungking

Yangtze R.

RYUKYU ISLANDS

OKINAWA

PACIFIC

TIBET

BHUTAN

INDIA

Taipei

OCEAN

E. PAKISTAN

Calcutta

Mandalay

BURMA

Canton

TAIWAN

Hong Kong
Macao

PESCADORES IS.

BAY OF

Rangoon ★

Hanoi
Haiphong

*G. of
Tonkin*

LAOS

HAINAN

BENGAL

Vientiane ★

N. VIETNAM

17°

THAILAND

Mekong R.

Hue

Da Nang

Bangkok ★

Qui Nhon

Manila ★ Quezon City

REPUBLIC

CAMBODIA

S. VIETNAM

OF THE

INDIAN

Phnom Penh ★

★ Saigon

Cebu

PHILIPPINES

SOUTH   CHINA   SEA

Davao

Jesselton

SABAH
(N. BORNEO)

Medan

FEDERATION   OF   MALAYSIA

Equator 0°

MALAYA

BRUNEI

WEST IRIAN
(NEW GUINEA)

Kuala Lumpur ★

Kuching

SARAWAK

0°

SUMATRA

★ Singapore

KALIMANTAN
(BORNEO)

SULAWESI
(CELEBES)

CERAM

OCEAN

Palembang

Bandjarmasin

R E P U B L I C   O F   I N D O N E S I A

Makassar

Djakarta ★

Bandung

JAVA

Surabaja

TIMOR

0   1000 miles

AUSTRALIA

the world's superstates. A Southeast Asia Defense Treaty
(SEATO), organized by the United States in 1954 as a counterpart
of NATO, proved to be neither popular nor effective. Only three
of the eight members of SEATO are Asian states (Thailand, Pakistan, and the Philippines); by 1967 both France and Pakistan had
virtually withdrawn from the alliance. Nor have the attempts of
Moscow and Peking to shape the political destinies of Asian countries been any more successful than those of the Western powers.
China's prestige among the peripheral states of the continent declined after the Sino-Indian border war of 1962 and reached a nadir
during the chaotic period of China's proletarian cultural revolution.
While the intervention of outside powers may have momentous
consequences for the peoples of Southeast Asia, its ability to effect
ideological change seems negligible. The destruction of the Indonesian Communist party—a significant rebuff to Peking—was an
internal affair, accomplished without any assistance from the West.
And it would be difficult to prove that the United States' enormous
military expenditure in Vietnam has restricted communism or advanced democracy in any part of Indochina. The most potent ideology among the states of Southeast Asia, as among those of Africa
and the Middle East, is nationalism. Ho Chi Minh rose to prominence not as a Communist but as a leader of the movement for national independence; in his struggle against the French he received
help from many non-Communists, including Nationalist Chinese.
The aspirations of Asians for both economic progress and independence were expressed perhaps most eloquently by Prince Norodom
Sihanouk of Cambodia, who set for his tiny country an almost im-
possibly difficult course. Proclaiming a policy of "active neutrality," he urged the great powers to respect a buffer zone in Indochina, declined Communist offers of military assistance, and in 1963
ended a United States aid program on the ground that its terms
were incompatible with his nation's sovereignty.

Not only the newer nations underwent radical transformations in
the period following World War II, but a number of the older ones
as well. Britain liquidated most of her empire, but she compensated
at least in part for this by internal progress. By 1965 her index of
industrial production had increased 30 per cent in a seven-year period. Unemployment had fallen to 307,000, less than 1.3 per cent of
the total labor force. An extensive National Health Service had been
set up, providing free hospital, medical, and dental service to all inhabitants regardless of need or economic status. The government of
Britain had been made more democratic with the provision permitting women to occupy seats in the House of Lords as well as in
the House of Commons, and with the reduction of the two-year
suspensive veto of the House of Lords to one year.

As had been true for more than a century, political evolution in
France was more tumultuous than in Great Britain. The French

Third Republic was a casualty of the war. It was replaced in 1946 by a Fourth Republic, designed to make cabinets less unstable. But the new government survived only twelve years; it was weaker than its architects intended. During its short existence more than a score of Premiers followed one another in quick succession. In 1958 a band of French generals, disgusted with the inability of the government to suppress a revolt in Algeria, flew to Paris, overturned the Fourth Republic, and supplanted it with a provisional dictatorship under Charles de Gaulle. A short time later a constitution, written by de Gaulle, was approved by the voters. It established the Fifth Republic with de Gaulle as its first President. Executive power was more highly concentrated than at any time since the reign of Napoleon III. The President was given authority to appoint the Premier, to dissolve parliament, and to assume dictatorial powers in a national emergency. De Gaulle proceeded to sponsor foreign policies quite different from those of his predecessors. Conceiving of the role of France in old-fashioned nationalist terms, he attempted to make the country the leader of a "Third Force" in Europe. He aspired to organize the nation as a formidable nuclear power and to repudiate the leadership of the United States in dealing with both Germany and the Soviet Union.

Changes in the political system of the United States during the postwar period resulted from both formal and informal processes. Exemplifying the former were four constitutional amendments. The Twenty-second Amendment prohibited any person from being lawfully elected President more than twice, and provided that no person succeeding to the office for more than two years could subsequently be elected President more than once. The Twenty-third Amendment gave to residents of the District of Columbia the right of suffrage in Presidential elections. The Twenty-fourth outlawed the requirement of a poll tax as a condition for voting in federal elections. The Twenty-fifth specified the conditions under which the inability of the President to perform the duties of his office could be determined, and provided for the exercise of Presidential powers by the .Vice President during such period of inability. Of equal consequence were the changes accomplished by ordinary legislation. During the administrations of Harry S. Truman, Dwight D. Eisenhower, John F. Kennedy, and Lyndon B. Johnson, Congress enacted numerous statutes that went far toward making the United States a welfare state. The Social Security System, originally established during the New Deal, was extended to include professional men and the self-employed. Unemployment insurance was expanded to cover practically all workers in industry, though almost none in agriculture. Minimum wages were raised from $.40 an hour in 1938 to $1.40 in 1967; agricultural workers were excluded from these benefits. In addition, Congress appropriated vast sums for highway construction, for loans to students, and for the relief of impoverished areas throughout the country. Most of this welfare legislation was enacted at the behest of the successive Presidents. Indeed, one of the outstanding features of United States history since 1933 was the growth in power of the national executive. Congress receded into the background as each new President, except Eisenhower, launched his special New Deal, Fair Deal, New Frontier, or Great Society program. Although some of their provisions encountered opposition, there was seldom much doubt as to their final passage. Postwar Presidents almost invariably had substantial majorities of their own party in Congress. Moreover, the prestige and power of the Presidential office were so high that it was difficult to deny the incumbent anything he demanded. As democratic opportunities multiplied and the standard of living rose, there seemed to be an increasing tendency to attribute such boons to the one man at the head of the government. As a consequence, the President of the United States soon emerged as the most powerful ruler in the Free World. Actually, his power at least equalled that of any of the dictators. It should be noted, however, that not all progressive measures emanated from the Chief Executive. The Supreme Court, in the postwar period, was the foremost champion of civil rights for the Negro and of freedom of the press, speech, and religion.

6. THE THREAT TO WESTERN HEGEMONY

No conclusion seemed more obvious, twenty years after World War II, than that the supremacy of the Western powers over the earth was approaching its end. Few powers existed any longer that could make a pretense of maintaining such supremacy. The colonial empires of the West European states had mostly disintegrated or been abandoned. Alone among Western nations, the United States had the wealth and the technological advancement to guide or control many peoples outside her boundaries. How long this would continue, no one could accurately predict. Although Soviet Russia had lost some of its earlier revolutionary dynamism, the Soviets still had ambitions to shape the destinies of underdeveloped nations in many parts of the world. Overshadowing Russia was the specter of an aggressive China, even more deeply committed to revolutionary goals in lands where poverty and disease stalked their victims interminably.

The decline of the Western empires and the rise of Russia and China

The menace of the big communist powers was not exclusively military or ideological. The underdeveloped nations generally, and especially the former colonies of Western empires, had been the chief victims of the population explosion. It was not the thundering hoofbeats of some modern Attila's cavalry that made these nations an easy prey to conquest but the "terrible patter of tiny feet." The population of the world was about 3 billion in the mid-1960's. Reli-

Plight of the underdeveloped nations

able estimates say that by 1980 it will be 4 billion. Eighty-five per cent of this increase will occur in the underdeveloped countries, which cannot support even their present populations. What will these hungry millions do? They will not starve peacefully and quietly as their ancestors might have done. They know there is a better life possible, and they will fight and riot, if necessary, to achieve it. Many of these countries have come to believe that China and Soviet Russia can do more to help them than the Western nations they think of as their former oppressors. National pride is a factor in their rebellion also, and, to a considerable extent, race. It is not a coincidence that most of the underdeveloped nations belong to the colored races, even though the Asian Indians are technically classified as Caucasian.

Yet the thesis that the West is bound to be toppled from its pinnacle is not indisputable. Even if we assume that the United States must almost alone bear the burden of maintaining Western hegemony, the cards are not necessarily stacked for her failure. The resources of America are so great and her technical skills so advanced that she could probably support the underdeveloped nations for a long enough time to enable them to feed themselves. This would involve supplying them not only with surplus food but also with farm machinery, and especially with fertilizers and the means of controlling their fantastic birthrates. Many obstacles would stand in the way. There is the danger of an overextension of American power into regions so distant and with such complex problems that effective control would be almost impossible. The people of India, for example, speak fourteen different languages, and the overwhelming majority are illiterate. Lack of foreign exchange prevents the governments of these countries from purchasing large quantities of grain from the outside, while free distribution might so profoundly disturb national economies as to make the remedy as bad as the disease. No panacea is readily available. Military containment of communist imperialism is no more than a partial answer. The "revolution of rising expectations" does not depend upon sparks from communism to kindle it into flames!

SELECTED READINGS

· *Items so designated are available in paperbound editions.*

· Almond, G. A., *The Appeals of Communism*, Princeton, 1954 (Princeton University Press).

· Aron, Raymond, *The Century of Total War*, Boston, 1955 (Beacon). The world today in historical perspective.

Barghoorn, F. C., *Soviet Russian Nationalism*, New York, 1956.

Berger, Earl, *The Covenant and the Sword: Arab-Israeli Relations, 1948–1956*, Toronto, 1965. Impartial.

Cady, J. F., *Southeast Asia: Its Historical Development*, New York, 1964.

Dallin, D. J., *The Changing World of Soviet Russia*, New Haven, 1956. A penetrating analysis from a conservative viewpoint.

Drucker, P. F., *The End of Economic Man*, New York, 1939. A really profound study of modern man's predicament.

Fleming, D. F., *The Cold War and Its Origins, 1917–1960*, Garden City, N.Y., 1961, 2 vols. A radical interpretation. Places the blame for the Cold War on the Western allies.

· Gatzke, H. W., *The Present in Perspective*, 3d ed., New Haven, 1965 (Rand McNally).

· Halpern, Manfred, *The Politics of Social Change in the Middle East and North Africa*, Princeton, 1963 (Princeton University Press).

Hammer, E. J., *The Struggle for Indochina*, Stanford, 1954.

Holborn, Hajo, *The Political Collapse of Europe*, New York, 1951.

Hoskins, H. L., *The Middle East*, New York, 1954.

Issawi, Charles, *Egypt in Revolution: An Economic Analysis*, New York, 1963.

Laski, H. J., *Reflections on the Revolution of Our Time*, New York, 1943. A discerning analysis not seriously marred by a Marxist viewpoint.

· Leckie, Robert, *Conflict: The History of the Korean War*, New York, 1962 (Avon). Emphasizes military history.

Lenczowski, George, *The Middle East in World Affairs*, Ithaca, N.Y., 1956.

Lie, Trygve, *In the Cause of Peace: Seven Years with the United Nations*, New York, 1954.

Low, Francis, *The Struggle for Asia*, New York, 1956.

Lyon, Peter, *Neutralism*, New York, 1963.

McCune, Shannon, *Korea's Heritage: A Regional and Social Geography*, Tokyo, 1956.

Macmillan, W. M., *Bantu, Boer, and Briton*, New York, 1963.

Mannheim, Karl, *Diagnosis of Our Time*, New York, 1944. A thoughtful study.

· Mosely, Philip, *The Kremlin and World Politics*, New York, 1961 (Vintage).

Neumann, Sigmund, *The Future in Perspective*, New York, 1943.

· Popper, K. R., *The Open Society and Its Enemies*, New York, 1962 (Torchbook). A vigorous comparison of the totalitarian and democratic philosophies.

· Reves, Emery, *The Anatomy of Peace*, New York, 1945 (Compass). The most eloquent of pleas for a world republic.

· Roberts, H. L., *Russia and America*, New York, 1956 (Mentor). An objective analysis.

Robinson, R. D., *The First Turkish Republic*, Cambridge, Mass., 1963.

· Seton-Watson, Hugh, *Neither War nor Peace: The Struggle for Power in the Post-War World*, London, 1960 (Frederick A. Praeger, rev. ed.).

Warth, R. D., *Soviet Russia in World Politics*, New York, 1963.

Wertheim, W. F., *Indonesian Society in Transition*, New York, 1956.

Williams, Philip, *Politics in Post-War France*, London, 1954.

Wilmot, Chester, *The Struggle for Europe*, New York, 1952.

Wilson, C. M., *Oil across the World*, New York, 1946.

Young, Crawford, *Politics in the Congo: Decolonization and Independence*, Princeton, 1965.

SOURCE MATERIALS

Roosevelt, F. D., "The Four Freedoms," *Congressional Record*, Vol. 87, pp. 46–47.

U.N. Dept. of Public Information, *Yearbook of the United Nations*.

Werner, M. R., *Stalin's Kampf*, New York, 1940.

CHAPTER 22

Twentieth-Century Culture

By far the most inportant consequence of the conceptual revolution brought about in physics by relativity and the quantum theory lies not in such details as that meter sticks shorten when they move or that simultaneous position and momentum have no meaning, but in the insight that we had not been using our minds properly and that it is important to find out how to do so. . . . This task is not to be accomplished by any "return" to the insights of the past. The insight that there is any problem here at all is devastatingly new in human history.

—P. W. Bridgman, "Quo Vadis"

Politically, economically, and socially the twentieth century thus far has constituted one of the most critical periods of modern history. It has been an age of wars and upheavals that have threatened the destruction of some of our most basic ideals and institutions. Some, in fact, did virtually go under in the devastating flood of barbarism and unreason that characterized much of the period. The early years of the century saw a continuation of many of the trends begun during the late decades of the nineteenth century. Perhaps one can say that this was true of ideals such as optimism, confidence in reason as an instrument of knowledge, and faith in the beneficence of science. To be sure, philosophies such as Pragmatism had attacked the old metaphysics hallowed from the time of Aristotle, and had cast doubt on the ability of the human mind to discover ultimate truth. Yet philosophers like F. H. Bradley could still write of the universe as a "star-domed city of God ruled by benevolent purpose," if only bewildered man would follow the proper methods of apprehending its reality. The novelist H. G. Wells and the playwright George Bernard Shaw exuded a sublime confidence in science and in social reform to reshape man's environment and to enable him quickly to solve his most serious problems. But there were rumblings of a distant thunder which forced men to question

Trends in the early twentieth century

685

their views along many of these lines. Early in the century Sigmund Freud evolved his psychoanalytic theory, which portrayed man's behavior as chiefly instinctual rather than rational. No longer could human nature be conceived as inherently good. The subconscious mind, with its egoistic impulses and suppressed desires, was more important than the conscious mind in determining man's thoughts and actions.

The year 1914 rather than 1900 must be regarded as the primary watershed dividing the cultural history of the contemporary world from that of the past. The philosophical tendencies toward skepticism and pessimism that had made their appearance during the early years of the century became really sweeping and dominant after 1914. The desperate and unprecedented conditions of World War I were in large measure responsible. Millions of young men who might have been the carriers of faith and hope died in the trenches. Civilians on both sides whipped up their hatred with atrocity stories and damned the cultural achievements of their enemies. The passions of the war distorted the thinking of countless individuals and led them to conceive of their world as chaotic and irrational.

1.   REVOLUTIONARY DEVELOPMENTS IN SCIENCE

Most of the foundations of contemporary science were laid at the end of the nineteenth century and the beginning of the twentieth. It was during that period that the atom was protrayed as a miniature solar system instead of a solid particle, that the phenomenon of radioactivity was discovered, and that the ether hypothesis was exploded. It was during the same period that psychoanalysis was founded, that the germ theory of disease was fully confirmed, and that the laws of heredity were formulated. A climax of the revolution in the physical sciences was reached with the publication of the Einstein theories. Originally issued in limited form in 1905, they were expanded into a more general application ten years later. Einstein challenged not merely the older conceptions of matter but practically the entire structure of traditional physics. The doctrine for which he is most noted is his principle of relativity. During the greater part of the nineteenth century, physicists had assumed that space and motion were absolute. Space was supposed to be filled with an intangible substance known as *ether*, which provided the medium for the undulations of light. The planets also moved in it like ships sailing in definite courses over the bounding main. The motion of the heavenly bodies was therefore to be measured by reference to this more or less static ether, just as the speed of a vehicle could be measured in terms of the distance traveled on a highway. But elaborate experiments performed by English and American physicists in 1887 virtually exploded the ether hypothesis. Einstein then set to work to reconstruct the scheme of the universe in accordance with an altogether different pattern. He maintained that space and motion, instead of being absolute, are relative to each other. Objects have not merely three dimensions but four. To the familiar length, breadth, and thickness, Einstein added a new dimension of *time* and represented all four as fused in a synthesis which he called the *space-time continuum*. In this way he sought to explain the idea that mass is dependent upon motion. Bodies traveling at high velocity have different proportions of extension and mass from what they would have at rest. Included also in the Einstein physics is the conception of a finite universe—that is, finite in space. The region of matter does not extend into infinity, but the universe has

Albert Einstein (*1879–1955*). From the portrait head by the noted American sculptor, Jo Davidson.

limits. While these are by no means definite boundaries, there is at least a region beyond which nothing exists. Space curves back upon itself so as to make of the universe a gigantic sphere within which are contained galaxies, solar systems, stars, and planets.

The Einstein theories had a major influence in precipitating other revolutionary developments in physics. By 1960 it had been discovered that the conception of the subatomic world as a miniature solar system was much too simple. The atom was found to contain not only positively charged protons and negatively charged electrons, but *positrons*, or positively charged electrons; *neutrons*, which carry no electric charges; and *mesons*, which may be either negative or positive. Mesons, it was discovered, exist not only within the atom (for about two millionths of a second) but are major components of the cosmic rays that are constantly bombarding the earth from somewhere in outer space. A recent hypothesis assumes the existence of a *neutral* meson that has a "life" of only one one-hundredth of a sextillionth of a second, but which, in disintegrating, is con-

More recent discoveries regarding matter and energy

The principle
of indeterminacy

verted into the energy that holds the universe together.

Even before the discovery of neutrons, positrons, and mesons the world within the atom had ceased, for many scientists, to be a world whose actions could be predicted on the basis of natural laws. In 1927 the German physicist Werner Heisenberg worked out his famous *principle of indeterminacy*, based upon his discovery that individual electrons do not appear to follow any definite laws of cause and effect, but jump from one orbit to another without apparent reason. He seemed therefore to be suggesting that the old mechanistic principle of universal causation was no longer entirely valid. The phenomena of the subatomic world could not be predicted with certainty but could be dealt with only in terms of *probability*, in essentially the same way as a life insurance company compiles actuarial statistics for millions of people. With the gradual acceptance of this hypothesis, the atom was reduced to a kind of "lawless abstraction" of which it was almost impossible to form a mental image.[1]

Releasing the
energy within
the atom

Several of the developments in physics outlined above helped to make possible one of the most spectacular achievements in the history of science, the splitting of the atom to release the energy contained within it. Ever since it became known that the atom is composed primarily of electrical energy, physicists had dreamed of unlocking this source of tremendous power and making it available for man. As early as 1905 Einstein became convinced of the equivalence of mass and energy and worked out a formula for the conversion of one into the other, which he expressed as follows: $E = mc^2$. E represents the energy in ergs, m the mass in grams, and c the velocity of light in centimeters per second. In other words, the amount of energy locked within the atom is equal to the mass multiplied by the square of the velocity of light. But no practical application of this formula was possible until after the discovery of the neutron by Sir James Chadwick in 1932. Since the neutron carries no charge of electricity, it is an ideal weapon for bombarding the atom. It is neither repulsed by the positively charged protons nor absorbed by the negatively charged electrons. Moreover, in the process of bombardment it produces more neutrons, which hit other atoms and cause them in turn to split and create neutrons. In this way the original reaction is repeated in an almost unending series.

Atomic fission

In 1939 two German physicists, Otto Hahn and Fritz Strassman, succeeded in splitting atoms of uranium by bombarding them with neutrons. The initial reaction produced a chain of reactions, in much the same way that a fire burning at the edge of a piece of paper raises the temperature of adjoining portions of the paper high

---

[1] It is noteworthy, however, that among the scientists who rejected this hypothesis was Einstein. He was reported, shortly before his death, to have expressed confidence that a new principle could be discovered which would reduce the whole universe to order and harmony.

enough to cause them to ignite. The potential of the neutrons employed in the splitting was only one-thirtieth of a volt, but the potential released was 200,000,000 volts. It was soon revealed that not all forms of uranium are equally valuable for the production of energy. Only the isotope 235, which forms only a tiny fraction of natural uranium, will split when bombarded with neutrons. Uranium 238, which constitutes over 99 per cent of the world supply, absorbs the neutrons and transmutes itself into neptunium and plutonium. The latter, however, behaves very much like uranium 235. That is, it does split and release great quantities of energy. More recently, the practice has developed of manufacturing plutonium in a structure known as an atomic pile, in which large quantities of uranium 238 are exposed to neutrons from uranium 235.

It is a sad commentary on modern civilization that the first use made of the knowledge of atomic fission was in the preparation of an atomic bomb. The devastating weapon was the achievement of a galaxy of scientists working for the War Department of the United States. Some were physicists who had been exiled by Nazi or Fascist oppression. By 1945 their work was completed, and in July of that year the first atomic bomb was exploded in a test conducted in the New Mexican desert near the War Department laboratory at Los Alamos. On August 6 the first atomic bomb used in warfare was dropped on the Japanese city of Hiroshima. A second bomb was unloaded on Nagasaki on August 9. The deadly effects of the new weapon almost passed belief. It was estimated that a single bomb had the explosive force of 20,000 tons of TNT. More than 100,000 people were killed in the two cities, large portions of which were literally wiped from the map. Man had at last acquired control over the basic forces of the universe, but whether he had created a Frankenstein's monster which might ultimately destroy him, no one could predict. Doleful queries were raised about what would happen in the future when the ability to produce atomic weapons would be no longer a monopoly of Anglo-Americans. This monopoly was brought to an end in the fall of 1949, when the U.S.S.R. exploded an atomic bomb. Since then Great Britain and France have acquired atomic weapons, and so has Communist China.

Atomic weapons

Even more disturbing were the first tests of a hydrogen bomb by the United States Atomic Energy Commission in November 1952. The tests were conducted at Eniwetok Atoll in the South Pacific, and according to reports an entire island disappeared after burning brightly for several hours. The hydrogen bomb, or H-bomb, is based upon fusion of hydrogen atoms, a process which requires the enormous heat generated by the splitting of uranium atoms to start the reaction. The fusion results in the creation of a new element, helium, which actually weighs less than the sum of the hydrogen atoms. The "free" energy left over provides the tremendous explosive power of the H-bomb. The force of hydrogen bombs is meas-

The hydrogen
bomb

An H-Bomb Mushrooms. The cloud spreads into a huge mushroom following a 1952 explosion of a hydrogen bomb in the Marshall Islands of the Pacific. The photo was made 50 miles from detonation site at about 12,000 feet. The cloud rose to 40,000 feet two minutes after the explosion. Ten minutes later the cloud stem had pushed about 25 miles. The mushroom portion went up to 10 miles and spread 100 miles.

ured in *megatons*, each of which represents 1,000,000 tons of TNT. Thus a 5-megaton H-bomb would equal 250 times the power of the A-bombs dropped on Hiroshima and Nagasaki. By 1962 both the Soviet Union and the United States were conducting experimental tests, including high-altitude explosions and devices of unparalleled destructive force. In 1966 China produced her fourth atomic bomb, this time in the form of a nuclear missile that flew 400 miles to its target.

The exploration of space

On October 4, 1957, the government of the Soviet Union inaugurated a new stage in man's control of his physical environment by rocketing into space the first artificial satellite, which began circling the earth at a speed of about 18,000 miles an hour. Though it weighed nearly 200 pounds, it was propelled upward higher than 500 miles. This Russian achievement gave the English language a new word—*sputnik*, the Russian for *satellite* or *fellow traveler*. A month later the Soviet scientists surpassed their first success by sending a new and much larger sputnik to an altitude of approximately 1000 miles. Sputnik II weighed more than half a ton and contained elaborate scientific instruments and even a live dog.

Orbiting the earth

These sputniks were simply the forerunners of others of greater significance. In April 1961, the Russians succeeded in sending the first man into orbit around the earth. Four months later the Soviets achieved an even greater triumph when they sent another of their army officers in a space capsule around the earth. He remained in orbit 25 hours and encircled the earth 17½ times. Meanwhile, scientists and military specialists in the United States had been working hard on the problem of space satellites. After a number of successes with animals and "uninhabited" capsules, they finally succeeded, on February 20, 1962, in launching the first American manned spaceship into orbit around the earth. The successful astronaut was **690** Lieutenant-Colonel John H. Glenn, Jr., and he encircled the globe

three times at a top speed of over 17,000 miles per hour. In 1966
United States Navy officer Richard F. Gordon left the cabin of his
spacecraft and walked in space for 44 minutes hundreds of miles
above the earth. All over the world these successful voyages were
hailed as events of capital importance. They at least promised a vast
extension of our knowledge of outer space and would doubtless prepare the way for exploration of the moon and eventually of distant
planets. But they also had sinister aspects. The purpose that inspired

Experiment in Space Flight.
Capsule containing Astronaut
John Glenn floats in the Atlantic Ocean after he had successfully completed three orbits
around the earth. February, 1962.

them was almost exclusively to gain military advantage. It was
assumed, for example, that giant space ships or artificial satellites
hurled into orbit might enable the nation that controlled them to
dominate the earth. The fact that the Russian vehicles were much
larger than the American indicated that the Soviets had rockets of
tremendous power, which might be used to propel intercontinental
ballistic missiles. A disturbing factor for the United States and its
allies was thus added to the armaments race between East and West.
Perhaps equally unfortunate was the fact that the talents of many
brilliant scientists were being drained into "practical" projects of
nationalist competition and were no longer available for the pure research that contributes most to the advancement of knowledge.

Notable advances in the biological sciences also occurred after
World War I. An outstanding one was the discovery of the viruses.
Viruses are organisms so small that they pass through ordinary fil- Advances in
ters. Only by means of special filters made of collodion films, or by biology
the use of ultraviolet or electron microscopes, can their presence be
detected. They are the cause of a multitude of dread diseases, includ- **691**

ing smallpox, measles, infantile paralysis, influenza, rabies, yellow fever, and the common cold. No one has yet been able to say whether
they should be classified as animate or inanimate objects. In some
ways they appear to have the properties of living creatures, including the capacity to reproduce. But they are closely dependent upon
their living host, and remain completely dormant except when they
come into contact with living tissue. They seem to occupy a kind of
intermediate stage between the inorganic and organic worlds, and
are sometimes referred to as "the bridge between Life and Death."
Perhaps Aristotle was right more than twenty-two centuries ago
when he wrote: "Nature makes so gradual a transition from the
inanimate to the animate kingdom that the boundary lines which
separate them are indistinct and doubtful."

Antibiotics

From time to time during the history of medicine, discoveries
have been made which can justifiably be described as epochal, in the
sense that they open up new and much greater possibilities for the
conquest of disease. One example was the discovery of vaccination
for smallpox by Sir Edward Jenner in 1796. Another was the development and proof of the germ theory of disease by Louis Pasteur
and Robert Koch about 1881. After 1918 a series of such epochal
discoveries laid the foundations for another new era of medical
progress. In 1935 a German named Gerhard Domagk discovered the
first of the sulfa drugs, which he called sulfanilamide. Soon others
were added to the list. Each was found to be marvelously effective
in curing or checking such diseases as rheumatic fever, gonorrhea,
scarlet fever, and meningitis. About 1930 Sir Alexander Fleming described the first of the antibiotics, which came to be known as penicillin. Antibiotics are chemical agents produced by living organisms
and possessing the power to check or kill bacteria. Many have their
origin in molds, fungi, algae, and in simple organisms living in the
soil. Penicillin was eventually found to be a kind of miracle drug
producing spectacular results in the treatment of pneumonia, syphilis, peritonitis, tetanus, and numerous other maladies hitherto frequently fatal. About 1940 the second most famous of the antibiotics
—streptomycin—was discovered by Dr. Selman A. Waksman.
Streptomycin seems to hold its greatest promise in the treatment of
tuberculosis, though it has been used for numerous other infections
that do not yield to penicillin, including the bubonic plague and
tularemia, or rabbit fever. Still other antibiotics are neomycin, also
discovered by Dr. Waksman; aureomycin, effective against Rocky
Mountain fever; and chloromycetin, valuable in the treatment of
typhus and typhoid fever. Many antibiotics are now used in powerful combinations against a wide variety of human ailments. Yet another category of so-called "miracle drugs" were the tranquilizers.
Introduced in 1955, they came to be used in the treatment of mental
disorders and accomplished wonders in making violent patients
more tractable. They thus eliminated to some extent the "snake

pits," the old-fashioned mental institutions with barred windows and locked doors. Although these drugs do not themselves effect cures, they help make the patient more accessible to other forms of therapy. Tranquilizers, of course, also gained comparatively widespread usage among the population at large as antidepressants and tension relievers.

Of almost equal importance with the discovery of new drugs has been the development of means of preventing disease. For the most part these have taken the form of vaccination. A characteristic example has been the development of two types of vaccination against poliomyelitis, or infantile paralysis. The first type was discovered by Dr. Jonas E. Salk of the University of Pittsburgh. Salk used "killed" viruses of the disease to assist the bodies of human beings to build up immunity against infection. About five years later Dr. Albert B. Sabin of the University of Cincinnati developed a second type of vaccination using "live" but weakened viruses administered orally. The respective advantages of the two types of vaccination continued for some time to be a matter of controversy. During World War II a remarkable insecticide was perfected which gave promise of the ultimate elimination of two of the most ancient enemies of mankind, malaria and typhus. Popularly known as DDT, it destroys the lice and mosquitoes that transmit these diseases. Recent years have witnessed also the development and wide though not universal acceptance of the fluoridation process for preventing tooth decay in young people. It consists of the simple expedient of adding sodium fluoride to the water supply of municipalities. So impressive was the progress in these and other aspects of preventive medicine that some scientists incautiously predicted that in the comparatively near future every infectious disease known to man would be finally and completely conquered. Their optimism received a shock, however, about 1960, when it was discovered that "new" bacteria, resistant to antibiotics, were making their appearance. Whether they were mutants or older organisms formerly held in check by the balance of nature and now released through the destruction of their natural "enemies" by antibiotics, their menace was serious. More recent studies even indicate that resistance to certain antibiotics may be transmitted from one strain of bacteria to another. There is apparently further cause to believe that the targets of DDT and other insecticides may be developing immunities to them.

No account of medical achievements since 1914 would be complete without mention at least of the following: the development of insulin by the Canadian scientist Frederick Banting for the treatment of diabetes; the perfection of radiation treatments for cancer; the discovery of new methods of detecting cancer and other diseases by the use of radioactive isotopes as "tracers"; the development of techniques for storing blood and blood plasma for transfusions; the

Preventive
medicine

Other medical
achievements

693

synthesization of cortisone (originally derived from the cortex of the adrenal gland) and its use in the treatment of rheumatoid arthritis; the discovery of the hormone ACTH and its application to asthma and to inflammatory diseases of the eye; the development of artificial kidneys and mechanical hearts to assist and even partially to supplant natural organs weakened by injury or disease; the discovery of atabrine as a substitute for quinine in the treatment of malaria; and the development of psychosomatic medicine based upon a recognition of the importance of anxiety, fear, and other psychological factors in causing ulcers, asthma, high blood pressure, and diseases of the heart. By 1965 the people of the world ought to have enjoyed the most abundant health since the dawn of medicine. Statistically, perhaps they did, taken as a whole. But many parts of the world still suffered from the health problems associated with war, social upheaval, poverty, and famine. Improved medical resources are of little immediate value to people who do not have money to buy them or doctors to administer them.

Developments in the social sciences

A record of scientific development in the twentieth century must include some reference to the social sciences. Most of these disciplines were already in existence when the century began, but an essentially new one was added, while the older ones underwent significant changes. The addition was anthropology. Originally a study of "races" and the physical characteristics of men, it was transformed into a study of *cultures* as well. The pioneers in this transformation were Franz Boas and Bronislaw Malinowski. After World War II most of the other social sciences were revolutionized by demands for "quantification." Economics tended to become "econometrics," sociology to become "sociometry," and psychology "psychometry." Everything, it was held, must be measured. The study of theories, institutions, and modes of the past was largely abandoned in favor of scientific surveys of what currently exists. It should be added that many leaders in these fields were not satisfied with mere measurement. Sociology and psychology, for example, were enriched by the discovery of the "mass mind" and the "alienation" of contemporary man. Both of these conceptions envisioned present-day civilization as degraded by the standards of the crowd and threatened by the negativism of unhappy multitudes who thought of themselves as aliens in a world they could neither understand nor control.

2. PHILOSOPHY IN THE CONTEMPORARY WORLD

Characteristics of contemporary philosophy

The history of philosophy since 1914 presents in large part a record of pessimism and confusion. To the majority of thinkers who lived during this period the events taking place around them justified the deepest anxiety. World War I seemed the beginning of a new dark age. Later the onrush of fascism and the plunge into a sec-

ond world conflict appeared to leave little hope that civilization would
ever recover. To be sure, few of the philosophers gave way to
despair, but an increasingly large number lost confidence in the ability of man to save himself without the support of authority or the
aid of supernatural powers. George Santayana fled from the materialist world in disgust and established himself for his declining years
in the Convent of the Blue Nuns in Rome. An even more spectacular change of views was accomplished by the English philosopher
C. E. M. Joad. Agnostic, advocate of polygamy and euthanasia, and
author of the Oxford Oath, which pledged its signers never to fight
under any circumstances for king and country, he turned before his
death in 1953 into a staunch upholder of original sin and a defender
of the Christian faith as a light to live by in a darkening world.

One of the most important of the philosophies that tended to give
a pessimistic view of man and his world was the Neo-Orthodoxy of
the Swiss-German theologian Karl Barth and the American Rein- **Neo-Orthodoxy**
hold Niebuhr. In form a system of theology, it presented profound
philosophical conclusions concerning the nature of life and the destiny of man. Barth and Niebuhr discussed the universe and its problems in something approaching Calvinist terms. They believed the
world to be governed by an all-powerful Deity, who controls all
things for His own inscrutable purposes. They considered man to
be a moral being, created in the divine image, and responsible to
God for the use that he makes of this life. Above all, they emphasized what they regarded as the fundamental fact of sin in the
world. Although man is capable of sympathy and benevolence, his
nature is sadly corrupted by pride and self-love. These commonly
take the form of a will to power, which is the primary source of
war, race conflict, tyranny, and exploitation. Sin can be conquered
only as men humble themselves before God, acknowledge the evil in
their own natures, and accept the redeeming power of the Christian
religion. By such means alone can they achieve that love and respect
for others which are the essence of democracy. The fatherhood of
God is the essential foundation of the brotherhood of man.

Similar in purpose to Neo-Orthodoxy but altogether different in
form and content was the Neo-Scholasticism or Neo-Thomism of
Jacques Maritain and his followers. This movement was not new **Neo-Scholasticism**
but, in the main, was a continuation of the Neo-Scholasticism of the
nineteeth century. Whereas Neo-Orthodoxy was exclusively Protestant, Neo-Scholasticism was predominantly Catholic. Both, however, came close to each other in their critical views of their own
religions. Niebuhr deplored the excessive freedom of conscience
permitted by Protestantism, while Maritain criticized the Catholic
tendency to rely too much on authority. Maritain and his disciples
turned back to the Scholasticism of St. Thomas Aquinas, which
they held had the supreme value of exalting reason and giving
wholeness and purpose to life. Nothing was left at loose ends by **695**

that philosophy to become a source of conflict and exasperation. The universe was governed by intelligent purpose, and everything could be explained by reason. But in the fourteenth century Scholasticism decayed; nominalism rapidly took its place, and the way was opened for the growth of individualism, materialism, and skepticism. Such concepts eventually destroyed man's confidence in himself as a reasoning creature, dethroned God as the ruler of the universe, and left little but anarchy and chaos. Man ever since has been at odds with himself, a restless and exasperated being who strives to conquer the world at the sacrifice of his soul.

The need for a return to faith

For the Neo-Scholastics, then, the salvation of the world depended upon the development of a Christian culture based on the wisdom of St. Thomas Aquinas. Nothing less, they believed, can give dignity to human nature and meaning to human life. Only by a return to faith in God as the creator and upholder of a rational universe can we escape the mood of despair so relentlessly pressing upon us. The time for this Christian revival has not yet come, however. Five centuries of human history cannot be liquidated in a single night. But it is to be hoped that some day the present period of agony and wretchedness will come to an end, and that a new era will dawn, guided by the spirit of the Angelic Doctor of the thirteenth century. Despite its medieval flavor, Neo-Scholasticism attracted many thinkers of the contemporary world. At one time or another it numbered among its followers such diverse intellects as G. K. Chesterton; Étienne Gilson, of the University of Paris; and Mortimer J. Adler, Director of the Institute for Philosophical Research in San Francisco.

Existentialism

The depths of pessimism in philosophy were reached by a movement known as Existentialism, the most popular form of which originated in France about 1938. Founded by Jean-Paul Sartre, a teacher of philosophy in a Paris *lycée* and subsequently a leader of the Resistance against the Germans, it takes its name from its doctrine that the *existence* of man as a free individual is the fundamental fact of life. But this freedom is of no help to man; instead, it is a source of anguish and terror. Realizing, however vaguely, that he is a free agent, morally responsible for all his acts, the individual feels himself a stranger in an alien world. He can have no confidence in a benevolent God or in a universe guided by purpose, for, according to Sartre, all such ideas have been reduced to fictions by modern science. His only way of escape from forlornness and despair is the path of "involvement," or active participation in human affairs. It should be noted that in addition to the atheistic Existentialism of Sartre, there was also an older, Christian form, which had its origin in the teachings of Sören Kierkegaard, a Danish theologian of the middle nineteenth century. Like its atheistic counterpart, Christian Existentialism also teaches that the chief cause of man's agony and terror is freedom, but it finds the source of this freedom in original

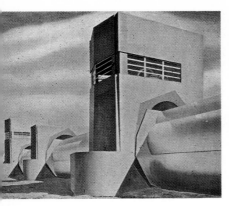

...Vater, Charles Sheeler (1883–). Sheeler, a Philadelphian, idealizes the industrial scene, which he detaches from humanity. (MMA)

Sea and Gulls, John Marin (1870–1953). A native of New Jersey, Marin was a gifted abstract painter. His objects are sometimes recognizable, sometimes not. He painted not the likeness of nature, but *about* nature. (MMA)

Barricade, José Clemente Orozco (1883–1949). The Mexican muralist Orozco was one of the most celebrated of contemporary painters with a social message. His themes were revolutionary fervor, satire of aristocracy and the Church, and deification of the common man. (Mus. Mod. Art)

The Persistence of Memory, Salvador Dali (1904–). The Spaniard Dali is the outstanding representative of the surrealist school. Many objects in his paintings are Freudian images. (Mus. Mod. Art)

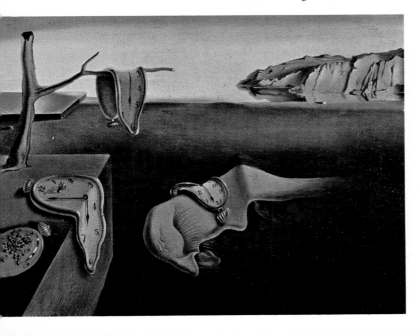

The Gulf Stream, Winslow Homer (1836–1910) Homer is most widely known for his marines. Though his genius was expressed particularly in watercolor, this oil won him great renown. (MMA)

Max Schmitt in a Single Scull, Thomas Eakins (1844–1916). A native of Philadelphia, Eakins painted with superb talent the places and people familiar to him. His work is warm and inspiring, but not profound. (MMA)

Roasting Ears, Thomas Hart Benton (1889–). Benton is one of a group of regional painters who portray scenes of the Midwest and South. (MMA)

Spring in Central Park, Adolf Dehn (1895–). Dehn is one of the most distinguished of American landscape painters. He paints indoors from sketches in order to escape the literalness of nature and to allow freedom for balance and rhythm. (MMA)

Portrait of Myself When Young, Ben Shahn (1898–). A native of Russia who grew up in Brooklyn, Shahn is concerned with communicating ordinary experience. His work combines the precision of photography with startling effects of proportion and size. (Mus. Mod. Art)

John Brown, John Steuart Curry (1897–1946). Born on a farm in Kansas, Curry depicted the beauty and majesty of his native region. *John Brown* is a portion of a large mural in the state capitol at Topeka. A prairie fire and a tornado in the background add fury to the fanaticism of the abolitionist, and symbolize the coming civil conflict. (MMA)

sin. It is not difficult to detect the influence of Kierkegaard and his followers upon the Neo-Orthodoxy of Karl Barth and Reinhold Niebuhr. Since 1930 the leading exponent of Christian Existentialism has been Karl Jaspers, philosophy professor at the University of Heidelberg.

At least two philosophers of the contemporary age retained their optimism amid the welter of gloom and uncertainty. One was Alfred North Whitehead. Born in England, the son of a clergyman of the Church of England, he spent the most fruitful years of his life as Professor of Philosophy at Harvard. Originally a mathematician, he turned to philosophy in an effort to harmonize modern thinking with the revolutionary discoveries of the new age of science. The system of thought he rapidly developed owed much to Plato, Kant, and Einstein. Like the first two, at least, he regarded intuition as just as valid a method of knowing as reason or sensory experience. He rebuked the hardheaded positivists who heaped scorn upon the mystic, the artist, and the romantic poet. A liberal in politics and in social theory, he had a firm belief in the certainty of progress. He had an abiding faith also in a benevolent God. But he refused to think of this God as a divine autocrat handing down tables of laws and punishing men eternally for trespassing against them. Instead, he conceived of Him as a God of love, as "the poet of the world, with tender patience, leading it by his vision of truth, beauty, and goodness." [2] The defect of most religions, Christianity included, has been to represent God as a God of power. God is not omnipotent, else He would be the author of evil. His primary function is to save human beings from the evil which necessarily arises in connection with their struggle for the good. Such was Whitehead's conception of a friendly universe in which God and man are partners in striving toward perfection.

The optimistic philosophy of Whitehead

The second of the philosophers whose thinking was basically optimistic was the American John Dewey. Born in 1859, Dewey had already achieved renown before 1918 as a philosopher of Pragmatism. He never abandoned his allegiance to that movement, but after World War I he gave more and more attention to specific human problems. In his celebrated *Reconstruction in Philosophy*, published in 1920, he urged that philosophy should abandon its dealings "with Ultimate and Absolute Reality" and "find compensation in enlightening the moral forces that move mankind." [3] Unlike most of his contemporaries, he retained a healthy confidence in the powers of the human intellect. He believed that man, making use of the resources acquired by reason and experience, could solve his own problems without any assistance from the supernatural. In common with the Humanists of the past, he considered human beings to be the most important creatures in the universe, and he refused to con-

The Humanism of John Dewey

[2] *Process and Reality*, p. 526.
[3] Pp. 26–27.

cede that their nature was corrupt or depraved. Amid the rising tide of totalitarian oppression in the 1930's, he stressed increasingly the importance of freedom. This, together with a belief in equality and in the capacity of men to form intelligent judgments when guided by experience and education, he held to be the essence of democracy.

The Pragmatism of John Dewey was one of the first of modern philosophies that can be classified as antimetaphysical. By some it has been called anti-intellectual, for it denies the possibility of finding conclusive answers to any of the great questions of life—the nature of the universe, the meaning of life, the possibility of a God as the source of the moral law and the architect of human destiny. Dewey had an able ally in Bertrand Russell, who continued the development of his New Realism into the twentieth century. One of Russell's disciples, Ludwig Wittgenstein, participated in the founding of Logical Positivism, the most extreme of all the antimetaphysical philosophies. Developed further by the so-called Vienna Circle, whose leader was Rudolf Carnap, Logical Positivism emerged as an uncompromisingly scientific philosophy. It is not concerned with values or ideals except to the extent that they may be demonstrable by mathematics or physics. In general, the Logical Positivists reject as "meaningless" everything that cannot be reduced to a "one-to-one correspondence" with something in the physical universe. In other words, they reduce philosophy to a mere instrument for the discovery of truth in harmony with the facts of the physical environment. They divest it almost entirely of its traditional content and use it as a medium for answering questions and solving problems. They are concerned especially with political theory, for they regard that subject as particularly burdened with unproved assumptions and questionable dogmas.

Included among the social and political philosophies after 1918 were the theories of some who despised democracy and therefore contributed to the deepening crisis. Foremost among them were the Italian Vilfredo Pareto and the German Oswald Spengler. Their forerunner was the Frenchman Georges Sorel, who has already been discussed as the founder of Syndicalism. For the most part, all of them agreed in their contempt for the masses, in their belief that democracy was impossible, in their anti-intellectual viewpoint, and in their admiration for strong and aggressive leaders. Spengler was, in many respects, more extreme than Pareto. Although he completed about 1918 an erudite and in some respects brilliant philosophy of history, which he entitled *The Decline of the West*, his later writings were as full of prejudice as the books of the Nazis. In his *Hour of Decision*, published in 1933, he fulminated against democracy, pacifism, internationalism, the lower classes, and the colored races. He sang the praises of those "who feel themselves born and called to be masters," of "healthy instincts, race, the will to possession and power." He despised the cold, analytical reasoning

Logical
Positivism

Antirationalist
and antidemo-
cratic philosophies

of urban intellectuals and called upon men to admire the "deep wisdom of old peasant families." Human beings, he maintained, are "beasts of prey," and those who deny this conclusion are simply "beasts of prey with broken teeth."

The years following World War II witnessed an increasing popularity of conservative political and social philosophy. The creeping shadow of communism was undoubtedly largely responsible, but the trend had been initiated while the U.S.S.R. was still an ally of the West. The paternity of the new movement should perhaps be ascribed to Frederick A. Hayek, an Austrian political economist who had taken up residence in London. In *The Road to Serfdom*, Hayek condemned all forms of collectivist interference with capitalism, on the ground that they would lead to socialism and eventually to communism or fascism. Destruction of economic freedom, he contended, must surely lead to the destruction of all freedoms, for the right of the individual to unhampered choice in the pursuit of tastes and interests is the very essence of freedom. A more strictly political variety of the new conservatism is exemplified by the work of Peter Viereck, Eric Voegelin, and Russell Kirk. All three espouse a philosophy essentially reactionary and antirational. Viereck, for example, describes himself as one who "distrusts human nature and believes (politically speaking) in Original Sin which must be restrained by the ethical traffic lights of traditionalism." According to Voegelin, Western society can be saved by venerating its tradition-rooted institutions and by abandoning the belief that knowledge, rather than faith, is the greatest good. Russell Kirk demands a revival of family piety, the defense of property, and recognition that a "divine intent rules society" and that "Providence is the proper instrument for change."

The New
Conservatism

3. LITERATURE IN THE CONTEMPORARY WORLD

Literary movements during the period of the depression and the two world wars showed tendencies similar to those in philosophy. Indeed, in many instances, it was difficult to tell where philosophy ended and literature began. The major novelists, poets, and dramatists were deeply concerned about social and political problems and about the hope and destiny of man. Like the philosophers, they were disillusioned by the brute facts of World War I and by the failure of victory to fulfill its promises. Many were profoundly affected also by the revolutionary developments in science and especially by the probings of the new psychology into the hidden secrets of the mind. Instead of a being created by God just "a little lower than the angels," man seemed now to be a creature just a bit higher than the apes. Finally, of course, literary men were influenced by the Great Depression and by the return to war in 1939. Both these developments led to a searching of methods and, among

Major tendencies
in literature

many writers, to a partial revision of objectives.

If there has been any one tendency preeminent above others that has marked the literature of the contemporary world it has been a revolt against "insubstantiality" and sentimentality. A cardinal legacy from the nineteenth century was symbolism, characterized by a sort of "art-for-art's-sake" attitude in poems and novels. Primary emphasis was given to the expression of delicate feelings, exquisiteness, and peculiar intuitions remote from ordinary experience. The mundane realities in the lives of flesh-and-blood human beings were largely ignored. Though symbolism was a child of romanticism, the parent movement did not entirely die out. It found

T.S. Eliot (1888–1965). Noted author of *The Waste Land* and *Murder in the Cathedral* in his London study. He was awarded the Nobel Prize for Literature in 1948. American born, he had been a citizen of Great Britain since 1927.

expression for a time in the novels of Rudyard Kipling. After World War I, however, its popularity rapidly faded.

Much of the literature of the interwar period revolved around themes of frustration, cynicism, and disenchantment. It was the era of the "lost generation," of young men whose ideals had been shattered by the brutal events of their time. Its mood was set by the early novels of Ernest Hemingway, by the poetry of T. S. Eliot, and by the dramas of Eugene O'Neill. In *A Farewell to Arms* Hemingway gave to the public one of its first insights into the folly and meanness of war and set a pattern which other writers were soon to follow. T. S. Eliot in his poem, *The Waste Land* (1922), presented a philosophy that was close to despair. Once you are born, he seemed to be saying, life is a living death to be ground out in boredom and frustration. The pessimism of Eugene O'Neill appeared to be somewhat different from that of his contemporaries. His tragedies depicted man not so much as a victim of society but rather as the pitiable slave of his own abnormal nature. Most critics would probably agree that O'Neill's greatest dramas were *Strange Interlude* (1927) and *Mourning Becomes Electra* (1931). Other tendencies manifesting themselves during this era were determinism and stream-of-consciousness writing. Theodore Dreiser brought determinism to a climax in *An American Tragedy* (1925). Deeply influenced by psychoanalysis, James Joyce became the leading exponent of stream-of-consciousness writing. His greatest novel, *Ulysses* (1922), was essentially a study of reverie rather than action.

The Great Depression of the 1930's forced a reexamination of the methods and purposes of literature. In the midst of economic stagnation and threats of fascism and war, the theory evolved that literature must have a serious purpose, that it should indict meanness, cruelty, and barbarism and point the way to a society more just. The new trend was reflected in the works of a diversity of writers. John Steinbeck depicted the sorry plight of impoverished farmers fleeing from the "dust bowl" to California only to find that all the good earth had been monopolized by big land companies that exploited their workers. Pervading some of the plays of Robert Sherwood and the novels of André Malraux was the strong suggestion that man's struggle against tyranny and injustice is the chief thing that gives meaning and value to life. A similar theme may be said to have characterized Ernest Hemingway's *For Whom the Bell Tolls* (1940). Here also was the strong implication that the individual, in sacrificing himself for the cause of the people, gives a meaning and dignity to life that can be achieved in no other way.

Influence of the
Depression:
literature with a
serious purpose

Literature with a serious purpose tended later to emphasize the lonely and tragic life of the common man and to protest ever more strongly against cruelty and injustice. A warm affinity for the plain folk of rural New England was expressed by Robert Frost, greatly beloved American poet. Nobel-prize winner William Faulkner devoted superb artistic talents to portrayals of crude elemental behavior in backward areas of the Deep South. The tragedy of World War II brought a series of novels dealing with the conflict itself, with the heroism of those who resisted Nazi tyranny, or with the brutality and inefficiency of military systems. Foremost among such writings were Norman Mailer's *The Naked and the Dead* and James Jones' *From Here to Eternity*. Both portrayed the coarseness and cruelty of military life with a ruthless realism. But along with these trends toward warm sympathy and stark realism as means of conveying hatred of injustice and oppression, there were also some new manifestations. One was a turning to religion to compensate for a sense of overwhelming tragedy or to prevent calamities which seemed certain to flow from allowing science to get out of control. Aldous Huxley, erstwhile prophet of the age of cynicism and sophistication, turned to Hindu mysticism in such novels as *After Many a Summer Dies the Swan* and *Time Must Have a Stop*. T. S. Eliot, who in the 1920's had found the universe a barren wasteland with no fruits but boredom and despair, now discovered that life could be meaningful when ennobled by the ageless truths of the church. His new mood was exemplified by *Murder in the Cathedral* and *The Cocktail Party*. In spite of the different directions of their thinking, most of the postwar writers seemed to have much in common. They were expressing with one voice their concern over the loneliness of man. They saw human beings in an age of mass thinking and mass actions as helpless and pitiable creatures. Embracing religion or lashing injustice and stupidity were merely different means of accomplishing the rescue of modern man from utter destruction by the forces around him.

Most of the literary moods of midcentury continued into the 1960's. Especially marked was the revolt against the complexities and cruelties of modern life. There was the same protest against injustice and maltreatment of the weak and unfortunate. The American Harper Lee exposed race prejudice in *To Kill a Mockingbird*, as did the South African Alan Paton in even stronger terms in *Cry the Beloved Country* and *Too Late the Phalarope*. More pronounced among recent literary trends was the protest against conformity and the extinction of individuality. This protest was most vigorously expressed by the Russian Boris Pasternak in *Doctor Zhivago*. The novel was an indictment of gregariousness and conformity, as exemplified by the Party Man and the Organization Man in the Soviet Union, and of their willingness to sacrifice self-respect for the sake of advancement and self-importance. Pasternak made his hero say, "Only individuals seek the truth." It is an ironic fact that so vigorous a defense of individual self-assertion should have come out of Soviet Russia. Symptomatic to an extreme of the individual's protest were two literary "movements"—the "Beat Generation" in America and the "Angry Young Men" in England. Although their literary merit may be debatable, the works of these writers all consider the individual in total conflict with a worthless "establishment" or "system," often by abandoning every contact with ordinary society. In the plays of Eugène Ionesco and Samuel Beckett, leading figures in the "theatre of the absurd," the individual is characteristically trapped in a nonsense world which moves with its own mad logic.

The Literature of protest

4. CONTEMPORARY ART AND MUSIC

As in literature, so in art the twentieth century was marked by revolt against exquisiteness and artificiality. In the closing decades of the preceding century this revolt had taken the form of a reaction against impressionism. The impressionists, as we have seen, had virtually abolished objects and ideas and had replaced them with suggestions and ingenious analyses of light. Cézanne and Van Gogh criticized the formlessness and insubstantiality of the work of the impressionists and held that the figures of the painter's art should be as solidly and completely molded as statues.

The revolt against impressionism

The work of Cézanne and Van Gogh, we have noted, led directly to *cubism*, the most revolutionary art of the twentieth century. It was developed about 1905 by Pablo Picasso, and continues to

Cubism

702

be a popular mode of artistic expression. Cubism began as an art of realism *par excellence*. It endeavors to present life, not in accordance with a nicely adorned conventional pattern, but as a jumble of arms, legs, heads, and bodies caught in motion and having no arrangement among themselves except that given by the observer. But disorder and disorganization are not for the cubist ends in themselves. They are intended partly to reflect notions of form—to repudiate the conception of art as mere prettiness.

*See color plates
at page 441*

An even more violent movement of rebellion against traditional standards of art and of life was *surrealism*, whose high priest since 1929 has been the Spaniard Salvador Dali. Originating about 1918 under the combined influence of the war and psychoanalysis, surrealism flourished during the age of nihilism that followed the armistice. The aim of its followers was not to represent the world of nature but to portray the reactions of the human mind. For this purpose they delved into the subconscious and attempted to depict the content of dreams and the weird impressions of reverie. This commonly resulted in a technique quite different from that of traditional art. In general, the surrealists paid little attention to the conventional standards of beauty and form. They argued that, in the light of the new psychology, naturalism was impossible if art were to have any value as an accurate expression of meaning.

Surrealism

*See color plates
at pages 696, 697*

For a time after 1930 the bizarre and anarchic painting of the extreme modernist schools suffered a substantial decline. Its place was taken to a large extent by a virile and popular art of the common man.[4] Among the chief representatives of the new movement were the Mexicans, Diego Rivera and José Clemente Orozco, and the United States painters Thomas Benton, Adolph Dehn, William Gropper, and Grant Wood. The fundamental aim of these artists was to depict the social conditions of the modern world and to present in graphic detail the hopes and struggles of peasants and toilers. While they scarcely adhered to any of the conventions of the past, there was nothing unintelligible about their work; it was intended to be art that anyone could understand. At the same time, much of it bore the sting or thrust of social satire. Orozco, in particular, delighted in pillorying the hypocrisy of the Church and the greed and cruelty of plutocrats and plunderers.

**The new art of
the common man**

Around 1950 another innovating movement in painting began to attract considerable attention. Known by different names, it is perhaps most accurately called *abstract expressionism*. Thus far its chief exponents have been Jackson Pollock, Willem de Kooning, and Franz Kline. So far as the past is concerned it owes most to expressionism, cubism, and surrealism. But the abstract expressionists prefer to repudiate nearly all the traditions of the past. They believe in innovation, experimentation, and the use of bold and startling de-

**Abstract
expressionism**

---

[4] The art of the common man is also called regional art, especially in the forms developed in the United States.

Mahoning by Franz Kline, a leader of the abstract expressionist school. Original in the Whitney Museum of American Art, New York.

vices to achieve effects. Some of the work of their minor disciples hardly appears to be painting at all, but seems rather a hodgepodge of daubs of paint interspersed with scraps of metal, bits of cloth and paper, and similar objects. Some who cannot draw achieve interesting results with coffee grounds and bread crumbs.

It was inevitable that music should reflect the spirit of disillusionment that reached a climax following World War I. The more original developments were closely parallel to those in painting. Most fundamental of all was the revolt against the romantic tradition, especially as it had culminated in Wagner. Many, although by no means all, composers went so far as to repudiate the aesthetic ideal entirely, relying upon complexity and novelty of structure or on a sheer display of energy to supply interest to their works.

Deviations from the classical and romantic formulas have been generally of two types, designated broadly as impressionism and expressionism. The former seeks to exploit the qualities of musical sound to suggest feelings or images. The latter is concerned more with form than with sensuous effects and tends toward abstraction. The most perfect exponent of impressionism was Claude Debussy, its originator, whose work was described in an earlier chapter. Even in France impressionism did not prove to be an enduring school. With Maurice Ravel (1875–1937), most celebrated of the composers who reflected Debussy's influence, it became less poetic and picturesque and acquired a degree of cold impassivity together with

The chief trends in contemporary music

Impressionism

704

greater firmness of texture.

Expressionism, more radical and more influential than impressionism, comprises two main schools: *atonality*, founded by the Viennese Arnold Schoenberg (1874–1951), and *polytonality*, best typified by the Russian Igor Stravinsky (1882–   ). Atonality implies
the repudiation of the concept of fixed tonal relationships; it abol-
ishes *key*. In this type of music, dissonances are the rule rather than
the exception, and the melodic line commonly alternates between
chromatic manipulation and strange unsingable leaps. In short, the
ordinary principles of composition are reversed. However, emancipation from the bonds of tradition has enabled the atonalists to give
undivided attention to the development of their own subjective
ideas with the utmost originality. They attempt, with some success,
to let musical sound become, not an object admirable in itself, but a
vehicle for expressing the inner meaning and elemental structure of
things. Odd as it may appear, some atonal works are deeply emotional in effect. They betray a kinship with symbolism and also
show the influence of the theories of the subconscious derived from
psychoanalysis. Most of the distinctive features of the atonal school
are vividly incorporated in Schoenberg's *Pierrot Lunaire*, the setting
of a symbolist text from the Belgian poet, Albert Giraud. This
fantasy, in which the singer intones her part in a special "song-
speech," somewhat between singing and reciting, has been described
as creating "a whole world of strange fascination and enchantment,
of nameless horrors and terrible imaginings, of perverse and poison-
ous beauty . . . of a searing and withering mockery and malicious,
elfish humor." [5]

Polytonality, of which Stravinsky is the most famous exponent, is
essentially a radical kind of counterpoint, deriving its inspiration
partly from baroque practices of counterpoint that were placed in

[5] Cecil Gray, *A Survey of Contemporary Music*, p. 176.

Igor Stravinsky (1882–   ).
Exponent of polytonality as a
form of expressionism in music.

705

the service of new ideas. However, it is not content simply to interweave independent melodies which together form concord, but undertakes to combine separate keys and unrelated harmonic systems, with results that are highly discordant. It is thus another example of revolt against the European harmonic heritage and differs from atonality more in technique than in ultimate aim. But while the atonalists, through their emotional expressiveness, have retained elements of romanticism, the polytonalists have tried to resurrect the architectural qualities of pure form, movement, and rhythm, stripping away all sentimentality and sensuous connotations. Stravinsky affirmed that his intention was to produce music in which acoustic properties were the only consideration and which would appeal to the physical ear alone. His coldly detached, anti-aesthetic experiments have much in common with cubism and similar tendencies in modern painting. In spite of this, however, Stravinsky's first really characteristic and widely heralded creations were composed in Paris for the Russian Ballet, a species of theatrical art which not only appeals to other senses than that of hearing but which also is intended to delineate human character and emotions. The application of his theories to such a medium conveys the sardonic impression of human beings who are mere automatons, manipulated by their own physical urges or by the grim hand of a mechanical fate. Stravinsky's style and interests have undergone successive changes; in recent years he has turned from the theater to more distinctly concert forms. Without sacrificing his intense individuality, he has achieved an increasing clarity of expression and an almost classical integration of structural design.

The twentieth century produced other great composers who, though touched by neoclassicism and the other prevailing trends, **Other twentieth-** went their own individual ways. Mention should be made of the **century composers** Hungarian Béla Bartók (1881–1945), the German Paul Hindemith (1895–1963), and the Russian Serge Prokofiev (1891–1953). In the meantime American music also came of age. After a period largely dominated by German romanticism, in the third decade of the twentieth century there emerged a "school" of music which, though representing various shades of modernism, can rightfully be called American. Aaron Copland (1900–   ), Samuel Barber (1910–   ), Roger Sessions (1896–   ), Quincy Porter (1897–1966), and William Schuman (1910–   ) can take their place among the best composers active in Europe.

It was no doubt inevitable that the great scientific advances of the past sixty years, especially in the fields of electronics and acoustics, **Electronic music** would have an impact upon the course of music. Since 1950 a number of composers have been exploring the new area of *electronic music*, which may be defined as "music based on techniques that generate, transform, and manipulate sounds electronically." In **706** France, the composers of *musique concrète* use magnetic tape to capture and then to recompose extramusical sounds (city noises, for example); these sounds are then modified by splicing or superimposing the tapes or by playing them at various speeds. In America, the laboratory for electronic music at Columbia University has used mainly conventional musical sounds and the human voice as raw material for experiments in tape-recorded music. Composers at the studio of the West German Radio in Cologne have developed a music utilizing sounds from an electric generator. The leading composer in this group is Karlheinz Stockhausen. The German

RCA Electronic Sound Synthesizer. At the Electronic Music Center of Columbia and Princeton Universities, in New York City.

school believes that the term "electronic music" is applicable only to compositions constructed out of electronically produced sounds, and, indeed, the majority of composers in this genre have come to concentrate on "pure" electronic sounds in recent years. It is far too early to decide whether electronic music, which eliminates the performer and enables the composer to reach the listener directly, is truly the music of the future, but it is unquestionably a significant product of our scientific age.

5. EPILOGUE

We have now come to the end of a long survey of the history of Western man and his civilizations from their earliest beginnings to the present. It is an appropriate time to ask ourselves a number of questions. What is the value of history? Do we learn anything from the study of history? Does history repeat itself? What is

What history is and means

707

the fate of our own civilization? Is it destined to decay and disintegrate, to succumb to barbarian invasions, either from within or from without, and to be replaced by a dark age?

Ever since the eighteenth century it has been fashionable in some quarters to be cynical about the meaning of history and to scoff at the value of studying it. For Herbert Spencer history was "worthless gossip." To Napoleon it was a "fable agreed upon." To Edward Gibbon it appeared at times to be "little more than a register of the crimes, follies, and misfortunes of mankind." The German philosopher Hegel maintained, in one of his darker moments, that "the only thing that peoples and governments learn from the study of history is that they learn nothing from the study of history." Actually, however, no one seems to take much stock in any of these disparaging doctrines. Every person who lives much above the animal level has constant recourse to the lessons of history. For all experience, whether recorded or merely remembered, is in reality history. In treating diseases the modern physician makes use of *historical* medicine. He may at times experiment with new remedies, but for the most part he relies upon treatments previously developed by research scientists or tested by past experience. The lawyer in defending his client and the judge in deciding cases turn back to the precedents established in similar litigation over a period of decades or even through centuries. The businessman, if he is to avoid severe losses, must take into account the trends of the market and the fluctuations of the economic cycle over a period of considerable length. All of these people and countless others would be as helpless as a ship without rudder or sails if it were not for the "lessons" of history.

But does history repeat itself sufficiently to enable us to predict the future? A large proportion of the philosophers of history have conceived of a uniform pattern characterizing the growth and decline of civilizations over thousands of years. Toynbee attributes the growth primarily to a condition of adversity and the decline to such factors as militarism and war, barbarization from within, and the rise of an "internal proletariat." By the last term he means a class like the city mob of ancient Rome who are "in" but not "of" a given society. Despised and disinherited, they nurse grievances against the society and gradually undermine it. Oswald Spengler saw the growth and decay of civilizations, or cultures as he called them, paralleling the four seasons or the life of an organism. Each had its spring or youth phase, its summer or early maturity phase, its autumn or late maturity phase, and its winter or senility phase.

Even in periods of the brightest optimism writers who have done much thinking about the meaning of history have generally assumed that decay and disintegration will follow prosperity and progress. For example, the Founding Fathers in the United States viewed the future of their own country with grave misgivings. So long as the nation remained predominantly agricultural, with an abundance of cheap land, all would be well. But increasing population in a few generations would result in the growth of large cities, with their slums, corrupt politicians, and a dependent mob ready to sell its votes to the highest bidder. The ultimate outcome would be the rise of Catilines and Caesars, who would seek, with the support of the proletariat, to overthrow the republic. In the late nineteenth century, when the age of science and industry in the United States was still facing the rising sun, Brooks Adams and his brother Henry described with accents of gloom the ultimate decay of Western culture. The former contended that every civilization passes through two stages, one dominated by fear and the other by greed. Fear stimulates the imagination and results in artistic production and great systems of religion. Greed subordinates everything to economic considerations. Marriage is avoided or postponed, the birthrate declines, and originality is stifled by an atmosphere of caution. Henry Adams sought to interpret civilization in terms of a scientific law—the second law of thermodynamics, or the law of the dissipation of energy. He predicted that the civilization of Western man would expend its vital force and die of exhaustion by 1932.

The fate of our own civilization

There seems little doubt that civilizations do grow old and die from a number of causes. A major one apparently is urbanization, carried to the point where a large proportion of the population is crowded into huge metropolitan areas. This condition adds so much to the complexity of social problems that human intelligence is unable to solve them. Crime, disease, boredom, insanity, corruption, poverty in the midst of plenty are only a few of these critical problems. Pollution of water and air threaten to make large portions of the earth uninhabitable. Excessive concentration of industry results in overproduction and leads to depressions and to exhaustion of natural resources. Whether our own civilization has reached this stage is a question impossible to answer. There are, of course, many ominous portents, but there are also signs of hope. Disease, at least in the form of the great pestilences, seems on the way toward extinction. If crime and corruption have not been eliminated, their nature and causes are better understood. Poverty is still with us, but standards of living for most of the masses have improved except where menaced by overpopulation, and more adequate provision is made for those who may suffer from want. Imperialism, at least of the type imposed by external conquest, seems on the wane, as exemplified by the freedom gained in recent years by India, Israel, Ceylon, Pakistan, Libya, Tunisia, Ghana, Indonesia, Morocco, Nigeria, and the Sudan.

The threat and the hope

The most serious threat to civilization wherever it exists is war. Throughout history its principal fruits have been inflation, impoverishment, revolution, and chaos. It has destroyed the best blood of nation after nation and left the physical and mental weaklings to become the fathers of the new generation. But even war must not be regarded as an insoluble problem. With the development of nuclear weapons it is coming to be regarded in widening circles as a logical monstrosity. Signs have multiplied that neither of the two great antagonists among the nations desires war or would deliberately take steps to make it inevitable. Despite all the prophets of doom, sanity has not been completely extinguished. Although progress is slow and faltering, the world does move. It is barely twenty centuries since human sacrifice was practiced by such a "civilized" people as the Carthaginians. It is only one century since slavery was abolished in the United States and serfdom in Russia. If we have not been able to solve all of our problems, we at least know what we need to do to dispose of a great many of them. The expansion of knowledge and the application of intelligence should provide us with the means of conquering most of the remainder.

SELECTED READINGS

· *Items so designated are available in paperbound editions.*

Barzun, Jacques, *Romanticism and the Modern Ego,* Boston, 1945. A discerning interpretation.

Bruun, Geoffrey, *The World in the Twentieth Century,* New York, 1948.

Burns, E. M., *Ideas in Conflict,* New York, 1960. A survey of contemporary political thought.

Colum, Mary, *From These Roots: the Ideas That Have Made Modern Literature,* New York, 1944.

· Copland, Aaron, *The New Music,* New York, 1968.

Craven, Thomas, *Modern Art: the Men, the Movement, the Meaning,* New York, 1934.

Gray, Cecil, *A Survey of Contemporary Music,* London, 1924.

· Hecht, Selig, *Explaining the Atom,* New York, 1947 (Compass, rev.).

Hogben, L. T., *Science for the Citizen,* New York, 1938.

· Jeans, Sir James, *The Universe around Us,* New York, 1944 (Cambridge University Press).

Lang, Paul, *Music in Western Civilization,* New York, 1941. An excellent, inclusive account.

Machlis, Joseph, *The Enjoyment of Music,* rev. ed., New York, 1963.

· Northrop, F. C. S., *The Meeting of East and West,* New York, 1946 (Collier).

Pritchett, V. S., *The Living Novel,* New York, 1947.

Randall, J. H., Jr., *Our Changing Civilization,* New York, 1929.

Salazar, Adolfo, *Music in Our Time,* New York, 1946.

Schapiro, J. S., *The World in Crisis,* New York, 1950.

· Schneider, H. W., *A History of American Philosophy,* New York, 1946 (Columbia University Press).

Singer, Charles, *A History of Biology,* New York, 1950.

· Slochower, Harry, *No Voice is Wholly Lost,* New York, 1945. Also available in paperback under the title *Literature and Philosophy Between Two World Wars* (Citadel, 1964).

· Snow, C. P., *The Two Cultures and the Scientific Revolution*, Cambridge,
1959. Also available in paperback under the title *The Two Cultures and a Second Look: An Expanded Version of the Two Cultures and the Scientific Revolution* (Mentor, Cambridge University Press, 1964).

Valentine, A. C., *The Age of Conformity*, Chicago, 1954. An expression of the point of view that democracy with its reliance upon mass opinion contains many dangers.

Ward, Harold, *New Worlds in Medicine*, New York, 1946.

· Wilson, Edmund, *Axel's Castle*, New York, 1958 (Scribner Library). An interpretative study of recent trends in literature.

· Wittels, Fritz, *Freud and His Time*, New York, 1948 (Universal Library).

SOURCE MATERIALS

Baumer, F. L. V., *Main Currents of Western Thought*, New York, 1952.

· Dewey, John, *Reconstruction in Philosophy* (Beacon, 1957).

· ———, *Liberalism and Social Action* (Capricorn, 1963).

· Niebuhr, Reinhold, *The Children of Light and the Children of Darkness*, New York, 1960 (Scribner Library).

Spengler, Oswald, *The Decline of the West*, Introduction, New York, 1945, 2 vols.

· Whitehead, A. N., *Science and the Modern World*, New York, 1926 (Mentor, 1949).

Rulers of Principal States, 1485-1964 A.D.

Holy Roman Emperors

Hapsburg Dynasty

Frederick III, 1440–1493
Maximilian I, 1493–1519
Charles V, 1519–1556
Ferdinand I, 1556–1564
Maximilian II, 1564–1576
Rudolf II, 1576–1612
Matthias, 1612–1619
Ferdinand II, 1619–1637
Ferdinand III, 1637–1657

Leopold I, 1658–1705
Joseph I, 1705–1711
Charles VI, 1711–1740
Charles VII (not a Hapsburg), 1742–1745
Francis I, 1745–1765
Joseph II, 1765–1790
Leopold II, 1790–1792
Francis II, 1792–1806

Rulers of France

House of Valois

Charles VIII, 1483–1498
Louis XII, 1498–1515
Francis I, 1515–1547
Henry II, 1547–1559
Francis II, 1559–1560
Charles IX, 1560–1574
Henry III, 1574–1589

Bourbon Dynasty

Henry IV, 1589–1610
Louis XIII, 1610–1643

Louis XIV, 1643–1715
Louis XV, 1715–1774
Louis XVI, 1774–1792
First Republic, 1792–1799
Napoleon Bonaparte, First Consul, 1799–1804
Napoleon I, Emperor, 1804–1814
Louis XVIII (Bourbon Dynasty), 1814–1824
Charles X (Bourbon Dynasty), 1824–1830
Louis Philippe, 1830–1848

713

Rulers of France (Continued)

Second Republic, 1848–1852
Napoleon III, Emperor, 1852–1870
Third Republic, 1870–1940
Pétain regime, 1940–1944

Provisional government, 1944–1946
Fourth Republic, 1946–1958
Fifth Republic, 1958–

Rulers of England

TUDOR SOVEREIGNS

Henry VII, 1485–1509
Henry VIII, 1509–1547
Edward VI, 1547–1553
Mary, 1553–1558
Elizabeth I, 1558–1603

STUART KINGS

James I, 1603–1625
Charles I, 1625–1649

COMMONWEALTH AND PROTECTORATE, 1649–1659

LATER STUART MONARCHS

Charles II, 1660–1685
James II, 1685–1688
William III and Mary II, 1689–1694
William III alone, 1694–1702

Anne, 1702–1714

HOUSE OF HANOVER

George I, 1714–1727
George II, 1727–1760
George III, 1760–1820
George IV, 1820–1830
William IV, 1830–1837
Victoria, 1837–1901

HOUSE OF SAXE-COBURG-GOTHA

Edward VII, 1901–1910
George V, 1910–1917

HOUSE OF WINDSOR

George V, 1917–1936
Edward VIII, 1936
George VI, 1936–1952
Elizabeth II, 1952–

Prominent Popes

Alexander VI, 1492–1503
Julius II, 1503–1513
Leo X, 1513–1521
Adrian VI, 1522–1523
Clement VII, 1523–1534
Paul IV, 1555–1559
Gregory XIII, 1572–1585
Gregory XVI, 1831–1846

Pius IX, 1846–1878
Leo XIII, 1878–1903
Benedict XV, 1914–1922
Pius XI, 1922–1939
Pius XII, 1939–1958
John XXIII, 1958–1963
Paul VI, 1963–

Rulers of Austria and Austria-Hungary

* Maximilian I (Archduke), 1493–1519
* Charles I (Charles V in the Holy Roman Empire), 1519–1556
* Ferdinand I, 1556–1564
* Maximilian II, 1564–1576
* Rudolf II, 1576–1612
* Matthias, 1612–1619

* Ferdinand II, 1619–1637
* Ferdinand III, 1637–1657
* Leopold I, 1658–1705
* Joseph I, 1705–1711
* Charles VI, 1711–1740
  Maria Theresa, 1740–1780
* Joseph II, 1780–1790

* Also bore title of Holy Roman Emperor

* Leopold II, 1790–1792
* Francis II, 1792–1835 (Emperor of Austria as Francis I after 1804)
Ferdinand I, 1835–1848
Francis Joseph, 1848–1916 (after 1867 Emperor of Austria and King of Hungary)

Charles I, 1916–1918 (Emperor of Austria and King of Hungary)
Republic of Austria, 1918–1938 (dictatorship after 1934)
Union with Germany (*Anschluss*), 1938–1945
Republic restored, under Allied occupation, 1945
Free Republic, 1956–

Rulers of Prussia and Germany

* Frederick I, 1701–1713
* Frederick William I, 1713–1740
* Frederick II (the Great), 1740–1786
* Frederick William II, 1786–1797
* Frederick William III, 1797–1840
* Frederick William IV, 1840–1861
* William I, 1861–1888 (German Emperor after 1871)
Frederick III, 1888

* Kings of Prussia

William II, 1888–1918
Weimar Republic, 1918–1933
Third Reich (Nazi Dictatorship), 1933–1945
Allied occupation, 1945–1952
Division into Federal Republic of Germany in west and German Democratic Republic in east, 1949–

Rulers of Russia

Ivan III, 1462–1505
Basil III, 1505–1533
Ivan IV, 1533–1584
Theodore I, 1584–1598
Boris Godunov, 1598–1605
Theodore II, 1605
Basil IV, 1606–1610
Michael, 1613–1645
Alexius, 1645–1676
Theodore III, 1676–1682
Ivan V and Peter I, 1682–1689
Peter I (the Great), 1689–1725
Catherine I, 1725–1727

Peter II, 1727–1730
Anna, 1730–1740
Ivan VI, 1740–1741
Elizabeth, 1741–1762
Peter III, 1762
Catherine II (the Great), 1762–1796
Paul, 1796–1801
Alexander I, 1801–1825
Nicholas I, 1825–1855
Alexander II, 1855–1881
Alexander III, 1881–1894
Nicholas II, 1894–1917
Soviet Republic, 1917–

Rulers of Italy

Victor Emmanuel II, 1861–1878
Humbert I, 1878–1900
Victor Emmanuel III, 1900–1946

Fascist Dictatorship, 1922–1943 (maintained in northern Italy until 1945)
Humbert II, May 9–June 13, 1946
Republic, 1946–

Rulers of Spain

Ferdinand { and Isabella, 1479–1504
and Philip I, 1504–1506
and Charles I, 1506–1516
Charles I (Holy Roman Emperor Charles V), 1516–1556
Philip III, 1598–1621
Philip IV, 1621–1665
Charles II, 1665–1700
Philip V, 1700–1746
Ferdinand VI, 1746–1759
Charles III, 1759–1788
Charles IV, 1788–1808

Ferdinand VII, 1808
Joseph Bonaparte, 1808–1813
Ferdinand VII (restored), 1814–1833
Isabella II, 1833–1868
Republic, 1868–1870
Amadeo, 1870–1873
Republic, 1873–1874
Alfonso XII, 1874–1885
Alfonso XIII, 1886–1931
Republic, 1931–1939
Fascist Dictatorship, 1939–

Principal Rulers of India

Babur (Mogul Dynasty), 1526–1530
Akbar (Mogul Dynasty), 1556–1605
Shah Jahan (Mogul Dynasty), 1627–1658
Aurangzeb (Mogul Dynasty), 1658–1707
Regime of British East India Company, 1757–1858

British *raj*, 1858–1947
Division into self-governing dominions of India and Pakistan, 1947
Republic of India, 1950–
Republic of Pakistan, 1956–

Periods of Chinese Rule

Ch'ing (Manchu) Dynasty, 1644–1912
Chinese Republic, 1912–1949
Communist Regime, 1949–

Periods of Japanese Rule

Sengoku Period, *ca.* 1500–1600
Edo (Tokugawa) Period, 1603–1867
Meiji Period (Mutsuhito), 1868–1912

Taisho Period (Yoshihito), 1912–1926
Showa Period (Hirohito), 1926–

Index

Guide to Pronunciation

The sounds represented by the diacritical marks used in this Index are illustrated by the following common words:

āle   ēve   īce   ōld   ūse   bo͞ot
ăt   ĕnd   ĭll   ŏf   ŭs   fo͝ot
fâtality évent   ôbey   ûnite
câre   makẽr   fôrm   ûrn
ärm
àsk

Vowels that have no diacritical marks are to be pronounced "neutral," for example: Aegean = ê-jē'an, Basel = bäz'el, Basil = bă'zil, common = kŏm'on, Alcaeus = ăl-sē'us. The combinations ou and oi are pronounced as in "out" and "oil."